A HISTORY OF
FENN COLLEGE

Sereno Peck Fenn

A History of Fenn College

G. BROOKS EARNEST

President of the College

Published by
THE FENN EDUCATIONAL FUND
OF THE CLEVELAND FOUNDATION
Cleveland : 1974

A History of Fenn College
Copyright © 1974 by G. Brooks Earnest
All rights reserved
Library of Congress Catalog Number 74-75204
Produced for the Fenn Educational Fund of the Cleveland Foundation
by Howard Allen, Inc., Publishers
Manufactured in The United States of America
at the Press of The Oberlin Printing Company
Designed by Merald E. Wrolstad

DEDICATION

This book is dedicated to four distinguished citizens of Greater Cleveland who were enthusiastically instrumental in the growth and development of Fenn College and its successor, the Fenn Educational Foundation, namely; Ellwood H. Fisher, first Chairman of Fenn's Board of Trustees, a trustee since 1932 who charted Fenn's direction in its early growth; Clayton G. Hale, a trustee since 1933, who served on and chaired many Trustee Committees, a dedicated helpmate to all Fenn's presidents and later, the second Chairman of the Board of Trustees of the Fenn Educational Foundation; Charles J. Stilwell, Fenn's second Chairman of the Board of Trustees, who tactfully led the Board through two changes of presidents, Fenn's largest fund raising campaign, and the College's largest acquisition of land and buildings, one of which bears his name, Stilwell Hall; Harry F. Burmester, Fenn's third, and last, Chairman of the Board of Trustees whose almost entire period of leadership was expended in the multiplicity of rigorous details involving the transfer of Fenn College to the State of Ohio as the nucleus of The Cleveland State University. Mr. Burmester was also the first Chairman of the Board of Trustees of the Fenn Educational Foundation. These four men accepted important responsibilities and exercised leadership qualities of the highest order in piloting the good ship "Fenn" through all kinds of seas. Cleveland will always be indebted to them.

C&p 1

PREFACE

All preeminent institutions should have their life works recorded in historical form. Fenn College's life, although brief (1923-1965), was filled with significant happenings which influenced, and for many years will continue to influence, the growth and development of Metropolitan Cleveland. The Fenn Alumni as well as those who completed part-time work in Fenn's evening division have been, and will continue to be instrumental in the advancements of the Cleveland community.

It would be impractical to include all of the many and varied highlights of Fenn College in one volume. The decision concerning what to include and what to omit was at times very exasperating. It is only natural that readers who have had many years of close contact with Fenn will look for certain anecdotes relating to their campus experiences. Obviously, there will be a number of disappointments, but these may be offset by the host of opportunities for pleasant reminiscing.

Historical firsts and affairs of the College involving policy were given the right of way. Many events, perforce, were sidetracked, but are available for reference in the files containing the important happenings of the College during the terms of all three of Fenn's Presidents. These files are in the office of the Fenn Educational Fund located in the suite of offices of The Cleveland Foundation at 700 National City Bank Building, Cleveland, Ohio 44114. Other archival material is available for reference in the Archives office, room 502, fifth floor, Library-Office Tower Building of The Cleveland State University.

Acknowledgement is made for the work of the late George B. Simon, Professor Emeritus of Speech, as Fenn's first Archivist in assembling historical records and artifacts of the College, and for the work of his successor, Professor Millard L. Jordan, who carried forward the archival research activity at Fenn and later at The Cleveland State University. Mention must also be made of Ethel Hamilton, Secretary to both Professors Simon and Jordan, who executed the tedious work of file prep-aration for all of the historical records, and who was always happily willing to provide archive material for the author's review.

Acknowledgement is made to Mathilda K. Duldner who was remark-ably adept in deciphering the author's handwriting in the preparation of the typed draft for this book.

But, extra special acknowledgement is made to Clayton G. Hale, Trustee of Fenn from 1933 to the dissolution of the College in 1965, who meticulously edited the author's draft as each chapter was completed. His memory of most of the events created a bit of reminiscing which ofttimes occasioned additional historical incidents to be added to the draft. The author is deeply indebted to Mr. Hale.

The author is also beholden to C. Howard Allen, Jr., who served as consultant in the publication of this book. His knowledge of the minute details concerning each step leading to the production of the final bound volume was invaluable. The many hours spent with him in proofreading and other important facets in gathering together all the elements in-volved in the publication of the book proved most helpful.

G. Brooks Earnest

CONTENTS

CHAPTER XVI

I

*The direction in which education starts a man
will determine his future life.*

Plato, 427–345 BC.

The progenitor of Fenn College was the Young Men's Christian Association, ofttimes referred to as the Association, the YMCA, or just the Y. The founding of the YMCA can be traced back to London, England, where George Williams, a dry goods clerk, together with J. Christopher Smith began a series of prayer meetings. The movement spread, and on June 6, 1844, a meeting was called to form a society to extend further this practice among London stores. Two weeks later, on June 20, 1844, at Smith's suggestion the name "The Young Men's Christian Association" was adopted. Williams, a young layman, twenty-three years old, was the guiding spirit in this new venture, and to this day he is credited as being the founder.

The first YMCA founded in the Western Hemisphere was at Montreal, Canada, on December 9, 1851, followed immediately by one in Toronto, both patterned after the Y in London.

The movement in the United States can be traced to Boston, Massachusetts, where, after a series of meetings beginning December 15, 1851, a constitution was finally adopted December 29, 1851, also patterned after the Y in London. In 1852 YMCA's were founded in Worcester and Springfield, Massachusetts; Buffalo, New York; Washington, D.C.; New London, Connecticut; Detroit, Michigan; and New Orleans, Louisiana. The following year, 1853, eleven additional YMCA's were founded in the cities of Baltimore, Alexandria, Chicago, Peoria, Louisville, San Francisco, Providence, Brooklyn, Lexington, Quincy, Illinois and Portland, Maine. In 1853, the Young Men's Society of Religious Inquiry founded in 1848 in Cincinnati, Ohio, merged with the YMCA

1

An organizational meeting for the establishment of a YMCA in Cleveland was held February 6, 1854. Those present were Dr. Aiken, Acting Chairman, S. B. Shaw, Secretary, Dr. Cleveland, S. H. Mather, Loren Prentiss, M. M. Battey, E. W. Roby, and E. F. Young. The actual founding date of the Cleveland YMCA is February 28, 1854, at a meeting in the First Baptist Church on Seneca Street, now West 3rd Street. A constitution was adopted containing this statement: "The name of this society shall be, The Young Men's Christian Association of Cleveland and its objects, the improvement of the religious and *intellectual* condition of men."*

J. B. Meriam attended the founding meeting of the Cleveland YMCA. The name Meriam has been prominent in YMCA history. This first J. B. Meriam was President of the Cleveland Y from 1879–1883. He was the uncle of J. W. Meriam, Chairman of the Board, and a great uncle of J. B. Meriam, Jr., President, of the Meriam Instrument Company, to whom Fenn College was indebted for the gift of the equipment in The Meriam Hydraulics Laboratory.

A vigorous existence was sustained from 1854 to 1863, but the demands of the Civil War and the expanding work of the sanitary and Christian missions caused suspension of the YMCA activity in 1863. The entire library was donated to the Cleveland Library Association with the express condition that the library would henceforth maintain a department of religious books. This era of the Y is known as the "Old Association," and its activities for this duration were mostly religious.

After this breach in the continuity of the YMCA from 1863 to 1867, the first meeting of the so-called "Modern Association" was called by C. E. Bolton on April 1, 1867, to organize a YMCA in Cleveland. No hint was given that the organization had previously existed from 1854 to 1863. At the third meeting of the group, April 29, the following excerpt from a new constitution was adopted: "The object of this Association shall be the improvement of the spiritual, *mental*, social and physical condition of Young Men by means of harmony with the Gospel."

The first mention of Sereno Peck Fenn occurred in the minutes of the meeting of July 8, 1867; he reported as a delegate to a meeting of

---

* *Underscoring* will be provided to emphasize the educational interests of the YMCA.

the YMCA in Montreal. The successor to the Cleveland YMCA School of Technology, Fenn College, was named in honor of Sereno Peck Fenn, who was born in Tallmadge, Ohio, on April 25, 1844, less than two months prior to the founding of the Y in London. He grew up on his father's farm and attended the district schools and for two years the Humiston Military Institute. He came to Cleveland in 1862 and enlisted in Co. B-164th Ohio Infantry in 1864 and was discharged later the same year. He was employed as a clerk in the freight department of the Big Four Railroad from 1865 to April 1870.

Henry A. Sherwin and Fenn became acquainted through their activities in the YMCA. Sherwin was undoubtedly greatly impressed with Fenn, for on April 1, 1870, Fenn joined the Sherwin-Williams Co. as a bookkeeper. He served this company for fifty years ending his career with it as Vice-President and Treasurer.

In 1892, at the age of 48, Sereno Peck Fenn was elected to the office of president of the YMCA. He held this office through a series of reelections until 1917—a span of twenty-five years, unequalled in the history of the Y to the present day (1974). Upon his retirement he was elected Honorary President, but he maintained his dedicated interest in the work of the Y. He gave considerable time and financial aid to the Educational Branch as will be described later.

On September 1, 1870, the Y Board of Trustees, at a meeting in the Y headquarters in the Hogan and Wade block, appointed Rawson, Falbey, and Irvine to a newly created Educational Committee. This committee was invited "to take into consideration and to provide for, if thought best, a series of free evening schools, lectures or classes for the benefit of young men coming with the Y or others who may desire to attend." Later at a meeting held February 9, 1871, the Educational Committee reported on the progress to date and recorded a vote of thanks to Professors Le Vasseuer and Esch for organizing and teaching free classes in French and German. The founding date of Fenn College, therefore, may well have been 1870; however, those officially concerned at a later date with the subject of a founding date for the college felt that such a conclusion would be unrealistic.

In 1871, Henry A. Sherwin was elected President of the Y, and later the same year, Lang Scheaff was engaged as the first full-time General Superintendent. This title was changed to General Secretary in 1873.

The oldest existing copy of the Cleveland YMCA Constitution was printed in 1871 and "the provisions declared unalterable, were those which stated the object of the Association," thus, "The improvement of the spiritual, moral, *mental*, social and physical condition of young men."

The classes in French and German evidently were only in operation from 1870 to and including 1872. Aside from Bible classes no educational program was mentioned in the Y Minutes until January 15, 1876, when the Board approved the following motion: "Steps should be taken to have a night school established with suitable teachers and paid from the school fund of the State of Ohio." No record of actual classes was found.

On November 16, 1878, the Board approved the erection of a gymnasium at 79 Public Square with funds then available and to be collected. Cost to individual members was $1.00 extra for organized classes in physical education (culture).

Joseph B. Meriam, President of the "Old Association," 1861–1862, became President of the "Modern Association" in 1879 and served to 1883. The YMCA and Fenn College owed much to his inspiring leadership. He was born in Randolph, Ohio, January 21, 1827, the son of a Presbyterian minister (his father served one parish in Randolph for sixty years, his entire ministerial life). After graduating from Western Reserve Academy at Hudson, Ohio, he came to Cleveland to assume the principalship of Shaw Academy (now Shaw High School in East Cleveland). He joined in partnership with a Mr. Morgan in the paraffin industry, later a refining industry. He became one of Cleveland's leading citizens and philanthropists. He died February 20, 1901, at the age of 74. Meriam C. Herrick, Admissions Director at Fenn College and a member of the Fenn Staff from September 1, 1938, to September 1, 1965, was a great nephew of Mr. Meriam.

For many years 1881 was considered the founding date of Fenn College. This founding date first appeared on the cover of the 1933 College Bulletin on the face of the College seal, centered in the vertical axis thereof and immediately below the emblem. Professor Emeritus George B. Simon in researching historical data for Fenn College was unable to determine by whom, when, and how the year 1881 was chosen as the year in which Fenn College was founded. Nevertheless the records do show that in the Fall of 1881 quasi-private evening classes were established in elocution, business training or bookkeeping, French, Latin, and art, on the premises of the YMCA. This same year the constitution was amended to create "A Board of Managers," a Y-controlling body which is still in operation today.

Thompson's history* states that: "the Annual Report presented in the Spring of 1882, listed the following classes offered by the Association: commercial law, bookkeeping, drawing, vocal music, German, Latin, lecture courses." There is no record as to the date of organization or duration of these classes. The Educational Committee appointed June 2, 1882, included H. M. Ingham, H. A. Sherman, and M. Lauer. There is no record, however, of official educational activities occurring until September 1887 when it was reported that there would be classes in Stenography by Professor Alfred Day, Vocal Music by Professor Fox, Freehand Drawing, professor to be appointed, and Orchestral Music by Professor Amme. On December 7, 1887, the General Secretary read his statistical report to the Board and for the first time the classes were given official recognition as follows:

> Shorthand classes   —   attendance 84
> Vocal Music   —   attendance 96.

Little can be gleaned from the Minutes of the Board during this era regarding the educational program. However, the Y periodical *Our Young Men* states that "the evening classes were established last year (1888), this becomes a first" (IV [1889]:8). The May 1889 issue carried the following quotation:

> Educational Classes—The season just closed was really the first actual test of the value of the evening class feature, as an attraction to young men. That this will be a permanent department of our work in the future and that special provision for its enlargement and permanency in the new building, will sufficiently answer the question, did it pay?

> | | |
> |---|---|
> | Total enrollment: | 97* |
> | German: | 26 |
> | Shorthand: | 42 |
> | Penmanship: | 31 |
> | Vocal Music: | 18 |
> | To finish the term: | 48 |

---

* *The Young Mens Christian Association* by Russell Thompson (Published by the Association in 1901).
* The total indicates there were multiple registrations.

The name of the periodical *Our Young Men* was changed to *"Cleveland's Young Men"* in 1890, and the June 1890 issue reported the following:

| | | Attendance | |
Subject	Instructor	Total	Average
Penmanship	E. L. Glick	442	18
Bookkeeping	W. H. Foote	478	20
Shorthand	M. G. Baxter	140	6
German	G. A. Ruelenik	233	12
Vocal Music	C. B. Ellinwood	206	10
Mechanical Drawing	J. W. Russell	146	7
French	Geo. Delon	209	9

Total enrollment 157   Newton M. Anderson Ch'm.

This is really the first instance of the promotion of a program of elementary status resembling continuity in education. In the Fall term of 1890 Frank L. Dyke taught penmanship. Later in 1893 he founded Dyke School which later became Dyke and Spencerian College and is now known as Dyke College.

The outstanding event of 1891 was the move into the newly constructed building on the southeast corner of Prospect Avenue and Erie Street (now East 9th Street). An open house was held the week of February 2. Sereno Peck Fenn was elected to the post of Director, and the Committee on Instruction and Lectures reported in June a total enrollment of 147 in seven evening classes. The average attendance of each class was ten at a total cost of $486. In addition five lectures were delivered on economic, historical, and scientific subjects, to a total attendance of 559.

Eighteen hundred and ninety-two was an important year in that Sereno Peck Fenn was elected President of the Y on May 31. The twenty-fifth anniversary of the Association was held this year (1867–1892), although the original founding date was 1854. Actually the centennial anniversary was commemorated in 1954, and there is a bronze plaque affixed to the Society National Bank Building, Public Square, to the right of the main entrance attesting to this fact. This was the site of the first building owned "in fee simple" by the YMCA.

From the very beginning, as displayed in all statistical reports, the educational activities of the Y were publicized under the symbol of the triangle, the three sides of which were dedicated to equality of service to the body, the mind, and the spirit of men.

The first inference of examinations, certificates, and diplomas appeared in 1893, as follows: "The first examination under the new system of grading took place February 21st 1893. Although 24 attended the requisite number of classes, only 15 were examined. Of this number 11 passed sufficiently high to take their first certificate. It is the purpose of the Association to give diplomas to any one who takes the full year and a half's course (3 semesters), and passes a satisfactory examination in all three with A grades."

Glen K. Shurtleff was elected General Secretary of the Board of Trustees in August 1893 and served in this capacity until 1909. He had a prime interest in educational activities of the Y. A classroom in the Central Y was later named in his honor.

It is of interest to note that "the second commencement exercises were held on Monday evening, April 23rd, 1894." Therefore, the first exercises were presumably held in 1893, but there is no record of them. W. H. Foote was engaged in 1894 as the first paid Educational Director. He served as such until 1899.

A State Committee surveyed enrollments in twenty-six institutions of higher education in Ohio in 1894 and reported that the Association's Evening College ranked second with an enrollment of 670 students. Only Ohio State University with an enrollment of 700 evening students surpassed the record of the Cleveland YMCA.

On February 27, 1895, Sereno Peck Fenn urged "the building of an annex to the main building (Prospect and East 9th) to meet the need of the educational and physical work." A mortgage on the main building was authorized and the annex was erected on East 9th Street.

There was a lapse in the record pertaining to the educational activities of the Y for the latter half of 1895, also for years 1896, 1897, and the first quarter of 1898. This undoubtedly came about because of the organization of The Cleveland Commercial University which was actually housed in the Y building. Forty courses were proposed divided among fourteen departments. After about three years of apparent competition with the Y educational program in the same building, the new University died a natural death. By the Fall of 1898 the Y educational calendar published the following courses:

1st, 2nd, & 3rd Mechanical Drawing   1st & 2nd Penmanship
1st & 2nd Electricity   1st Algebra
1st & 2nd Bookkeeping   English Correspondence
Literary Science   Spelling
1st & 2nd Steam Engineering   Spanish
1st Stenography   1st & 2nd Chemistry
1st, 2nd & 3rd Arithmetic   Geometry
Freehand Drawing
First Aid

W. H. Foote resigned as Educational Director during the summer of 1899, and George P. Kurtz was appointed as his successor. Kurtz, an alumnus of Adelbert College of Western Reserve University, served until May 10, 1900. T. T. Long succeeded Kurtz and served until April 1902.

Perhaps the genesis of the very friendly relationship between industry and Fenn College can be traced to the following unsigned article printed late in 1899, the closing year of the nineteenth century. "One firm who sent eleven of its employees to the classes, presented each one of them with a sum of money equal to his class fees, for a Christmas present."

The first mention of an Alumni Association is found in 1900. All men who completed a course in the evening classes and received a grade entitling them to a certificate were eligible for membership. An organizational dinner meeting was held in Society Hall (Y Building) April 27, 1900. Dinner was served at 25 cents a plate. A goodly number of graduates were present to meet with members of the Educational Committee and the Faculty. Harry McKnight was elected as the first president, S. S. Robinson as vice president and Clifford Franklin as Secretary. E. S. Babcock, J. P. Henry, Arthur Frazier, and William Shively were elected to the Executive Committee. The forerunner of class banquets took place March 27, 1903. The dinner, also at a cost of 25 cents per student, was termed to be "the end of a perfect day."

A total of 30 different courses were scheduled for the first term and 34 for the second term in 1901. Four clubs were organized, namely: debating, camera, Shakespeare, and current topics. E. C. Morey succeeded T. T. Long as Educational Director in the summer of 1902. Director E. C. Morey edited a weekly news article directed to the students and for the most part of an "inspirational nature." A few, however, were informative to the lay public. His name disappeared from the records after February 5, 1904, and in the fall of that year, M. N. Fowler was engaged as employment secretary. He soon became the fifth Educational Director.

In May 1904, Fowler announced a new course in Automobile Instruction. The increase in the manufacture and use of motor vehicles had created a demand for a new line of mechanical knowledge. The instruction was executed by George S. Case of Case School of Applied Science (father of George S. Case, Jr., Trustee of Fenn College from 1948 to 1959). Some thirty students enrolled in the first class, and this was the beginning of a specialized class of instruction in automotive engineering that was to be part of the institution for many years.

The schedule for the evening classes starting January 3, 1905, carried 39 courses of study including the day, hour, and the cost per term. For the first time the format of the schedule began to resemble a college bulletin. A sufficient number of the courses leaned toward departmental status. In fact, one could almost allocate such courses to Departments of Business, Engineering, and Art.

The Educational Director Fowler suggested on January 4, 1906: "the advisability of continuing the movement for industrial education." The Automobile School as of January 25 was enjoying the most successful year to date; fifty men were enrolled. In fact, the very first day-time classes were in the Automobile School.

The Minutes of the Board for April 19, 1906, carry the following:

A letter from A. B. Williams, Secretary, Central Department was read to the Board of Trustees.

At a meeting of our Committee of Management held this noon, the establishment of a *Day School* as a part of the Association's educational scheme was discussed. It was finally moved and carried that the project be approved [this undoubtedly refers to a motion that $3,000 be expended for alterations to enlarge class room area], that the Educational Committee be requested to secure guarantors up to the amount of a possible $600 deficit, payable April 1, 1907 and that the budget of the Educational Committee be increased $1,300 to cover the enterprise.

A. B. Williams, Sec'y
E. W. Palmer
F. S. McGowan
Frank A. Scott

Approved:

Day School opened September 10, 1906, with the following departments represented: Stenographic, Business Training, Mechanical Engineering, English, and College Preparatory. The growing institution created a need for an all-inclusive name. Accordingly, the Y house organ, *Cleveland's Young Men*, of mid-1906 carried the following article:

> The educational activities of the Young Men's Christian Association now are known—as seen in the composition of this issue—as "*Association Institute*". This name was adopted in order that the Day and Evening Schools and tributary organizations might be known by a single comprehensive name, rather than by an unlimited number. Association is calculated to incorporate every branch of educational work.

The evening classes of the Association Institute began October 1, 1906, to cover a period of three terms of 12 weeks each instead of the previous two 10-week terms per year.

The Automobile School introduced a new course in electrical vehicles during the Winter term starting January 9, 1907. Mr. A. N. Bentley, M.E., from Cornell University was in charge.

The Association Institute had a total enrollment of 740 in the fall of 1907 which was an increase of 210 over the previous Fall. The Day School had an enrollment of about 60 and the ages ranged from 14 to 40.

On March 25, 1908, the "All School Dinner" was dignified to the status of "All School Banquet." Dr. Charles S. Howe, President of Case School of Applied Science, delivered the address on "the significance of evening education." The cost of the dinner was 50 cents, double the cost of the "All School Dinner" in 1903.

Judge Frederick A. Henry was duly sworn in as a Trustee of the Association on April 28, 1908, and subsequently became president thereof, serving from 1936 to 1938. He took a very active part in the educational branch of the Association. YMCA General Secretary Glen K. Shurtleff, who had taken office September 1893, died in January of 1909. He was succeeded by Robert E. Lewis, who served in this office until 1928. Joseph H. Peck, who joined the Y Staff in 1897, became assistant treasurer May 4, 1909, and remained in active service until 1938. His major contribution to the educational branch rested on his keen sense of financial responsibility in maintaining a respectable balance between income and expenditures.

On May 19, 1909, Sereno Peck Fenn was reelected President of the Y, and on June 22 of the same year the following five committees were filled by appointment: Executive, Finance, Departments, Property, and Church Cooperation. The educational activities were placed under the jurisdiction of the Committee on Departments which provokes the assumption that the educational program was not of sufficient importance to warrant the establishment of a committee whose services would be devoted exclusively to the field of education.

There were four Day Schools in 1909, the objectives were as follows:

The School of Commerce and Finance
"Prepares for a business career: for accounting, bookkeeping, stenography, and of general office positions."

The Technical School
"Prepares for industrial life, for drafting and electrical positions."

The Preparatory School
"Prepares for colleges, commercial, technical, law, medical, dental or high school."

The Special School
"For young men and boys who feel out of place in public schools; who have lost time through sickness; who are too big for their grade; etc. The tuition rates are low and include all Association privileges" (This was termed the "Department of Misfits" and there were 19 in the first class).

The School of Commerce and Finance became the School of Commerce, Accounts and Finance and later the School of Business Administration of Fenn College. The Technical School became the YMCA School of Technology, and later the School of Engineering of Fenn College. The Preparatory School became the Nash Junior College and later the School of Arts and Sciences of Fenn College. The Special School really had no successor at Fenn College.

In December 1909 the Board took an option to purchase the lot at the southeast corner of Prospect Avenue and East 22nd Street, and a campaign was started immediately to raise $500,000 for the construction of a new headquarters building.

The December 1909 report of the new Educational Department carried the following statements:

The Fall term of the Day School was ended by a dinner and an afternoon of contests and class rivalry in the gymnasium. The musical part of the dinner program was given by the well known Hruby Brothers, three talented young men who have given up their concert tour this year in order to attend the Special Department of our Day School. (The three Hruby Brothers referred to were Frank, Alois and John, in all there were six brothers in the family, all musical. Five of the brothers played at one time in the Cleveland Orchestra, accompanying such artists as Caruso, Kreisler and Paderewski. The Hruby Conservatory of Music was a very popular school of music which in the mid 1940's had an enrollment of 750 students. Frank Hruby, Jr., who has been Music Critic for The Cleveland Press for seventeen years informed the author that his father, still living in 1974, informed him that the three brothers, who had been giving concert tours in United States and Europe—violin, cello and piano—cancelled their concert tour in 1909 to study German and English at the YMCA. Because of their many tours in the United States and Europe, especially Germany, they wanted to become more proficient in English and German).

Other students in the Day School are making big sacrifices and working many hours a day in order to secure an education. One young man sells newspapers in the morning and has a street lamp lighting route in the afternoon. Another boy runs an elevator from five in the evening until one o'clock in the morning. A man, twenty-eight years of age, works in the steel mills from 6:00 p.m. until 7:00 a.m., comes to the Day School until eleven thirty and uses only the afternoon for sleep. A man fifty-three years of age, having to give up his former work as a railway conductor because of a physical injury, is preparing for an office position. A younger man, married and with children in the public schools, is spending six months in the technical classes to fit himself for a promotion. A young man, born in Finland, whose home is in the large Finnish Colony at Ashtabula, has come to spend three months studying English in the Special Department. One of the Chinese proprietors of the Mandarin Restaurant spends one hour each afternoon studying English under Mr. Fox. [It appears that Fenn College's forerunner practiced semi-cooperative education under the title of "Special Department.]

The total expenses for the academic year 1908–1909 were $13,445.11. The income for the year was $9,775.53. Therefore, the deficit for the year was $3,669.58. No explanation was given for the manner in which this deficit was covered. The following year, however, was better, the income being within $1,198.41 of the total expenses.

In 1910 a new course was added to the curricula through the new Cleveland School of Accountancy managed by Pace and Pace of New York City as a part of the educational program of the YMCA. Trustees of the YMCA voted unanimously on March 28, 1910, to pay $135,000 for the Childs property on the southeast corner of Prospect Avenue and East 22nd Street as the site for a new Y building of at least 250 rooms. Mr. Oscar M. Miller succeeded M. N. Miller as Educational Director about April 1, 1910.

The April 1910 minutes of the Educational Department stated:

> During the month the Educational Director had a communication from the Hill-Clutch Company asking if some plan of co-operation could be arranged so that the apprentices and young mechanics of their firm can be instructed in evening classes, mainly at the expense of the Company.
>
> The kind of instruction which apprentices need is that which will particularly help in understanding the principles of machine construction and shop mathematics. A *Co-operative Plan* whereby the practical training is obtained in a commercial shop and the theory in a special school is now known to be the most effective way of making thoroughly trained mechanics.
>
> Believing that more than one firm would be interested in such a proposition, the Director has been calling on the superintendents of other shops. These superintendents very heartily favor any plan that will give these young men more education. Another firm, the Cleveland Twist Drill Company, has already asked to have twelve of their young men admitted if we decide to inaugurate such classes. [This is just another example of the conception of the *co-operative plan* by the Educational Department of the YMCA in 1910, thirteen years in advance of the actual founding of Fenn College and its cooperative program of higher education.] For the record, the new apprenticeship *cooperative plan* was inaugurated and its costs were entirely subscribed by the Twist Drill Company, The Hill-Clutch Company, the Cleveland Foundry Company and the Peerless Motor Car Company. By the end of the first year of operation of this plan the following sponsors were added to the list: Cleveland Punch and Shear, Ferro Machine and Foundry, National Acme, Rauch & Lang, Baker Motor, Cleveland Wire Spring, Re-

liance Electric, American Multigraph, National Carbon, Osborn Manufacturing Company and P. A. Geier & Co.

The Board of Trustees voted to accept the working drawings for the new headquarters building (at Prospect Avenue and East 22nd Street) as submitted by the architect on December 24, 1910. The building was to have a maximum cost limit of $500,000. The contract for construction was approved May 24, 1911. Ground had already been broken for the new headquarters building on the previous April 20.

The following excerpt is from an editorial in the *Cleveland Leader* of September 23, 1910, under the headline "The YMCA Classes":

> While it is not so much in the spotlight as the schools and colleges, there is one institution in Cleveland which is doing an educational work (not possible for them) that deserves attention. It is the Young Men's Christian Association.

The Executive Committee of the Board of Trustees authorized the purchase of the farm land now known as Centerville Mills Camp on June 7, 1911. Possession was taken on November 18 of the same year. In later years the incoming Freshmen at Fenn College spent a weekend at the YMCA Centerville Mills Camp as a get-acquainted session prior to the start of the Fall term.

Seemingly, a bit of salesmanship was included in a memo dated December 28, 1911, by attempting to entice new students through offering a special tuition inducement. Note the following:

> *Two weeks free to new students*
>
> The tuition fees pay for 15 weeks after January 15th, but all new students will be given the first two weeks in January without cost—seventeen full weeks at the price of fifteen.

Miss Almeda J. Rothrock entered the employ of the Y on January 15, 1912, while the headquarters was still located at Prospect and East 9th Street. She served the Y and Fenn College faithfully and well. She was confidential secretary to the Educational Director and subsequently to Dr. C. V. Thomas while he was President of Fenn College.

The new "Cleveland Cooperative Apprentice School" opened February 1, 1912. The school was designed to instruct young men in the shops and factories to become skilled mechanics. The unique feature was the provision that the tuition was paid by the employers who also permitted the apprentices a half day off per week, on full pay, to attend classes at the Y. Note how the word *cooperative* comes into play even during the early years of the Y's educational activities. The early establishment of friendships between the Y and Cleveland industry undoubtedly paved the way for cordial reception of the college credit co-op program when it was instituted in 1923.

Charles E. Adams, second Vice President of the Y, at the April 1912 meeting of the Corporation eulogized President Sereno Peck Fenn for his twenty years of unselfish service to the community in general and in particular to the YMCA. "When Mr. Fenn was elected President of the Association in 1892," so Adams said, "the educational department taught 9 subjects and had an enrollment of 247, while in 1912, student enrollment totalled 1121, and 37 subjects were taught." Forty-four different subjects were offered in the Fall of 1912. Table 1 records a number of statistics concerning the Evening School.

TABLE 1

EVENING SCHOOL STATISTICS

Year	Number Students	Number Classes (Evening)	Total Expense	Total Income	Loss — or Gain +
1901–02	1,019	25	$ 4,669	$ 2,169	—$2,500
1902–03	745	33	4,546	2,420	— 2,126
1903–04	534	31	4,788	2,695	— 2,093
1904–05	688	39	5,084	3,110	— 1,974
1905–06	703	39	5,647	3,953	— 1,694
1906–07	965	41	12,368	11,356	— 1,012
1907–08	1,271	44	21,281	16,801	— 4,480
1908–09	898	38	24,966	19,970	— 4,996
1909–10	812		12,445	11,247	— 1,198
1910–11	915	32	16,495	16,777	+ 281
1911–12	1,121	38	22,932	22,731	— 201
1912–13	1,580				
1913–14	1,603				

Starting with Friday, December 27, 1912, there followed seven days of program termed inauguration week. Sunday, December 29, was the day set aside for the actual dedication ceremonies of the new headquarters building at Prospect Avenue and East 22nd Street.

The following is an excerpt from William Ganson Rose's book *Cleveland: The Making of a City*:

There was jubilation at the dedication of the new YMCA building, December 29, at the corner of East 22nd Street and Prospect Avenue, because a fund-raising campaign had left the structure, costing $759,767, debt-free. Speakers included Bishop William A. Leonard, Dr. Henry Churchill King, President Sereno P. Fenn, Charles E. Adams, chairman of the building committee, and Secretary Robert E. Lewis.

Not much information is available for the year 1913 concerning the Educational Department. An article dated August 21, 1913, noted that,

the day time operation of the Educational Division falls within the confines of 3 schools, which are now designated as sections as follows:

> The Commercial Section
> The Technical Section
> The Preparatory Section

Evidently the Special School instituted in 1909 was dropped about this time.

The winter teaching schedule of January 1914 shows 51 elementary and advanced classes due to open January 19, and interestingly enough it offers discounts for cash at the time of enrollment.

The date of organization of the first Day School basketball team is unknown. The first mention of such a team reports that early in February 1914 the Day School defeated East Tech 24 to 9 in basketball.

The Apprentice School under the direction of H. C. Bayliss, Assistant Educational Director, continued to prosper in 1914 with the financial aid and hearty cooperation of seventeen representative industrial corporations of Cleveland.

Adrian D. Joyce, then General Manager of Sales of the Sherwin-Williams Co., addressed the class in salesmanship May 21, 1914, on the occasion of their annual banquet. Thirty-six years later, in 1950, Joyce was elected a Trustee of Fenn College, and at the commencement convocation held May 29, 1953, he received the honorary degree of "Doctor of Business Administration" (D.BA.) from Fenn College. Joyce died August 8, 1954, and left a bequest of $10,000 to Fenn College.

On September 1, 1914, Louis W. Hunt, a recent June graduate of the University of Michigan, joined the faculty in the field of chemistry. He later became chairman of the department and served in this capacity until his resignation August 31, 1939.

A name that lived long with the educational activities of the Y and Fenn College was G. Hamlin Mouck. He, too, joined the faculty in September 1914 as a supervisor of the accounting system installed in the "Cleveland School of Accountancy" managed by Pace and Pace of New York. Mouck resigned in 1916 to join the Security Discount Co. He was later appointed to the Y-Tech Board of Governors and taught part-time in the evening school. On September 1, 1936, he was appointed a full-time member of the faculty of Fenn College. He retired with Professor Emeritus of Accounting status on June 8, 1956, and passed away May 20, 1967, at his home in Franklin, Pennsylvania. In the book entitled *The Story of Accountancy*, copyrighted in 1954 by the Ohio Association of Certified Public Accountants, there appears this tribute: "Undoubtedly more students have been taught accounting by Professor G. Hamlin Mouck of Fenn than by any other teacher in Cleveland for he has been teaching continuously since 1914. Many of our early CPA's and private accountants studied under Professor Mouck. He is and always has been held in high respect by his students."

Oscar M. Miller resigned as Educational Director on August 14, 1914, and Richard J. Hoddinott was immediately appointed Acting Director. On April 1, 1915, Mr. Hoddinott was appointed Educational Secretary and Director.

During the school year 1913–1914 there were 1,251 students in the night school and 352 in the day school for a total of 1,603. There were 11 full-time teachers and 40 on a part-time basis. One day school student was appointed to West Point and one to Annapolis. Friends of the Educational Department contributed a total of $1,569 toward its operation.

The following statement appeared in a Y house-organ published early in 1915:

Manufacturers Support School

The school year in the Association School for Apprentices opened February 1. The attitude of the Cleveland employers towards the school is well illustrated by the fact that although many of them are running their plants with reduced forces, a majority of them are keeping the same number of apprentices in the school as was the case last year.

The Cleveland School of Accountancy held its annual banquet April 13, 1915, at the Hotel Statler. Eighty men were in attendance. The full course in accounting was acknowledged to be the "best preparation offered in the United States for those desiring to study in fitting themselves for examination for the degree of Certified Public Accountant under the laws of the various states."

President Sereno Peck Fenn appointed E. A. Scott, W. H. Prescott, and E. H. Baker as a committee of three to examine the budgets of the several departments for the fiscal year 1915–1916. E. H. Baker, Jr., became a Trustee of Fenn College in 1932 and was appointed an Honorary Life Trustee November 20, 1956, and passed away August 8, 1962.

Professor George Simon is credited with this statement: "They [Y Tech Instructors] were men with a mission and their fields of action and usefulness were circumscribed only by the limitations of the tools given them for the execution of tasks assigned them." A special reference to one manifestation of instructor interest occurs in an article published August 26, 1915, as follows:

> An electrical course which surpasses anything obtainable elsewhere and equipment that is far ahead of many other schools is offered to prospective students by the day school for the coming year. This course which will start new classes September 7th, now covers two years time, has been placed in the hands of N. H. Brown. He has combined his technical, scholastic and practical experience towards a reorganization of the course.

On October 7, 1915, under the title "State Recognized Y School" in *Cleveland's Young Men* (Vol. XXX) the following quotation is of record:

> The Preparatory School of the Central Y achieved new honors last week when it gained recognition from the State Educational Department . . . in a letter received by the Educational Department (Y) from Frank W. Miller, Superintendent of Public Instruction, it was stated that all work done in the school at the Y would receive full credit by the state. . . .

It was reported in the *Red Triangle* of September 1, 1915, that Mr. C. M. Finfrock was appointed Dean of the evening school beginning the fall of 1915. He became the first person to hold the title of Dean in the Educational Division. Dean Finfrock later became Dean of the Law School at Western Reserve University.

Evidence is somewhat vague, but it points to the very first Student Council meeting as being held on or about October 15, 1915.

Four hundred of the day and night school students held their annual banquet on Thursday evening, December 2, 1915. The occasion was highlighted by a panel of speakers including Dr. Charles S. Howe, President of Case School of Applied Science, Dr. Charles F. Thwing, President of Western Reserve University, and J. M. H. Frederick, Superintendent, Cleveland City Schools. Each speaker complimented the Y "for the educational opportunities it offered to those who for the most part were unable to take advantage of either or both the elementary and the high schools."

Early in 1916 the University of Michigan notified the Y Educational Department that the Day School had been placed on its accredited list. About the same time a committee was appointed to study and plan for the creation of a retirement program for the Y employees including the instructing staff.

Cecil Vincent Thomas, who later became the first President of Fenn College, joined the staff of the Educational Department of the YMCA July 5, 1916, as Assistant to the Principal of the Day School, Assistant to the Educational Secretary, Instructor of English to the foreign born and Mathematics to the regular students. He had just graduated from The Ohio State University with a degree of Bachelor of Science in Education, specializing in mathematics. On September 1, 1916, he was appointed to the Office of Director, Evening Division, YMCA Schools. Later in the year on December 23, 1916, he was married to Sylvia May Moore of Ada, an alumna of Ohio Northern University.

On November 28, 1916, the Y Board secured options on three lots to the south and southeast of the Y building. A portion of this new property was later used in 1929 for the location of the Fenn Building and the remainder for a parking lot.

The following is excerpted from the December 28, 1916, issue of *Cleveland's Young Men* under the title "Day School Team Has a New Coach": "The basketball team of the Central Y Day School has a new coach, and he is a capable one, too. His name is Carl V. Weygandt, and he is a student at Western Reserve University Law School. He will also teach English in the Day School." Mr. Weygandt later served twenty-nine years as Chief Justice of the Supreme Court of the State of Ohio. Justice Weygandt was elected to the Board of Governors of the Cleveland YMCA School of Technology in 1928 and became a Trustee of the Y in 1929. He resigned his trusteeship in the Spring of 1933 to accept the robes of Chief Justice.

The first student edited paper was published in January 1917. It was called *The Day School News*. Jack Ludwig was Editor-in-Chief, James Thybere, Assistant Editor, and Walter Lanson, Cartoonist. No copies are available for reference of historical events.

The January 24, 1917, Minutes of the Y Board of Trustees carried the following very important letter:

> My dear Mr. Lewis:
> In consideration of our conversation of a few days ago in regard to the great and eminent needs of our Association, both in the Central Department and some of the Branches, and the necessity of providing relief in additional facilities at the earliest possible date, I hereby agree to contribute toward the accomplishment of this end, through plans which will be duly approved by the Trustees of the Association the sum of one hundred thousand ($100,000) dollars in cash or equivalent securities. The same to be paid as and when additional subscriptions shall have been made and paid within three years from this date, for not less than three hundred thousand ($300,000) dollars.
>
> Signed, S. P. Fenn

The three years evidently passed by without success in raising the total specified, for according to Archivist George B. Simon's research on this subject, Fenn later paid his $100,000 to the Y, and it was distributed in varying amounts between March 3, 1928, and January 7, 1929, at which time his total obligation was discharged. Through Dr. C. V. Thomas, Simon learned that the entire $300,000 specified in Fenn's letter was duly contributed by friends of the Association and approximately $210,000 went into construction of the Fenn Building in 1928. More about this later.

On April 6, 1917, President Woodrow Wilson appeared before Congress and, subject to its confirmation, declared that a state of war existed between the United States and Germany. Later in April under the command of Captain C. V. Thomas the boys of the Day School were organized along military lines into companies of 125 each. The gymnasium was used as a parade ground and fundamental tactics were taught with the aid of wands instead of guns. It so happened that C. V. Thomas had about four years of military training at Ohio Northern University plus some post graduate training in military manoeuvres at The Ohio State University.

The 49th Annual Meeting of the Association was held in the Auditorium of the Central Y Building on Wednesday, May 2, 1917, at 2:00 p.m. Judge Frederick A. Henry, a Trustee, paid high tribute to the faithfulness, loyalty and self-sacrifice of Fenn in his service to the Association as President over a period of twenty-five years. Ambrose Swasey succeeded Fenn as President. However, Fenn was elected to the new office of Honorary President for life. Ambrose Swasey served for one year, and Charles E. Adams succeeded him.

The Day School on August 23, 1917, expressed pride in its alumnus Frank E. Boldizar who had later graduated from the Cleveland School of Law and at the age of 22 was admitted to the Bar of Ohio as the youngest attorney in the state.

Commencement was held Thursday evening, August 16, 1917, at which diplomas were received by 23 graduates of the Preparatory, Business, Technical, and Elementary Schools.

Thirty-one different courses were taught during the first nine months of the 1917–1918 academic year. A total of 2,014 different students were enrolled. This is the first time enrollment exceeded the 2,000 mark. The distribution of areas of instruction is given in Table 2.
The discrepancy between total enrollment of 2,014 and class assignments of 2,573 was explained by a note which said, "Some students were pursuing two or more courses."

Vance Chamberlin, graduate of Case in 1916, joined the Y staff as a part-time instructor for the Summer Term of 1918. He taught trigonometry to the Naval Reserves. This was the beginning of a long association with the Y and Fenn College. He continued as a part-time instructor in the Evening Division, largely in the field of marketing, until December 1, 1946, at which time he was appointed to the Day Division faculty on a full-time basis as Assistant Professor of Marketing. September 1, 1948, he was appointed Acting Chairman, Department of Marketing, and on September 1, 1951, he was promoted to Associate Professor of Marketing and Chairman of the Department. He received his full professorship September 1, 1955, and retired as Professor Emeritus of Marketing from The Cleveland State Universty in June 1966.

An important decision was made by the Education Committee in August 1918 to admit women to a restricted list of classes. That fall 24 women enrolled in Accounting and a number of women students enrolled in Advertising, Applied English, Credits, and Traffic.

TABLE 2

DISTRIBUTION OF AREAS OF INSTRUCTION FOR 1917–1918

		Enrollment	Total
I.	Collegiate—Night Classes only:		
	a. Cleveland School of Accounting	277	
	b. Cleveland School of Salesmanship	129	
	c. Cleveland School of Commerce	310	
	d. Cleveland School of Engineering	155	
		—	
			871
II.	Preparatory:		
	a. Business	368	
	b. Cleveland Co-op Apprentice School (day)	35	
	c. College Preparatory School (day)	60	
	d. College Preparatory School (night)	383	
	e. Technical (day)	61	
	f. Technical (night)	379	
		—	
			1,286
III.	Pre-preparatory:		
	a. Day	54	
	b. Night	362	
		—	
			416
	TOTAL		2,573

The September 16, 1918, report to the Educational Committee had a significant bit of news which later proved to be the harbinger of an important era in the history of Fenn College:

> The outstanding success of our work during the summer has been the Naval Auxiliary Reserve School. The successful planning and carrying out of this project has been almost entirely due to Mr. Thomas, Director of Business and Preparatory School and the School of Commerce and Engineering. As a recognition of this splendid piece of work we feel he should be promoted to a position of larger responsibility as Associate Educational Secretary, with

responsibility covering the entire Educational Department but still to have active promotion of the two special schools of which he is now director.

This was the beginning of a new way of life for C. V. Thomas in that he apparently carried on his shoulders the responsibilities of two jobs right up to his death in 1947.

Here is another interesting paragraph from the same report:

Sam Hakola, one of the graduates of the Y Preparatory School in August, is now enrolled in the Colorado School of Mines. He was admitted on a scholarship worth $200 per year which was won by merit, and which was the only scholarship granted to the State of Ohio. Through the financial aid of one of our committee-men, Sam has been enabled to enter college this fall without being obliged to wait a year. . . . Day School opened this morning with a very fine enrollment, and for the first time in our history we have employed, as a regular instructor a woman teacher, made necessary by the war exigency.

The Educational Department on November 12, 1918, reported to the Educational Committee that:

The conclusion of peace will materially change our work in many regards. The demand for purely war courses will now be eliminated. This will mean a curtailing of income from these sources. On the other hand, it is quite possible that the end of the war will remove the element of uncertainty that has existed in the minds of many men during the past two years, and will assist enrollments in certain classes which were not so popular during war time.

The reconstruction period will bring many new opportunities to the Association [YMCA] Schools. What should be the objective of the Association School during the next five years? There is a need in Cleveland for a strong school of commerce. There is also a need for a strong night engineering school, and all of our former educational activities will be open to us in a larger measure than ever before.

In January 1919 an anonymous Cleveland banker established the first scholarship of record. It was a $37 gift earmarked for an outstanding and worthy student engaged in the study of bookkeeping.

The first instance in which C. V. Thomas signed the Minutes of the Educational Committee was April 29, 1919. He had been elected Secretary at a special meeting of the Educational Committee held April 16. He succeeded R. J. Hoddinott, and his salary was set at $2,400 per year. Hoddinott resigned April 30 to become Advertising and Promotion Manager of the Garfield Bank.

In May 1919 the Day School organized its first senior class composed of graduates of all departments and elected Paul Horasta as its President. A staff was elected to prepare and publish the "first School Annual." Those elected were: Wm. Hunt, Oscar Torreson, Paul Horasta, Frank Fredericks and Leopold Kushlau.

On July 8, 1919, Almeda J. Rothrock was reported as having joined the staff January 15, 1912, and that her length of service had been outstanding. The report further stated: "When facts are desired we consult her." She became Secretary to C. V. Thomas September 1916, and following his death she became Secretary to Arthur P. Loegler, Director of Finance. On September 1, 1948, she became Payroll Clerk in the Department of Finance. She retired to Tuscon, Arizona, August 29, 1958, where she died November 28, 1966.

John L. Severance presided at the June 1919 Commencement Exercises, and Fred W. Ramsey delivered the address.

An article authored by C. V. Thomas and published September 25, 1919, noted the following: "Nearly 500 more students have enrolled at the Y so far this year, than for the same period last year." As a result of this extraordinary increase in enrollment three additional classrooms were constructed on the ninth floor of the Central building and four new ones in a building on Carnegie Avenue owned by the Y. In addition a new Electrical Laboratory was installed in the basement of the Central building.

Shades of the 1950–1960s appear in the October 13, 1919, report of the Educational Department, thus: "Mr. Glaze and the engineering staff have done a fine piece of work in the Electrical Laboratory. The walls have not been painted, but in the main the Electrical Laboratory is in excellent condition." Mr. Glaze was Superintendent of Buildings for the YMCA. The coincidence arises from the fact that his grandson, Harold Glaze, became Superintendent of Buildings and Grounds for Fenn College in August, 1955 and still held this office for The Cleveland State University in 1974.

A report of the Educational Department to the Educational Committee December 16, 1919, read as follows: "Mr. Lewis called a meeting of the Executive Committee of the Board of Trustees consisting of Franklin G. Smith, Charles E. Adams, F. W. Ramsey, S. P. Fenn, J. L. Severance and D. C. Wills. This Committee authorized the borrowing of funds ($35,569) sufficient to purchase machines and tools which were being advertised by the Salvage Division of the Ordnance Department."

Samuel Ward and P. F. Ellsworth were engaged to teach in the School of Engineering in 1920, Ward as an Instructor and Ellsworth as Director of the School.

On May 18, 1920, the Board of Trustees approved a YMCA retirement plan which was submitted by Sereno Peck Fenn. When Fenn College and the YMCA agreed on a legal separation early in 1951 many of the so-called "old timers" elected to remain in the YMCA retirement program rather than transfer to the Teachers Insurance and Annuity Association adopted by Fenn as a private College.

Secretary Thomas is authority for the statement in mid-1920 "that the 3603 students now enrolled, an increase of 19% over last year has broken all records, . . . and that 124 paid instructors taught 59 different classes." The Day Y Preparatory School was accredited by the North Central Association of Colleges and Secondary Schools in 1920. Also during the year 1920 the Educational Department made a number of requests to the Y Board of Trustees that negotiations be made with the owners of the Johnson Building and adjacent Edwards Building for classroom usage for the expanding enrollment. The Edwards Building was rehabilitated later in the year. The new Machine Shop School was opened at Chester Avenue and East 23rd Street in July 1920. An interior photo of the shop was reminiscent of a bygone day. All machines were belt driven from line shafts so the interior view was a veritable sea of belts.

Leyton E. Carter, A.B., Oberlin '14, joined the faculty of the YMCA Schools in October 1920. He did graduate work at Columbia from 1914 to 1917 and taught Political Science at Western Reserve University from 1917 to 1920. He became Chairman of the Cleveland Foundation in 1928 and a Trustee of Fenn College in 1933. He taught many classes in Government in the Evening Division of Fenn College and was very active in civic affairs. He died November 16, 1953.

An important personage who was to rise high in academic circles in Ohio, Howard W. Jones, joined the teaching staff of the Y Schools September 1920 as Physical Director and Instructor of Mathematics and Drafting. He had just graduated from Hiram College in June. He later served as Principal of the Preparatory School and resigned August 15, 1928, to accept the position of Assistant to the President of Hiram College. He later became President of Youngstown University and retired from that office about 1965.

The December 1, 1920, Report of the Educational Department carried the following important history:

> At the last regular meeting of this committee the privilege of incorporating the YMCA Schools was approved. Since that time the Educational Committee has been actively at work on the form of incorporation. Suggestive articles of incorporation have been drawn up, together with by-laws, and these are being worked over by the Educational Committee. The following was adopted at the last regular meeting: "The Cleveland School of Commerce and Technology of the Young Men's Christian Association", as the school name. This name includes both the Business Administration and the Engineering courses offered by the Schools. Correspondence with Detroit, Boston, Portland, Oregon and Baltimore indicates that this step is one of the most helpful that the schools have taken thus far. The results accruing from similar actions in the above cities have been most helpful in establishing the schools in the minds of the general public.

The following officers were elected to constitute the incorporators: Franklin G. Smith, President; F. W. Ramsey, Vice President; D. C. Wills, Treasurer; Robert E. Lewis, General Secretary; W. R. Green, Chairman, Educational Committee. The purpose of incorporation was to give entity to the school and to make it possible to make application for degree granting power. Quoting from C. V. Thomas's October 11, 1920, report of the Educational Department: "After degree granting power, we believe that the next move should be an organized aggressive effort to secure endowment and an adequate school building and other physical equipment." His sights were high, and his goals were met in due course. This was the first mention on record of becoming a degree granting institution.

On February 2, 1921, the Y Board of Trustees accepted formally the recommendations of a Special Education Committee that (1) the Y

Schools be organized into a separate branch of the YMCA; (2) all educational activities of the Y be conducted and controlled by this branch under a Board of Governors; (3) the new branch become effective April 1, 1921. This was an important milestone in the history of Fenn College, for at this stage the Y Board of Trustees finally took cognizance of the growth, development, scope, and civic influence of its Educational Division in duly officially granting formal recognition and status to its schools.

The Operating Committee met February 25, 1921, and appointed the following men to the first Board of Governors of the new educational branch:

W. R. Green, Chairman	R. J. Hoddinott
George W. Bodenhorn	Clinton M. Horn
B. L. Britton	Franklin T. Jones
M. D. Coate	G. Hamilton Mouck
O. K. Forn	E. M. Preston
C. M. Finfrock	Fred T. Jones
G. M. Gottshall	C. V. Thomas, Sec'y Pro-tem

On March 2, 1921, the Board of Governors took action changing the name of the Educational Branch of the Cleveland Young Men's Christian Association to "The Cleveland School of Technology." At this same meeting Dr. Thomas was elected Secretary of the Board of Governors. Regular monthly meetings were held by the Board of Governors and a complete report on academic matters was presented at each meeting. For instance, the following is the report for March 22, 1921:

Attendance	
Regular day classes	232
Machine Shop—Day Division	74
Machine Shop—Evening Division	63
Business & Preparatory	337
Commerce	452
Engineering	289
Accountancy	285
Extension	90
Total	1,822

Number of different subjects taught	47
Number of paid staff and teachers	117
Number of full time faculty	10
Total attendance student hours all sessions	52,849
Number of classes of groups meeting regularly	138
Number of different class sessions	1,480
Number of new students enrolled during the month	333

Obviously the preparation of these monthly reports entailed considerable paper work since this was many years prior to the computer age. At this same March 22, 1921, Board of Governors meeting, a Committee on Standards was appointed "whose particular province it should be to correlate the courses of the school into a unified curriculum and to study the problem of degree granting power."

At the meeting of the Board of Governors on July 19, 1921, Chairman W. R. Green reported that degree granting power was received for the Business Administration Course. G. Hamlin Mouck, Board Member, was highly complimented for his efforts toward this end. In the discussion, emphasis was placed upon the opportunity which this power presented. "The Secretary [Thomas] was instructed to arrange a meeting of some members of the Board with one or two members of the Chamber of Commerce who would be dispositioned to present the Business Administration curriculum to the Chamber of Commerce clientele. During the discussion of curriculum activities, emphasis was placed upon the value of the course in Human Relations and the portent of the course. It was the feeling of the Board that this beginning should be followed through in a very thorough way." One-half century of time has not altered this trend of thought.

The first commencement exercise held in other than the YMCA building took place on Thursday evening, May 26, 1921, in the Euclid Avenue Baptist Church; 1,128 were in attendance.

In the summer of 1921 Case School of Applied Science offered a $600 scholarship to a student in one of Cleveland's private schools making the highest grade in a competitive examination. George J. Goudreau, a student in the Preparatory Department of the Cleveland School of Technology, carried off the highest honors and later graduated from Case. He, likewise, served as an instructor in Mathematics at the Y for two and a half years starting in August 1924. He later became President of G. J. Goudreau and Co. in real estate and building development in Cleveland.

Beginning on September 9, 1921, the Cleveland School of Technology offered a five-year course in Business Administration of three terms each year. This was the first college type curriculum of the school to receive authorization by the State Department of Education (Ohio) for the granting of a degree (Bachelor of Commercial Science, B.C.S.). This was an Evening Division program, not Day Division.

It is not unreasonable to assume with the information on hand that, at this stage in the history of the Cleveland School of Technology, the members of the relatively new Board of Governors of the Educational Branch were evidently becoming impatient with the trial and error educational methods employed for many years and were now insisting on an educational pattern and policy more nearly related to the accepted standards of the day.

For the fall of 1921, records show the Automobile School enrollment to be 73 and J. C. Nichols as Supervisor of enrollment and promotion. Nichols, a graduate of Columbia University, had joined the teaching staff in September 1920 as Instructor in Mechanical Drawing and Shop Mathematics. He later became Dean of the Faculty of Fenn College, and for about one year following the death of C. V. Thomas in November 1947, he served as Acting President.

An October 18, 1921, report to the Board of Governors contains the following statements:

> The opening of the first semester of the five-year curriculum in Business Administration augurs well for this course. Approximately 45 men are attending Economics, English and Mathematics classes. This curriculum, combined with the accounting training, should soon establish its worth.
>
> The organized curricula in our Engineering School offer the greatest opportunity for engineering training now afforded in Cleveland (*Sic*). Some method in selling the various engineering organizations the educational work of the Cleveland School of Technology should be found. Boston and, more recently, Detroit have begun cooperative day engineering schools. There is a field for this type of education in Cleveland.

To quote from the December 22, 1921, report of the Cleveland School of Technology to the Board of Governors:

An inspector of the North Central Association of Colleges and Secondary Schools studied our Evening Preparatory School and later notified us that this department of our work had been placed on the recognized list of the Association. This is the first time that such recognition has been given to an evening preparatory school in Ohio. It means that students from our Evening Preparatory School will enter college on the same basis as those coming from any day high school.

Your secretary [C. V. Thomas] believes that now is the psychological time to tie to the YMCA an institution that will do for Cleveland what the Ohio Mechanics Institute does for Cincinnati. The Cleveland School of Technology should become for Cleveland what other privately endowed and controlled institutions have become in many large cities. The *University of Cleveland* is well on its way. Does not this school and this Board have a responsibility to Cleveland which should be accepted?

The Operating Committee of the Y met January 25, 1922, to review the financial status at the close of the year, December 31, 1921. The Cleveland School of Technology reported an income for the year of $148,503.69 and expenses of $160,432.05 for a deficit of $11,028.36 Most of this loss was chargable to the Machine Shop and Automobile Schools.

In May 1922 a new Committee on the Occupation of the Field was appointed to "report specifically upon the future policy of the Association in regard to its educational work." The committee reported on June 28 in joint session with the Board of Governors. A series of recommendations was proposed including a building campaign to raise money for new "Engineering Shops and Laboratories." The Executive Committee of the Board of Trustees met September 20 and recommended that the architectural firm of Hubbell and Benes be engaged for the design and construction of a new building and the remodeling of any others. The Board also considered the perpetual lease of the Johnson Building directly adjacent to the Y on the east side and assigned a special committee the power to act on the terms presented.

At the Commencement Convocation held May 29, 1922, eighty-nine graduates received diplomas and eight hundred and twenty-three received certificates, the latter for the completion of short courses. Willis L. Hotchkiss was one of the diploma recipients. He graduated from Western Reserve University Law School in 1929 with an LL.B. having previously received his A.B. He joined the Fenn Faculty as Assistant to the Dean in September 1931 and resigned in 1933 at which time he was Associate Dean of the School of Business Administration. He later received a degree for graduate study at Yale University and became the Director of the Chicago Regional Office of the Anti-Trust Division of the U. S. Department of Justice.

The activities of the Machine Shop School and the Automobile School were merged in July 1922 under the name: "The Trade School of the Cleveland YMCA School of Technology." The subjects taught in this school were:

Acetylene welding	Automobile ignition
Electric welding	Machine Shop Practice
Automobile mechanics	Tractor mechanics

1922 brought to a close a long era of growing pains relating to educational activities of the YMCA. From the initial record (1870) of the first classes in French and German (tuition free) taught by Professors Le Vasseuer and Esch to the year 1923, at which time the administration was prepared to springboard into an era stressing college curriculum, a band of loyal, dedicated men at the Trustee, Educational Committee, and Faculty levels provided an educational structure for many students which met the pre-college educational and vocational needs of this span of years.

II

Practice is the best of all instructors.

Publilius Syrus, c. 42 BC.

The year 1923 was the start of a new and very important era in the history of The Cleveland YMCA School of Technology, frequently referred to as Y-Tech. Considerable discussion ensued at each board meeting concerning a new policy for the Day Engineering School. A visit was made to Akron University by Thomas and Ellsworth to secure information relating to its Cooperative Engineering School.

Enrollment, income, and expense data obtained from Northeastern University in Boston and Akron University showed that for about the first four years the Cooperative Engineering School at each university operated on a deficit budget. A report to the Board of Governors dated January 18, 1923, showed a projected deficit of $1,887.50 for the first year of operation of a Junior Cooperative Engineering School at Y-Tech. Director C. V. Thomas also reported that "Cleveland affords a great field for this type of school. The YMCA has an educational organization that can, by slight adaptation, put such a plan of training into operation. The YMCA has the class rooms and facilities, unused during the day, for conducting a cooperative school. If there is a need for a school of this type in Cleveland, and if there is a conviction that the YMCA is the logical organization to conduct such a school, we believe the deficit budget problem can be solved."

The resolution of the cooperative program did not restrict occasions of levity. In a letter of invitation to the Annual Student Dinner scheduled for February 14, 1923 (St. Valentine's Day), addressed to members of the Board of Governors, Member Fred T. Jones urged them to attend the dinner and bring some outside guests at the expense of the school. The following paragraph from the letter practically clinched one's decision to attend: "The Program set up by the Student Council is excellent. Starting with a dinner served by the Brandt Company, seasoned with music by one of Johnson's orchestras, the program is off. This will be followed by 35 minutes of entertainment by the Regal Sextette, which will be in the form of light opera and musical comedy. This will be followed by Mr. Parlette's popular lecture on 'The University of Hard Knocks'. The floor will be cleared and dancing will follow for those who desire it." Of course, the letter was signed by Director C. V. Thomas.

In September 1923 a Special Committee composed of Board Members Ryan, Ingalls, and Finfrock presented data on the work done for the YMCA by the Y Trade School. This particular school had an enrollment of 777 men students in academic year 1922–1923. The quarters, equipment, and time of instructors were used to a maximum. However, this was only one of the following types of education sponsored by the YMCA during that period:

1. Elementary School for Adults (day)
2. Day High School for Adults
3. Day Trade School for Adults in a limited number of courses
4. Day Technical School for Adults in a limited number of courses
5. Night Elementary School for Adults
6. Night Trade School in a limited number of courses
7. Night Technical School in a limited number of courses
8. Night Pre-Engineering School in four courses
9. Night Business Administration School

It is interesting to note that during the Summer of 1923 officials of Western Reserve University (W.R.U.) proposed that the YMCA cooperate with them in conducting courses in chemistry. The suggestion entailed the teaching of General, Qualitative, and Quantitative Analysis courses at the YMCA and the Organic and Advanced General courses at W.R.U. The students would provide their own transportation between campuses and full credit would be transferable. The very first mention of the start of the new cooperative program was in a report of the Cleveland YMCA School of Technology to the Board of Governors dated September 26, 1923. It was as follows: "The Day Cooperative Engineering School will have an enrollment of 14 men, 7 to a section. They are unusually high grade. The school feels it is on a solid foundation in this division." Other comments from the same report are as follows:

> Oscar Torreson came to the Y Night School to study English to help him in his clerical work. This school showed him how he could finish his high school and go to college. He graduated with the highest honors at Case this year. The Carnegie Research Foundation selected him for special astronomical research work in Australia.
>
> George Goudreau came in to study electricity. He transferred to the high school division. In competitive examinations he won a four-year scholarship at Case. Last commencement he was awarded the physics prize given to the best student of Physics at Case.
>
> The Y High School (Day & Night) is a member of the North Central Association of Colleges and Secondary Schools. This means an annual inspection of our teaching staff, laboratories, library facilities, length of courses, etc.
>
> W.R.U., Case, and Ohio State University send students to us who apply to them for college entrance but who do not have sufficient credits. The Cleveland Board of Education gives us weekly the names and addresses of all boys who drop out of the public high schools, with the understanding that we shall get in touch with them regarding our night high school.
>
> The Boston, Detroit, Chicago, Youngstown and a few other YMCA's operate regular Arts Colleges. The Cleveland Y has not felt that it should get into this field, but that one of the universities should do this work.
>
> Y-Tech has not emphasized degree granting powers in the sense that many YMCA's have. We offer only one course leading to a degree. Detroit offers six and Boston, seven.
>
> A few men have withdrawn from the school because of the embarrassment which they said it was to them to have us call them out of classes regarding their tuition payments. However, in order for us to break even for the year it is necessary that we take in at least $1800 between December 21 and 30.

For many years the founding date of Fenn College was considered to be 1881. In 1956 it was changed to 1923, the year the first college credit day classes were established, but this is discussed more fully in a later chapter. The enrollments in the various schools of The Cleveland School of Technology in the Fall of 1923 were as follows:

Accounting School	157
School of Commerce	292
Elementary School	264
School of Engineering	397
Preparatory School	442
Trade School	264
Total	1,816

Forty-three men were enrolled in the Freshman Class of the "new" School of Business Administration in the Night School. It was stated that "Mr. Carter and Mr. Eckelberry have made the standards in this school so high and the work so difficult that six or seven of the 43 have not been able to stand the pace. The instruction is of college level of difficulty in every respect. We believe that this division is on such a basis that Cleveland as a city will soon recognize that it has a Night School of Business."

Preparatory to inaugurating the college degree program in Business Administration a survey was made of the number of male students enrolled in the various institutions in Cleveland. The following list of schools shows the number of students enrolled in bookkeeping, accounting, auditing, and record keeping courses:

Cleveland Business University	125
Cleveland Association of Credit Men	85
Knights of Columbus	364
American Institute of Banking	595
Public Schools (day)	1,400
Public Schools (night)	375
YMCA	926
Dyke	100
Spencerian	400
Other business schools and courses	300
Total	4,670

Strange as it may seem Y-Tech had a football team in the Fall of 1923. Football suits and other paraphernalia were underwritten by members of the Board of Governors. Thornbury was the coach, and Heininger was the captain. The win-loss record is unavailable but a report of the football banquet noted: "two cakes were donated by Kaase, one of the football players. His people are the owners of the Kaase chain of bakeries."

The December 21, 1923, meeting of the Board of Governors was held in honor of Bodenhorn, who had served over ten years on the Board. Bodenhorn was leaving Cleveland and had submitted his resignation. Green, Chairman of the Board, read a letter from the members of the Board of Governors expressing their good will and appreciation. Members present were: Green, Bodenhorn, Fred T. Jones, Finfrock, Richard J. Hoddinott (The Collver-Miller Co.), Mouck, Ryan, Lewis, Ellsworth, Howard W. Jones, Roth, and Thomas. Attached to the Minutes of this meeting were the following statements:

> The objective of The Cleveland YMCA School of Technology is to provide educational opportunities for older boys and young men in a Christian educational institution.
> a.   The school operates twelve months in the year. Semesters open in September, January and June.
> b.   The students pay 95% of total operation costs. The Community Chest pays the other 5%.
> c.   The school meets the standards of accrediting bodies in the respective fields, such as, the High School is a member of the North Central Association of Colleges and Secondary Schools; the Evening Business Administration School is granted the degree granting power by the State Department of Education.
> d.   The school cooperates with other organizations. It conducts the educational work for the Real Estate Board, the Credit Men's Association, the Life Underwriters, and others.
> e.   The total different subjects taught during 1923 was 96.
> f.   The total number of paid teachers during 1923 was 157. The total number of full time staff, other than teachers was 18, and the total number of different students during the year was 4,274.
> g.   Religious emphasis is introduced into the school through the attitude and motives of the instructors; assemblies for all students; discussion groups and Bible classes for groups of students; personal interviews with students.

The 1923 Cleveland Foundation Year Book cited a great need for the coordination of the evening education in Cleveland. A Commission was formed composed of representatives from Case, W.R.U., The Cleveland YMCA School of Technology, and twelve other institutions. Considerable time was spent on the study of existing curricula offered in the evening by the several institutions located in Cleveland. Curricula in Business Administration received the greatest attention. One of the recommendations of the Cleveland Foundation was that a "Greater University" program be established and a number of the larger institutions merge their programs to be more effective.

The commission's final recommendations included the following: the establishment of a School of Business Administration with its own dean and faculty; a four year baccalaureate degree program with a Master of Business Administration following the fifth year of study; the curriculum to be broadly cultural and sufficiently technical; provision for certificate courses; provision for admission of special students; the faculty to also constitute the Bureau of Business Research; the arrangement for transfer of credits; an off-campus advisory board of business men; and appropriate funding in support of the school.

The Board of Governors of Y-Tech agreed that such an affiliation with a Greater University would promote the best interests of Cleveland. The Board of Governors adopted a resolution recommending to the Board of Trustees of the YMCA that action be taken which would lead to the affiliation of Y-Tech with the "Greater University" contemplated in the Cleveland Foundation Survey of Higher Education. It was further recommended that the land owned by the Medical Library Association on Prospect Avenue be used as the future home of the downtown University Center.

Dean Frederick B. Robinson, School of Business and Civic Administration, The College of the City of New York, was engaged as a consultant to study the affiliation of several institutions in Cleveland to provide better higher education. After several visits to Cleveland and careful study, Dean Robinson recommended that quick action be taken by at least two of the Boards of Case, W.R.U., and Y-Tech and then an Executive Committee and a lay Advisory Council be appointed. At a meeting in the Union Club, December 6, 1924, attended by President Howe of Case, President Vinson of W.R.U., Secretary Lewis and Director Thomas of Y-Tech, Eckstein Case, Newton D. Baker, Charles E. Adams, W. H. Prescott, and Dean Robinson of C.C.N.Y., it was formally moved by Newton D. Baker and unanimously passed that Dean Robinson submit his plan for the organization of an Evening University in writing, including budgeting recommendations.

The Cleveland YMCA School of Technology went on the air for the first time in January 1925 with a course in English taught by Professor Barclay Leathem over station WHIC. Further radio courses planned included government, civics, history, and mathematics. The radio listeners were asked to do certain home work and mail it to the school for correction. The beginning of each evening was allotted to a discussion of the responses.

The Minutes of the Board of Governors meeting of June 24, 1925, carry these two excerpts: "A committee composed of Messrs. Hoddinott, Hamilton and Fred T. Jones was appointed to study the advisability of lengthening our Cooperative Engineering course to five or six years. This committee is to study the additional expense and total load which action would incur," and "Messrs. Eckelberry, Mouck and Jones were appointed to select the Director of the newly united Commerce and Accountancy School into one school."

The 1925 Board of Trustees of the Cleveland YMCA was composed of the following men, each one important to the history of Cleveland:

Charles E. Adams—The Cleveland Hardware Co.
Judge George S. Addams—Juvenile Court
A. F. Allen—The American Steel and Wire Co.
Elbert H. Baker—The Plain Dealer Publishing Co.
Claude E. Clarke—Attorney
J. S. Crider—The Stuyvesant Motor Co.
Louis D. Cull—The Cleveland Chain & Mfg. Co.
Cyrus S. Eaton—Otis & Co.
S. P. Fenn—The Sherwin-Williams Co.
R. J. Frackelton—The Chandler and Price Co.
E. M. France—State Mutual Life Assurance Co.
Thomas W. Garvin—Real Estate
Wm. R. Green—The Guardian Savings & Trust Co.
Hon. Frederick A. Henry—Snyder, Henry, Thompson, Ford
    & Seagrave
Fred T. Jones—Johns-Manville, Inc.
H. D. King—The Cleveland Trust Co.
Robert E. Lewis—General Secretary, Y.M.C.A.
W. H. Prescott—Saginaw Bay Co.

F. W. Ramsey—The Cleveland Metal Products Co.

Frederick A. Reading—The Western Reserve Woolen Co.

Paul E. Ryan—Minerva Pottery Co., Minerva, Ohio

John L. Severance—Standard Oil of Ohio and other companies

Franklin G. Smith—The Osborn Mfg. Co.

Ambrose Swasey—The Warner & Swasey Co.

David W. Teachout—The A. Teachout Co.

H. M. Tomkins—New York Central Railroad

Ralph S. Tyler—The Chandler & Price Co.

Malcolm B. Vilas—Attorney

D. C. Wills—The Federal Reserve Bank

Dr. F. Q. Blanchard—Euclid Avenue Congregational Church

Ellsworth resigned from the Engineering School in August 1925, and J. C. Nichols became the new Director. At the same time Sperry, formerely superintendent of the Automobile Division, became Director of the Trade School, and Hiram Folkman of Garfield Heights succeeded Thornbury as coach of the day athletic teams and assistant to Howard Jones in the Preparatory School.

By late summer of 1925 the welding course in the Trade School was becoming nationally known. The President of the Chicago Steel and Wire Co. had asked permission to send one of his men to the Y-Trade School for training, and a number of inquiries for admission had come in from Detroit, but the enrollments in all welding classes were filled for the Fall Semester. Comparable figures for enrollments, and other statistics at the beginning of the Fall Quarters for 1924 and 1925 are given in Table 1.

TABLE 1

ENROLLMENTS AND OTHER STATISTICS FOR THE
CLEVELAND YMCA SCHOOL OF TECHNOLOGY

| | *Enrollments* | | | *Other Statistics* | |
	1924	*1925*		*1924*	*1925*
Accountancy	116	110	Subjects taught	108	95
Commerce	181	228	Paid teachers	100	102
Elementary	72	57	Full-time staff		
Engineering	280	312	(other than teachers)	20	17
Preparatory	341	427	Students (counted once)	1,659	1,517
Trade School	89	90	Student Hour Attendance	53,737	50,261
Total	1079	1224			

Shades of college campuses of 1969 are found in the November 16, 1925, Minutes of the Board of Governors, as follows: "It was moved by Mr. Eckelberry and seconded by Mr. Dibble that the President of the Student Council be invited to attend the Board of Governors' meetings at the discretion of the Chairman of the Board and the Educational Director."

It might be conjectured whether any teaching effort that has groped its way along through so many revisions and methods (with more to come) was really needed in the first place; but sufficient evidence was becoming available that the confidence sustained in young men of basic intelligence, and above all, "high motivation," was profoundly affecting many of their lives, and consequently, the life of Cleveland.

A study was made in 1925 of the walks-of-life of former Y-Tech students who were in class during the years 1904–1905 and 1906. The numbers and categories were as follows:

30 presidents	11 civil, electrical & mechanical
24 vice presidents	engineers
19 secretaries	4 attorneys
16 superintendents	3 teachers
9 managers	2 dentists
11 secretary-treasurers	14 foremen
8 treasurers	12 draftsmen
6 auditors	11 machinists
15 retail store owners	9 carpenters
6 carpenter contractors	5 pattern makers
5 contractors	5 electricians
5 small manufacturers	4 plumbers
2 brokers	5 auto mechanics
2 wholesalers	4 painters
2 real estate operators	3 brick layers
2 garage proprietors	44 clerks
41 salesmen & advertising men	29 unskilled workers
2 chemical engineers	21 operating engineers
8 architects	——
4 physicians	515 Total

The following quotation is from the Minutes of the final meeting of the Board of Governors of Y-Tech for the fiscal year 1925, held December 21:

Mr. McMillin as President of the Student Council was asked to make a statement to the Board. He pointed out the regard which the students have for the instruction they are receiving, but he also indicated the great need for equipment and adequate class and laboratory space. He stated that the students questioned the advisability of increasing the enrollment further until provision was made for taking care of the present student body.

The Board approved the idea of the Department of Religious Education in the Day High School and authorized the Educational Director (C. V. Thomas) to proceed to work out the problems involved and to present to the Finance Committee any unusual financial conditions arising from this new development.

Dr. Beardsley Ruml of the Rockefeller Foundation was a consultant in 1925 to a group of Clevelanders known as "The Cleveland Conference For Educational Cooperation." Philip R. Mather was the first Secretary of the Study Committee for the conference; Newton D. Baker succeeded Mather in 1926. Serving with Baker were J. H. Wade, H. G. Dalton, E. M. Williams, Lewis B. Williams, James R. Garfield, and W. H. Prescott. The objective of the conference was to plan adequately for adult educational needs in Cleveland, at all levels and both day and evening.

The Cleveland Foundation directed by Carlton K. Matson made an Educational Survey on the education of Cleveland youth covering a ten-year period 1916–1925. This survey revealed that thirty-three percent did not go beyond grammar school and eighty percent did not graduate from high school. It was these disillusioned, disappointed young men and women who looked to the YMCA for another chance.

The survey further recommended: "that a joint committee of the faculties of Case School of Applied Science, the YMCA, and the John Huntington Polytechnic Institute be appointed to study and coordinate the respective fields which these institutions will cover in regard to evening and day work and report the same to their respective Boards, and that all unnecessary duplication of work in these institutions be avoided."

The Cleveland Conference for Educational Cooperation re-affirmed the suggested Greater University organization for Cleveland. A special committee composed of three trustees from each of the institutions, Case, W.R.U. and the YMCA, chaired by Newton D. Baker, was appointed to study the recommendations of the consultant regarding the evening and extension work. The committee recommended that a Board of Trustees be created for the establishment and operation of the evening and extension work in the City of Cleveland. . . . This Board of Trustees should be incorporated with the usual powers of the trustees of an educational institution, its purpose being to function in the arts, sciences, technical courses, business administration, etc., of university grade for the benefit of students who would otherwise be deprived of the privilege of the usual day courses of university instruction, but should be careful in securing its Articles of Incorporation to provide that the institution so formed is established with a view to its becoming an integral unit in the Greater University which is now in process of creation.

Near the end of 1925 the idea of creating a Greater University was dropped because Dr. Charles S. Howe, President, Case School of Applied Science and Dr. W. G. Leutner, Dean, Western Reserve University and Acting Director of Cleveland College, refused to carry out the recommendations of the Cleveland Foundation Survey for Higher Education and the consultants, Ruml and Robinson.

On January 18, 1926, the Board of Governors of Y-Tech approved acquiring the Medical Library building for school purposes beginning September 1926. This building was directly east of the Edwards Annex and the third building east of the Central Y. It provided twelve additional class rooms, an auditorium seating 250, and a 40' x 60' basement for the electrical laboratory.

The Evening Division Student Council in 1926 was under the leadership of S. H. Scharschmidt, Maintenance of Way Engineer for the New York Central Railroad. The most active element in the Council was the Committee on Education. Scharschmidt later became Chief Bridge Engineer of N.Y.C.R.R. and passed away in 1969.

The question of lengthening the three-year Day Cooperative Engineering School into a five-year program had been before the Board of Governors on three occasions. Finally on February 15, 1926, the board, after considerable discussion, approved the extension thereof to a five-year bachelor degree program. The program was to start September 1926. At this same meeting Director C. V. Thomas was asked to formulate a list of possible team workers and captains for a fund raising campaign for a new building. This was the first mention of the conception of a new building that later became the "Fenn Building."

The first student news publication in the history of the school was published as Vol. I, Number 1, under the date of March 1, 1926. It is reproduced here in full:

THE CLEVELAND Y.M.C.A.

SCHOOL OF TECHNOLOGY

–BULLETIN–

VOLUME I	MARCH 1, 1926	NUMBER 1

ALTHOUGH forty-five years have passed since the school was first organized, this is the first news publication which the school has issued. The school seems to have grown to the point where such a bulletin is necessary. The present issue and those to follow hope to accomplish several things.

The students in five departments, attending classes as they do during the day and on separate evenings, have very little opportunity to know any department beyond the one in which they are enrolled. The students in the Engineering School who attend classes in the Main building on Tuesday and Thursday evenings know very little about the classes in the School of Commerce, Accounts and Finance, which meet in the adjoining buildings on the same evenings. Usually they know even less about the classes in the Y-Preparatory School and the Trade School which meet on other evenings.

The present bulletin is being published in order to make information about school activities more available to the students in the separate departments. Special lectures and the organization of clubs which will be of interest to the entire student body will be announced in these columns. The Student Council is arranging visits to various manufacturing plants and the schedule of these visits will be published.

In addition to current school news the next few issues will contain facts regarding the development and present organization of the school. These facts will be of interest to former students.

The Annual Student Banquet

The Honorable Frank B. Willis, United States Senator from Ohio, has accepted the invitation of the school to address the Student Banquet at the Hotel Statler on March 6th. His subject will be "America and the World Court."

The dinner will be served in the ballroom and in adjoining dining rooms. The Canfield Glee Club, formerly known as the Cambrian Welsh Male Chorus has been engaged. Easton's Orchestra will play during the evening and for the dance which follows the regular program.

All arrangements for this banquet are being made by the Student Council and its Social Committee. Mr. W. G. Pinkerton, City Sales Manager for Swift & Co., is Chairman of the Social Committee; other members of this committee are, C. P. Andre, S. M. Wilson, H. M. Griffin and F. E. Bradner. Mr. P. A. McMillin, Superintendent of the City Hospital and President of the Student Council will act as toastmaster.

Not in a Day

Organized twenty-five years before two-cylinder automobiles invaded our highways, the school began to teach five subjects to a handful of students. Adult education was hardly more than an idea. The man or woman who had finished college was stamped as a member of the "upper classes;" those who had completed high school were "well educated."

The few evening classes that were organized were at once popular. The novelty of the idea seemed to be a part of the attraction, however, for after the first two years the attendance decreased. It was not until 1887 that the enrollment rose above the five hundred mark.

Inspection Trips

About 115 men from the YMCA Schools visited Nela Park last Saturday afternoon on the second educational trip of a series planned by the educational committee of the student council. The party met at the school and at the lodge at Nela Park and were conducted through the Historical Exhibit and the Nela School of Lighting by Mr. Kirk Reid, a former instructor in Electricity.

Two weeks before about 70 men visited the Orange Street Terminal. Other trips are being planned to the White Motor Company and the Cleveland Automobile Company. A trip to Detroit is also being planned for the month of May.

Mr. S. H. Scharschmidt, Maintenance of Way Engineer with the New York Central R.R., is chairman of the Educational Committee. Other members of this committee are R. C. Bednar, G. V. Shaw, H. M. Taylor and J. B. Collins.

In 1905 the bicycle crossed our horizon. The two-cylinder automobile followed and before the smoke had cleared away modern transportation had arrived. Modern large scale production methods and specialized tasks in office and shops followed.

These changes in industry and therefore changes in our daily lives made part-time education more and more necessary. The specialized knowledge which was soon required in credit and advertising and other departments was not given in public schools. There was a demand for an evening school in which men who worked in shops and offices during the day might study technical and business subjects in the evening.

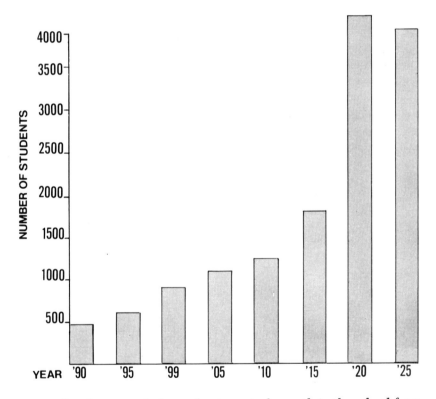

The above graph shows the numerical growth in the school from the time the school was organized. Until 1910 the school increased in size slowly. People seemed to need to be educated to the idea of part-time education. However, between 1910 and 1915 the enrollment nearly doubled. Between 1915 and 1920 it more than doubled.

For many years the attendance has remained fairly constant, some years going to nearly 5,000, but in later years it rose to 7,000.

City Manager William R. Hopkins wrote the following in March 1926 to William R. Green, Chairman of the Y-Board of Trustees:

> The YMCA School of Technology is in my opinion, the finest educational work in the City of Cleveland. It helps people who know just what they want and who want it badly enough to struggle and sacrifice to get it. By helping them it raises the whole standard of proficiency in every line of endeavor. It strengthens the professional sense, the sense which contributes both to happiness in labor and to the fruitfulness of labor. It deserves the heartiest support of everyone who is really concerned in the future of the city and its people.

The above was quoted in a number of YMCA communications.

J. C. Nichols, after consultation with area representative industrialists and engineers and a study of college catalogues, established a five-year curriculum for the five-year Cooperative Engineering program. Nichols had made a location survey of past and present students to determine the relationship of the school to individual firms. Following is a sample of the study using the Warner & Swasey Co. as an example:

> 14 employees in school
> 28 employees who have completed courses
> Group includes Assistant Treasurer, Assistant to the President, Treasurer, Secretary, Chief Accountant, Acting Credit Manager, Chief Draftsman, several foremen, draftsmen, machinists and clerks.

Similar information was compiled for The National Carbon Company, The Cleveland Trust Company, The Sherwin-Williams Company, The American Steel and Wire Company, The Cleveland Twist Drill Company, and others.

Although the class of 1927 was considered the first graduating class of Fenn College (The Cleveland YMCA School of Technology), actually one student, J. Lindsay Smith, Credit Manager, The Foster Bolt and Nut Company, received the first baccalaureate degree conferred by the school at a commencement dinner held at the New Amsterdam Hotel in May 1926. Smith had a number of acceptable transfer credits upon entrance to the school and therefore completed his graduation requirements in advance of his regular class.

The July 28, 1926, report of the school to the Board of Governors carried the following paragraph of significant prediction which proved to be an understatement:

Co-operative Engineering School Enrollment

This department is securing a very wholesome enrollment, Mr. Nichols is requiring all students to pay $65.00 before they are considered as enrolled. Thus far over 20 men have paid. Last year to date only 10 had enrolled. There is every indication that this school is now getting a real start. In a few years it will be one of the largest departments of the school. Many new firms are co-operating for the first time this year.

It was reported at the same meeting that the building campaign was progressing satisfactorily. General planning had reached the stage of deciding whether it would be desirable to construct a new building without frills at 35c per cubic foot or one with a few frills at 45 to 50c per cubic foot.

A total of $209,000 to be used for the new building was pledged in late July 1926 by members of the Board of Trustees, present and former students and faculty, and Sereno Peck Fenn's pledge of $100,000.

Dean Eckelberry of the School of Commerce, Accounts and Finance (later, Business Administration) announced his resignation in August 1926 to accept a new opportunity in Detroit, Michigan. He became a member of the Y school faculty in 1919 and Dean of business administrative activities in 1922. Credit was given him for the progress of the school of Commerce, Accounts and Finance during his era of responsibility, especially the undergraduate degree program.

The Cooperative Engineering School opened its new five-year program in the Fall term in 1926 with an enrollment of 71 as compared to 30 for the previous three-year program in the Fall of 1925. The Medical Library building was occupied for the first time by the school in October. New drafting tables were purchased representing the first tangible results of the campaign for the new building and equipment.

The fall term of 1926 had a total enrollment of 1098 (day and evening) distributed as follows:

Commerce	269
Elementary	36
Engineering	299
Preparatory	400
Trade School	94

However, the net operating loss for the first nine months of 1926 was $31,872, and for the first time question was raised whether twenty or so of the leading industries in Cleveland should be approached for an annual underwriting of $500 to $1,000 each inasmuch as they were the group benefiting most from the school and paying the least. Cleveland College of W.R.U. had already established a precedent for this procedure and was securing an annual guarantee of between $20,000 and $30,000. Question was also raised as to whether the school can request underwriting from firms as long as the Y receives aid from the Community Fund. Nevertheless, there were many Cleveland firms with fifteen or more employees attending Y classes and it would be very expensive for these firms to provide similar educational benefits on their own premises.

The concentrated building campaign efforts coupled with the problems of balancing the annual operating budget created the need for an exploration concerning what programs should be offered by Y-Tech and how much space would be required to provide adequately for such programs. Should the school continue its very diversified programs of trying to provide an education for all types of vocational and undergraduate college level programs or should diversity be minimized to permit growth of prestige?

The subject of educational status was being discussed at frequent intervals, including the upgrading of the Evening Division professional curricula to provide sufficient credits for a baccalaureate degree program. It was conceded that educational status would be accelerated by functioning at the college level. The year 1926 closed with a number of committees studying the future of Y-Tech. The actual deficit for the school year was $18,424.

January 4, 1927, was a dark day in the history of the YMCA and its School of Technology, the day of Sereno P. Fenn's death. No single Clevelander had before or since given so much of his time and talents to the Y and its educational program.

About this time the subject of Junior Colleges was permeating discussions throughout the United States. A number had already sprung up in the metropolitan areas. The Y-Tech's evening programs approximated the curricula of these programs. With a little modification these curricula could be designated as Junior College Programs. On January 28, 1927, the Board of Governors unanimously approved the Junior College plan as presented by Director C. V. Thomas.

As the result of committee study on the subject of diversification the Board of Governors of Y-Tech recommended to the Board of Trustees of the YMCA on February 15, 1927, that certain elements of the Trade School be combined with the Engineering School and the remaining course work be phased out as rapidly as possible. The Trade School had its start after World War I when the U. S. Government offered to educational institutions certain machinery and equipment for fifteen cents on the dollar. About this time Y-Tech had requests from the U.S. Veterans' Bureau for trade school instruction. The Trade School consisted at first of a course in Machine Shop. Later Welding, Automobile Mechanics, Battery, and Ignition were added. The school had in attendance during 1920, 166 students; 1921, 483 students; 1922, 777 students; 1923, 762 students; 1924, 602 students; 1925, 667 students; and 1926, 624 students. In addition to training many wounded and other ex-service men who were granted scholarships, it had been the only school in Cleveland where men might learn acetylene and electric welding, battery building, and ignition. It also operated the only large machine shop in the city and the only long and comprehensive automobile course for men. From 1924 through 1926 it had been used by the State Industrial Commission for the rehabilitation of men injured in industry. Fifty-five such men had been trained in the Trade School.

However, because of the laboratory equipment needs, the nature of the almost personal instruction, the insurance requirements, rental, heat, light, and power bills, the greatest loss of the entire school in 1926 occurred in the Trade School, i.e. $14,202. Inasmuch as it was not the type of curriculum where the tuition could be increased to defray the expenses, the board elected to drop this activity. This was a very important step in further upgrading of the curricula in spite of the fact that there was need for this type of vocational training in Cleveland. All Y Trade School classes were finally suspended in May 1927.

1927 marks the beginning of fraternities and clubs at Y-Tech. The Cooperative School students organized "The Cleveland Cooperative Engineers." Two fraternities were started in the Business Administration School. These were in addition to the Friendship, Debating, Speakers, and Dramatic Clubs conducted by the Student Council.

In April 1927 the members of the Board of Governors of the Cleveland YMCA School of Technology were as follows:

W. R. Green, Guardian Trust Co., Chairman
Fred T. Jones, The Johns-Manville Co., Vice Chairman
James E. Campbell, The Sherwin-Williams Co.
Charles C. Dibble, Northwestern Mutual Life Insurance Co.
Harold K. Ferguson, The H. K. Ferguson Co.
Scott Hamilton, The Wadsworth-Addison Co.
Richard J. Hoddinott, The Cleveland Trust Co.
E. W. Kempton, The American Steel & Wire Co.
J. H. Lesh, Forest City Structural Steel Co.
G. Hamlin Mouck, The Security Discount Co.
Harris W. Roberts, The Plain Dealer Publishing Co.
William J. Semple, City of Cleveland Finance Director
Lawrence A. Tucker, National City Bank

The "Survey of Higher Education" financed by the Cleveland Foundation and executed by educational experts reported the following in May 1927:

Of all the evening education in Cleveland, that of the Young Men's Christian Association is outstanding. It has done remarkably progressive and effective work in the field of adult evening classes, and has done far more for Cleveland than any other agency.

It will be observed that the Young Men's Christian Association has all levels of work, some elementary, some secondary, and some of collegiate grade; furthermore, these courses cover not only the common branches of general education, but also certain vocational, trainee, and professional courses of study. In short, the Young Men's Christian Association has endeavored to the best of its ability to met the actual needs of the workers or the under-opportunitied young men.

A report submitted in 1927 to the Special Committee of the Operating Committee of the Y-Tech Board of Governors divided the educational activities into four stages starting with 1881. This may be the reason the original founding date of Fenn College of 1881 was conceived. The four stages of educational development were as follows:

1881–1900—a series of lectures or unit courses of short duration
1900–1912—unit courses extended in length and more thorough in content.
1912–1921—certain unit courses combined in curricula, largely a grouping of subjects; beginning of schools within the department.
1921–1927—courses of study planned to meet the educational needs of men; Schools, such as Night Preparatory, Day Cooperative Engineering and Evening Junior College, organized.

Director C. V. Thomas prepared the following report for a Board of Governors meeting held July 19, 1927:

The Junior College and Cooperative Engineering Schools

Over a year ago information regarding the Junior College movement was presented to this Board and the preliminary steps were taken leading to the organization of our Junior College work. The new catalogs carry outlines of seven Junior College programs. It is well that we keep in mind the fundamental educational philosophy underlying these courses. Dean Seashore of the College of Commerce, Accounts and Finance gives the argument from the point of view of an Arts College Dean. Your secretary believes that the tendency in education is toward making all of life educational, hence the removing of education from within the four walls of a class room. In other words, education in the future will more and more interpret the experience of the past in terms of the present activities of individuals. Mr. Hoddinott has often referred to one of the distinctive features of this school—that is its contact with industry. The Junior College and the Cooperative Engineering School are advance steps in tying this institution into the industrial activity of the city. Experience on the job is supplemented and interpreted by instruction in the class room.

We need also to keep in mind that education is much broader than vocational preparation, but that the dominant and perhaps most essential need of the young adult of the type that we serve is vocational preparation. Experience is showing that interest in the so-called cultural courses and the study of the "humanities" follows vocational preparation. The individual sees that success is dependent upon breadth of understanding, attitudes, etc., which are not obtained from a study of technical facts. There is a very big idea back of these vocational Junior College programs. It is worthy of our best effort in giving an interpretation of it to the young men of Cleveland.

The Cooperative School is having a most worthy growth. The indication is that there will be one hundred Freshmen enter this school this fall.

Because of the institution of the new Junior College program and the accelerated growth of the day Cooperative Engineering program much study was given to the subject of increasing library facilities. Urgency for this study stemmed from recommendations from accrediting agencies, especially the North Central Association of Colleges and Secondary Schools. The Cleveland Public Library agreed to cooperate fully in the loan of circulating books and supplementary reference material, but they strongly advised that the Y find space for a library and engage a librarian. This appeared to be one of the most important needs at this point in the history of Y-Tech.

The first group (six men) to complete the four-year (48 weeks per year) Business Administration School degree program was graduated Friday evening, September 2, 1927. Col. Leonard P. Ayres, Vice President and Economist, The Cleveland Trust Bank, was the commencement speaker. This was the first formal commencement of The Cleveland YMCA School of Technology. The first graduates of the School were:

> Harold J. Chopard, Bachelor of Business Administration
> William J. Franz, Bachelor of Business Administration
> Stanley C. Rex, Bachelor of Business Administration
> Clarence L. Ross, Bachelor of Business Administration
> Benjamin J. Smith, Bachelor of Business Administration
> Ross W. Emerson, Graduate of Business Administration

A special committee consisting of Hoddinott and Thomas of the Board of Governors and McMillin, President of the Student Council, and Student Council members S. H. Scharschmidt and William R. Lenga was appointed to study the establishment of a Student Activities Fund. The following recommendation was presented to the Y-Tech Board of Governors August 8, 1927, and received unanimous approval:

That each student be charged $1.00 per semester, the fund resulting to be used to promote student activities. The fund so raised to be spent as follows: Not to exceed 50% to be used for purchasing books, magazines and supplies for a school library, and not to exceed 50% is to cover the cost of a school paper, athletics and other activities.

The Day Cooperative Engineering students through their official organization, "Cleveland Cooperative Engineers" felt that their department of the school should have a distinctive name. The president of the group, G. A. Scherry, wrote J. C. Nichols on September 30, 1927, requesting that consideration be given to a name for the department which would identify it as a college. The Board of Governors on October 17 took no definite action on the request but expressed the opinion that "it would be wrong in principle to give any particular department of the school a distinct name."

The fiscal year of the YMCA and all of its departments, including Education, was the calendar year. Table 2 presents the summary of the proposed budget for the year 1928 with the actual income and expense statement for 1926, plus the budget for 1927, and an estimate as to how 1927 might close after four months of actual experience.

The year 1928 was the most important year to date in the history of Y-Tech. It started out with the re-organization of the Board of Governors into special committees to study policy matters relating to (1) the Preparatory School, (2) the Engineering School, (3) the Commerce School, (4) the promotion of public relations for the entire school, and (5) the financial operation of the college. Inasmuch as $56,165.55 had been paid by January 30, 1928, on the $109,000 pledged by trustees, faculty, and students toward the new building, a special committee was appointed to be responsible for the anticipated building activities. At least a portion of the $100,000 to be forthcoming from the S. P. Fenn estate would be available in 1928, so it was imperative that the actual construction of the new building get under way as early as possible. It was urgent that the building be available for the opening Fall Term of 1928.

The Annual School Banquets were now being held in the ballroom of the Hotel Statler. Nine hundred sixteen people were in attendance at the banquet held February 18, 1928; it was the largest educational banquet ever held in Cleveland.

TABLE 2
SUMMARY OF BUDGET FOR 1928

INCOME

	1926 Actual	1927 Budget	1927* Estimate	1928** Proposed
School of Commerce Tuition	28,907.	35,250.	27,659.	30,000.
Elementary School Tuition	3,924.	4,925.	3,442.	3,500.
School of Engineering Tuition	31,029.	27,600.	34,641.	40,000.
Preparatory School Tuition	33,874.	33,700.	32,318.	34,000.
Trade School Tuition	30,906.	36,000.	9,952.	...
	128,730.	137,475.	107,922.	107,500.
Commerce Miscellaneous	165.	250.	85.	100.
Elementary Miscellaneous	18.	75.	15.	20.
Engineering Miscellaneous	269.	400.	200.	200.
Preparatory Miscellaneous	234.	300.	100.	150.
Trade School Miscellaneous	9,630.	12,000.	2,990.	...
General Miscellaneous	1,721.	1,800.	1,400.	1,400.
Book Store Sales	16,608.	16,000.	14,198.	15,000.
Membership	10,004.	10,000.	8,170.	9,000.
Total Income except Contributions	167,384.	178,300.	135,080.	133,370.
Contributions***	14,376.	15,671.	25,857.	15,630.
Gross Total Income	181,760.	193,971.	160,937.	149,000.

EXPENSE

	1926 Actual	1927 Budget	1927* Estimate	1928** Proposed
School of Commerce	34,786.	37,347.	32,885.	34,500.
Elementary School	6,888.	7,000.	6,657.	6,000.
School of Engineering	36,152.	37,600.	38,427.	44,500.
Preparatory School	41,252.	38,500.	40,760.	41,000.
Trade School	50,953.	45,124.	19,992.	...
Trade School Stock	5,242.	5,600.	...	...
General	...	...	...	...
Book Store	16,213.	12,800.	14,046.	14,000.
Membership	9,056.	10,000.	8,170.	9,000.
Total Expense	200,184.	193,971.	160,937.	149,000.

* Actual for 4 months plus estimate for 8 months.

** Column 4 is the amount of income required to operate the departments of the school on an equitable basis. It is doubtful if these amounts can be realized from tuition only. We ask, therefore, the privilege of underwriting the income budget from a limited number of friends of the Young Men's Christian Association. This seems to be the only way to obtain the necessary income since the Welfare Federation has informed the Association that it cannot make larger appropriations than it has in the past.

*** Actually received (1926) or needed to balance the budget.

The Bayless-Kerr Advertising Agency was engaged by the board on February 27, 1928, to manage and prepare all advertising for the school. Their fee was $200 per month. Gerald S. Wellman, Denison University alumnus, who had worked for the Boynton Advertising Agency was engaged to assist in general office activities relating largely to internal promotion and registration of students.

Considerable self-analyzing resulted from the studies of the special committees. One study suggested the following four plans for critique as to the future policy of the Cleveland YMCA School of Technology:

1. Limit the collegiate offerings to the Junior College work only and carry on all other training and secondary school activity.
2. Limit the collegiate offerings to the Cooperative Engineering School only and carry on all other training and secondary school activity.
3. Eliminate all courses excepting the cooperative Engineering offerings.
4. Continue as is, making adjustments as approved by the Board.

Plan 4 was most preferable and was selected by the Board. Suggestions were made to the finance committee to study ways and means of increasing the income to the school.

Another study, by the faculty and administrative staff titled "A Self-Survey of The Cleveland YMCA School of Technology," raised questions for the Board of Governors to discuss. Typical questions were as follows:

1. What should be the optimum enrollment?
2. What is Cleveland's need for adult education?
3. Is the cost of the Y-Tech to the community average or less than average?
4. Does Y-Tech offer a distinctive service?
5. Would a reduction or increase in enrollment solve the financial problem?
6. Should the YMCA hold its position in education in view of the entry of many strictly educational agencies into the educational field?
7. Should the YMCA pioneer in other types of educational activities?
8. Should the new school building be erected immediately?

9. What is the solution to the school's financial problem?
   a. It was recommended that the Y trustees obtain an annual underwriting for Y-Tech for $15,000 to assist in meeting each years deficit. (Mr. Baker of the Plain Dealer indicated the P.D. would be glad to annually underwrite the Y-Tech to the extent of $500.).

At the February 27, 1928, Board of Governors meeting it was decided that it was absolutely essential that the new building be ready for the September opening of the Fall Term, two reasons being: It would be the first year for the fourth year of study for the five-year Cooperative Engineering School and there was an immediate need for the new mechanical, electrical, and materials testing laboratories; and indications were that at least one hundred forty new cooperative Engineering students would enter the freshman class and the existing laboratories and drafting facilities were entirely inadequate to accommodate this enrollment.

The Board of Trustees of the YMCA authorized construction of the new building on February 27, 1928, based upon early site selection.

Judge Carl V. Weygandt, who, as indicated previously, had coached the Central Y Day School basketball team in 1916 while a student at Western Reserve University, was elected to the Board of Governors on February 27, 1928. He had entered the practice of law in 1918, was Judge, Court of Common Pleas, Cuyahoga County from 1924 to 1930; Judge, Court of Appeals of Ohio, 8 Appellate District from 1930 to 1933; at which time he was elected to the high office of Chief Justice of the Supreme Court of the State of Ohio at age 45. He presided in this office without interruption through December 31, 1962.

The location of the new building was finally decided by the Y-Tech Board of Governors at the March 26, 1928, meeting. The site selected was behind (south of) the Johnson Building with a one-story connection between the two buildings and with an enclosed connecting ramp between the Johnson Building and the Central Y Building. Question was raised whether certain floors of the new building should be assigned to specific schools. The Commerce School originated this subject in requesting the first floor space through Dean Stacey R. Black.

The enrollments reported for the year 1927 were as follows:

College of Commerce	987
College of Engineering	865
Preparatory School	754
	———
Total	2606*

The first athletic carnival or meet conducted by Y-Tech was held in April 1928 under the auspices of the Student Council and Athletic Commission. Boxing, wrestling, basketball tournaments, and foul-shooting events took place. The athletic activities of the school increased appreciably over any previous year to date.

The *Plain Dealer* of April 29, 1928, carried a story on Oscar Torreson (mentioned earlier), a former Y-Tech student. About ten years previously Torreson entered Y-Tech for a course in Business English. He had dropped out of school following the eighth grade and had taken a business course. The faculty of Y-Tech encouraged him to complete his high school, and he did this through intermittent attendance at both day and night classes. Through a competitive examination he earned a scholarship to Case and made an excellent record in the Department of Physics. The news story related his proposed 100,000 mile cruise as the chief investigator and executive officer for the Carnegie Institute in Washington, D.C. The members of his staff were to study marine life, electrical storms, ocean currents, and other oceanic conditions relating to magnetism. He had just completed a cruise to Australia working on the same problems. The author knew Torreson well as a student at Case.

Late in April 1928 the Executive Committee of the Board of Trustees of the YMCA let the contract for the new educational building to The Van Blarcom Company for $148,000 amounting to about 32c per cubic foot. This did not include the architect's fee nor the contractor's bond. The total estimated cost amounted to about $160,000, which was greater than planned, but it was decided to proceed because of time and need, although this overall building cost would materially reduce the amount of money available for furnishings and equipment. Anyway, it appeared compelling to proceed with the building and work out the problem of furnishings and equipment at a later date.

---

* This does not include the Junior College and a few other Evening Division programs for a grand total of 3603 students.

The first student annual (yearbook) edited by the Student Council of Y-Tech was published in June 1928. This was the first publication of the school showing pictures of the students and their activities.

Paul E. Williams was engaged in July 1928 as Principal of the Y-Tech Preparatory School. He succeeded Howard W. Jones who resigned to become Assistant to the President of Hiram College. Williams had graduated from Ohio Wesleyan University, was a member of the first twenty-five thousand troops to go to France in World War I, and had a background of experience in personnel work in industry and education.

Closing in on the completion date of the new building, Clarence F. Deeter, a department secretary of the YMCA Central Branch, requested the return of space on the second floor which had been used for classrooms for many years. He planned to establish greatly needed transient dormitories. The Executive Committee of the Board of Governors agreed to this transfer. A review of space usage by Y-Tech as of September 1, 1928, was as follows:

19 classrooms in the Fenn Building*
6 classrooms in the Johnson Building
10 classrooms in the Edwards Annex
2 classrooms in the Central Branch Building
1 large drawing room in the Medical Library Building
8 laboratories in the Fenn Building*
2 laboratories in the Central Branch Building
Total of 48 class rooms and laboratories

The Board of Trustees officially dedicated the new Fenn Building September 13, 1928. The wives of the Board of Governors assisted with the decorations and refreshments. Many compliments and congratulations were received, especially from the faculty and students. The actual cost of the building including extras, survey of plat, bond, architects fees, and payment to the superintendent of construction total $168,193. Campaign, plus furnishings and equipment expenses brought the grand total to $201,700.25. This was greater than anticipated and

---

* This was the first instance in which the new building was designated with the name *Fenn*; therefore, it is assumed that sometime during July 1928 the Board of Trustees of the YMCA took action on naming the new building in honor of the man who had given much of his substance for many years to the Cleveland YMCA and its educational activities.

to complicate the problem further there was a shrinkage in the receipts from the building fund pledges. This created a reduction in funds planned for furnishings and equipment of an amount approximating $20,000. It was decided to attempt to secure this additional amount from a few individuals and firms.

The completion of the new Fenn Building again raised the question of accreditation of the college-grade work. The two accrediting agencies under consideration were the North Central Association of Colleges and Secondary Schools and the Ohio College Association. Accreditation was essential to be eligible for acceptance of transfer of student credits from one college to another. Each accrediting agency has minimum standards relative to endowment, teaching loads, laboratory equipment, library facilities, required number of credits for graduation, faculty scholarship, and a number of intangible items. At the November 13, 1928, meeting of the Y-Tech Board of Governors action was taken to appoint a sub-committee to work out the problems involved, realizing that there were areas which did not meet the minimum standards, and also realizing that securing accreditation would not be accomplished in a brief space of time.

William R. Lenga reported as the retiring president of the Student Council (at the same Board of Governors meeting) on the student activities for the year and was complimented for having completed the most successful year of the Council to date. Lenga later joined the United States Steel Corporation and retired in 1968 as Assistant Secretary.

Also reported at the same Board meeting were the following statistics for October, 1928 and 1927.

	October 1928	October 1927
Total—different students in attendance	1,456	1,241
Total—different classes meeting	217	206
Total—different class sessions	2,120	2,006
Total—different subjects taught	105	104
Total—different instructors paid	85	89
Total—instructor hours	2,675	2,472
Total—student hours attended	40,487	31,143

The December 12, 1928, meeting of the Board of Governors contained this statement presented by J. C. Nichols concerning the intelligence ranking of the cooperative engineering students: "The median score for the 120 freshmen who entered our Cooperative Engineering School this fall was 179 compared with a median score of 175 for 2279 freshmen in sixteen Ohio colleges. Fifty-five per cent of our entering freshmen rank in the upper half of all entering freshmen reported."

Dr. Goodwin B. Watson of Columbia University was engaged as a consultant to the faculty of the Day Prep (High) School. The enrollment of this school had been averaging approximately eighty for several years. The objective of the classroom work under research was to build character growth in the student. Dr. Watson stated that the Cleveland Y-Prep School was the first school to actually apply his modern educational theories in the classroom.

Director C. V. Thomas summed up the progress in 1928 as follows:

> Y-Tech moved ahead in 1928. No year has produced as many forward steps at Y-Tech as the year just closed.
>
> Fenn Hall was erected.
>
> The Cooperative Engineering College more than doubled its enrollment.
>
> Number of cooperating firms increased to 60.
>
> Number of high schools feeding students to Y-Tech increased to 70.
>
> Student activities reached a new high peak.
>
> The first school annual was published.
>
> The athletic program was greatly expanded.
>
> Y-Tech Courier was published for first full year.
>
> September enrollment was 18% greater than for September, 1927.
>
> The nine Junior College programs in the College of Commerce and the Evening Engineering Division had their first full year of operation.
>
> The Vocational Junior College was one of the first in the United States for employed adults.
>
> Y-Tech's new library was a 1928 must, leading to future accreditation.
>
> Action was taken by the YMCA Board of Trustees to establish more adequate financial support for the school.
>
> The Character Education program in the Day High School was carried forward by engaging Dr. Goodwin B. Watson of Columbia University as a consultant.
>
> New fraternities were organized.
>
> New method of teaching started in School of Commerce.

The Y-Tech Board of Governors at the January 9, 1929, meeting requested that the Board Commerce School Committee study the possibility of introducing a cooperative education program in the day Commerce School.

As of January 1929 the amount collected on the Fenn Building program was $178,000. The total pledges amounted to $209,000. The total cost of building, furnishings, and equipment to date was $203,000, and this did not include greatly needed equipment in the mechanical and chemistry laboratories. The collection of the remaining pleges was the first order of business.

Related to expanding enrollments and added building facilities was the program of engaging and retaining professional faculty and staff members. Accreditation by national and state agencies would enhance a faculty member's status in the community, but more than that it would enhance the prestige of the school in the eyes of the public. Director C. V. Thomas wrote the following to the Board of Governors in January 1929: "The public does not think of the school as having a purpose and a philosophy back of its work and as being really seriously at work on educational ideas." Even the two major institutions of higher learning in Cleveland would not accept the transfer credits of the Cleveland YMCA School of Technology (*sic*).*

The 19th Annual Student Banquet was held Saturday, March 2, 1929, in the north wing of the Public Auditorium. The dinner meeting was held on one floor followed by dancing on another. A total of 1,200 attended including students, faculty, administration, Board members, high school principals and vocational counselors, representatives of industries, and friends. The banquet was related to the 75th anniversary of the founding of the YMCA in Cleveland (Diamond Jubilee Anniversary). Edmund Vance Cooke, a student in the first classes of the Cleveland YMCA, was the principal speaker and an effort was especially made to urge former students to attend. William Ganson Rose, in his book CLEVELAND, *The Making of a City*, reported that "When the YMCA in 1881 added Greek, French and Elocution to its curriculum, the latter attracted Edmund Vance Cooke. He entertained his listeners with read-

---

* It will be observed that the terms Y.M.C.A., Y., YMCA, as well as Tech., Y-Tech, Technology and other variations, appear over the years, varying somewhat in relation to the formality or informality of the material quoted or referred to. This writer has faithfully accepted and recorded what he has found without presuming to alter or even amend it.

ings from Shakespeare and later earned wide renown as Cleveland's best known poet. He died December 18, 1932."

Miss Willingham was engaged in the Fall of 1928 as the first librarian of Y-Tech. The Fenn Building contained the first all-school library. Miss Willingham reported for the February 13, 1929, meeting of the Board of Governors that the number of students using the library increased from a maximum day use of 58 in December 1928 to 130 in January 1929. At the same meeting Judge Weygandt urged that the school participate in the Ohio High School Athletic Track Meet scheduled for March.

Statistical and financial data comparisons varied considerably from month to month and semester to semester. Tables 3 and 4 are taken from reports of Director C. V. Thomas to the Board of Governors:

TABLE 3

COMPARISON OF ENROLLMENTS AND VALUE OF CONTRACTS FOR JANUARY AND FEBRUARY, 1926–1929

As reported at the Board of Governors meeting on March 13, 1929

School	Enrollments				Value of Contracts			
	1926	1927	1928	1929	1926	1927	1928	1929
Commerce	203	145	118	185	$ 8,929	$ 5,927	$ 6,181	$ 6,839
Engineering	206	174	185	307	10,442	8,230	8,137	12,898
Preparatory	218	149	200	233	9,115	6,533	8,027	9,683
Totals	627	468	503	725	$28,486	$20,690	$22,345	$29,420

TABLE 4

COMPARISON OF ENROLLMENTS AND VALUE OF CONTRACTS FOR AUGUST, SEPTEMBER AND OCTOBER, 1927–1929

As reported at the Board of Governors meeting on October 23, 1929

School	Enrollments			Value of Contracts		
	1927	1928	1929	1927	1928	1929
Commerce	323	354	378	$ 26,140	$ 25,409	$ 24,926
Engineering	402	585	893	33,703	54,403	81,771
Bookstore	467	488	512	35,399	33,699	44,631
Totals	1192	1427	1783	$ 95,242	$113,511	$151,328

Note the significant increases in the Engineering School, not only between the different periods of the year, but especially between 1928 and 1929.

Forty-four students were graduated from the Preparatory School and 22 from the College of Commerce and Engineering in June 1929. Two of the latter were women. This was the first commencement for the Junior College, an Evening Division program.

As of June 1929 former students of Y-Tech who were then presidents of Cleveland firms numbered 133; vice presidents, 116; and secretaries and/or treasurers, 318. In reflecting upon the statistics it does not seem out of place to repeat that the pioneering probing of the teaching effort that was occurring at this institution was an early recognition of other than the orthodox pattern of reaching and affecting men of native intelligence and uncommon motivation, thereby assisting them and the city of Cleveland in fuller utilization of their and its native potential.

The first alumni reunion in the history of the school was held preceding the June 1929 commencement. The first officers elected were: President, Cecil B. Whitcomb, Secretary of the Cleveland Stock Exchange; Secretary, Charles H. Hudson, The White Motor Company; Treasurer, Harrison Hunter, Treasurer of Telling Belle Vernon Company.

The fifth year of the engineering cooperative program was to be given for the first time in the fall of 1929. This entailed enlarging the engineering faculty by four competent professional engineers and the acquisition of considerable laboratory equipment which had been postponed because of the high original cost of construction of the Fenn Building. Fifteen firms were approached to endeavor to raise $45,000, the estimated cost of the needed equipment. The first company approached was the Warner & Swasey Company and its officers agreed to contribute $3,500 plus a polishing machine worth $250. Throughout the history of Fenn College the Warner & Swasey Company contributed more money to the operation, equipment, and building development of the college than any other company.

On June 28, 1929, a special committee of the Y-Tech Board of Governors recommended to the Board that, as a result of two years of study and trial of the character education type of teaching in the Y-Preparatory School under the counsel of Dr. Goodwin Watson of Columbia University, the junior and senior years of the Day High School be conducted on a co-op basis. Millard L. Jordan was a member of this special committee. The Board of Governors approved the recommendation of the special committee to go into operation the following fall term.

Professor Jordan started teaching at Y-Tech on a part-time basis in the evening Preparatory School in February 1926. He became an Instructor in Sociology in 1928, Dean of Nash Junior College in 1932, Associate Professor (Fenn College) in 1934, Professor in 1937, and Chairman of the Department of Sociology in 1941. He retired as Professor Emeritus August 31, 1965, and succeeded George Simon as Archivist of The Cleveland State University.

The first Y-Tech picnic was held at Euclid Beach Park on Saturday, August 24, 1929. It was arranged by the Student Council.

The Board of Governors, on August 26, 1929, approved the appointment of Homer E. Woodling, a graduate of Butler College. He was engaged to teach economics and other business courses in the College of Engineering, to coach the College of Engineering basketball team, and as an assistant to Stacey Black in the College of Commerce. Professor Woodling was affectionately known as Woody by all the students and faculty at Fenn College. He became Athletic Coach, Instructor and Director of Student Activities, January 1931; Assistant Professor of Physical Education, September 1936; Associate Professor of Physical Education, July 1937; Professor of Health and Physical Education, September 1941; Chairman, Department of Health, Physical Education and Recreation, July 1946; and retired from The Cleveland State University in 1966, where the gymnasium in the new CSU Physical Education Center was dedicated in his name October 20, 1973.

On many occasions Director C. V. Thomas wrote about how valuable to the young man was the service provided by the Cleveland YMCA School of Technology. He drew his examples from actual happenings at the School. All his reports to the Y-Tech Board of Governors were verbose and oft-times repetitive to stress the points he found of considerable importance. As Secretary to the Board of Governors his Minutes of the meetings were just the opposite, with very few words to describe each subject on the agenda and any action thereon. Of course, his report to the Board of Governors, which constituted the agenda, was always attached to the Minutes; and thus, in a very real manner, he was teaching his board his concepts for the school's operation.

To give the reader some insight as to Director Thomas' style of writing and his homey manner of expressing himself, the following is quoted from an undated report written in September or October 1929:

I. *Helping Young Men Find Themselves*

The increasing number of high school graduates, together with the changes in industrial processes, is resulting in a larger and larger number of young men who are at sea regarding what their purpose in life should be. Mothers and fathers, together with the boys, are asking us to help the boys find themselves. A typical case will illustrate.

A boy graduated from Cleveland Heights High School with excellent grades but without any clear idea of what he should do. His mother phoned for an appointment. The boy and the mother came to the office. At the close of the interview the boy was given Dr. Strong's Vocational Interest blank, together with our own booklet which contains about four hundred questions for him to answer. Filling out these two blanks requires about six hours' work. When they were returned to us, they were checked against the vocational interest records of successful people in various lines of activity and it was found that this boy had the interests of engineers. The father and the boy came to the office for a second interview. It became clear to the boy and his parents that his interests did lie in construction and engineering activities. He is now a freshman in the College of Engineering.

Cases of this nature are multiplying very rapidly. They require a great deal of time but the results indicate how valuable to the young men the service is.

II. *Introducing New Types of Education to Cleveland*

(a) *Co-operative Engineering*

Six years ago your educational secretaries discussed the co-operative type of engineering education with Dr. Howe of Case School of Applied Science and representative heads of Cleveland industries. Case was not interested in such a program but the manufacturers expressed a real interest in it. The application of modern educational principles showed the great value of the cooperative plan of education in developing young men.

The first year we began school we had 14 students—7 at work and 7 in school; the next year 32 were enrolled; the next year 128; last year 205; this year 325. Only young men who graduate in the upper 2/3 of their high school classes and who give evidence of ability and willingness to do hard work in industry are accepted for this cooperative program. In our student body are graduates of 104 high schools, including all high schools of Greater Cleveland, many Ohio high schools and high schools located in North Dakota, New York, Massachusetts, Indiana, Pennsylvania, together with six students from foreign countries. These students are spending their alternating five-week work periods in 65 firms. The first men will be graduating from this college in June.

The cooperative kind of education is being recognized rapidly. The Association* is doing an excellent service in introducing co-operative education to Cleveland. There is perhaps no more effective way for the Association to integrate itself into the industrial life of the community than through this type of activity.

(b) *Vocational Junior Colleges*

Two years ago the Association, after months of thinking and conference with educational leaders, announced a new type of educational program known as the Vocational Junior College. The educational philosophy back of this type of college is that the high school graduate who does not expect to enter the professions should be given an opportunity to obtain vocational preparation. Instead of requiring him to spend his first two years in the study of History, Philosophy, Foreign Languages and other courses, his education is immediately focused upon his vocation. If he desires to be a draftsman or mechanical man, his education consists of Higher Mathematics, Mechanics, Strength of Materials, etc. The Association has eight Vocational Junior College programs in operation. Students attend classes 3 evenings per week 3 hours per evening 40 weeks per year for 3 years. They earn 60 semester hours of college credit. They are graduated with the title of Graduate in Mechanical Engineering or Business Administration, specializing in Accounting, etc.

At the end of the three years many of them will have seen the real meaning of education and will continue with their broadening and cultural subjects, which would have been of no interest to them before they obtained their vocational preparation.

---

* YMCA.

The response to this program has been most gratifying. The Society for the Promotion of Engineering Education had representatives here twice last year studying our work. They stated that it was the best set-up they had yet found. Industries have seen the value of it. One Cleveland industry has 15 men in this program at the present time. There are over 100 freshmen in the Engineering Junior College set-up this fall.

(c) *The Co-operative High School*

Sixteen and seventeen year old boys twenty years ago were doing "chores" on the farm or in other ways developing work habits in much larger numbers than at present. It is the conviction of your educational secretaries that a great need in secondary education is the relating of school activity to life experience through actual work; that work experience is one of the elements that should be included in preparation for college and later life. This conviction was tested against the thinking of Dr. Watson of Teachers' College, Columbia, representatives of the North Central Association of Colleges and Secondary Schools, parents of boys, etc. The result was the beginning this fall of the first Cooperative High School preparing boys for college anywhere in the United States.

The boys spend 3 weeks in school and 3 weeks at work. A [member of] Department of Coordination visits them at their work, counsels with them about their experience, helps them to interpret life outside the classroom and relates their classroom work to their work experience. We have 34 boys on this plan.

The North Central Association of Colleges and Secondary Schools, after a thorough examination of the set-up, wrote that they have never seen a plan like it but that they could find nothing wrong with it and that they would approve it. We believe that a type of educational program on the secondary or high school level has been begun here which will be used quite generally within the next five years.

III. *Making the Purpose of the Y. Function for the Students*

(a) One of the many unique features of the Young Men's Christian Association is that it has a variety of activities, each of which attract young men to the organization. Some come through the "door" of gymnasium interest, some through the "door" of a place to live. Many enter through the "door" of a desire to learn. Within the Association, however, there is a common set of purposes which must function on all groups. There are the development of the social possibilities of the man, the keeping of his physical self sound and the enriching of his spiritual self and helping him find an adequate philosophy of life.

Y-Tech is making progress in making the purposes of the Y function. The developing of social qualities largely centers in self-directed student activities. The Student Council represents all the classes and groups of the school. There are clubs, fraternities, choral societies, dramatic groups—all organized and directed by students. Committees of the students arrange visits to Cleveland industries, dinners, dances, banquets, etc.

(b) *Physical Development*

Arrangements have been made with the Central Branch whereby students who carry six hours or more of work per week are given free use of the gymnasium and swimming pool. All others may use the physical facilities on Tuesday and Friday evenings without charge. There will be this year at least 16 basketball teams and swimming teams. Wrestling, handball and boxing tournaments will be conducted. The school employs two men who develop athletic and gymnasium interests in the students and supervise their tournaments.

(c) *Spiritual and Character Growth*

In common with churches and other character-building and religious organizations, the Association is faced with new conditions in this field. The purpose of religion has shifted from preparing for another world to enriching present living. Science has developed a vast amount of new knowledge regarding character. Much of the protection which young men had twenty years ago in their home life has been removed and instead we have the influences of the radio, the movie and the automobile. Religion is no longer thought of as a compartment of life but as a reality which permeates the whole of life.

* * *

In the Summer of 1929 the Board of Trustees of the Buffalo YMCA decided to drop its program of cooperative engineering education because of financial difficulties. Representatives of the Cleveland Y-Tech staff were invited to Buffalo to meet with their students and evaluate their laboratory equipment. As a result of this trip twenty of Buffalo's second and third year co-op students came to Cleveland to complete their course work. They returned to Buffalo each co-op period to continue their original employment plans. In addition six boys from Buffalo came to Cleveland Y-Tech as freshmen in the Co-op Program. Also Y-Tech was able to obtain $3,400 worth of equipment from the Buffalo Y for $1,220.

The question was raised in the August 26, 1929, meeting of the Board of Governors concerning the advisability of having girls attend Y-Tech. A special committee was appointed to study the matter and report at a later board meeting.

Three new courses were started in the Fall of 1929: Chemistry for Nurses with an enrollment of 23, Steel Treating with an enrollment of 25, and Auto Salesmanship with an enrollment of 34. There was likewise an increase in the demand for technical courses such as Drafting, Radio, and Practical Electricity. It was necessary to limit and eventually close enrollment in these three courses because of lack of space and laboratory equipment.

For the first time, at the Board of Governors meeting of October 23, 1929, the subject of creating a scholarship fund was discussed. The concensus of the members was that the student should pay for his education, but they requested Director Thomas to report at a later meeting on the details of establishing and operating a scholarship fund.

Student resentment was arising again in the college-level programs concerning the lack of proper distinction between the college and the non-college activities. For the first time it was suggested that the college area should be known as Fenn College of The Cleveland YMCA School of Technology. The Board was unanimous at their October 23, 1929, meeting that the college-level work should be given collegiate recognition. On a motion by Hoddinott and second by Mouck a committee was appointed to prepare a statement to be presented to the Board of Trustees of the YMCA citing arguments in favor of the college-level work being distinguished by a specific name.

In early December 1929 the Executive Committee of the Board of Trustees of the YMCA approved the name "Fenn College of The Cleveland YMCA School of Technology" which was henceforth referred to directly as Fenn College. The following undated, unsigned statement was included in the Minutes of the Board of Governors:

> The Board of Trustees of the Cleveland Young Men's Christian Association upon the recommendation of the Board of Governors of The Cleveland YMCA School of Technology has approved the

unification of the college [level] work of the Association under
one title—The Fenn College of The Cleveland YMCA School of
Technology.

The advantages of this coordination lie in the opportunity to
unite all students who are attending college [level] courses offered
by the Association. At present one group of students attend a Day
Cooperative Engineering Division, another an Evening College of
Commerce and still another an Evening College of Engineering.
There has been no means of developing loyalty of all these groups
around the entire college grade program of the Association.

The name Fenn College was selected because of the great influence which Mr. Sereno P. Fenn has had upon the development
of the educational work of the Cleveland Association. During the
twenty-five years that Mr. Fenn was President of the Cleveland
Association [YMCA] he gave liberally in both time and money
to the development of the school. It was through his initial gift
of $100,000 that it was possible to obtain a fund large enough
to erect the Fenn Building, the present main class room and laboratory building of the Association. The Cleveland Young Men's
Christian Association purposes to carry forward in Fenn College
the ideals of Christian character and growth in young men for
which Mr. Fenn stood.

The new Fenn College will bring together 850 college grade
students. Athletics, social activities, school publications, commencement exercises, etc., can be conducted much more efficiently and
effectively when the present group of college students are united
into one organization. The high school and the non-college grade
vocational courses of the Association will be continued as the Preparatory and Vocational courses of The Cleveland YMCA School
of Technology.

* * *

There was considerable discussion at the December 11, 1929 meeting,
of the Board of Governors concerning the advisability of establishing
a Day Division Cooperative College of Commerce. The Commerce
Committee of the Board had been exploring the subject for several
months and reported they were agreed: (1) that the cooperative program of higher education is sound; (2) the program would be beneficial
to certain types of young men; (3) that such a school would not compete
with any program of Fenn College nor any other school in Cleveland;
and (4) that it would supplement the Day Division Cooperative Engi-

neering Program and the Evening Division Commerce Program. The Board, on hearing and discussing the report of the committee, voted unanimously to put the program into effect as early as possible after curriculum and financial operations were resolved. A committee composed of Green, Fred T. Jones and Thomas was given power to act on the effective starting date.

Action was taken at the same meeting to add a course in Metallurgy to the Cooperative Engineering Program. This was the first day division course in Metallurgy.

Also, a report was given by Director Thomas on the progress of the Character Building Program in the Day Preparatory School. Dr. Goodwin B. Watson, Consultant to the program, reported after his fifth visit to the school that: "Y-Prep has done more than any other secondary school in the United States in leading boys to an understanding of social problems—the vital problems of work, leisure time, poverty, wealth, etc. Its new program is making use of character building principles which have proven sound. Probably only Lincoln High School, a part of Teachers' College of Columbia, exceeds Y-Tech in its plan of operation." Dr. Watson was Associate Professor of Education at Columbia University Teachers' College.

At the close of the fiscal year, December 31, 1929, the following administrative staff and faculty members were engaged in full-time service for Fenn College:

Administrative Staff

Cecil V. Thomas, Executive Secretary and Director
Stacy R. Black, Dean, Department of Business Administration
Joseph C. Nichols, Dean, Department of Engineering
Maurice E. Nichols, Associate Dean, Evening Engineering Division
Paul Edgar Williams, Principal, Preparatory School
Gerald S. Wellman, Registrar

Faculty

John W. Armstrong	Charles W. Francis
Landis R. Bradfield	William E. Hitchcock
Ross C. Brown	Louis W. Hunt
Rudolph T. Damstedt	Millard L. Jordan
William C. Davis	Isbell F. McIlhenny
Donald C. Fabel	Russell R. Steele

Floyd R. Stewart   Arthur Wald
Byron E. Toan   Samuel Ward
Frank J. Tomich   Homer E. Woodling

Members constituting the first Board of Governors of Fenn College as of December 31, 1929 were:

William R. Green, Chairman, Guardian Trust Co.
Fred T. Jones, Vice Chairman, Johns-Manville Corporation
James E. Campbell, The Sherwin Williams Co.
Harold K. Ferguson, The H. K. Ferguson Co.
A. Scott Hamilton, The Smitley-Hamilton Co.
Richard J. Hoddinott, The Collver-Miller Co.
Edward W. Kempton, The American Steel & Wire Co.
Parker A. McMillin, City Hospital
G. Hamlin Mouck, Security Discount Co.
Harris W. Roberts, Washington Times
William J. Semple, Standard Oil of Ohio
Lawrence A. Tucker, Attorney
Carl V. Weygandt, Judge, Court of Common Pleas

The end of the calendar year 1929 not only brought to a close a prominent decade henceforth referred to as the "roaring twenties," but also terminated a period of extremely significant and accelerated progress and growth in the history of Y-Tech and Fenn College. The expression *terminated* is used because 1930 was the beginning of the depression years of the thirties, springboarded by the stock market crash of October 29, 1929, the day since referred to as "Black Friday." Fenn College weathered the Depression, but it took intensely frugal management and operation plus extraordinary patience and considerable sacrifice on the part of the administration and faculty.

III

*Human history becomes more and more
a race between education and catastrophe.*

Herbert George Wells, 1866–1946.

The Board of Governors authorized Director Thomas at its January 15, 1930, meeting to make application to the Supreme Court of Ohio for accreditation as an institution where students preparing for the study of law may obtain their necessary credits to become eligible to register for the Bar Examination. Successful completion of 60 semester hours of Business Administration or Engineering courses constituted eligibility for the examination.

Although the Fenn Building was only a little over a year old, preliminary planning was already under way for the construction of another building. The Fenn Building, furnishings, and equipment costs had not all been met because outstanding pledges had not been paid. E. J. Hart was engaged by the Board to call upon people who had not fulfilled their pledges. The effect of "Black Friday" had not yet caught up with the local economy.

The general planning for the new building took into consideration the use of the Fenn Building for the laboratory, drafting room, and design purposes for which it was best suited. The proposed new building would contain classrooms, large lecture rooms, library, faculty and staff offices, bookstore, and stock rooms. Its proposed location was on the Carnegie Avenue end of the Johnson property, immediately south of the Fenn Building.

Director Thomas was most anxious to convince the Board of Governors of the space needs and wrote thus: "Again, the growth of our student body has resulted in the following reactions from our faculty and students regarding our present space needs: We need 12 additional

73

classrooms, we have outgrown our Qualitative and Quantitative Chemistry Laboratories, our High School Physics Laboratory is not large enough, stock rooms for Physics and Chemistry are not large enough, both Chemistry and Physics Lecture Rooms are too small (both should be at least twice the present size), our Metallurgical Laboratory space is far too small, the Testing Materials Laboratory is inadequate, the Electrical Laboratory is in need of more space, our Drafting Rooms in the Fenn Building are too small for efficient operation and our Library has outgrown its space." Note how many different expressions he used to stress the lack of space.

Many members of the faculty and staff were being called upon to speak before groups, particularly in churches and schools. The Board of Governors discussed the extent of the contact with the public at the February 19, 1930, meeting and felt that the college was making excellent progress in bringing about a better understanding of its work on the part of the public, although Dr. Thomas had the opinion that the progress was far too slow.

Dr. William E. Wickenden, the new President of Case School of Applied Science, was the speaker at the Annual Student Banquet held March 1, 1930, at the Hotel Statler.

"The Envoy," the 1930 yearbook, was planned, developed, financed, and published by the Student Council. It had over sixty group pictures and was dedicated to S. P. Fenn.

It was reported at the April 23, 1930, meeting of the Board of Governors that the Supreme Court of Ohio had approved the accreditation of Fenn College as an institution qualified to prepare students to take the Ohio Bar Examinations.

Because of the anticipated growth in enrollment in the fall term of 1930, several new faculty members were engaged. Among them were: Marion B. Tolar, Assistant Professor and Head, Department of Mathematics, and Alex Rexion, Coordination Department staff member. Professor Ward was reengaged and later retired as Emeritus Professor of Civil Engineering August 31, 1949. Professor Tolar later became Professor, Head, Department of Mathematics, and his wife also taught mathematics. He resigned August 31, 1955. Rexion remained until December 1944, at which time he resigned.

Miss Willingham, Librarian, gave the following report to the Board of Governors on May 26, 1930:

1. Total number of books increased from 1,600 as of November 1, 1928, to 2,496 as of December 31, 1929.
2. During 1929 a total of 2,221 books were borrowed from the Cleveland Public Library.
3. During 1929 the library was visited by 17,379 persons.
4. During 1929 the number of books issued for outside use was 4,721.

The Y-Preparatory School commencement was held June 13, 1930, with Dr. Harold Phillips the speaker. The Fenn College commencement was held June 19, 1930, with Dr. Frank Slutz of Dayton as the speaker. The first group of Fenn co-op students to complete the five-year program in Engineering, ten in number, received their diplomas. Receiving the degree of bachelor of science, they were:

Kenneth J. Burke	Carl F. Mueller
John W. Glover	Robert Mulhauser
Theodore W. Hartman	Vernon R. Roy
Elliott F. Hoff	George A. Scheny
Michael L. Kraing	Lawrence W. Ulrich

Nine of the ten graduates accepted full-time engineering positions with the firms which had provided work experience (co-op jobs) for them during their college years.

The Fenn College Graduating Class of 1930 presented a bronze plaque in memory of S. P. Fenn to the Board of Trustees of the YMCA at the June 19, 1930, commencement convocation. The plaque was later affixed to the first floor corridor wall of the Fenn Building.

Sometime during July 1930, Director C. V. Thomas wrote the following related to the basic concepts of the educational programs under the aegis of the YMCA:

> The philosophy underlying The Cleveland YMCA School of Technology is the integrating of the basic purposes of the Young Men's Christian Association with the best theory of modern education. It is the conviction of the administrative and governing groups of this institution that the bringing together of the principles for which the Young Men's Christian Association exists with modern concepts of education provides a most unique service to young men and to Cleveland. The purpose of the institution is to permeate all of its educational activities with that which will stimulate young men to work out a meaningful philosophy of life.

Some specific objectives of Fenn College and of the Y-Preparatory School—the two divisions of Y-tech—are:

(1) To stimulate young men to mental growth. The institution believes that there is a type of mental growth suitable to everyone and that the abundant life cannot be achieved unless a continuous mental development occurs in the individual.

(2) To assist young men in thinking through their vocational objective. The specialization of types of work due to industrial development, together with the increase in the percentage of young men who are living in urban communities, results in confusion on the part of young men as to what their vocation should be. It is the purpose of the Young Men's Christian Association to assist young men in finding a challenging vocational objective.

(3) To aid young men in planning their educational programs. Often individuals believe that there are 'short cuts' to a given objective. Such persons need counsel as to the steps which they must take if they are finally to achieve their purpose. The rapid growth of Adult Education has also resulted in an urge on the part of large numbers of people for some type of mental activity, although they are often hazy as to the kind of study they should pursue. This institution seeks to introduce people to the 'different intellectual worlds' which they may explore.

(4) To provide classroom instruction adapted to the interests and needs of employed adults. Y-Tech desires to use and to assist in the development of methods of instruction which apply modern theories of what education is and how educational growth occurs.

(5) To aid young men in locating employment opportunities which will enable them to continue to grow because of their work experience.

The basic educational concepts underlying Fenn College and the Y-Preparatory School are:

(1) Education is a growth process.

(2) Education is a continuous life-long opportunity and responsibility.

(3) Education—some type of Growth—is for everyone.

The application of these concepts results in the cooperative type of education which produces growth in the individual by integrating life experience with the laboratory and classroom teaching; the Vocational Junior College which offers higher educational opportunity to young men according to their interests and needs; and in the emphasis which the institution places upon Adult Education—a growth continuous process.

In proportion to the ability of the institution to make these concepts operative in the lives of young men is it possible for the school to assist young men in more abundant living, and thus the purposes of the Young Men's Christian Association and the theory of modern education are united.

The first inventory ever executed by the Cleveland YMCA School of Technology was completed in August 1930. The value of all furnishings, equipment, instruments, and supplies totaled $81,842.

TABLE 1

A RESUMÉ OF THE THREE MAIN AREAS OF ACTIVITY
OF THE ENGINEERING DIVISION OF FENN COLLEGE
FOR THE ACADEMIC YEAR 1929–1930

I. *Co-operative Engineering (Day School)*

(a) Courses offered:
    Mechanical Engineering
    Electrical Engineering
    Structural Engineering
    Chemical Engineering
(b) Entrance Requirements: High School education
(c) Length of course: 5 years
(d) Credit given: B.S. Degree
(e) Purpose: To develop production executives
(f) Number of students: 280
(g) Number of industries cooperating: 68

II. *Junior Engineering College*

(a) Courses offered:
    Mechanical Engineering
    Electrical Engineering
    Structural Engineering
    Chemical Engineering
(b) Entrance Requirements: High School education or
    equivalent
(c) Length of course: 3 years
(d) Credit given: "Associate in Science"
(e) Purpose: To raise the level of workmen to executives
    and designers

(f) Number of students: 135
(g) Median age: 20
(h) Type of work these students are doing
(The following is an analysis of the Freshman class)
Office work: 5
Drafting: 14
Apprentices: 7
General shop work: 20
Stock clerks: 3
Designers: 2
Other types of work given include:
Inspector
Salesman
Die maker
Truck driver

III. *One and Two Year Vocational Courses*

(a) Purpose: To train men in a particular phase of industrial work
(b) Entrance requirements: None
(c) Credit given: Certificate
(d) *Courses Offered*

Courses Offered	*Length*	*Students*
Mechanical Drafting	2 years	96
Structural Drafting	2 years	20
Architectural Drafting	2 years	29
Practical Electricity	1 year	54
Structural Design	1 year	10
Blue Print Reading	½ year	19
Building Estimating	1 year	19
Radio Telegraphy	½ year	28
Radio Construction	½ year	65
Show Card Writing	½ year	17
Steam Engineering	½ year	11
Qualitative Analysis	1 year	5
Steel Treating	½ year	19
Heating & Ventilating	1 year	13
Concrete Construction	1 year	11
Shop Mathematics	(mostly students taking other courses)	

The following analysis of students in the *Mechanical Drafting* gives some idea of who is reached by such courses:

Median age: 22

Average hours attending per week: 6

Previous Education:

Number	*Amount of Education*
15	8 years
17	9 years
22	10 years
12	11 years
25	12 years
2	1 year college
1	3 years college

Type of work they are now doing:

Construction: 2

Drafting: 10

Apprentices: 5

Office: 19

General shop work: 24

Machinists: 14

Pattern makers: 2

Tool makers: 2

Other occupations represented:

Assistant Treasurer

Assistant Foreman

Compositor

Millwright

Stationary Engineer

In the Fall of 1930 the freshman class in the Cooperative Division of Fenn College numbered 218: 161 in the Engineering section and 57 in the Business Administration section. The budget was built on an anticipated 160 in Engineering and 40 in Business Administration so the freshman enrollment exceeded the budget by 18 students.

The minutes of the September 17, 1930, meeting of the Board of Governors carried an item on the first Flag Rush between the sophomores and freshmen, also on the publication of the first Fenn Handbook prepared and sponsored by the Student Council. The establishment of a Scholarship Loan Fund had been discussed at previous board meetings, and a committee had been appointed to study the matter. The committee reported a plan at this September meeting which was acceptable to the board. The usual amount of the loan was $200, and the student was obligated to obtain a co-signer for the note and a life insurance policy which was assigned to the Scholarship Loan Fund of Fenn College. The note was payable prior to three years from date of graduation at an interest rate of 6%. The loan fund was originally funded by contributions. The first contribution of $200 to the fund was made anonymously by the father of one of Fenn's students.

The enrollment in the Cooperative divisions increased more rapidly than available job opportunities. The board members were requested in the Fall of 1930 to help find jobs for about fifty students; 312 students had found jobs. Of course, with the passage of time into the depression years, the job situation deteriorated considerably.

Authorization was approved at the November 12, 1930, meeting of the Board of Governors to organize a group of approximately thirty leading Cleveland executives in business and industry to promote co-operative education in Cleveland. Perhaps just as important was the prestige these men would bring the College through their association with Fenn and having their names linked with the College. This was the forerunner of the "Members of the Corporation" formed in 1951 numbering approximately eighty for essentially the same reason.

A group of educational leaders of Cleveland was organized in 1930 to study technical education in the community. Dr. Wickenden, President, Case School of Applied Science was appointed chairman. Dr. Wickenden raised four questions for discussion at the first meeting of the group. Following are the questions and the response prepared by Director C. V. Thomas; also a chart to aid the committee in its study of the YMCA educational program.

> *Question 1*—What is the philosophy upon which the Young Men's Christian Association bases its educational program? In other words, why does it conduct a school?
> *Answer*—The basic purpose of the Young Men's Christian Association is to assist young men in achieving the abundant life; that the organization believes that the all-around growth—including the physical, mental, spiritual and social elements in a young man—must occur if the abundant life is to develop. Young men must however be approached from the angle of their immediate interest.

Regardless of what an individual's particular interests may be, it is the Association's purpose to stimulate him to grow in all of the phases of his life. The result is that the Association must have an educational program in order to attract a large group of young men whose immediate interest is in education, and it must have an educational program to complete its four-fold service to young men.

Question 2—Why does the Association offer Cooperative Education? What does the Y consider to be the philosophy beneath cooperative training?

Answer—There are two major reasons why Cooperative Education is included in the program of the Cleveland YMCA School of Technology. (1) The Co-operative plan assists high school graduates who desire to enter industry and commerce to obtain an education and at the same time get practical experience. (2) The administration of the school believes that Cooperative Education expresses a most fundamental educational concept—namely, that Education is a Growth Process. The Association believes in Cooperative Education because it thinks that it is a most excellent plan for producing educational growth in young men. The cooperative plan requires that the student integrate what he learns in college with what is going on in life as he contacts it through his alternating five-week work periods.

In summary the Association conducts Cooperative Education *First* because it knows that it helps young men and *Second* because it believes that the plan is educationally sound.

Question 3—Why does the Association conduct a Day High School since there are so many good high schools in Cleveland?

Answer—Again there are two reasons. The school knows many boys who have found themselves because of the Day High School opportunity. The Day High School is one of the means whereby the basic purposes of the Association in relation to older boys is achieved. Because of the necessarily large classes in the public high schools which makes a personal relationship between the boy and teacher most difficult, many boys do not make the progress in the public high schools which they should make. The boys tend to build wrong attitudes. They fail to obtain from their high school the kind of growth which an adolescent boy should have. Parents prefer to send them to a school such as our Y-Prep School where classes have from ten to fifteen pupils and where there is a very close understanding between the teacher and the boy.

In addition to the help which the school gives to individual boys the Association believes that the Day High School should be conducted because of laboratory work which is going on in it. For the last three years the Day High School has been a laboratory where Dr. Goodwin Watson and Dr. John P. Herring—two specialists in the field of Character Education—have been introducing the principles of their character growth psychology in a secondary school. Both educational processes and the content of what is taught have been radically changed.

In summary the Association conducts a Day High School because it knows that boys are advantaged by the small classes, the influence of the Christian motivated teachers and because it believes that it is in a strategic position to make a contribution to Character Development in Secondary Education.

Question 4—What is the "Educational Bank" in which credits earned in the Evening Junior College of Engineering can be deposited?

Answer—The Evening Junior College of Engineering is designed for the high school graduate who has gone to work in industry. The curricula in Engineering teach these high school graduates mathematics, mechanics, strength of materials, etc., they need in order to advance in their jobs. At the same time the courses are so organized that they can get college credit for the work they do. When occasionally a boy desires to transfer these credits to some other college, the following procedure is used.

A letter is written the college which gives information about the subjects which the young man has studied, the number of clock hours that he studied each of the subjects, the qualifications of the instructors under whom he studied, the textbooks used, etc. The college then figures the number of credits to which the individual is entitled based upon the number of hours that he has studied in this school. The number of hours required in some colleges is such that the student gets full credit for certain subjects; in other subjects he gets only that proportion of credit which is represented by the number of hours he has studied in this school.

Chart I exhibits a host of factual data concerned with many elements of Y-Tech for the year 1930.

THE CLEVELAND Y.M.C.A. SCHOOL OF TECHNOLOGY

| | FENN COLLEGE | | | | Y-PREP SCHOOL | |
| | ENGINEERING | | BUSINESS ADMINISTRATION | | | |
	DAY CO-OPERATIVE	EVENING	DAY CO-OPERATIVE	EVENING	DAY	EVENING
NUMBER OF DIFFERENT STUDENTS IN 1930	433	1107	60	686	250	637
MEDIAN AGE OF STUDENTS	18+	22+	18+	23+	17+	21+
NUMBER OF INSTRUCTORS	21	37	6	25	8	24
ENTRANCE REQUIREMENTS	GRADUATION UPPER 2/3 OF H.S. CLASSES, AND EVIDENCE OF ABILITY TO SUCCEED ON COOPERATIVE PLAN.	H.S. GRADUATION FOR JUNIOR COLLEGE COURSES. NECESSARY MATHEMATICAL AND ENGLISH ABILITY TO CARRY UNIT TECHNICAL COURSES.	GRADUATION UPPER 2/3 OF H.S. CLASSES. PERSONALITY THAT GIVES INDICATION OF SUCCESS ON COOPERATIVE PLAN.	H.S. GRADUATION FOR REGULAR CURRICULUM STUDENTS. ADULTS WITHOUT H.S. EDUCATION MAY ENTER UNIT COURSES, IF THEIR BUSINESS EXPERIENCE INDICATES THEY HAVE A FOUNDATION FOR BENEFITTING FROM THE COURSE.	EIGHTH GRADE. COOPERATIVE PROGRAM REQUIRES JUNIOR STANDING FOR ENTRANCE	EIGHTH GRADE.
LENGTH OF TIME REQUIRED FOR COMPLETION	FIVE YEARS. 48 WEEKS PER YEAR.	JUNIOR COLLEGE – 3 YEARS AT 40 WEEKS PER YEAR. UNIT COURSES – 1/2-2 YEARS AT 32 WEEKS PER YEAR.	FIVE YEARS. 48 WEEKS PER YEAR.	JUNIOR COLLEGE – 3 YEARS AT 40 WEEKS PER YEAR. SENIOR COLLEGE – 6 YEARS AT 40 WEEKS PER YEAR.	FOUR YEARS.	FIVE YEARS AT 40 WEEKS PER YEAR, PLUS 2 SUMMER TERMS.
LENGTH OF TIME IN OPERATION	SEVEN YEARS	CURRICULUM COURSES 10 YEARS. SOME OF UNIT COURSES 25 YEARS.	THREE MONTHS	CURRICULUM COURSES 17 YEARS. SOME OF UNIT COURSES 30 YEARS.	NINETEEN YEARS.	CURRICULUM WORK 13 YEARS. UNIT COURSES 49 YEARS.
NUMBER OF FIRMS COOPERATING WITH THE DAY DIVISION.	80	~	22	~	12	~
INTELLIGENCE RANKING OF STUDENTS.	MEDIAN SCORE FOR 3000 FRESHMEN IN OHIO COLLEGES IN 1922 BASED ON O.S.U. TEST WAS 127. MEDIAN SCORE FENN COLLEGE FRESHMEN SAME TEST WAS 133. 43% OF FRESHMAN CLASS GRADUATED UPPER 1/3 OF THEIR H.S. CLASS. COMPARISON OF FENN STUDENTS ON IOWA PLACEMENT FORM "A" IS ATTACHED.	MEDIAN SCORE JUNIOR COLLEGE GROUP 134 ON O.S.U. TEST LAST YEAR.	NORMS NOT YET AVAILABLE ON O.S.U. TEST USED THIS YEAR.	ON O.S.U. TEST FORM 13, MEDIANS OF OHIO COLLEGES WAS 179. THIS GROUP 181.	ON CLEVELAND CLASSIFICATION TEST, MEDIAN FOR Y-PREP WAS 104.3. MEDIAN FOR CLEVELAND PUBLIC SCHOOLS ON SAME TEST WAS 100.7	BASED ON THE OTIS. C TEST. THIS IS A NORMAL DISTRIBUTION GROUP.
PERCENTAGE OF TEACHERS WHO HAVE DEGREES BEYOND THE BACHELOR DEGREE.	70%	74% IN JUNIOR COLLEGE STAFF.	60%	41%	25%	50%
PERCENTAGE OF TEACHERS WHO HAVE HAD ONE OR MORE YEARS OF INDUSTRIAL EXPERIENCE.	81%	90% IN JUNIOR COLLEGE STAFF	100%	100%	~	~

SUMMARY OF FINANCIAL OPERATIONS FOR 1930

EXPENSE $234,000.
REC'D FROM STUDENTS $199,275.
INCOME REQUIRED FROM OTHER SOURCES THAN STUDENTS $34,725.

PERCENTAGE OF EXPENSES PAID BY STUDENTS = 85.2%

At the December 17, 1930, meeting of the Board of Governors it was reported that because of the demand for cooperative education it would be necessary to start, for the first time, a third section in the Engineering and Business Administration day co-op classes. The new section would register on February 2, 1931, and attend classes twenty weeks without break, then join the sophomore class in September.

Dr. Watson of Columbia University, who had been a consultant for the Preparatory School for three years, recommended that the school should have a distinctive name which would give it entity and around which the loyalty of the students might be developed. The name Nash School was approved by the Board of Governors for submission to the YMCA Board of Trustees. Augustus Nash for many years had a special interest in the Preparatory School. It was especially fitting that the school be named in his honor for his thirty years of active and dedicated service as Secretary of Religion for the YMCA from 1898 to 1928. He had died June 23, 1929, at the age of 66. A meeting room in the Central YMCA was named in his honor prior to his death.

Also at the December 17, 1930, meeting of the YMCA Board of Trustees twelve men were suggested for membership on the Board of Governors of the educational branch. Among those selected was Ellwood H. Fisher, "an able young man who will probably have increasingly large responsibilities with The Fisher Brothers organization." This was an understatement for he not only became president of that company, and chairman of the Fenn College Board of Trustees, but he also became one of Cleveland's most active civic leaders. More about him later. Another selectee was John A. Greene, General Manager of the Ohio Bell Telephone Company; "our school would be very greatly advantaged by having a man of the type of Mr. Greene." He later became President of the Ohio Bell Telephone Company and later resigned from the Fenn College Board of Trustees in 1936. The quotations about the above two men were made by Director C. V. Thomas.

Because of the increase in enrollment, financial operations, and the problems of collections, the new office of "Finance Director" was established in January 1931. Stacey R. Black, who had been Dean of the Department of Business Administration, was appointed as the first Finance Director of the school. This change in Black's duties created others. J. C. Nichols was placed in charge of the Day Cooperative programs in Engineering and Business Administration. Paul R. Anders, Acting Director of the Evening Business Administration School, was given the additional duties as Associate Dean of the Fenn College Day Cooperative Division.

Director and Mrs. C. V. Thomas were given a surprise party on February 24, 1931, by the Board of Trustees of the YMCA and the Board of Governors of Y-Tech. The surprise was the announcement of a fully pre-planned trip to Europe with all expenses paid. Many visitations to universities were included in the itinerary.

The first and only fire of any consequence in the history of the school occurred March 25, 1931, in the Edwards Building. This building was used for classrooms, faculty offices, and the first official headquarters for the Department of Coordination. The total cost to repair the damage was $3,650.

Strange as it may seem, the question arose again as to whether girls should be admitted to the Cooperative Department of Business Administration. John A. Greene and Hoddinott reported at the April 15, 1931, Board meeting for the special committee appointed to make a survey. Interviews with prominent Clevelanders resulted in a tie vote. Upon a show of hands the Board was about evenly divided on the subject, so the chairman put the problem into the hands of the committee with power to act. The committee reported on May 29, 1931, as follows:

1. As a general rule women will not be admitted to the Day Cooperative Business Administration School.

2. There may be a few special cases where admitting of women would be desirable. The Director is therefore authorized, personally, to approve the admission of women, on the condition that the total number, at any one time, will not exceed five. These exceptions will be made only in case of unusual circumstances and a real desire to attend the school will not by itself be sufficient reason.

3. If the Director feels that more than five should be admitted, he will refer the matter to the Board of Governors before taking action.

4. The presence of women will be merely incidental to the operation of the school and no effort will be made to modify the courses in order to fit their needs.

5. Before being accepted, for admission, any woman should be advised that the Employment Department of the school is not equipped to find positions for them so that no organized effort toward placing them can be promised.

It was also reported at this same Board meeting that Joseph S. Kopas, Fenn College, '31, was a new member of the Department of Coordination and that George Simon of The White Motor Company and part-time teacher in the Evening Division was also being considered for the same department.

As of April 15, 1931, there were 49 members on the Day Division faculty and staff and 67 part-time teachers in the Evening Division.

The tragic death of Manning H. Fisher, April 26, 1931 (father of Ellwood), was recorded in the Minutes of the YMCA Board of Trustees. Ellwood H. Fisher had previously accepted membership on the Board of Governors of Y-Tech. He was officially sworn in October 22, 1931.

At the May 20, 1931, meeting of the Board of Governors, congratulations on behalf of the Board were sent to co-op freshman William R. Miller for winning a $500 scholarship in a contest conducted by The American Chemical Society. Miller graduated from Fenn College with a B.S. in Metallurgy in 1934 and later became Chief Metallurgical Engineer for the American Steel and Wire Company. He was president of the Fenn Alumni Association in 1938, and received the Alumni Distinguished Service Award in 1958. He served as an Alumni Trustee for two terms from 1953 to 1959.

Randolph C. Randall was appointed as an Instructor in English at the May 20, 1931, Board meeting. He later became Chairman of the Department of English from which he retired at The Cleveland State University in 1969.

For some time, members of the Board of Governors questioned the advisability of continuing the Day Preparatory School (high school) on the same campus with Fenn. It was felt that it should have a different environment than a college campus. Knebel suggested that the following Euclid Avenue residences be considered for a possible location for the Preparatory School: Rockefeller at East 40th, Wade at East 40th, Cox at 3411, Payne at 2445, Sanders at 3133, Mather at 2605, and the new East End Y Building when erected. A committee was appointed to study the situation and report back. The committee presented a progress report at the June 24, 1931, meeting, stating that accreditation of Fenn College was questionable when housed with a secondary school.

Also at the June 24 meeting of the Board of Governors, action was taken to file the necessary copies of curricula with the State Department of Public Instruction requesting degree granting power in the Evening Division of Fenn College in Engineering and Business Administration by extending the then current three year program to six years. Official approval was given by the State as reported to the Board of Governors on July 15, 1931.

At the same meeting it was reported that the freshmen in Cooperative Engineering are now experiencing a six weeks surveying camp at Hiram under the tutelage of Samuel Ward, Virgil Hales and Joseph Kopas. The group surveyed land for Hiram College, the Village of Hiram, and the County Surveyor's office. This summer-surveying practice session was later conducted at Hiram House near SOM Center and Harvard Roads. Each year a topographic map was extended to provide eventually a complete topographic map of the entire area as reciprocity for use of the area for practice surveying.

The effect of the Depression was beginning to work a hardship on the Preparatory School, the vocational short term course enrollments for the Fall term, and procurement of co-op jobs. It was also creating a problem in balancing the budget for 1931. By June the Executive Committee of the Y-Board issued instructions to the school administration to close fiscal year 1931 without a deficit and, at the same time, postponed indefinitely a planned capital fund campaign. Action was taken at the September 23, 1931, meeting of the board to appoint a committee to develop a way to increase the student loan fund.

Director Thomas also reported at the September 23 board meeting that "Fenn College has now the beginnings of a real fraternity row on Prospect Avenue across the street and just east of the Medical Building. A co-op fraternity moved into one house and two other fraternities moved into another house." One of these was the Pi Sigma Tau organized as a local at Fenn which later became a chapter of the national fraternity, Phi Sigma Delta. Further quoting Director Thomas: "We believe that such developments are an asset to an institution of our type in that they enable the boys who are working and do not have as much opportunity for social life as regular college students, to get the development which comes from association in a fraternity house."

The registrations for the Fall terms of 1930–1931 were as follows:

	1930	1931
Day Co-op Engineering	178	194
Day Business Administration	24	39
Day High School	241	137
Evening Engineering	380	250
Evening Business Administration	236	172
Evening High School	241	137
Total	1143	834

Note that the greatest loss in enrollment occurred in the Day High School and the Evening programs, undoubtedly the result of the Depression.

With the year 1881 the assumed founding date of the school, 1931 became the 50th anniversary date. Ellwood Fisher was appointed chairman of the committee to plan an appropriate celebration. He reported at the October 14, 1931, meeting of the Board of Governors that October 29 and 30 were set for the occasion. Students arranged a Mardi Gras for the evening of October 30. Charles E. Adams was toastmaster for a luncheon on October 30 which was well attended by the business and industrial leaders of Cleveland. The Alumni staged a dinner for October 29 at which former City Manager Hopkins and Edmund Vance Cooke, both former students of old Y-Tech, were the speakers. William Lenga, President of the Alumni Association, was in charge of the affair. It was reported in the Minutes of the board meeting of November 12, 1931, that through Fisher the Fleischman Yeast Company sponsored a half-hour program over WTAM and that the largest crowd ever to occupy the Central Y building attended the Mardi Gras.

By October 1931 Director Thomas reported to the Board of Governors that every effort should be made to establish a Student Loan Fund of a minimum of $8,000 to aid upper-class students who were unable to pay their tuition for the Fall term and also unable to find work. The students were to sign notes for their tuition and reimburse the school as early as possible. By November 25, 1931, a total of 18 students had received loans or scholarships in a total amount exceeding $17,000. These were largely taken care of by tuition remission. The Board of Governors took steps to raise a loan fund of $20,000 through solicitations.

Dr. Cecil V. Thomas, first President of Fenn College

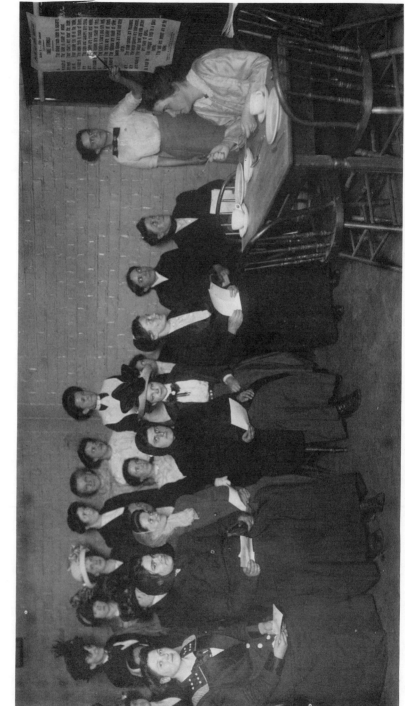

Special class for the instruction of the foreign born (circa 1895)

Class in Accounting at Y-Tech—1919

Class in Typing at Y-Tech—1919

Class in Physics at Y-Tech—1920

Class in the Electrical Engineering Laboratory at Y-Tech—1920

Students in Day Division at Y-Tech—1920

Class in Bookkeeping at Y-Tech—1920

Class in English at Y-Tech—1926

Library in Y-Tech Building (later Fenn Building)

The Edwards building at left; the Johnson Building with Y-Tech (Fenn) Building at the rear Central Branch, Cleveland YMCA, extreme right.

Engineering students in front of Edwards Building—Y-Tech—1928

View of Y-Tech (Fenn) Building, Johnson Building, Edwards Building and Medical Building with YMCA, Central Branch, in background.

Nash Junior College Faculty—1932

Left to right: Dr. Tuttle, O'Konski, Anderson, Mrs. Tolar, Super, Tomich, Williams, Mulhauser, Dr. Jordan

Fenn College Faculty—1935

BACK ROW Dilley, Tuttle, Rexion, Robinson, Francis, Bush, McAlpine, Pasuit, Randall
CENTER ROW Christian, Jordan, Hotchkiss, Fabel, Kopas, Berger, Ward, Hunt, Margolis
FRONT ROW Mrs. Tolar, Davis, Anders, Nichols, Simon, Hales, Lumer

Fenn Tower with stores on Euclid Avenue—1936

Fenn Tower—1947

Varsity Swimming Team—1940

Robert Busbey; front row, third from right. Coach Raymond Ray; standing, second from left.

The Ellwood H. Fisher Swimming Pool, sixth floor of Fenn Tower (Robert Busbey coaching).

Board of Trustees of Fenn College—1939

Clockwise: Fred C. Baldwin, John L. Irvin, George V. Woodling, Elbert H. Baker, Jr., Dr. C. V. Thomas (President of Fenn College),
Joseph W. Meriam, Ellwood H. Fisher (Chairman), Richard G. Roth, John S. Crider, Leyton E. Carter,
Jacob D. Cox, Jr., John C. Sanders, Clayton G. Hale

The name *Board of Governors* was changed to *Board of Managers* in October 1931.

On November 25, 1931, it was reported by the Board of Managers that the enrollment in the Day Division of Fenn College was larger than either John Carroll University or Baldwin Wallace College and two-thirds as large as Case School of Applied Science. The board also reported that the students at Fenn through their tuition fees paid eighty-five percent of the total cost of their education. Down through the years, to the transfer of Fenn College to the State, this percentage was not greatly reduced.

Historically, the December 2, 1931, meeting of the YMCA Board of Trustees proved to be very important. The following recommendations of the Board of Managers were approved by the Trustees:

1. The elementary grades and the first year of the Day High School program be discontinued.

2. The three years of high school remaining be extended to include two years of college work in the field of Liberal Arts. (This was in effect the beginning of the School of Arts and Sciences of Fenn College.)

   a. It was felt that the move should be made towards a higher level of academic work and this new program would enable the school to pioneer in introducing to Cleveland a five-year program for adolescents from ages of 16 through 20. In addition, and of tremendous importance during this era, this proposed reorganization would entail a savings in the 1932 budget of $7,000.

3. The new five-year program area be called the "Nash Junior College of the YMCA of Cleveland."

   a. The objectives of the new program included the philosophy, methods and purposes for which Augustus Nash lived.

   b. A school encompassing the education of 16- to 20-year-old youth would be a fitting memorial to Nash.

   c. The Trustees felt it should have the full name including, "of the YMCA of Cleveland" as did Fenn College to make sure that twenty or so years hence they would not have a unit of the Y in operation which might develop a tendency to disassociate itself from the Y. (It should be noted here that this concern became a reality just twenty years later, in 1951, when Fenn College, through mutual consent, broke parental ties with the YMCA and became a private college.)

4. As soon as practicable the name, *Cleveland YMCA School of Technology* be dropped.

The first "Report of Fenn College and The Nash Junior College of the YMCA to the Board of Managers" was presented by Director Thomas on December 16, 1931. He reported the following:

(a) The members of the staff have spoken to 55 audiences since September 1, to a total of 4,900 people.

(b) Total number of inches of newspaper publicity in one academic year was 692 compared to 511 the preceding year.

(c) Ashland College defeated Fenn College in basketball by a score of 24 to 22. Fenn College defeated Youngstown by a score of 21 to 20. Members of the Board should attend some of the home games in order to see the student body and understand the spirit within the school.

(d) The number of books and periodicals withdrawn from the library during the year 1931 exceeded those withdrawn during 1930 by 53%.

The 1931 fiscal year ended with a deficit approximating $22,000. It was voted to amortize the deficit over the first six months of 1932. A special committee was appointed to study the 1932 budget and reduce expenses in any manner to prevent another deficit year. The Great Depression of the early nineteen thirties was looming its ugly head on the educational horizon.

E. H. Baker, Jr., was sworn in as a Trustee of the YMCA on February 3, 1932. He was also elected to the Board of Managers of Fenn College and later, the Board of Trustees. For his many years of loyal service, he was elected an Honorary Life Trustee of Fenn College November 20, 1956. He died August 18, 1962.

The Finance Committee of the YMCA met June 6, 1932, at which time they considered reducing the faculty and staff of Fenn College and Nash Junior College. However, they finally decided to carry the personnel through the school year at reduced salaries and where possible to urge certain persons to accept other offers of employment.

Following is a sampling of reduction in salaries proposed to a few individuals who were associated with Fenn College for many years:

| | Annual Rate | |
	1931	1932
Paul R. Anders, Dean, Commerce School	$3000	$2700
Burl H. Bush, Instructor	2000	1800
William C. Davis, Instructor	2850	2565
Donald C. Fabel, Instructor	2850	2565
Virgil D. Hales, Instructor	2700	2430
Millard L. Jordan, Ass't Principal, Prep School	2600	2340
Joseph C. Nichols, Dean, Co-op School	4700	4230
Maurice E. Nichols, Dean, Evening Engineering School	3300	2970
Lad A. Pasuit, Instructor (part time)	1500	1350
Randolph C. Randall, Instructor	2800	2520
Alex Rexion Coordination Department	2400	2160
Almeda J. Rothrock, Secretary to Director	2100	1890
George B. Simon, Coordination Department	2600	2340
Cecil V. Thomas, Director	5500	4950
Donald R. Tuttle, Instructor	1700	1530
Ola I. Twerell, Cashier	1320	1188
Samuel Ward, Instructor	3600	3240
Gerald S. Wellman, Promotion Director	3000	2700
Homer E. Woodling, Coach, Co-op School	2400	2160

Before the end of 1932 further problems arose relative to maintaining faculty salaries.

Malcolm B. Vilas was sworn in as a Trustee of the YMCA on March 18, 1932. An honorary degree, doctor of laws, was conferred on him at the 1963 commencement convocation of Fenn College.

Harold H. Burton was sworn in as a Trustee of the YMCA April 19, 1932. He had long been active in the East Cleveland Branch of the Metropolitan Y. He served as Law Director and Mayor of the City of Cleveland. He served his country in World War I rising from first Lieutenant to Captain and was the recipient of the Belgian Croix-de-Guerre and the U.S. Army Citation Certificate. During World War II he served as a United States Senator from Ohio. He served as a Trustee of Fenn College from 1934 to 1955 (he had studied Accounting at the College in previous years) and an Honorary Life Trustee to the time of his death October 28, 1964. He served as Justice of the U.S. Supreme Court and while in this office received the honorary degree, doctor of laws (LL.D.) through the authorized investiture by Clayton G. Hale on June 5, 1952, in his Supreme Court chambers.

At the April 27 meeting of the Board of Managers action was taken to permit students to attend college on a full-time basis when cooperative employment was impossible to obtain. The Depression was working a hardship on the cooperative program of higher education.

Fifty-five men graduated from Fenn College at the June commencement of 1932. Among this group was Clayton G. Hale who graduated from the Evening Division School of Business Administration.

At the July 27, 1932, Operating Committee meeting Chairman Fred W. Ramsey revealed the gloomy financial situation and stated that in the judgment of the Executive Committee, further salary and wage cuts were inescapable. It was reported that business was bad, unemployment was on the increase, and banks refused to make loans. An honorary degree, doctor of laws, was conferred on Ramsey at the Fenn College Commencement Convocation in 1958.

Just when the school's financial affairs were at a very low ebb W. A. Johnson, whose mother owned the Johnson property (now joined to the Fenn Building and the Central Y), notified the YMCA that effective October 1, 1932, the rent on the property would be increased from $6,000 to $8,000 per year. This occasioned a number of meetings of the Executive Committee and after much discussion the matter of further negotiations was placed in the hands of a special committee with instructions to do everything in its power to secure a readjustment of terms.

To give the reader a glimpse of the fiscal difficulties encountered on the approach of the Fall Semester in 1932, the following is an excerpt of a letter of August 5, from Director Thomas to Fred W. Ramsey.

> The present expense budget for 1932 is $211,200 as compared with $252,280 in 1931, a reduction of $41,080. The above expense figure for 1932 includes the 1931 deficit of $21,843. The difference between the operation expenses of 1931 and 1932 is therefore $41,080 plus $21,843 or $62,923. The expense reductions are quite excessive in the Advertising, Equipment and Maintenance, Postage, Printing, Salary and Supply items. They are possible only in an emergency such as now exists.

The largest reduction has been made in salaries—a total of $40,-393. This item breaks down as follows: Approximately $14,000 was produced by a 10% straight salary cut made on everyone as of January 1st. Another $9,750 is due to the reduction of our staff by six full time men. Some of these men left the organization in March; others as of June. $2,500 came from reduction in part time staff. $5,200 represents the second 10% reduction, beginning as of July 1st. . . .

In order to absorb the 1931 deficit of $21,843 and the reduction in Community Chest income of $6,198, as well as to balance this year's operations, it is necessary for the school to show a net of $49,884 in excess of 1931 actual. In seeking to accomplish [this] the operating expenses have been reduced by $62,923, as compared with 1931. If the income for 1932 can be held to within $13,000— or $16,880 if the student loan money is obtained, then the $49,884 better operation in 1932 will be achieved. The income is the problem ahead.

Paul E. Williams, Dean of the Nash Junior College reported to the board on August 17, 1932, that credits from both the Day and Evening Division were transferable to any high school and that graduates were admitted to colleges without examination. It was also reported at the same meeting that since Fenn had been in operation 84 credit transcripts had been sent to 40 different colleges and that 73 transfer students had been accepted by Fenn. Dale Cox (editorial writer for the *Cleveland Plain Dealer*) made this comment in October 1932 in speaking about Fenn College and the Nash Junior College: "There is not anything comparable to it from an educational standpoint in all Cleveland. I should think this would give you YMCA men particular satisfaction." Dale Cox was elected to the Board of Managers on November 30, 1932.

At a joint meeting of the Board of Trustees, YMCA and the educational Board of Managers held November 10, 1932, the following was reported by Director Thomas:

1. The first Junior College of Liberal Arts to be organized in Cleveland began at Nash Junior College on September 12, 1932. Students can complete the first two years of liberal arts work and transfer to other colleges. The New York Times September 18, 1932, Sunday edition carried a story about this new program under the heading "A REALISTIC CURRICULUM."

    2.   Fenn has cooperative relationships with more than 80 Cleveland and Northern Ohio industries. Members of its field staff contact regularly more than 1,000 industries.

    3.   Of the 55 men who received degrees at Fenn last June, 36 had positions upon graduation—a most unusual record of employment for college graduates this year.

    4.   2803 students attended Fenn and Nash last year. They were taught by 103 instructors.

    5.   Included in the 1932 expense reductions is $8,953 of December salaries (80% for the month) which the staff will not receive. This is in addition to the two straight 10% salary reductions made on January 1st and July 1st respectively.

    6.   The Educational Branch has $10,000 in Notes Receivable from students receiving help from the loan fund, from which it has no cash receipts.

These were dire times to say the least and the major portion of board meetings was spent in discussing ways and means of reducing the annual deficit. A special committee was appointed at the November 18 meeting of the Y Trustees' Executive Committee, composed of members from both the Board of Trustees and the Board of Managers to seek funds for the Educational Branch.

At the November 30, 1932, meeting of the Operating Committee it was reported that "for the first 10 months of 1932 the college was $26,432 better off than the preceeding year although the loss was $22,237, but this included $18,240 of last year's deficit." This semi-favorable report was made possible because the faculty and staff were helping subsidize the students tuition (education) by the drastic reductions made in their salaries.

Ellwood H. Fisher was sworn in as member of the Board of Trustees of the YMCA at a meeting of the Board held December 28, 1932. Fisher enjoyed a long continued friendship and close personal association with Fenn College and its successor in 1965, the Fenn Educational Foundation, and in 1971, the Fenn Educational Fund.

During the Christmas holidays of 1932 a special meeting of seven hundred students from throughout the United States was held in Chicago. Carl Geiser, a senior student at Fenn, was one of the students elected at that meeting to represent the students of the United States at a World Congress on the Elimination of War held in Uruguay in January 1933.

At the close of 1932 Director Thomas drafted the following concerning the Purpose, History, Students, Faculty and Curriculum of Fenn College:

I. *Purpose*

The purpose of Fenn College is to equip young men to live usefully and more abundantly. The college is unique in the close contact it maintains between the classroom and the conditions and requirements of commerce, industry and life. Young men receive the following services:

(1) The college teaches them the knowledges, skills and attitudes they will require when earning a living.

(2) The college aids young men in choosing their vocations wisely and in planning the educational programs which will prepare them for their life work.

(3) The college studies the individual student and gives attention to his interests and needs.

(4) The college stresses the *growth* of the individual student rather than the mere transfer of information to him.

(5) The college stimulates the individual to develop what will be for him a meaningful philosophy of life.

The achievement of these goals is the objective of the administration and faculty. Evidences of the growing success of the college in accomplishing the above results in the lives of young men are increasing. The fact that 36 out of 55 men who graduated from Fenn College last spring had jobs when they graduated is an indication of how under present employment conditions the school is equipping students to earn a living.

The college finds that few young men have a definite vocational objective which continues throughout their school experience. By means of Vocational Interest and Aptitude Tests and by the use of other tools, together with numerous conversations between the young man and members of the staff and faculty, the student is helped to think through what his vocation is to be. Vocational Guidance at Fenn is a process and not an event.

Likewise, young men are known as individuals at Fenn. Often the factors which will determine the success of a young man are those which do not emerge in the usual classroom experience. Points of view, attitudes toward work and life, are effected through personal mutual understandings which occur when working with young men as individuals. The development in young men of

the ability to deal with problems and situations is the purpose
of Fenn College, rather than to make them "storage tanks" for
facts, the use or value of which students often do not understand.

Fenn students are stimulated to think. Persons who visit Fenn
often remark about the maturity of the students. Since Fenn students are the same age as other college students, the visitors are
referring to the maturity of thinking occurring in the classrooms.

And lastly, Fenn College is stimulating young men to develop
their philosophies of life. The school seeks to keep young men
thinking about the "Whys" of life. The more or less childish "rah
rah" expressions often found among college students is largely replaced at Fenn by a searching, inquiring attitude about basic life
values.

II. *History*

The first educational classes to be organized by the Cleveland
Young Men's Christian Association were started in 1881—51 years
ago. From the beginning the Association has conducted its educational program at the educational level of the young men who
form the membership of the institution. In 1881, since the great
majority of young men had an education equivalent to the sixth
or seventh grade, the Association offered courses in Arithmetic,
English [and] Elementary Bookkeeping, on the sixth and seventh
grade level. Now, when the great group of young men who form
the clientele of the Young Men's Christian Association are high
school graduates, the organization conducts the large part of its
educational program on the collegiate level. Although the offerings
of the curriculum have advanced throughout the years, yet the
purpose of the Association has endured.

Another characteristic of the educational work of the Cleveland
Young Men's Christian Association has been its "pioneering" nature.
The first extensive adult educational program in Cleveland began
at the Y. The first Americanization work for foreign born men
was started by the Y. The first apprenticeship education for Cleveland industries originated at the Y. The first accredited evening
high school plan in Cleveland developed at the Y. Now the Association is introducing to Cleveland the cooperative plan of education
which brings together school and industry; the semi-professional
junior college on the accredited basis; and new methods in classroom procedures designed to adapt education to changing conditions.

From a few evening students in 1881 the work has grown to the extent that its day college students number five hundred or more each year. (More day college students are attending Fenn than are registered at Baldwin-Wallace, John Carroll or Hiram. The day college registration at Fenn this fall is 75% of the day registration at Case.)

Again, during the 51 years the program of study of students has changed from one or two courses to the present time when the large majority is pursuing curricula which extend over three, four, five or more years.

III. *Students*

During 1932, 1827 different persons have attended the Day and Evening Division of Fenn College. Although a few of the Fenn College students are less than 18 years of age and some are more than 25, yet the large group is between the ages of 18 and 25. About one-half of the day students live in Cleveland. The other half have graduated from "middle class" homes. They are a superior group intellectually. The freshman class who entered Fenn this fall made a median score of 176 on the same psychological test on which 181,000 college freshmen made a median score of 145. The evening students work in Cleveland industries and offices during the day and study at Fenn in the evening.

IV. *Faculty*

The Fenn College faculty resembles that of other colleges in many ways. The factors that have been used in their selection have resulted in certain characteristics in the teachers which are different. For example, the larger group of Fenn teachers have had experience in commerce and industry doing the kind of work about which they are teaching students. Fenn College encourages its students to inquire about the application of theories. Only teachers who have had practical experience can satisfactorily answer such questions.

Again, Fenn College teachers are "learners" regarding how they may improve their teaching. In addition to faculty discussions led by persons who visit the school to stimulate faculty thinking, the teachers are for themselves exploring new ways by which growth may be brought about in their students.

Also, Fenn teachers obtain greater satisfaction from observing the development of their students than they do from the subjects they teach. Subject matter is a means; young men are the end

Among the faculty are many who have been teachers in other colleges but who transferred to Fenn because of their desire to participate in the type of education Fenn fosters. Others have come directly from commerce and industry. The Fenn faculty consists at present of 27 full time and 48 part time teachers.

V. *Curriculum*

The major fields for which Fenn College students are preparing are Business and Engineering. Although the content of the courses offered is in total similar to that in other colleges preparing for the same occupations, yet a basic difference is found in the ways by which courses are taught. Fenn students are increasingly beginning with their interests and needs and developing the curriculum out of their growing experience, the teachers acting as guides.

Out of the classrooms and from contacts with the administrative staff and the school as a whole come the stimulation for the development of a philosophy of life.

Paul E. Williams, Dean of the Nash Junior College drafted the following to supplement Director Thomas' above statement to have a complete story of Fenn College and Nash Junior College:

I. *Purpose*

The Day Preparatory Division of Nash Junior College is unlike any other school in Cleveland or Ohio. It is ranked among the upper 5% of progressive schools of the United States. It performs three services.

(1)   The school provides education on a secondary level for deserving and ambitious boys 15 to 18 years of age, adapted to their interests and needs, at a nominal tuition cost.

(2)   The school serves as a demonstration center for the application of the principles of progressive education designed to build character and good citizenship.

(3)   The school adjusts its services to special community needs, such as the conducting of an enlarged summer school this year when the public schools were unable to operate their summer session.

Many boys fail to develop in the usual mass education processes. They need the personal attention which is possible in a student body where classes are small. In the Preparatory Division of Nash Junior College every pupil is known personally by both the administration and faculty. Because of this relationship and the methods of instruction followed, changes occur in the interests and in the citizenship and home attitudes of boys who attend the school.

Likewise, progress in education generally requires centers where demonstrations of the application of progressive educational theory occur. This school is such a center. Students of education state that the methods used in this school place it in the upper 5% of all schools where new methods and subject matter suited to present day life situations are used. A primary objective is to develop an educational process which will result in a greater amount of character growth.

II. *A Brief History*

The beginnings of what is now the Day Preparatory Division of Nash Junior College started in 1913 when the educational program of the Cleveland Young Men's Christian Association first included day classes.

In 1919 the work had so developed that it met the standards of the North Central Association of Colleges and Secondary Schools. Since that time it has continuously been a member of that Association.

In 1928, under the leadership of Dr. Goodwin B. Watson of Teachers College Columbia University, changes looking toward the making of the school a more positive factor in the development of character in boys and young men began. During the next three years at regular intervals Dr. Watson visited the school. With the staff and faculty he brought about changes in what the school taught and in the methods by which the instruction was given.

Later Dr. John P. Herring of New York further developed the points of view which Dr. Watson had introduced. During the last two years he has spent an average of four weeks each year in the school.

Dr. Watson's contribution was largely one of stimulation and suggestion; Dr. Herring's one of method and evaluation.

The resignation of Gerald S. Wellman was announced at the January 4, 1933, meeting of the Board of Managers. He had done much to promote and interpret Fenn College and Nash Junior College to the high schools, business, industry, and the general public. He left Fenn to enter Cleveland industry, but later became a Vice President at Case Institute of Technology. From there he became Special Assistant to the President of Baldwin Wallace College.

Several "old timers" of Fenn College have already been mentioned. Perhaps here at the beginning of 1933, at this point in Fenn's history, it would be most appropriate to repeat the names of a number of people who were instrumental in the development of Fenn over the period when the institution was known as Fenn College.

First there was Director C. V. Thomas to whom much credit is due for his leadership, devotion, spiritual guidance, and seemingly inexhaustible efforts on behalf of the educational program of the YMCA. He must be credited with the introduction of the co-op college program in Cleveland. Those that follow are listed in alphabetical order and not in sequence of importance, but they were all stalwarts in a large portion of, or perhaps the entire life of Fenn College.

Paul R. Anders became Dean of the School of Business Administration, the Senior Dean at Fenn. The Day and Evening Division of Business Administration developed largely through his earnest efforts. His special devotion to the Evening Division Business Administration activities resulted in its outstanding growth to an enrollment of 40% of that for the entire Evening Division which in Fenn's later years averaged 5000 per year. He was faculty advisor to the Beta Alpha fraternity, a Fenn local which later became a Fenn chapter of Tau Kappa Epsilon, a national fraternity of which Dean Anders was a member at Knox College, his alma mater. He, together with George Simon were instrumental in the establishment of the first Fenn sorority, the Iota Tau Lamba. They were both considered honorary members thereof. Dean Anders retired in 1964 but returned to assist in the transfer of Fenn to The Cleveland State University (C.S.U.), without pay. He died Sunday, December 11, 1966, at the age of 72 while watching the Dallas-Washington pro football game on television in his home.

Burl H. Bush, a graduate of the U.S. Naval Academy, came to Fenn in September 1931 as Instructor in Mechanical Engineering. He became Assistant Dean of Engineering in 1934 and Dean of Engineering in 1937. In June 1941 he left to serve his country in World War II as an Engineering Duty Officer and remained in the Navy on the West Coast following the war as a Commander in charge of various engineering design, research and service departments. He returned to Fenn College February 21, 1962, to again assume the duties as Dean of Engineering again and remained in this capacity until his retirement from C.S.U. in August 1972.

William C. Davis joined the faculty in September 1928 as Instructor in Electrical Engineering. He rose to the rank of Chairman and Professor, Department of Electrical Engineering in 1943. He organized and developed an outstanding electrical engineering laboratory which received extensive usage in the Day and Evening Divisions and by the Technical Institute students. Much of the development he did himself. He died in June 1956.

Donald C. Fabel became a member of the faculty just one month ahead of Professor Davis, i.e., August 1, 1928. He rose from the rank of Instructor to Chairman and Professor, Department of Mechanical Engineering, by 1940. He had a leave of absence from January 1, 1941, to June 1, 1946, during which time he served in the U.S. Army in World War II rising to the rank of Colonel. In 1949 the chairmanship of the Department of Metallurgy was added to his duties. In 1958 this latter responsibility was dropped from his office, and in 1962 he resigned the chairmanship of the Department of Mechanical Engineering to take on duties as a teaching professor. He retired as Professor Emeritus of Metallurgy and Mechanical Engineering from The Cleveland State University in June 1966.

Virgil D. Hales joined the faculty on April 4, 1929, as Instructor in Mechanical Drawing. He became Associate Professor and Chairman of the Department of Engineering Drawing in September 1945. He designed the new drafting desks which furnished the drafting rooms in the new Foster Mechanical Engineering Building in 1947. The same type of drafting desks were used in furnishing the drafting rooms in the new Stilwell Hall in 1960. Professor Hales died June 8, 1963.

Millard L. Jordan started as a part-time instructor in the Evening Preparatory School in February 1926. He became a full-time Instructor of Sociology in July 1928. For a time he served as Associate Dean of the Nash Junior College. By 1941 he rose to the rank of Chairman and Professor, Department of Sociology. On August 31, 1965, he retired as Professor Emeritus of Sociology and became Archivist for The Cleveland State University succeeding George Simon in this post.

Joseph C. Nichols became teacher in Day Prep School of Y-Tech on January 1, 1920, Director of the Trade School, Y-Tech January 1, 1921. He was appointed Director of the Engineering School on April 1, 1922, and held the office as Dean, Department of Engineering from September 1, 1926, to August 31, 1931. He was also appointed Dean,

Day Cooperative Division in January 1931 and Dean of the entire Day Division in 1934. He became Dean of the College on January 1, 1935, and upon the death of Dr. Thomas he was appointed Acting President from December 1, 1947, to September 1, 1948. He resigned as Dean of Fenn College on April 30, 1951.

Maurice E. Nichols, brother of Joseph C. came to Y-Tech as a part-time instructor. He became a full-time instructor in the Trade School October 1, 1925, and Co-ordinator in Y-Tech August 1, 1927. In 1929–1930 he was Director of Engineering for the Evening Division and was appointed Dean of Engineering for the Evening Division in 1932. He resigned in June 1937 to work with the American Steel and Wire Company. Then on November 16, 1959, he returned to Fenn College as an Industrial Coordinator in the Department of Cooperative Education. He retired from C.S.U. in June of 1968 to become a full-time industrial arbitrator.

Lad A. Pasiut joined the Fenn Faculty in January 1931 in the Department of Chemistry. He taught Freshmen Chemistry and became an expert in Organic Chemistry and Micro-Biology. He was very research oriented especially concerning farm produce. Well liked by his students and his colleagues on the staff, he retired August 31, 1962, to spend winters in Florida and summers in travel.

Randolph C. Randall was engaged as an Instructor of English on August 1, 1931. He rose in rank to Professor of English in 1934 and was appointed Chairman of the English Department August 1, 1941. He held this office until June 30, 1969, at which time he retired to revert to part-time teaching as a Professor of English at C.S.U.

Max B. Robinson, a student of Professor Herman Schneider, the father of the Cooperative Program of Higher Education at the University of Cincinnati, joined the Fenn staff in August 1933 as Director of Cooperative Education. In June of 1940, upon Dean Bush's departure for service in World War II, Robinson was appointed Acting Dean of Engineering and when Dean Bush remained in the Navy for several years, Acting Dean Robinson was named Dean of Engineering. Then in September of 1946 he was appointed Dean of Cooperative Education and held this office until August 31, 1959, when he retired as Dean Emeritus of Cooperative Education.

George B. Simon was part-time instructor in both the Day and Evening Divisions from February 1928 to 1937. During this period he was also a Coordinator in the Co-op activity of the school and Instructor of Speech. From January 1, 1936, to retirement in August 1952, he rose to the rank of Associate Professor of Speech. Upon retirement he was immediately re-engaged as the first Historian and Archivist of Fenn College. With the aid of a Committee on the History of Fenn College, he established an archives office and many historically significant articles are stored there. Professor Simon researched the Minutes of the Boards of Trustees of the YMCA, Y-Tech and Fenn College and recorded a number of volumes of the entire history of Fenn College and its predecessor in chronological order. Professor Simon retired for the second time on August 31, 1964, and died June 17, 1967.

Donald R. Tuttle joined the Fenn faculty in September 1930 and was principally assigned responsible teaching and administrative duties in the English Department of Y-Prep and Nash Junior College. He was appointed Instructor in English for Fenn College in 1933 and rose to the rank of Professor of English in 1948. For the academic year 1942–1943 he was Acting Director of Testing and Guidance and for the year 1946–1947 he was Vocational Counselor in the Department of Personnel Development. He was very active in the Ohio College Association in establishing quality education in the field of English in secondary education. His colleagues in higher education gave him full credit for the splendid results of his efforts. Professor Tuttle left Fenn in August 1963 to take up work in Washington for the Department of Health, Education, and Welfare.

Ola I. Twerell came to Y-Tech as a young girl newly graduated from Spencerian College. She was assigned to bookkeeping in the Bookstore. She became cashier and manager of the Bookstore and Business Office for Fenn College in 1936 and Manager of Purchasing in 1954. She died on March 15, 1967. Probably no more loyal and dedicated individual ever worked for Fenn College. Miss Twerell spent hours of her own time to take care of planning for commencement receptions and other social affairs. Through her year-round efforts in gathering gifts she was instrumental in the success of every Staff Christmas Party.

Samuel Ward with previous teaching experience at Case School of Applied Science came to Fenn in 1920 as an Instructor in Civil Engineering. He soon became Chairman of the Department of Civil Engineering and in 1939 was appointed Chairman of the Department of Mechanics and Materials which was an offshoot of the Department of Civil

Engineering. He was active in the Community Chest for thirty years. He retired May 25, 1949, and moved to North Carolina where he died in 1971.

Homer E. Woodling joined Fenn as Director of Physical Education on August 1, 1929. He also assisted in courses in Business Administration. He rose through the ranks to Chairman and Professor of the Department of Health and Physical Education on July 1, 1946. During his lengthy career at Fenn he coached in all branches of sports, but toward his later years he concentrated on baseball and golf. While few Fenn athletic teams had winning seasons, nevertheless Woody, as he was affectionately known by everyone, always did the best he could with the talent available and the difficulties encountered in conducting an intercollegiate sports program with a relatively small student body engaged in a cooperative program of higher education alternating three months of academic work on campus with three months work on an outside job. Professor Woodling retired from Fenn October 31, 1964.

Some of the above biographical material may be a partial repetition of previous references to these individuals, but it bears repeating for this distinguished group.

Charles A. Dilley was appointed at the February 20, 1933, meeting of the Board of Managers to succeed Wellman in promotional and public relations activity. Dilley remained at Fenn until October 1, 1941, when he joined the Clevite Corporation and later became Executive Director of the Clevite Foundation.

The Day Division enrollment for the new Winter semester (1933) was slightly greater than the previous year, but the Evening Division enrollment had declined considerably because of the difficulty in finding work to pay for tuition fees.

Fenn College acted as host to an Intercollegiate Swimming Meet held Saturday, March 25, 1933. Entries included teams from Wooster, Case, Ohio State University, Western Reserve University, Ohio Wesleyan University, and Wittenberg University.

An Open House was held at Fenn College and Nash Junior College on March 31, 1933. Seniors in local high schools were invited to visit the laboratories and witness exhibits of work done by the co-op students in various industries, also to visit the fraternity houses and attend the final intramural basketball game. A total of 2,200 guests were in attendance.

For the first time in the history of Fenn the graduating class sponsored and financed a buffet dinner, reception, and smoker hosting the Board of Managers and Faculty. A splendid turn-out was reported and the occasion gave the students a wonderful opportunity to become better acquainted with the members of the Board and Faculty.

The Board of Managers approved an experiment on March 20, 1933, to establish ten evening "study clubs" for unemployed men between 16 and 25 years of age. Ellwood Fisher, then vice president of the Y Board of Trustees was chairman of the special committee which recommended the clubs. The subjects taught or discussed on occasion of meetings of these groups over an eight-week period were psychology, salesmanship, bookkeeping, current history, blue print reading, mathematics, art appreciation, letter writing, economics, and public speaking. In addition, several rooms were cleared in the basement of the Edwards Building to provide space for a series of workshops, the purpose being to provide hand tools, simple equipment, and materials where men could do carpentry and electrical work. None of these activities offered the same type of instruction as programmed in the regular classes in the Evening Division.

The financial situation in 1933 grew acute as the months went by. President Roosevelt ordered a bank holiday on March 6. Special Committees were appointed for each branch of the Central YMCA to study ways and means for operating the remainder of 1933. Ellwood Fisher was chairman of the Educational Branch.

After extensive consideration Fisher's committee recommended that beginning April 1, 1933, the faculty and staff receive 75% of their normal salaries until August 31, and that the cash receipts of the months September and October form the basis for determining what proportion of the 25% not paid during the five preceding months can be repaid to the faculty and staff. This meant that the status of the faculty and staff salaries for the five-month period was contingent on enrollment and ensuing income. Even to pay the 75% proportion of the salaries and other obligations a loan of $35,000 was necessary.

The Board of Trustees on April 17, 1933, authorized a United Membership Campaign. "Mr. Clayton G. Hale, a graduate of Fenn's Evening Business Administration Division and a teacher of Insurance in the Business Administration School was appointed to be the general chief of the Educational Division Campaign." The objective of the Educational Branch was to raise $2,500 for the Student Loan Fund for the dual purpose of aiding needy students and providing payroll funds. Within seven weeks, under the leadership of Mr. Hale and through the cooperation of Board members, team workers, staff, faculty, and students, the goal was way over-subscribed to the tune of $4,151.50 of which $2,607.87 was in cash.

Frankland F. Stafford and Harry White were elected to the Board of Managers at the May 12, 1933, meeting of the Board. Stafford was then elected Chairman of the Board at the June 7, 1933, meeting. He immediately appointed the following committees:

Coordination	Finance	Promotion & Publicity
J. A. Greene, Chairman	J. E. Campbell, Chairman	Dale Cox, Chairman
Leyton E. Carter	W. R. Green	Clayton G. Hale
Ellwood H. Fisher	G. H. Mouck	Nelson Rupp
Nelson Rupp	W. A. Rowe	
Harry White	W. J. Semple	

"Mr. Stafford also announced that he had invited Mr. Clayton G. Hale and Mr. Leyton Carter to become members of the Board. A motion approving their selection was made and unanimously carried."

Alex Rexion announced at this same meeting that "of the 88 recent graduates, 56 had been placed in industry." This was quite an achievement considering the status of unemployment in 1933.

The first six months of 1933 were unlike any similar period in Cleveland's eighty year history. It was said that a crisis no longer brought consternation or alarm. In fact, those in responsible positions seemed almost disappointed to awaken in the morning to discover that another crisis was not in the offing that day. The Cleveland YMCA was in an economic drought. The following statistics illustrate the appalling economic situation:

	1931	1933
Number of full-time employees	233	191
June payroll	$45,906	$17,106
Operating expenses (1st 6 months)	$562,067	$330,245

Within two years the payroll for the month of June was cut 64% and the faculty and staff of the Educational Division of the Y experienced still a greater percentage in reduction. In spite of this job and salary crisis the enrollment for the Fall Semester of 1933 in both the Day and Evening Divisions increased about 20%. In some instances savings and loan passbooks quoted by investment houses were accepted for a limit of 50% of the tuition on the basis of the market value of the books.

As a result of the increase in enrollment the Board of Managers voted at the August 21, 1933, meeting to engage a new man in the Department of Coordination. It was reported at the October 16, 1933, meeting of the Board that Max Robinson had been appointed head of the Department. This was the beginning of his long association with Fenn College.

The need to borrow $35,000 to start the Fall Semester of Fenn College created the need for a committee to study the matter. Following is the report of the committee chaired by W. L. Hotchkiss:

> The question of securing and safeguarding the repayment of this loan becomes of paramount importance. Obviously, no person or organization will venture to advance the sum needed unless he is reasonably sure of the safety of the investment. Can such assurance be given at present—either to such prospective investors or to general creditors who do business primarily with Fenn College?
>
> The school is now legally constituted as the Educational Branch, known as Fenn College, of the Cleveland Young Men's Christian Association. This educational work is conducted by the Cleveland Association through authority given it in O.G.C. 10027 which states,
>
> > "The Association may conduct such work and organize such departments as are deemed by its Trustees necessary to attain the purposes of the organization, and organize through its Trustees under such rules as they adopt, branches which may become coordinate parts of the Association."
>
> Funds of the Educational Branch go through the general financial offices of the Cleveland Association. While these funds may be segregated on the books of the general office for bookkeeping purposes, they become for legal purposes not the funds of the Educational Branch but the funds of the Cleveland Association as a whole. This is further evidenced by the fact that all of the funds of the different branches including the Educational Branch are deposited to the General Association account. This fact gives rise to certain special problems insofar as the Educational Branch

is concerned. The Educational Branch is practically 80% self-supporting. The other branches of the Association are only about 20% self-supporting and must look to general community aid through the Welfare Federation for the balance of their support.

If a condition should arise in which the Association as a whole, or any individual branch, should be in such financial straits that creditors' claims for work done, or any other obligations for any of the individual branches, were turned into court judgments, then the real property and working capital of the whole Cleveland Association would be subject to the satisfaction of such judgments. Thus no matter how strong a financial status the Educational Branch might show on the books of the Cleveland Association by virtue of segregated book accounts, its assets both real and personal could be levied upon as part of the Cleveland Association property. Thus a loan made to furnish working capital for the Educational Branch and going into the General Association account, or even into a segregated Association bank account, would be in a hazardous position by virtue of the fact that it would legally be the property of the whole Cleveland Association.

To place a mortgage on the property used by any one branch to secure a loan made for the use of that branch might arouse the suspicions of general creditors of the Association and result in a deluge of legal actions to protect creditors' claims arising out of transactions involving several or all of the branches.

In view of the very real possibility of such financial difficulties, it may be well for the Cleveland Association as a whole and the Educational Branch as a part, to look for safeguards which will protect the position of a financially strong and virtually self-supporting branch and enable it to secure working capital with which to carry on its functions.

One feasible way out is suggested by O.G.C. 10031 POWER TO STATE ASSOCIATIONS

> "The State Association may incorporate and exercise the privileges of this chapter. When so incorporated and organized, it may receive Young Men's Christian Associations into affiliation and may pass upon all applications for the incorporation of such Associations, causing to be affixed thereto a certificate of its approval."

Acting under this suggestion, the Educational Branch of the Cleveland Young Men's Christian Association could be incorporated as a separate, independent legal entity, and not a branch of a parent Association.

Such separate Association could be known as "Fenn College of the Young Men's Christian Association." It would therefore be from the legal standpoint an Association entirely distinct and separate from the Cleveland Young Men's Christian Association. Its property would be held in its own name and be acquired by deed of its personal school quarters from the Cleveland Young Men's Christian Association. It would have its own Board of Trustees. It would have its own separate banking account. Its obligations would not be a liability of the Cleveland Young Men's Christian Association, and vice versa.

While there would be two Young Men's Christian Associations in Cleveland and two legal entities, there is no reason why the spiritual and personal ties and associations should not remain the same as at present. While there would be two Boards of Trustees, the two could be interlocking as to personnel. One General Secretary could serve in a dual capacity as General Secretary of the Cleveland Young Men's Christian Association and of Fenn College of the Young Men's Christian Association. The present internal financial relationships as to membership fees, house charges, etc., could be handled as they are now. Association objectives and leadership would remain the same as they now are, but the financial and legal status of the two would be clarified and strengthened.

S/ W. L. Hotchkiss

This is the first intimation of the perspective that perhaps it would be advantageous to Fenn College to be a separate entity with its own Board of Trustees. This was to happen sooner than the committee which prepared the above report expected and for additional reasons.

Director Thomas reported at the October 16, 1933, meeting of the Board of Managers on the wisdom of seeking accreditation with the North Central Association. Fenn College had been developed in accordance with the kinds of education which seemed to be most needed with the available resources, although some decisions did not lead directly to the meeting of accrediting agency standards. Teachers were sought with experience and point of view, rather than for being equipped with a Ph.D. degree.

No difficulties had been met in executing student transfers to universities of note. The teaching loads, however, because of economic pressures exceeded North Central Association (N.C.A.) standards. The library requirements of N.C.A. were in excess of Fenn's number of volumes on hand. The financial requirements of N.C.A. also exceeded Fenn's annual income. Director Thomas was authorized to contact individuals acquainted with the attitudes of accrediting bodies and report back to the Board.

The November 13, 1933, Minutes of the Board of Managers carried Ellwood H. Fisher as Chairman of the Board. This is the first reference signifying his appointment to this office. It was reported at this meeting that because of the bad economic situation the enrollment in Nash Junior College was declining. A special committee was appointed by Fisher to study the feasibility of continuing this particular educational activity of Fenn College.

The special committee reported at the December 6, 1933, meeting of the Board that continuance of the Nash Junior College was inadvisable. Six alternatives were presented as follows:

I.   Continue the school as at present.
II. Drop the Day High School and concentrate on the first two years of Junior College.
III. Drop the Day High School and extend the two years of Junior College into a complete college program by means of integrating the present Nash curricula with present Fenn Courses, making a general curriculum leading to the B.S. or the A.B. degree.
IV. Eliminate the Day Nash program.
V.   Extend the present two-year Nash program into a four-year Nash program.
VI. Reorganize the entire day work and place the freshmen and sophomore students in two-year Junior College programs, then enter them into Engineering, Business or other curricula after the first two years.

Arguments in favor of number III were as follows:

(1) This change would simplify promotion and would make possible a unified program under the name of "Fenn".

(2) This move would not increase the teaching cost and would decrease promotion cost.*

(3) This move would tend to decrease direct administrative cost.

---

* "Some changes in the faculty would probably be required. Some reductions would be made and two persons other than those now on our staff would probably be needed in the Social Sciences."

(4) This move would bring to Fenn the good will that goes with a liberal or general curriculum. It would tend to remove the idea that Fenn is a business college or a trade school.

(5) This move would retain the part of the Nash program that seems to have the greatest possibility for growth.

(6) All the day work of the institution would be on the college level.

This was a very important meeting for it undoubtedly was the beginning of the School of Arts and Sciences at Fenn College. The Day High School was dropped at the end of the school year 1934.

The fiscal year end report showed that in addition to repayment of $5,388 of the 1931 deficit, the school balanced the operating budget. This brought the re-payment of the 1931 deficit to a total of $11,000, but most of it was financed by the reduction in faculty salaries. In other words the faculty voluntarily subsidized the operation of the college to the tune of $70,000 for the year 1933.

A survey made by the *Plain Dealer* showed that only two non-tax-supported colleges in Ohio, Oberlin and Western Reserve University, had more male students in the Fall of 1933 than Fenn College.

At the January 17, 1934, meeting of the Board of Managers a special committee recommended that the quarter-plan be adopted, effective September 1934. The advantage was many-fold. It made it possible to spend a longer time in class and laboratory activity as well as on co-op jobs in industry. The four twelve-week change periods produced less confusion than the ten periods of five weeks each. It made it possible to remain in industry long enough to get worthwhile experience. Also, employers were more apt to give students jobs for twelve weeks than the on-going five week program.

In reorganizing for the quarter-plan, the number of weeks of class and laboratory work required for a degree was raised from 115 to 132. This was more in keeping with requirements in other colleges and universities. Because of this time-grid increase the tuition was also increased from $200 to $235 for two quarters' work. Students who were unable to obtain Co-op work were permitted to attend a third quarter at no increase in tuition.

Figure 1 is a facsimile of an announcement of staff changes prepared by Director Thomas on January 30, 1934.

Clayton G. Hale, Chairman of a special committee to organize another Student Loan campaign, reported at the February 21, 1934, meeting

FENN COLLEGE
OF THE CLEVELAND YMCA SCHOOL OF TECHNOLOGY
2200 PROSPECT AVENUE

OFFICE OF THE DIRECTOR   **CLEVELAND, OHIO**   January 30, 1934   PHONE
                                                                                    PROSPECT 2200

Statement of Changes in Organization
    and Staff Relationships of Fenn College

The following changes in organization and in the assignment of personnel
are designed to make effective the policy adopted by the Board of Managers
to bring about the unification of the work of Fenn College and Nash
Junior College:

(1) Beginning February 1st, Mr. Paul E. Williams becomes Assistant to the
Director of Fenn College. He will have responsibility for extending the
relationships of Fenn College with the high schools of Greater Cleveland;
for continuing and developing the participation of Fenn College in radio
programs; for increasing the amount of educational service given by Fenn
College to industries and organizations within their own plants and offices;
for working with groups of alumni in the organization of educational and
other activities; as well as additional duties which will arise in the
general administration of the college.

(2) Mr. J. C. Nichols becomes the Dean of the Day Division of Fenn
College which includes the Division of Engineering, the Division of Business
Administration and the Division of Liberal Arts. Mr. Nichols will have
associated with him the following persons who will be Associate Deans in
their respective divisions:
        (a) Livingstone Hotchkiss will continue as Associate Dean of Fenn
College responsible for the Day Division of Business Administration.
        (b) Marion B. Tolar becomes the Associate Dean of Fenn College
responsible for the Day Division of Liberal Arts. In addition Mr. Tolar
will continue as Head of the Mathematics Department of Fenn College.
        (c) Burl H. Bush becomes the Associate Dean of Fenn College
related to the Day Division of Engineering.

(3) Mr. Millard L. Jordan becomes the Acting Principal of the Day and
Evening High School Division, as well as instructor in the Department of
Social Sciences.

Although the above changes are to be effective as of February 1st, yet it
is recognized that time will be required to bring about all of the necessary
adjustments.

                                        C. V. Thomas, Director

of the Board that Gerald S. Wellman had agreed to be Chairman of the
campaign and Ellwood H. Fisher, to be head of the Special Gifts Committee. The goal was again to be $2,500. The drive was most successful
in that the receipts were more than double the goal.

   At the same meeting Wellman and Dilley presented a sketch of a
proposed Student Union Room in what had been historically known
as the Medical Library Building. The Student Councils of the Day

and Evening Divisions had offered to raise funds to rehabilitate the room. The board approved the idea and expressed hope that the students would be successful in their venture.

A new program of aid to needy students was inaugurated early in 1934 by the U. S. Office of Education known as the Federal Emergency Relief Association (F.E.R.A.). Only students who were financially unable to attend college were eligible for work on the campus for full college expenses. In addition the Federal Government would submit to the college monthly a sum of money equal to $15 $\left(\dfrac{\text{full time student enrollment}}{10}\right)$. By a process of competitive examinations and interviews 35 of a total of 120 were selected for admission to Fenn College. Here is an excerpt from Director Thomas' report to the Board of Managers for the February 21, 1934, meeting:

Fenn Forward

Jesus once said, "The harvest is great but the laborers are few." The truth of this statement in relation to this institution was never as evident to your secretary as now. In the midst of the greatest need which young men and women have had in the last thirty years or perhaps longer, Fenn College finds itself facing these young men and women with small vision, a limited number of persons who are willing to lose themselves in providing the conditions necessary to make possible the kind of futures which these young men and women so much want and to which they are entitled.

How can this institution, with its plan of education, its capacity to help young men meet life, find the type of persons who will throw themselves into this adventure? This institution must have first place in the hearts as well as the minds of more persons who themselves have capacity and who have vision of Cleveland as it can be and of the kind of citizens whom our city of tomorrow must have.

The young men and women in Philadelphia, for example, have Temple University. 12,000 are attending. They have Drexel and other similar schools in addition to the regular college programs such as the University of Pennsylvania. Young men and women in Boston have Wentworth Institute, Franklin Union and other institutions in addition to the universities. These institutions are so financed that the young men and women who wish to attend them can do so without paying high fees. The instructors who teach in them can themselves live, and the buildings and equipment are attractive and modern.

Your secretary [Director of the College] has been wondering much the last few weeks whether we shall be guilty of permitting young men and women in Cleveland to perish because of the lack of vision on the part of the Board and paid leadership of Fenn College. We have one of the greatest setups for abundant service in Cleveland—in my opinion because of our philosophy and educational program, one of the greatest in the country. The young men who go through school here fit into life. They get jobs. They have a philosophy. They are the finest assets of Cleveland. There are 1400 of them in school right now. There should be 12,000 of them.

This statement is not a cry of distress nor one of alarm. It is rather an expression of grief that in the midst of so great possibilities, so little is being done. Fenn needs men—men for its Board of Managers—citizens who see in it their greatest opportunity for creating an institution which will be a fountain of the abundant life. Wherein are we failing? What can be done?

The College, through the courtesy of Samuel P. Halle, began using the vacant lot on the northeast corner of Euclid Avenue and East 30th Street for athletic purposes. In a letter of appreciation to Halle under date of May 1, 1934, C. V. Thomas signed his name as "President" of Fenn College. This was the first inference that his title of "Director" had been changed. This change undoubtedly took place because of the projected reorganization changes and the planning for accreditation. There is no Minute reference relating thereto.

A commission of the North Central Association of Colleges and Secondary Schools finally reported the results of its efforts over a five-year period to revise the standards of accreditation of colleges. At the May 16, 1934, meeting of the Board, President C. V. Thomas reported that eleven committees of the faculty and staff were "hard at work on various phases of the report," and that a twelfth committee composed of Board members should be appointed to study the section dealing with Administration.

The following letter explicitly portrays Director C. V. Thomas' philosophy on education. It contains a group of powerful assertions which could not be better expressed thirty-five, forty, or fifty years following the date of the letter. Note the letter is addressed to Harold Burton, an attorney, who had taken some course work in the evening at old Y-Tech. He later became Mayor of Cleveland and U.S. Senator, ultimately Justice of the Supreme Court of the United States.

May 25, 1934

Mr. Harold Burton, Chairman
Committee on Citizenship Training
Room 339 Board of Education Bldg.
Cleveland, Ohio

My dear Mr. Burton:

The questionnaire regarding Citizenship Training in Fenn College has been filled out and returned. We shall also be glad to have any member of your organization visit the school at any time.

I have the conviction however that Citizenship Training in a period such as the present is far more fundamental than the subjects we teach, the texts we use or the lectures we give. I don't believe we can succeed in helping train pupils to be good citizens unless we search for some of the basic causes of the present non-social acts of individuals and groups, and then remake our education in the light of our findings of the causes of bad citizenship. I personally agree with the general import of the report of the Social Studies Commission of the American Historical Association, which states that the present tensions in society are caused by the transition from a more individualistic type of economic and social life to an era which requires cooperative action. The report points out that the tensions between individuals and groups results in non-social acts of wide and fundamental types.

If the report is correct—and it is in agreement with much of the best thought throughout the world—then education has some most basic adjustments before it. For example, the purposes for which education is conducted must in many ways be changed. Instead of our practices in schools training persons to be competitive, we must develop people who are cooperative in spirit and who know the techniques of cooperation as well as the present generation has known the methods of competition. Making this change means facing our grading systems, the uses made of the normal distribution curve of intelligence, athletic programs, etc.

Again we have done a little in developing persons who have the tendency and the ability to plan. Our schools have been too much developing people who live to pass the examinations to go into the next grade. Planning vs. drifting becomes a major objective in education if we are going into a more cooperative type of society. Another objective has to do with whether we are essentially concerned about Production or Distribution. The great emphasis in our schools for the last thirty years has been on teaching the physical sciences and related subjects, with the thought that such information will be helpful in production. But we are now told that we are in an economy of abundance age rather than scarcity, hence the problem of distribution becomes a major one. Another change in purpose is doing something about the philosophy of success. Acquisition from, or contribution to society, which? We have talked some about contribution to, but I fear our practices have been more in terms of sensitizing individuals to *getting* rather than *giving*.

In addition to the question of objectives, the philosophy of what education is is involved. Kilpatrick points the problem out by referring to the different concepts of "learn." If "learn" means in our school practice the transferring of information, then it is essentially giving to persons in the present the facts of the past. Dr. Whitehead in a publication several years ago pointed out that such a process results in turning out of static minds in a changing world. If "learn" means, on the other hand, the adjustment of individuals to their changing society and that the individual and his environment are inseparable, then education becomes different from much of our present practice. It seems to me that if we are interested in developing citizens for a period of transition, the concept of "to learn" which is based upon essentially the transferring of facts from books and teachers to pupils, is false and we shall have to find out how to practice the kind of education that conceives of "learn" as helping the individual to adjust to ever-changing environment. Those who hold that "learn" means adjustment, question a great deal all the machinery of the modern educational program which assumes that what the pupil learns can be measured in much the same style that the Newtonian type of physicist has assumed, that all that is real consists of units of matter which are massy and movable. Such a concept of physics leaves out color, odor, etc., as unreal. Likewise education which is developed on the basis of measuring quantities is likely to leave out personality, attitudes, philosophy, which in citizenship training are most central.

Finally, an education for citizenship in a changing society will require an examination of classroom methods if the purposes outlined above are to be achieved. Schools will need to be so organized that they are person-centered and not subject-centered. The present necessity of having one teacher inform five or six sections of thirty-five to forty pupils each is from my point of view not compatible with the development of good citizens, if we are really in earnest. Likewise the present will need to replace the past as the point of reference to the pupil. Obviously as the implications of the present are explored, the past will be involved, but the past must be secondary to the present. Again, the solution of problems rather than the memorization of data will characterize schools that are concerned about developing citizens in the present society. Also teachers who can help pupils understand the present must have contact with life. I personally believe that good citizenship training requires that teachers have perhaps one year out of five free from classroom duties for purposeful experience.

Other changes in organization and method could be mentioned, but this statement is already far too long. I have written this letter however because of my conviction that training citizens requires major educational adjustment. Fenn College is at work on some of these problems. Many difficulties arise as the staff, faculty and students attempt together to define their purposes, and adjust their methods. We are eager to see the report of your committee and shall be pleased to participate in any program that may be recommended for the future.

Sincerely yours,

s/ *C. V. Thomas*, President

Baccalaureate Service was held June 17, 1934, at the Euclid Avenue Baptist Church, East 18th Street and Euclid Avenue. The speaker was Dr. Charles W. Gilkey, Dean of University Chapel, University of Chicago. Commencement was held on June 20 at the Baptist Church of the Master, Euclid Avenue and East 97th Street. R. I. Rees, Assistant Vice President, American Telegraph and Telephone Company of Philadelphia, delivered the address. A Board meeting was held just prior to commencement to hear reports of committees on criteria of the North Central Association of Colleges.

The August 15, 1934, meeting of the Board of Managers of The Educational Branch YMCA (Fenn College) was an historical occasion.

It was here that Chairman Fisher presented the report of the special committee of the Board of Managers appointed to study and recommend a plan of organizational relationship between the Board of Managers and the Board of Trustees of the YMCA. The recommendations forthcoming were based on the requirement of the North Central Association that no Board of Control for a college be in a secondary position to another Board of Control.

Accordingly, Fisher reported that a plan be developed which would place the control including the operation of Fenn College in a Board of Trustees of Fenn College, the members of which would also be members of the Board of Trustees of the YMCA. The committee had suggested that there be approximately fifteen members on the new Fenn College Board, one-third of whom would be, at the beginning, members of the then present Y Board and the remainder, persons elected to the Y Board from the present Board of Managers of Fenn College. These recommendations were unanimously approved and the necessary steps to consummate this organization were outlined, namely:

1. Meeting of the corporation of YMCA to effect change in by-laws.
2. Appointment of a nominating committee.
3. Election of new Board members.

At this same meeting J. C. Nichols presented a request by the faculty that the school subsidize one-half the annual dues for faculty members of national professional societies. The Board approved the request with a total school expense budget of $225 and general distribution to the several professional fields. One of the guide lines of the North Central Association was active membership in professional society affairs.

Dr. Blake Crider of W.R.U. was appointed to the faculty in September 1934 as Instructor in Psychology. He became Associate Professor in September 1936, Chairman, Department of Psychology in September 1941, and Professor, Chairman, Department of Psychology in April 1943. He retired from C.S.U. in 1970.

The enrollment for the entire school for the fall term of 1934 was 22% over that for 1933. The Day Cooperative registration increased 20%, the Evening Commerce, 43%, the Evening Engineering, 24% and the Evening High School showed no increase. The number of young people recommended to the school by graduates, former students, members of the Board of Trustees, Board of Managers, and other friends far surpassed any previous year.

"The Frontiers of Learning" was the subject of a radio series over WGAR that Director Thomas led off on September 10, 1934, and that terminated December 6 following a schedule of 39 subjects and speakers. Figure 2 is a facsimile of the folder announcing the program.

The October 17, 1934, meeting of the Board of Managers was a very important one. It was here that Chairman Ellwood H. Fisher submitted the report of the Board of Managers for transmittal to the Board of Trustees of the YMCA. Here is his report:

A Recommendation of the Board of Managers of the Educational Branch to the Board of Trustees of the Young Men's Christian Association of Cleveland

The development of the educational program of the Young Men's Christian Association in Cleveland, especially during the last ten year period, has required many adjustments to meet the new conditions and relationships which have arisen. Whereas ten years ago our educational program consisted almost wholly of evening classes with a shifting student body, now 75% of the volume of education in our Fenn College occurs during the day. Both the day and evening courses extend over a period of three to six years. Ten years ago our educational work was largely on the high school level. Today it is almost entirely on the college level. These developments have raised many problems of laboratories, relationships with other institutions of higher learning, membership in college accrediting bodies, and financial and endowment needs.

The changes during the last ten years have perhaps been more rapid than those which occurred in other periods of our fifty-four years of operating educational classes, yet the adjustments to meet the educational level and needs of young men which have been occurring during the last ten years are like those which the Cleveland Association have always met. When in 1881 the Cleveland Association started its educational program, the large group of young men who desired to study were 6th grade graduates. Our courses were on the 6th grade level. When about 1900 the average young man who came to the Association had finished the 8th grade, our courses became of high school grade. Beginning about 1924 the majority of the young men who came to our classes were high school graduates. At the present time almost all of them are. Just as an adjustment from the 6th grade to high school education was necessary about 1900, so the adjustment from high school to college level has become necessary during recent years.

The Frontiers of Learning

A RADIO SERIES

under auspices of

FENN COLLEGE

▸

Beginning September 10, 1934

OVER W G A R

Each Monday, Tuesday, and Thursday, 10:30 P. M.

▸

FREE SCHOLARSHIPS GIVEN
Further Details Inside Cover

Scholarships

FENN COLLEGE offers three scholarships to the persons who present the first, second and third best papers outlining the materials given in the talks during the entire broadcast, and indicating the ways by which they propose to keep on learning.

The first scholarship offered is for two years in either the day or evening division of Fenn College.

The second scholarship is for one-semester day or evening division in Fenn College.

The third scholarship is for two subjects for one semester in the day or evening division of Fenn College.

Three people will be appointed to judge these papers and award the scholarships.

The winners of these scholarships may begin their work immediately after the first of the year, January, 1935.

Fenn College broadcasts

are designed to aid men and women who wish to acquaint themselves with the trends in the various fields of knowledge.

Each talk of the series will trace events in the different fields of knowledge during the last ten (10) years, and what effects they have had upon our present standards of living.

Suggestions will be given on how adults may acquire more knowledge in the fields of business, engineering, and liberal arts.

These subjects are discussed by men qualified through experience to speak with authority.

On Monday evenings subjects in the field of business will be discussed.

On Tuesday evenings technical subjects will be discussed.

On Thursday evenings subjects in the realm of liberal arts will be presented.

See back of folder for information regarding scholarship.

Schedule of Broadcasts

Why keep on learning?	C. V. Thomas	Sept. 10
The newest frontiers in Employment	M. B. Robinson	Sept. 11
The newest frontiers in Financing further learning	S. R. Black	Sept. 13
The newest frontiers in Business Methods	P. R. Anders	Sept. 17
The newest frontiers in Engineering	J. C. Nichols	Sept. 18
The newest frontiers in Culture	M. B. Tolar	Sept. 20
The newest frontiers in Economics	A. O. Berger	Sept. 24
The newest frontiers in Chemistry	L. W. Hunt	Sept. 25
The newest frontiers in Psychology	B. Crider	Sept. 27
The newest frontiers in Marketing Methods	H. D. Kerr	Oct. 1
The newest frontiers in Aeronautics	S. Ward	Oct. 2
The newest frontiers in History	M. L. Jordan	Oct. 4
The newest frontiers in Law	W. L. Hotchkiss	Oct. 8
The newest frontiers in Metals	C. W. Francis	Oct. 9
The newest frontiers in Poetry	C. Anderson	Oct. 11
The newest frontiers in Business Finance	H. A. Gotschall	Oct. 15
The newest frontiers in Production	D. C. Fabel	Oct. 16
The newest frontiers in Music	L. Nowak	Oct. 18
The newest frontiers in Cities	L. E. Carter	Oct. 22
The newest frontiers in Electrical Engineering	W. C. Davis	Oct. 23
The newest frontiers in Insurance	C. G. Hale	Oct. 25
The newest frontiers in Government	J. J. Joseph	Oct. 29
The newest frontiers in Patents	G. V. Woodling	Oct. 30
The newest frontiers in Prose	D. R. Tuttle	Nov. 1
The newest frontiers in Advertising	K. W. Akers	Nov. 5
The newest frontiers in Physics	W. Poppy	Nov. 6
The newest frontiers in Modern Languages	F. J. Tomich	Nov. 8
The newest frontiers in Personal Selling	I. W. Brandel	Nov. 12
The newest frontiers in Air Conditioning	B. H. Bush	Nov. 13
The newest frontiers in Reading	Eliz. W. Willingham	Nov. 15
The newest frontiers in Industrial Problems	M. E. Nichols	Nov. 19
The newest frontiers in Public Speaking	G. B. Simon	Nov. 20
The newest frontiers in Sociology	L. A. Tucker	Nov. 22
The newest frontiers in Accounting	G. H. Mouck	Nov. 26
The newest frontiers in Radio	H. S. Scott	Nov. 27
The newest frontiers in Dramatics		Nov. 29
The newest frontiers in Taxes	H. C. Cox	Dec. 3
The newest frontiers in Construction	V. D. Hales	Dec. 4
Ways to keep on learning	A. Rexion	Dec. 6

Broadcast ends December 6, 1934.

It is because of the problems which grow out of the operation
of education on the college level that the Board of Managers of
Fenn College have been studying the relationship of the college
to the Board of Trustees of the Young Men's Christian Association.
As a result of this study, and for the reasons given below, and
after consultation with the officers of the Board of Trustees of
the Young Men's Christian Association, the Board of Managers
make the following recommendations:

> That the control of Fenn College be a direct responsibility
> of the Board of Trustees of the Young Men's Christian As-
> sociation;
>
> That the Board of Trustees of the YMCA empower a section
> of its body to be responsible for Fenn College;
>
> That the number of Trustees at Large of the Young Men's
> Christian Association of Cleveland be increased to approxi-
> mately thirty-five (35) and that the personnel of the Trustees
> assigned to Fenn College consist of approximately ten (10)
> new persons to be elected to the Board of Trustees of the
> Young Men's Christian Association and five (5) persons who
> are now members of the Board of Trustees of the YMCA;
>
> That the present Board of Managers resign as of the date,
> if, and when, this recommendation becomes effective.

Reasons for the recommendation are:

> (1) The growth of the college has created budget, personnel,
> public relationships, equipment problems of such impor-
> tance that they should be the direct responsibility of the
> Board of Trustees of the Young Men's Christian Association.
>
> (2) The requirements of the North Central Association of
> Colleges and Secondary Schools that no Board of control
> of a college be in a secondary position to another Board
> would to a considerable degree be met by the change recom-
> mended.
>
> (3) The change would make the Board of Trustees respon-
> sible for an activity which is city-wide and is different in
> many ways from those activities directed by Branch Boards
> of Management.

The Board of Managers at their meeting on August 15th unanimously recommended that the above change occur. They, individually and as a group, desire to be of every service possible in
furthering the educational program of the Association. They believe that the meeting in an adequate way of some of the problems

which are now before the educational program of the Association, will open opportunities for educational service to young men greater than any which the Cleveland Association has thus far had.

Ellwood H. Fisher

Chairman Board of Managers of the
Educational Branch

Dated: Saturday, September 15, 1934

Also at the October 17, 1934, meeting of the Board of Governors there was considerable discussion concerning the appropriate time to seek membership in the Ohio College Association and the North Central Association of Colleges and Secondary Schools. The following statement on accreditation and the two accrediting associations was submitted by President Thomas:

Some Values of Accreditation

Accreditation is a "stamp" of quality.

Accreditation facilitates the transfer of students to other colleges.

Accreditation gives status to faculty members among college teachers.

Accreditation removes irritations that come from those who use the lack of accreditation as a means of disparaging the work of a college.

Accreditation tends to increase the enthusiasm of students and alumni for their college.

Accreditation increases and enriches the relationships of a college with other institutions of higher learning.

Accrediting Associations

The Ohio College Association.
More than 40 Ohio Colleges belong. Membership to date largely based upon size of endowment, number of Ph.D's who are heads of departments, library facilities and general tone of a college.

The North Central Association of Colleges and Secondary Schools.
Universities and Colleges in the North Central States belong.
At its annual meeting in April 1934 the Association stated:
"In its accrediting procedures the Association intends within the general patterns of higher education to observe such principles as will preserve whatever desirable individual qualities member institutions may have. While it is necessary to emphasize cer-

tain characteristics that are recognized as basic—such as the competence of the faculty, the representative character of the curriculum, effective administration, standards of student accomplishment and financial adequacy—it is regarded as of prime importance also to protect such institutional variations as appear to be educationally sound. Even in these basic matters it is clear that considerable divergence from average or optimum conditions may occur without perceptibly detracting from the essential educational worth of an institution. Uniformity in every detail of institutional policies and practices is believed to be not only unnecessary but undesirable."

Questions Before Fenn

(1) Should it make application for admission to the Ohio College Association and the North Central Association?

(2) How can the less favorable conditions at Fenn, as compared with those of other colleges, be improved—namely

(a) The endowment situation, both the amount of income from endowment and the evidence of permanence of the endowment income now received.

(b) The freedom from non-educational controls. (The recent action of the Board of Trustees of the Young Men's Christian Association is directed toward the meeting of this problem.)

(c) The Library. Both the number of books in the library and the annual expenditure for the library are inadequate.

(d) The number of Ph.D's on the faculty. (This problem is lessened by the inclusion in Fenn's faculty of many men who have had professional experience in the fields which they teach.)

(e) Buildings. (A prominent leader in the field of higher education recently stated that the greatest weakness that the college has to the superficial observer is its buildings.)

Inasmuch as it was essential that application be filed prior to November 1 with the secretary of the North Central Association or postpone such application for about one year, the Board instructed Director Thomas to proceed with filing such application. The new accreditation policy of the North Central Association required applying institutions to state their objectives and then give evidence that they have the personnel, equipment, curriculum, and finances to attain the objectives.

The Faculty, for the first time, prepared a statement, "Objectives of Fenn College" which was adopted by the Board on December 5, 1934. The text is quoted here:

OBJECTIVES OF FENN COLLEGE

I. *Institutional Development*

In the charter granted to the Young Men's Christian Association of Cleveland in 1867, Section III of the Articles of Incorporation states: "The purpose for which said Incorporation is organized is the improvement of the spiritual, moral, mental, social and physical conditions of the young men by means in harmony with the spirit of the Gospel."

The Young Men's Christian Association of Cleveland seeks to provide personnel programs and facilities which will enable young people to achieve this purpose in the setting of contemporary life.

The focal interest of many young people who comprise the clientele of the Association is mental development. Fenn College is the division of the Young Men's Christian Association of Cleveland which seeks to assist them in achieving this development through the medium of education.

The Young Men's Christian Association of Cleveland has sought from its beginning to adjust the level of its educational offerings to the needs of persons who come to it. When the educational work now known as Fenn College was founded in 1881, the educational attainment of the average young person was below high school level; consequently the programs of instruction offered were of the elementary and trade school grade.

As the level of education of young people moved upward, the standards of the educational offerings of the Young Men's Christian Association were likewise raised. By 1923 a majority of the young people seeking education through the Young Men's Christian Association were high school graduates. This condition required that the educational program be then raised to the college level. By 1930 the Trustees of the Association authorized that its formal educational division be known as "Fenn College."

II. *General Educational Objectives of Fenn College*

Fenn College seeks in its general educational objectives

1. To awaken and stimulate in students a desire to understand themselves and the world about them.

2. To assist students in choosing their vocations and in planning the kinds of education that are most suitable to their interests, needs, abilities and resources.

3. To assist students in developing those skills and attitudes and acquiring such knowledges as will enable them to deal effectively with the whole range of life experiences.

4. To stimulate students to recognize social, economic and political problems and to seek to apply Christian principles of thought and action to their solution.

5. To develop in students the tendency to use, and skill in the use of, analytical methods and factual data in the solution of the problems which confront them.

6. To assist in the discovery and development of the types of course content, student experience and methods of instruction best adapted to fulfill the purposes of the college.

III. *The Purposes of the Day Division of Fenn College*

In addition to the general educational objectives of Fenn College, the Day Division seeks

1. To make available in Cleveland the opportunities and advantages of cooperative education on the college level. More specifically:

    (a) To combine theory and practice, study and work, learning and doing, as an integral part of the educational experience itself.

    (b) To provide students with the opportunity to determine their aptitudes and develop their adaptability for various kinds of work.

    (c) To make it possible for many deserving and capable young men to obtain the benefits of a college education who would otherwise be unable to do so.

    (d) To provide direct opportunity for cooperation between the college and business and industry.

2. To provide the kinds of work experience while the students are in college that will tend to lead to immediate induction into employment upon graduation.

3. To provide training on the college level in the fields of Engineering and Business Administration.

4. To provide in the Liberal Arts program a general educational training and the foundations for certain types of professional study.

IV. *The Purposes of the Evening Division of Fenn College*

The responsibilities of a college in an urban community include providing educational opportunities for employed adults. To meet this obligation Fenn College maintains an Evening Division, which has the following objectives in addition to those stated for the entire school:

1. To prepare young men and women employed during the day for successful and socially useful careers in Business and Engineering fields.

2. To afford an opportunity to persons employed in business and industry to acquire or re-study specialized skills or knowledges which from time to time they need in meeting the demands of their work.

3. To maintain facilities by which adults may in their leisure time study themselves and their relationships to society, and obtain growth in self-expression in oral, written and other creative forms.

Fenn College seeks by means of the personnel employed; the clientele admitted, the facilities provided, the course content selected and the methods of instruction used, to attain the foregoing objectives.

Stacey Black, Finance Director, reported at the December 5, 1934, meeting of the Board of Managers that $2,500 to $3,000 would have to be raised prior to December 31 to balance the annual budget. He emphatically reported that the board should forthwith face up to methods of balancing the fiscal budget *other than by the adjustment of Faculty salaries.*

Two very revealing statistical analyses were made during the fall of 1934; the first was a comparison of American Council of Education Psychological Test scores. One hundred sixty Fenn College Freshmen took the test. It is worthy of note that the Fenn score exceeded the national median score in all brackets; only 15 of the 203 colleges and universities which gave the tests to a total of 40,229 students had a median score higher than that at Fenn. This echoed most commendable admission standards. Table 2 also shows the median scores in the three brackets for a number of select colleges and universities.

In addition a study was made of student enrollments beginning with the first Day Division college Fall admission in 1923. (See Table 3.) The figures are actual through the Fall of 1934 and projected through

TABLE 2

A COMPARISON OF AMERICAN COUNCIL OF EDUCATION PSYCHOLOGICAL TEST SCORES

I. *A Comparison of Fenn Scores with Scores for All Colleges*

	Median score for lowest quarter of the students	Median score for middle half of the students	Median score for highest quarter of the students
40,229 freshmen from			
203 colleges in U.S.	116	160	208
160 Fenn College Freshmen	154	186	224

II. *Scores Made in Some of the Other Colleges*

Akron	124	163	201
Antioch	168	200	236
Case	164	205	236
Colgate	147	179	214
Lehigh	145	180	220
Rollins	107	163	205
Tufts	148	180	216
Valparaiso	104	138	176
Washington & Jefferson	110	143	190
Dartmouth	170	203	239
Coe	118	151	192
Northwestern	142	179	224

the Fall of 1939. It is interesting to note from the following tabulation that the average increase in Freshmen enrollments approximated fifty percent in many years, about 65% of Freshmen became Sophomores, about 60% of Sophomores became Pre-Juniors, about 70% of Pre-Juniors became Juniors, and about 90% of Juniors became Seniors.

The Y.M.C.A. Board of Trustees took action December 12, 1934, approving the recommendations of the Board of Managers to establish a Board of Trustees of Fenn College. The following were elected to membership on the new Board:

PERSONNEL BEING PROPOSED FOR THE BOARD OF
TRUSTEES OF FENN COLLEGE

From the Present Board of the Y.M.C.A.

Ellwood H. Fisher, Chairman, The Fisher Bros. Company
Harold H. Burton, Andrews, Hadden & Burton
Jacob D. Cox, Jr., The Cleveland Twist Drill Co.
Cyrus S. Eaton, Otis & Company
John A. Greene, Ohio Bell Telephone Company
Hon. Frederick A. Henry, Geauga Lake, Ohio
Harry D. Sims, The Chandler & Rudd Company
Ex-Officio:
    A. G. Knebel, General Secretary Y.M.C.A.
    David W. Teachout, The Teachout Company

From the Former Board of Managers of Fenn College

E. H. Baker, Jr., Locke Machine Company
James E. Campbell, The Sherwin-Williams Company
Leyton E. Carter, The Cleveland Foundation
Dale Cox, The Cleveland Plain Dealer
Clayton G. Hale, Hale & Hale

Additional Nominations

Eugene W. Kettering, The Winton Engine Company
Richard Roth, William Taylor & Company

The new Board of Trustees of Fenn College (henceforth referred to as the board) met for the first time December 21, 1934, called to order by Chairman Ellwood H. Fisher. Standing Committees were established and the personnel appointed with the following acting as Chairmen:

1. Budget and Current Finance   J. E. Campbell
2. Instruction and Personnel   Clayton G. Hale
3. Capital Needs   Ellwood H. Fisher
4. Public Relations   Dale Cox

Thus began a new era in the history of Fenn College. The end of 1934 brought to a close two most important steps, the formation and installation of a new independent board and the application for accreditation to the North Central Association; 1934 must be considered one

Table 3
STUDENT ENROLLMENTS IN DAY DIVISION COLLEGE

	'23	'24	'25	'26	'27	'28	'29	'30	'31	'32	'33	'34	'35	'36	'37	'38	'39
ENGINEERING																	
Freshmen	14	20	24	48	62	121	135	160	180	210	250	290	330	330	330	330	330
Sophomores		10	10	12	33	40	87	87	104	117	136	162	188	214	214	214	214
Pre-Juniors			8	9	11	25	40	70	70	85	82	108	129	150	171	171	171
Juniors						11	16	28	49	49	58	58	77	90	105	119	119
Seniors							10	14	25	44	45	52	52	70	80	94	107
TOTAL	14	30	42	69	106	197	288	359	428	505	571	670	776	854	900	928	941
COMMERCE																	
Freshmen								40	60	80	100	120	150	150	150	150	150
Sophomores									26	40	52	65	78	97	97	97	97
Pre-Juniors										20	32	40	50	62	77	77	77
Juniors											14	22	28	33	43	54	54
Seniors												12	18	25	30	38	48
TOTAL								40	86	140	198	259	324	369	397	416	426
GRAND TOTAL								399	514	645	769	929	1,100	1,223	1,297	1,344	1,367

of the most important years in Fenn's history. It bears mentioning, and in some cases reiterating, here a number of important events or developments which took place that year:

Organization

1. The Faculties of Fenn College and Nash Junior College were consolidated.
2. All Day classes on the secondary school level were discontinued in June.
3. The new Board of Trustees was established.

Program

1. The 12-week quarter replaced the 5-week period in the Day Division Cooperative program.
2. The fifth year of the Day Business Administration program was offered for the first time.
3. A Production Laboratory was organized.
4. The freshman Liberal Arts course was started.
5. The Evening Division programs were strengthened.

Extra Curricular Activities

1. A reorganization of faculty responsibility was effected.
2. A Fine Arts Department was started.
3. The Fenn Glee Club gave its first concert at Severance Hall.
4. *The Perspective*—a literary magazine—was started.
5. The Fenn Debaters joined the Association of Northern Ohio Colleges.

In Study of Purposes of Fenn

1. The Faculty prepared the objectives of Fenn College for future guide-lines and transmittal to accrediting agencies.

This chapter had originally been planned to include the years 1930 through 1939, but, although most of this chapter covered the depression years, it included a host of progress and historical events, especially during 1934. Therefore, this chapter ends with the first meeting of the newly organized and appointed Board of Trustees of Fenn College.

IV

*For which of you, intending to build a tower,
sitteth not down first, and counteth the cost,
whether he have sufficient to finish it?*

Luke xiv, 28.

The new Constitution and By-Laws (a requirement for accreditation) were approved at the first board meeting in the new fiscal year, held January 23, 1935. The proposed annual budget was also approved, but it still contained a 10% salary "reserve." Action was taken to review the budget operation each succeeding sixty days, "with the purpose of repaying the reserves as early as possible." It was reported that in 1934 faculty salaries were finally paid on the 100% basis for the first time since 1931, and that the existing 100% basis was 81% of the 1931 scale.

It was also reported that John Dale Russell of the University of Chicago and Father Schmitalla of St. Louis University had tentatively been selected by the North Central Association to inspect Fenn College, but a question had been raised in the Association's office concerning the advisability of an inspection by the Association of an Ohio college which had not already become a member of the Ohio College Association. Questionable areas of inadequacy for membership in the Ohio College Association and accreditation by the North Central Association included the following:

1. Library: insufficient number of volumes.
2. Faculty tenure and ranking system: there were no contracts for tenure and a total lack of policies for appropriate ranking of the faculty in the usual four categories.
3. Inadequate classroom space and laboratory equipment.

152

4. Insufficient number of faculty with Ph.D. status.
5. Lack of endowment.
6. Lack of a four-year Liberal Arts degree program in operation.

A request was therefore made that the Ohio College Association (O.C. A.) inspect Fenn College.

On February 19, 1935, four representatives of O.C.A. made a thorough survey of Fenn and even prior to submitting a formal report expressed favorable comment regarding the quality of the student body and specific laboratories and courses of study.

Various committees of the board had been studying ways and means of upgrading certain areas of the college, both academic and physical, to bring them up to standards which would be acceptable by accrediting bodies. There was an extreme need for urgency and committees were meeting often to present recommendations at each board meeting.

Clayton G. Hale, Chairman of the Personnel Committee of the Board, presented the recommendations of his committee at the February 27, 1935, board meeting. These dealt with the policy of faculty tenure, form of agreement with faculty members, classification of faculty, and review of faculty status and rank. These recommendations were unanimously adopted so an impressive start had been made toward complying with customary college personnel standards.

The two representatives of the North Central Association visited the campus on March 1 and 2, 1935. They were most prompt in submitting their report to the Administration. President Thomas presented the following résumé of their findings before the Board on March 27, 1935:

The Survey of Fenn College by the North Central Association
The usual practice of the North Central Association of Colleges in surveying a college and indicating the further developments that should be made previous to the institution's becoming a member of the Association was followed in relation to Fenn College. Of the 51 colleges which filed applications to the North Central Association this year 4 were admitted. Three of the 4 had been members of the Association previous to this year and the 4th had its first survey four years ago. All of the institutions which had their first surveys this year were advised regarding their outstanding characteristics and the types of developments which the North Central Association believes advisable. The report regarding Fenn made by the persons who surveyed the college includes the following statements:

Your examiners found Fenn College a most interesting institution. The authorities of the college should be congratulated on the educational daring that has characterized their experimentation with a new type of collegiate program. The institution is carrying out a most challenging experiment on the effect which intensive student guidance has, not so much upon his education in the more technical sense as rather upon his self-development in the broadest sense of that word. The outstanding characteristic of the college is the measure of attention which is given to the individual student and the evaluation of the student's experience while on cooperative placement. In maintaining these features, the college shows some secondary characteristics which are sufficiently unique to merit very special attention.

The college also as a consequence of its objectives, experiments with curriculum courses, some of which are distinctive enough to offer contrasts with ordinarily accepted curricula and courses. Those who studied this college as visitors of the North Central Association naturally found this situation intensely interesting. . . .

The recommendations for the improvements of Fenn College include the bringing together of the records now kept in the Dean's offices into a central Registrar's office—the further functionalizing and centralizing of the administration of the college—the adjusting of the accounting procedures to conform more closely with recommendations recently made to all colleges—the including of all special funds, such as Laboratory funds, in the regular budget of the college—the increasing of the percentage of income secured from other than tuition fees—the closer controlling of intercollegiate athletics by a faculty committee—the increasing of the number of books in and of the seating capacity of the Library—the providing of more adequate facilities for Biology and to a certain extent for Chemistry—the improving of some parts of the physical plant—*the discontinuing of the balancing of budgets by means of salary reserves as in 1932 and 1933.*

The recommendations contained no reference to the improvement of instruction, curriculum, placement, or the quality of the personnel service. The report states, "The instruction is characterized by practicability and vigor."

Contained in the report are numerous suggestions for the development of the college which will be of great value. The survey is a further step in the continuous study which Fenn College has been making of itself since 1927. Just as Dr. Goodwin Watson,

Dr. John P. Herring, Mr. T. H. Nelson and Dr. Arthur J. Klein have through their visits to and study of Fenn been of great value in bringing about the educational methods which the North Central report commends, so the survey provides a chart for some future steps. The Board of Trustees and faculty will examine each of the suggestions in the light of their probable effect upon the achievement of the purposes of the college and will determine the steps required to put those which are desirable and feasible into operation. The authorization by the Board of Trustees in their March meeting for the establishment of a central Registrar's office was the first outgrowth of the North Central Association survey.

President Thomas also reported at the March 27, 1935, meeting that the Liberal Arts Division of Fenn which was started in 1932 for students who did not wish to specialize in a professional program and also to enrich the curriculum of the entire institution had been approved by the State Department of Education to grant the Bachelor of Arts degree. It was necessary to have students in the third year of the program prior to applying for the privilege of granting degrees.

The Personnel Committee recommended at this same meeting and the board approved that: (1) the functions usually assigned to a Registrar's office be brought together, and that the Office of Registrar be established not later than September 1, and (2) the functionalization of the administrative activities of the Day Division be increased as rapidly as possible. These conformed to recommendations of the North Central Association.

Certain steps had already been taken toward a functional type of organization, such as:

1. Assignment of the responsibility for the preparation of catalogues, advertising and other forms of promotion to one individual.
2. Appointment of a Finance Director.
3. Appointment of a Head of the Department of Coordination.
4. Appointment of a Director of Athletics.
5. Appointment of a Director of Student Activities.

However, there were areas which needed functionalization, such as:

1. Appointment of a Director of Admissions.
2. Appointment of a Dean to select and supervise faculty activities.

    3. Planning of programs of study and educational supervision of students by Associate Deans of the three departments of the Day Division.

It was pointed out at the April 17, 1935, board meeting that during the Depression many high school principals of Greater Cleveland sent their most able graduates, who lacked financial resources, to Fenn College for competitive examinations. A select group of 132 of these students was later enrolled at Fenn because of the popularity of the Co-op program. Their first year's tuition was subsidized by tuition remission, and henceforth they were able to earn most of school expenses via co-op jobs. Furthermore, most of these students had jobs upon graduation because of their co-op work.

Action was taken at the May 8, 1935, meeting of the board appointing G. H. Mouck as Professor of Accounting, effective September 1935. Also at this same meeting it was announced that Dr. Charles F. Kettering, President of General Motors Research Corporation, would be the commencement speaker on May 23.

One of the graduates of the class of 1935 was Alfred G. Hose, who later served as an Alumni Trustee on the Fenn College Board, as Secretary of the Board of Trustees of the Fenn Educational Foundation, while Vice President of the Lindsay Wire Weaving Company. He was later elected as a Trustee of the Foundation.

Action was also taken at the May 8, 1935, board meeting to discontinue the Evening Preparatory School as of August 1935.

An Honorary Degree, Doctor of Laws, LL.D., was conferred on President C. V. Thomas by Baldwin-Wallace College at its commencement on June 10, 1935.

To further the progress on the functional organization of the staff, Chairman Hale of the Personnel Committee moved for adoption at the June 26, 1935, board meeting the following:

    1. J. C. Nichols appointment to Dean of the College.
    2. M. E. Nichols appointment to Dean of Engineering.
    3. P. R. Anders appointment to Dean of Business Administration.
    4. M. B. Tolar appointment to Dean of Liberal Arts.
    5. W. L. Hotchkiss appointment to Registrar.
    6. Miss Ann Sharow appointment to Assistant to the Registrar.

With the need for an enlarged Library and space for housing the newly created functional offices, it was essential that a study be made on total space requirements plus ways and means of the financing thereof. Chairman Fisher reported on the action of the Executive Committee in relation to new building space at the June 26, 1935, Board meeting and Vilas reported that he had visited F.H.A. and several banks to determine the possibility of obtaining funds for further Fenn College building space from government loans.

Malcolm B. Vilas was an active member of the YMCA Board of Trustees for many years. The Honorary Degree, Doctor of Laws, LL.D. was conferred on him by Fenn College in 1963.

The following enrollment statistics were presented at the October 1, 1935, meeting of the Board of Trustees for the entire school for the month of September:

1927: 949	1930: 1,330	1933: 909
1928: 1,125	1931: 1,024	1934: 1,101
1929: 1,412	1932: 792	1935: 1,261

It appeared that the September 1936 enrollment would be an all-time high for Fenn and in anticipation of this, Chairman Fisher and President Thomas went to New York City to present the building and equipment needs of Fenn to the YMCA General Education Board. They were well received, and it was suggested by a General Education Board member that they return later in the fall with additional information about Fenn's specific needs.

The question of accreditation arose again at the November 6, 1935, meeting of the board. The following was reported on the progress thus far:

Possible Action in Relation to Accreditation

The question is often asked regarding when Fenn College expects to renew its applications for membership in the North Central Association and the Ohio College Association. The following summarizes the changes that have occurred within the college since the North Central recommendation:

—A central registrar's office has been set up.

—Unification of the Day and Evening Divisions under a centralized administration has been effected.

—The Library: Space enlarged; additional books obtained; clerical help added; study of use made by Fenn students of other libraries started.

—Budget: Chart of Accounts adjusted to collegiate regulations; Laboratory funds included; Department Heads consulted regarding the needs of their departments.

—Athletics: Participation by co-op students in athletics reduced to three years; Participation in Night teams regulated; Faculty Committee placed in charge; Gate Receipts now under control of the Finance Department.

—Health: A more complete Health Service established; Students pay $3.00 each for additional service.

—Testing and Guidance: Plans for providing information secured from Testing to the Placement, Instruction and other departments of the college more fully developed.

—Improvement in Marking and Grading System effected.

—New members of faculty have been engaged on the basis of teaching both day and evening, rather than day only and extra instruction in the evening.

—Number of hours instructors are teaching slightly reduced.

Problems raised by the accrediting bodies which have as yet not been dealt with:

—Too small a percentage of total income received from other than tuition sources.

—The use of salary reserves to balance budgets.

—The need for improvement of plant and equipment, especially the replacement of the old houses and the improvement of equipment in the Physics, Botany and Chemical laboratories.

—The decrease of teaching load of the faculty.

—The right of the college to receive and hold property.

The list of both things accomplished and the things yet undone could be extended, but the above includes the major items. At least three possibilities are before the college in relation to its accreditation move:

(1) To again this year request accreditation from both the Ohio College and the North Central Associations;

(2) To request accreditation from either the Ohio College or the North Central Association;

(3) To make no approach for accreditation this year.

Accreditation is one of the three major problems before the college. The best strategy in relation to it must be followed. What is the recommendation of the Board in relation to seeking accreditation this year?

Problems of the pirating of faculty were prevalent even in the mid-thirties as shown in this excerpt from Chairman Clayton G. Hale's Personnel Committee report to the Board of Trustees on November 6, 1935:

The Resignation of Dr. T. M. Pitkin

Dr. Pitkin, who was appointed Assistant Professor of History last August, has recently been appointed a Regional Supervisor of Historical Research under the general direction of the National Park Service, and has filed a letter of resignation with the college asking for his release as of November 27th, the end of the first quarter of the college year. He is to receive $2600 and his travel expenses. His appointment at Fenn called for a salary of $1800 for three quarters of employment.

Although Dr. Pitkin did not inform the college that he had filed an application for appointment in the above service until after the telegram of appointment had come to him, and although the college is embarrassed by the necessity of changing instructors in the middle of a school year when the opportunity of locating a high type of individual is very limited, yet the Personnel Committee believes that the only action the college can take is to accept the resignation.

The Personnel Committee therefore recommends to the Board of Trustees that the resignation of Dr. Pitkin be accepted, with the understanding that Dr. Pitkin be informed that the resignation is regretfully accepted, and that the Board of Trustees is not happy that a relationship supposedly established for the school year is thus severed.

The Personnel Committee requests that it be given authority pro tem to approve the appointment of the successor to Dr. Pitkin upon the recommendation of the staff, the appointment to be approved finally by the Board of Trustees at a later meeting.

The Personnel Committee desires to call to the attention of the Board of Trustees a problem which the college will increasingly face unless it finds a way to raise its salary scale.

Some members of the Board will recall that a year ago Dr. Robert Holzer was called from Fenn to the University of California at a larger salary. About a month ago another member of our full time faculty was approached by a state institution to join its staff. An offer of $400 more per year for three quarters of instruction was made to this individual. Probably the only factor that kept

Fenn from having to replace this man, after the school year had
begun, was the fact that the appropriation to the state institution
is somewhat in doubt for the next year and the administration
of the state institution could not make a commitment beyond the
present year.

The Personnel Committee believes that Fenn has selected and
has drawn to it some younger faculty men of promise, and that
unless some means can be found for raising the salary levels—
especially of some of our younger and lower paid men—that the
effectiveness of our work will decrease through the loss of more
of our personnel.

Although the year 1935 ended without success in gaining accredita-
tion, the two investigators from the North Central Association, Father
Schmitalla and Dr. John Dale Russell instilled some optimism in the
Administration through the following excerpt from their report:

Anyone who is concerned with the educational processes of today
cannot but find in the Fenn College program a somewhat startling
challenge to conventional thinking. The authorities of the college
should be congratulated on the educational daring that has characterized their experimentation with a new type of college program.
The institution should be encouraged to continue its quest for
accreditation, and should be assured that its general objectives
place it within the field of interest of the North Central Association.

President Thomas' Annual Report for the year 1935, his first full year
as President, delineates a year of substantial progress. It bears publication herein:

ANNUAL REPORT OF FENN COLLEGE
FOR THE YEAR 1935

Prepared for the Board of Trustees of the College

To understand the work of Fenn College requires that one have
a background of its purposes and the social setting in which it
operates. In Cleveland and Northeastern Ohio large numbers of
high school graduates desire to equip themselves for earning a
living and for being effective citizens. These Fenn seeks to assist
in the following ways:

—To awaken and stimulate a desire to understand themselves
and the world about them.

—To assist them in choosing their vocations and in planning the kinds of education that are most suitable to their interests, needs, abilities and resources.

—To assist them in developing those skills and attitudes and acquiring such knowledges as will enable them to deal effectively with the whole range of life experiences.

—To stimulate them to recognize social, economic and political problems and to seek to apply Christian principles of thought and action to their solution.

—To develop in them the tendency to use, and skill in the use of, analytical methods and factual data in the solution of the problems which confront them.

—To introduce and orient them into business and industry—to help them in finding the right job opportunity.

For the achievement of these purposes Fenn College exists. Faculty, equipment, all facilities and resources of the institution, are centered upon these aims. The following summary of the work and development of the college for 1935 is a statement of some of the important factors by which the purposes were realized.

Personnel of Fenn College During 1935

2490 young men and women attended Fenn College during 1935. 1170 were studying in the Business Administration Division, 1243 in the Engineering, and 77 in the General Arts and Science Division. 659 of them came to Fenn during the day and 1831 attended during evening hours. The median age of the day students was 20 years; that of the evening students, 23 years. 135 persons constituted the faculty. In addition to the students and faculty, the executives and employment managers of more than eighty industries and business organizations were members of the field faculty of Fenn. They were the supervisors of the Fenn students while they were on their cooperative jobs.

Some Significant Developments

During 1935 many developments designed to facilitate the achievement of the purposes of the college occurred. The following is a brief summary of those changes:

In Administration—During the year the Day and Evening Divisions were placed under a unified administrative control. The academic administration was vested in a Dean of the College, a Dean of

Engineering, a Dean of Business Administration and a Dean of Arts and Sciences—whose responsibilities extended over both the Day and Evening Divisions.

A central Registrar's office was established. Academic records which had previously been kept in the Deans' offices were brought together under the supervision of a Registrar for the College.

The Chart of Accounts of the College was changed to conform to the recommendations of the National Committee on Standard Reports for Institutions of Higher Education. This both facilitates comparisons of the operation of Fenn with other institutions of higher learning and improves the financial control within the college.

In Finance—The expense of operating the college in 1935 was $231,209.41. The income from all sources was $231,971.17. Of this amount the students paid $212,912.22 and endowment and gifts provided $19,058.95.

Although the students provided 91.7% of the total income which, in comparison with higher educational institutions generally is excessively high, yet during 1935 Fenn received $1,604.12 more from endowment and gifts than the previous year.

The Chart of Accounts previously referred to unified the financial operation of the college as contrasted with the previous method which set up three units of financial operation, each expected to balance its income with its expenses. The new Chart of Accounts also provided for the inclusion of all laboratory, library and other educational expenses in the total budget of the college.

In Library Facilities—During 1935 some important developments occurred in the Fenn College Library. Shelving capacity was increased by more than 100%, the seating capacity by 50% and the book content by 55%.

A full time student assistant was added to the staff. A new charging system was installed.

2695 books were added to the collection owned by the college. These, together with the 1400 books supplied by the Cleveland Public Library, made a total of 8629.

A survey of the use made by students of Fenn College of the library showed that 1½ times as many books were drawn from over forty libraries as were drawn from the Fenn Library, although the Fenn Library predominates as a source of reference material and periodical reading.

In Physical Plant—The development of Production and Chemical Engineering laboratories began in 1935. Equipment was added to the Physics, Chemical, Metallurgical and Electrical laboratories.

The reception room and the student union rooms were redecorated and refurnished.

In Faculty—The policy of employing new faculty members on the basis of teaching for Fenn College either day or evening, rather than teaching a full day schedule and adding evening work, was adopted.

The provisions of faculty tenure were clarified and strengthened. The average teaching load was decreased. Faculty participation in the formation of educational policies was extended.

In the Curriculum—The number of majors in the Arts and Science Division was decreased, and the offerings for each major strengthened. The number of curricula in the Engineering Division was reduced from six to four and the hours of technical course content for each curriculum was increased. Advanced courses were added in Physics, Mathematics and English.

In Instruction—Major attention was given to evaluation of different methods of instruction. Dr. Ralph Tyler and Dr. Arthur J. Klein of Ohio State University visited the college and assisted the faculty in developing Measurement techniques. A study of Grading and Marking Systems was made by the Business Administration faculty. The Blended Curriculum in the Arts and Science Division was carried into its second year and additional steps taken in its evaluation. All full time faculty members participated in the preparation of a statement showing the methods of instruction being used by different faculty persons. Questions regarding how to improve methods and how to measure the results of the methods were listed and discussed.

In Academic Administration—The method and content of the orientation courses offered in the three divisions of the school were studied and an orientation program for all freshmen was evolved. Academic records were centralized in one office. Visits to other institutions for the purpose of studying systems and forms were made, and based upon the information obtained, an academic record system was developed.

The time of personnel for the conducting of psychological and testing programs, and for relaying information thus secured to the

Coordination Department and the instruction staff, was increased. A plan of faculty conferences dealing with the work of each individual student in the light of information available in the Personnel Office was developed and placed in operation.

In Athletics—The control of intercollegiate athletics was placed in the hands of a faculty committee. Eligibility requirements were set up for evening school teams. Day Cooperative students were limited to three years' participation in intercollegiate games. The control of gate receipts was placed in the business office of the college.

In Student Health Service—The time available to Fenn students by the school physician was increased. The amount of information regarding the physical condition and health of students was enlarged, and methods were developed for extending the use of the information in the classrooms. A clinical infirmary service was included in the Student Health Program.

In Student Welfare—Additional records dealing with the amount of participation of students in extra-curricular activities were kept and further steps taken to control the amount of such participation.

The Scholarship Committee broadened the basis for the granting of scholarships.

The placement of Cooperative students and graduates improved. A survey of graduates in October showed that 95% of all graduates were employed. The percentage of employment of Cooperative students exceeded 90.

In Financial Aid to Students—198 persons received Student Loan, Scholarship and N.Y.A. aid totaling $18,119.00 in value. By means of the cooperative plan a high percentage of the day students were enabled to earn a considerable part of their college expenses, and thus continue their education. Evening students almost entirely finance their education from their earnings during day hours.

Opportunities and Problems Ahead

The developments during 1935 and the continuing increase in the number of individuals coming to Fenn create both opportunities and problems. Cleveland greatly needs expansion of the kind of education which Fenn provides. Such "Public Service Institutions" as Temple University in Philadelphia, New York University in New York City, and Northeastern University in Boston, illustrate the type and size of institutions which Cleveland must soon have.

In the meantime the buildings of Fenn College are crowded. The old houses in which half of the education is conducted are being used for purposes for which they were not intended. Buildings, equipment, more adequate financial support, combined with the program and purposes of Fenn, will produce in Cleveland a service to the youth, the value of which it is difficult to encompass. Furthermore, by the work-and-study plan a large percentage of of the cost can and will be covered by the youth themselves. Business, industry, the social and political structure of the city, demand that youth have the opportunities which the Fenn program expanded to meet the needs of the city can provide. This is the problem that confronts Fenn College.

Cooperation—The Heart of Fenn's Program

During 1935 the spirit which makes Fenn College possible was further developed. More persons found opportunity for self-expression and creative activity than in previous years. The Board of Trustees, the staff, the faculty, the alumni and the employers of Fenn students, all seeking to achieve the purpose of the college, are the foundations upon which it has developed and upon which its future rests.

—C. V. Thomas, President

Much of the board committee activity during January and February 1936 centered around space and laboratory equipment requirements and discussion of ways and means of raising the funds to provide the additional physical needs. Also time consuming was the preparation of the 1936 annual budget. The budget was approved at the January 22 meeting of the Board. Stacey Black, Finance Director, also reported at this board meeting that Fenn ended the fiscal year 1935 in the black by an amount of $761. Dr. Major B. Jenks was officially appointed as Assistant Professor of History. He later became Dean of the School of Arts and Sciences of Fenn College, and still later, for The Cleveland State University, Executive Assistant to the President.

The board on January 22 had authorized Knebel, Black, Dilley, and Thomas to contact Carlton G. Ketchum, noted college capital fund raising consultant, to determine whether Fenn was ready for a large fund drive. Ketchum stated on February 13 that if men of the ability of the Fenn Board believed in Fenn sufficiently to give the effort necessary to put this type of program across, and if the actual programs of the College could be so skillfully interpreted that the Trustees and those whom they would rally to their group could make it understood, that over a period of twelve to fifteen months, in his opinion, the funds could be secured. The general campaign organization got under way March 20.

Charles A. Dilley was promoted to the office as Special Assistant to the President, at the February 26, 1936, board meeting with the responsibility for the appropriate interpretation of Fenn College, specifically to individuals, foundations, and corporations. His duties also included Recording Secretary of the Board.

The Finance Committee recommended at the March 16, 1936, board meeting that the goal for the Scholarship Library and Equipment Fund Campaign be $10,000. The Board voted to reduce the goal to $8,000 with half the goal to be sought by the Board members and the remaining half by a general campaign organization under the leadership of Gerald Wellman.

The board also approved, on March 16, the appointment of Dr. Hyman Lumer as an Instructor in Biology, Hygiene, and Health.

This special announcement by Chairman Fisher and President Thomas concerns two very important people in the history of Fenn College, Stacey R. Black and his successor as Director of Finance, Arthur P. Loegler.

Announcement Regarding the Resignation of Mr. Stacy R. Black and the Appointment of Mr. Arthur P. Loegler

The Resignation of Mr. Black

Everyone connected with Fenn College will greatly regret the decision of Mr. Black to return to business. Mr. Black has done an unusual job of organizing the Finance Director's Department and of developing the business operations of the college to a high level of efficiency. For the last several years he has expressed his purpose to re-enter business and an opportunity has now come which makes the move desirable. He is to be a member of the executive staff of General Dry Batteries, Inc. He will continue at Fenn until the latter part of April and will be available in the months and years to come for counsel and suggestions regarding the problems that arise in the Finance Director's office. Just as everyone regrets his going, all are pleased that he has his present opportunity.

The Appointment of Mr. Loegler

The Personnel Committee of the Board of Trustees have been for a number of weeks seeking a person to take over the work of Mr. Black. Based upon an analysis of the types of work done in the Finance Director's office and the qualities that an individual doing this work should possess, the Personnel Committee have chosen Mr. Arthur P. Loegler to be the Finance Director of Fenn College. Mr. Loegler is beginning his work as of Monday, March 30th. Mr. Loegler comes to Fenn from the position of administrative assistant in the CCRA organization. Several of our group will remember him as a Warner & Swasey man. While at the Warner & Swasey Company Mr. Loegler held positions as assistant employment manager, chief of the estimating department, sales representative of Warner & Swasey Company on the West Coast and assistant in the advertising department. When the Relief load in the County was developing so rapidly, he was asked by Mr. Stockton Raymond to set up the budgeting and control systems for the organization and was later asked to become the administrative assistant. In addition to his diversified practical experience, Mr. Loegler is a graduate of the Warner & Swasey Apprenticeship School and holds a Bachelor of Science degree from Case School of Applied Science. Mr. Loegler's family consists of his wife and a fourteen year old daughter.

Just as we regret to have Mr. Black sever his active relationship with Fenn, so we welcome Mr. Loegler to our organization.

Ellwood H. Fisher, Chairman
Board of Trustees
C. V. Thomas, President

March 30, 1936

Loegler proved to be an outstanding asset to the college and remained as Finance Director until his sudden death on April 1, 1958.

Dr. William A. Patterson was appointed as an Instructor in Mathematics at the April 21, 1936, board meeting, effective September 1, 1936. He became Assistant Professor, Mathematics, and Director, Student Activities, on September 1, 1939; Acting Registrar and Assistant in Personnel Development on December 1, 1944. Then after spending about a year and a half with the Ohio Rubber Company he became Registrar on July 1, 1946; Associate Dean of Engineering and Registrar on February 1, 1952; Dean of Engineering on April 4, 1953; Provost and Dean of Engineering on June 1, 1960; Provost on February 21, 1962; and upon transfer of Fenn to the State, he became Budget Officer for The Cleveland State University and retired June 30, 1971. He was a most efficient administrator, a good organization man, and always held the respect and confidence of his colleagues.

Authorization was given at the April 21, 1936, board meeting for the chairman to appoint a Special Committee on Organizational Relationships. Leyton E. Carter was appointed Chairman and E. H. Baker, Clayton G. Hale, and John W. Eckelberry (Legal Assistant) with Carter constituted the committee. This committee made a preliminary report to the Board at the June 3, 1936, meeting:

> *A Preliminary Report to the Board of Trustees of Fenn College by the Special Committee appointed to study Reorganization Relationships of the College*
>
> I. The committee desires to stress at the very beginning the importance of recognizing that any consideration given to the advisability of incorporating the college has for its purposes the carrying forward of the educational program of the Young Men's Christian Association in the most effective manner.
>
> Just as the progress in education generally has made developments in the educational program of the YMCA advisable, so present conditions require consideration of separate incorporation. It is probable that the present educational program of the Association could not be if the educational work had not been organized into a Branch, if the Fenn Building had not been provided, and if the present organizational status had not been developed.
>
> Just as the steps previously taken have not involved radical changes but have been natural outgrowths of previous developments, so the incorporation of the college naturally would be a next step which would make comparatively little difference in the actual operation of the college. Precedent for separate incorporation has occurred at Chicago, Youngstown, Boston and perhaps other cities.
>
> The *advantages* of incorporation are chiefly the following:
>
> —Giving proper status to the degree granting function of the college.
> —Assuring educational accrediting bodies that the college has freedom to maintain proper academic standards.

—Making it possible for donors who desire to assist the educational program of the Association to give funds to the college as such.

—Meeting the requests of students and prospective students who desire to attend a college rather than a school which is in a secondary relationship to another organization.

Some of the possible *disadvantages* are:

—If the development were not properly understood, individuals might develop the attitude that the college and the Young Men's Christian Association were being separated.

—If such a viewpoint did develop, it might result in a lack of active cooperation between persons related to the Association and the college.

It is the opinion of your committee that the above disadvantages are largely theoretical, and that separate incorporation will bring to the educational work of the Young Men's Christian Association and to the Association itself many advantages.

II. Some Principles related to Incorporation recommended by your Committee.

(1) The Board of Trustees of Fenn College should be elected by the members of the Corporation of the YMCA in the same manner that the members of the Board of Trustees of the Association are elected.

(2) The President and the General Secretary of the Young Men's Christian Association should be ex officio members of the Board of Trustees of Fenn College.

(3) The By-Laws of Fenn College should be so developed that the present tie-in of financial relationships—such as the banking of money, the issuing of checks, etc.—will be continued.

(4) The President of the College should be a member of the Cabinet of the General Secretary of the Young Men's Christian Association.

III. Your committee has given some consideration to a Constitution and By-Laws and will bring to the Board a proposed statement of Constitution and By-Laws if the Board thus desires. The committee wishes to know the Board's reactions to the above principles and needs suggestions regarding additional principles.

Members of the Board who attended the luncheon given by Mr. Eaton to Dr. Russell will recall that Dr. Russell stressed the clarification of organization relationships as one of the three major problems before the Board of Trustees. He also indicated that the time to make such adjustments is when there are no problems involved.

Your committee believes that incorporation of Fenn College should be effected as rapidly as policies involved can be determined. The committee hopes that such incorporation can be effective by the beginning of the next college year.

The first intimation that the building later known as the Fenn Tower was being considered for the future expansion of Fenn's physical facilities is found in the Minutes of the Board meeting of June 3, 1936. The Minute is as follows together with the Minute on the action taken on Chairman Carter's "Special Committee" report:

> *Report of the Special Committee Appointed to Study the Possibility of Relocating the College in Another Building*—The report was made by Mr. Greene, Chairman of this committee. Judge Henry raised the fundamental issue involved in the Town & Country Club Building, inquiring about the history of the project and the history of the building ownership. Dr. Thomas and Mr. Knebel answered these questions. Mr. Greene asked if it would be in order to accept the report of the committee and asked that Mr. Fisher investigate how the building might be acquired. Mr. Knebel suggested that a committee be appointed to enter into conference with the Central Branch to see what this move would do to the Central Branch. Mr. Cox suggested that a study be made to see how the money might be raised for the remodeling which would be necessary. Mr. Cox made a motion which included the three suggestions mentioned and it was carried.

> *Report of the Special Committee Appointed to Deal with Organization Relationships*—The report was made by Mr. Carter, Chairman of this committee. After the reading of this report Judge Henry moved that the report be received, that the recommendations be approved, and that the committee be authorized to draw up Articles of Incorporation as soon as possible; also that the report be presented to the Board of Trustees of the Young Men's Christian Association. Mr. Carter seconded this motion and it was so ordered.

Chairman Fisher and President Thomas visited the Reconstruction Finance Corporation (R.F.C.) offices in Washington and had conferences with a number of persons recommended by Oscar L. Cox, head liquidator of the Union Trust Company. They reported on their visit

The first organization chart for the newly proposed incorporation of Fenn College

MEMBERS OF THE CORPORATION

CHART OF ORGANIZATION
OF FENN COLLEGE

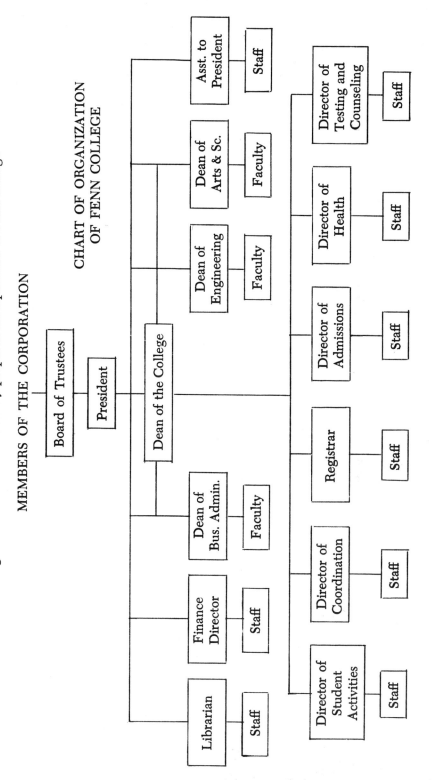

at the June 24, 1936, meeting of the Board. The R.F.C. officials indicated that their appraised value of the Town and Country Club Building (Tower) exceeded the figure Chairman Fisher believed the college could and would pay. By letter of June 22, 1936, however, R.F.C. requested that Fenn's proposal be clarified. It was the opinion of the members present that the building would greatly strengthen the college because it provided many facilities which the college needed and which it would probably be unable to obtain for many years. Chairman Fisher indicated that no official answer could be given R.F.C. without action of the Fenn College Board and the YMCA Board in unison. He was requested to discuss the situation with the YMCA Board and report back at a later meeting.

The question of submitting an application for visitation by inspectors of the Engineer's Council for Professional Development (E.C.P.D.) was also discussed at the June 24, 1936, board meeting. It was decided to request visitation for inspection in the fields of Chemical, Electrical, and Mechanical Engineering.

The first draft of the proposed By-Laws for Fenn, if separately incorporated, was also submitted by John Eckelberry at this same meeting.

The new Articles of Incorporation and Regulations for Fenn College were approved by the Fenn Board at their August 26, 1936, meeting. The board instructed its chairman to present the document to the Board of Trustees of the YMCA with the request that the Y Board transfer to the Fenn Board the title to classroom, laboratory, and office equipment then in use by the college.

The Fenn Board also instructed the administration of the college to prepare statements required for degree granting privileges for submittal to the State Department of Public Instruction, and further, to submit to the Secretary of State all essential communications from both the Fenn and Y Boards upon authorization of the Y Board of the Articles of Incorporation.

Chairman Fisher presented the correspondence dealing with the R.F.C. regarding the Tower, and the President was authorized to write R.F.C. expressing the board's interest in the Tower and indicating that the board believed that $300,000 was the total amount which the college could raise for purchasing, equipping and otherwise making the building available and usable for college purposes.

President Thomas presented the comparative statistics regarding enrollments and financial income at the September 23, 1936, Board meeting that are presented in Table 1.

TABLE 1

COMPARATIVE STATISTICS FOR ENROLLMENTS
AND FINANCIAL INCOME

School	Enrollments		Value of Tuition Contracts	
	1936	1935	1936	1935
Day Co-op	357	331	$ 78,212	$ 71,132
Evening B. A.	450	332	22,389	18,774
Evening Engineering	464	355	31,433	25,415
Laboratory Fees and Misc. Income			13,883	10,432
Total	1,271	1,018	$145,917	$125,753

The evening jump in attendance of 33% marked the third consecutive year in which the increase in evening enrollments was more than 20%. The enrollment in the Freshman Co-op Day Division was 158 as compared with 137 in 1935. Two-thirds of the Freshmen came from Greater Cleveland high schools; 25 Freshmen came from other Ohio high schools, 5 from New York, 4 from Pennsylvania, and 1 from Montana.

The first constitution of The Faculty of Fenn College was adopted October 26, 1936.

It was necessary to rent space in the Plymouth Building on the northwest corner of Prospect and East 22nd Street for the expanding enrollment. The space was needed for drawing and classroom instruction. Pleasant arrangements were also made with Dean Chester B. Emerson of Trinity Cathedral to holds assemblies of Day Division students in the Trinity Cathedral Hall.

Chairman Fisher reported that the Board of Trustees of the YMCA had approved the new Articles for Incorporation and Regulations and the transfer of title of classroom, office, and laboratory equipment to the Board of Fenn. The essential documents were all signed and transmitted to Columbus.

Official approval was received sufficiently early from the State Department of Public Instruction and the Secretary of State so that at the October 28, 1936, meeting of the Fenn Board all of the necessary actions were taken to conform with the Articles of Incorporation, such as: the Adoption of the Code of Regulations; election of the new corporate officers; election of the President of the College; appointment of an Executive Committee; appointment of a committee to develop By-Laws; appointment of a Nominating Committee for nomination of potential Trustee electees at the first annual meeting of the Corporation; and the appointment of Faculty and Staff (existing members appointed to respective positions). The existing officers were elected, President Thomas was reelected, John S. Crider, Treasurer of the YMCA was elected Treasurer of Fenn College, thereby giving legal status to maintaining the existing accounting procedures. Leyton E. Carter, Clayton G. Hale, and E. H. Baker were appointed to prepare By-Laws. Chairman Fisher and President Thomas were appointed members of the Nominating Committee. Discussion then ensued regarding the engagement of an architect to develop plans for Fenn's future building needs. Chairman Fisher was authorized to appoint a committee to study Fenn's physical needs and make recommendations at a future meeting.

The "Articles of Incorporation" and the "Regulations" of Fenn College which were approved by the State Department of Public Instruction and the Secretary of State are quoted here in full:

ARTICLES OF INCORPORATION OF FENN COLLEGE

The undersigned citizens of the State of Ohio, desiring to form a Corporation not for Profit, hereby subscribe to and acknowledge the following Articles of Incorporation:

(1) The name of said Corporation shall be, "Fenn College."

(2) The place where said college is to be located or its principal business transacted shall be the City of Cleveland, County of Cuyahoga and State of Ohio.

(3) The purpose for which said Corporation is organized is to maintain a college; to provide education designed to meet the cultural, vocational, spiritual, social and physical needs of youth; to confer degrees and to have and to use all other powers provided by law for colleges; and to do any and all things necessary or convenient for the accomplishment thereof.

(4) The names and addresses of the Trustees who will serve until the first annual meeting of the Corporation are:

Elbert H. Baker, Jr.   21849 Parnell Rd, Shaker Heights, Ohio
Harold H. Burton   13509 Drexmore Rd, Cleveland, Ohio
James E. Campbell   1748 Lee Rd, Cleveland Heights, Ohio
Leyton E. Carter   19610 Kinsman Rd, Shaker Heights, Ohio
Dale Cox   Hemlock Point, Chagrin Falls, Ohio
Jacob D. Cox, Jr.   3411 Euclid Ave, Cleveland, Ohio
Cyrus S. Eaton   Northfield, Ohio
Ellwood H. Fisher   2683 Ashley Rd, Shaker Heights, Ohio
John A. Greene   2566 Wellington Rd, Cleveland Heights, Ohio

Clayton G. Hale   16710 Lakewood Hts Blvd, Lakewood, Ohio
Frederick A. Henry   Geauga Lake, Ohio
Eugene W. Kettering   17897 Lake Ave, Lakewood, Ohio
A. G. Knebel   1961 Ford Drive, Cleveland, Ohio
James L. Myers   2841 Weybridge Rd, Shaker Heights, Ohio

Richard G. Roth   2901 Drummond Rd, Shaker Heights, Ohio

Harry D. Sims   2866 West Park Blvd, Shaker Heights, Ohio
David W. Teachout   Berkshire Rd, Gates Mills, Ohio

STATE OF OHIO
COUNTY OF CUYAHOGA   ss.

Personally appeared before me, the undersigned, a Notary Public in and for said County, this 23rd Day of September, A.D. 1936, the above named Ellwood H. Fisher, Frederick A. Henry, A. G. Knebel, Leyton E. Carter, Clayton G. Hale and Elbert H. Baker who each severally acknowledged the signing of the foregoing Articles of Incorporation to be his free act and deed for the use and purposes therein mentioned.

WITNESS my hand and official seal on the day and year last aforesaid.

(signed)

_____

Notary Public
Joseph H. Peck, Notary Public
My Commission Expires
Sept. 29, 1936

STATE OF OHIO

COUNTY OF CUYAHOGA   ss.

I, JOHN J. BUSHER, Clerk of the Court of Common Pleas within and for the County aforesaid, do hereby certify that Joseph H. Peck whose name is subscribed to the foregoing acknowledgment as a Notary Public, was at the date thereof a Notary Public in and for said County, duly commissioned and qualified, and authorized as such to take such acknowledgment; and further, that I am well acquainted with his handwriting and believe that the signature to said acknowledgment is genuine.

IN WITNESS WHEREOF, I have hereunto set my hand and affixed the seal of said Court at Cleveland, this 29 day of September, A.D. 1936.

JOHN J. BUSHER, Clerk.

by   , Deputy Clerk.

REGULATIONS OF FENN COLLEGE

Membership in Corporation	1. The membership of this Corporation shall be confined to those persons who are members of the Corporation of the Young Men's Christian Association of Cleveland, Ohio, and any of such persons may become members of this Corporation by signing the Membership Book of this Corporation.
Annual Meeting of Corporation	2. The Annual Meeting of the members of the Corporation for the election of Trustees and transaction of other business shall be held shortly following the adjournment of the Annual Meeting of the Corporation of the Young Men's Christian Association of Cleveland.
Special Meetings of Corporation	3. Special Meetings of the members of the corporation may be held on the call of the Chairman of the Board of Trustees, or the written request of not less than five of the members of the corporation.
Notice of Meetings to Members of Corporation	4. At least three days previous to a meeting of the corporation written or printed notice of the meeting shall be mailed or delivered to each member.

Quorum of Corpo-
ration Meetings

5. At any meeting of the members of the corporation ten shall constitute a quorum.

Suspension of
Members of
Corporation

6. Any member of the corporation may be suspended or expelled by a three-fourths vote of the members of the corporation at any meeting; provided however that thirty days notice in writing addressed to his last known place of residence shall be given such member of the charge preferred against him, and he shall have the privilege of appearing personally at the meeting and answering the same. No charges shall be entertained unless preferred in writing and signed by at least three members of the Board of Trustees. If a member shall fail to attend two consecutive meetings of the corporation, his membership may be terminated by a vote of the majority of the Trustees present at any regular meeting.

Trustees—
Number and
Term of
Service

7. The powers, property and affairs of this corporation shall be exercised, conducted and controlled by a Board of twenty-seven Trustees. The Board of Trustees shall be composed as follows:

(a) Twenty-four shall be elected from and by the members of the corporation, not fewer than eleven of whom shall be members of the Board of Trustees of the Young Men's Christian Association of Cleveland, Ohio. They shall retire by rotation, four in each year. When the first Annual Meeting is held, the members of the Board of Trustees shall be elected as follows: Four to serve for one year; four for two years; four for three years; four for four years; four for five years; four for six years. Thereafter four shall be elected each year.

(b) The President, the Treasurer and the General Secretary of the Young Men's Christian Association of Cleveland shall be ex officio members of the Board of Trustees.

(c) Following the incorporation of Fenn College, the Board of Trustees as constituted immediately preceding the incorporation shall continue to serve as the Board of Trustees of Fenn College until the first Annual Meeting of the Corporation.

Vacancies in the Board of Trustees

8. Any vacancy in the Board of Trustees caused by death, resignation or otherwise shall be filled by the remaining members thereof, by a majority of the entire membership of the Board.

Nomination and Election of Trustees

9. The Board of Trustees shall appoint a committee to nominate Trustees whose election shall occur at the Annual Meeting of the Corporation.

Executive and Other Committees

10. The Trustees shall appoint five or more of their own number who, with the President, shall constitute an Executive Committee to superintend and act upon all business requiring immediate attention during the intervals between the meetings of the Board of Trustees, and the Trustees may by By-Laws provide for the appointment of other committees and officers and define their duties.

Officers and Duties

11. The officers of the Board of Trustees shall be a Chairman, one or more Vice-Chairmen, a Secretary, a Treasurer, and such other offices as the Trustees may from time to time elect, and shall perform the duties usually incident to their respective offices. The Chairman, Vice-Chairmen, Secretary and Treasurer of the Board of Trustees shall be the Chairman, Vice-Chairmen, Secretary and Treasurer of the Corporation. The Chairman and Secretary of the Board of Trustees of Fenn College as immediately preceding the first annual

meeting of the corporation shall act as temporary chairman and secretary at the first annual meeting of the corporation.

Election of Officers and Terms of Office

12. All officers shall be chosen by the Trustees annually at their first meeting after the Annual Meeting of the Corporation and shall hold office until their successors are elected. The Chairman, Vice-Chairmen, Secretary and Treasurer shall be, and the other officers may be, chosen from among the Trustees.

President— Election of

13. The President of the college shall be elected by the Board of Trustees. He shall be the chief administrative officer of the college and shall have general supervision and direction of all divisions and departments within the college. He shall be the official medium of communication between the Board of Trustees and the officers of administration, the faculties and the students, respectively.

Duties of the Secretary

14. The Secretary shall make and preserve minutes of all meetings of the Corporation and Trustees; shall be custodian of all records of the Corporation and shall send out all notices required by the Regulations or By-Laws of the Board of Trustees.

Duties of the Treasurer

15. The Treasurer shall perform the usual duties pertaining to his office except in those instances in which some other officer or officers of the Board of Trustees, or an officer, officers, or employees of the college or other individuals are authorized by the Board of Trustees to act for him.

Amendment of Regulations

16. These regulations may be amended, repealed or added to by the assent of two-thirds of the members present at a meeting held for that purpose, notice of the proposed change having been incorporated in the notice of the meeting.

The December 9, 1936, meeting of the board was held in special joint session with members of the Fenn Faculty and Staff; 63 persons were present. President Thomas reported that while in Columbus appearing before the State Department of Public Instruction the suggestion had been made to him that Fenn consider becoming a "Teacher Training" institution. The cooperation of the Cleveland Board of Education for provision of practice-teaching facilities would be needed. Application had been made for these privileges, and they had been granted by the Board of Education.

The subject of the joint session between the Board and the Faculty and Staff dealt with the following subjects: growth in scholarship of faculty, growth and development of student body, participation in professional society and community affairs, reduction in teaching loads, graduate institutions attended by faculty over last two years, and a three-quarter teaching year rather than the existing four-quarter year.

The final board meeting for 1936 was held December 15. Here finally, a remaining back-log of 1931 Faculty salary deficit amounting to $1,797, originally scheduled to be paid in 1937, was authorized to be paid from 1936 income. After six years the 1931 deficit was paid in full. The board voted to rent an additional 1,068 square feet of space in the Plymouth Building. This would bring the total rental space therein to 2,347 square feet and the total rental cost to $1,980 per year. The board also discussed the possibility of a long term lease with option to purchase the Tower. Some of the pros and cons expressed were as follows, together with information related to the possible use of the Tower:

For

(1) The building would make available to the college within the next few months space which the college greatly needs. (It is questionable how long the college can turn young men away from classes. The condition of the old houses now used for classroom purposes makes good education most difficult to achieve.)

(2) The building would provide the college with gymnasium, club room, library and dormitory space which the amount being suggested for the erection of a building for Fenn College would not in any way provide. (The college would be obtaining a building with facilities which it could not look forward to securing for many years to come.)

(3) The building would give a concreteness and objectivenes to the coming financial campaign. If the campaign objective included funds for the alteration and furnishing of the building in question and a sum which would be used to provide income for the college until such time as purchase was made, there would probably be a community-wide response greater than if a similar amount of money is to be raised for the erection of a new building.

(4) The building in question would give a status to Fenn College. It would provide a "lift" to the institution which it would be difficult to match in almost any other way.

(5) The increase in demand for training on the part of the youth of Cleveland and the emphasis upon such training which industries are beginning to make, combined with the size of the present Fenn College enrollment, make the determination of the policy regarding building development both opportune and serious. The Board of Trustees must soon determine its policy in relation to the building program of Fenn.

Against

(1) The college would be accepting a financial responsibility much greater than at present.

(2) The college would be removed from as close proximity to the Central Y. Building as at present, although the Engineering Laboratories would be continued in the present Fenn Building.

(3) The building was not designed for educational use. It would require alteration and would at best not have the classroom layout that a building expressly designed for educational purposes would possess.

(4) A long term lease would not give the college ownership. It would have the problem before it of either future purchases of the building, or of re-location.

Information Related to the Possible Use of the
Town & Country Club Building by Fenn College

I. *General Description of the Building*

The building is 21 stories in height. The first 8 floors are designed for club activities, including a complete physical department layout. The 9th to 18th floors inclusive provide 122 bedrooms and 14 parlors adjacent to bedrooms. Each bedroom has a private bath. The 19th and 20th floors were laid out for service purposes although they include some space suitable for certain kinds of usage by groups. The 21st floor is given over chiefly to a solarium. The basement is used for a large billiard room, and numerous refrigeration and mechanical service machinery.

II. *Estimated Cost of Operating the Building*

A study of the probable cost of heating, lighting, cleaning and providing the other elements in a maintenance operation shows that the total cost without providing for repairs and upkeep would be $47,753.00. If 5c per sq. ft. is allowed for upkeep, an additional $8,900.00 would be added, making a total of $56,653.00. This amount is equivalent to 31.8c per sq.ft. If the operating cost is figured at 35c per sq. ft., the maintenance cost would be $62,300.00.

III. *Possible Sources of Income to Meet Operating Expenses*

(1) Membership fees now paid to the Central Branch
of the YMCA by Fenn College ....$ 9,000.00
(2) Rent now paid for the use of the Medical Library
and Edwards House 2,000.00
(3) Reduction in House charges paid Central Branch
if the Medical Library, Edwards House and
possibly Johnson House were not used 2,500.00
(4) Net earnings from dormitory rooms
122 rooms @ 6.00 per week average,
for 50 wks $36,600.00
Less additional service cost for
operating 13,000.00   23,600.00

(5) Net increase from additional student fees
25% increase in tuition fees on
present $178,000.00 .... $44,500.00
Less 20% increase in instruction
costs on $131,000.00 .... 26,200.00   18,300.00

TOTAL $55,400.00

If the figure of $56,650.00 is used, the net cost per year on above bases would be $1,250.00.

IV. *Space Which the Building Would Provide*

The above calculations are based upon the retaining of the Fenn Building for laboratory, drawing room and other engineering purposes; hence the House and Maintenance charges on this building are not included in the above figures. The proposed building would be the headquarters for the college and would provide Library, Assembly and Physical Department facilities. It would also be the location for Business Administration and Arts and Science classes, together with some of the non-laboratory Engineering classes.

The space which the Town and Country Club Building would provide is as follows:

(1) *The first 8 floors*

    27 classrooms seating at one time 715 students
     1 student lounge
     1 library space 3½ times the size of our original library
     1 assembly hall
     1 large drawing room
     1 laboratory space 41 x 32
     1 laboratory space 71 x 41
     1 laboratory space 26 x 83
     1 complete equipment for physical activities including showers, hot room, locker rooms, etc.
     1 gymnasium
     1 swimming pool
     3 handball courts
     2 squash courts
     1 laboratory space 32 x 47
     1 laboratory space 67 x 42
     1 laboratory space 39 x 88

Note: Many of the above laboratory spaces do not have daylight. They would require artificial lighting at all times.

(2) *The 9th to 18th floors inclusive*

    111 single bedrooms with bath and clothes closet
        (The single bedrooms are large when compared with the usual YMCA bedroom.)
     11 double bedrooms with bath and clothes closet
     14 parlors adjacent to the bedrooms

    ———

    136 rooms TOTAL

(3) A Solarium and other spaces on the *19th, 20th and 21st floors*

V. *Cost of Remodeling and Furnishing*

Cost of furnishing 136 rooms ....$ 13,600.00
> (Figures based upon the Central Branch experience in furnishing rooms. Their costs are $87.00 per room. This figure is based on $100.00 per room.)

Cost of covering floors and hallways in Dormitory Floors 2,000.00
> (Estimate only.)

Cost of putting the building in its original condition 15,000.00
> (Estimate only.)

Cost of removing partitions, placing partitions in other locations and otherwise adjusting the building to Fenn College needs 15,000.00
> (Estimate only.)

Cost of additional furniture, floor covering, library stacks, etc. 54,400.00

TOTAL $100,000.00

At the December 30, 1936, meeting of the Finance Committee it was recommended that President Thomas be authorized to engage an architect to make a study of the adaptability of the Town and Country Club (Tower) Building for college purposes, at an expense of $150.00.

In a number of instances following Board meetings President Thomas would take interested board members on a tour of the potential classrooms and laboratories. It is appropriate that this history of Fenn College for the year 1936 close with the thoughts expressed by Dale Cox, *Plain Dealer* columnist, subsequent to experiencing one of these tours.

The year 1937 was a banner year for Fenn College. In keeping with the quotation at the beginning of this chapter from Luke XIV, verse 28, the Fenn Trustees were not about to build a "tower," but to buy one already built, and they still had to sit down and determine a method of financing.

Dercom had been engaged to determine the adaptability of the Town and Country Club Building for college use. He reported at the February 3, 1937, meeting of the board that the first nine floors of the tower would provide 53 classrooms, laboratory, and library spaces; administrative offices, gymnasium, swimming pool, and other facilities. The total

The Young Men's Christian Association of Cleveland

October 9th
1 9 3 6

My dear Judge Henry:

Ellwood Fisher and I had dinner the other evening with a group of Trustees, and then took them on a tour of our Fenn College. Dale Cox, well-known Plain Dealer columnist, himself a Trustee, has written me about the visit. His letter embodies what I am confident we all sensed as we walked through the corridors, looked into classrooms, visited the various buildings in which the evening students are housed.

Some day I hope you and other Trustees who have not had this opportunity may enjoy a similar experience. Believe me, it was an experience which registers and makes one feel that we have a responsibility which somehow must be met.

A. G. KNEBEL.

"This letter to you is an expression of some compelling thoughts of mine following an experience this week in touring the busy halls and classrooms of Fenn College on a typical operating night. Such a tour, I am confident, could not fail to impress anyone with the quality and scope of the educational work being carried on by this educational auxiliary of the Young Men's Christian Association.

"I can only say that the tour opened my eyes to the real volume of education being carried by the institution, and I have been associated with it for several years as a member of its governing Board of Trustees.

"Wise, old Benjamin Franklin said of the educated man: 'If a man empties his purse into his head, no man can take it away from him. An investment in knowledge always pays the best interest.'

"It seems to me that in a peculiar sense Fenn College is serving hundreds of young men and women who have Benjamin Franklin's idea of education. They are emptying their purses into their heads. And in a majority of cases their purses are slim in material possessions. These young men and women come to Fenn College partly because they feel that they will receive a maximum of education in return for what they are able to empty into it from their purses. That is because the college operates under the cooperative plan of education, permitting students to earn most of their educational expenses from work they perform in cooperating industrial plants and businesses.

"I believe Dr. Franklin would approve of this cooperative plan of education. It instills thrift and promotes enterprise and self-reliance, and surely these were Franklinian virtues. The 371 students now enrolled in the day cooperative division of the college are employed in more than 80 firms, while the 1,420 students attending the night classes have jobs with more than 500 firms. The big majority of these students come from the middle and lower economic brackets, and therefore merit, it seems to me, the especial encouragement of the community.

"It is about the furtherance of this community support that I wish to comment.

"The college has been overwhelmed this fall with the largest enrollment in
its history, nearly 2,000 men and women. This is a gain of from 300 to 400 over the
previous registration peak, reached in the prosperity year of 1929.

"Classes have been crammed into every available classroom and laboratory.
The numerical size of many classes has been stretched beyond the point of maximum
teaching efficiency. But it was better to do that than turn away eager young people
seeking an education, seeking, as Franklin said, to empty their purses, however
meager, into their heads.

"But despite every effort that the administration and faculty could make,
despite an expansion of teaching quarters into nearby old houses and into the
adjacent Plymouth Building, many young people had to be turned away from Fenn this
autumn because there was not room to accommodate them. They had to be denied the
opportunity which Franklin and all wise men since have deemed the best investment
man and his society could make.

"It was an inspiring sight to see the Fenn educational plant at the peak
of its operating load last Monday night. Every classroom occupied as early as 7
o'clock in the evening. Every laboratory in use. Almost every piece of laboratory
equipment in use. Not even enough chairs to seat all the students in some classes.
Lights blazing from every window, like a busy factory producing goods for an
insatiable market. Old stairways in the nearby houses groaning under the tread
of student feet. Instructors and students doing a heroic job of education in a
plant which long since would have been written off and abandoned as outgrown and
obsolete by any self-respecting industrial enterprise.

"Standing outside these busy buildings at the conclusion of the tour,
and seeing that steady blaze of light from classrooms and laboratories, I could
not fail to catch the vision of the real need and the challenging, mighty future
which lies ahead for Fenn College if only it is able to supply the physical plant
to accommodate the volume of students that seek its services.

"I could vision the old houses to the east of the main college building
replaced by a thoroughly modern educational building running through from Prospect
to Carnegie Avenue, perhaps a modern factory-type building if you please, in any
event a building so constructed as to obtain a maximum educational benefit for a
minimum of investment. It would be large enough to accommodate the hundreds of
students now huddled in over-crowded classrooms and laboratories, and other
hundreds as well.

"Fenn needs to have an educational plant equipped to handle double its
present volume of education. As surely as the world moves on, that volume will
be doubled over the next decade or so.

"The community needs to cooperate in the meeting of this demand. It needs
to pour some of the money from its well-filled purse into the heads of its young
citizens. There is no investment it can make that will return better dividends.

"'Look out for the boy who begins by sweeping out the office,' said Andrew
Carnegie. Look out today for the youth who is determined, even though having only
a slim purse, to get an education. These are the youth coming to Fenn College.

                                        DALE COX. "

report included the major problems involved, estimated cost of remodeling, cost of classroom furnishings and equipment, cost of furnishing the dormitory rooms, square feet of classroom space available, and the number of students which both the Tower and the Fenn Building would seat at one time.

Following a discussion of comparative costs involved in building a new structure versus remodeling the Tower, action was taken by the board to propose to R.F.C. that title to the Tower be transferred to Fenn College on the bases of the College paying all back taxes (approximately $178,000) and executing the necessary alterations for college use (approximately $150,000), for the consideration of One Dollar—the above action based upon clearance with the Building Department, City of Cleveland, and the State of Ohio relative to the use of the Tower for college purposes.

President Thomas reported at this same meeting that Fenn had been certified by the State Department of Education to institute a new Teachers Training Program. Arrangements had been made with the public schools for practice teaching facilities.

C. D. Williams was appointed as an Associate Professor in Civil Engineering at the March 24, 1937, board meeting. He had formerly been associated with the New York Central Railroad in the design of bridges. It was later through Professor Williams' untiring efforts over many months that the planning, designing, and drafting for the rehabilitation and adaption of the Tower for college purposes was successfully culminated. He later became Chairman of the Department of Structural Engineering at Fenn, and he was co-editor with Professor E. C. Harris on several structural engineering textbooks. He became head of a consulting firm in Augusta, Georgia, and later served as a Director and one of four vice-presidents for the American Society of Civil Engineers. He was a recipient of the Fenn Alumni Distinguished Service Award in 1960.

Miss Willingham, the first librarian of Fenn, had been most instrumental in the development of library facilities toward qualifications required by accreditation agencies. She resigned in February 1937 and was succeeded by Roland Mulhauser.

Burl H. Bush was appointed Dean of the School of Engineering at the April 27, 1937, meeting of the Board. He succeeded Dean M. E. Nichols, who had joined the staff in 1922, and who resigned to take charge of Industrial Training for The American Steel & Wire Company. Nichols returned to Fenn in 1959 as a Coordinator in the Department of Co-operative Education. E. A. Brown, John Irvin, James Hamilton, and Allen Perry were elected to the Board of Trustees. Of this group, only Allen Perry served through to 1965, the time of transfer of Fenn College to the State of Ohio.

The graduating class of 1937 consisted of a number of individuals who later became active in Fenn Alumni affairs or were honored as distinguished alumni. Wilson B. Creveling was elected Alumni Trustee serving from 1959 to 1962, and he received the Alumni Distinguished Service Award in 1967. Hiram Brown was a recipient of the Alumni Distinguished Service Award in 1956, one of the first three to receive this award. C. D. Williams received the Alumni Distinguished Service Award in 1960. Milton J. Wurzbach was elected Alumni Trustee and served from 1956 to 1957 when he was transferred to Pittsburgh by the U.S. Steel Corporation. He was also a recipient of the Alumni Distinguished Service Award in 1962. Alex Jamieson joined the U.S. Air Force as a career man and upon retirement in 1960 became a Coordinator in the Department of Co-operative Education at Fenn and later, C.S.U.

Nicholas R. Rimboi, Jr., graduate in Electrical Engineering, Fenn Class of 1934, was appointed Secretary of the Engineering School at the May 11, 1937, board meeting. He became Supervisor of the newly established Technical Institute (evening program only, in 1938, and in 1946 he was appointed Director of the Technical Institute (T.I.), which office he held through to the transfer of the College to the State, following which, he became an Administrative Assistant in the Department of Buildings and Grounds.

The Board of Fenn College and the Executive Committee of the YMCA met in joint session June 25, 1937. There was considerable discussion concerning the effect of moving the Fenn College activity to another location, such as the Tower. It was decided by the YMCA representatives present that some adjustments in the operation of the Central Branch would be necessary, but within a year or so the Branch would be "advantaged by such a development." Following further discussion on the present ownership of the Tower, probable future use thereof and its appraised value, it was judged that use of the Tower by Fenn would be an asset to Cleveland, would assist the College, and would be most helpful to the development program of the YMCA. It was voted that Chairman Fisher appoint a committee of five to follow-up on Tower developments with the view that if it can be secured for a price within the potential resources of the College, the Board should take whatever steps are necessary to obtain the building. The architect's plans had already been presented to the Building Department of the City of Cleveland and to the State of Ohio and with a few slight alterations both agencies approved the revised plans. A contractor had estimated the cost of executing these alterations to be $136,500.

Dr. Harold E. Morgan was appointed as Instructor in Physics, effective September 1, 1937. He was promoted to Assistant Professor September 1, 1939, and Acting Chairman, September 1, 1942. He served in the U.S. Signal Corps from June 1943 to February 1946, returning to Fenn as Associate Professor, Physics, and in 1949 he was appointed Acting Chairman. He was promoted to Chairman and Professor, Department of Physics September 1, 1950, which office he held at the time of transfer of Fenn to the State. He later retired from his administrative duties at C.S.U. to do teaching only.

Jerome Thralls, Special Representative for R.F.C., notified President Thomas on July 1, 1937, that the "Tower" building would be sold by the U.S. District Court, Eastern District of New York, July 9, 1937, at 2:00 p.m. The sale was to take place in Room 224 of the U.S. Court House, Washington and Johnson Streets, Brooklyn, N.Y., and that no bid less than $250,000 would be considered. Thralls seemed to feel a preference for Fenn as a prospective buyer, indicating that it would be preferable for Fenn to negotiate with the R.F.C. after the sale, rather than deal with the court. One group had indicated interest in bidding on the property. Thrall suggested that the R.F.C. would bid the building in for an amount R.F.C. felt it could get for it if R.F.C. could be certain that Fenn was interested to this extent. After several important meetings of the Special Building Committee, the Fenn Board of Trustees, and the Executive Committee of the YMCA, it was agreed to send the following letter to Thralls under date of August 16, 1937.

The Reconstruction Finance Corporation
33 Liberty Street
New York, N.Y.

Attention: Mr. Jerome Thralls,
Special Representative

Gentlemen:

In the letter dated July 6th the Board of Trustees of Fenn College reviewed the study that the college had made of the possible use of the National Town and Country Club Building in Cleveland by the college. The letter outlined the practical value to young men and women and to Cleveland as a city which the use of the building by Fenn College would have. The letter expressed the hope of the Trustees to purchase the building and outlined two plans, either of which seemed to be possible. The Trustees however at that date were not in a position to make a definite proposal.

Since July 6th the Board of Trustees of the college have been studying the two major problems involved—First, the determination of the maximum financial obligation which the college can assume and continue to occupy the building permanently; Second, the working out of a plan by which the raising of the funds needed to purchase the building can be most readily achieved. The following proposal to the Reconstruction Finance Corporation is the result of such consideration:

$500,000.00 is the maximum obligation which the college can assume in relation to the National Town and Country Club Building—this sum to include tax liens, repairs, alterations and furnishings. In order to work out the financing of the obligation the Trustees ask the Reconstruction Finance Corporation for an Option under the following conditions:

—The Reconstruction Finance Corporation to give the college an option to run to June 30, 1938 unless taken up previous to that date;

—The Trustees of the college to pay the Reconstruction Finance Corporation $5,000.00 for the option and an additional $100,000.00 when and if the option is exercised;

—The Trustees of the college to assume the obligation of the back taxes amounting to approximately $178,000.00 plus the 1937 taxes which will be approximately $31,000.00;

—The Trustees of the college to remodel, repair and otherwise put the building into condition for college use at an estimated cost of $136,000.00;

—The Trustees of the college to furnish the building at an estimated cost of $50,000.00 ——

—— making a total obligation of $500,000.00.

The foregoing offer is made by a responsible group of Cleveland citizens who are confident that the financial support required will be secured. The option arrangement as suggested by a representative of the Reconstruction Finance Corporation provides the college the period of time required to raise the money. In fact Fenn College, the Young Men's Christian Association and Cleveland as a City cannot afford to enter into an Option Agreement and not exercise the Option.

The Board of Trustees of the college make the offer with the conviction that the use of the National Town and Country Club Building by Fenn College is in keeping with the basic purposes for which the Reconstruction Finance Corporation was established. The building if used by the college will be a great social and economic asset to Cleveland. Society will thus benefit from the investment that it has made in the building.

The Trustees therefore present this offer, not as representatives of an institution only but as citizens of Cleveland who desire that the assets represented by the National Town and Country Club Building be used for a purpose which from a social and economic viewpoint cannot be excelled.

Sincerely yours,

Ellwood H. Fisher, Chairman
Board of Trustees
C. V. Thomas, President

After several communications between R.F.C. and Fenn College the following telegram was sent to Thralls by President Thomas on August 23, 1937.

August 23, 1937

Mr. Jerome Thralls
Reconstruction Finance Corporation
33 Liberty Street
New York, N.Y.

Board approved plan per conversation   STOP
Letter and check follow.   STOP

C.V. Thomas

This author feels that the following chronological outline by President Thomas ably and succinctly summarizes the history of important events leading to the purchase of the Tower:

Information Regarding Negotiations which Preceded taking of an Option on the National Town and Country Club Building by Fenn College

—Fenn College has at no time been in competition with any organization for the purchase of the property.
—The Board of Trustees of Fenn College first discussed the use of the property with officials of the RFC in the spring of 1936.
—A few weeks later Cleveland newspapers announced that the Club Realty had arranged to purchase the property and to make it available to the Ohio Club, and that the Ohio Club would occupy the building by October 1936. A detailed statement regarding the organization of the club was given.
—Fenn College Trustees discontinued further consideration of the property until the spring of 1937.
—In April 1937 the Trustees of the college again discussed the property with RFC officials, and were informed that a proposal from the college would be welcome.
—Early in July announcements were made in Cleveland and New York papers that the property would be sold at public auction on July 9th. The RFC bid the property in at the sale at the upset price of $250,000. No other bids were offered.
—Following the public sale RFC officials indicated that they would be glad to confer with the Trustees of Fenn College regarding a plan which would make it possible for the college to purchase the property.
—On August 13th the Executive Committee of the Board of Trustees of the Young Men's Christian Association and of Fenn College prepared a proposal and instructed a committee to present it to the RFC officials.
—The proposal was given to the RFC representatives on August 17th.
—The RFC asked that they be permitted to study the proposal in the light of the conditions they must require to sell the property.
—On August 18th a proposal of the RFC outlining the conditions under which they would dispose of the property was made to representatives of the Board of Trustees of Fenn College, and it was agreed that the college would have one week to determine

its decision regarding the proposal. The check taken with the proposal of Fenn College was retained by the RFC, subject to return to the college if the proposal submitted by the RFC was not accepted.

—The committee of the Fenn Board discussed the RFC proposal with other members of the Board and with representative citizens. They were encouraged to proceed with the plan and to confer with the RFC about details.

—The morning of August 23rd representatives of Fenn phoned RFC officials asking that a few details in the RFC proposal be changed and they were informed that the RFC officials would telephone Washington regarding the changes and would give an anwer by noon of the 23rd, the hour when the Board of Trustees of Fenn met for the consideration of the proposal. The answer of the RFC officials was affirmative.

—The Board of Trustees of the Young Men's Christian Association and of Fenn College heard the proposal of the RFC as amended by telephone conversations and accepted the proposal.

—A wire notifying the RFC that the plan was accepted was sent on the afternoon of August 23rd.

—A letter containing a check for the additional amount called for in the proposal was sent to the RFC on the afternoon of August 23rd.

—C. V. Thomas

At a November 24, 1937, joint meeting of the Boards of Trustees of Fenn College and the YMCA it was reported that $186,988 had been pledged toward the purchase of the Tower, of which $134,966 had already been paid. Because of this enthusiastic response action was taken to exercise the option on the property and the officers were instructed to pay R.F.C. the second installment of $35,000 toward the $50,000 first payment on the $250,000 purchase price. The Certificate of Resolution is as follows:

Certificate of Resolution by Trustees of Fenn College to Purchase National Town and Country Club Building from Reconstruction Finance Corporation

C. V. Thomas, President, and Charles A. Dilley, Secretary, of Fenn College of Cleveland, Ohio, an Ohio college corporation with its principal office located at Cleveland, Ohio, do hereby certify that a meeting of the Trustees of said corporation was duly called and held on the 24th day of November, 1937, at which meeting a quorum of its Trustees were present, and that by the affirmative vote of a majority of its Trustees the following resolution was adopted:

"BE IT RESOLVED by the Board of Trustees of Fenn College: That the option granted by Reconstruction Finance Corporation to Fenn College to purchase the property known as National Town and Country Club, situate, lying and being in the City of Cleveland, Cuyahoga County and State of Ohio, at the northeast corner of East 24th Street and Euclid Avenue, fronting approximately 228 feet on East 24th Street and 83¼ feet on Euclid Avenue, together with the building thereon consisting of a twenty-two story brick, stone and steel building, with all other property real, personal and mixed, lawfully pertaining thereto, for the price of $250,000.00 payable as in said option provided (including the sum of $15,000.00 already paid as and for the consideration of said option), and with future installments of said purchase price to be secured by purchase money mortgage as in said option provided, be and the same is hereby affirmatively exercised for the purchase of said property by Fenn College from the Reconstruction Finance Corporation on the terms aforesaid, by special or limited warranty deed from said vendor to said vendee, conveying and warranting a good merchantable title free of any incumbrance except such as existed prior to the acquisition of title by the vendor.

"RESOLVED FURTHER, that the Chairman of the Board of Trustees and the President of Fenn College be and they are hereby authorized in its name and behalf to execute its promissory note or notes for the future installments of said purchase price together with the purchase money mortgage to secure said notes; to deliver said notes and mortgage to the Reconstruction Finance Corporation on receipt of its deed of conveyance as aforesaid; and to do and perform all other things necessary or convenient to consummate said purchase."

In witness whereof said C. V. Thomas, President, and Charles A. Dilley, Secretary, of said Fenn College of Cleveland, Ohio, acting for and on behalf of said corporation have hereunto subscribed their names and caused the seal of said corporation to be affixed this 8th day of December, 1937.

s/C. V. Thomas, President

s/Charles A. Dilley, Secretary

Through communication with John A. Zangerle, Cuyahoga County Auditor, by President Thomas, and with the help of Charles Cowan and Ellwood Rasmussen (later Secretary, Central Branch, YMCA), it was reported at the board meeting of December 9, 1937, that the valuation of the Tower property had been reduced in the amount of $340,000 for the year 1936, that $25,640.49 worth of taxes had been paid to date, and that the total unpaid taxes amounted to $117,678.09. Thus far there had been a saving of $35,000 on the amount to be paid as back taxes.

At the same meeting, Charles J. Stilwell, President, The Warner & Swasey Company, was not only elected to the Fenn Board of Trustees, but was also appointed Chairman of the Building Committee of the Board. He had recently been elected to the Board of Trustees of the YMCA to fill the vacancy caused by the death of Ambrose Swasey, former President and Chairman of the Board of The Warner & Swasey Company. Stilwell later became Chairman of the Fenn Board, but there will be a lot more about him later. Dr. Frank H. Ferris, Walter Halle, and Cyril P. Deibel were invited to membership on the Fenn Board. Gerald S. Wellman was elected General Chairman of the Fenn College Building Campaign, and J. H. Burke, who had been the maintenance man for the National Town and Country Club, was retained on the same basis by Fenn. He later became Superintendant of Buildings and Grounds.

This being the last Board meeting for the fiscal year, Loegler reported that the college would close the year approximately $7,000 in the black.

If one were to choose a significant highlight for the year 1937, it would have to be the astuteness of the board in acquiring the Tower for an upset price of $250,000 plus delinquent taxes approximating $146,000 for a total approximating $396,000 in contrast to the cost of erection in 1930 of $1,500,000 and the actual mortgage held by the R.F.C. on the building in 1937 of $1,156,000.

Prior to the end of December 1937 Professor C. D. Williams, Chairman of the recently appointed Faculty Committee for planning space allocations in the Tower, was requested to establish an office in the new building and act as liaison and planning official for study of adaptation of the space for academic usage. As later noted this assignment and its time consuming obligations were responsible for a breakdown in Professor Williams' health from which, however, he made speedy recovery.

Charles J. Stilwell presented his first report as Chairman of the Board Property Committee at the January 3, 1938, board meeting. It included essential steps to be taken to occupy the first two floors of the Tower by February 1. Much of the building was completed at this point. Even the light bulbs had been distributed throughout the rooms in their cartons ready to be inserted in the fixtures. The building was broom cleaned.

The resignation of Trustee John A. Greene was accepted with deep regret. Greene requested release from Trustee activity because of health and increasing responsibilities at the Ohio Bell Telephone Company.

Upon recommendation of Trustee Dale Cox early in 1937, Dean Anders and the Faculty of the School of Business Administration made a statistical analysis of the business conditions in Cleveland. Their study covered the years 1924–1937. Their results were published as Volume I, Number I of *The Cleveland Business Review*. Copies were distributed at the February 3, 1938, meeting. This was the forerunner of annual publications of some particular study on the part of the faculty and students of the School of Business Administration up to the transfer of Fenn College to the State.

President Thomas read a statement of appreciation from the Faculty and Administrative Staff of the college for the history-making events of the past year. Chairman Fisher pointed out the importance of President Thomas to the campaign for capital funds to liquidate the Tower building debt and suggested that the Finance Committee consider the matter of the college carrying insurance on the life of Dr. Thomas.

According to the Minutes of the February 23, 1938, board meeting, the 23rd Annual Banquet was scheduled for February 26, in the ballroom of the Hotel Cleveland. The banquet was dedicated to the new Tower and Mayor Harold H. Burton (Fenn Trustee) was the principal speaker.

The Cleveland Rotary Club, on February 24, 1938, turned its program over to Fenn College. Chairman Fisher spoke on the growth of the college and introduced the Trustees present.

It was also reported that the first regular classes were held in the new Tower Monday evening, January 31. "The expressions on the faces of the students who had previously been meeting in the Plymouth Building and the classrooms in the old houses on Prospect Avenue needed no interpretation." The renovation, equipping, furnishing, moving, and planning costs to prepare the Tower for partial occupancy amounted to approximately $10,700.

It was also reported at the February 15, 1938, board meeting that A. C. Ernst, Managing Partner of Ernst & Ernst had requested that Chairman Fisher furnish him with a broad general statement of the program in Business Administration which Fenn provides with any proposals for future modifications. The following is the statement adopted by the Board March 23 which was submitted to Ernst:

Statement of Purpose
The School of Business Administration
Fenn College

Recognizing that our modern business and industrial organization exercises over the happiness of most of our population a pervasive power dangerous when in the hands of individuals unfamiliar with economic laws or motivated by immediate and selfish desires,

The School of Business Administration of Fenn College is dedicated to the preparation of young men and women for competent and socially useful participation in life and in business.

In viewing this objective, the school proposes in its administration and instruction to continue and increase its effectiveness in:

(a) Giving a thorough grounding in economic history and laws, and in the general principles of business.

(b) Supplying adequate training in the techniques and elemental practices of business to ensure competency in their practice, and provide for specialized training in the major fields of business.

(c) Introducing students to the literature of business and to sources of information; developing the tendency to use and skill in the use of analytical methods and factual data in the solution of problems.

(d) Developing an understanding of the respective functions, responsibilities, and rights of capital, management and labor in our industrial structure.

(e) Maintaining a close cooperation between school and industry, that the problems of the latter be the concern of the former and that teaching may be more vital and learning more purposeful.

(f) Instilling the desire to develop the capacity for improvement, not only in terms of material efficiency, but of greater uprightness in business relationships.

(g) Inculcating the dignity of sound business operations and the responsibilities of authority; a realization of the stewardship with which each is charged with respect to his fellows.

(h) Establishing the duty of every one to perform well and cheerfully his part as a member of the community whose prosperity he thus advances and shares.

(i) Assisting students in determining and developing their individual aptitudes so that each may serve society best by the exercise of his greatest talents, fully developed.

(j) Recognizing that in the training of persons for most effective participation in business, it is essential that general knowledge and a broad understanding be developed, a curriculum is thought desireable which will aim at a knowledge of history; an understanding of people, of political, legal and social institutions and practices; an appreciation of the arts; a capacity for self-expression.

(k) Encouraging the development in each student of a personal philosophy in terms of which a life may be planned and carried to fruition.

On the basis of the above statement and action of the Board, Ernst contributed $50,000 to the College to help make such instruction available to youth. This was the largest gift the College had received since Sereno Peck Fenn's gift of $100,000.

The board authorized the conferring of degrees on 78 candidates on May 16, 1938. Dr. Carl F. Wittke, Dean of Oberlin College, was the commencement speaker on May 20 at the Euclid Avenue Baptist Church. Fenn College conferred an Honorary Degree, LL.D. on Dean Wittke at the 1955 Commencement.

Several of the 1938 graduates have been active in Fenn Alumni affairs. Harold A. Harriger served as President of the Alumni Association in 1943. H. Martin Huge served as an Alumni Trustee from 1955 to 1958 and received the Alumni Distinguished Service Award in 1959. Edward J. Hrdlicka, Jr., was a star basketball player during his undergraduate years. He was the first Fenn Alumnus to be elected as an Alumni Trustee, serving from 1951 to 1954. He received the Alumni Distinguished Service Award in 1959, served as President of the C.S.U. Alumni Association in 1968, and was appointed to the Executive Board of the Fenn Educational Fund in 1972.

Professor Williams was authorized May 16, 1938, to proceed with the working drawings for the basement, first four floors, and the dormitories of the Tower. The Department of Physics had to be moved to the fourth floor of the Tower to make room for the expansion of the Department of Chemistry in the Fenn Building.

It was reported at the June 20, 1938, board meeting that Trustees James A. Hamilton and Harry D. Sims had submitted their resignations. Hamilton moved out of Cleveland and Sims had a health problem. Also at this same meeting the titles of the degrees granted by the School of Engineering were changed through recommendation of the Society for the Promotion of Engineering Education. As an example rather than Bachelor of Science (with a major in Civil Engineering) the new title was to be Bachelor of Civil Engineering.

As the result of a fund raising campaign conducted by the YMCA, Fenn College received a pro-rated share of $285,000. This meant that after Fenn met its obligations to R.F.C. and to back taxes, approximately $66,000 would be available for alteration on the Tower.

The Fenn Tower was dedicated Friday evening, September 9, 1938. Visitors numbered 3,214. A luncheon for a group of prominent citizens was held at noon. Following is the program and a portion of the dedication ceremony:

DEDICATION OF FENN TOWER
Friday Evening, September Ninth
Nineteen Hundred and Thirty Eight

✿   ✿   ✿   ✿   ✿

Presiding .... Ellwood H. Fisher
Chairman of the Board of Trustees
of Fenn College

"Fenn Tower" .... The Chairman

"The Significance of Fenn Tower to Cleveland"
.... Honorable Harold H. Burton
Mayor of Cleveland

"The Relation of Fenn Tower to Business
and Industry" .... A. C. Ernst
President of The Cleveland
Chamber of Commerce

Presentation of Key to Fenn Tower .... Elbert H. Baker, Jr.
Member of the Property Committee
of the Board of Trustees

Dedication Response .... Led by the President of the College
Dedicatory Prayer .... Dr. Frank H. Ferris
Minister, Fairmount Church

WE DEDICATE FENN TOWER

Leader—To Young Men and Women who desire to understand themselves and the world about them.

Response—*We dedicate Fenn Tower*

Leader—To awaken and encourage youth to equip themselves for productive and socially useful living.

Response—*We dedicate Fenn Tower*

Leader—To providing tools, personnel and experiences whereby young men and women may choose their vocations more wisely and may plan the kinds of education that are most suitable to their interests, needs and abilities.

Response—*We dedicate Fenn Tower*

Leader—To assist youth in developing those skills and attitudes and acquiring such knowledges as will enable them to deal effectively with the whole range of life experiences.

Response—*We dedicate Fenn Tower*

Leader—To stimulate youth to recognize social, economic and political problems and to seek to apply Christian principles of thought and action to their solution.

Response—*We dedicate Fenn Tower*

Leader—To develop in students the tendency to use and skill in the use of, analytical methods and factual data in the solution of the problems which confront them.

Response—*We dedicate Fenn Tower*

Leader—To assist in the discovery and development of the types of course content, student experience and methods of instruction best adapted to fulfill the purposes of Fenn College.

Response—*We dedicate Fenn Tower*

Leader—To make available education which combines theory and practice, study and work, learning and doing, as an integral part of the educational experience itself.

Response—*We dedicate Fenn Tower*

Leader—To provide direct opportunity for cooperation between College and Business and Industry.

Response—*We dedicate Fenn Tower*

Leader—To give young men and women experience in practicing good citizenship and in bringing about community betterment.

Response—*We dedicate Fenn Tower*

Leader—To assist youth in discovering and enjoying the values of the beautiful, the artistic and the cultural.

Response—*We dedicate Fenn Tower*

Leader—To make available facilities and persons which will stimulate youth to find a workable, meaningful life philosophy.

Response—*We dedicate Fenn Tower*

Leader—To enable youth to develop their potential capacities and become Cleveland's greatest assets.

Response—*We dedicate Fenn Tower*

Leader—To aid young men and women to know how, through the increasing understanding and the enlarging purposes of man, God seeks to establish His Way of Life among Men.

Response—*We dedicate Fenn Tower*

Meriam C. Herrick was appointed Acting Director of Admissions at the September 28, 1938, board meeting. His title and duty changes were as follows: September 1, 1940, Assistant Director of Admissions and Director of Student Activities; October 1, 1941, Director of Admissions and Student Activities; September 1, 1949, Director of Admissions; September 1, 1960, Associate Director, Admissions and Records; September 1, 1961, Dean of Students. He resigned from C.S.U. as Dean of Students in 1966, and died of a heart attack September 27, 1971.

George V. Parmelee, an alumnus of Fenn, was appointed at the same board meeting as Instructor in Mechanical Engineering. He remained at Fenn until 1944 at which time he joined the American Society of Heating and Ventilating Engineers in their Cleveland research laboratory. He left there in 1955 to become a consultant on air-conditioning in Saudi Arabia. In January 1963 he was re-engaged at Fenn as Professor and Chairman, Department of Mechanical Engineering, and held this same status for C.S.U. after the transfer of Fenn College to the State.

For the second time the subject of a three-quarter teaching year was discussed by the Board of Trustees. The subject arose many times in the future, but nothing was done about it until 1956 at which time the three-quarter teaching year was adopted.

Dr. Thomas had been elected General Secretary of the YMCA and the question arose as to his ability to serve also as President of Fenn. The Personnel Committee of the Board under chairmanship of Clayton G. Hale was instructed to seek suitable candidates for the College position. Qualifications were established by the committee. Finally it was decided that Dr. Thomas should be retained as President, that he be provided with an assistant, and that Dean Nichols be assigned additional duties with the approval of the Trustees.

TABLE 2

FALL REGISTRATION STATISTICS

	Enrollment		Value of Tuition Contracts	
School	1938	1937	1938	1937
Day Co-op	502°	386°	$112,952	$ 80,777
Evening Business Adm.	894	873	36,740	36,726
Evening Engineering	703	942	33,560	49,294
Total	2,099	2,201	$183,252	$166,794

° Does not include Group "B" students on Co-op jobs.

The Evening Division Engineering enrollment, as shown in Table 2, dropped because of greater unemployment in Cleveland's industry in 1938. Much discussion ensued at this October 25, 1938, Board of Trustees meeting because of lack of projected operating income and also of capital funds to rehabilitate the Fenn Tower. Drastic cuts were made in budgeted expense items for the remainder of the year, even to the extent of eliminating further expenses for office supplies, car mileage, all extra meals, part-time salaries, and memberships in professional societies. The greatest single source loss of income resulted from an $11,000 reduction from the Fenn Trust Fund.

The final board meeting for 1938 was held December 7. The one highlight of this meeting was the report that, through the efforts of Malcolm Vilas, Ellwood Rasmussen, and Charles Carran, the Ohio State Tax Commission, upon recommendation of John Zangerle, County Auditor, had exempted the Fenn Tower from further taxation. This was a good note on which to end the year.

The first board meeting in 1939 was held on January 13. Chairman Fisher announced that the capital fund needs were real and important and it was the responsibility of the board to raise at least $40,000 in 1939 to meet the capital fiscal obligations.

Also at this same meeting, J. C. Sanders, Resident Partner of Ernst and Ernst, and Fred C. Baldwin, Attorney, were elected Trustees of the College. The members of the Fenn College Board of Trustees as of January 13, 1939, were as follows:

Fisher, Ellwood H., Chairman
The Fisher Brothers Co.

Baldwin, Fred C.
Garfield, Baldwin, Jamison,
Hope & Ulrich

Brown, Elmer A.
Standard Oil Co.

Burton, Hon. Harold H.
Mayor of Cleveland

Campbell, James E.
The Sherwin-Williams Co.

Carter, Leyton E.
The Cleveland Foundation

Cox, Dale
International Harvester Co.

Cox, Jacob D., Jr.
The Cleveland Twist Drill Co.

Crider, John S.
Retired

Eaton, Cyrus S.
Otis & Co.

Hale, Clayton G.
Hale & Hale Co.

Irvin, John L.
The Cleveland Press

Kettering, Eugene W.
Electromotive Corporation

Myers, James L.
The Cleveland Graphite
Bronze Co.

Perry, Allen T.
Harshaw Chemical Co.

Roth, Richard G.
Wm. Taylor Son & Co.

Sanders, J. C.
Ernst and Ernst

Stilwell, Charles J.
The Warner & Swasey Co.

Thomas, Dr. C. V., President
Fenn College

Ex-officio
Frederick A. Henry, President
YMCA

A. G. Knebel, General Secretary
YMCA

The operating budget for fiscal 1939 totalling $378,000 was approved at the January meeting of the board. This was the largest operating budget thus far in the history of Fenn College.

The following were approved for tenure at the February 18, 1939, meeting of the board:

Walter R. Goetsch, Registrar and Assistant Professor
Major B. Jenks, Associate Professor
William A. Patterson, Assistant Professor
Vasily D. Brian, Assistant Professor
Chester A. Tudbury, Assistant Professor
Urban F. von Rosen, Associate Professor
Robert F. Yeager, Instructor

The Annual Student Banquet was held February 11 at the Hotel Statler. The students dedicated it to Chairman Fisher who had been so instrumental in procuring the Fenn Tower.

Early in March of 1939 the college had visitation inspections from Dr. John Dale Russell (for the North Central Association) and Dr. Bland L. Stradley (for the Ohio College Association). These were visitations to check the progress Fenn was making to qualify for accreditation in these two organizations.

A major in Home Economics, effective in the Fall Quarter in the School of Arts and Sciences, was approved by the board on March 3, 1939. Also at this same meeting the board approved the purchase of a $25,000 insurance policy on the life of Dr. Thomas. The YMCA Board had previously taken out a $25,000 ordinary life policy on Dr. Thomas.

The Special Capital Accounts Committee reported that there was an urgency in raising funds for remodeling and equipment for the Fenn Tower plus the liquidation of the mortgage and back taxes. It was recommended that a special brochure be prepared, stating the needs, for board members to hand to corporation presidents during a personal visit to discuss Fenn's problems. At the same time a written statement would be included to list said corporation employees who were graduates of Fenn plus the present undergraduates who were co-oping with the company.

Fenn had been holding Annual Open Houses, but April 28, 1939, was the first such event which included exhibits in the new Fenn Tower.

Exhibits and on-going classes were also displayed in the Fenn Building on Prospect Avenue. The Women's League, the Fenn Women's Board, and the Home Economics Class served refreshments and the evening was capped by the final intramural game in basketball between Kappa Delta Phi of the Day Division and The Barons of the Evening Division.

The board held a meeting at noon of the same day at which it was reported that Professor Max Robinson had recently been elected President of the Ohio Section of the Society for the Promotion of Engineering Education, and that the 1940 Annual Meeting of S.P.E.E. would be held at Fenn College.

A letter was read to the board from John G. Henninger, Treasurer of the Day Division Student Council, disclosing a surplus of about $1,000 for the year and offering this amount to the Board if they would agree to match it for improvements to the student lounge. Action was taken to accept and match this generous offer and to express the board's appreciation to the Day Student Council.

Personnel Committee Chairman Hale submitted the resignation of Professor C. D. Williams to the board. Professor Williams had seriously affected his health in his months of diligent planning for rehabilitation of the Fenn Tower. The board returned the resignation for further consideration.

There were 104 graduates in the class of 1939, the largest thus far in Fenn's history. They were distributed as follows:

		Day Co-op Div.	Evening Div.
Engineering	53	35	18
Business Adm.	39	29	10
Arts & Sci.	12	12	–
	—	—	—
Total	104	76	28

This was also the largest number of Evening Division graduates in any class thus far. The 76 Day Division graduates came from an entering class of 174 in 1934. They were employed by 40 different co-op firms in 1939. The 28 Evening Division graduates came from a student body approximating 1,800 evening students, employed in 474 Cleveland industries.

Many 1939 graduates have been loyal, active Fenn Alumni. Raymond B. Aufmuth was elected an Alumni Trustee in 1961 and received the Alumni Distinguished Service Award in 1964. Lysle D. Cahill received the Alumni Distinguished Service Award in 1966. George V. Darchuk was active in Alumni fund raising, and he was President of the Cleveland Society of Professional Engineers in 1968. Ernest C. Harris was one of the draftsmen for Professor Williams on the Tower building planning. He joined the Fenn Faculty as an Instructor in Civil Engineering in March 1942 and became Chairman of the Department in May 1946, then Chairman, Department of Civil Engineering and Engineering Mechanics in December 1952. He resigned from C.S.U. in December 1967. He was a recipient of the Alumni Distinguished Service Award in 1962. Edward Trela taught in the Fenn Technical Institute for about thirteen years. He then became Assistant Professor, Department of Metallurgy in 1965. He was promoted to Associate Professor by C.S.U. in 1969. Paul R. Balliett became a Methodist Minister. He was very active in the Fenn Alumni Association and was a recipient of the Alumni Distinguished Service Award in 1968. John G. Henninger was elected an Alumni Trustee in 1963, serving until 1969, at which time he was elected a Member of the Fenn Educational Foundation. He received the Alumni Distinguished Service Award in 1965. Vernon Davis, following a stint in the U.S. Air Force joined Fenn as Assistant Finance Director in October 1952. He was appointed Finance Director in September 1958 and served in this capacity until the transfer of Fenn to C.S.U. He then became Finance Director and Assistant Treasurer of C.S.U. He was elected an Alumni Trustee of the Fenn Educational Foundation (F.E.F.) in 1970 and a member of the Executive Board of the Fenn Educational Fund in 1973. Theodore J. Wilner was a recipient of the Alumni Distinguished Service Award in 1968.

Upon recommendation of Dean Bush, Fenn had made application to Engineers Council for Professional Development (E.C.P.D.) in 1937 and upon inspection was directed to further develop several areas of academic status to qualify for accreditation. At the June 30, 1939, meeting of the Trustees approval was given to increase the length of the Engineering curriculum from eleven to twelve quarters. This was in keeping with one of the recommendations of E.C.P.D. Also at this meeting it was reported that A. M. Dudley of the Westinghouse Company in a semi-official capacity for E.C.P.D. had visited Fenn again and was very impressed with the substantial progress and development made by the college over the two-year period. He suggested that Fenn renew its application for accreditation by E.C.P.D. in 1940.

A special committee composed of Fisher, Sanders, Stilwell, Glen Smith, and Dr. Thomas met September 25, 1939, to discuss ways and means of obtaining capital funds and the creation of an endowment fund to aid in annual operational needs. A ten-year program was proposed with specific annual contributions suggested from corporations, alumni, individuals, and foundations. When the Fenn Building was opened in 1928, the enrollment demands soon exceeded the available space. There was a repetition of the enrollment experience following the opening of the Fenn Tower, except in the latter case, there was space available but no funds to rehabilitate it for college use. To take positive steps toward resolving the financial problems, Chairman Fisher reported at the October 20, 1939, board meeting that the special committee recommended: (1) attorneys who prepare wills of leading Cleveland citizens be informed about Fenn and its needs, and (2) industrial and other civic leaders be invited to the Tower (in small groups) to let them see the new physical facilities and to inform them of Fenn's financial needs and obligations.

Henry J. Tremmel was elected a Trustee at the October 20, 1939, meeting, and he served in this capacity until his death, February 15, 1953.

Also at this meeting it was reported that: (1) a Nurses' Training Course was started jointly with St. Luke's Hospital, (2) an Airplane Pilot Training Program was started in cooperation with the Civil Aeronautical Authority, (3) a girls' dormitory had been established in the New Amsterdam Hotel, and (4) following a recent visit from three members of the Ohio College Association (O.C.A.), the Executive Committee of O.C.A. agreed to recommend Fenn College for membership at the April 5, 1940, O.C.A. meeting. This latter information was to be kept confidential until the meeting date. The board also approved that the Department of Civil Engineering would henceforth be known as the Department of Structural Engineering.

The last board meeting of 1939 and the decade of the thirties was held December 27. The year ended on several happy notes. Whereas it appeared at the October 20 meeting that the year would end about $12,000 in the red, a number of adjustments in the budget were made and some unanticipated income was received so Trustee Baker, chairman of the Board Finance Committee, was able to report a balanced operation for the year.

Other items of particular interest reported were: (1) The installation of restaurant equipment in the grill by The Telling-Belle Vernon Company on a permanent loan basis. (2) The contribution of $5,000 by the Warner & Swasey Company toward capital account. This was in addition to a previous recent gift of $10,000. (3) The re-application to North Central Association for inspection and accreditation.

The board also approved a resolution by Hale that inasmuch as the actual cost of construction of the Fenn Tower was $1,672,137.44 and based on appraisal studies by three separate agencies the then present sound value of the building was estimated to be $1,200,000, that this sound value be accepted and the difference from the actual cost to Fenn College be accredited to capital surplus retroactive to December 31, 1968.

The faculty at the close of 1939 totaled 56 full-time and 76 part-time. Nineteen members of the full-time faculty were doing graduate work. Six articles, two books, and one play were published. Eleven faculty members held offices in ten learned or professional societies. Six of these presented ten papers at society meetings. Thirty-eight faculty members held 92 memberships in 66 different societies. Fifteen members were serving on Boards of Directors or consulting. Thirty-five courses, new to the faculty who taught them, were developed during the year. Of the 783 Day Division students, 575 lived in Greater Cleveland, 156 in other areas of Ohio and 52 were from out-of-state; 231 were in the School of Business Administration, 432 in Engineering, and 100 in Arts & Sciences. There were 101 women students in the Day Division. The Health Service of the college had 1,123 consultations with students and 377 physical examinations were made by the college doctor. A total of 165 students received financial aid totalling $19,104. Earnings from co-op work averaged $400 per student. Three hundred eighty-eight students from the Day Division participated in one or more of twelve different types of intramural programs. The library experienced its largest year in circulation of 19,877 books. The total number of books at the end of 1939 was 11,977. Total assets at the end of the year were $1,529,138.85.

So we come to the end of another era in Fenn's history, somewhat similar to the end of the era of the twenties, i.e., a growing enrollment; the recent occupation of a new building, yet an almost immediate lack of classroom, laboratory, and office space; the problem of financing the new building; the problem of balancing the annual budget; the quest for faculty members with advanced degrees and professional experience; and the striving for all the necessary elements leading toward accreditation by the important academic and professional accrediting agencies. At the end of each decade the students exhibited added pride in their college, more favorable attention had come to Fenn from the public, and interest in the college had increased on the part of the alumni and others who had special contacts with the institution. Now what about the next ten years? But remember the advice found in the Bible under Luke XIV, 28 "For which of you, intending to build a tower, sitteth not down first, and counteth the cost, whether he have sufficient to finish it."

V

More than an end to war,
we want an end to the beginning of all wars.

Franklin D. Roosevelt.
From an address written for the Jefferson Day Dinners Broadcast,
April 13, 1945, the day after he died at Warm Springs, Georgia.

A new war was on the horizon at the beginning of the decade of the forties. Colleges and universities were being called upon by the federal government to accelerate instruction in various types of defense activities: Civil Defense; Civilian Air Corps; Engineering, Science, Management and War Training (E.S.M.W.T.) courses, and special highly technical, long and comprehensive seminars in structural design against bomb and fire damage. Fenn was already engaged in teaching ground school courses to students electing an option offered by the Civil Aeronautics Authority (C.A.A.) which proved to be the start of more vigorous training programs.

But the first meeting of the year (and the decade) was by the Board Personnel Committee and a few other select Trustees on January 16, 1940. The subject did not concern war, but something much more important to the College—the choosing of a permanent President. Chairman Fisher presided and spoke on the background of Fenn. He then called upon Clayton G. Hale, Chairman of the Personnel Committee, to review the work of the augmented Committee. Hale reported that back in May 1938 Dr. Thomas, President of Fenn, had also accepted the General Secretaryship of the YMCA, following which the Personnel Committee, after due deliberation and upon recommendation of the board, sought a new President for Fenn College. Three or four prospects were approached and in the meantime the rehabilitation and occupation of the Fenn Tower held the full attention of the board. Also, in the

210

meantime, the three or four presidential prospects had all accepted excellent new positions, proving the high caliber of men sought. A portion of the Minutes of this meeting which were drafted by Hale, who served also as Secretary pro tem, follows:

Mr. Fisher then called for a comprehensive discussion of the entire situation, including other possible candidates, effect upon the school of continuing the present situation indefinitely, a reconsideration of choosing an inside man rather than selecting someone from the outside and especially someone not familiar with Cleveland conditions, various relationships which must be kept in balance between the College and the Y, the overload now being borne by Dr. Thomas, the problems of the College in relation to the problems which confront the Y, and all other angles. He required each man present to express himself fully and without restraint. This was done freely by all present, and the meeting was characterized by its earnestness and intentness.

From this came the conclusions, shared in by all, that (1) it is unfair to Dr. Thomas and unwise both for the College and the Y to continue the present situation indefinitely; (2) the selection of a permanent President is an essential step in dealing with the other problems of the College; (3) the accomplishments heretofore recited are currently making progress toward fulfillment under Dr. Thomas' efforts, even though his time is divided; (4) the past history and present progress and future possibilities of the College are completely interwoven with Dr. Thomas (the man); (5) the experience of the Committee in applying to other men the measuring stick of the list of qualities sought after brought the Committee back to Dr. Thomas himself time after time; (6) the importance of Dr. Thomas accepting the Secretaryship of the Y at the time and under the circumstances then prevailing is admitted, but that crisis is past and the fact remains that the Presidency of the College is not now and has not been vacant but has been and still is held by Dr. Thomas; wherefore the Committee voted unanimously that it now renders as its first and only official report to the Chairman of the Board of Trustees the conviction that Dr. C. V. Thomas again devote his full time to the continued development of the College, and that Mr. Fisher be requested to present this action suitably to the persons and bodies affected by this action with view to consummating this recommendation at the earliest feasible time and with the co-operation and blessing of those others whose problems would thus be deprived of the guidance of Dr. Thomas.

The meeting was declared adjourned at 2:25 o'clock P.M. although the men continued to discuss the subject further and generally expressed the feeling that ways must be found to accomplish this decision and that every effort should be made to assist the YMCA in making possible the fulfillment of this important action.

The first 1940 meeting of the full board was held February 23. The following officers were elected:

> Ellwood H. Fisher, Chairman
> Charles J. Stilwell, Vice Chairman
> Charles A. Dilley, Secretary
> John S. Crider, Treasurer

It was reported that Professor C. D. Williams, because of his proven unusual ability in structural design, was appointed a member of Committee on Structural Engineering Standards for the American Railway Engineering Association. Karl D. Kelly was appointed Assistant Professor of Mathematics, effective September 1940. He had been teaching in the Evening Division for several years. Action was also taken to waive tuition for children of full-time Faculty attending Fenn, effective September 1940.

The Fenn College Glee Club under the direction of Jacob E. Hines offered a selection of songs at the April 17, 1940, evening meeting of the board. A number of wives of the board were present (members of the Women's Board of Fenn College). Dean Anders reported that "The Cauldron" had won a prize as one of the best college newspapers of all classes. Dr. Thomas was asked to convey the board's congratulations to the Editor, Jay W. Collins. Collins appears again later. The highlight of the evening, however, was the announcement by Dr. Thomas that Fenn had been accepted as an accredited member of the North Central Association of Colleges and Secondary Schools. He cited twelve areas of progress reported by the examiners, since their visit five years previously. However, he also cited twelve areas in which the examiners felt strongly that there should be further development in order to hold accreditation. The examiners were Father Alphonse Schmitalla of St. Louis University and President Hopkins of Wabash College.

A new salary scale was adopted at the May 15, 1940, Personnel Committee meeting. The comparisons of the old and new scales for the four academic ranks are:

	Old Scale	New Scale
Professors	$2400–$3600	$2700–$4200
Associate Professors	2100– 2900	2100– 3300
Assistant Professors	1900– 2600	1900– 2800
Instructors	1500– 2200	1500– 2200

It must be remembered that this scale is for an eleven-month teaching schedule and not the usual nine-month teaching schedule prevalent in non-co-op institutions. Furthermore, a faculty member was expected to teach in both the Day and Evening Divisions. One quarter's leave of absence every three years was set as a policy for both the Faculty and the Administrative Staff. The new salary scale and "leave" policy were adopted by the board at its May 22, 1940, meeting.

The candidates for degrees recommended at the May meeting included several Fenn Alumni who have been active in the Alumni Association or who have earned distinction. Jay W. Collins, mentioned earlier as Editor of "The Cauldron" received the Fenn Alumni Distinguished Service Award in 1958, was an Alumni Trustee of the College 1954–1957, was President of the Alumni Association in 1966, and served on many fund raising programs. He became Executive Director of the Euclid General Hospital. He was elected a Member of the Corporation of the Fenn Educational Foundation in 1969. Eleanore J. Bouquard was President of the Fenn Alumni Association in 1942 and recipient of the Alumni Distinguished Service Award in 1963. She became a Senior Counselor at W.R.U. William F. Bland was President of the Fenn Alumni Association in 1945. He became Personnel Management Advisor of the McGraw-Hill Publishing Company in New York. Richard S. Huxtable was a member of the Fenn Board of Trustees from 1944 to 1950 and served as Chairman of the Development and Building Committees during the planning and construction of the Claude Foster Mechanical Engineering Building.

An Honorary Bachelor of Letters degree was conferred on Professor George B. Simon at the Commencement Convocation, May 19, 1940.

It was reported at the August 19, 1940, board meeting that four groups of students had received Ground School training since spring under the auspices of the C.A.A. and that two other groups would start in September.

Waiver was given on tuition charges for children of full-time YMCA Secretaries for the first two years at Fenn. The same limitation was placed on children of full-time Faculty and Administrative Staff members. It was felt that the income from co-op work should be employed to pay tuition for the last three years.

Considerable time was spent by the board on the subject of resolving the capital needs of the college. The problem was two-fold: (1) to secure $13,000 to finance rehabilitation of the 10th floor in the Tower for classroom and office use, the 14th and 15th floors for dormitory use and the gymnasium and swimming pool, and (2) to secure approximately ninety additional $200 gifts needed to meet 1940s R.F.C. and tax obligations. Action was taken to proceed with the Fisher-Thomas plan to approach one hundred twenty-five corporations and individuals for $200 each, and a limited number of larger corporations for a larger amount each to finance the essential remodeling of the Tower. The Trustees were to carry the major responsibility for the fund raising.

The Minutes of the Board meeting of September 10, 1940, show that seven classrooms plus office space for the Dean of Arts & Sciences, his secretary, and four members of the faculty were ready for occupancy on the 10th floor of the Tower at the start of the Fall Quarter. Also, that the coming Sunday *Plain Dealer* would carry a special article on Fenn College on the first page of the feature section, and that equipment worth $11,000 had recently been received from the Federal Government for use in the Aeronautical Laboratory.

President Thomas called to the attention of the Trustees that a telegram had been received from the War Department inquiring of the interest of Fenn College in the establishment of a Signal Corps Training Program for an area including Ohio, Indiana, Kentucky, and West Virginia. The program was to be set up in Cincinnati or Cleveland, and Fenn College was the preferred location. It was proposed to train 300 Radio Operators and 200 Radio Mechanics each year for five years. An estimated budget of income and expense was prepared including remodeling of additional space in the Tower for class and dormitory rooms. The college was to be responsible for board and room and the educational program. The Army would pay up to $11 per week per student for board and room and would meet reasonable instruction, maintenance, and equipment costs. It was conceived that the 6th, 7th, 8th, and 9th floors in the Tower should be rehabilitated to provide classroom and office space.

After consideration of the pros and cons and at the suggestion of Stilwell, Dr. Thomas summarized his position on the subject as follows:

(1) "It might be a protection against the ravages of the draft and war upon our present and potential student body"; and (2) "The adoption of this program by Fenn might be thought of as a part of its institutional responsibility in the program for National Defense." Action was taken to invite Lt. Col. Stoner to Fenn to discuss the conditions under which the Trustees would be willing to undertake the program and a definite decision to do so was made at a later Board meeting.

About the same time Dean Bush was also developing new training programs for men employed in defense industries. Congress had appropriated nine million dollars for the establishment of Engineering, Science, Management and Defense Training (E.S.M.D.T.) courses in colleges and universities. College enrollments in general were on the verge of considerable reduction by the draft, but Fenn's enrollment was increasing because of the new Tower Building. Programs approved for establishment at Fenn early in 1941 were:

Engineering Drawing	Materials Inspection and Testing
Production Engineering	Tool Engineering
Non-metals materials testing	Stress Analysis
Production supervision	Structural Detailing

For many years the employees of the Warner & Swasey Company attended Fenn as part of their apprenticeship program with the Company. At the suggestion of Stilwell and on approval of other officers of the Company and representatives of the College a new four-year college level program for apprentices was established. The Warner & Swasey Company deposited $20,000 with Fenn from which the College drew expenses for tuition, books, activity fees, and other necessary academic supplies for apprentices accepted by Fenn. From time to time the Company replenished the fund.

It was reported at the December 27, 1940, board meeting that it was estimated the College would end the fiscal year with a net gain of approximately $8,700. Also, that fifty-two corporations and individuals had contributed $12,050 to date toward debt reduction, and three individuals and three corporations had contributed $13,000 toward "building" development. The Fenn Women's Advisory Board financed the development of two lounges for co-ed students at a cost approximating $2,000. Mrs. Philip Bliss contributed $5,000 for improvement of some part of the Tower and it was decided to apply it to the development and furnishing of an additional dormitory floor. The 14th was selected and a plaque installed on the wall in recognition of her generosity. It was known as the Bliss Dorm Floor henceforth.

The year 1940 had a number of highlights, but the three that stood out academically were: (1) the acceptance to membership (accreditation) by the North Central Association; (2) membership in the Ohio College Association; and (3) the approval of the graduates of the Engineering School for registration by the Ohio State Board of Registration for Professional Engineers and Surveyors. Three milestones had been earned by Fenn College. In addition to these, however, the College for the first time became a member of The American Council on Education, The Association of Urban Universities, and The American Association of Business Teacher Training Institutions.

According to the February 14, 1941, board Minutes, 59 Warner & Swasey apprentices were enrolled in their first Evening Division class. Reliance Electric and Engineering followed the lead of Warner & Swasey and started an apprentice program at Fenn. At the same meeting Ellwood H. Fisher was re-elected Board Chairman and Charles J. Stilwell was re-elected Vice Chairman and the following were elected as new Fenn Trustees:

> Edward T. Bartlett, The Cleveland Trust Company
> James H. Coolidge, McDonald-Coolidge Company
> Clarence L. Collins, Reliance Electric and Engineering Co.
> C. William Poe, The C. W. Poe Company
> Dr. Robert M. Stecher, City Hospital
> Clarence M. Taylor, The Lincoln Electric Company
> Dr. Nathan Van Stone, The Sherwin-Williams Company

In addition to the above, the Fenn Board was composed of the following Trustees:

> Elbert H. Baker, Jr., Locke Machine Co.
> Fred C. Baldwin, Attorney
> Leyton E. Carter, Cleveland Foundation
> Jacob D. Cox, Jr., Cleveland Twist Drill Co.
> Cyrus S. Eaton, Otis & Company
> Clayton G. Hale, Hale & Hale Co.
> James L. Myers, Cleveland Graphite Bronze Co.
> Allen T. Perry, Harshaw Chemical Co.
> John C. Sanders, Ernst & Ernst
> Henry J. Tremmel, North American Fibre Products

Jay C. Whitehair, Whitehair & Whitehair
George V. Woodling, Woodling & Krost
John David Wright, Thompson Products, Inc.
Hon. Harold H. Burton, U.S. Senate, Washington, D.C.
Eugene W. Kettering, Electromotive Corporation,
   La Grange, Illinois
John S. Crider, Ex-Officio, YMCA
Joseph W. Meriam, Ex-Officio, YMCA
Dr. C. V. Thomas, Ex-Officio

The E.S.M.D.T. courses were growing in popularity. Whereas original plans were for nine sections totaling 180 students, the demand necessitated expansion of the program to eighteen sections totaling 360 students, and there was still a large waiting list. Employees from 96 different corporations and businesses sought the training.

The long awaited opening of the physical education floors of the Tower took place the evening of February 19, 1941. The swimming pool was dedicated as "The Ellwood H. Fisher Swimming Pool." It was "unveiled," according to the Minutes, and Fisher turned the pool over to the Director of Physical Education, Professor Homer E. Woodling. The Women's Advisory Board arranged an informal reception following the dedication ceremony. The entire affair was in recognition of the interest, devotion and years of leadership which Fisher had given to the development of Fenn College.

The increase in cost of operation of the Tower and the increased services being provided the students (such as the swimming pool and gymnasium, vocational guidance and testing, increased placement obligations, plus the increased Faculty and Staff salaries, and the fact that there had not been an increase in endowment resources) forced the decision by the board on March 21, 1941, to increase the Day Division tuition from $225 to $250 per year effective September 1, 1941. This was in keeping with the experience at many other colleges. When questioned by a Trustee concerning Fenn's objective to take care of the financially handicapped, Dr. Thomas pointed out that the College's contribution in the Cleveland area was achieved not so much through a low tuition scale as through the cooperative plan which enabled the upperclass men to earn more money than obligated by tuition and fees.

Fisher suggested at this same meeting that consideration be given to holding a civic luncheon to celebrate the 60th Anniversary of the College (assuming the founding date to be 1881). He had hoped to use such a celebration as an event to amortize Fenn's debt obligations amounting to:

$ 90,000   to R.F.C.
  73,000   toward back taxes
  18,000   to YMCA for capital account debt

$181,000   Total

It was finally decided to have a dinner and reception for Dr. Thomas in honor of his twenty-five years with the YMCA educational activities and the College instead of a celebration dinner for a 60th anniversary date which was in question.

The following list of the ten Cleveland companies having the largest numbers of employees attending Fenn during the Spring term is noted in the May 16, 1941, Minutes of the Board:

Thompson Products, Inc.	129
The Warner & Swasey Co.	116
American Steel and Wire Co.	67
Lincoln Electric Co.	35
Aluminum Company of America	35
Republic Steel Corporation	35
General Electric Company	32
Weatherhead Company	32
Cleveland Graphite Bronze Company	29
National Acme Company	25

The military draft had been affecting the student enrollment, but the time had arrived when the faculty members with Reserve Officer status also were becoming vulnerable to call. The following excerpt from the same Minutes states some specific instances:

Calling of Members of the Faculty into Service
Professor Donald Fabel, Head of our Mechanical Engineering Department, and Joseph Borg of our Structural Engineering Department—Reserve Officers—have been called to active duty.
     One of the most serious problems now confronting the college is the future status of Dean Burl H. Bush of the School of En-

gineering. Following his graduation from Annapolis, Dean Bush took an advanced degree in Mechanical Engineering at the University of Iowa. He came to Fenn in 1931 and was appointed dean of Engineering in 1937. His present responsibilities include the organization and supervision of an Engineering program that is providing instruction for 1500 regular engineering students, the direction of the Engineering Defense Training program with an enrollment of 400 students, and the supervision of the C.A.A. program. He is making a very important contribution to National Defense.

Soon after Dean Bush tendered his resignation from the Naval Reserves, a representative of the Navy visited the college. The information he secured was presented to a committee of the Navy and Mr. Bush was informed that he would not be called previous to July 1, 1941. Dean Seaton, the Director of the Engineering Defense Training in Washington has requested the Navy to permit Dean Bush to remain in his present position because of his value in National Defense Training. Unless something additional can be done, it is probable that Dean Bush will be called for service on July 1st. This is a major personnel problem.

Several graduates of the class of 1941 have been active in Fenn Alumni affairs. Clifford L. Graves served on the Fenn Faculty for several years. He received the Alumni Distinguished Service Award in 1964. He was elected a Member of the Fenn Educational Foundation in December 1970. William J. Easton, Jr., was president of the Fenn Alumni Association in 1948 and has been active in alumni fund raising programs. William J. Pugh was president of the Alumni Association in 1955 and 1956. He is the only Fenn Alumnus who served as president for two terms. He received the Alumni Distinguished Service Award in 1963 and was elected to the Advisory Committee of the Fenn Educational Fund in December 1971. He was always very loyal to his Alma Mater. Thomas R. Toomey was elected to the Board of Trustees as an Alumni Member December 11, 1969, and Richard J. Verba was president of the Fenn Alumni Association in 1959. He, too, was active in fund raising campaigns for the Association.

On the evening of May 20, 1941, a group of special guests and members of the Fenn family held a reception in The Mid-Day Club honoring both Dr. Thomas for his twenty-five years of loyal dedicated service to the educational activities of the YMCA, and the 1941 graduates.

In attendance were 72 hosts, 77 special guests, 75 Faculty members, 112 graduates, and 5 YMCA Executive Secretaries, for a total of 341 persons. Stilwell served as Chairman of the dinner meeting. The Very Reverend E. D. Horne, S.J., President of John Carroll University gave the Invocation. The Warner & Swasey Glee Club provided music entertainment. William J. Pugh, President of the Senior Class (mentioned above) responded to a statement from Stilwell concerning the graduates. Board Chairman Ellwood H. Fisher presented Dr. Thomas a Resolution for his twenty-five years of service to the YMCA College activities and Nat Howard, then Editor of the *Cleveland News*, expressed the greetings and congratulations from the group to Dr. Thomas.

The fear that Fenn was about to lose Dean Bush to the U.S. Navy came true. On June 23, 1941, he was called into active duty, and Max B. Robinson was appointed Acting Dean of the Engineering School for the duration. The following is a memorandum which Dr. Thomas sent to the Faculty over date of August 15, 1941.

> *To the Faculty of Fenn College:*
>
> Within a month the school year of 1941–42 will have begun. You will be glad to know that during the summer the following developments have occurred:
>
> *Physical*————A new General Chemistry Laboratory has been installed on the 3rd floor of the Fenn Building; the entire 18th floor of Fenn Tower has been developed into a Home Economics Department; a new laboratory for the use of the Structural Engineering Department, faculty offices, and the Downtown Office of the Weather Bureau have been located on the 17th floor of the Tower; the 14th floor (the Philip E. Bliss Floor) is ready for Dormitory use; additional administrative offices have been provided on the 2nd floor of the Tower.
>
> *Personnel*————The following adjustments of responsibilities are in effect:
>
> Acting Dean of the Engineering School—Max B. Robinson
> Junior Dean of the Engineering School—Marion B. Tolar
> Dean of the College of Arts & Sciences (as well as Registrar)—
>   W. R. Goetsch
> Secretary of the Department of Coordination—James W. Griswold
>   New personnel has been added in the Departments of English, Mathematics, Coordination, Engineering Defense Training and

Electrical Engineering. These persons will be introduced at the Fall Faculty Meeting on the evening of September 12th.

Developments in program, the enlargement of the Engineering Defense Training activities, and other items, will also be announced at the Fall Faculty Meeting. Although the operations of the draft and the great increase in industrial employment will affect the enrollment, yet the college believes that balancing factors will result in a registration approximately the same as a year ago.

In common with other colleges, Fenn has the responsibility to help young men and women think clearly about the personal and national defense values involved in continuing their education. The long view of the necessity for education in terms of the individual is clear but needs to be reemphasized with certain individuals. The value of higher education viewed from the angle of National Defense was recently expressed by Colonel Burgess, representing the Training Division of the Army. He stated: "The War Department has felt and still feels that a good schooling of mind and body is the positive source of strength in any event; that the college world in carrying out its normal role is making the most important and necessary contribution to National Defense.

In the same connection, General Hershey of the Selective Service Board said that he was unalterably opposed to lowering the age limit of twenty-one for men called by Selective Service. As you know, upperclassmen in the College of Engineering and in other technical fields are securing deferment to complete their college education.

Your active cooperation in interpreting the significance of college education under present conditions will be helpful to individuals, to Fenn, and to our total National Defense Program. Please keep the date of September 12th for the Fall Faculty Meeting.

s/C. V. Thomas

August 15, 1941

Some of the new personnel referred to in the above memorandum included Walter H. Van Voorhis, Instructor in Mathematics. He was promoted to Assistant Professor in May 1946; to Associate Professor in January 1947; to Professor in September 1949; and to Chairman, Department of Mathematics in July 1955. He remained at C.S.U. until his retirement in 1971. Miss Pauline Bloomquist, Instructor in Secretarial Studies, was promoted to Assistant Professor in September 1942; Chairman of the Department in April 1943; Associate Professor and Chairman in September 1950. She, too, remained at C.S.U. through to retirement in 1973. Chester W. Topp, Instructor in Mathematics, was promoted to Assistant Professor in May 1946; to Associate Professor in September 1949; and to Professor in September 1956. He received his Ph.D. from Case in 1951. He was transferred from Fenn to C.S.U. in September 1965. Emil Stefancic, Library Assistant, was appointed Acting Librarian for the year September 1948 to September 1949, then Assistant Librarian until September 1955, at which time he was made Librarian. He transferred from Fenn to C.S.U. in September 1965.

The 1941 Spring and Summer Programs in E.S.M.D.T. and C.A.A. totaled 16 courses and a total enrollment of 765 students. Ninety-one companies were represented in the student body. The overall cost of this instruction was $50,190.91.

It was reported in the Board Minutes of September 12, 1941, that Robert W. Schindler from the faculty at Case had been appointed Assistant Professor, Electrical Engineering, effective at the beginning of the Fall term. He was promoted to Associate Professor in June 1945, Professor in June 1952, and on the death of Professor Davis, to Professor and Chairman, Department of Electrical Engineering in July 1956. He transferred from Fenn to C.S.U. in September 1965 and resigned as Chairman in September 1968. Schindler, however, remained on the faculty as professor until retirement in 1973.

Dilley's resignation was accepted with considerable regret at this same September 12 meeting. He had accepted a position in the Personnel Department of The Cleveland Graphite Bronze Company. Herrick was assigned to Dilley's duties and served in the dual capacity as Director of Admissions and Director of Student Activities. He, likewise, took over Dilley's assignment as Secretary to the Fenn Board of Trustees.

The Athletic Committee of the faculty reported to the board on the need for an outdoor athletic field close to the College for intramural rather than inter-collegiate activities. The subject brought to the attention of the board that an exploration be made of the properties to the East and North of the Tower to determine whether an option could be exercised thereon to protect the College in case there would be plans for the future use of this property which would be detrimental to Fenn. The Executive Committee was given power to act.

Also at the September 12, 1941, board meeting, Dr. Thomas presented information about the enrollments for years 1937–1940 (see Table 1) and new building developments for the fall term.

Building Developments

During the summer the following building and equipment facilities have been obtained:

—A General Chemistry Laboratory providing locker space for 240 students has been made available in the Fenn Building on Prospect Avenue.

—The Home Economics Department has been moved to the 18th floor of Fenn Tower, where modern cooking and sewing laboratories have been developed.

—A Stress Analysis Laboratory has been made available and located on the 17th floor of Fenn Tower.

—Office space and equipment to provide for the Health Service of the college are now located on the 5th floor. ($500 to purchase equipment was provided by the White Trust Fund.)

—The three handball courts on the 8th floor are being made ready for drawing room and classroom use by opening the windows, painting the walls and purchasing the drawing tables and chairs required.

—Faculty offices for the E.S.M.D.T. staff will be located in the former kitchen on the 2nd floor, and other faculty offices have been made ready on the 17th floor.

Only the 15th and 16th floors yet remain for development. They are dormitory floors. It may also be possible at a later date to make use of the 19th and 20th floors and the solarium on the 21st floor.

It was also reported that Fenn's physical facilities were distributed in the following catagories:

Rooms	Number
For instruction purposes	84
For physical education purposes	5
For Faculty & Administration Staff offices	68
For general student services	6
For dormitory usage	60
Total	223

TABLE 1

A TABLE FROM THE REGISTRAR'S ANNUAL REPORT GIVING THE NUMBER OF DIFFERENT STUDENTS ENROLLED EACH OF THE LAST FOUR YEARS

Year	Day Bus.	Eve Bus.	Total Bus.	Day Engr.	Eve Engr.	Total Engr.	Day Arts	Eve Arts	Total Arts	Total Day	Total Eve	Total College
1937–38	176	1191	1367	380	1201	1580	109	–	109	665	2392	3057
1938–39	251	1109	1360	432	1169	1601	100	–	100	783	2278	3061
1939–40	263	1228	1491	450	1103	1553	118	–	118	831	2331	3162
1940–41	276	1400	1676	514	1589	2103	154	–	154	944	2989	3933*

* During 1941, 800 additional students studied in the E.D.T. programs, and 130 were enrolled in the C.A.A. program. These added to the 3,933 students in the regular courses of the college make a total enrollment of 4,863.

The final 1941 meeting of the Board was held November 25. Dr. Thomas reported the following:

> The evening Division, Co-op and E.S.M.D.T. students worked at 914 different places of employment. 54 of the firms had 20 or more employees registered at Fenn, with Thompson Products leading with 306, and American Steel and Wire second, with 208. There were 1470 E.S.M.D.T. students in 35 courses with a total of 55 class sections.
>
> Two representatives of the North Central Association made a routine inspection following two years of membership.

Chairman Fisher reported that the adjoining property to the north of the Tower fronting on East 24th Street was up for Sheriff's sale at approximately $24,000. Also, that the property east of the Tower, with an 83-foot frontage on Euclid Avenue and a depth of 400 feet had a sale price of $40,000. The matter was referred to the Executive Committee for study and recommendation.

Dr. Thomas felt the possibility of expansion needed more rigorous study; therefore, a joint committee was appointed by Chairman Fisher consisting of members of the Board of Trustees, faculty, and the administration "to study the situation and make a report."

The first two paragraphs of Dr. Thomas' Annual Report to the Board of Trustees for the year 1941 are as follows:

> In common with all institutions, Fenn College faced during the year 1941 many new situations and demands. The determination of policies and their translation into on-going and new programs of study, faculty and student personnel practices, plant facilities, budget requirements, and community relationships, constituted the major new concerns of the Board of Trustees, the administrative staff and faculty of the college. The report which follows summarizes the more significant developments of the year and indicates the emerging trends of the college.
>
> Although the volume of education provided by the regular programs constituted 90% of the volume of work done, yet participation in education related specifically to National Defense necessitated adjustments in almost all areas of the operation of the institution. The college sought to make its contribution to National Defense needs through both its on-going offerings and through special training given in cooperation with the Civil Aeronautics Authority and

the U.S. Office of Education in Engineering Defense Training programs. The location of the college in a large industrial center presented many opportunities to make contributions to the training and upgrading of National Defense workers.

Dr. Thomas went on to stress the following highlights of the year:

1. Many new areas were made ready for student and faculty use in the Tower.
2. All divisions of the College experienced their greatest enrollment of all time.
3. Forty percent of the Day Division Students came from outside the Greater Cleveland area.
4. There were increasing enrollments from western Pennsylvania and New York. There were 5 students from outside the United States.
5. Eleven full time persons were added to the faculty making the total 64. Twenty-one E.S.M.D.T. instructors were employed from outside the College.
6. Twenty faculty members pursued graduate study. Eight earned advanced degrees.
7. Publications by faculty members included three text books and 15 articles in professional journals.
8. 25 Faculty members were officers or served on committees of professional societies.
9. The School of Engineering revised its curricula to comply with E.C.P.D. standards.
10. The School of Business Administration instituted a three-year certificate program in Traffic Management in the Evening Division.
11. 113 degrees were conferred at commencement.
12. 2378 volumes were added to the library. The circulation increased 18% over the previous year.
13. Student personnel services increased many-fold. The Department of Testing and Guidance administered 7,300 psychological, aptitude, personality and other tests which were given to 865 people.
14. The Co-op Department experienced wonderful cooperation in placing 300 students in 24 different firms.
15. The average monthly earnings of the Co-op students were as follows:

School of Arts and Sciences	$76
School of Business Administration	$84
School of Engineering	$105

16. The College weekly newspaper, *The Cauldron*, for the second consecutive year was one of ten college publications to receive the coveted award, "All American Pacemaker."
17. The College physician made 1500 examinations and treatments of students.
18. 60% of the Day Division participated in intramural sports.
19. Seven new Trustees were elected to the Board.
20. Faculty salary scales were increased.
21. Gifts for capital purposes totaled $38,600.
22. The year's obligations for R.F.C. debt reduction, interest and planned developments on the Tower were met.
23. The income slightly exceeded expenditures for a successful 1941 budget operation.

A good year in many ways but 1941 now led to 1942 and the problems created by World War II and Pearl Harbor which adversely affected all institutions of higher learning. It is amazing that nowhere in the Board Minutes or other records on file is a reference made to Pearl Harbor.

The first Board meeting of 1942 was held on January 16. The first order of business was the reporting of the good news that Fenn was elected to membership in the Association of American Colleges (A.A.C.) at the Association's annual meeting in Baltimore on January 2.

The Advisory Committee of the North Central Association which recently reported to the Board of Review of the Association was comprised of the following members: John Dale Russell, Professor of Education and Dean of Students, Division of Social Sciences, University of Chicago; C. J. Freund, Dean of the College of Engineering, University of Detroit; and Chare E. Griffin, Dean of the School of Business Administration, University of Michigan. Their report pointed out eleven areas where Fenn College made splendid progress in the two intervening years between inspections. Their Conclusions and Recommendations were very enlightening and must have pleased Dr. Thomas and the Trustees tremendously:

> Fenn College is a distinctive institution, different in many respects from the typical college of its size. It has deliberately

adopted many unusual features in order to provide a unique type of service to its students. In the judgment of the Committee the institution has been successful in adapting its program to the needs of its environment. The Committee believes that Fenn College must be judged in the light of the fixed policy of the North Central Association, to consider institutions with regard to their success in achieving their individual objectives rather than with regard to their conformity to any standard pattern. On this basis Fenn College must be considered a successful institution.

The Committee believes that Fenn College is worthy of accreditment by the North Central Association. The institution has no more need for special supervision over its general program from the North Central Association than most of the colleges on the accredited list. The Engineering curriculums, however, have not yet been approved by the Engineers Council for Professional Development, although progress toward meeting the standards of that body is being made.

The Committee recommends that Fenn College be continued on the accredited list of the North Central Association without special supervision, but that a report be required five years hence with respect to the progress made in obtaining recognition for the engineering curriculums. It is further recommended that this special Supervisory Committee be discharged.

Strange as it may seem, the adaptation of Fenn's program to the needs of the environment was one of the adverse criticisms of the Review Committee of E.C.P.D. in the 1950s. This latter committee felt that Fenn over-adapted its program for the needs of the community and neglected needs of other United States geographical areas.

Dr. Thomas and Dean Nichols attended a National Conference of College and University Presidents on Higher Education and the War in Baltimore on January 3–4, 1942. A number of resolutions and recommendations were adopted which were quite interesting in comparison to the attitudes and loyalties of a number of college and university presidents during the war in Viet Nam. Following is a portion of the Preamble and one of the recommendations:

Preamble

In the present supreme national crisis we pledge to the President of the United States, Commander-in-Chief of our nation, the total strength of our colleges and universities—our faculties, our students, our administrative organizations, and our physical facilities. The institutions of higher education of the United States are organized for action, and they offer their united power for decisive military victory, and for the ultimate and even more difficult task of establishing a just and lasting peace.

All the needs to win a total war cannot be accurately defined now. Nor can total present and future resources of trained power be fully appraised. New areas of need and of potential service will develop as the months pass. We pledge our unstinted effort to meet these needs as they arise.

The surest and quickest route to victory is the full, energetic, and planned use of all our resources and materials. Where shortages may develop, both efficiency and the principles of equality require that the government take steps in advance to allocate resources to meet total needs, with a fair distribution of sacrifice. This is at present being done with material such as rubber, aluminum, and tin. It is clear that productive man power is also an area in which critical shortages are already evident.

Recommendation
Acceleration of Educational Programs

It is important to retain as far as practicable a degree of uniformity among colleges and universities in such matters as calendar changes and credits, while making adjustments in the interests of acceleration. Recognizing the increasing demand for men and women trained in technical skills and in professions essential to total war and the consequent need for preparing them for such service at the earliest possible time, and further recognizing that basic education should be completed prior to induction through Selective Service at the age of 20, we recommend that:

1. All institutions of higher education give immediate consideration to ways and means for accelerating the progress of students through such extension of the annual period of instruction and such adjustments of curricula as may be consistent with national needs and with educational standards, and as may be possible with available resources.
2. Desirable acceleration of programs of higher education should be accomplished without lowering of established standards of admission to college.
3. An immediate study be made by the National Committee on Education and Defense and the United States Office

of Education Wartime Commission of desirable articulation in the academic calendars of the secondary schools and the colleges to facilitate acceleration of total educational progress.

As the result of the above recommendation the faculty, under the leadership of Dean Nichols, submitted a plan to the Trustees at the January 16, 1942, meeting whereby the Day Division Co-op Program would continue, but in order to conform to the National Conference suggestion, it would be accelerated so as to permit the Day Co-op students to earn a degree in three years and eight months. This was effected by eliminating vacations, extra days for registration and final examinations. The plan called for five terms of ten weeks each year. Students who were granted permission to waive the co-op program could earn their degrees in two years and ten weeks. The faculty recommendation actually and amazingly decreased the usual annual faculty vacation period from four weeks to two. Freshmen were permitted to enter in June, September, and February. The board approved the program.

The April 7, 1942, Board Minutes carry the report that Clayton G. Hale, Chairman of the Board Personnel Committee, had accepted an assignment with the U.S. Navy in Washington. The board took action to retain him on the board as a member on leave.

In addition to the war training efforts in which the College was already involved a contract was executed with the U.S. Army Signal Corps to institute a program for 60 male students in which they would attend classes 44 hours per week for 24 weeks and would be replaced at the end of that time by another group of 60 students. The College was to house and feed these students. The program became effective Monday, April 13, 1942. With the start of this new program the over-all volume of war training courses provided by the College amounted to approximately thirty percent of the total volume. This caused concern and several Trustees feared that this additional expansion of Federal Government sponsored courses might weaken or lower the standards of the regular on-going college work. A special committee was appointed to advise President Thomas concerning additional requests for war training courses.

The 1942 Commencement was held Sunday, May 17, in the Euclid Avenue Baptist Church with Chairman Stilwell presiding. Ninety-nine graduates received diplomas. One of the graduates, Helen B. Lobdell, was one of three Fenn Alumni in 1956 who were the very first to receive the Fenn Alumni Distinguished Service Award. Since the recipients were selected by a committee of Fenn Alumni and Faculty, being amongst the first three awardees was a signal honor.

Another 1942 graduate, Emil Perout, became an Instructor in Metallurgy at Fenn in 1946, took graduate work for his M.S. at the University of Cincinnati from September 1, 1948, to September 1, 1949. Perout returned as Instructor in Metallurgical Engineering, but left in November 1950 to enter industry. He returned as Assistant Professor in April 1958, became Associate Professor and Chairman, Department of Metallurigical Engineering in September 1963. He did work toward his doctorate at Stevens Institute of Technology during the period June 14, 1965, to August 31, 1966, returning to The Cleveland State University in the same capacity as he left Fenn College.

As the fall of 1942 approached it was not only the students and faculty who were being called to the service of their country, but the Trustees as well. The Minutes of the Board meeting of September 4, 1942, show that in addition to Clayton Hale, Ellwood Fisher, Fred Baldwin, Edward Bartlett, and Jay Whitehair were temporarily located outside of Cleveland in some phase of war effort. Minutes of Board meetings were sent to these individuals. Likewise, copies of *The Cauldron* and *Alumni Bulletin* were sent to former students and alumni in the armed services.

The September 2, 1942, issue of *The Cleveland News* carried the following editorial:

War Training Tower

Opening of the school season marks another achievement by Fenn College. The last two floors of Fenn Tower have been remodeled as dormitories, so that the college will open next Tuesday with the entire 22 floors in use for the first time.

It was four years ago that the structure, built in pre-depression days for the Town and Country Club, but never occupied, was taken over by Fenn College. Nothing now remains of the original interior arrangement. Card rooms have become the Physics Department, the women's dining room a library and the bowling alleys a classroom for 60 Signal Corps men.

Fenn is proud of its job of reclamation, and we think it deserves to be. It is doubtful whether any other college is so completely devoted to training war workers. Fenn is headquarters for more than 7,000 students, all of whom are learning skills that the government needs.

Fenn had made many adjustments to comply with requested training for service in the armed forces. A résumé of this activity is as follows:

1. Junior Engineers Aide course for Signal Corps. Fenn received its second group of 60 men in this 24-week program of 44 hours per week of instruction in October 1942.
2. For two years the College had been conducting primary and secondary courses in Pilot and Glider Training under the auspices of the Civilian Pilot Training Authority. A new section of 30 students began September 7.
3. The College provided specialized training in Radio Instruction for over 500 persons. The Electrical Laboratories operated 15 hours a day for 7 days each week.
4. Courses designed to prepare men and women for specialized employment in War Production industries. No record of number of students was available.
5. E.S.M.D.T. courses which to date had registered a total of 4,410 students, second only to the University of Toledo among all colleges in Ohio, in the number of students authorized to receive instruction.

In fact, the volume of war emergency education which Fenn provided was among the largest of all colleges in the United States. Difficulties arose, however, in obtaining satisfactory funds from the government for proper maintenance and overhead charges. Loegler made a cost study (on a basis of student-hour cost) and accompanied Stilwell to Washington to obtain the proper apportioning of funds to these classifications. They were successful.

Dr. Thomas reported at the September meeting that $51,560 had been contributed by corporations and individuals to reduce Fenn's indebtedness which on January 1, 1942, had amounted to a total of $170,-000.

Dr. Sara Ruth Watson was appointed Instructor in English at the September 1942 board meeting. She had been teaching on a part-time basis for two years. She was promoted to Assistant Professor on January 1, 1945, to Associate Professor in September 1948, and to full Professor on September 1, 1956. She transferred to C.S.U. in 1965 and remained there until her retirement in 1970. Miss Watson was the daughter of a prominent Cleveland consulting engineer, Wilbur J. Watson. In addition to being an Elizabethan scholar she had many talents: a student of the violin and harpsichord, a contributor of many book reviews, Secretary of the Milton Society of American, and a member of the American Society for the Advancement of Science. She taught History of Bridge Engineering to the Civil Engineering students at Fenn, authored and collaborated with her father, her sister Emily, and in addition Dr. David B. Steinman on several books on the history of bridges and famous engineers. She was the only female ever to receive the History and Heritage Award of the American Society of Civil Engineering (1973).

The final board meeting for 1942 was held November 10. General strategy was planned for the year ahead. Problems involved included a decline of thirty percent in enrollment in the Evening Division and strong possibility of the drafting of 18 and 19 year-old males into the armed forces. In addition, the long hours being scheduled for industrial employees worked further hardships on the Evening Division. The strategy of the Administration and Faculty was first of all, to maintain the basic structure of the College, make adjustments where needed to meet war needs, but to sustain the core of the institution so that the structure of Fenn would be available for the years following the war emergency. This meant that entrance requirements, scholastic standards, conditions for graduation, and the Co-op plan be continued for those young men and women not called into service.

Other parts of the strategy included continuing the specialized course work for the armed forces, war production workers, and, as called upon, regular college courses for persons in uniform.

It was announced at this last meeting of the year that it appeared the income would exceed the expenses for the year by approximately $12,700 and that 57 gifts totalling $74,060 in capital funds had been received to help amortize the debt on the Tower and $20,000 borrowed from the YMCA.

Although Fenn, in 1942, had the largest enrollment to date in its history, over 7,000, it was a temporary condition due to the large special war training programs. In the Day and Evening Divisions regular college enrollments were declining because of the draft, which resulted in decreasing class sizes in the pre-war basic college credit programs.

This brought frustration to the Trustees as they entered 1943, a year which imposed much planning and the exercise of serious decisions, but at the end of the year the Administration and the Trustees made wise decisions and carried on the affairs of managing Fenn College superbly.

The first Board meeting for 1943 was held on January 11, at which time it was announced that Dr. John Dale Russell would be the guest speaker at the "All Fenn Family Night," January 13. His subject was "Higher Education in the Days Ahead."

The accelerated program begun in 1942 advanced the date of the first of three commencements to be held in 1943 to January 31. Ninety-one graduates received diplomas. Among the group were several who have distinguished themselves as Fenn Alumni and/or have been active in alumni affairs. Maurice J. Struchen was especially honored as one of the first three to receive the Alumni Distinguished Service Award in 1956. He was president of the C.S.U. Alumni Association in 1970 and at that time held the office of President of the Society National Bank of Cleveland. He was elected a Member of the Corporation of the Fenn Educational Foundation in 1969. He was elected a Trustee of C.S.U. in 1970 and Chairman, C.S.U. Board of Trustees in 1973. Donald E. Wise received the Alumni Distinguished Service Award in 1966, and was elected to the Advisory Committee of the Fenn Educational Fund in 1971. James P. Mason was president of the Fenn Alumni Association in 1955. Alberta M. Prasse and Alfred R. Deptula were members of the Fenn Faculty for a few years.

The Cleveland Foundation presented $2,500 from the Beardslee Trust Fund to the 1943 operating expenses of Fenn. Henceforth, to 1965, the year of the transfer of Fenn to the State, Fenn received a grant from this fund by vote of the distribution committee of the Cleveland Foundation.

In preparing the budget for the year 1943, highly desirable but not absolutely necessary expenditures were deleted. Many faculty and staff members were assigned to instruction and supervision of war training courses to relieve the regular operating budget. It was estimated that income from the Day and Evening Divisions would be approximately fifty percent of that in 1941, and the income from E.M.S.W.T. would drop from $181,000 to $150,000. Other income areas would approximate the 1942 income. With all these precautions the budget for 1943 was

$57,000 out of balance. The budget was approved by the board for a period of only sixty days because of so many uncertainties. If developments with government training programs faltered during this interim a special board meeting was to be called.

As of the January 11, 1943, Board meeting, all but $115,000 of the $540,000 to purchase and equip the Fenn Tower had been retired. The Board agreed to continue with the capital fund campaign to liquidate this debt, notwithstanding the problem of balancing the budget for the year. As of February 1943 the Board of Trustees of Fenn College was composed of the following:

Chas. J. Stilwell, Acting Chairman, The Warner & Swasey Company

Elbert H. Baker, Jr., Locke Machine Company

Leyton E. Carter, The Cleveland Foundation

Clarence L. Collins, Reliance Electric & Engineering Co.

James H. Coolidge, Thompson Aircraft Products Co.

Jacob D. Cox, Jr., Cleveland Twist Drill Co.

Cyrus S. Eaton, Otis & Company

James L. Myers, Cleveland Graphite Bronze Co.

Allen T. Perry, Harshaw Chemical Co.

John C. Sanders, Ernst & Ernst

Dr. Robert M. Stecher, City Hospital

Clarence M. Taylor, The Lincoln Electric Co.

Henry G. Tremmel, North American Fibre Products

Dr. Nathan E. Van Stone, The Sherwin-Williams Co.

George V. Woodling, Woodling & Krost

John David Wright, Thompson Aircraft Products Co.

OUT-OF-TOWN

Ellwood H. Fisher, Chairman, Major, Chicago Depot Quartermaster Corps

Fred C. Baldwin, Garfield, Daoust, Baldwin & Vrooman; Lieutenant, U.S. Army

Edward T. Bartlett, Cleveland Trust Company; 1st Lieutenant, U.S. Army

Harold H. Burton, U.S. Senate, Washington, D.C.

Clayton G. Hale, The Hale & Hale Company; Executive offices of James Forrestal, Under Secretary, Navy Department, Washington, D.C.

Eugene W. Kettering, Electromotive Corporation, LaGrange, Illinois

C. William Poe, The C.W. Poe Co.; National Administrator, War Production Board

Jay C. Whitehair, Whitehair & Whitehair; Lt. Colonel, U.S. Army

EX-OFFICIO

John S. Crider, YMCA

Joseph W. Meriam, YMCA

Dr. C. V. Thomas, Fenn College & YMCA

Shortly after the January board meeting Dr. Thomas was asked to provide the government with additional information regarding class and laboratory space, personnel, housing, and messing. On January 25, 1943, Air Corps representatives from Maxwell Field and Engineers from Cincinnati and Pittsburgh visited the College. They indicated that Fenn's instruction "bottleneck" was the Department of Physics and that the College would be limited to a maximum of 600 Army Air Corps students. The Administration actually learned that Fenn was selected for the Army Air Corps training program through an article in the Sunday, February 7, *New York Times* which carried a list of 281 U.S. colleges selected for the program by the Army, Navy, and War Manpower Committee. Fenn was one of fifteen Ohio colleges selected.

The selectees were assigned to Fenn from camps for five months of classes in English, Mathematics, History, Geography, Physics, and Physical Education. In addition, they were to obtain ten hours of flight instruction at the Cleveland Airport and also to be drilled in Military Tactics. The first contingent of 300 arrived Sunday afternoon, February 28, 1943, and the second group of 300 arrived April 1. The entire contingent was housed in the former Spencerian College building, at 3200 Euclid Avenue, which was obtained on a rental basis at $2,000 per month. It was estimated that two five-month groups of 600 selectees would take care of the necessary capital expenditures for the group. Messing arrangements were made in the third floor student lounge and in the grill room of the Tower with Mrs. Alice J. Lewis, Manager of the Food Service for Fenn, in charge. Dean Anders was assigned the responsibility and title of "Coordinator of the Army Air Corps Training Program."

The new Air Corps program was a most important adjunct in financially remedying an unbalanced budget for the year. This program together with four other war-training programs brought 3,250 special students to the campus. With this large volume of war-training effort it was difficult to maintain the basic structure of the College and the esprit de corps of the regular students. This was somewhat of a typical problem of the time within many colleges in the United States. The major dilemma was adequate class size and economic use of laboratories at the Junior and Senior class levels. This created a hardship in the retention of the professional ranks of specialized engineering backgrounds in the Faculty.

Herrick, Admissions Director, was officially appointed Secretary of the Board of Trustees at the March 23, 1943, meeting. Also at this same meeting authorization was given to house an overflow of Army Air Corps students in the banquet hall of the Masonic Auditorium at 36th Street and Euclid Avenue, and to use the residence on the Euclid frontage of the Spencerian barracks as a recreational center for the Cadets.

The June 15, 1943, meeting of the board was largely one of reporting of information. Some of the items include (1) The field on the northeast corner of 30th Street and Euclid Avenue, and the one immediately east of the Tower were graded for drilling by the Air Corps. The Cadets marched in formation to and from classes and the dining hall. (2) Each Air Corps student received ten hours of flight instruction. There were twenty-two planes and fifteen instructors assigned to the College. (3) The Infirmary on the fifth floor of the Tower was expanded and a 24-hour (3 shift) nursing schedule was put into effect. (4) The College had been given a rating of "very satisfactory" by Captain Gould, Acting Assistant Inspector General for the District. However, Captain Frye of the Intelligence Department gave the Fenn detachment a rating of "Exceptional." (5) Dean Anders reported the annual operation of the Army Air Corps program would approximate $520,000. (6) Captain Thompson, officer in charge at Fenn reported that "the Fenn contract had been lived up to as well or better than in any college in Ohio."

The second commencement for the year 1943 was held on June 30 in the First Methodist Church. Only twenty-four graduates were in this class as the result of accelerating the usual June group of seniors to graduation the previous January. Earle H. Daringer, who graduated magna cum laude, was elected to the office of President of the Alumni Association for the year 1947.

Although the country was in the midst of World War II and Fenn was strenuously bending its efforts toward providing knowledgeable man-power to aid in the winning of the war, the administration and faculty were far-sighted enough to start preparing for conducting extensive rehabilitation training programs for returning soldiers. Fenn already had such training experience following World War I, but it was on a vocational level at that time. Public Law No. 16, which was already in effect, provided for federal government subsidy of all academic expenses and limited subsistence expenses for a maximum of four years of college education. Dr. McCracken, a special representative of the U.S. Office of Education, upon visiting Fenn, recommended the Testing and Guidance facilities, the Health and Physical Education Service, the Co-operative Plan of Higher Education and the wide variety of educational services as especially suitable for consideration by the Administration for undertaking the government's program for rehabilitating World War II Veterans. The administration concurred in this recommendation and a faculty committee was appointed to prepare for engagement in the Veterans Program at the appropriate time.

In September 1943 *Fenn Newsletter* No. 1 was published. The complete copy of this newsletter is quoted.

Two individuals are mentioned in this *Fenn Newsletter* issue, namely: Alex C. Jamieson, who was decorated for valor in the Tunisian Campaign, and E. Philip Earl, who had just been engaged as an Instructor in Physics. Colonel Jamieson returned to Fenn June 10, 1953, as a Vocational Counselor in the Department of Cooperative Education and remained in this department following the transfer of Fenn to C.S.U. He also served for a time as Director of Student Guidance and Director of Counseling and Testing. He was elected to the Fenn Advisory Committee of the Fenn Educational Fund in 1973.

Philip Earl became Assistant Professor of Physics on February 15, 1946, Assistant Professor of Engineering Drawing in 1954, Associate Professor of Engineering Drawing in September 1955, and Associate Professor of Engineering Graphics in the Department of Mechanical Engineering in September 1963. He remained in this position following the transfer of Fenn to C.S.U. and retired from C.S.U. in 1972.

At the September 3, 1943, meeting the board discussed the policy relating to Fenn's participation in the rehabilitation of ex-service men

FENN NEWSLETTER

No. 1   Edited by Publicity Department, Fenn College, Cleveland, Ohio   September, 1943

FENN MEN ON THE BATTLE FRONTS

```
┌─────────────────────────────────────────┐
│              * IN MEMORIAM *              │
│                                           │
│   Robert Bigham           Otto Loesch     │
│   William Vanselow        Curtis Black     │
│                                           │
│           Killed in the service           │
│             of their country              │
└─────────────────────────────────────────┘
```

Decorated for Valor:

Thomas G. Monahan, Jr., Lt.j.g. USN, in Solomon Islands.
Don Billington, Lt.s.g. USN, U.S.S. Enterprise, Pacific.
Alex C. Jamieson, Major, USAAF, Tunisian campaign.

Missing in Action:

Robert C. Heller, 1st Lt., USAAF, 22,

> son of Mr. and Mrs. Paul W. Heller, 1362 Lakewood Avenue, Lakewood, in a raid over Gelsenkirchen, Germany. Lt. Heller was piloting a Flying Fortress. He had enlisted November 7, 1941 and received basic training in Texas. He was commissioned July 3, 1942. A graduate of Lakewood high school, he had completed two years at Fenn when he entered service.

Alexander R. Lukich, 2nd Lt., USAAF, 25,

> son of Mr. and Mrs. Peter Lukich, 10701 Clifton Road, in a raid over the Southwest Pacific. He was co-pilot of a B-25 medium bomber and had been in the Pacific area since July 20. Lt. Lukich joined the army air corps in January, 1941. A graduate of Brunswick high school, he received a scholarship to Fenn, where he studied Civil Aeronautics.

Decorated for Valor and Prisoner of War:

Carl G. Jones, 1st Lt., USAAF,

> awarded the Air Medal and three Oak Leaf Clusters. Lt. Jones, navigator on the Flying Fortress "Yankee Raider" was shot down in a raid over Bremen, Germany on April 17, 1943.   He has been interned at Stalagluft III and is reported uninjured and in good health.

Prisoners of War:

Francis J. Meyers, 1st Lt. USAAF, 22,

> son of Mr. and Mrs. Frank Meyers, 3457 E. 99 St., a bombardier on a Flying Fortress. Lt. Meyers was shot down in an attack over the Ruhr. A graduate of John Adams high school, he was a student at Fenn when he entered the service.

Kenneth L. Selway, 2nd Lt. USAAF, 23,

> son of Mrs. Bessie A. Shoer, 780 E. 91 St., shot down in the bombing of Kiel. A graduate of East Tech, he was a student at Fenn when he entered the army air force in April, 1942.

Outstanding Alumni:

    Frederick C. Grambo, promoted to Lt. Colonel, 364th Fighter Group, Army Air
        Drome, Glendale, California.
    Stanley J. Czyzak, promoted to Major at 26, 10th USA Air Force, A.P.O. 884,
        c/o New York.

Fenn Faculty in Service:

    Aaron L. Andrews, A.F. V-7, USNR, Physical Education Instructor,
        USNR Midshipmen's School, Johnson Hall, New York, 27, N.Y.
    William Avery, USA, Spanist Instructor.
    Burl H. Bush, Lt.s.g., USN, Dean of School of Engineering,
        8709 Sundale Drive, Silver Springs, Md.
    Bruce T. Brickley, Ensign USNR, Assistant Director of Admissions,
        c/o Armed Guard Center, S. Brooklyn, N.Y.
    William T. Christian, Pvt. USA, Associate Professor of English,
        Battery A, 55th F.A., Building 6219, Camp Roberts, California.
    Jay Collins, 2nd Lt. USA, (Staff) Publicity and Promotion.
    Donald C. Fabel, Lt. Col. USA, Chairman Department of Mechanical Engineering,
        2701 Pershing Avenue, Davenport, Iowa.
    Benton E. Jones, USA, Instructor of English, Air Training School.
    Harry D. Morris, Lt. USNR, College Physician,
        Medical Corps, V (S), Navy Yard, Charleston, S. C.
    Emil Stefancic, Assistant Librarian,
        Air Cadet Barracks, Louisville, Ky.
    Chester W. Topp, Ensign USN, Mathematics Instructor,
        Ft. Schuyler, N.Y.
    Walter R. VanVoorhis, Lt., Assistant Professor of Mathematics,
        P.A.A.F., Pecos, Texas.

* * *

Fall Enrollment

    Regular college enrollment, day and evening, will probably be half the 1942 figure when classes start on September 7, according to Dr. Walter K. Goetsch, Registrar.   Last September Fenn had 492 college day students and 1,162 college evening students.   In addition 512 were enrolled in the Technical Institute and 4,200 in ESMWT. The total enrollment was 6,366.*

New Faculty

    Alva B. Crobaugh to Assistant Professor of Economics. Held same position at Alabama Institute of Technology, Auburn, Alabama. A.B. 1925 and A.M. 1926, Leland Stanford University. Married. Will live at 2636 St. James Parkway, Cleveland Heights. Brother of Dr. C. J. Crobaugh.

    E. Philip Earl to Physics Instructor in ATS. Formerly part-time (evening) at Fenn and full-time Lakewood high school. M.A. Western Reserve University, B.S. Case School of Applied Science. Married, has three children. Lives at 15297 Lanning Avenue, Lakewood.

    Thomas Dwyer to Assistant Finance Director. Formerly with Cincinnati Retail Credit Company. B.B.A. Fenn, 1935. Married, has one daughter. Lives at 8017 Decker Avenue.

    Dorothy Green to Assistant Librarian. Formerly in library departments of Western Reserve University and Hamilton College. M.A. Ohio State. Lives at 8820 Euclid Avenue.

---

*Does not include 840 ATS students this year.

PROBLEMS OF THE POSTWAR WORLD

By Dr. Clyde J. Crobaugh

It is now apparent that the winning of a military victory over the Axis is more certain and much easier than the solution of the postwar problems that are bound to arise. The military objectives are definite, the measures for carrying them out are exact and known, but the postwar problems are uncertain and not subject to precise planning.

Probably most postwar problems fall into two groups: first, those that are of a broad nature and concern nations as a whole; second, those that are specific and which relate to particular industries or individual companies.

Some of the over-all postwar problems may be briefly described as follows:

There is the problem of the declining rate of population growth which has set in particularly in the industrial nations. One of the most significant statements in the famous Beveridge report is found on page 154 and states - "With its present rate of reproduction, the British race cannot continue; means of reversing the recent course of the birth rate must be found." On the other hand, the populations of the oriental countries are increasing and will remain a problem after military victory. Given the same technology, in the long run numbers will decide world issues.

There is also the problem of providing full employment after the war. Nearly sixty million people are gainfully employed at the present time because of the urgency of the war and the government market for goods. What will happen when the government no longer buys fifty per cent of the commodities produced? Will there be a market for these goods that will keep the people fully employed? Technology has made it possible for us to turn out an abundance of goods.

One other broad problem is of a fiscal nature. It concerns the matter of taxation and the public debt. Full employment and a high level of national income will be needed after the war to meet the heavy taxes and to pay the fixed charges on the public debt.

Many of the specific postwar problems concern particular lines of businesses. Some companies face a serious reconversion task; that is, changing back to peacetime production. Other companies have less of a reconversion problem, but are faced with the job of rebuilding sales organizations abandoned because of the war.

Business in general is concerned with the problem of government control. How long after the war will the wartime restrictions remain? When will business be able to return to more of the free enterprise system? These are but a few of the vital postwar problems.

* * *

Editor's Note: The Fenn newsletter will feature in each issue a faculty member currently rendering an outstanding public service. This issue features Dr. Crobaugh, chairman, Department of Marketing, who has become an outstanding authority in the field of postwar planning and problems. His courses are attended by many company executives. As the result of his work many inquiries come to Fenn regarding Dr. Crobaugh's course outlines and bibliographies. "Sales Management" featured Dr. Crobaugh's postwar marketing course in a recent issue. He was recently elected a director of Northwestern Ohio Chapter, American Marketing Association.

DEAN NICHOLS APPRAISES CURRENT DEVELOPMENTS

* * *

As Fenn College faces the school year 1943-1944, our major and immediate purposes might be variously stated.   Certainly among them would be the following: to help <u>win the war</u> — to <u>maintain basic programs</u> of on-going education, both as a service to those attending now and as a nucleus for expansion in the days ahead — to help <u>rehabilitate</u> returning <u>service men</u> — to identify emerging needs and to <u>plan educational programs</u> and procedures designed to meet them — not opportunism in the narrow sense, but educational adjustment and reconstruction in the broader and more basic sense — to <u>reduce</u> the <u>debt</u> of the college so that funds will be available for further <u>development</u> and <u>expansion</u> <u>after</u> the war.

The fulfillment of these and other objectives should enable the college to <u>keep intact its faculty</u> and provide challenging work, as nearly related to our respective fields as is possible.

Fenn Today — A Few Items

<u>The Army Air Force Trainees</u>: On August 1, Fenn <u>quota increased</u> to 750... More than 25% of the instructional load being carried by regular faculty... Otherwise schedules would have been reduced by declining enrollments... Administration costs, building operation and maintenance expenses are charged to the ATS program on proportional basis... In items of over-all operation, <u>this program</u> <u>more than replaces the training services formerly needed for our regular day</u> <u>student body</u>... <u>Fenn</u> College is already <u>more widely</u> and more favorably <u>known</u> as a result of this program.

<u>Rehabilitation Training</u>: General Marlin of the U.S. Veterans Administration at Brecksville has sent sample contract forms to Fenn College to cover the cost of placing returned service men in training... The <u>Veterans Administration will</u> <u>pay</u> the prevailing tuition rates for these students - that is, $250 per school year... Two students have already applied for admission... This activity may take on significance in terms of the number of students involved in the day division before the school year we are now entering comes to an end... There is every indication that the <u>Government will be</u> most <u>generous</u> in its provisions for the continued education of men returning from service.

<u>Faculty Roster for the Fall Includes the Following</u>: In the regular college and ATS, 70... Part-time regular college and ATS, 100... Total, 170... This does not include more than 100 additional persons teaching one or more ESMWT courses either on or off the campus.

<u>Fall Commencement, September 26</u>: Originally it was decided to have two commencements - one in the fall and one in the spring. The fall commencement was originally set for November 15, at the end of the fall quarter. It develops that a number of students soon to complete their graduation requirements will be called to the service before that time. At the request of the seniors, fall commencement has been moved ahead to September 26. It will be held in the First M.E. Church at 3:30 in the afternoon and will be preceded by a <u>reception in</u> the <u>Panel Room</u>.

We move into the new school year with evidence that <u>Fenn's training</u> <u>facilities</u> will be <u>used to</u> the <u>maximum</u> and that the means for keeping our budget in balance will be available. — J. C. Nichols, Dean.

PRESIDENT THOMAS REVIEWS WORK, AIMS OF FENN TRUSTEES, ADMINISTRATION

* * *

Fenn College, in common with all other institutions of higher learning, has faced a dual responsibility during the last two or three years. The college had the obligation to make those adjustments which would enable it to participate in the war effort and also to effect the type of organization and operation that would maintain the essential structure of the college during the war period. This dual responsibility has been a chief concern of the Board of Trustees and the Administration of the college.

Beginning in 1939, Fenn contacted the U. S. Office of Education in Washington about the services that would be expected of colleges if and when war occurred. Fenn was one of the first colleges to participate in what is now known as the ESMWT Program. During the last school year Fenn ranked first among the colleges in Ohio in the volume of ESMWT training. Likewise, when the armed forces determined that a limited number of institutions of higher learning would be used for the training of men in uniform, Fenn took steps to be included among the institutions selected for such training.

Teaching, housing, feeding and providing medical care to a large number of Army Air Corps trainees necessarily has brought to the college many new problems. That the program has been effectively administered is evidenced by the increase in the quota of Fenn from 600 to 750 trainees. The institution was told that Fenn was asked to increase its quota because of its superior rating among the colleges participating in the training.

To meet the organization and administration demands of the Army Air Corps program, and to maintain the essential structure of the college necessitated the definite assignment of administrative responsibilities. Dean Joseph C. Nichols was asked to give major attention to the maintaining of the on-going college, and Dean Paul R. Anders was given responsibility for administering the Army Air Corps program.

Again, in common with other institutions, Fenn has faced during the last year new problems in balancing its operating budget. The services to the armed forces, careful management of the on-going college program, and skilful administration by the Finance Director, have enabled the college to maintain a balanced budget. A recent analysis and forecast indicates that the operating budget of the college for the year 1943 will be approximately $890,000 and that it will be in balance.

The Board of Trustees has been constantly in touch with the on-going operations of the college and has participated in the determination of policies. Through the combined work of the Trustees and the Administration, the capital indebtedness of the college has also been greatly reduced. Only $80,000 of the $250,000 due to the RFC because of the purchase of Fenn Tower remains to be paid. Likewise, tax authorities have received to date all but $11,000 of the $136,000 which the college assumed when the Tower was purchased. It is hoped that all indebtedness of the college may be cleared during the immediate months ahead. — C. V. Thomas, President.

Off-Campus Program

At its peak last year the off-campus program included 40 classes for 1,000 people in 15 plants. More than 2,500 persons were enrolled during the full school year. With the fall program just getting under way, James W. Griswold, Field Director of ESMWT, announces a new course has been started at Pump Engineering for 15 girls employed in the drafting room. They have a classroom inside the plant and attend classes three hours per day, three days per week. An inspection course has just been concluded at Nottingham Equipment Works, General Electric Co. for 14 girls. Four of them have already been promoted to final inspection work. Ten girls have just started a mechanical drawing course at Fenn and are receiving pay from these companies: Steel Improvement and Forge,   Pump Engineering, Iron Fireman and Leese-Neville Co.

Wartime Changes

No faculty members are reported to have continued their studies during the summer vacation.   Some worked part-time in war industry, others taught the aircrew trainees.   Professors Joseph Sutliffe (Chemical Engineering), George V. Parmelee (Mechanical Engineering), Virgil D. Hales (Mechanical Drawing), and Robert W. Schindler (Electrical Engineering) taught Physics; Robert Leininger (Chemistry) taught Mathematics.

Three outstanding members of the Engineering faculty who formerly taught day courses full-time are now working days in war industry and teaching evening courses.   They are C. D. Williams, Professor of Structural Engineering, now engineer and stress analyst at Fisher Bomber Plant;   Oscar Hoffman, Associate Professor of Structural Engineering,   now analyst at Cleveland Pneumatic Tool; Ernest C. Harris, Structural Engineering instructor, now structural engineer at Fisher Body.

25 to 30 engineering students this fall will be men who were attending other colleges but are now engaged in war work in Cleveland and are enrolling at Fenn to continue their engineering education.   Several are from Purdue.

A pat on the back to Dr. Willard Poppy, head of the Physics Department, which furnished twice as much instruction to army aircrew students as any other department.

Personals

Ruby and Robert Leininger accepting what they thought was an appointment in California, but being sent to Springfield, Mass....   Florence Boticki, secretary in War Training Office,   resigning to enter war industry at Marquette Metals... Dean M. R. Robinson returning from the State Committee meeting of ESMWT institutional representatives at Columbus...   M. C. Herrick, Director of Admissions, up to his neck in applications this week, taking a ribbing from   Ensign Bruce Brickley, who writes that he is having less trouble in the Middle East.

The Fenn Newsletter will be issued monthly
or at six-weeks intervals.   Please send or
phone information now for October issue.
Suggestions and helpful criticisms welcomed.
                    - Wayman Thomasson
                      2200 Prospect
                      Phone PR 2200

under the auspices of the U.S. Veterans Bureau. The following action was approved:

> The Board authorized the college to enter into a contract with the Rehabilitation authorities to accept their students, with the understanding that the college has final authority to accept or reject individual applicants and that the contract calls for no specific number of students.

At this same meeting the subject of appropriate dormitory facilities for girls was discussed. The New Amsterdam Hotel was not proving satisfactory, and furthermore, it was limited in capacity for future enrollments. Action was taken to rent the former Women's Club, a residence adjacent to the Masonic Temple at 3635 Euclid Avenue. Through a later gift for furnishings from Mrs. Phillip E. Bliss, the girls,' dorm was named Bliss Hall.

There were 25 graduates in the third class to be graduated in 1943. Richard Zimmerman of this class was later honored in 1961 as a recipient of the Alumni Distinguished Service Award. Frank J. Gallo later joined the Fenn Faculty in November 1946 as Instructor in Structural Engineering. He became Assistant Professor of Structural Engineering September 1951, Assistant Professor of Civil Engineering and Engineering Mechanics in December 1952, and Associate Professor of Civil Engineering and Engineering Mechanics in September 1962. He held this rank following the transfer of Fenn College to the State of Ohio. He was active in the Cleveland Section of the American Society of Civil Engineers.

Fenn Newsletter No. 2, issued in October 1943, carried the following news items:

Fenn Men in Service of Their Country

Killed: Robert H. McMurray, 1st Lt. USAAF August 21, somewhere in China.

Robert P. Cseplo, Sgt., August 23, Battle of Munda, New Georgia Island.

John Cooley, Pfc., Air Transport Command, September 5, plane crash in Missouri.

Missing: Harold H. Johnson, Pilot USN, in Aleutian area. Awarded Air Medal for distinguished Service in Aleutian Campaign.

Prisoner: Robert C. Heller, 1st Lt. USAAF previously reported
missing, now held in Germany.

Registration for the Fall Quarter was as follows:

	Day Division	Evening Division
Arts and Sciences School	60	191
Business Administration School	44	500
Engineering School	73	520
Total	177	1211

Probably half of the Day Division enrollment was Freshmen; therefore, the War-Training courses were particularily welcome in making possible classroom teaching to keep the Day Division Faculty occupied, although in most instances the subjects were not of their usual professional specialities.

"Marion D. Cooper was appointed Assistant Professor, Electrical Engineering. He formerly served in the Research Department, General Electric Company and taught part-time in Fenn's Evening Division. Received his B.S. in E.E. from the University of Wisconsin in 1908, and his M.S. in E.E. from Case School of Applied Science in 1939." Professor Cooper was promoted to Associate Professor in July 1946, and Professor in May 1948. He retired August 31, 1963, but taught on a part-time basis for both Fenn College and C.S.U. to June 1966.

"Mrs. Edwin L. Battle is Hostess in Panel Hall. The atmosphere and conduct in the lounge now reflect her personal charm and friendliness." Mrs. Battle remained as student Hostess in Panel Hall until the mid-fifties.

For some unknown reason the Board of Trustees did not meet from September 3, 1943, until January 12, 1944. Inasmuch as 1944 apparently was the year of adjustment between war and post war conditions, it seems most appropriate that a new chapter be started with that year.

VI

*I am not willing that this discussion should close
without mention of a true teacher.
Give me a log hut, with only a simple bench,
Mark Hopkins on one end and I on the other,
and you may have all the buildings, apparatus
and libraries without him.*

James Abram Garfield, 1831–1881.
Address to Williams College Alumni,
New York, December 28, 1871.

The YMCA was in the throes of a fund-raising campaign during 1943, and it was reported at the January 12, 1944, board meeting that should the campaign be a success Fenn would stand to receive a pro-rated share sufficiently large to clear all capital debts, including an operating debt of $92,000 due the YMCA resulting from loans made by the Y to the College for machine shop training during the Post War I period for which the federal government did not reimburse the College. It was hoped that in addition to liquidating these debts sufficient working capital would be available so that the College would not have to borrow from the Y during the first eight months of each year.

Dr. Thomas reported at the February 17, 1944, board meeting that the Army Air Corps Training Program was on the wane, and that 136 men would be departing each month, which would bring the terminal date for the program sometime in June. Letters were sent to Senators Burton and Taft to endeavor to extend this training program despite possible criticism from the public and press against any effort to keep government war-projects existing beyond the time of need.

Considerable discussion ensued at this same meeting concerning the pros and cons of initiating Day Division Technical Institute (T.I.) train-

247

ing for returning veterans. Dr. Thomas felt that, if Fenn did not offer this type of training, Ohio State University would open a special branch for it in Cleveland. A joint Trustee-Faculty Committee was appointed to study the advisibility of entering into a T.I. day program.

The proposed budget for 1944 ($418,374) failed to balance by $79,-913. Chairman Stilwell requested President Thomas to restudy the budget with his staff for areas in which estimated expenditures could be reduced, and he asked the Trustees to study ways in which the estimated income might be increased.

Dr. Thomas presented to the Board the following outline "Fenn College—The Long View and Adjustments for the Post War Period."

I. *The Long View*
Basic Assets

1. The college has demonstrated its ability to make adjustments to emerging educational needs with the consequent public expectancy that Fenn will be a leader in making such adjustments.

2. The college has had experience in conducting a program of education that includes many elements of the types of education that will be needed in the years just ahead, such as—

    a. Curricula that combine a liberal education with a vocational cutting tool;

    b. Provision for work experience as a part of the educational process;

    c. Processes for the testing and guidance of the individual student;

    d. A faculty that has taught mature students as well as younger high school graduates;

    e. Curricula "streamlined" in part to meet the demands of mature students.

3. The college has a physical plant unique and strategically located that includes classrooms, laboratories, library, office, physical education and dormitory facilities.

4. The institution has academic status because of accreditation by the North Central Association.

5. The Board of Trustees are vitally interested in the college and have the relationships and influence to help it meet its opportunities.

6. The institution has a close relationship with the industrial and business life of the city through cooperative, evening and E.S.

M.W.T. instruction; through gifts to the capital needs of the college; through special services of the faculty to companies; and through interchange of ideas between the faculty and industry and business.

7.   Much good will exists within Cleveland, along with a considerable understanding of the college outside of the city.

8.   The need and potential demand in Cleveland for the type of education Fenn provides will far exceed the enrollment of the college in the period before the war.

Some Unmet Needs

1.   Teaching and administrative loads must be lightened.

2.   Additional operating income must be secured from endowment or other sources.

3.   A classroom-auditorium building should be provided.

4.   Additional laboratory, classroom and library facilities must be obtained.

5.   Working capital to cover inventories and provide for "peaks and valleys" in income should be secured.

6.   A continuous study of curricula and course offerings to meet changing educational needs and opportunities is always essential, but most necessary now.

7.   Likewise alertness to and use of more effective processes and methods of education are required, such as—visual aids and other developments.

The development, present status and future opportunities of Fenn College are embodied in "Hats off to the past and coats off to the future."

II.   *The Year 1944*

1.   1944 is a year of adjustment from War to Post War conditions.

2.   The points of view the college has toward making these adjustments are:

   a. It is gratified that it has had opportunity to participate in the war training program, which has enabled the institution to render essential training service;

   b. It has placed the college in the "main stream" of higher education in the United States;

   c. The college is grateful that the developments of the war make reductions in training possible. Fenn in common with other institutions and individuals hopes above every other concern for the quick termination of the war;

d. The announcement of the gradual reduction and discontinuance of the Army Air Corps training makes adjustments possible over a period of months rather than overnight;

e. The termination of the Army Air Corps training program will result in the analysis, planning and action required to place the college in position to meet its post war opportunities and responsibilities.

3. *Some Advantages Fenn Has in Making Adjustments*:

a. If all Army Air Corps training and E.S.M.W.T. training were eliminated, the volume of education being provided at Fenn during 1944 would equal that of 1935. Included in the ongoing education program are: 200 DAY students and 1200 to 1500 EVENING students.

b. In addition the present Fenn program includes: A large volume of E.S.M.W.T. education, the continuing operation of the Army Air Corps program during the first few months of the year; the use of the college for training men returning from the armed services has begun and it is evident that Fenn will be asked to provide an increasing volume of education in this field; a growing volume of special services to industry for which the college is reimbursed.

4. *Steps in the Program of Adjustment*

An analysis of the educational programs to be conducted and number of students involved is being translated into instruction and faculty requirements. These requirements will then be analyzed in terms of the income and expense involved.

The steps necessary to meet the instruction and financial requirements of 1944, and to maintain and develop the college for the post war period will be determined after they are studied.

Both the welfare of the institution and of individuals will be included as adjustments are effected. Information about adjustments and plans as they are determined will be provided to members of the organization.

The adjustments necessary in 1944 and the building necessary for the years ahead will require the suggestions, cooperation and assistance of all the members of the organization—Trustees, faculty and administrative staff—both in their respective fields of responsibility and in relation to the entire institution.

—C. V. Thomas

February 3, 1944

The first of two commencement convocations in 1944 was held at the Euclid Avenue Baptist Church, Sunday, April 16. There were 56 graduates in the class of which 36 were from the School of Engineering, 11 from the School of Arts and Sciences, and 9 from the School of Business Administration.

Chester J. Kishel of this class graduated with a B.S. in Mechanical Engineering. He obtained his B.S. in Industrial Engineering from Fenn in 1947, and joined the faculty as Assistant Professor of Mechanical Engineering in June 1948. He received his Ph.D. in Engineering Administration at Case in 1959. He became Associate Professor in September 1954 and Professor in September 1962. Kishel served as a consultant for Michigan State University for two years (1963–1964) at the University of Sao Paulo, Brazil in charge of the installation of a large computer and the training of the faculty in its use. He transferred to the faculty of C.S.U. in 1965.

The joint Trustee-Faculty Committee on the advisibility of organizing a Day Division Technical Institute through its chairman, Leyton E. Carter, reported its deliberations at the April 24, 1944, board meeting. Again much discussion ensued following which the board passed unanimously the adoption of the report and authorization to institute a Day Division Technical Institute. This action was based largely on the premise that there would be a great number of returning veterans, not qualified for college work, but in need of the type of education at the technical institute level, and there would be a need for certificate holders of such a program in Cleveland's industries. At the same time it was recognized that Fenn's Engineering Programs must eventually be accredited by the E.C.P.D., and that Fenn's reputation as an institution of collegiate standing must not be jeopardized by the organization of a Day Technical Institute.

At this same board meeting Dr. Thomas reported that Fenn had already been requested to aid in the testing, guidance and counseling of returning veterans. Joseph Kopas, in charge of the vocational testing and guidance program at Fenn and as a consultant at several industries devised a program for the Trustees' study and discussion. Chairman Stilwell appointed a joint Fenn-YMCA committee to work with Kopas to prepare a plan for presentation to the Veteran's Administration. The joint committee reported at the July 5, 1944, meeting of the board, recommending the establishment of a Testing and Counseling Center mainly for returning veterans. The recommendation was accepted on a six-month trial basis with the understanding that the Center was to be self-supporting. This was the beginning of a long association with the Veteran's Administration in its testing program.

Dr. Thomas informed the board that Fenn had received an Award of Merit for its part in the 53rd College Training Detachment Air Crew (Army Air Corps).

Elbert H. Baker, Jr., Chairman of the Finance Committee also reported that $1,300,000 had been received to date in the YMCA Capital Campaign. This represented about ninety percent of the goal. Of this amount $180,000 were designated for Fenn College. It was voted unanimously to pay the R.F.C. $20,000, representing the remaining debt on the purchase of the Fenn Tower. It was also voted to postpone payment of the $92,000 owed the Y from the World War I Machine Shop class activity in order that the College meet existing needs growing out of World War II conditions.

The Board meeting of October 11, 1944, proved to be a very full and active one. Following are a number of the items considered:

General information presented by Dr. Thomas:

SUMMARY OF THE YEAR 1943–1944
Number of Students

	Men	Women	Total
College	822	785	1607
Technical Institute	406	105	511
Army Air Forces	1404	—	1404
E.S.M.W.T.	?	?	3090
			6612

Faculty (including Administrative Staff)

	Men	Women	Total
Full Time Basis	59	14	73
Part Time Basis	183	11	194
	242	25	267

Operating Costs (Calendar Year 1943)

Administration and General Expense	$ 59,180
Resident Instruction	167,051
Library	9,146
Plant Operation and Maintenance	82,242
Capital Outlay, Plant and Equipment	6,544
Bond and Other Debt Retirements	76,608
Interest on Loans	8,772
Scholarship and Student Aid	6,022
Residence and Dining Halls	34,874
Auxiliary Enterprises	34,733
Federal Contract Courses	589,177
Total	$1,074,349

Outlook for Enrollment for the Present Year

Day College	250
Evening College	1500
E.S.M.W.T.	1500
Day Technical Institute	50
	3850

Seventy-eight returned veterans were enrolled in the Day and Evening Divisions for the Fall Term.

$283,000 were allocated to Fenn from the YMCA Centennial Campaign. The $20,000 debt on the Tower and the $92,000 debt to the Y were paid. The remainder was used for building alterations and other developments.

Eugene W. Kettering and C. William Poe resigned from the Board of Trustees, having taken up residence out of Cleveland.

Cyrus S. Eaton and Dr. Nathan E. Stone were not renominated to the Board because of their inability to attend meetings over the past two years.

The second commencement for 1944 was held at Trinity Cathedral on December 3. Although there were only fourteen graduates in this class, two members, Clyde H. Haynes and Robert C. Waltemade, served as presidents of the Fenn Alumni Association, Haynes in 1950 and Waltemede in 1953.

The following letter from Charles B. Henderson, Chairman of the Board, R.F.C., Washington, D.C. closes the chapter on the procurement and financing of the Fenn Tower, certainly an admirable milestone in Fenn's history resulting from the leadership of Dr. Thomas.

The final board meeting for the year 1944 was held on December 22. It was reported that Dr. M. B. Jenks was assuming the duties as Acting Dean of the School of Arts and Sciences because Dean W. R. Goetsch was leaving for an 18-month study at the University of Iowa. Dean J. C. Nichols took over the administration of the Department of Education, formerly under the guidance of Dean Goetsch. Dr. W. A. Patterson became Acting Registrar. These duties were also under Dean Goetsch's direction.

Dr. Thomas advised the board that he had received a letter from Henry G. Tremmel stating that the trustees of the Foster (Claud H.) Trust Fund had agreed to contribute $10,000 to Fenn for specific use in expanding the equipment facilities of the Production Laboratory, the area occupied to be dedicated henceforth and known as the Claud H. Foster Mechanical Hall. The board took action in accepting the gift and agreeing to the terms inasmuch as there was some veiled information that there would be a future contribution from the same source. This proved to be the case, as indicated later.

The newly established Personnel Development Testing Laboratory had tested and counseled more than a thousand individuals, mostly veterans, by the end of the year 1944.

The following new Trustees were elected at the December 22, 1944, board meeting:

Vernon Stouffer (remained a Trustee to a term ending in 1962)
Richard S. Huxtable (resigned in 1951)
Herbert P. Ladds (remained a Trustee to his death, April 6, 1963)

RECONSTRUCTION FINANCE CORPORATION
WASHINGTON

December 16, 1944

Mr. C. V. Thomas, Esquire
President, Fenn College
Cleveland, Ohio

Dear Mr. Thomas:

Mr. Thralls recently advised me that you have liquidated the obligation arising out of the purchase of the Cleveland National Town and County Club for the use of Fenn College.

I want to take this occasion to congratulate you and the Board of Trustees for the fine progress you have made and to wish you and Fenn College continued success in your work.

With kind personal regards, and wishing you compliments of the season.

Sincerely yours,

Charles B. Henderson

The last item in the Minutes of the final 1944 board meeting concerned a request from the faculty that a joint Trustee-Faculty Committee be appointed to "Study the objectives of the College with special reference to ACADEMIC PURPOSES." The generation gap between 1944 and the early 1970s displays a difference in Trustee thinking and the resolution of such a request. The December 22, 1944, Minutes resolved the faculty request as follows:

Mr. Stilwell indicated that this sounded like a policy-forming committee which seemed to be the purpose of the "Institutional Purposes Committee" (a Board committee). He further indicated that his personal viewpoint would be that policy-forming is the business of the Board of Trustees, and that while he would not oppose such a committee, he would prefer that the Faculty act by reporting to the Board.

This would have been "front page" news in 1970.

The year 1945 proved to be another difficult year for Fenn; some problems were similar to those of past years and some were entirely new and different. It certainly was not an easy year for President Thomas. One of the problems was lack of enrollment of regular Day Division students. The returning veterans and 4Fs joined by an increasing number of women students were estimated at 400 for 1945. This is compared with 900 in 1941. The veterans, however, were on a four-quarter per year basis (not co-op), resulting in an increased tuition income from these students. Another problem encountered was a deficit budget for the year amounting to $48,763. Nevertheless there was such a full agenda at the first board meeting for 1945 that the budget item was postponed until the next meeting.

Fred C. Baldwin, John Sanders, Jay C. Whitehair and George V. Woodling were re-elected to six-year terms at this first Board meeting.

Inasmuch as there had not been a meeting of the Fenn Corporation for several years, legal counsel advised that one be held to "recognize, ratify and approve a Board of Trustees consisting of individuals with terms of office." Accordingly a meeting of the Fenn College Corporation was held prior to the Board meeting on February 17, 1945, at which the following Trustees and terms of office were set forth:

> Trustees whose terms expire in 1951
> Fred C. Baldwin
> John C. Sanders
> Jay C. Whitehair
> George V. Woodling
>
> Trustees whose terms expire in 1950
> Edward T. Bartlett
> Harold H. Burton
> James L. Myers
> Vernon B. Stouffer

Trustees whose terms expire in 1949
  Allen T. Perry
  Chas. J. Stilwell
  Henry G. Tremmel
  Dr. Nathan E. Van Stone

Trustees whose terms expire in 1948
  Jacob D. Cox, Jr.
  Clayton G. Hale
  Ellwood H. Fisher
  Richard S. Huxtable

Trustees whose terms expire in 1947
  James H. Coolidge
  Clarence L. Collens
  Herbert P. Ladds
  Dr. Robert M. Stecher

Trustees whose terms expire in 1946
  Elbert H. Baker, Jr.
  Leyton E. Carter
  Clarence M. Taylor
  John David Wright

Ex-Officio Members of the Board of Trustees
  The President
  The Treasurer
  and the General Secretary of the
  Young Men's Christian Association [of Cleveland]

Legal action was also taken at this meeting to "ratify and approve all action previously taken by the Board of Trustees and Executive Committee of the Corporation." The following resolution was unanimously passed:

> RESOLVED that the members of this Corporation hereby ratify and approve all action previously taken by individuals serving this Corporation as members of the Board of Trustees, as members of the Executive Committee and any other committee of the Corporation, including action taken by any individuals who are no longer serving the Corporation in such capacities.

At the Board meeting, following the Corporation meeting, the following officers were elected for the year 1945:

Ellwood H. Fisher, Chairman
Charles J. Stilwell, Vice Chairman & Acting Chairman
John S. Crider, Treasurer
M. C. Herrick, Secretary
Dr. C. V. Thomas, President

Considerable time was spent in discussing the report of the Committee on By-Laws, chaired by James H. Coolidge. The report was referred back to the committee for further study. Again following long deliberation by the board at its March 14, 1945, meeting the By-Laws were approved for adoption as modified.

The board authorized the establishment of a Recognition Committee (to be designated Section 15 of Article VII of the Constitution of the General Faculty) composed of the President of the College, a Trustee, and a faculty member (elected by the faculty). The committee was to "study the nature of memorials, awards and honors which the College may appropriately establish or bestow at commencements and upon other occasions in recognition of service to the college, the community, or society." The committee was empowered to choose at least one person to be honored at each commencement, beginning May 1945, to determine the nature of recognition to be given and take all necessary steps in arranging for its bestowal.

The deficit ($48,763) budget for 1945 was finally approved at the March 14 Trustee meeting. Stilwell, Acting Chairman, suggested that the Finance Committee study possible ways in which income could be increased or expenses decreased. Jacob D. Cox, Jr., indicated that as a member of the committee, he did not see any way expenses could be decreased.

John David Wright, in reporting for the Special Financial Campaign committee, indicated that at least $20,000 was in sight toward balancing the 1945 budget.

Stilwell appointed the following Standing Committees of the Board for 1945:

Standing Committees of the Board of Trustees

Executive: Charles J. Stilwell, Chairman
Clarence L. Collens
James L. Myers
Clarence M. Taylor
John D. Wright

Finance: James H. Coolidge, Chairman
          Elbert H. Baker, Jr.
          Richard S. Huxtable
          Herbert P. Ladds
          John C. Sanders
Personnel: Clayton G. Hale, Chairman
            Allen T. Perry
            Dr. Robert M. Stecher
            Vernon B. Stouffer
            George V. Woodling
Institutional Leyton E. Carter, Chairman
Purposes: Henry G. Tremmel

Fenn was experiencing considerable difficulty reconciling settlement with the government on the contract with the U.S. Air Force. The government proposed to pay Fenn $582,107.14, whereas the College submitted its actual costs for the program as $619,524.42. The $37,417.28 difference resulted in the following areas:

Library	$ 3,874.97
Plant operation	7,218.19
Administration	26,324.12

An all-day meeting was held on April 10, 1945, in the office of Robert F. Bingham of Thompson, Hine and Flory, legal counsel for the College. Two U.S. Air Force representatives, Trustees John C. Sanders, Elbert H. Baker, Jr., Clarence M. Taylor, Dr. C. V. Thomas, plus Arthur P. Loegler and Dean Paul R. Anders were in attendance. The contracting representatives of the U.S. Air Force claimed to be bound by the provisions of Manual M-102 and other Army directives rather than the contract itself. The manual was issued seven months after the contract was executed between Fenn and the Air Force.

One of the considerations in the original contract was that all reductions in actual costs below estimates and rates must be passed on to the government. Because of good management and organization Fenn was able to effect a savings of $57,361.55 in feeding the Air Force students (under the original contract rate), but this savings had to be passed on to the government. The government, however, refused to pay the excess costs in the library, plant, and administration operations even though Fenn could prove these actual costs by recognized accounting procedures. No profit was being sought—just actual out-of-pocket costs. When the College representatives asked that the officer who had been in charge of the program at Fenn be produced to testify that he had not only authorized an increase in the number of showerheads, but had ordered the College to install them, the Review Board admitted that they knew of his whereabouts, but refused to call him to testify or disclose his location to the College representatives.

The meeting closed with the Air Force representatives' promise to secure a ruling on the Contract Settlement Act of 1944 which authorized the contracting agency of the government to provide full and just compensation to the contractor irrespective of agency directives. The A.F. representatives felt the act did not apply to "Training Contracts."

Several months later, on August 16, 1945, C. V. Thomas, A. P. Loegler, P. R. Anders, J. C. Sanders, and R. F. Bingham met with the Joint Army and Navy Board for Training Unit Contracts at the Pentagon, Washington, D. C. The Board was chaired by Dr. Robert B. Stewart of Purdue University. Dr. Thomas again emphasized that Fenn was not claiming the contract price as stipulated by the original contract but was asking for reimbursement only of its costs. Nor was Fenn seeking to obtain a balanced budget for the year. Even if the Air Force paid Fenn the $37,417.28, Fenn would experience a deficit year.

The records show that Dr. Stewart was antagonistic and prejudiced and that he had already made up his mind. He happened to be one of the college representatives who prepared Manual 102 (after Fenn had signed its original contract). There was considerable confusion in the discussion prompted by Dr. Stewart. Finally, Dr. Thomas stated "that he could not understand why the government was not bound on the original contract if Fenn was, and why the government, for its convenience, could refer to and use the terms of the original contract but could refuse to let Fenn do likewise." Dr. Stewart asked Dr. Thomas if he wanted the record to show that remark. Dr. Thomas said he did, for it was how he felt and what actually was happening. The negotiations over this non-renegotiable pre-manual contract ended with the chairman of the Review Board stating that Fenn's only recourse would be to refuse to agree to the findings, in which event the Fenn file would be placed at the "bottom of the pile and they would see to it that it would not be reached for further review for ten years."

The final outcome of Fenn's negotiations with the Air Force was made in October 1945. Fenn received $6,441.32 additional allowances from the government, which resulted in Fenn subsidizing the Air Corps Training Program by an amount of $31,054.06.

The Minutes of the meeting of the Personnel Committee of the Board held April 30, 1945, include the following statement recommended by Chairman Hale:

> The Personnel Committee would like to make a point to the Board of Trustees that this particular committee, perhaps more than any other of our standing committees, feels the need for clarification of our long term institutional purposes in order that teaching emphasis may properly accomplish such major objectives as may be prescribed by the Trustees.

Dr. Thomas indicated at this same meeting that the Trustees needed to face the necessity and rightness of continuing to secure funds for annual operating budgetary needs. Because of the service which Fenn renders through its Co-op program, industries should feel they are partners in this higher education endeavor and provide financial support annually to maintain this important service. Dr. Thomas referred to this as "living endowment" as the College lacked money endowment.

Fenn's Trustees on May 25, 1945, unanimously agreed to purchase land adjacent to the Tower facing 300 feet on East 24th Street, with a depth of 83.25 feet, for $18,000. It was listed on the tax duplicate for $38,340. The immediate need for this property was for parking.

Word was received from the U.S. Maritime Commission that one of the new ships being built for the Commission was to be named the *S.S. Fenn Victory*. This article by Charlotte Rood in the March 2, 1966, *Nite Shift* (the Evening Division student newspaper) gives a splendid history of the ship:

FENN IS STILL AFLOAT
by Charlotte Rood

Fenn was one of the selected colleges during World War II to have a Victory ship named after it. The ship was a 10,800-ton cargo carrier built by the U. S. Maritime Commission and launched at Richmond, California, on June 20, 1945. This was a Victory type of ship which was equipped with a turbine gear power plant rated at 6,000 h.p. and was designed to be much faster than the Liberty type which it replaced.

The Maritime Administration is responsible for maintaining the National Defense Reserve Fleet which is comprised mainly of WW II-built Liberty and Victory ships. These vessels are preserved to prevent any shortage of shipping capacity that might hamper American military operations in any part of the world. Sometimes they are needed and used to relieve shortages of shipping capacity caused by sudden rises in the demand for commercial shipping services.

These Victory ships were named for American colleges and universities having a student body of more than five hundred. The order of assignment followed the chronological order of the dates of founding. As an interesting side note, State universities were ineligible to have a ship named after then, because only schools with one main word in its name would be short enough and would sound right.

Fenn Victory was built by Permanente Metals Corp. at Richmond, California, and was used in WW II, Korea, and in civilian needs of transporting American foreign aid cargoes in 1945–49 and 1956–57.

Gifts from the college to a ship were wanted at the time of launching and could include plaques, books, phonographs and records, and games. A plaque with an appropriate history of the college and a picture of the Tower was planned by Mr. Herrick and Dean Anders; the 50–100 books for the library: Mr. Nichols; Victrola records: the Cauldron Staff; and the collection of games and game equipment: Mr. Woodling.

When it was learned a ship bearing the name S. S. Fenn Victory would definitely be launched, it was felt certain things should be done. The following inscription on parchment with a picture of the school was mounted in a glass frame aboard the ship.

Fenn College
Founded in 1881
in
Cleveland, Ohio
A truly American institute, democratic
in ideals and tradition, dedicated to
truth and to service.

A copy of the plaque can be seen in the Archives Office.

Dean Bush of the Engineering School (then Lt. Cmdr. Bush) was present at the launching. A lady member of the Canadian Parliament christened the ship with a bottle of champagne.

A letter from the Master, G. E. Melanson, under date of August 4, 1945, was received by President Thomas thanking the college for their gifts and adding the plaque had been placed in the officers' salon. He mentioned the gifts had been in constant use and the Fenn Victory was one of a few ships that had received such an abundant number of articles recently.

Since September 16, 1957, S. S. Fenn Victory has been laid up at the Mobile, Alabama, Reserve Fleet site. Her home port is still San Francisco.

On December 9, 1965, the Navy's Military Sea Transportation Service asked Maritime to reactivate twenty-five more Victory ships from the reserve fleet because of increasing requirements of our commitment in Southeast Asia. Since that time, the S. S. Fenn Victory is again serving her country in the same fine traditions that Fenn College served her community.

In addition to Dean Bush, Lts. Henry W. Bricker, William C. Fuller, and Karman Duchon (with his wife Edna, also a Fenn graduate) were in attendance at the launching.

On December 12, 1965, Mr. Nicholas Johnson, Maritime Administrator, wrote to Dr. G. Brooks Earnest, President, Fenn College, that on December 9, 1965, the *S.S. Fenn Victory* was reactivated and committed to service for S.E. Asia cargo requirements.

As an aside, the *S.S. Fenn Victory* collided with and sank the *S.S. Diamond Knot*, August 13, 1947, in the entrance to Puget Sound. Damage to *S.S. Fenn Victory* was $13,000—damage to *S.S. Diamond Knot* was 154 cases of canned salmon plus ship—about $5,000,000. The canned salmon was later salvaged.

The nineteenth commencement of Fenn College was held the evening of May 25, 1945, at the Euclid Avenue Baptist Church. Professor Charles T. Holman of the University of Chicago was the speaker. There were 39 graduates; Charles R. Day was President of the class. Day became News Director of Radio Station W.G.A.R. and later, Regional Public Relations Director, Ohio Bell Company, was a recipient of the Alumni Distinguished Service Award in 1962. He was an Alumni Trustee (1958–1961) of Fenn College and was elected a Member of the Corporation of the Fenn Educational Foundation in December 1969.

The 1945 Fall enrollment as reported at the October 10 Board meeting was as follows:

		Fall Enrollment	
		1945	*1944*
Day Division		288	191
Evening Division:	Arts & Sciences	325	247
	Business Administration	804	575
	Engineering	717	567
	Total	2134	1580

	Day Div.	*Evening Div.*	*Day & Eve. Div.*
Percentage increase	51%	33%	35%

Returned Veterans enrollment:	Day Division	93
	Evening Division	244
	Total	337

It was reported that Fenn's Veterans testing activity was the largest in this area of Ohio.

The Federal government set about to dispose of its surplus office furnishings and classroom and laboratory equipment, with an office located in each state. Ohio's was located in Columbus. Dr. Vasily Prian, Acting Chairman, Department of Mechanical Engineering was the College's designee as contact man with the faculty and the Columbus office. Here again, Claud H. Foster offered $10,000 for the purchase of surplus Mechanical Laboratory equipment if it was the latest and best of its type.

By the date of the final board meeting for 1945 on December 28, there were 190 Veterans in the Day Division and 310 in the Evening Division for a total of 500. The Personnel Development Department had tested and counseled 2,123 Veterans and 347 other individuals from industry. The total income from this operation was $56,658 for 1945. The Department also tested all Fenn students, absorbing an expense approximating $7,000. It was a profitable department for the College. Dr. Thomas reported that Fenn's Testing and Guidance Center for Veterans had grown to be the largest in the United States, with New York University second.

On December 16, 1945, Justice Harold H. Burton of the Supreme Court of the United States offered the College thirty-nine volumes entitled *Definitive Writings of George Washington* covering everything Washington wrote except his diaries. The board accepted this gift at the December 28 meeting with thanks and appreciation for the gift and for the many years of faithful service which Justice Burton rendered the College. Dr. Thomas reported also that the Army Air Forces Training Command had recently offered Fenn College the opportunity to apply for an Army Air Force ROTC Unit. The Trustees requested the administration obtain further details.

Dr. Thomas also reported that the College was within $3,500 of a balanced budget for the year and that he expected it to be balanced by year's end.

The resignations from leaves of absence of Deans Burl H. Bush and Walter R. Goetsch were accepted with regret. It was reported that Bruce T. Brickley, Emil J. Stefancic, and Donald R. Tuttle had returned from service. Dr. William A. Patterson was appointed Registrar. Dr. Major B. Jenks was appointed Dean, School of Arts and Sciences, and Max B. Robinson was appointed Dean, School of Engineering.

Since this was the first meeting attended by Chairman Ellwood H. Fisher after he returned from serving his country, he congratulated and thanked the Trustees for their faithful work and service to Fenn during the war years, and reported that he was very happy to be "back on the job."

The board met as the Corporation on February 15, 1946, and voted the recommendations of the Nominating Committee, i.e., Baker, Carter, and Taylor be re-elected to a six-year term to expire in 1952; that Vollmer W. Fries be elected to the same term; and Robert F. Bingham be elected to fill a vacancy existing on the term ending in 1951.

At the board meeting following the Corporation meeting, the following slate of officers was elected:

Charles J. Stilwell, Chairman
Clarence M. Taylor, Vice Chairman
Ellwood H. Fisher, 2nd Vice Chairman
Meriam C. Herrick, Secretary

The following resolution was then unanimously adopted:

That this Board express its great appreciation and gratitude for the long, highly efficient and loyal service of Ellwood H. Fisher as Chairman of this Board, and its sense of greater confidence in facing the future because of Mr. Fisher's willingness to continue service on this Board.

It was reported that the Guidance Department, because of its increased testing and counseling activities, had grown to forty full-time employees.

To assist in closing the 1945 fiscal year slightly in-the-black a total of 131 companies and individuals gave $58,200 to the College.

By the time of the Board Executive Committee meeting on April 26, 1946, Dr. Thomas pointed out that because of lack of physical space and numbers of qualified faculty members, Fenn could admit only about 55% to 70% of the qualified students applying for admission. The Committee requested the following:

> 1. That the College should explore the possibilities of securing additional facilities and personnel to assist in meeting the present higher educational demand, with the understanding that such facilities secured be of a temporary nature.
>
> 2. That a long term plan be developed for the College which would include the study of the size of enrollment which the College should plan to have, the personnel that would be required, the buildings, laboratories and other facilities that would be needed, and the financial resources that would be necessary.

This two-part request kindled a lengthy discussion that a study be made on the conditions under which Fenn might acquire the property to the east of the Tower and whether there were any buildings in close proximity which might be utilized temporarily for academic or gymnasium purposes.

By March 1946 there were 1,159,761 college students in the United States of which 417,324 were Veterans. The U.S. Office of Education forecast that by fall there would be 1,850,000 college students of which 700,000 would be Veterans.

The demand for college admissions in Ohio had also increased and it was estimated admissions would be as high as 99,000 by the fall of 1946. Only 72,000 students could be accommodated in Ohio's 63 colleges. College enrollments had increased two and one-half times each twenty years since 1900. Only Fenn College and Ohio State University in Ohio used their plants on a 14-hour day basis. The need for additional faculty members was great.

These national and state statistics caused much concern to the Trustees of Fenn, and they looked for answers to the reports of their two requests made on April 26 to the Executive Committee. They realized that with the influx of Veterans and the demand for additional faculty throughout the state, Fenn's position would become increasingly difficult on a competitive basis, especially with the salary schedule existing at Fenn which became effective in April 1945.

The Personnel Committee of the Board, chaired by Clayton G. Hale, studied the manpower and salary structure of the College. A special committee composed of Fisher, Wright, and Stouffer accepted the assignment to visit buildings near the campus with the view of temporary usage.

Following several meetings and a detailed comprehensive study, the Personnel Committee recommended to the Board on May 3, 1946, that a new faculty salary schedule be adopted as follows:

		Existing Scale
Academic Deans	$4,500 to $6,000	— — —
Professors	3,500 to 5,000	$3,200 to $5,000
Associate Professors	3,000 to 4,500	2,700 to 4,000
Assistant Professors	2,700 to 4,000	2,400 to 3,300
Instructors	2,000 to 3,300	2,000 to 2,700

In the past year twenty-two new members had been added to the faculty. Eight members had returned from service to their country and four more were returning within a month. However, seven former members who had been in service submitted their resignations to Fenn. The full-time faculty totaled seventy-two at the time of this board meeting and the Administration Staff nine, with a total annual payroll for these eighty-one members of $275,357. Action was taken to increase this amount annually by $25,183, effective July 1, 1946.

Fisher reported that Baker, Cox, and he had visited the League House to determine whether it could be used for housing students at Fenn. It was estimated that a fair purchase value would approximate $85,000 and that it would cost about $35,000 to put the entire building into good operating condition, including making ready for use 24 suites for married couples and 98 for single men. One of the drawbacks to financing this venture was that the building, located between Prospect and Carnegie Avenues, was in the path of the proposed Innerbelt Freeway. After much discussion the matter of the purchase of the League House was tabled.

Another building in the neighborhood was considered at this same meeting: the Towne Club on the south side of Prospect Avenue about a block east of the YMCA. It was formerly the K. of C. Gymnasium. During the war years the Navy leased the building. It had the advantage of providing Fenn with the type of physical facilities which the College needed, especially with its growing enrollment. Such needs were, auditorium space, basketball and other field house type of space, space. for music, dramatics, and recreation such as billiards, ping-pong, and bowling. Fisher had visited the Towne Club and was very enthusiastic about its possibilities of providing Fenn with intercollegiate and intramural athletic space. He had, however, discovered that the owner was asking exorbitant rent for the structure and that it, too, was in the path of the proposed Innerbelt Freeway. Nevertheless, the following action was taken: "That the officers of the college be authorized to negotiate for a lease of the Towne Club for a sum not to exceed $7,500 gross per year for a term of ten years with such renewal terms as may be available." This action was rescinded at the June 18, 1946, meeting of the Board when it was voted to inform the owners of the Towne Club that the College was not interested in acquiring the property under the conditions submitted by them.

Dr. Thomas reported at the May 3, 1946, board meeting that the spring term enrollment included 737 Day Division and 2,810 Evening Division students of which 1,998 or 56% were Veterans. Also, that an analysis of employees of the 1071 firms represented in the Evening Division showed the following with employees attending Fenn:

> 6 firms had more than 50 employees
> 11 firms had from 25 to 49 employees
> 17 firms had from 15 to 24 employees
> 81 firms had from 5 to 14 employees

The 1946 commencement was held on May 24 at the Euclid Avenue Baptist Church. Dr. Kirtley Mather, Head of the Geology Department of Harvard University gave the address. Fifty-six students graduated.

Action was taken at the Board Executive Committee meeting of June 18, 1946, to engage an architect for advice on removing the original first floor stores and windows on the Euclid Avenue frontage of the

Tower in order to provide for additional interior space for office and bookstore supply needs and to enhance the appearance of the building.

The enrollment forecast for the fall of 1946 presented a problem concerning space and the number of faculty. A special Board Executive Committee meeting was called for August 8 at which authorization was given to the Administration to erect two quonset huts (24 x 60 ft. each) directly north of the Tower at a total cost of $17,375 including heating, lighting, and blackboards. Each quonset hut was divided so, all told, there were four classrooms, each 24 x 30 ft.

Dr. Thomas reported at the September 23, 1946, meeting of the board that the fall term enrollment included 1,220 Day Division and 3,600 Evening Division students and that the faculty had grown to 102 day and 120 part-time evening. One-third of the day faculty had been appointed in the last seven months. An additional available elevator in the Tower had to be put into service to accommodate the expanded enrollment. Also the Administration was authorized to rent suitable space for basketball practice.

During the Summer, James W. Griswold, Head of the Department of Cooperative Education, resigned to become the Business Officer at Park College. Dean Robinson, who had been serving as Dean of Engineering, was appointed Head of the Department of Cooperative Education. Dr. Sholto M. Spears, a Civil Engineer and a former Lt. Col. in the Army was appointed Dean of Engineering. The office of Junior Dean of Engineering (filled by Professor Tolar) was discontinued, and Professor Tolar was asked to devote his full time to the Department of Mathematics.

Once again, Fenn was experiencing accelerating growing pains. It needed the following: development of its laboratories to meet instructional requirements; an auditorium and additional classrooms; an enlarged library; more land for expansion of physical facilities; accreditation by The Engineers' Council for Professional Development, The Association of American Universities, and The American Association of Collegiate Schools of Business and Finance (both operating and capital). Accordingly a Committee on Long Term Planning was appointed at the September 23, 1946, Board meeting specifically for the planning for physical needs.

The following constituted the 104 administrative officers, faculty, and staff of Fenn College and their professional status as of September 1, 1946.

Name and Position

Paul R. Anders, A.B., Dean, School of Bus. Administration

Robert B. Auld, M. Ed.,†* Instructor, English

Richard G. Bauman, B.S.,* Instructor, Ind. Chem.

Arlene Bernon, B.A., B.L.S., Cataloguer, Library

Pauline Bloomquist, B.A.,† Chairman, Dept. Sec. St., Asst. Prof. Sec. Studies

Arthur P. Boblett, B.S.,* Instructor, Mathematics

Bertha L. Bottle, Hostess, Panel Hall

Eleanore J. Bouquard, B.B.A., Vocational Counselor

Bruce T. Brickley, M.A., Asst. Dir. of Admissions

Marie E. Center, A. H.,† Instructor, Sec. Studies

William Cherubini, Ph.D.,† Instructor, English

Marion D. Cooper, M.S., Associate Prof. Elec. Eng.

Blake Crider, Ph.D.,† Chairman, Dept. Psych., Professor, Psychology

Clyde J. Crobaugh, Ph.D., Chairman, Dept. Mktg., Professor, Marketing

William C. Davis, B.S., Chairman, Dept. E.E., Professor, Elec. Eng.

Frank DeMarinis, Ph.D.,† Asst. Prof. Biology

Thomas L. Dotson, M.A.,† Vocational Counselor

Thomas N. Dwyer, B.B.A., Asst. Finance Director

E. Philip Earl, M.A.,† Asst. Prof. Physics

Russell R. Ehrhart, A.B.,* Industrial Coordinator

Donald C. Fabel, M.S.,† Chairman, Dept. Mech. Eng., Professor, Mech. Eng.

John A. Froebe, LL.B.,†* Instructor, Accounting

Geraldine Gallagher, M.A.,* Instructor, English

James E. Ginther, M.A.,* Instructor, English

Rose E. Goodman, M.A.,* Instructor, Mathematics

Archie B. Gould, Instructor, Mech. Eng.

Clifford L. Graves, B.A., Vocational Counselor

Gerald U. Greene, Sc.D., Chairman, Chem. & Met. Eng., Professor, Chem. & Met. Eng.

---

* Denotes individuals who were engaged by the College in 1946.

† Designates those individuals, which total 33 or about 33%, who were still with Fenn College in 1965, at the time of transfer to C.S.U. and joined C.S.U. for at least one year.

V. Richard Gulbenkian, M.A.,† Instructor, English

Raymond R. Gutzman, M.S.,* Instructor, Mathematics

Virgil D. Hales, Chairman, Dept. Eng. Drg, Assoc. Prof. Eng. Drawing

George D. Hall,* Instructor, Chem. & Met. Eng.

Earnest C. Harris, B.C.E.,† Chairman, Dept. Struc. Eng., Asst. Prof. Struc. Eng.

Elijah H. Hartley, B.S.,* Vocational Counselor

Meriam Clay Herrick, A.B.,† Director of Admissions, Dr. Student Activities

Major B. Jenks, Ph.D.,† Dean, School of Arts & Sci., Chairman, Dept. Hist. & Pol.

Millard L. Jordan, M.A.,† Chairman, Dept. Sociology, Professor, Sociology

Karl David Kelly, M.S., Assoc. Prof. Mathematics

Elvan E. Kintner, M.A.,* Instructor, English

Joseph S. Kopas, M.A., Dir. Dept. Pers. Develop., Professor, Pers. Develop.

George A. Leech, M.A.,† Vocational Counselor

James A. Lemon, M.A.,* Instructor, Mathematics

Arthur P. Loegler, B.S., Director of Finance

Phyllis J. Lowndes, B.B.A., Instructor, Sec. Studies

Hyman Lumer, Ph.D., Chairman, Dept. Biology, Assoc. Prof. Biology

Lee A. Marshall, M.A.,* Vocational Counselor

Walter B. McClelland, B.B.A.,* Instructor, Accounting

Frank H. McGar, Jr., B.A.,* Instructor, Mathematics

John G. McGrew, Ph.D., Chairman, Dept. Economics, Assoc. Prof. Economics

George McKinnon, Jr., B.S., Instructor, Physical Ed.

John W. McNeill, M.A.,† Chairman, Dept. Management, Assoc. Prof. Management

Foster T. Miller, M.A.,* Vocational Counselor

William T. Moorman, B.S.,* Asst. Prof. Mech. Eng.

---

* Denotes individuals who were engaged by the College in 1946.

† Designates those individuals, which total 33 or about 33%, who were still with Fenn College in 1965, at the time of transfer to C.S.U. and joined C.S.U. for at least one year.

Harold E. Morgan, Ph.D.,† Assoc. Prof. Physics

G. Hamlin Mouck, B.S., Professor, Accounting

Joseph C. Nichols, Ed.D., Dean of the College, Chairman, Dept. Education

Ambrosia C. Noetzel, M.S., Chairman, Dept. Home Ec., Assoc. Prof. Home Ec.

Edward Noyes, Ph.D.,* Asst. Prof. History

David G. Parker, B.B.A.,†* Instructor, Economics, Asst. in Bus. Admin. Office

Lad A. Pasiut, Ph.D., Assoc. Prof. Chem. & Met.

William A. Patterson, Ph.D.,† Registrar

Jane Pease, A.B.,† Instructor, Women's Phys. Ed.

Dwight L. Penney, B.S.,†* Instructor, Eng. Drg.

Emil Perout, B. of Met. E.,†* Instructor, Metallurgy

Edwin A. Pfeil,* Instructor, Mech. Eng.

Willard J. Poppy, Ph.D., Chairman Dept. Physics, Professor, Physics

Alberta M. Prasse, B.S., Instructor, Mathematics

Randolph C. Randall, M.A.,† Chairman, Dept. English

Raymond Ray, B.S. in Ed., Asst. Prof. Physical Ed.

Kenneth L. Raymond, B.L.S., Librarian

Ruby V. Redinger, Ph.D., Asst. Prof. English

Richard J. Reed, B.S.,* Instructor, Mech. Eng.

Nicholas R. Rimboi, B.S.,† Director, Tech. Institute & Eve. Eng. Admissions

P. J. Robechek, A.B., M.D.,* College Physician

Max B. Robinson, M.E., Dean of Cooperative Education

Robert W. Schindler, M.S.,† Assoc. Prof. Elec. Eng.

Gene Schott, B.S., R.N.,* College Nurse

Julius J. Schreiber, M.A., Vocational Counselor

Eunice Shanaberger, B.S.,* Dean of Women

George B. Simon, Litt. B.,† Assoc. Prof. Speech

Walter G. Sites, M.A., Asst. Director Dept. of Personnel Development

---

* Denotes individuals who were engaged by the College in 1946.

† Designates those individuals, which total 33 or about 33%, who were still with Fenn College in 1965, at the time of transfer to C.S.U. and joined C.S.U. for at least one year.

Richard B. Small, M.A.,†* Instructor, Mod. Lang.

Sholto M. Spears, Ph.D.,* Dean, School of Engineering

Emil J. Stefancic, B.L.S.,† Asst. Librarian

Joseph W. Sutliff, M.A., Assoc. Prof. Chem. Eng.

H. Walter Sykes,* Instructor, Eng. Drawing

Horace R. Thayer, S.B., M.S.,* Asst. Prof. Mech. & Mat.

Demetrios E. Theodore, Ph.D.,†* Asst. Prof. Economics

Cecil V. Thomas, M.A., LL.D., President

Theodore V. Thomas, B.A.,* Vocational Interviewer

Blanche Hall Tolar, M.A., Assoc. Prof. Mathematics

Marion B. Tolar, M.S., Chairman, Dept. of Math., Professor, Mathematics

Frank J. Tomich, M.A., Assoc. Prof. Mod. Lang.

Chester W. Topp, A.M.,† Asst. Prof. Mathematics

Donald R. Tuttle, Ph. D., Assoc. Prof. English

Walter R. Van Voorhis, Ph.D.,† Asst. Prof. Mathematics

Joseph J. Velky, B.S.,* Instructor, Chemistry

William von Reichbauer, LL.B., Asst. Prof. Accounting

Urban F. von Rosen, C.P.A., Chairman, Dept. Acctg., Professor, Accounting

John W. Walter, B.B.A.,* Asst. in Admissions Dept.

Samuel Ward, M.S., C.E., Chairman, Dept. Mech. & Mat., Professor, Mech. & Matls.

Sara Ruth Watson, Ph.D.,† Asst. Professor, English

Bertram W. White, B.A.,* Vocational Interviewer

Homer E. Woodling, M.A., Chairman, Dept. of Health and Physical Education, Professor, Health & Physical Education

Dr. Thomas was thoroughly liked by all and held the esteem and high respect of all his associates. This was one reason that there were few personnel problems at Fenn during his regime with the Y and the College. There was one problem which flared up, however, in 1946. Dr. Hyman Lumer, Chairman of the Department of Biology, was the subject of some unfavorable publicity in the summer of 1945 in a publication called *League for Justice*, published by one John P. Moran,

---

* Denotes individuals who were engaged by the College in 1946.

† Designates those individuals, which total 33 or about 33%, who were still with Fenn College in 1965, at the time of transfer to C.S.U. and joined C.S.U. for at least one year.

Director. The statement alleged that Dr. Lumer was the Chairman of the Educational Committee of the Communist Party of Ohio. This statement was refuted immediately in a letter from Dr. Lumer to Moran. Another similar statement, however, occurred in the November 1946 issue of the same publication. After several conferences with Clayton G. Hale, Chairman of the Board Personnel Committee, and President Thomas, Dr. Lumer chose to resign from the College rather than take legal action against Moran because of the published allegations or to assist the College itself in taking the matter up with the post office department over the possible misuse of the mails. It so happened that not too many years following this episode, Dr. Lumer was ascertained to be affiliated with the Communist Party of the United States.

The need for expansion was raised again at the board meeting held on December 12, 1946. Ellwood Fisher reported that two properties were available, one with a 155-foot frontage on Euclid Avenue, extending through to Chester Avenue and the other, known as the Warter's property, adjacent to the Tower with an 83.25-foot frontage on Euclid Avenue extending north to the eastern extension of the north Fenn College property line. The former had a sale price of $90,000 and the latter $50,000. The board voted to proceed with the purchase of the Warter's property financed over a twenty-year period.

The following new appointees were approved at this same Board meeting:

> George Smith, Assistant to Dean of Engineering and Assistant Professor, Electrical Engineering
> Vance Chamberlin, Assistant Professor, Marketing
> George Srail, Assistant Professor, Speech and Dramatics
> Alvin Rood, Assistant Professor, Mathematics
> Robert Truelsch, Instructor, Engineering Drawing
> Alfred Deptula, Instructor, Mechanics
> Frank Gallo, Instructor, Structural Engineering

Professor Chamberlin, an alumnus of Case, had been a part-time instructor in Fenn's Evening Division since June 1918. He became Professor and Chairman, Department of Marketing in 1955. He retired from C.S.U. in August 1966. Professor Srail became Professor and Chairman, Department of Speech and Dramatics in 1962, and transferred to C.S.U. in the same capacity in 1965. Professor Gallo became Associate Professor, Department of Civil Engineering and Engineering Mechanics in 1962 and also transferred to C.S.U. in the same capacity in 1965.

The financial report for the year 1946 showed that with an overall expenditure of $950,900; there was a gain in income over expense of $32,011.

The Long Term Planning Committee, chaired by Clarence M. Taylor, met December 18, 1946. Dr. Thomas served as Secretary and the following Minutes reflect the many facets of concern and the substance of thought presented by those in attendance:

> Present: Clarence M. Taylor, Chairman; Charles J. Stilwell; Ellwood H. Fisher; Leyton E. Carter; James H. Coolidge; Vollmer W. Fries; Richard S. Huxtable; and C. V. Thomas.
>
> The Chairman indicated that some members of the committee had previously met, and that there had been considerable discussion about *The Basic Purpose of Fenn College*. He stated that the discussion had included the advisability of making Fenn almost entirely a Day Cooperative College; the need for offering Evening instruction; and the possibility of concentrating the work of the college on the rather specific educational needs of industry and business. He indicated that no conclusion had been reached; and that the committee was in process of learning about the factors that should be considered in formulating the purpose of the college.
>
> The Chairman had previously asked the President of the college to prepare a statement outlining some of the elements that should be included in a long term planning program. This statement was then reviewed by the committee.
>
> The first item dealt with *The Purpose of Fenn College* as prepared by the faculty of the college. In summary the statement indicated that the purposes of Fenn College are to provide the Cooperative Plan of Education on the college level in the Day Division, and to furnish educational opportunities for employed persons in the Evening Division. . . . After considerable discussion, the committee tentatively approved this statement as presenting the purpose of the college.
>
> *The Curricula* was the next item reviewed. It was indicated that the college now provided curricula on the college level in Engineering, Business Administration and Arts & Science, and that these curricula are offered in both the Day and the Evening Divisions. It was also indicated that a Technical Institute program is conducted in the Evening Division on the non-college level,

for the purpose of assisting employed persons who need to acquire specialized skills and knowledges. . . . The committee requested that the term "non-college" be changed to "non-college credit" level, as a description of the Technical Institute program.

A lengthy discussion followed about *The Number of Students that the College Should Enroll in Future Years*. It was indicated that both national forecasts of growth in college enrollment and the rate of growth of Fenn College to date indicate that if facilities, personnel and finance can be provided, the enrollment in 1950–51 will probably be 2000 DAY and 8000 EVENING students. Many considerations were given to what the size of the student body should be. . . . The committee tentatively approved the inclusion of an enrollment of 2000 DAY and 8000 EVENING students as the number of persons which the college should seek to instruct at any one time.

Information about *The Faculty* was then reviewed. It was stated that the present faculty consists of 108 full time and 196 part time persons—and that if and when the enrollment approximates 10,000 students, the faculty required would be 154 full time and 280 part time persons, on the basis of the present faculty-student ratios. . . . The committee expressed the opinion that provision should be made for the increasing of faculty salaries, to the end that the institution would be able to attract and retain a high quality of teaching personnel.

The *Budget* of the college was then considered. It was pointed out that the budget for 1947 will approximate $1,200,000, and that of this amount $24,500 is budgeted to be received from endowment and gift sources—or approximately 2%. It was stated that colleges usually receive from 20 to 50% of their income from endowment or gift sources, and that the chief factors which have enabled Fenn College to operate with a small endowment income are a unified administration of the Day and Evening Divisions; the use of the plant from early morning until late at night; the advantages of the cooperative plan; and the requiring of faculty members to teach four quarters per year.

A lengthy discussion followed regarding the recommendation that an *Endowment and Gift Income* equal to 10 to 15% of the budget of the college was required to place the institution in a sound operating position. Some members of the committee expressed the hope that ways could be found to enable the college to operate without a considerable amount of endowment and gift income.

It was pointed out that tuition fees cannot be raised beyond those which other educational institutions charge without affecting the enrollment of the college, and that the clientele with which the college works usually have limited financial resources. It was also indicated that since 70% of the cost of operating the institution is made up of salaries, and that the institution must necessarily pay the approximate amounts which other colleges pay if it is to secure trained high quality persons—that over a long period of time it would be very difficult to operate the college without an increase in its endowment and gift income.

A discussion followed about *the advisability of seeking support from industries* on the basis of paying the college an amount per employee studying at the college—such as the present practice of some corporations providing the college Fifty Dollars per employee who is studying at the institution.

After a thorough consideration of the above and other factors, the committee approved the principle of increasing the endowment and gift income to an amount approximately 10 to 15% of the annual budget. A break-down of the amount that would be required included a possible $50,000 per year from corporations; the increasing of the present $25,000 per year from endowment to $50,000 through additional grants from trust funds and a larger endowment; and securing $25,000 to $50,000 per year from alumni and friends of the college.

The next item considered was the *Physical Plant* that would be required in the years ahead. A statement was made which indicated the number of classrooms and laboratories, drawing rooms and other facilities which the college now has. It was indicated that one of the problems confronting the institution is providing sufficient laboratory space and equipment to teach adequately the present freshman students when they become upperclassmen.

The statement indicated that the three major building needs are:

an Engineering Laboratory-Classroom building

an Auditorium—Classroom building

and a Gymnasium—Student Union building

The committee recognized that the first step in the expansion of the physical facilities is the acquisition of additional land which was authorized at the last meeting of the Board of Trustees.

Many questions then arose regarding *The Budget Problems which would confront the College If and When Additional Facili-*

ties were required. The following requests were made by the committee:

(1) That the Business Office of the college prepare statements which would include the probable financial operation of the institution

(a) during 1947 (the operating budget for the year)

(b) the probable budget of the college if the student body becomes 2000 DAY and 8000 EVENING students—and if the three additional buildings mentioned above are secured

(c) the position of the budget of the college during the interim between present operations and the situation that would exist under (b)

This analysis is to include as much provision as can be foreseen for meeting the imminent laboratory needs that the present student body will require in the immediate years ahead.

It was also requested that an *Architect be secured* to sketch the locations of the three proposed buildings on the land which the college now owns and which it hopes to acquire in the near future.

The committee adjourned to reconvene when the information to be prepared by the Business Office and the sketch to be drawn by the Architect become available.

—C. V. Thomas

A year of tremendous growth in the student body, faculty, and staff, 1946, by and large, had turned out to be a good year for Fenn.

VII

Nor, in truth, would the honours of illustrious men
continue after death, if their own spirits
did not make us preserve a longer remembrance of them.

Marcus Tullius Cicero, 106–42 BC. *De Senectute* XXII.

Although the shortest in the book, this chapter is one of the most difficult to write because so much happened in the year 1947. Board
committees were meeting frequently on subjects and activities vital
to the future of Fenn College, consequential decisions were being fash-
ioned, and the board was just on the brink of putting them into effect
when the illustrious leader of the educational program at the YMCA
and at Fenn College, Dr. C. V. Thomas, died in his office on November
28, 1947. His "own spirits" still "preserve" in the hearts of all who
knew him well and were associated with him at Fenn, "a long remembrance of" his "honours" after death.

As of January 1, 1947, a total of 116 people were in the administration,
faculty and other staff offices at Fenn, distributed as follows:

Administration	12
Professors	14
Associate Professors	15
Assistant Professors	21
Instructors	35
Personnel Development and others	19
Total	116

Apropos of the expansion in student enrollment during 1946, this total
of 116 is compared to a total of 67 faculty and staff on January 1,
1946, a 73 percent increase.

The Federal Government had by now set up War-Surplus Property Offices in each state. Colleges and universites were given preferential treatment. By February 5, 1947, Fenn had acquired 98 items for laboratories and offices with a fair value of $61,155.40 for a net cost of $4,279.03. In transit and promised were 44 additional items with a fair value of $20,141.95 for a proposed net cost of $392.52.

The Fenn Corporation met for its annual meeting on February 28, 1947. Bartlett, Collens, Coolidge and Ladds were re-elected to six-year terms expiring in 1953. The following tabulation represents the membership in the Board of Trustees and their respective term expirations at the close of this meeting:

Term Expires in 1948
Jacob D. Cox, Jr.
Richard S. Huxtable
Henry G. Tremmel
Charles J. Stilwell

Term Expires in 1949
Ellwood H. Fisher
Clayton G. Hale
James L. Myers
Allen T. Perry

Term Expires in 1950
Harold H. Burton
John C. Sanders
Robert M. Stecher
Vernon B. Stouffer

Term Expires in 1951
Fred C. Baldwin

Robert F. Bingham
George V. Woodling
John David Wright

Term Expires in 1952
Elbert H. Baker, Jr.
Leyton E. Carter
Vollmer W. Fries
Clarence M. Taylor

Term Expires in 1953
Edward T. Bartlett
Clarence L. Collens
James H. Coolidge
Herbert P. Ladds

Ex-Officio Members
John S. Crider
Joseph W. Meriam
Dr. C. V. Thomas

At the board meeting following the Corporation meeting incumbent officers of the board were re-elected, as follows: Charles J. Stilwell, Chairman; Ellwood H. Fisher, Vice Chairman; John S. Crider, Treasurer; and M. C. Herrick, Secretary.

Fisher reported the completion of the transaction for the purchase of the Warter's property (immediately east of the Fenn Tower with 83.25 foot frontage on Euclid Avenue, extending north to the eastern extension of the north property line of the College) for $50,000 at three percent interest, calling for annual payments approximating $3,300, including principal and interest, over a 20-year period. This property was almost paid in full at the time of the transfer of Fenn to the State in 1965. Fisher also reported that the Payne-Bingham Company was desirous of selling the property adjacent to the Warter's property with 155-foot frontage on Euclid Avenue extending north to Chester Avenue. It was voted to purchase the property for $90,000 and to place a mortgage on the Fenn Tower for this amount. It was also voted, at this meeting, to expend $7,444 to provide a larger Organic Chemistry Laboratory in the Fenn Building.

In carrying out the authorization to purchase the Payne-Bingham Company property and to place a mortgage on the Tower, it was necessary to name specific individuals to execute the various documents. The Board Executive Committee met February 3, 1947, in order to do so and passed a resolution granting Charles J. Stilwell and Dr. C. V. Thomas authority to sign such documents in accordance with Board action.

The second meeting of the Long Term Planning Committee was held February 24, 1947. The following report of this meeting exhibits the trend of thought of the committee members respective to the immediate and long range physical needs of the College:

Present:

Clarence M. Taylor, Chairman; Messrs. Leyton E. Carter, James H. Coolidge, Richard S. Huxtable, Charles J. Stilwell, C. V. Thomas, Arthur P. Loegler—and upon invitation, Mr. Michal Kunic.

Introductory Statement—The committee has had two lengthy meetings in addition to a preliminary meeting of some members of the group. The first regular meeting was held December 18, 1946 and the second on February 24, 1947. Each meeting extended over a period of three and one-half hours. The committee had been instructed by the Board of Trustees to work upon *a long term plan* for the development of Fenn College. The committee recognizes that the conclusions and recommendations which follow are subject to further consideration. A summary of the findings of the committee are:

1. *Purposes of the College*—The purposes of Fenn College have been—and the committee recommends that they continue to be—

TO PROVIDE the Cooperative Plan of Education on the college level in the DAY Division, and TO FURNISH educational opportunities for employed persons in the EVENING Division. A distinguishing characteristic of the purposes of the college is that [which] seeks to combine classroom and laboratory learning with work experience.

2. *Curricula*—The committee recommends that the college should seek to carry out its purposes by providing curricula on the college level in Engineering, Business Administration and the Arts and Sciences, and that these curricula be offered in both the DAY and EVENING Divisions. The college should also continue to conduct a Technical Institute in the EVENING Division on the non-college level for the purpose of assisting employed persons who need to acquire specialized skills and knowledges.

3. *The Size of the Student Body*—After a consideration of the forecast of growth in college enrollment, the need for an extension of higher educational opportunities in Greater Cleveland, and the rate of growth of Fenn College to date, the committee recommends that the college should seek to provide faculty and facilities that will make possible an enrollment of 2000 DAY and 8000 EVENING students. It is expected that if facilities can be provided, the college will attain these enrollment figures within the next five years.

4. *Faculty*—The committee was informed that the present faculty consists of 116 full time and 196 part time persons. Based upon an increase in the number of faculty members proportionate to the increase in the number of students, the committee believes that the faculty should be increased to 154 full time and 280 part time persons to instruct the proposed enrollment. The committee also highly recommends that provision be made for the increasing of faculty salaries, to the end that the college will be able to attract and retain a high quality of teaching personnel.

5. *Operating Budget*—The operating budget for 1947 will approximate $1,200,000. Of this amount $24,500 is budgeted to be received from endowment and gift sources, or approximately 2%. The committee was informed that colleges usually obtain from 20 to 50% of their income from endowment or gift sources, and that the factors which enable Fenn College to operate with a small endowment income are chiefly—a unified administration of the DAY and EVENING Divisions; the use of the physical plant from early morning until late at night; the advantages of the cooperative

plan; and the requiring of faculty members to teach four quarters per year.

After a thorough consideration of many factors related to the income and expense of the college, the committee recommends that an effort be made to provide from 10 to 15% of the operating budget of the college from endowment and gift sources. The committee believes that the additional support that should be sought may be obtained as follows: $50,000 per year from corporation gifts (based upon a payment to the college in proportion to the number of employees studying at the institution); the increase of the present endowment income of $25,000 per year; and an additional $50,000 per year from alumni and friends of the college. The committee recognizes that this is a long term recommendation and will require a period for developing the sources of the income proposed.

6. *Physical Plant*—The committee reviewed the classroom, laboratory and other physical facilities of the college. The problems that will confront the institution during the next few years because of the need for larger laboratories to instruct the upperclassmen as they move ahead from freshman and sophomore years, were considered by the committee. The needs which the college has for additional plant facilities and which should be included in the long term plan of the institution are an engineering-laboratory-classroom building, an auditorium-student union-classroom building, a gymnasium-fieldhouse building. The committee recommends that the college include in its long term planning these buildings to meet the needs of the institution.

7. *Additional Land Adjacent to the College*—The committee is pleased by the recent acquisition of additional land east and north of Fenn Tower. The approximately four and one-half acres of land which the college now owns will provide building and campus space which the Long Term Planning Committee believes to be adequate for the next major development of the institution.

8. *An Architect's Plan for the Development of the Physical Plant of the College*—The committee requested that an architect prepare a sketch of the location of buildings needed by the college, placed upon the land which the institution has recently acquired. The committee has studied this plan and recommends it to the Board of Trustees as an outline of a general program of development for the college. The approval of the general plan by the Board would be a next step in the development of an understanding of the needs and broad expansion program of the institution.

9. *A More Immediate Building Program*—Although the committee recommends the Long Term Building Development Program outlined in the architect's plan, yet the committee believes that the problems immediately confronting the college require that first attention be given to (*a*) the acquisition of the Engineering-Laboratory Unit and (*b*) a structure, perhaps semi-temporary in nature, which would make possible the bringing together of students into an assembly hall and provide facilities for basketball and other recreational activities. (Such a building might be obtained from the War Assets Administration.) It could be located where the permanent Gymnasium-Fieldhouse Building will ultimately be constructed.

10. *Capital Costs*—a. *For the Complete Long Term Plan*: Estimates of the costs of the buildings needed can only be very rough. Statements have been made by architects that the types of buildings proposed could probably be built at today's prices for about $1.00 per cubic foot. Costs of equipment and furnishings require usually 25 to 35% of the cost of construction. Based upon these rough estimates, the cost of the three buildings would be:

The Engineering-Laboratory-Classroom
Building

572,000 cu.ft. @ 1.00 per cu.ft.	$572,000	
Furnishings and equipment (1/3 of the cost of building)	190,000	
Architect's fees and other costs	50,000	$ 812,000

The Auditorium-Student Union-Classroom
Building

624,000 cu.ft. @ 1.00 per cu.ft.	$624,000	
Furnishings and equipment (25% of cost of building)	156,000	
Architect's fees and other costs	50,000	$ 830,000

Additional Classrooms, Laboratories &
Offices Unit

206,000 cu.ft. @ 1.00 per cu.ft.	$206,000	
Furnishings and equipment	51,000	
Architect's fees and other costs	20,000	$ 277,000

Gymnasium-Fieldhouse Building
  627,000 cu.ft. @ 1.00 per cu.ft. $627,000
  Furnishings and equipment   100,000
  Architect's fees and other costs   50,000 $ 777,000

                        Total $2,696,000

b. *For the Most Immediate Requirements*:

The Engineering-Laboratory-Classroom
Building
  572,000 cu.ft. @ 1.00 per cu.ft. $572,000
  Furnishings and equipment   190,000
  Architect's fees and other costs   50,000 $ 812,000

A Semi-Temporary Auditorium-Fieldhouse
Unit
  The cost of such a unit will depend very
  much upon whether or not it can be secured from War Surplus sources. Further
  investigation is required before an estimate
  of the cost of this structure can be made.

11. *Operating Budget Requirements*—The committee requested
Mr. Coolidge as Chairman of the Finance Committee to work with
Mr. Loegler, Finance Director of the college, in the preparation
of estimates of the operating budget requirements of the college,
based upon the recommendations of the committee regarding the
future size of enrollment and additional facilities required. . . .
                    Respectfully submitted,
                        The Long Term Planning Committee
                        Clarence M. Taylor, Chairman
                        Leyton E. Carter
                        James H. Coolidge
                        Vollmer W. Fries
                        Richard S. Huxtable

Enrollment, budget and space need analyses were prepared for three
plans as follows: (1) present Day and Evening enrollments (1947);
(2) 1,500 Day and 3,700 Evening enrollments with minimum additions
or improvements to existing laboratories and maximum use of classrooms; and (3) 2,000 Day and 8,000 Evening enrollments including

necessary buildings to provide normal facilities as compared with other colleges, to meet the needs of this size student body. The study showed a net gain of $43,928 for plan 1, a net loss of $32,893 for plan 2 and a net loss of $162,616 for plan 3.

The Personnel Committee of the Board met February 27, 1947, to study a plan for revision of the salary structure at Fenn which had been prepared by Dean Nichols in concert with the three academic Deans and other officials of the College. The need for increase in salary schedules emanated from four chief considerations: (1) teaching and administrative loads at Fenn were somewhat heavier than at most colleges; (2) the Fenn Faculty taught four quarters per year instead of the usual three at most colleges; (3) living costs in Cleveland were somewhat higher than in smaller communities; and (4) Fenn's salaries had consistently been lower than those at most colleges. The Committee recommended an annual increase of $30,350 (approximately 8 percent) effective April 1, 1947. This represented an average of about $285 per individual per year for the 107 faculty and staff members involved. The specific increases, however, *were* granted on the basis of the consideration of each individual's academic and professional efforts. The adoption of the new salary structure was officially passed by the Board at its meeting held March 6, 1947. President Thomas reported that with this new salary revision Fenn's average salary had increased 49 percent above that of 1941.

The report of the Long Term Planning Committee, with architect's renderings, was submitted at this same board meeting. It engendered considerable discussion concerning national statistics on future college enrollments, absorption of increased numbers of college graduates by business and industry, limiting Evening Division activity to college level students only, ratio of Day to Evening students, increase in endowment and operating subsidy, and whether the architect's renderings were the recommendations of the Committee. The board finally adopted the report as the long-range policy of the board as conceived at that date. Then a new Building Committee of five Trustees was immediately appointed to initiate definite plans for physical expansion of the College. Richard S. Huxtable was appointed chairman, and Bartlett, Coolidge, Fisher, and Taylor were the other four appointees.

This new Building Committee held its first meeting on April 12, 1947, and decided to engage an architect who had some experience in school or college design, specifically, one properly qualified for over-all planning from site location to preparation of working drawings and specifications. It was agreed that a rather complete development of the plans for the engineering-laboratory-classroom building should be the first priority by the newly engaged architect.

This committee also discussed the need to replace the store windows on the Euclid Avenue front of the Fenn Tower. This rehabilitation had been approved by the board about a year previously, but nothing had ever been done about it. Architect Joseph Ceruti was engaged to prepare working drawings for the replacement of the store windows.

The Building Committee met again at noon of May 6 and voted to recommend to the board that for security reasons a new fence be constructed around the boundary of the property recently purchased to expand Fenn's campus. Burke, Superintendent of Buildings and Grounds, estimated the fence in place would cost about $3,600.

A number of local architects were considered and the members of the committee met with them to discuss the development of the over-all campus planning and preparation of the working drawings. It was decided to recommend the firm of C. B. Rowley & Associates, Inc. to the board. It was also decided to recommend to the board that a topographic survey of the new campus area be prepared by the Engineering School of the College, with the general idea in mind that the property should be graded to the level of the East 24 Street sidewalk. Also, that the old house on the Warter's property be razed and the topographic survey include filling in and leveling off the area occupied by said house. The Board of Trustees, at a meeting held May 16, 1947, approved the above recommendations of the Building Committee.

Dr. Thomas reported an offer from the Cleveland Automobile Club to share equally in the cost of the topographic survey and construction of the fence between the two properties. He also reported that the College had now received an accumulation of war surplus property valued at $150,101.86 for a net cost to the College of $5,531.18. Promised or in transit were additional items valued at $15,349.30 which would cost the College $469.53.

Leyton Carter suggested that steps be taken to better illuminate the main entrance to the Tower and Elbert Baker, Jr. suggested that the Building Committee investigate ways by which the Tower can be identified from Euclid Avenue.

The last Fenn College Commencement over which Dr. Thomas presided was the largest graduating class to that date in Fenn's history; it also had the largest number of women graduates. The majority of the male graduates had served in World War II. All told, there were 156 graduates of which 23 were women. The Baccalaureate Service was held at the First Methodist Church and its minister, Dr. Harold Lancaster, delivered the sermon. Commencement was held at the Euclid Avenue Baptist Church, and Dr. William Edwards Stevenson, President of Oberlin College, delivered the address, entitled, "Today's Challenge." Little did "Tommy" (Dr. Thomas) realize that this was to be his last Fenn Commencement and his final "charge" to a Fenn graduating class.

George R. Kingsbury, of the 1947 class, became President of the Fenn Alumni Association in 1951.

It was reported at the July 7, 1947, meeting of the Building Committee that the Euclid Avenue store fronts of the Tower had been replaced, to appear just like the remainder of the building, at a cost of $7,650 which was considerably under the original estimate of $10,000.

The following memorandum and statistical material was mailed to the Board of Trustees by Dr. Thomas at the close of his last full academic year at Fenn College:

> The information on the enclosed sheets will be of interest to you. Members of the Board who were not included in the personnel of the Building Committee will be pleased to know that the Building Committee is moving forward with the following developments which have been authorized by the Board of Trustees; plans for razing the old residence east of the Tower, and for leveling the land recently purchased by the college; fencing the property of the college after the land has been leveled; and working with the architect's office in developing plans and outline specifications for a new Engineering-Laboratory-Classroom building, and an overall development plan for the long term building needs of the college.
>
> In the not too distant future the Building Committee hopes to be able to present to the Board of Trustees as a whole the plans for building developments.
>
> You will be glad to know that the college continues to obtain valuable equipment from the War Assets Administration. An estimate of the fair value of the equipment secured within the last few months exceeds Two Hundred Thousand Dollars.

Present indications are that the enrollment of the college will be at its maximum capacity during the coming school year, and that the quality of service of the institution will likewise be further increased during the year ahead.

The present school year closes this Friday (August 1st) and classes will be resumed in the Day Division immediately following Labor Day, and in the Evening Division one week later.

July 29, 1947

DEVELOPMENT OF FENN COLLEGE

A. The 10-Year Period 1937 to 1947

	1937	*1947*	*%* *Increase*
1. Growth in Student Body			
Number of Day Coop Students	665	1,675	252
Number of Evening Students	2,392	4,991	208
Total Student Body	3,057	6,666	212
2. Growth in Operating Budget	$341,000	$1,200,000	350
3. Value of Buildings, Land, and Equipment	$ 75,000	$1,451,682	

4. Property and Equipment Acquired
   Fenn Tower
   Land north and east of the Tower (approximately 4 acres)
   Laboratory equipment for Engineering, Science and Business instruction which has a value in excess of $300,000

5. Some Significant Educational Developments
   Full-time faculty increased from 45 to 123
   Accredited by the North Central Association of Colleges and Secondary Schools
   Direct services to industries through Personnel Development department greatly expanded
   Evening College Programs in Engineering, Business Administration and Arts and Sciences fully organized

B.   The 10-Year Period 1947 to 1957

(Based on a Report of the Long-Term Planning Committee of the Board of Trustees)

1.   Growth in Student Body*

	1947 (actual)	1957 (projected)	1957 (actual)
Number of Day Co-op Students	1,675	3,000	1315
		2,000 in College	930
		1,000 at Work	385
Number of Evening College Students	4,991	8,000	5164
Total	6,666	11,000	6479

2.   Operating Budget* $1,200,000 $1,800,000 $2,154,815

3.   Value of Property and Equipment* $1,450,000 $4,000,000 $4,499,515.65

4.   Buildings and Equipment to be Acquired
>   An engineering-laboratory-classroom building
>>   An auditorium-student union-classroom building
>>   A field house-physical education-recreation building
>>   An equipment-laboratory and classroom for added buildings
>>   Present Fenn Building on Prospect Avenue to be converted to chemistry, chemical engineering and metallurgy purposes
>>   All of the third floor of Fenn Tower to be used for library purposes

5.   Some Educational Objectives
>>   Further development of the cooperative method of education, including more complete integration of Instruction and Work experience

---

* Apropos of items B.1, B.2, and B.3 above, the reader may question the large decrease in the actual 1957 enrollments (B.1) as compared to those estimated; and the respectable increases in actual Operating Budget (B.2) and the Value of Property and Equipment dollars (B.3) from those estimated. The estimated statistics for ten years hence were made without benefit of the effect of all unforeseen intangibles which arose during the ten year period. It must be remembered that the late days of the depression, the decrease in birthrate, the early years of World War II, the interference with normal student enrollment, the improvement in admission and other academic standards of the College, plus other factors brought to mind by the above statistics could themselves be the subject of a separate study.

Continuation of improvements in the selection and development of the faculty of the College

Effect an organization that will make possible a continuing
close relationship with the individual student as the student body expands

To show the actual for 1957 the figures are noted to the right of the
estimated statistics B-1, B-2, and B-3.

At the Building Committee meeting on August 18, 1947, it was decided, for the sake of economy, to just level off and cinder the land
adjacent to the Tower, instead of grading it level with the sidewalk
on East 24th Street. Also, it was decided to go ahead with fencing
the East, North, and 24th Street boundaries and postpone the Euclid
Avenue frontage until plans for the proposed engineering-laboratory-
classroom building were more complete. Two alternate plans for this
proposed building were submitted by the architect at this meeting.
Each approximated 775,000 cubic feet, and the estimated cost thereof
was $970,000. Following considerable discussion, it was intimated, for
the first time, that there was a prospective donor for a building providing
these same specific functions, who proposed a gift of approximately
$500,000 for the building.

Accordingly, the members of the Building Committee requested the
architect to prepare preliminary plans for a building which would cost
about $500,000 to be located on the easterly side of the Euclid Avenue
frontage, between the Fenn Tower and the property of the Cleveland
Automobile Club.

The Division of Building and Housing of the City of Cleveland surprised the board through a notification dated September 3, 1947, that
the center open stairway in the Tower from the first to seventh floors
was a fire hazard and must be enclosed with masonry walls and self-
closing fire doors. Also, that the two former dumb waiter shafts had
to be firestopped with concrete, all storage be confined to the basement,
the lobby be segregated from all adjacent usages by masonry walls
and self-closing fire doors, and that all exit signs must conform with
city standards. This obligated the expenditure of funds, entirely unantic-
ipated in this modern building—so recently designed as a club and
residence hall with dormitory facilities—and not only strained an already tight budget, but required considerable ingenuity in devising
ways of physically complying with the demands of the City.

The Building Committee met at the Union Club on September 8, 1947, to view the newly revised plans developed by the architect. The building had a frontage of 100 feet on Euclid Avenue, a depth of 99 feet on the first floor, and 63 feet on the second and third floors. This totaled about 337,000 cubic feet. It was proposed that perhaps a second, similar in size, building be planned between this building and the Tower.

The Committee was informed that the possible donor wanted to complete the details necessary to processing the gift, and had his legal counsel prepare an agreement citing the conditions under which he would make the gift. After counselling with Harold Clark, an attorney attending a meeting in an adjacent room at the Union Club, the Committee went on record as approving the terms of the agreement. This called for a date when the actual construction would begin and upon consulting the architect the Committee set the date as "not later than July 1, 1948." Dr. Thomas signed the minutes of this meeting, but he did not live to witness the ground-breaking, let alone the fruition of this particular goal and dream of his.

The policy always followed by Dr. Thomas was to prepare a comprehensive agenda for each board meeting. The work of Meriam C. (Bud) Herrick, Secretary of the Board, was facilitated thereby, for much of his Minutes could be copied from the agenda supplemented with the action of the Board.

The last meeting of the Board attended by Dr. Thomas was held September 19, 1947. Herewith are the Minutes of the meeting in full:

Present:

Chairman Stilwell; Trustees Baker, Bartlett, Fisher, Huxtable, Meriam, Taylor, Thomas, Woodling. Also Messrs. Herrick, Loegler, Nichols, Patterson and Thomasson.

The meeting was called to order by Chairman Stilwell at 4:35 P.M.

1. Minutes of the meeting of May 16, 1947 were approved as distributed.

2. It was moved, seconded and passed that the Chairman appoint a committee to draft a resolution expressing the regret of the Board at the passing of Mr. Robert F. Bingham.

3. Dr. Thomas presented the following information (contained in the agenda) regarding the opening of the college year:

		This Year	Last Year
a. *Number of Students*:			
Day: Attending college during			
Fall Quarter		1390	1220
On Co-op Jobs		180	50 (approx)
		1570	1270
Evening		3650	3500
	Total	5220	4770

b. *Faculty*:

The present faculty consists of 116 full time and 155 part time persons. Twelve (12) full time individuals joined the faculty this fall.

Additional Facilities:—A new organic chemistry laboratory, an additional electrical engineering laboratory, and an X-ray laboratory, were made available this fall. —Much additional laboratory equipment has been secured. The fair value of equipment obtained to date from war assets sources exceeds $234,000. Some of this equipment has been stored for future use.

4. Mr. Huxtable presented the report of the building committee, explaining that the Building Committee had done a great deal of work since the last meeting of the Board, and that some of the action taken would have been presented to the Board if meetings had been possible. He explained the need for immediate action and hoped that all of the committee action would be approved by the Board. He then read the report of the Building Committee.

It was determined that the action of the Building Committee at the meeting of July 7th had already been authorized, and copies of the minutes of this meeting are attached to the records.

Confirming the action of the Building Committee at the meeting of August 18th, the following approvals were given:

a. Mr. Fisher moved and Mr. Baker seconded that the expense of approximately $2,000 for providing temporary parking space for cars be approved. This was passed.

b. Mr. Fisher moved and Mr. Bartlett seconded that the decision of the committee to proceed with the fencing of the easterly side of the property, and at the present ground level to fence the Chester Avenue frontage and to continue the fence around the property including the 24th Street side. This was passed.

c. Mr. Fisher moved and Mr. Taylor seconded that the Board approve the authorization to let the contract for the razing of the old house east of Fenn Tower to the firm which would pay the college $410. This was passed.

At the conclusion of the reading of the report of the August 18th meeting, blue prints of the proposed new engineering building were passed around to members of the Board.

Mr. Huxtable explained briefly the gift of $500,000 and the decision of the committee to consider two separate buildings therefore, rather than the original one. . . . Mr. Baker wondered whether the foundation of this three-story building would allow for the adding of floors in the future. Dr. Thomas explained that for school purposes three floors were all that were allowed by the building code, and that therefore this was not necessary.

Mr. Huxtable then proceeded to read from the minutes of *the meeting of September 8th*, and indicated that Mr. Fisher would take up the details of the $500,000 gift a little later.

Concerning the communication from the Division of Building and Housing of the City of Cleveland, Mr. Loegler explained that all of the fire wells of the building would have to be enclosed. . . . Mr. Fisher said that at the committee meeting he had felt that the college should comply with those alterations which could be done immediately, and that time should be asked for to study the problem of enclosing the stair wells. Since that time however he has been appointed to organize a Fire Prevention Committee for the City of Cleveland. He indicated that this was part of a national program which would be organized on the basis of State, County and City Committees. He described the causes of the La-Salle Hotel fire and now feels that there is necessity for taking all needed precautions. He suggested that the Board appoint a committee to check into the total Fenn Tower situation and to recommend elimination of *any* hazard which might exist. . . . Mr. Stilwell concurred and wondered if this could be referred to the Building Committee.

Mr. Stilwell asked Mr. Loegler what could be done immediately —and Mr. Loegler indicated that the construction of a fire tower at the north end of the basement should be done, and that the dumb waiters at the north end of the building should be closed off.

Mr. Fisher then moved and Mr. Baker seconded that the matter of any fire hazards existing in Fenn Tower be referred to the Building Committee for very careful attention. This was passed.

5. Mr. Fisher told the Board of a meeting with the donor of a $500,000 gift to Fenn College—and Mr. Stilwell then wondered if Dr. Thomas could read the agreement in full which had been made with the donor. Dr. Thomas then read the entire agreement. . . . Mr. Huxtable moved and Mr. Bartlett seconded that the acceptance of this gift, according to the agreement, be approved. This was passed.

6. Mr. Loegler explained the necessity for filing an authorization for access to a lockbox of Fenn College at the Cleveland Trust Company, and distributed copies of the resolution. . . . Mr. Taylor moved and Mr. Fisher seconded that this Resolution be approved, and that any two of the following persons be authorized to sign for access to the safe: C. V. Thomas, Charles H. Franklin, Arthur P. Loegler. This was passed.

7. Presentation of the architect's plans for the engineering-laboratory-classroom building—Approval of the overall specifications for the proposed new engineering building. . . . Mr. Fisher expressed the feeling that if the administrative staff O.K.'s the specifications of the engineering-laboratory-classroom building, the Board should concur and authorize the architect to proceed so that the construction of the building may be started by June 1, 1948.

Mr. Fisher indicated that the architect favored not breaking ground before May 1, 1948 because of the winter conditions. . . . Mr. Stilwell and Mr. Taylor felt that construction should get under way earlier. The Building Committee was asked to discuss with the various builders the advisability of building during the winter, and Mr. Huxtable indicated that he would do this immediately.

It was stated that the architect, Mr. Spencer, said it would take two months to get the detailed plans prepared. . . . Mr. Baker then moved and Mr. Fisher seconded that the Board approve the plans as presented and approved by the Building Committee at their meeting on September 8, 1947. This was passed.

8. Financial operation of the College for the first 8 months of 1947—Mr. Loegler read from the statement which was distributed to members of the Board and is attached to these minutes. . . . The Board generally was pleased at the favorable financial statement.

At this point Mr. Fisher left the meeting.

9.   Other Items: Dr. Thomas mentioned that the loan of $250,000 from the Cleveland Trust Company for operating purposes had been repaid in full.

Mr. Baker and Mr. Taylor asked about the condition of the Fenn Trust Fund, and Mr. Bartlett expressed the feeling that income from the fund would continue. . . . Mr. Meriam expressed the opinion that income from the fund might increase but that there were many demands from various groups for participation in the fund.

Mr. Loegler reported that Government payments to the college are being made more promptly.

Dr. Thomas expressed appreciation to the Board for the part they had in the presentation of his portrait.

The meeting adjourned at 5:54 P.M.

s/M. C. Herrick, Secretary

This was the first and only intimation in any Minutes relative to the oil portrait of Dr. Thomas. The former Fenn Archives (now C.S.U.'s) through Archivist Millard L. Jordan, aided by Mrs. Ethel Campbell provided the following information: The oil painting was by Rolf Stoll of the Cleveland Institute of Art. It showed Dr. Thomas seated in full academic costume. It was presented at a special meeting September 5, 1947, in Panel Hall of the Tower. Dean J. C. Nichols, acting for the Recognition Committee of the Board and Faculty, presented the portrait to Board Chairman Charles J. Stilwell, who received it for the institution. One anecdote of this important ceremony, which the author learned from Professor Jordan, was a comment made by Dr. Thomas when Dean Nichols was reading a rather lengthy biographical sketch of the President. Dr. Thomas turned to Mrs. Jordan, seated beside him and, with a whimsical, yet serious smile, said to her, "It sounds like an obituary, doesn't it?"

The Building Committee of the Board at its meeting on October 29, 1947, reviewed the site plan and plans and elevations for the new building. The architect was complimented on the attractiveness of the building. The architect reported that the working drawings and specifications would be available by February 1, 1948. About two weeks after this meeting the architect provided the members of the Committee with perspective sketches of a proposed site plan for the future placement of buildings on the then existent campus property. See Figure 1

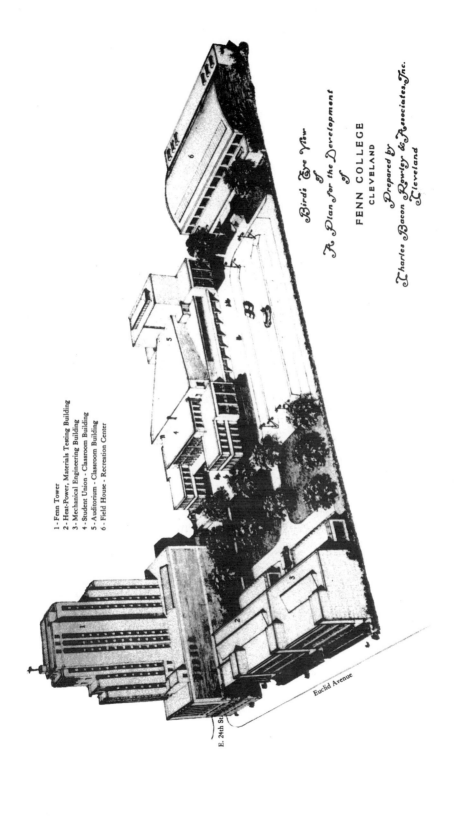

Bird's Eye View
of
A Plan for the Development
of
FENN COLLEGE
CLEVELAND

Prepared By
Charles Bacon Rowley & Associates, Inc.
Cleveland

1 - Fenn Tower
2 - Heat-Power, Materials Testing Building
3 - Mechanical Engineering Building
4 - Student Union - Classroom Building
5 - Auditorium - Classroom Building
6 - Field House - Recreation Center

Euclid Avenue

E. 24th St.

which shows architect's sketches in which the proposed first new building is number 3.

At this Building Committee meeting it was decided that in addition to executing the alterations in the Tower requested by the City of Cleveland, a fire alarm system should be installed in the building with an emergency power unit. It was recommended that periodic fire-drills be conducted to practice vacating the classrooms, laboratories, offices, and dormitory rooms.

The final meeting attended by Dr. Thomas was with the Executive Committee of the Board held Wednesday, November 26, 1947. He died of a heart attack two days later sitting at his desk in his office on the ninth floor of the Fenn Tower. The Minutes of this Executive Committee meeting were signed by Stilwell:

Present:

Messrs. Baldwin, Collens, Fisher, Myers, Taylor, Stilwell, and Dr. Thomas.

During the lunch period, Dr. Thomas reviewed as matters of general information total enrollment of students as approximately 5,350. He reported also that the Operating Budget of $1,336,000 for 1947 will be in balance with several thousand dollars to be carried over into 1948, but that the accounting for the year was not far enough advanced for him to make a more accurate report.

In Mr. Huxtable's absence, Dr. Thomas presented to the committee, in connection with the report of the Long-Term Planning Committee of March 6, 1947, the reduced photostats of the ground plan and the bird's-eye view of the whole college plan as developed by the Long-Term Planning Committee. He then presented for Mr. Huxtable the estimates of the various units in the whole program, which are based on present cost estimates and which total $3,506,000.

The Committee then discussed the practicability of making a year-end approach in the hope that we may secure some additional capital funds from corporations which could be included in their year-end appropriations. After some discussion, it was unanimously agreed by the Committee that Dr. Thomas should instruct the Public Relations Department to proceed at once with general publicity to be released to the Cleveland PLAIN DEALER for next Sunday's edition (this material being already prepared under Dr. Thomas' advice) and that the publicity be immediately followed by letters which were to go out over the name of the President and the Chairman to a list of companies who have in the college students to the number of 20 or more. It was specifically understood that the immediate efforts to raise year-end contributions should be with the idea of applying such funds to the reduction of the $115,000 loan on land purchased for the building of new buildings.

A discussion then took place concerning further efforts on the part of the Public Relations Committee in providing printed material carrying information concerning the long-term plans of the college, illustrations of long-term development, and other facts. The question was also raised concerning the preparation of a motion picture which would represent the work and the aims of the college.

Upon a motion which was carried unanimously, the Committee authorized Dr. Thomas to instruct the Public Relations Department to proceed immediately with the preparation of a comprehensive booklet to be presented in dummy form to the Board for authorization of the final appropriation.

After considerable discussion, it was the feeling of the Committee that until plans were developed further for the next move in connection with the long-term plan, the making of a motion picture should be postponed, but generally the idea was heartily approved. The suggested delay was both because of timing and cost.

There were no other items of business, but before adjournment Dr. Thomas raised the question of the division of his salary. At the present time, the salary is paid $10,000 by the YMCA and $5,000 by the college. The President suggested that if it met with the approval of the Committee and because of the increasing amount of time that he is devoting to Fenn and the decreasing amount of time to the YMCA, he felt the division should be on a fifty-fifty basis as of the first of January.

The President further pointed out that the YMCA was arranging for a new Assistant Secretary who has been called and accepted the Assistant Secretaryship as of January 1, but further that he would wish to continue a fair proportion of his time at the YMCA until the new Assistant Secretary had been sufficiently acclimated to assume the duties—which is the plan in prospect.

The Executive Committee heartily agreed with Dr. Thomas' suggestion, and Mr. Stilwell was asked to instruct Mr. Coolidge of the change to become effective January 1, 1948.

s/*Charles J. Stilwell*, Chairman

The following quoted letter also signed by Charles Stilwell contains the last letter dictated by Dr. Thomas within the hour before his death.

> On Wednesday, before Thanksgiving, the Executive Committee of Fenn College had its last meeting with Dr. C. V. Thomas, at which time final approval was given to specific plans for the future development of the college.
>
> The Committee recommended to Dr. Thomas that he send letters to the heads of companies having considerable number of employees attending Fenn, in order to inform them that an important unit of the forward plan will be built in 1948 on land which the college owns but has not yet paid for.
>
> The following, therefore, was dictated by Dr. Thomas one hour before his death Friday noon, November 28th, and is reproduced in this letter to you:
>
>> You will be pleased to know that the employees of your company listed on the enclosed sheet are studying in the Evening Division of Fenn College this Fall. They are among the 5,350 students now enrolled at the college.
>>
>> The rapid rate of growth of Fenn has continued this year. Only by the use of Quonset huts and over-normal scheduling of classrooms and laboratories can the present student body be accommodated.
>>
>> A special committee of the Board of Trustees has given long and careful study to the need for new buildings to provide for the growth of the college, and help in meeting the community need for expanding Higher Education facilities. On an enclosed sheet you will see the results of their planning—a development program requiring, at present costs, the expenditure of approximately $3,500,000. A Cleveland citizen has recently given $500,000 to pay for one of the engineering buildings.
>>
>> During the present year, the college has acquired land necessary for the development, and now owns about four and one-half acres at East 24th and Euclid Avenue. The cost of the additional land was $115,000.
>>
>> Because of the educational services which Fenn provides to employees and in other ways, the Board of Trustees believe that industry and business will assist the college in its development. A first step in this program is enabling the college to pay for the land recently acquired. One corporation last week,

learning of Fenn's land and building needs, voted $5,000 on account for the development program. It was understood that the $5,000 would be credited to a larger account which the company will furnish for the complete development.

This letter is being sent to you with the hope that some assistance to Fenn may be provided from the 1947 operations of your organization. The first $115,000 received will be used to pay for the additional land.

What Fenn College is today, is largely due to the cooperation and support which your company, along with others of Greater Cleveland has provided. The Board of Trustees greatly appreciate this assistance and respectfully request your continuing support of the work and development of the college.

I commend Dr. Thomas' letter to you with the hope that you will give it careful consideration.

> Sincerely yours,
> Charles J. Stilwell, Chairman,
> Board of Trustees

Thus ended an era of extraordinary growth of the educational branch of the YMCA and Fenn College under the leadership of Dr. C. V. Thomas. From the time he joined the YMCA on July 5, 1916, with the titles of Assistant to the Principal of the Day School, Assistant to the Educational Secretary, Instructor of English (to the foreign born) and Mathematics (to the regular students), to the date of his death at age 55 on November 28, 1947, he worked prodigiously to provide the educational "cutting tool" to upgrade the student, subject to hardships, in his efforts to develop himself scholastically. Thirty-one years, four months, and 28 days of "yeoman to executive" leadership service to the youth of Greater Cleveland, a record unsurpassed by any other academician in Cleveland's history. This was too great a man of distinction to not have his name carved into a living memorial on the Fenn Campus, now C.S.U.

All during the author's fourteen-year stay on the Fenn Campus, friends of Dr. Thomas (and especially Dean Anders) would repeat his gems of wisdom. However, one of the finest tributes to Dr. Thomas was written two days following his death by Gerald S. Wellman, who had served on Fenn's staff as Registrar from 1928 to 1933 and later served many years as Assistant to the President of Baldwin Wallace College. Following is Mr. Wellman's tribute:

A MAN YOU COULD BELIEVE IN
By
Gerald S. Wellman
November 30, 1947

Ever since Friday noon I've been trying to analyze the hold that C. V. Thomas had upon me and upon thousands of others like me.

The most important fact about "Tommie," I have decided, is that he was a man you could *believe in*. He accomplished miracles in his too brief lifetime because he multiplied himself and his enthusiasms through the loyalty and energies of his staff, the lay members of boards and committees and each new friend to whom he voiced his earnest concern that young men and boys have their opportunity to grow to their full capacity.

Youth lost a great champion when Dr. Thomas died—youth of all colors and creeds, for he made no distinctions. His mind was uncluttered with racial prejudice or intolerance of any kind. He saw the man's potential, the individual at his maximum capacity for growth, and he dedicated his life to satisfying for as many thousands as possible that need for growth. He was never impatient with people as individuals, but only with smallness and pettiness that so often blocked off the approaches to worthwhile objectives.

When will we ever know all the human stories that made up a part of each day's work? The encouragement here—the loan out of his pocket there—the chance, always the chance extended to someone to realize the capacity that was in him. Who could do more with a handshake or a few words in passing, to bring back a surge of self-confidence because a man like Dr. Thomas cared that much?

Was there ever more drive and determination behind a pair of dark brown eyes? Or more sparkling humor just below the surface that would not be denied frequent expression? His laughter came from deep within the man, bathing everyone around him in its humor and contagious good feeling. When did he ever bother another with personal problems? Always it was the big job—more opportunities for more people for which he enlisted cooperation. He could put a point across in three minutes to which another would devote an ineffective hour. He could lead a conference at a comfortable yet earnest pace, wring out of the minds of others convictions and conclusions and sum it all up in a few dynamic sentences that nailed together a solid platform of ideas. He needed no ghost-writer for his speeches. His keen mind cut through to the heart of any problem and restlessly drove toward specific action to correct it. He would have been a great man in any profession or activity. He never regretted the one he chose. It consumed him day and night with the challenge of unfinished tasks and unexplored areas of social consequence.

He respected the time of busy men, yet he never hesitated to take their time to win help and money for something he believed in. There were hundreds of busy men in Cleveland who could never say "No" to Dr. Thomas. Their belief in him embraced any cause he himself believed in, yet he never assumed the fact or traded upon it. He always marshalled his argument in so brief and compelling a manner as to utterly dissolve any fortress of resistance.

Was there ever a man more skillful in planting the seed of an idea for another to adopt and express while he modestly joined the hands to reap the harvest? His humility could only be described as Christlike. Personal glory and applause never got through to his inner ear. There he only listened for the echoes of men's attitudes toward causes bigger than themselves, enlarging opportunities for others. He knew when these tones rang true and for the men who rang true he had work—for the others a challenge and an invitation that was always open.

Because they knew he never spared himself, because of the deep sincerity of the man, he won a working response from others. Only because of this could he accomplish in a short working lifetime of thirty years his incredible achievements in the educational and social life of this city. Never could it be more aptly said that the institutions he headed were the lengthened shadow of one man, yet such an inference invariably brought from him the quick retort that if that were true he had failed. He did not fail. Into that lengthened shadow have merged the growing figures of men to whom he gave responsibility, encouragement, self-confidence and a vision. And the great enterprises in personal growth and brotherhood to which he gave his life will forever be living memorials to his character and genius.

He was one of the few men in each generation who make a difference. For a little while, as time is measured, his driving force —with all its magnetic attraction for the best efforts of others— made important gains in the battle toward racial understanding, universal brotherhood and enlarged opportunities for men and boys to grow to full stature. Will there be enough of us whom he trusted to hold and extend those gains? To the extent in which we succeed we will add significance and luster to his life and justify the faith a truly great man had in us.

This chapter closes on the unusual calendar date, November 28, 1947, the day after Thanksgiving, ordinarily a holiday in academic circles. But, "Tommy" was working. This was the way he would wish his departure from earthly ties and obligations, but it should not have happened at his early age. Fenn, the YMCA, and Cleveland lost a man with great leadership qualities, a humanitarian, a substantial citizen, a religious as well as an educational preceptor. His many friends and associates will never forget him. At the beginning of this chapter is a most appropriate quotation by Marcus Tullius Cicero. Reread it.

VIII

*I have built me a monument
more lasting than bronze.*

Horace, 65–8 BC. *Odes,* Book III line 41.

The above quotation epitomizes a thought Dr. Thomas probably never considered in his modesty. But, he was a master builder of an educational system and plant. He was the father of the Cooperative Program of Higher Education in Cleveland. As an educational leader, he was a builder of men. So, Fenn College and The Cleveland State University is a living memorial to him. Would that he could see the impact of his early dreams in the 1920s on the near downtown area of Cleveland between Euclid and Chester Avenues and west of the Innerbelt Freeway.

A Memorial Resolution was prepared by Messrs. Fisher, Huxtable and Stouffer and mailed to Mrs. Thomas. Mrs. Thomas' reply was as follows:

December 17, 1947
Lakewood, Ohio

To the Board of Trustees of Fenn College,

The children and I wish to thank the members of the Fenn College Board for their helpfulness and also their expressions of sympathy during these days of shock and sorrow in the losing of the presence of our beloved father and husband.

For the years of cooperation and loyalty to my husband and his life work, I thank you all.

For the many happy experiences he had had among you, I thank you.

For the encouragement, inspiration and friendship, I thank you.

305

Without your assent and helpfulness, his work could not have been accomplished. So the credit for the progress of Fenn College is, in a large measure, due to the strength of this group's interest.

I am sure, if he could speak today, it would be something like this poem, entitled "Progress":

"Could we but see the pattern of our days,
We should discern how devious were the ways
By which we came to this, the present time,
This place in life; and we should see the climb
Our soul has made through the years.

"We should forget the hunts, the wanderings, the fears,
The Wastelands of our life and know
That we could come to no other way or grow
Into our good without these steps our feet
Found hard to take, our faith found hard to meet.

"The road of life winds on and we like travelers go
From turn to turn until we come to know
The truth that life is endless and that we
Forever are inhabitants of all eternity."

That I may help in some way to carry on is a sincere wish.

Very sincerely
(Mrs. C. V.) Sylvia M. Thomas

Mrs. Thomas had broached the subject with Stilwell of the establishment of a Chair of Philosophy as a memorial to Dr. Thomas. At a meeting of the Executive Committee at Chairman Stilwell's home on December 17, 1947, it was the consensus of the committee that any effort at this time to obtain funding to endow a Chair of Philosophy, desirable as it might be as a living memorial, would seriously interfere with the accomplishment of the building program instituted by Dr. Thomas and which he considered "the most pressing need." Stilwell was requested to present this phase of the discussion to Mrs. Thomas with the hope that she may be reconciled to postponing the effort toward a living memorial to a later date—"perhaps several years in the future." For unknown reasons, a living memorial to Dr. Thomas never developed.

Dr. Thomas' death was such a shock to all, that it overshadowed the then recent deaths of Trustees J. C. Sanders and R. F. Bingham.

Resolutions for these two men were authorized at the December 23, 1947, meeting of the board, the first meeting of the board following Dr. Thomas' death. The board at this meeting rededicated its efforts to carrying out the plans and dreams envisioned by the late Dr. Thomas. Paraphrasing Abraham Lincoln, "it is for us, the living, to rededicate ourselves to the unfinished task to which he gave his full measure of devotion," the board named Dean J. C. Nichols Acting President and appointed a special committee composed of Clarence L. Collens, Chairman, Ellwood H. Fisher, Clayton G. Hale, Richard S. Huxtable, and Robert M. Stecher to seek a new president.

The following was reported at the December 23, 1947, board meeting:

a. By Faculty action, all students entering Fenn after September 1, 1947, were required to follow the Co-op Program.

b. According to a survey by *The Cleveland Press*, Fenn was second among the Cleveland colleges in volume of education for veterans.

c. On the basis of Intelligence Tests, entering students at Fenn ranked twenty-third among 350 colleges using the American Council on Education (ACE) Psychological Tests. This rating placed Fenn students in the upper thirty percent indicating a superior student body. This drew favorable comments from the Board.

d. Fenn was highly complimented in being invited to prepare and present programs over three Cleveland radio stations (WTAM, WEWS and WSRS). The basketball game between Fenn and W.R.U. on December 8, 1947, was the first to be televised in Cleveland.

e. The proposed budget for 1948, $1,475,000, was the largest to date in the history of Fenn. The increase in enrollment in 1948 required the appointment of eighteen additional Faculty members.

This was the last meeting of the year 1947 for the board or for any Fenn committee, a dire year for Fenn College.

Dr. Thomas exercised the policy of summarizing educational information for presentation to the board in memorandum form. It was his custom to define some of the local and national trends affecting the the colleges. He completed the following memorandum just two days before his death and it was mailed to the Fenn Trustees near the end of the year.

HIGHER EDUCATION—A 20th CENTURY COLOSSUS

A great historical development of the 20th century is the growth of higher education in the United States. It is all the more significant since there is no parallel growth in the rest of the world. For instance, in Birmingham, England, an industrial center the size of Cleveland, there is one university and only 1600 students.

In the United States today, there are 2,338,226 college students (26,000 in Greater Cleveland—5,350 at Fenn) compared with 2,078,095 last year and 1,360,000 in the pre-war peak year of 1939–40. *By 1960 and after*, 3,000,000 students and upwards will attend college annually, according to best authority.

Peak veteran enrollment is expected in 1949–50. At the present time, 110,739 veterans are attending colleges in Ohio, and approximately 1,300,000 in the nation—an increase of 3.9% over last year. Enrollment of non-veterans increased 21.8%.

John Dale Russell of U.S. Office of Education estimates enrollment will level off at 2,477,000 in 1951–52, but mount to 2,924,000 in 1959–60. Enrollment in 1965 is expected to be still higher.

Contrary to popular belief, government subsidy of veterans is not *the* cause of high enrollment, but only a contributing factor. Surveys indicate that the average veteran would have entered college anyway. Russell estimates 3,000,000 would have enrolled by 1950 without the G.I. Bill.

Some factors responsible for the new "plateau" in enrollment: "Going to college is tending to become part of the social pattern." . . . "College education is getting to be contagious . . . is likely to become as common as secondary education used to be." . . . "Like keeping up with the Joneses, it's going to be increasingly difficult *not* to go to college"—quotes from educators.

Increasingly, business and industry are making college education a factor in the job-advancement of key personnel. Welfare agencies and institutions of all kinds require a college degree as a pre-employment requisite. . . . Some industries are turning to college-trained foremen. . . . Most Cleveland industries prefer employees who attend evening classes. (Some 1400 Cleveland industries have 3,750 employees attending Fenn College evening classes—250 firms provide job opportunities to 1600 Fenn day students alternating three-month periods of work and study.)

A business recession or a rise in the subsistence pay of veterans attending college under the G.I. Bill would set thousands more scrambling for college entrance. The present pay of $65 for unmarried and $90 for married veterans is low enough to be a deterrent to college entrance. Only *2,270,186 of 5,182,523* veterans who indicated intention of taking G.I. education already have enrolled. More veteran students, due to the high cost of living, will find part-time jobs more necessary this year. Savings are gone.

At the turn of the century, one person in 30 who finished high school attended college. The ratio was 1 to 16 in 1930, 1 to 7 in 1940, 1 to 5 now and estimated 1 to 3 after 1960.

The college boom raises two controversial issues: (1) Costs and (2) Subsidy.

In privately controlled institutions the average tuition fee has increased since 1939 as follows: Arts & Sciences 29.3%; Engineering 32.8; Dentistry 56.1. "Never before had so many men and women wanted to go to college; and never before had the price of college education been higher," TIME magazine commented.

In publicly controlled colleges and universities, average tuition fee for state residents increased 31.4% in Business Administration; 45.5 in Graduate Schools; 56.3 in Law. Another source estimates that the average cost per student has gone up 41% since 1939. Sharpest rise is in room and board: the average in 1939, $608; this fall, $860.

Warned the U.S. Office of Education: When Government has spent its $15 to $20 billion under G.I. Bill, colleges will either have to cut prices or accept only well-to-do students—"a counter-democratic tendency."

In "Financing the Future of Higher Education," a study by Dr. Thad L. Hungate, Columbia University, annual cost of higher education by 1965 will be $3 billion . . . increased costs and larger enrollments will have changed the pattern of educational support . . . as a result, 2/3 of total college cost should be borne by public funds and 1/3 by the student . . . students who cannot meet any part of the college expenses should have full cost borne by State. Student's share would be repaid out of his future earnings.

In this way, personal qualifications, not ability to pay, would become the only standard of admission. An opposite point of view is expressed by Dr. James B. Conant, president of Harvard: The emphasis on a college education for everyone creates the danger of a "white-collar proletariat," an army of unemployed, because many more will desire professional work than our society can afford.

Many educators are convinced that the privately controlled institutions of higher learning can continue to play an important role in American society. They contend that government subsidy, at best, is an indirect threat to academic freedom.

Tub-thumpers for subsidy hold that college status is economic status, that the "forgotten boy and girl who do not come under the G.I. Bill" should also have their opportunities for college training.

Widely-held opinion is that Government will finance the education of worthy and capable students under a *POST G.I. BILL* to eliminate discrimination against children of low-income families.

Tuition never has covered college costs, not even now with higher rates and government aid. If you are buying hats at $1 each and selling them at 90c each, you aren't going to make more money by selling more hats. If the college has to advance 10% of the cost of each student enrolled, increased enrollments mean higher losses. Fenn College has about the same endowment for 1,600 day students now that it had for 700 a few years ago.

College endowment is concentrated in only a few colleges. Only 9% of the 1,400 colleges and universities in the nation hold 81% of all endowment funds.

Colleges and universities entering into extensive fund-raising campaigns throughout the nation are seeking the staggering total of $1,200,000,000, an average of $1,700,000 for each of the 700 liberal arts schools. (Fenn College requires $3,500,000 to meet its urgent building needs.)

Some 400 colleges thus far have raised $350,000,000. A majority of the colleges say they are having less difficulty raising funds. Extensive drives had been discontinued during the war.

The $1,200,000,000 total sought would be used as follows: Building and equipment $385,000,000; teachers' salaries $309,000,000; general endowment $214,000,000; scholarships $121,000,000; miscellaneous $200,000,000.

Reversing a trend that began soon after the war, the flow of foreign students to this country is practically at an end. Soviet Union, however, is spending large sums to attract foreign students, especially from Eastern Europe.

One Soviet university set aside a special building for foreign students, gave them better food and sleeping quarters than their own people.

Difficulty in getting American dollars reduced the number of foreign students in this country 40% this year over last. Great Britain and Ireland sent 150 in 1946, but only 23 this year. France dropped from 179 to 36.

Fulbright Act makes an estimated $140,000,000 available for American students and teachers to study a year abroad—in 22 countries, not including Russia. Money will be spent over a 20-year period. No students have as yet been exchanged, and none will be until the beginning of the 1948–49 academic year.

The supply of college instructors coming from graduate schools is still inadequate, but tremendous graduate school enrollments indicate supply soon will be catching up with demand.

A survey reveals that the colleges will need 67,000 new full-time staff members by next September; 89,000 by 1950, and 140,000 by 1959. Lowest estimate anywhere is 28,000 by next September. The ratio of students to teachers considered desirable since 1900 was 10 to 1. The "emergency" ratio now is about 16 to 1.

The 2,338,226 students now are squeezed into an educational plant designed for some 1,600,000. Government estimates that colleges need an additional 90,000,000 square feet of classroom space now and a total of 300,000,000 by 1950. Before the war, colleges had about 165 square feet of space per student for all instruction purposes. This year they have about 83 square feet. War and Navy Departments required 120 square feet as a minimum for the war-time training program.

Peak veteran load on the labor market will be reached in 1950 when the largest number of G.I. Bill graduates will leave college. Mature, serious-purposed, they will be expecting employment at the high level of their preparation, but already various professions and occupational fields are filling up. A national survey is needed to determine numbers of graduates, the fields they will enter, and the employment conditions expected. A major social as well as economic problem will result if nothing is done and thousands face disillusionment.

For the first time in history, the world is witnessing the beginnings of an experiment in higher education for the masses. The ultimate, educationwise, to the free man may be attained in this century unless the forces of destruction intervene. It behooves educators, then, to guard zealously the great experiment that somehow has fallen abruptly into their hands because only in America will we have this opportunity.

It is enigmatic, however, that this century of education's greatest progress and development is also ". . . the most destructive, the least conducive to social safety, the least productive of human happiness. . . ." Obviously, just learning is not enough; a truly educated man must have a personal and vital life philosophy.

Fenn College, through its combination of classroom theory and work experience, its emphasis upon the individual and its purpose to aid students in developing a life philosophy, seeks to make its contribution to its students and to society.

s/C. V. Thomas, President

December 1947

Special attention is called to the second and third paragraphs from the end. These could have been written in 1970, perhaps more appropriately than in 1947.

No committee or board meetings were held in January 1948. The Long Term Planning Committee held its first meeting for the year at noon, February 5, 1948. This committee had been charged with determining ways and means of carrying out the Development Program.

The committee conceived the following plan for raising the necessary $3,525,000 to finance the proposed building and equipment program:

1. A few large gifts from educational foundations, individuals, etc. $2,200,000
2. Gifts from seventy-five large industrial firms and individuals varying from $5,000 to $50,000 each   975,000
3. A general campaign including small firms, individuals, faculty, alumni, Trustees, and general public   350,000

Total $3,525,000

It was decided to present this plan at the February meeting of the board and to recommend that steps be taken immediately to secure funds in the first group without waiting for the selection of a new president, the reason being that there was intense competition in educational fund raising at that period.

While campaigning for funds in the first group, it was planned to organize and develop interpretative materials including architectural renderings of plans and elevations of proposed buildings plus equipment needs. In this effort a fitting memorial to Dr. Thomas was to be established. This never took place.

The Building Committee met the afternoon of February 5, 1948, to view for the first time the working drawings of the new Mechanical Engineering Building. Chairman Huxtable requested that Burke, Superintendent of Buildings, Dean Spears, and Dean (Acting President) Nichols study the plans and submit suggestions for changes or additions at a meeting to be held a week later.

The Finance Committee of the Board met on February 12, 1948, and reported that $62,344.45 had been contributed to the Building Program of Fenn as of February 1, 1948.

The Annual Corporation meeting was held February 17, 1948, at which time Jacob D. Cox, Jr., Richard S. Huxtable, Henry G. Tremmel, and Charles J. Stilwell, whose terms expired at that meeting, were re-elected to six-year terms expiring in 1954. The two vacancies on the board resulting from the deaths of Sanders and Bingham were not filled at this meeting. A Nominating Committee was appointed to make recommendations to fill these vacancies at the next board meeting.

The board met immediately after the Corporation meeting and the following officers were re-elected for the year 1948:

Charles J. Stilwell, Chairman
Clarence M. Taylor, Vice Chairman
Ellwood H. Fisher, Vice Chairman
Meriam C. Herrick, Secretary
John S. Crider, Treasurer

It was reported at this meeting that 212 graduates of Fenn had gone on to graduate study in fifty different universities, and the records showed that to date, 64 had earned advanced degrees. The analysis made by Dr. W. A. Patterson, Registrar, showed that 29% of the graduates from the School of Arts and Sciences, 6% from Business Administration, and 5% from Engineering had gone on to graduate study.

The board was informed of the outstanding record of Fenn's Swimming Team—nine victories to one defeat. This success was largely due to one individual, a sophomore named Robert Busbey who had already captured all the Fisher Pool records (including all visiting contestants) for all the free-style events. Busbey joined the Faculty as an Instructor, Department of Health and Physical Education on September 1, 1951, became Assistant Professor in 1955 and Associate Professor in 1963. Upon transfer of Fenn to the State, following the retirement of Professor Woodling, he was appointed Director of Athletics and Acting Chairman, Health and Physical Education at C.S.U. He was also the Varsity Swimming Coach.

Nineteen hundred and forty-eight marked the silver anniversary of the founding of the Cooperative Program of higher education in Cleveland. The board on February 17, 1948, expressed favor in celebrating this anniversary later in the year, perhaps in conjunction with showing a new college president to the Cleveland public.

The board authorized the Building Committee to seek bids for the new Mechanical Engineering Building and also gave the Executive Committee authorization to approve a bid and order the construction to begin.

Chairman Stilwell asked and received the board's permission to appoint Vernon Stouffer as Chairman of the Personnel Committee to replace Clayton G. Hale, whose poor health had forced him to become inactive for an indefinite period. Leyton E. Carter replaced Hale on the committee to select a new president. The Selection (president) Committee together with an Advisory Committee from the Faculty had screened the biographical backgrounds of some sixty candidates and reported that they were meeting weekly in order to attempt to have the office filled by the Fall term.

The Building and Executive Committees of the Board met jointly March 22, 1948, to review the contractor's bids on the proposed Mechanical Engineering Building. Four of the six contractors invited to bid submitted firm bids on the project. The lowest bid was $469,908 submitted by Alger-Rau, Inc. Bids ranged to a high of $539,000. But none of the bids included architects' fees or laboratory equipment, and the committee was trying to keep total costs to $500,000. Therefore, the three low bidders were requested to revise their bids based on certain specified changes and deletions. After considerable deliberating and additional changes and deletions the A. M. Higley Company resubmitted the lowest bid of $445,000 which was accepted for contract performance. Acting President J. C. Nichols was authorized to sign the contract in the name of the College. The building as designed contained approximately 350,000 cubic feet divided into the following physical facilities:

> 8 classrooms, accommodating 272 students
> 2 drafting rooms, accommodating 65 students
> 1 mechanical shop, accommodating 35 students
> 2 offices
> 1 locker room
> 1 tool room
> 1 women's rest room
> 1 men's rest room

Nichols pointed out that these facilities provided about half the instructional facilities required at one time for the existing enrollment in Engineering.

The board met April 6, 1948, and approved the recommendations of all committees including the letting of the building contract to the A. M. Higley Company. It was reported at this meeting that six new appointments had been made to the faculty, that Finance Director A. P. Loegler was convalescing from a recent heart attack and that the following editorial was in the March 26, 1948, *Cleveland News.*

New Building Marks Progress at Fenn

Further evidence of the growth of Fenn College is shown with the announcement that ground will be broken May 1 for a mechanical engineering building, which will cost just under $500,000 and will be the first of five projected units. The institution, even under crowded conditions, has been providing a fine service.

With the expansion program, Fenn shortly will be making greater contributions to the community.

The *News* congratulates the college on its achievements and sees brightness, real progress and optimism for civilization in its plan for the future.

It was also reported that sophomore Robert Busbey recently competed in the A.A.U. swimming meet at New Haven, Connecticut, and qualified as a candidate for qualifying meets for the U.S. Olympic Team.

And again, the subject of a memorial for Dr. Thomas was discussed at this meeting. The Minutes read thus:

The Determination of a Memorial for Dr. Thomas—The question of a Memorial for Dr. Thomas is raised quite frequently, both by individuals and by interested groups. While this matter may not be decided finally until more definite decisions are made regarding the Development Program itself, is it desirable that a committee be appointed to study this question and make recommendations to the Board? Perhaps the committee might consist of members of the Board of Trustees, representatives of the staff of the college, and a representative of the Women's Advisory Board.
"Mr. Stilwell felt, and the Board concurred, that the Executive Committee should give serious consideration to this matter of a Memorial to Dr. Thomas and should at least start it off and give it direction."

No Memorial was ever named at Fenn College in honor of Dr. Thomas. The only material recognition of his existence is his oil portrait hanging in Panel Hall of the Fenn Tower at C.S.U., and this was financed by close friends of Dr. Thomas and unveiled at a ceremony in his honor while he was still alive.

The following factual information and statistics relating to Fenn's development program was also presented at the April 6, 1948, board meeting (this was a long and important board meeting lasting three hours and ten minutes):

I. LOCAL TRENDS IN COLLEGE ENROLLMENT

A. College enrollment in Greater Cleveland (March 1948)

Institution	Total	Day	Evening (Part Time)
Western Reserve	13,206	6,543	6,663
Fenn	5,271	1,671	3,600
John Carroll	2,154	1,677	477
Case	2,062	1,459	513
Baldwin-Wallace	1,776	1,659	117
Ursuline	252	252	–
Notre Dame	250	250	–
TOTALS	24,971	13,601	11,370

B. Ten-year enrollment trends with percentages of increase

Institution	1936–37	1946–47	Percentage Of Increase
Western Reserve	9,191	16,484	79%
Fenn	1,851	4,739	155%
John Carroll	554	2,024	266%
Case	789	1,600	103%
Baldwin-Wallace	751	1,560	108%
Notre Dame	169	272	61%

C. Enrollment trends of different types of colleges nearby

Institution	1936–37	1946–47	Percentage Of Increase
Akron	1,532	6,716	338%
Fenn	1,851	4,739	155%
Toledo	3,292	7,500	128%
Pittsburgh	10,294	22,871	122%
Antioch	715	1,082	51%
Oberlin	1,805	2,109	17%

D. Interpretation: Fenn College, in spite of limited physical facilities, takes care of 22% of all the students attending colleges in the Greater Cleveland area—and 32% of the part-time students (Evening College).

Fenn College is the second largest college or university in the Greater Cleveland area—one out of every four college students goes to Fenn.

The Fenn enrollment increase of 155% during the past ten-year period is topped by John Carroll University with 266%. John Carroll is a denominational university and does not offer technical training.

There is a definite trend toward larger urban universities, especially those offering technical training. The increase in enrollment at the University of Akron (338%) more than doubled the Fenn increase.

The University of Pittsburgh has almost as many students as Western Reserve University, Fenn College and Case Institute of Technology combined (22,871). The City of Pittsburgh has other fine colleges as well, including Carnegie Tech and Duquesne University.

You cannot have a great city without great colleges.

To be great, colleges must have buildings and equipment adequate for the task.

With its development program, *Fenn College builds to meet Greater Cleveland's growing needs.*

II. NATIONAL TRENDS IN COLLEGE ENROLLMENT

A.   Fenn College enrollment trends as related to the national trend (1920–1960).

        —See following chart.

B.   College enrollments in the nation's seven largest cities in 1947.

New York City	151,992
Chicago	40,226
Philadelphia	40,649
Detroit	36,135
Los Angeles	28,276
Boston	36,668
Cleveland	22,305

C.   Interpretation: In the United States today, there are 2,338,226 college students compared with 2,078,095 last year and 1,360,000 in the pre-war peak year (1939–40).

Peak veteran enrollment is expected in 1949–50. Contrary to popular belief, government subsidy of veterans is not *the* cause of high enrollment, but only a contributing factor. Surveys indicate that the average veteran would have entered college anyway.

U.S. Office of Education estimates college enrollment will level off at 2,477,000 in 1951–52, but mount to 2,924,000 in 1959–60. Enrollment after 1960 is expected to rise steadily, paralleling the population growth.

Fenn College enrollment more than doubled during each of the past ten-year periods, 1927–37 and 1937–47. 1927–1039; 1937–2229; 1947–5210.

Fenn College growth *IS* in line with the national trend and does reflect the need for an enlarged college plant in Cleveland.

The growth of urban universities reflects population trends. In 1790 only 5% of the U.S. population lived in cities and towns. It was 10% in 1840, 35% in 1890 and 57% today.

The Association of Urban Universities (49 member institutions, including Fenn College) represents only 5% of the total number of four-year colleges (1200) but the small group enrolls 25% of the four-year college students in the nation.

FENN COLLEGE ENROLLMENT TRENDS AS RELATED TO
NATIONAL ENROLLMENT TRENDS (1920-1960)

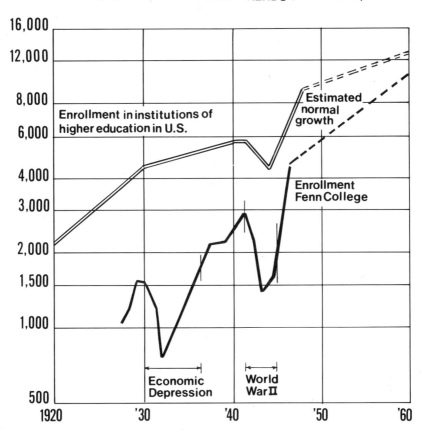

Although Fenn College students come from 6 nations and 14 states, *95% of the student body is from the Greater Cleveland area.*

A gift to Fenn College is an *INVESTMENT* in the future of Cleveland—in the social stability and cultural progress of the *city in which we live.*

Cleveland is the nation's sixth city in population, but the total enrollment of all the Greater Cleveland colleges combined is less than the enrollment of New York University alone. (45,125)

Boston has seven colleges and 36,668 students.

You cannot have a great city without great colleges.

THE RELATIONSHIP BETWEEN TRENDS IN ENROLLMENT AT
FENN COLLEGE AND THE CLEVELAND PUBLIC SCHOOLS

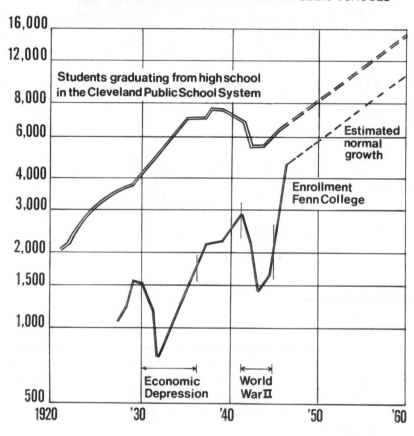

FENN COLLEGE ENROLLMENT & PLANT EVALUATION AT TEN-
YEAR INTERVALS. (Based on a report of the Board of Trustees)

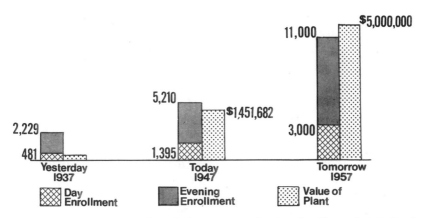

A. Fenn compared with five major Cleveland colleges (1948 data)

(Full-time Day students only)

Institution	Book Value Of Plant And Equipment	Full-Time Enrollment	Value Of Plant And Equipment Per Student
Case	$ 3,958,000	1,549	$2,555
Western Reserve	11,628,000	6,543	1,776
John Carroll	2,400,000	1,677	1,431
Baldwin-Wallace	2,250,000	1,659	1,356
Fenn	1,600,815	1,671	958

B. Fenn compared with three different types of Ohio colleges

Institution	Book Value Of Plant And Equipment	Full-Time Enrollment	Value Of Plant And Equipment Per Student
Oberlin— private college	$6,000,000	1,727	$3,407*
Antioch— work-study	1,700,000	800	2,125*
Toledo— tax-supported	4,000,000	2,976	1,344*
Fenn	1,600,815	1,671	958†

---

* 1946 data.
† 1948 data.

C. A chart based on a report of the Long Term Planning Committee of the Board showing Fenn College enrollment and plant evaluation at ten-year intervals

D. Interpretation: Fenn College has 22% of all the college students in Greater Cleveland *but only 7% of the college plant and equipment.*

National investment ($2,752,780,163) in physical plant per college student is approximately $1,800 (U.S. Office of Education survey). The Fenn investment is $958, only about half the national average.

Case Tech's plant investment per student is 266% higher than Fenn's.

Oberlin, a liberal arts college only (no engineering school), has a plant investment per student 356% higher than Fenn's.

Among 317 leading colleges requiring the same psychological examination of entering freshmen (1946–47), Fenn students ranked 21st from the top.

Of the 1,394 Fenn graduates, 212 are known to have entered graduate schools.

In other words, Fenn College ranks *HIGH* in enrollment. . . .

HIGH in the quality of its students . . .

but *LOW* in buildings and equipment.

V. CONCLUSIONS

The planned growth of Fenn College as outlined by the Long Term Planning Committee *IS* in line with the national trend as well as the local need.

The Greater Cleveland area, by comparison with other large cities *DOES NOT* have adequate college facilities to serve the cultural, professional and industrial needs of a great city.

Fenn College in pioneering a dynamic, modern idea in Higher Education—the work-study plan—is not in competition with any other local college or university. Its peculiar area of service is largely business and industry where special needs for trained personnel are met.

In bringing to fruition the plans of former President C. V. Thomas and the Trustees as expressed in the development program, Fenn College builds to meet Greater Cleveland's growing needs.

The day of interdependence of universities and urban growth is firmly established.

All planning to establish a $4,000,000 Development Program was executed. The need was originally established by Dr. Thomas. The objectives had been defined by the Long Term Planning and Building Committees together with Dr. Thomas. The task facing the board was to set up an organization. In the past the board depended on Dr. Thomas to recruit an organization to run the campaign. He spearheaded the effort and raised a large share of the money.

The methods of interpretation of Fenn to business and industry and special events were conceived by the board and College staff. The following represents conclusions drawn by the committee in charge of spring-boarding the $4,000,000 Development Program (notice how Dr. Thomas' name appeared in almost everything prepared for the planning for the future of Fenn):

> At Fenn College, the need for additional facilities is great and urgent. The College carries 22% of the load in the Cleveland area with only 7% of the total college plant.
>
> Education *never stops* at Fenn College. Extensive courses covering a wide range of cultural and vocational, as well as technical interests are available day and night throughout the year *to students of all ages*. The opportunity to learn is welcomed by a large percentage of the city's population.
>
> Fenn supplies industry and the professions with *Educated Manpower*, adds to the social, political and economic stability of the community and follows a typically American philosophy which President C. V. Thomas stated as follows:
>
> "Higher Education as offered at Fenn College is in keeping with the best American traditions of free enterprise, enabling students to earn and produce while they learn. As work-study students, they are never withdrawn from production."
>
> The educational objectives Dr. Thomas shared in common with the heads of some other large urban colleges and universities were these:
>
> 1. A liberal education for *all* students to the end that they may live fuller, more useful and more gracious lives, and may better shoulder the duties of responsible free citizenship.
>
> 2. Thorough professional and technical education to meet the demands of industry, commerce, government, and to supply agencies of culture and public service with competent personnel equipped with understanding of our complex and dynamic industrial society.

3. Continuing educational services for adults that they may more effectively carry on their occupations, further enrich their personal lives, and better understand our domestic and world problems.

4. Scholarly research to enhance the productive capacities of the city and region, to widen the horizons of scientific knowledge, and to deepen the understanding of human values.

The ground-breaking ceremony for the new Mechanical Engineering Building was held May 17, 1948, at the site. Governor Thomas J. Herbert of Ohio and Mayor Thomas A. Burke of Cleveland spoke on the significance of Fenn's building program to the state and the city respectively. Stilwell, Huxtable, Higley (contractor), and Dr. Nichols also took part in the ceremony. The program carried the following statement:

> The Mechanical Engineering Building, for which ground is being broken today, was made possible by a $500,000 gift, donated anonymously by a Cleveland citizen with a "conviction regarding the cooperative education program which Fenn College provides."

At the May 24, 1948, board meeting, action was taken to make the Cooperative Plan compulsory for all students. During and immediately following the war the plan was of necessity on an optional basis. A few days previous to this board meeting the School of Engineering had been inspected by four representatives from the Engineering Council for Professional Development (ECPD). Four departments were inspected: Mechanical, Electrical, Metallurgical, and Structural Engineering. The board approved the reappointment of 46 faculty members, the appointment to indefinite tenure of 11, the promotion in academic rank of 8, leaves of absence for 9 and 11 new appointments to Faculty status. John David Wright submitted his resignation from the board, but action was taken to ask him to continue as a member although he may not be able to attend meetings regularly.

The 22nd Commencement of Fenn College was held May 28, 1948. It was the first Fenn commencement held at Severance Hall. The speaker was Nat Howard, editor of the *Cleveland News*. The graduating class of 212 was the largest to date in Fenn's history: 187 Day Division and 25 Evening Division students. Of this class 182 were veterans, 102 were married and had a total of 68 children, 95 entered college before the war and had their education interrupted, and 87 transferred to Fenn from other colleges.

Several members of this class have been active in alumni affairs. Philip B. Perry, who graduated *summa cum laude* was president of Fenn Alumni Association in 1964. He received the Alumni Distinguished Service Award in 1968. He served as an Alumni Trustee from 1968 to 1971. He was appointed Vice President Operations, The Cleveland Electric Illuminating Company in 1970. In 1972 Mr. Perry was elected to the Executive Board of the Fenn Educational Fund. Paul G. DuBois was president of the Fenn Alumni Association in 1963. John S. Lamppert received the Alumni Distinguished Service Award in 1969. William F. Kerka joined the Fenn Faculty as Assistant Dean of Engineering in 1961 and was an Associate Dean in 1973 for C.S.U.

A special meeting of the board was called July 2, 1948, to hear the report of the Presidential Selection Committee. Ellwood Fisher, in the absence of Clarence Collens, Chairman, reported for the committee. Following a recitation of the work of the committee and the Faculty Advisory Committee, Fisher formally presented the name of Dr. Edward Hodnett as the unanimous choice of both committees. Dr. Hodnett was then elected formally as the second president of Fenn College. He actually assumed the office on September 1, 1948. Dr. Hodnett, an alumnus of Columbia University and member of the Department of English faculty for eight years, Dean of the College of Arts and Sciences of Newark University for two years, Vice President of University of Massachusetts for two years, and Advisory Editor of Columbia University Press for six years, came to Fenn with high recommendations from the faculty at the University of Newark and Columbia University.

It was reported at the July 30, 1948, Board meeting that Professor Harris and former Professor C. D. Williams received the First Prize ($5,000) in the J. F. Lincoln Award contest for their publication of a new textbook in structural design. It was also reported that Robert Busbey, Fenn's first candidate for the Olympic swimming tryouts missed by a fraction of a second in qualifying for the U. S. team.

Action was taken to establish a new Department of Philosophy in the School of Arts and Sciences with Dr. Ruby Redinger as Chairman. Huxtable reported that Dr. (Boss) Kettering had tentatively accepted an invitation to speak at the twenty-fifth Anniversary of Cooperative Education in Cleveland in November, and if this was not possible, it was hoped that Dr. Hodnett could obtain the services of Dr. Dwight D. Eisenhower, then President of Columbia University.

TABLE 1

1948 FALL ENROLLMENT STATISTICS COMPARED WITH 1947

DAY DIVISION

	In School	Fall 1948 *On Co-op*	*Total*	*In School*	Fall 1947 *On Co-op*	*Total*
Arts & Science	205	25	230	217	19	236
Business Administration	493	65	558	460	52	512
Engineering	861	155	1016	718	124	842
College	1559	245	1804	1395	195	1590
Men — 1451	Women — 108			Men — 1264	Women — 131	
Veterans — 1068				Veterans — 1191		

EVENING DIVISION

	Fall 1948	Fall 1947
Arts & Science	517	473
Business Administration	1642	1770
Engineering	648	707
College	2807	2950
Technical Institute	748	865
Total	3555	3815
Day plus Evening totals	5359	5405

The October 28, 1948, board meeting was the first attended by the new President Hodnett, and the business transacted was from his first prepared board agenda. It was reported that the estimated income would slightly exceed the expenses for the year. Dr. Hodnett reported nineteen new appointees to the faculty for the Fall term plus a new Building Superintendent, George Whalon, who succeeded Burke. Whalon proved to be a most knowledgeable and effective Superintendent. He was well informed on mechanical and electrical equipment, materials, and cost estimates. He was liked by all members of the faculty and staff. Dr. Hodnett was well acquainted with Whalon in Massachusetts and persuaded him to come to Cleveland. But his family refused to move to Cleveland, and after living alone in the Tower dormitory until August 1955, Mr. Whalon decided to move back to New England and join his family. He became Superintendent of Buildings and Grounds for the new campus of Colby College at Waterville, Maine.

Faculty members appointed at this meeting who later held the following key positions at Fenn were:

Samuel H. Berwald, Professor of Accounting

Anna B. Hisey, Director of Music

Chester J. Kishel, Professor, Mechanical & Industrial Engineering

W. J. Moore, Jr., Chairman, Department of Sociology and Director of Religious Education

Emil Stefancic, Librarian

On his first occasion to appear before the Board, Dr. Hodnett informed those present that he had made every attempt to talk with as many people as possible, both inside and outside the College. He then made the following comments, according to the Minutes, concerning his impressions and convictions:

A. He [Dr. Hodnett] does not accept expansion as necessarily desirable.

1. Bigness of the college in number of students, number of faculty, number of buildings, etc., is not necessarily good; Fenn's job is to size up and meet the needs of the community.

2. There is a need to build up the women enrollment and the Arts and Sciences school as a hedge against a possible financial depression or national emergency.

3. Other factors should be considered in planning for Fenn's future such as the fact that only two out of four high school graduates who should go to college now do so and that one out of these two who attend drop out before obtaining their degree; that other cities have adopted the 6-4-4 plan of public education, meaning two additional years of high school, and that some such plan might be developed in Cleveland.

B. He would prefer to concentrate first on strengthening the college educationally:

1. There is a need for improving the professional standing of the faculty.

2. There is a need for more personal attention for our students:

a. Admission should be based on interviews, and personality and promise of future usefulness to society should be real factors.

b. There is need for more adequate individual guidance after a student is admitted.

c. There needs to be further refinement of the operation of the Cooperative Plan. Dr. Hodnett commented that he is increasingly more enthusiastic about the Cooperative Plan as he talks with people around Cleveland.

    3.   The financial position of the college needs strengthening.

    a. 98% dependence on yearly fees is hazardous.

    b. The increase in the number of students does not help the financial picture of the college.

    c. More buildings will increase expense.

C.   Nevertheless the present facilities are so woefully inadequate for the present needs that action is necessary:

    a. Dramatics—no stage, props, etc.

    b. Music—no studio, listening rooms

    c. Auditorium—no opportunity to get together

    d. Centralized student personnel services needed

    e. Separate faculty lunchroom

    f. Library seating capacity inadequate

    g. No place for students to study

    h. Additional engineering labs and office space needed

    i. Student Union—to house student activities

    j. General secretarial office for efficiency

    k. More seminar rooms

    l. More classrooms—75% of use considered satisfactory; ours is very much higher

Conclusions:

A.   Fenn has both immediate and future needs, but as Dr. Thomas indicated, many of the development campaign needs are also immediate ones. Dr. Hodnett emphasized that we must keep working on the future needs and plan for them now in terms of

    1.   Increase of school population indicated in the future.

    2.   Increase in demand for college education in the future.

B.   Contributions from business and industrial concerns for the current fiscal year should be sought to pay off the $100,343.21 still owed for the land adjoining Fenn Tower recently purchased for the new buildings.

The Silver Anniversary of Cooperative Education in Cleveland was celebrated November 18, 1948. It was divided into three parts: A morning assembly was held at the Euclid Avenue Baptist Church. Dr. Hodnett presided. Dr. J. C. Nichols spoke on the topic "Twenty-five Years of Co-operative Education at Fenn." Anniversary awards for outstanding achievements were presented to:

H. Martin Huge, 1938, Electronics

Kenneth J. Burke, 1930, Engineering and Management

Joseph S. Kopas, 1931, Personnel Administration

Dr. Hezzleton E. Simmons, President, University of Akron addressed the assembly on "The Cooperative Way of Higher Education."

An afternoon discussion was held in Panel Hall, Fenn Tower. Dr. Hodnett served as moderator and the following served on the panel:

> Max B. Robinson, Dean of Cooperative Education, "Cooperative work as Educative Experience"
>
> Arthur V. Pohm 1950, Electrical Engineering and John R. Smart 1950, Business Administration, "Cooperative Education as Viewed by Students"
>
> Kenneth J. Burke 1930, Assistant Chief Engineer, National Dairy Company, "Cooperative Education as Viewed by an Alumnus"
>
> Leonard Giles, Personnel Director, Lincoln Electric Company and Fred J. Marker, Manager Industrial Relations, Cleveland Plant, Swift and Company, "Cooperative Education as Viewed by Employers, as it Relates to Personnel Policy, Selection and Training."

An evening dinner meeting was held in the Rainbow Room, Hotel Carter. Board Chairman Charles J. Stilwell presided. The meeting was sponsored by the Cleveland Chamber of Commerce. George W. Codrington, Director of the Chamber and Vice President, General Motors Corporation, Cleveland Diesel Division, welcomed those in attendance. Dr. Hodnett responded to Codrington's remarks. The principal speaker of the evening was Dr. Charles F. (Boss) Kettering, Research Consultant, General Motors Corporation, one of America's outstanding inventors and research scientists. Among many important research successes and inventions attributed to Dr. Kettering's genius are the self-starter which revolutionized the automobile industry, the Delco Farm Lighting System which gave the farmers indoor and outdoor generated electric illumination, and antiknock fuels. The following is a quotation from his address before those assembled:

> If you have any idea what a great advantage it is to have a cooperative school in a large city, especially a diversified city like Cleveland, you will certainly appreciate Fenn College. I think if you went all over and sized up every great city in the United States, you couldn't find one that offered the opportunity or wide

advantages to industry that you have in this city. I think it is more diversified in every type of industry than any other city in the world, and so you have a valuable place in which to have cooperative education. You need to train back and forth. How will you do it? By having men give talks, by visiting plants, or by having cooperative education? Cooperative education helps solve the question both of production and how to make a living.

An accounting of the Silver Anniversary proceedings ends with this paragraph: "Thus came to a successful end a red letter day in the history of Fenn College. Cooperative education in Cleveland was placed on a firmer foundation in the minds of those concerned academically as well as those who employ co-op students."

There were no further board meetings in 1948. And so the year ended with a new president in the harness and three additional important reasons for a joyous, optimistic, and enthusiastic entrance into 1949, namely: the "provisional" accreditation of both Day and Evening Divisions of the School of Engineering on October 28, 1948, by the Engineers Council for Professional Development; the celebration of the Twenty-fifth Anniversary of Cooperative Education at Fenn College at which Dr. Charles F. Kettering spoke so tellingly; and the progress being made in construction of the new Mechanical Engineering Building which was scheduled for completion April 1, 1949.

The first board meeting of 1949 was held at the University Club on January 17. A deficit budget for the year was approved with an estimated income of $1,466,506 and estimated expenditures totaling $1,538,204. This included an increase of $50 per annual tuition charge per Day student and an increase amounting to approximately $1.50 per semester credit hour in the Evening Division. This tuition increase was questioned by Trustee George Woodling whose concern was that this action would endanger Fenn's competitive standing "particularily since there was pressure to have a tax-supported college in Cleveland." Mind you, this was 1949—not 1964 when such great pressure really did spring up. Mr. Woodling also emphasized the need for bettering the public relations with students and alumni.

Dr. Hodnett presented his first Annual Report for fiscal 1948, although he had been a member of the staff for only the last four months thereof. Here are some excerpts therefrom:

The college is in sound condition. It has a particular educational job to do, and it is doing it honestly and thriftily.

Without Fenn and the other fine colleges in Cleveland, the taxpayers would willy-nilly be supporting a municipal institution.

In terms of the long-range development plans it is important to realize that the building program outlined by Dr. Thomas is as vitally necessary for 1000 as for 1500 or more students.

As one means of achieving more public support, I propose (1) that the Corporation of Fenn College be expanded to include fifty or so more members representing the industrial, business, and professional leaders of Cleveland and (2) that 'Friends of Fenn,' an organization of unlimited membership, be created.

Beyond meeting immediate needs, strong efforts should be maintained constantly to build endowments. The security of Fenn in the future lies in such efforts.

We need to seek out more ways in which to serve Cleveland and to channel the rich cultural, technical, and human resources of Cleveland to flow freely into the College.

Education is a slow and complex growth. It is not easy to see when the growing is going on, or say whether it is going well or no. A fine, serious student body, a loyal, dedicated faculty, a dynamic Board of Trustees, and one of the world's most prosperous and civilized cities are assurance that Fenn will progress in ways that matter.

The Annual Meeting of the Fenn Corporation was held March 21, 1949. Fisher, Hale, Perry, and Stecher were re-elected as Trustee members of the class of 1955. George S. Case, Jr., was elected as a Trustee member of the class of 1950 to succeed the late John C. Sanders and Dr. Hodnett was elected to the class of 1951 to succeed the late Robert F. Bingham. John David Wright's resignation was accepted with regret.

The board met immediately following the Corporation meeting and the following officers were elected:

Charles J. Stilwell, Chairman
Richard S. Huxtable, First Vice Chairman
Ellwood H. Fisher, Second Vice Chairman
Joseph C. Nichols, Secretary
Arthur P. Loegler, Secretary, Finance Committee

Through an inadvertence J. S. Crider was not officially elected Treasurer until the May 19, 1949, meeting of the board. Herrick had requested that he not be re-elected to the office of Secretary because of the increase in the promotion work in the Admissions Office to meet the accelerated recruiting program.

Action was taken to assess tuition and fees in the Day Division on a quarterly basis rather than an annual basis.

Dr. Hodnett announced that the date for dedication of the new building was set as September 12, 1949. The name of the donor was still kept anonymous to the general public. Dr. Hodnett also reported on important items of personnel, new courses, cooperation with business and industry, research, and professional activities of the three schools, and he presented a special report on development plans. He based his report on the answers to these three questions: (1) What are our objectives? (2) What is Fenn's area of general distinction? (3) How shall our efforts be organized? Trustee Woodling "expressed the view that the Board was seeking not so much questions—as answers to questions, and hoped something more definite would be forthcoming at the next meeting of the Board."

Dean Nichols reported that the swimming team had won 11 dual meets and lost only 4. Robert Busbey set 17 pool records in opponents' pools and 4 in the Fisher Pool at Fenn. He won 43 first places in diving in 45 meets over a three-year period.

At the request of Dr. Hodnett a special Corporation Meeting was called on May 19, 1949, in advance of the board meeting to amend Article 7 of the Regulations of Fenn College to include a 28-man Board with the President of the College, and the President, Treasurer, and General Secretary of the YMCA as ex officio members. After considerable discussion, and at the suggestion of Stilwell the proposal was withdrawn by Dr. Hodnett.

At the board meeting immediately following, Coolidge outlined the financial operation of the Women's Dormitory (Bliss Hall), indicating that since October 1943 it has incurred a net loss of $15,568 and that the loss for 1949 would approximate $6,620. It was voted that because of the interest of the Fenn Women's Advisory Board in this academic activity their advice in this matter should be sought. They used Bliss Hall occasionally for teas and other similar events; it was adjacent to the Masonic Auditorium at Euclid Avenue and East 36th Street. Approval was voted to place the non-academic personnel on a five-day week.

The 23rd Commencement of Fenn College was held in Severance Hall on May 27, 1949. Dr. Mark C. Schinnerer, Superintendent, Cleveland Public Schools, delivered the Commencement Address the title of which was, "Let's Take Stock." There were 52 graduates in Arts and Sciences, 154 in Business Administration, and 192 in Engineering for a total of 398.

Nicholas V. Di Cello, *cum laude* graduate from this class served as President of the Fenn Alumni Association in 1962 and John R. Lowe, Jr., served as President in 1965. Richard J. Egan and Andrew P. Slivka served on the faculty for a few years.

The dedication of the new Claud Foster (for a long time, the anonymous donor) Engineering Building started with a luncheon in the Fenn Tower. Fred M. Zeder, Vice Chairman, Chrysler Corporation and close friend of Mr. Foster was the principal speaker. Richard S. Huxtable, Vice Chairman, Fenn Board of Trustees and Chairman of the Building Committee, and Dr. Sholto M. Spears, Dean, School of Engineering, were also called upon by moderator Ellwood H. Fisher to speak. Foster presented the key to the building to Dr. Hodnett following which, afternoon tours of the building were conducted. In the evening, representatives of Technical Societies and Educators of Greater Cleveland were guests at a buffet supper and then conducted on tours of the new building. The following Sunday afternoon, September 18, 1949, a general open house of the new building was held for the general public to visit and inspect this new modern facility provided through the generosity of Mr. Claud Foster.

The program for the dedication carried the following statement by Foster:

> My philosophy of life finds its natural expression in the lives of typical Fenn students, young people who work hard and earn their own way. I believe the Fenn Plan of Cooperative Education is selective enough to sort out students who can make the best use of their education, the ones with self enterprise and real ability. Later as college graduates they don't have to waste time trying to locate in the right job, they have the right job waiting.

Beneath the large photograph of Foster which was, at his request, placed in the first floor lobby of what was later to be known as Foster Hall, is this inscription followed by his signature: "You cannot tell anyone else how to make things unless you have first made them with your own hands." Claud H. Foster was an unusual man. He was raised on a farm in what is now part of the City of Cleveland. He was a musician, machinist, designer, inventor, manufacturing administrator, salesman, and an expert golfer, a truly remarkable man. He founded the Gabriel Company in 1904, invented and manufactured the Gabriel automobile horn, and Gabriel Snubber shock absorber. He sold the company in 1925 and retired from Chairman of the Board in 1928 at age 55. He received an Honorary Degree, L.H.D. from Fenn College in 1953.

On July 31, 1952, Foster, at age 79, invited the heads of sixteen Protestant, Catholic, and Jewish hospitals and orphanages and 94 other guests to a dinner at the Hotel Statler. Following the dinner he surprised everyone present by presenting securities and checks ranging from $35,000 to $775,000 to the sixteen institutions. All told he gave away $3,879,680.79 that evening. He remarked, "Too many institutions get their money from dead men, I wanted to see them get it." The only restriction placed on the gifts was that they be used for capital purposes, buildings, and equipment.

Claud H. Foster had previously given $509,203 to Fenn College to build the Foster Engineering Building and $550,000 to the YMCA to build the Brooklyn-Parma Branch. He later gave 732 organs to churches scattered throughout the United States. He died in the Bellevue, Ohio, Hospital on June 21, 1965, following a long, lingering illness resulting from an automobile accident while he was on his way to present an organ to a church in Ohio.

The final board meeting of 1949 was held November 30. It was reported that from estimated income and expenditures for the month of December it would appear that the College would close the fiscal year in "a plus condition approximating $2,219." Action was taken on six Faculty resignations, eight new appointments including R. Malcolm Sills of Massachusetts as Librarian, two re-appointments, five promotions, and two leaves of absence.

A new Joint Committee on Relations with YMCA (a task committee) had been previously appointed including Myers, Dr. Carter, and Fries from Fenn and Fred Ramsey, Ray Livingston, and Louis Peirce from the Y. Myers, Chairman of this committee reported that they had discussed the subject of faculty retirement and that they intended to study further the problems of Fenn-Y relationships.

Dr. Hodnett presented his first year-end report as President. Following are a few excerpts:

> We are ending the first complete fiscal year since I became President with a balanced budget in view. The present estimated actual income for the year 1949 is $1,443,703, and the estimated actual expense is $1,441,484. We are proud of this showing because we are making it by wiping out an anticipated deficit of $71,000 by means of careful management in all departments and cooperation from all hands.
>
> In spite of these economies, Fenn has moved ahead. Faculty salaries have gone up and are now in line with those of comparable undergraduate institutions. The post-war shifting of faculty is about ended. A young, alert faculty and a hard-working student body are cooperating with the administration to make Fenn a better college in every way.
>
> The great advance of the year, of course, was the September opening of the Claud Foster Engineering Building with its splendid new equipment. Occupancy of this building relieved the pressure for space in other classroom buildings and permitted some much-needed improvements in our laboratories.
>
> Registration in the Day Division dropped from 1804 in September 1948 to 1629 in September 1949, but in the Evening Division it rose from 3515 to 3755. Fenn still serves over 5000 students.
>
> During the past year, also, the Fenn co-op work-study plan has returned to normal after the dislocation of the War and heavy veteran enrollments. For the past quarter (September to December) 368 students were out on co-op jobs. This quarter (December to March) they will be in College and their opposite numbers will be out covering the same jobs.
>
> You are all aware of the financial problems facing all independent institutions of higher learning. Fenn, like Case, Carroll, and Reserve as well as Yale and Harvard, must find funds to make up the difference between expense and income from student fees and various auxiliary enterprises (bookstore, research, etc.). If Fenn and the other independent colleges and universities do not find these funds, the plain indication is that many times more money will be demanded from corporations and individuals to underwrite nearly-free instruction in tax-supported institutions.
>
> We cannot run Fenn on student fees. We cannot permit control of higher education to slip into the eager hands of the bureaucrats

by default. We must secure wider voluntary financial support from both corporations and individuals. We must keep Cleveland a citadel of private citizens.

A brief meeting of the board was held January 17, 1950, principally to review the proposed budget for the year. The budget, as submitted for $1,438,657, was approved, and Dr. Hodnett reported that it did not include any new facilities which were greatly needed. He also reported that the year 1949 was closed with an actual surplus of $8,326.

The recommendation of the Personnel Committee was approved that the position of Director of Public Relations, which was vacated by Thomasson, be filled with a full-time appointee with the new title of Assistant to the President. A few months later (June) H. Richard Taylor was appointed to this post.

The Nominating Committee indicated that it had no report to submit. It was agreed the encumbents would remain in office until their successors were elected. Perhaps a little explanation is in order. Back on April 22, 1946, Chairman Stilwell wrote Dr. Thomas that he preferred "to be dropped from the Chairmanship of the Board at the end of the year." In 1947, no Nominating Committee had been appointed, and in Chairman Stilwell's absence the incumbent officers were elected for another term. Dr. Thomas died in November 1947 so Stilwell continued as Board Chairman through the selection of the new president, Dr. Hodnett. In December 1948, however, Stilwell warned Dr. Hodnett that he would accept the chairmanship for only one more year, with the understanding that it would be his last year as Board Chairman. Then on February 20, 1950, he wrote Dr. Hodnett the following:

> The Nominating Committee appointed at the last meeting of the Board has indicated to me that they have canvassed the subject of a new Chairman of the Board with several members, and up to the moment without reaching a definite arrangement; therefore, they will appear at today's Board meeting without a report.
>
> I have agreed with the Nominating Committee that in case they do reach the Board meeting without a definite report, I will continue in office in accordance with the by-laws until such time as they can secure a new Chairman; but for the record I prefer to have it understood, and with you as well, that this resignation is to become effective in any event not later than May 1, 1950.

Circumstances arose which induced Stilwell to change his mind. Administration versus faculty-alumni unrest, the subsequent resignation of Dr. Hodnett, the appointment of a new president, and the rapid development of Fenn College evidently rekindled Stilwell's interest in Fenn to the degree that he did not finally retire as Board Chairman until February 26, 1960.

The Minutes of the February 20, 1950, board meeting closed with the following two paragraphs:

> Mr. Fisher urged each member of the Board of Trustees to keep close to the College and to take the responsibilities as a Trustee seriously.
>
> Mr. Rasmussen asked that the Minutes carry a statement of appreciation for the service which Mr. Stillwell has rendered the College as Trustee and Chairman. This suggestion was approved by a rising vote that was unanimous.

Every so often the subject of a three-quarter versus the existing four-quarter year cropped up, but nothing much was done about it until 1950 when, on approval of the board, Dr. Hodnett presented an optional plan to the faculty granting each faculty member the option of electing a three-quarter teaching year at a reduction of one-eighth of his existing salary. Upon taking a poll of the regular teaching faculty only 14 of a total of 89 voted to accept such option. Because of the uncertainties of mobilization in the future, the Board Personnel Committee on November 21, 1950, decided not to take any further action on the three-quarter teaching year.

The Board of Trustees on May 2, 1950, took the following action concerning academic rank for non-teaching members of the College staff:

> Professional non-teaching members shall be assigned rank indicating the equivalent academic rank of their positions. For instance, the Librarian might be described "with rank equivalent to that of full professor." Since the equivalent rank would be evaluated on the basis of a man's qualifications, from time to time it might be increased, just as the teacher might be promoted. This designation does not grant tenure status to non-teaching staff members.

Again, the Nominating Committee was invited to present its report at this May 2, 1950, meeting. Here is an excerpt from the Minutes of the meeting:

The Chairman asked for the report of the Nominating Committee, consisting of Mr. Fries, Mr. Baldwin and Mr. Tremmel.

Mr. Tremmel reported as follows:

For Chairman of the Board—no nomination

For First Vice Chairman—Mr. Huxtable

For Second Vice Chairman—no nomination

Mr. Tremmel asked that since the Committee had worked long and diligently and had been unable to determine upon a slate of Officers for the Board, that the Committee be relieved of this responsibility and that the matter be placed in the hands of the Executive Committee.

After some discussion, it was moved by Mr. C. M. Taylor and seconded that the report, including the recommendation, be approved. At this point, Mr. Carter moved that the report be tabled. This was seconded by Mr. Bartlett. After some discussion, the motion to table was defeated 8 to 5. At this point Mr. Huxtable asked that his name be withdrawn from the nomination report.

The Chairman then asked that he be allowed to refer this matter to the Executive Committee. Accordingly, Mr. Baldwin moved that the nomination of Officers for the Board be referred to the Chairman, the Executive Committee and such other members of the Board as the Executive Committee chooses to include. This motion was seconded and adopted.

The 1950 Commencement was held at Severance Hall and James F. Lincoln, President, The Lincoln Electric Company, gave an address titled "Opportunity." Pertinent information concerning the graduating class is shown in Table 2.

TABLE 2

CLASS OF 1950

School	Day	Evening	Men	Women	Cum Laude	Magna Cum Laude	Summa Cum Laude	Total
A. & S.	39	1	27	13	3	0	2	40
Bus. Ad.	119	17	126	10	4	0	1	136
Engineering	197	17	210	4	7	2	2	214
Totals	355	35	363	27	14	2	5	390

Veterans: 327
Non-veterans: 63

Robert F. Busbey, accomplished swimmer of this class (mentioned earlier) joined the Fenn Staff in the Department of Physical Education and Health. He later became Director of Athletics and General Service Programs in Physical Education at C.S.U. Percy B. Bray, graduated *magna cum laude* and was a recipient of the Alumni Distinguished Service Award in 1969. Arthur V. Pohm, graduated *summa cum laude* and was a recipient of the Alumni Service Award in 1967. James M. Madigan became an Instructor in the Department of Chemical Engineering for a few years. John F. Cleary organized the Cleary Construction Company and executed a number of small Buildings and Grounds contracts for Fenn College.

The first inference of a change in the administrative staff was in the Minutes of a joint meeting of the Board Executive and Personnel Committees held September 7, 1950. It was as follows: "It was moved by Mr. Coolidge, and voted, that the appointment of Professor G. Brooks Earnest [of Case Institute of Technology] as Dean of the School of Engineering, effective February 1, 1951, be approved by the Committees and presented to the Board of Trustees for final action." This action was approved at the December 4, 1950, meeting of the board.

Considerable business was transacted at the September 25, 1950, board meeting. The dinner and meeting lasted from 6:00 to 10:15 p.m. Much of the time was spent in a new plan proposed by H. R. Taylor, assistant to the President, to provide for the expansion of the membership of the Fenn Corporation to include at least one representative each from approximately fifty major civic, business, industrial, and professional groups. Names of individuals and suggestions of firms were recommended by Taylor and reviewed by the board for organized contact thereof and to explain the plan to the proposed individuals and obtain their acceptances to join the Fenn Family as Corporate Members.

The board then went into executive session to discuss certain inter-family problems which had arisen. As the result of this executive session the following statement was released to the Cleveland news media on September 26, 1950.

> The resignation of Dr. Sholto M. Spears, Dean of the School of Engineering, to take effect October 1, 1950, has been requested by the Board of Trustees of Fenn College, it was announced last night by Charles J. Stilwell, Chairman of the Board, following a trustees' meeting at the University Club.

"The Board of Trustees takes this action with much reluctance and regret," Mr. Stilwell stated. "We believe that new leadership is needed in the Engineering School, in order to straighten out misunderstandings that have quite unnecessarily arisen and persisted in that school. Fenn College has made excellent progress, especially in the field of engineering, during the past two years, and the members of the Board of Trustees are solidly behind the plans for the future. We are confident that Fenn is entering a period of increased educational stature, and we count on the loyal cooperation of all members of the faculty and administrative team to assure its progress."

"Dean Spears was notified of the intention of the Trustees last June," Mr. Stilwell added. "The trustees were not prepared to make any announcement concerning his successor," he said.

The office of Dean of the College was terminated by the board effective November 1, 1950. Dr. J. C. Nichols, encumbent for fifteen years, chose to resign and was given a leave of absence with pay for six months, to May 1, 1951, and leave of absence without pay until he obtained permanent employment.

There were growing tensions regarding the administration of the College. Vice Chairman Fisher presided at the December 4, 1950, meeting of the board, although Chairman Stilwell was in attendance. H. R. Taylor was elected Secretary of the Board to succeed Dr. Nichols, and Adrian D. Joyce, Chairman of the Board of the Glidden Company was elected a Trustee, Class of 1951. Mary J. Magee was appointed as College Nurse (she graduated from Fenn with a Bachelor of Science degree in 1952) and she held this position through 1967, two years after the transfer of the College to the State of Ohio. Michael J. Phillips was appointed Assistant Professor of Structural Engineering. He was promoted to Associate Professor, Civil Engineering and Engineering Mechanics in 1952 and held this same title for C.S.U. He retired in June, 1972. The board voted to expand the membership of the Fenn Corporation to approximately fifty business, industrial, and professional individuals in various walks of life, and that a meeting of the new group be held in the Spring of 1951.

This was the final board meeting for 1950, a strategic year in the history of Fenn. In fact, it was the last year that the College employed the calendar year as its fiscal year. The uninformed would wonder why Fenn's academic year September 1 through August 31 included parts of two fiscal years. It really created difficulties in college accounting. But, inasmuch as the College was a creation of the YMCA it was mandatory that it follow the identical fiscal year of the Y. The change, was made in 1951 when Fenn College embarked under its own sail.

All colleges have their ups and downs, but during 1950 and 1951 Fenn experienced more downs than ups. One of the ups, however, was the acceptance of the report of the Special Joint Committee of Fenn-YMCA Trustees at the first board meeting in 1951 held on January 15. This committee was appointed by both boards to examine the relationships between the two organizations with a view to recommending measures to resolve certain questions concerning areas of responsibility and lines of authority. The committee held eight meetings, examined the records, and conferred with members and officers of both Boards.

To review briefly, back in 1934 the Branch status of Fenn became too unwieldy and after much study a separate Board of Trustees was established for the College. In 1937, largely due to policies of accrediting agencies the College was separately incorporated as an educational institution under the laws of the State of Ohio. The purpose for which the Corporation was organized was to "maintain a college; to provide education designed to meet the cultural, vocational, spiritual, social and physical needs of youth; to confer degrees and to have and to use all other powers provided by law for colleges; and to do any and all things necessary or convenient for the accomplishment thereof."

Following is an excerpt from the report of the special Joint Committee:

> In the view of the Committee, separation as to operations, government and control has in fact been accomplished, and acceptance of the fact of separation need not mean the breaking of the spiritual bonds, or the dimming of the sense of common aim and purpose that all desire to preserve. On the contrary, we believe that the full implications of the independent status of the College should be willingly recognized and accepted by the Association, and that this acceptance will:
>
> Provide the atmosphere in which these spiritual bonds can be strengthened; permit a cooperative, working relationship, consistent with the facts of the position, and far more satisfying and fruitful than is possible in the present confusion; lead to deeper, closer unity in a common service to youth on the basis of mutual consent; reveal more clearly than now appears the privileges and

advantages to both residing in close cooperation; simplify planning for wise and equitable use of joint resources and facilities, placing financial responsibility where it reasonably belongs; and open the way for long-term planning for permanent financial security of the College; the achievement of self-support in terms of earnings, endowments, and contribution income.

Under the concept of free and independent proprietorship and a status of separate and complete autonomy enjoyed by both bodies, the opportunity for a closer drawing together for the purpose of serving youth will be enhanced rather than diminished. To this end, it is proposed:

That a Committee of Joint Counsel be established as a permanent feature, with membership drawn from the two boards of trustees, with chairmen alternating annually, as between the representatives of the College and the Association.

This Committee should have no administrative function, but should confine its work to discovering, devising, and fostering measures of cooperation so that both institutions may express more effectively their common concern for the welfare of youth.

In the opinion of the Committee, the College should not depart from the spiritual heritage of the Association. Good colleges are always concerned with the mental, moral and physical development of their students, and Fenn is, and should be, no exception. In addition to this legacy from the Association, Fenn has a second heritage—of educational liberalism, which came from Dr. Thomas, and which is responsible for most of the distinctive features which the College now has.

Fenn does not want to change its objectives—it merely wants the freedom to pursue those objectives in the most effective way possible.

The problem that confronts the College is an intensely practical problem. Fenn has become a large and complex institution, involving thousands of people and millions of dollars, and, as such, it should be administered according to the best established principles for institutions of higher learning. Good administrative procedures will not make an institution great, but bad procedure may make it difficult to achieve greatness.

The adjustments which Fenn had to make to achieve the status of self-support were many. The orderly transition to private status was made with the complete cooperation of the YMCA officials. Some of the items needing change of management or fiscal operation were as follows:

1. New retirement program for new faculty and staff.
2. Fenn to establish its own accounting department.
3. Change title of Fenn Building (adjacent to the Y. on Prospect Avenue) to the College.
4. Rental charge to Fenn on Johnson property.
5. Maintenance charge on above mentioned Fenn Building.
6. Rental charge on Cleveland Medical Library Association property. (classroom and laboratory space)
7. Fenn establish its own telephone switch board.
8. Fenn discontinue payment of student and faculty memberships to the Y.
9. Fenn discontinue free tuition for children of YMCA employees.
10. Fenn discontinue use of YMCA gym facilities.
11. YMCA discontinue all financial support of Fenn College including pro rated share of the S.P. Fenn Trust Fund.
12. The College free to establish its own rules and regulations and appoint its own Trustees and Corporate Members.

The Joint Committees felt that in consideration of the past relationship between the YMCA and the College, and the desirability of maintaining a close tie in the future, it would be wise and helpful for the President of the Y to be an ex-officio member of the Fenn Board. Chairman Stilwell was authorized to appoint the Fenn members to a Fenn-YMCA Committee of Joint Counsel as recommended in the Special Joint Committee report, noted above. He also appointed a pro-tem Committee to draft a new Code of Regulations, consisting of Carter, Myers, Fries, Bartlett, and Baldwin.

Professor G. Brooks Earnest took office as Dean of Engineering on February 1, 1951. Soon thereafter he was elected to the office of President of the Cleveland Society of Professional Engineers (C.S.P.E.).

The first Fenn Corporation meeting as a private college was held February 12, 1951. The new Code of Regulations for the College was approved. The Annual Meeting was changed to October, the Board membership was established as at least 27 Trustees, the Presidents of Fenn and the YMCA were elected ex-officio members of the Board, and it was decided that one Trustee should be elected from the Alumni of the College.

The Board of Trustees met following the Corporation meeting and elected Coolidge as Treasurer of the Board. It was also voted not to renew the lease on Bliss Hall (Women's dormitory) on September 12, 1951, because of the deficit in operations of $25,227 over the past seven years. There had been considerable use of Bliss Hall by student organizations, but not enough to justify the continuing deficit.

The first meeting of the Fenn-YMCA Committee of Joint Counsel was held March 28, 1951. Members present were Elbert H. Baker, Chairman, Carr Liggett, Vice Chairman, Fred Baldwin, George S. Case, and Alfred E. Gibson, and by invitation H. B. Bentsen, Clarence F. Deeter, Dr. Edward Hodnett, Arthur Loegler, and E. J. Rasmussen. Rasmussen and Hodnett were elected Secretary and Assistant Secretary respectively.

It was reported that Fenn Faculty members in the YMCA retirement program would be permitted to continue their status as long as they remained at Fenn College.

April 1, 1951, was set as the deadline date for the segregation of bookkeeping and cash. Ernst and Ernst, internationally known firm of certified public accountants with headquarters office located in Cleveland, was to determine the best bookkeeping plan for Fenn.

Fenn was to assume the payment of the Johnson property lease ($6,000 annually) and the Fenn Building lease was assigned to Fenn with the stipulation that the YMCA had the right to approve or reject any sale or other disposition of the building. (The building reverted to the YMCA upon the transfer of Fenn's physical assets to the State of Ohio in 1965). Fenn was also to assume payment of the $1,500 annual Medical Building lease and $300 annually for Fenn's portion of the adjacent parking area.

Action was officially taken at the April 25, 1951, meeting of the board to adopt the academic year September 1 to August 31, and a proposed budget for an eight-month period with a deficit of $80,658 terminating August 31, 1951. The Cleveland Trust Company was designated as the bank for Fenn College Funds. The report of the Committee of Joint Counsel Fenn-YMCA was accepted. May 24, 1951, was set as the date for the first meeting of the newly formed (expanded) Corporation, and it was reported that twenty-two representatives had accepted membership. Fisher recommended that the lease on Bliss Hall (Women's dormitory) be terminated prior to November 12, 1951.

The Personnel Policies of Fenn College constituted as a private college had to be entirely redrafted. These policies were approved by the Board on April 25, 1951. It was reported at this same meeting that the Veterans Administration would discontinue its contract for testing veterans on June 30, 1951. This was a blow to the Personnel Development Department because three-fourths of the $41,800 annual budget of the department came from the Veterans Administration. All members of the department were released excepting the four professional members.

After much preparation, May 24, 1951, the day of the first Corporation Meeting arrived. Campus tours, with students and Faculty assisting, were conducted from 3:30 to 5:00 p.m. All laboratories were exhibited. A social hour was held at the Hotel Statler starting at 5:30 p.m. with the banquet starting at 6:30 p.m. The evening program consisted of the following:

Presiding, President Hodnett

Welcome to new Corporate Members, Ellwood H. Fisher.

Greetings from the City of Cleveland, Mayor Thomas A. Burke.

Greetings from Education, T. Keith Glennan, President, Case.

The Product of Co-operative Education, Edward J. Hrdlicka, Fenn Alumnus 1938, Vice President, Hydraulic Equipment Company.

Introduction of Speaker, Herbert P. Ladds, Trustee, Fenn College, President, National Screw and Manufacturing Company.

Speaker, J. Warren Kinsman, Vice President, E. I. du Pont de Nemours & Co., subject, "Mutual Dependency."

Introduction of new Corporate Members, Mr. Fisher.

Response, James W. Corey, New Corporate Member, President, Reliance Electric & Engineering Company.

The inside front cover of the program had the following quotation from the late Dr. Thomas: "An institution of higher learning must be a living, dynamic organism if it is to adjust its curricula and program of education to the needs of young men and women of society." The inside back cover had the following quotation from President Hodnett: "At Fenn we believe in education correlated with reality—reality that embraces the humblest facts about making a living and the highest aspects of a man's reasons for living. We believe that such education will be dynamic. It will not be education for passive self-improvement. It will be education for Action."

The twenty-fifth commencement of Fenn College was held at Severance Hall on May 25, 1951. Trustee Adrian D. Joyce, Chairman, Board of Directors, The Glidden Company, delivered the address entitled "The Dignity of Work." Michael Shuga of this class joined the Fenn Faculty as Instructor, Structural Engineering in 1952. He became Assistant Professor, Civil Engineering and Engineering Mechanics in 1956, Associate Professor in 1961, Acting Chairman of the Department during 1963–64 and later Chairman of the Department for C.S.U. in 1970. He died March 22, 1971. Philip M. Forniti of this class taught for many years in the Technical Institute of Fenn College.

Unfortunately, President Hodnett, indeed a scholarly man, was encountering serious administrative faculty, staff, and alumni problems. These were culminating in resignations which were attracting the attention of the newspapers and open criticism from Fenn's sponsors to the severe detriment of the College. Very unexpectedly he submitted his resignation as President of Fenn College to Stilwell on July 9, 1951, to accept the chairmanship of the Department of English at Ohio University. The board, immeasurably astonished at this turn of events, accepted his resignation on July 12 and at the same time adopted the following resolution in its appreciation of Dr. Hodnett's services to Fenn.

> Be It Known That Dr. Edward Hodnett as President of Fenn College from September, 1948 to the present, has displayed the utmost of intelligent and capable leadership in administering the affairs of the College, and a high degree of loyalty and devotion to the faculty and students. His noble efforts to keep the College intact during a period of national crises confronting all colleges, and at the same time further Fenn's development of quality education to enable its graduates to better meet the requirements of employment and society, has gained the admiration of the Fenn Corporation, the Fenn Board of Trustees, the Alumni, the Faculty and Students, and the City of Cleveland. With deep gratitude, the Trustees of Fenn College adopt this resolution in their appreciation for the outstanding services of Dr. Edward Hodnett.
>
> *In testimony whereof, the seal of the College is hereunto affixed. Dated at Cleveland, Ohio, this 12th day of July, 1951.*
>
> s/Charles J. Stilwell, Chairman

Action was taken at the July 12, 1951 board meeting authorizing Chairman Stilwell to appoint a Trustee Committee to investigate candidates for the position of President of the College. The Personnel of the Committee was announced at the September 11, 1951, meeting of the board: Leyton E. Carter, Chairman, Adrian D. Joyce, Vernon B. Stouffer, Robert M. Stecher, and Henry G. Tremmel.

In the meantime, an Interim Committee was appointed by Chairman Stilwell to administer the affairs of the College. This Committee consisted of Dean Paul R. Anders, Chairman, Dean G. Brooks Earnest, Dean Major B. Jenks, Dean Max B. Robinson, Arthur P. Loegler, Finance Director, and H. R. Taylor, Director of Public Relations.

The Fenn-YMCA Committee of Joint Counsel met August 20, 1951, and the main order of business was the reconciliation of the separation of funds of Fenn and the YMCA and the cancellation of the Medical Library Building lease by the College. After much deliberation it was decided that Fenn owed the YMCA $16,218.69 as the result of a deficit created in 1944 in connection with the Y Centennial Fund Campaign. Approval of this payment was granted at the September 11, 1951, board meeting.

It was reported at this same board meeting that President J. W. Wunsch of the Silent Hoist & Crane Co., Inc. of Brooklyn, New York, contributed $5,000 as a permanent fund, the income from which was to be used for prize awards for students preparing the best papers on the subject of "Materials Handling." A Board of Review selected by the Trustees of Fenn was to decide as to the winners of the award.

The new By-Laws of Fenn College were also approved by the board on September 11, 1951.

The Reliance Electric and Engineering Company established an $80,000 Co-op scholarship program at Fenn in 1951 to develop and educate engineers for the Company. The program was to establish 32 scholarships for high school graduates of northern Ohio who would study at Fenn and Co-op at Reliance Electric and Engineering Company in a stepped-up plan of training.

The Annual Meeting of the Fenn College Corporation was held October 8, 1951. Thirty-one Members were present. The annual reports of various elements of the College were given by the Deans and Directors.

Kenneth A. Akers, Fred C. Baldwin, George S. Case, Jr., and George V. Woodling were elected to the Trustee Class of 1957. Jay Iglauer was elected to the unexpired term of James L. Myers, who had resigned after serving faithfully as a Fenn Trustee for fifteen years. Edward J. Hrdlicka, graduate of Fenn, was elected as the first alumnus to serve for a one year term as Alumni Trustee.

James W. Corey, President, Reliance Electric and Engineering Company, spoke briefly on the company's scholarship program. Elmer L. Lindseth, President, Cleveland Electric Illuminating Company, was the principal speaker of the evening. His subject was: "Industry's Responsibility to Higher Education."

The final Fenn Board of Trustees meeting for the year 1951 was held December 10. Two Trustee resignations were accepted at this meeting, namely: Henry G. Tremmel, who had served for 12 years and Richard S. Huxtable, who had served for 7 years. Each of these men were appointed Honorary Members of the Fenn Corporation.

Chairman Stilwell reported that he had received an unofficial proposal from Western Reserve University and Case Institute of Technology to discuss possible measures of consolidation. The Cleveland Foundation was requested through Chairman Stilwell to conduct a survey concerning the current over-all academic facilities vs demand for higher education in Cleveland. The Cleveland Foundation agreed to conduct the survey and appropriated $75,000 toward the project, pending appointment by the three colleges concerned of a joint committee which would supervise the survey. In point of fact, however, this survey never did take place.

The close of 1951 was the terminus of another era in Fenn's history. The second President of Fenn College had come and gone in a brief period of three years, but probably the most important event in the history of Fenn College, up to that time, took place under his guidance and near the end of his regime, i.e., the establishment of Fenn as a private college. This was a giant step for the Board of Trustees.

Fenn's separation from the YMCA was at first more nominal than real, for the two organizations had functioned independently since 1936. But it did involve a sentimental break, because the College had been fostered by the YMCA since its birth and cherished the relationship. The separation really came about because the functions of the growing College and of a YMCA were too dissimilar and the connection between them, no matter how friendly, had lost its original purpose and had become increasingly awkward to carry out.

This achieved independence from its parent organization, was a milestone in the further growth to maturity. Hopes, fears, doubts, and dreams began to shape events which brought Fenn eventually to a fully accredited, independent degree granting institution.

IX

*There is nothing more difficult to take in hand,
more perilous to conduct, or more uncertain
in its success, than to take the lead
in the introduction of a new order of things.*

Nicolò Machiavelli, 1469–1527.

The remaining chapters should normally be the easiest to set forth because they constitute the era in which the author was president of Fenn College. In starting the drafting thereof, however, it appears that the reverse might be true for two reasons: There could easily be the urge to include the happenings at the College in greater detail, and there could also be the impulse to glamorize this particular era. The author will endeavor to continue the setting down of Fenn's history with the same policy heretofor adopted in drafting all historical events, quoting more from documents and relying less upon judgment or opinion.

The initial board meeting of 1952 was held on January 28 at the University Club. Dr. Carter submitted the report of the Trustee [presidential] Selection Committee. The following is abstracted from the report:

> After deliberation and appraisal of the excellent qualifications of the several members of our top level administrative staff, your Committee voted unanimously (Mr. Stouffer being absent on vacation) to recommend to this Board the appointment of G. Brooks Earnest, present Dean of the School of Engineering, as Acting President of Fenn College.
>
> If the first task of your Committee—that of solving the matter of the appointment of an Acting President—is presently resolved,

your Committee can address itself in an unhurried and thorough manner to the task of exploring, sifting, scrutinizing and evaluating qualifications and experience of persons from near and far who appear worthy of consideration as potential candidates for the permanent presidency of Fenn College.

The board unanimously approved the report of the Selection Committee and "that Dean Earnest be appointed as Acting President of the College."

Chairman Stilwell reported that a committee to supervise the joint survey on higher education in the Greater Cleveland area had been appointed. The members of this committee were W. R. Burwell, Chairman, Mark C. Schinnerer, Ray M. Gidney, Frank E. Joseph, Mrs. Robert H. Jamison, George S. Dively, and William I. Ong. This committee added the area college presidents to its membership and soon engaged Dr. John D. Millett, Professor, Public Administration at Columbia University, as its Consulting Director. C. De Witt Hardy was Associate Director. Dr. Millett was appointed President of Miami University in 1953 and Chancellor of the Ohio Board of Regents in 1964. He was a recipient of an honorary degree, Doctor of Laws, LL.D. from Fenn College at the 1953 commencement at which he delivered the address. DeWitt Hardy succeeded Dr. Millett as Director of the Commission.

This important survey committee continued its work as the Cleveland Commission on Higher Education and in 1956 was entirely reorganized with Ralph M. Besse (then Vice President, the Cleveland Electric Illuminating Company) as the chairman. The commission was then composed of the five college presidents and six lay members. The commission became and still is a powerful advisory body in the field of higher education in the Greater Cleveland area.

A resolution in memory of the late John S. Crider was approved by the board at the January 28, 1952, meeting. Crider, a YMCA representative, served as an ex-officio member of the Fenn Board of Trustees from 1936 to 1950.

On February 5, 1952, the Executive Committee of the board approved the recommendation of the author that Dr. William A. Patterson, Registrar, be appointed Associate Dean of Engineering and Registrar, effective February 1, 1952.

On the Euclid Avenue side of the Tower on the sixth floor were two rooms, each two stories high. They were originally designed as squash courts and were never completed, although they were being used as classrooms. They had bare red-tiled walls, no windows, inadequate lighting, heating, and ventilation. On the suggestion of the acting president, the board approved remodelling these two rooms to four rooms by adding a structural floor system on the seventh floor, finished walls, ceilings, and windows. The four rooms were completed, adequately lighted, heated and ventilated, providing pleasant classroom space all at a cost approximating $12,000. Seating space was thereby provided for an additional ninety students.

Chairman Stilwell announced at the March 31, 1952, meeting of the Board that Ralph L. Dickey and Dr. James C. Hodge had been duly elected Trustees of the College by letter ballot, also that Acting President Earnest had been elected President of the Heights Chamber of Commerce. At the same meeting, at the request of the acting president, the new office of Dean of Women was authorized. Mrs. Selma Montasana, who had been teaching physics, was appointed to this new office. During the years of her tenure the number of co-eds and the co-ed and sorority activities increased manyfold. She had equal voice with other administrators of the College and was a permanent member of the Administrative Staff reporting directly to the President.

The retirement of George B. Simon, effective August 31, 1952, as Associate Professor Emeritus of Speech was authorized by the board at the March 31 meeting. He was re-employed November 1, 1952, as the first Archivist of the College and held this post until his second retirement on August 31, 1965. He died June 16, 1967. He was in demand as a speaker, especially at alumni affairs, right up to the end of his life. He did considerable research on the history of Fenn and drafted a chronological sequence of the important college happenings. He requested and obtained from many sources representative pictures, printed College booklets, trophies, periodicals, and other memorabilia which rested in the Archives office, located off the Library in Stilwell Hall. It was subsequently moved to the fifth floor of the new University Tower building of C.S.U.

Acting President Earnest appointed a Joint Faculty-Trustee Committee to establish more specific criteria for the awarding of honorary degrees. This committee reported sufficiently early to permit selection of candidates for the next commencement. Justice Harold H. Burton (mentioned earlier), Charles J. Stilwell, and Ellwood H. Fisher were approved for the Doctor of Laws, LL.D., and Elmer L. Lindseth for the Doctor of Engineering, D. Eng., at the March 31, 1952, board meeting. Stilwell asked that his name be withdrawn.

At the May 21, 1952, Trustee meeting, authorization was granted to appoint four Corporation Committees of four members each, as advisory to the three schools and the Department of Cooperative Education. Each committee was to assist a respective dean and his faculty to improve the services of the College to the student body and to the Cleveland community.

The twenty-sixth commencement convocation of Fenn College was the first commencement which Acting President Earnest presided. It was held May 23, 1952, at Severance Hall. Elmer L. Lindseth delivered the address titled "Not by Bread Alone." There were 221 graduates distributed as follows: Arts and Sciences, 28; Business Administration, 62; and Engineering, 131. The first honorary degrees were conferred by Fenn at this convocation.

Cecil L. Dobbins of this class later returned to Fenn for a few years as a Coordinator in the Department of Cooperative Education, he then became associated with the University of Akron.

It was announced at the July 28, 1952, meeting of the board that tentative approval of the Elementary Education curriculum proposed for beginning in the Fall Quarter of 1952 (subsequently to become C.S.U.'s College of Education) had been granted by Harold E. Bowers of the State Education Department.

The proposed operating budget for fiscal year 1952–1953 was approved at this meeting. The amount required from gifts and grants to balance this budget was $220,402.

The board also unanimously adopted a resolution in memory of Fred C. Baldwin, Fenn Trustee from 1938 to 1952, who died July 21, 1952.

By way of review, the following milestones occurred in Fenn's history during the first year and a half G. Brooks Earnest spent on the campus:

1. Fenn became a completely independent college.

2. The Fenn Corporation reorganized to represent business, industry, and the professions.

3. Curricula in Electrical, Mechanical, and Metallurgical Engineering were for the first time favored with full accreditation by the Engineer's Council for Professional Development (E.C.P.D.).

4. The Structural Engineering curriculum was expanded to be known as Civil Engineering.

5. Fenn's first honorary degrees were conferred.

6. Fenn Alumni held their first "Annual Contribution" campaign.

7. The first full-time Dean of Women was appointed.

8. The Co-op program in Elmentary Education was instituted.

9. The College Archives office was established.

The first board meeting in the new academic year was held at the University Club on September 22, 1952. The Trustee Presidential Selection Committee reported the following at this meeting:

Report of Trustees' Selection Committee of Fenn College

Board members have noted with satisfaction the performance of Mr. Earnest as acting president of the College. The general morale appears excellent. Cooperation and team play of staff have never seemed better. The faculty—while always a fine and loyal body—has, so far as is known, been in good spirit and more united than ever in its endeavors to provide conscientious and increasingly better instruction and guidance to the student body.

With the aid of resourceful staff members, a vigorous and intelligent program of student recruitment and advancement of the College with the public has gone forward under Mr. Earnest's leadership. Favorable comments in the community concerning his leadership have been heard repeatedly by board members.

While enrollment and financial difficulties have not been eliminated—as scarcely could be expected—excellent progress has been made. At the opening of the new year a spirit of hope, and growing confidence that the most difficult days of financial stress and depressed enrollment may well be over, appears warranted, particularly if good leadership and high morale are sustained.

Several important improvements and betterments have been made in the College buildings such as the refurbishing of the Oak Room, new classrooms and new lighting in various places including the main foyer and other well considered expenditures upon the physical plant. These evidences of faith in the future and awareness of the value of keeping the plant facilities in efficient and attractive condition are further evidences of good management and forward-looking leadership.

Engineering Drawing in Fenn Tower, about 1944. Professor Virgil D. Hales standing in center.

Claud Foster, industrialist, inventor and philanthropist

Foster Hall in foreground, on Euclid Avenue
Fenn Tower in background, fronting on East 24th Street

Long Term Planning Committee— Fenn College Board of Trustees—1947
CLOCKWISE Ellwood H. Fisher, Dr. C. V. Thomas, Leyton E. Carter, Vollmer W. Fries, Richard S. Huxtable (Committee Chairman), Clarence M. Taylor

CLOCKWISE Charles Kettering, Vice President, General Motors Corporation; Edward Hodnett, President Fenn College (1948-1951); T. Keith Glennan, President, Case Institute of Technology; George W. Codrington, President, Cleveland Diesel Division, General Motors Corporation

Portrait of Dr. C. V. Thomas.

J. B. Meriam and Professor C. D. Williams in the Meriam Hydraulics Laboratory

Ellwood H. Fisher, first Chairman of the Board of Trustees of Fenn College

Dr. Joseph C. Nichols, Dean of Fenn College and Acting President
from December 1, 1947 to August 31, 1948

Dr. Edward Hodnett, second President of Fenn College
from September 1, 1948 to August 11, 1951

Within the several past weeks there has been considerable discussion—informal and spontaneous—among various board members that it would be timely for the Trustees' Selection Committee to meet, appraise progress, and consider whether or not it would be appropriate and timely to recommend that the acting presidency be terminated and Mr. Earnest be made President of the College.

At the suggestion of our Board Chairman, Mr. Chas. J. Stilwell, a meeting of the Trustees' Selection Committee was recently called to consider the appointment of Brooks Earnest as President of the College. The Faculty Advisory Committee was also called into consultation. That committee was asked for its judgment and advice as to the timeliness and wisdom of recommending that the acting presidency be terminated and that Mr. Earnest be appointed president. The Faculty Committee considered the matter among themselves, away from the Trustees' Committee.

The Faculty Committee reported that, with the exception of one member thereof, it was agreeable to its members that Mr. Earnest be appointed president if such was the desire of the Board of Trustees; that it would not question the wisdom or timeliness of such action and that their loyalty and support of Mr. Earnest as president would be freely and wholeheartedly assured. (The dissenting member made it clear that his support and cooperation would be given inasmuch as he did not lack confidence in Mr. Earnest's character, integrity and desire to serve the College faithfully.)

The Faculty Committee further was of the opinion that the appointment of Mr. Earnest as president would meet with general approval on the part of the faculty and administrative staff of the College and that, to its knowledge, loyal support of him as president and leader of the College would be forthcoming.

It was agreed that no machinery exists whereby a poll of the faculty members upon the matter could be conducted even though such might be deemed desirable. Furthermore, it was pointed out that the members of the Faculty Advisory Committee had been elected by the faculties of the Engineering, Business Administration, and Arts and Sciences Schools and the administrative staff to *represent* these bodies in an advisory capacity to the Board of Trustees which is responsible—and inescapably so—for the appointment of a President for the College.

A meeting was held today with the alumni advisory committee. It was not deemed expedient to hold such meeting at an earlier time.

Mr. Chairman and members of the Board of Trustees, your committee is happy and proud to recommend unanimously the appointment of G. Brooks Earnest as President of Fenn College as of this date.

If this recommendation is accepted it is further recommended that Mr. Earnest be formally inducted into such office by an appropriate inaugural ceremony to be held as soon as adequate arrangements can be made.

Respectfully submitted,

Kenneth Akers

Edward T. Bartlett

Adrian D. Joyce

Robert M. Stecher, M.D.

Vernon Stouffer

Leyton E. Carter, Chairman

September 22, 1952

The Minutes record that "Dr. Carter moved and Mr. Akers seconded that Mr. G. Brooks Earnest be appointed permanent President of Fenn College" and "Motion approved unanimously."

The enrollment statistics for the Fall Quarters for the years 1951 and 1952 are shown in Table 1.

The Fenn College Corporation meeting was held at the University Club on October 13, 1952. Elbert H. Baker, Jr., Leyton E. Carter, Vollmer W. Fries, and Clarence M. Taylor were re-elected to the Trustee class of 1958. Howard F. Burns was elected to fill the unexpired term of Trustee Fred C. Baldwin, deceased, and Edward J. Hrdlicka was re-elected for a one year term as an Alumni Trustee. Thirty-two were present.

TABLE 1
FALL QUARTER ENROLLMENTS
FOR 1951 AND 1952

| | Enrollment | |
	1951	1952
Day Division	690	607
Evening Division	3660	3710
Total	4350	4317

Instead of a principal speaker the meeting consisted of a series of annual reports, as follows:

Arthur P. Loegler, Finance
William A. Patterson, Registrar
Meriam C. Herrick, Admission
Major B. Jenks, School of Arts and Sciences
Paul R. Anders, School of Business Administration
William A. Patterson, School of Engineering
Nicholas Rimboi, Technical Institute
Max B. Robinson, Cooperative Education
George A. Leech, Personnel Development
Foster T. Miller, Student Activities
H. R. Taylor, Jr., Development

President Earnest, Summary for the academic year, 1951–1952

The Trustees met December 11, 1952, at which time several important actions were taken. Vernon H. Davis was appointed as Assistant Finance Director, and Professor Emeritus George B. Simon was engaged as Archivist. Dean Max B. Robinson was appointed Dean of Personnel Services with all department chairmen carrying responsibilities relating to student services reporting to him instead of to the President, as theretofore. A three-year agreement was made with the Fenn Alumni to establish a permanent Alumni Office on the campus for the Fenn College Alumni Association. Following is a portion of the report prepared for submission to the Board:

> I.   In the past year the 3,000 Alumni of Fenn College, through the Alumni Association, have displayed a growing and constructive interest in the welfare of the College. Factors leading to this position are: (1) More mature leadership and representation in the Fenn Alumni Association; (2) A nation-wide trend toward official alumni support of operating costs of colleges and universities; and (3) Sincere cooperation and assistance in alumni affairs by the administration.
>
> II.   This interest has been highlighted by the inauguration of the Fenn College Alumni Scholarship Fund, sponsored by the Alumni Association. Monies received in their annual solicitation from Alumni will be used to finance a portion of the College's existing scholarships. Goal for the 1952–53 campaign is $10,000, which indirectly will contribute to the College's operation. Accord-

ingly, scholarships to the extent of funds received will be known as the C. V. Thomas Scholarships and will be limited to entering freshman.

Other increased activities by the Alumni Association include an annual Homecoming Dinner and Dance and monthly luncheons.

III. This growing interest of the Association has been closely observed by the Administration; it is apparent that to enable the Association to attain its goal in each specific phase of activity as well as embark on new activities, a permanent alumni office with full-time Alumni Secretary must be established.

IV. Recommended: That the College and the Alumni Association participate in a three-year agreement, beginning about February 1, 1953, for the purpose of establishing a permanent alumni office for the Association, according to the following suggested agreement:

1. The College will pay the annual salary for one Alumni Secretary who will perform duties as the executive director of the Alumni Association; the College will pay the annual salary of one clerical secretary; and the College will provide adequate office space including basic furniture, heat and light.

2. The Fenn College Alumni Association will assume all other expenses incurred in the operation of the Alumni Office including fund-raising campaign costs, office supplies, publication and mailing of the *Fenn Grad,* and the expense account of the Alumni Secretary.

3. The Fenn College Alumni Association will pay to the College annually, at the close of the Association's fiscal year, all monies received by the Association in any fund-raising efforts, minus expenses incurred in the operation of the Alumni Office as described in paragraph 2, and 10 percent of net income which will be deposited in the Association's bank account. The income received by the College will be used for financing Alumni Scholarships only.

4. The Alumni Secretary will report to and work full-time for the Alumni Association in Alumni affairs. It is assumed that the willingness of the Alumni Association to assist the Admissions Office in new student recruitment will be continued, with the Alumni Secretary assuming direction of this program.

5. Annually, on or about the anniversary date of this agreement, representatives of the College and the Alumni Association will

meet to re-examine the agreement for any modifications or changes.

At this December meeting the Trustees also decided to invest $200,000 of the cash reserve in short-term securities and to appropriate $1,000 to conduct a survey including preliminary architectural drawings (elevations and floor plans) for a multi-purpose building. They further authorized $5,000 for the inauguration of President Earnest on May 9, 1953.

A comprehensive study was prepared for the physical needs of the College based upon the following projected enrollment forecasts:

	1960	*1968*
Day Divisions	1,500	2,000
Evening Divisions	4,000	4,000
Total	5,500	6,000

It was believed that for facility-use balance, the Evening Division enrollment should not exceed 4,000 for a Day Division enrollment up to 2,000. The actual enrollment in 1960 was 1,580 Day students and 5,317 Evening students for a total of 6,897. Note that the policy for limiting Evening students was changed in the interim since (1952). Comparisons are not feasible for the year 1968 inasmuch as Fenn College no longer existed. For the sake of the uninformed reader, Fenn made a gift of its physical assets, its faculty, and staff to the State on September 1, 1965, as the nucleus for The Cleveland State University.

Complete area needs for all expanded elements of the college were projected as 156,565 sq. ft., and it was suggested that the multi-purpose building be 120 ft. x 143 ft. and eight stories high plus a basement. This would be the same height as the main portion of the Tower so it was recommended that the building be placed adjacent to the Tower on Euclid Avenue with floor connections to the Tower and to the Foster Building.

The first board meeting in 1953 was held on April 6. Action was taken to grant an Honorary Doctor of Engineering degree to President T. Keith Glennan of Case Institute of Technology and an Honorary Doctor of Commerce degree to Minton M. Anderson, Treasurer of the Aluminum Company of America at the Inauguration Convocation of President Earnest on May 9, 1953. Dr. Glennan was the principal speaker at the Convocation in the Music Hall of the Public Auditorium, and Anderson was the principal speaker at the dinner assembly, for the members of the Fenn Family and guests, held at the University Club that evening.

On suggestion of President Earnest action was also taken to charge the Board Development Committee with the task of making a study regarding the adaptation to college use and the financing of the Motors Realty Company property occupied by Ohio Motors Company, located on the west side of East 24th Street between Euclid and Chester Avenues. Action was also taken to allocate the invested income from the $10,000 gift from the estate of the late Trustee Jacob D. Cox, Jr., to the establishment of the Jocob D. Cox Memorial Scholarship Fund. Cox had passed away in February 1953.

Shortly after assuming the presidency, Earnest noticed that the windows on the northwest side of the Tower at the eighth-floor level were always very dirty; all other Tower windows were clean. Upon checking with Whalon, Superintendent of Buildings and Grounds, it was determined that false ceilings had been hung in three squash courts on the eighth floor, back in the late thirties, to turn the squash courts into classrooms of one-story height. The Board approved President Earnest's recommendation to place a structural floor system at the ninth floor, similar to what had been done on the seventh floor on the Euclid side, thus adding three more classrooms accommodating another ninety additional students. Three doors were placed in the ninth-floor corridor, and three windows were placed in the north wall of the north room. The cost for these three new classrooms was approximately $20,000. Thus within two years five classrooms and 180 new student stations had been added to the Tower area by placing floor systems in five former squash courts.

Joseph Ceruti, architect, was again called upon by the Trustee Development Committee to provide architectural studies of the College's physical facilities and to prepare a graphic presentation of proposed new physical needs to include space organization studies, site plan indicating location of new facilities, and the study of existing facilities and their relation to a future program. The committee also voted an additional $4,000 to the $1,000 authorized at its December 11, 1952, meeting to perform adequately the architectural studies. The board, on April 6, 1953, approved the above recommendations of the Development Committee. The Development Committee also reported that as of March 31, 1953, the College had received contributions totalling $138,865.47, which exceeded the experience at the same date in 1952 by $30,846.05.

The board also was obliged to approve a program to tuck-point, caulk, and waterproof all exterior surfaces of the twenty-story Fenn Tower. Considerable deterioration had taken place since the building was constructed, resulting in some damage to its interior. Furthermore, when window openings were broken in to place new windows in the rehabilitated squash courts, it was discovered that the original grouting of the entire exterior brick was of inferior quality. Daylight could be seen through a number of ungrouted openings. This introduced a serious negative factor into the College finances, and the repairing of one exterior wall was put into each following year's budget, totalling $75,000. The board also approved an expenditure of $5,000 for new ultra-high frequency equipment for the Electrical Engineering Laboratory. It was especially needed to keep pace with the advances in this special field and to uphold Fenn's reputation for high quality instruction in Electrical Engineering.

The following report was presented to the Board by President Earnest on April 28, 1953:

> Mr. Joseph Ceruti, architect engaged February 24, 1953 to render architectural services for a Fenn College building program has met with all Deans and Department Heads relative to their planned needs. The composite area requests amount to 200,000 square feet at an estimated cost of $20.00/sq. ft. to produce *new*, therefore, the total cost would amount to $4,000,000. Assuming that we could reduce the requested space needs by 30,000 square feet resulting in 170,000 square feet gross, the total cost would be $3,400,000.
>
> To convert the present Ohio Motors Building to educational purposes and add all facilities to the exterior which cannot feasibly be incorporated in the structure it is estimated that the costs would be as follows:

Cost of property with buildings	$1,000,000
Cost of conversion of existing building	1,987,500
Cost of new facilities	600,000
Cost of conversion of Tower (floors 8,9,16,17)	90,000
Total	$3,677,500

The Ohio Motors Building contains 180,000 square feet. The new facilities include a gym-auditorium combination and a girl's dormitory which add 30,000 square feet for a total of 210,000 square feet.

The actual value of the property minus the buildings is estimated at $550,000 which would bring the net building cost to a total of $3,127,500.

Since the cost of direct purchase and conversion of the Ohio Motors property is lower by about $1,000,000 for approximately the same amount of area and would add approximately 70% more acreage to the Fenn campus, and further, inasmuch as a tentative study of space usage indicates that it would be possible to utilize the building for educational purposes, it is recommended that the Board of Trustees give every consideration to the purchase of the property.

The following excerpt from the April 28, 1953, board meeting acknowledges the action taken on the above recommendation:

Mr. Earnest reviewed the study in recent weeks regarding the possible purchase of the Motors Realty Company property, and the feasibility of converting the four-story building to educational use. Mr. Earnest recommended that the College purchase the property.

Mr. Collens moved, and Mr. Iglauer seconded that the College be authorized to purchase the Motors Realty Company property at a cost not to exceed approximately $1,000,000, and that officials of the College be further instructed to make every effort to negotiate a lease agreement satisfactory to the College.

Motion approved unanimously.

Mr. Stilwell appointed a special campaign committee to organize the fund raising efforts for the purchase of the Motors Realty Company property.

Ralph Dickey, Chairman
Kenneth W. Akers
James C. Hodge
Adrian Joyce
C. M. Taylor
E. H. Fisher
James H. Coolidge, Alternate

Mr. Stilwell instructed the committee to appoint at least three additional members of the Fenn Corporation.

As a result of the above action of the Board, Mr. Stilwell, Chairman, mailed the following letter to 150 Cleveland corporations the day following the Board meeting.

Dear Mr. —:

I am reporting to you of important action taken last night at a special meeting of the Fenn College Board of Trustees.

We want you to know for three reasons. First, you are a partner of Fenn College; second, we know you would have voted as we did; and third, we need your immediate help.

To give a little background—five months ago, the Trustees directed that a comprehensive survey be made by the College with an architect to determine Fenn's physical needs for the next ten years. The first phase of that survey, to determine the additional space requirements, revealed that an estimated 200,000 square feet will be needed to meet our increasing educational responsibilities to the community and your company.

This orderly survey was interrupted three weeks ago when the Ohio Motors property, directly West of the College, including the four-story building on East 24th Street, came on the market.

After three weeks of constant study, the Trustees came up with these facts. Acquisition of the Ohio Motors property would . . . increase Fenn's land area by 68%, provide a four-story reinforced concrete building with 180,000 square feet, all adaptable to educational use, and, present Fenn the last opportunity for expansion since it is bounded on the East by the Automobile Club and proposed freeway, on the South by Euclid Avenue, and on the North by Chester.

Last night, the Trustees voted unanimously to purchase the property for approximately $1,000,000. We know you will agree it was a business proposition too good to pass up. A new building would cost over twice as much, and in addition, deplete our valuable parking area adjacent to the Tower.

We're determined to raise the entire amount at once to avoid costly financing. With every one of Fenn's 150 corporate friends participating, we can meet the obligation.

We know we can count on your company for financial support. Within a few days you will hear personally from a Fenn Trustee or staff member, giving you more details, and asking for your active help.

Sincerely yours,
Chas. J. Stilwell, Chairman
Fenn College Board of Trustees

The response from the above letter and the contacts made by the Trustees and the Administration was tremendous. Industry and business, especially those firms who had been long-time employers of Fenn's co-op students, immediately came to the support of the College. The special committee charged with the negotiations with the Motors Realty Company worked fast. In fact, in less than one month following date of Stilwell's letter requesting financial support, the board met to take action on the purchase of the Ohio Motors Building. Witness the following Minutes of the Board meeting held May 12, 1953:

Present:
Stilwell, Fisher, Baker, Bartlett, Carter, Collens, Coolidge, Iglauer, Joyce, Stecher, Burns, Earnest, Loegler, and H. R. Taylor, Jr.

I. Mr. Burns reviewed the negotiations of the last ten days in respect to the proposed purchase of approximately one-half of the Motors Realty Company property on the west side of East 24th Street between Euclid and Chester Avenues, the part to be purchased being the 4-story building and a parcel of land approximately 113 feet fronting on East 24th Street and 134 feet on Chester Avenue. The property to be purchased upon the following terms:

A gross purchase price of Six Hundred Fifty Thousand Dollars ($650,000.00). All taxes, rent, insurance, and charges for utilities to be prorated as of the date of transfer. The purchase price to be paid as follows: Ten Thousand Dollars ($10,000.00) upon the signing of the contract, Ninety Thousand Dollars ($90,000.00) on the transfer of the property; the balance of Five Hundred Fifty Thousand Dollars ($550,000.00) to be financed by purchase money note and mortgage to the Seller in the sum of Five Hundred Fifty Thousand Dollars ($550,000.00), with interest at four and one-half per cent (4½) per annum. Said mortgage to be payable as follows: Two Hundred Twenty-five Thousand Dollars ($225,000.-00) six months after date of transfer. Thereafter quarterly payments to be made of Sixty-five Hundred Dollars ($6,500.00), plus interest, and the entire balance to be due ten (10) years after date of transfer.

The Motors Realty Company is to grant an option to the College to purchase the remaining portion of the Motors Realty Company's property, namely, the northwest corner of Euclid Avenue and the East 24th Street, having a frontage of approximately 220 feet on Euclid Avenue and a frontage of approximately 208 feet on East 24th Street, for the sum of Three Hundred Thousand Dollars

($300,000.00), said option to give the College the right to purchase said property on July 1, 1968, or in certain events at an earlier date, all as more fully set forth in the proposed contract which was submitted to the meeting. The Motors Realty Company is given the right to require the College, by proper notice, to exercise the option at the end of five (5) years from the transfer, or at any time thereafter.

In connection with said purchase, the College agrees to give a lease to The Ohio Motors Company for a term of two (2) years from the date of purchase, said lease to cover the entire basement and second floor of the 4-story building and all of the first floorspace in said building, except the space now occupied by Automotive Center, Inc., of approximately 7500 square feet, said lease to be at a minimum rental of Twenty-four Thousand Dollars ($24,000.00) per year. Said contract contemplates that the College will secure title to a 3-foot strip of land immediately adjoining the property retained by The Motors Realty Company, Inc. on the west and having a frontage of approximately 3 feet on Euclid Avenue and extending back between parallel lines approximately 384 feet from the Payne-Bingham Company and convey said property to The Motors Realty Company, said 3-foot strip to be subject to the same option as the other property retained by The Motors Realty Company.

II. Mr. Joyce moved, and Mr. Fisher seconded a motion that the President and Secretary of the Board be authorized to sign a contract for purchase of The Motors Realty property in accordance with the above. Motion approved.

III. Mr. Fisher moved, and Mr. Baker seconded authorization of appointment of a committee to complete negotiations for the strip of land, 3 x 384 feet, on the east boundary of the Payne-Bingham Company. Motion approved.

Mr. Stilwell appointed Mr. Burns, Mr. Earnest and Mr. H. R. Taylor, Jr. to that committee.

IV. Mr. Fisher moved, and Mr. Bartlett seconded, that the recommendation of the Special Campaign Committee, calling for a Phase I Fund Drive with a three-year goal of $1,500,000 be approved, and that the committee re-study the possibility of planning a program which could in certain instances be interpreted as a two phase program with a total goal of $3,500,000. Motion approved.

The first and only inauguration of a Fenn College president was held May 9, 1953, in Public Music Hall. Charles J. Stilwell, Chairman of the Board of Trustees, presided. Dr. Yoder P. Leith, Pastor, Forest Hill Church, Presbyterian, delivered the invocation. Greetings were presented by the following:

> William A. Quallich, President, Day Division Students, from the Students
>
> Paul R. Anders, Dean, School of Business Administration, from the Faculty
>
> Madison H. Dods, President, Fenn Alumni Association, from the Alumni
>
> Mark C. Schinnerer, Superintendent, Cleveland Public Schools, from Secondary Schools
>
> Curtis Lee Smith, President, Cleveland Chamber of Commerce, from Business and Industry
>
> John S. Millis, President, Western Reserve University, from the Delegates
>
> Thomas A. Burke, Mayor, City of Cleveland, from the City of Cleveland

The Fenn College Choir under the Direction of Professor Anne B. Hisey provided the music. Dr. T. Keith Glennan, President, Case Institute of Technology, delivered the address entitled, "These Changing Days in Higher Education." Honorary Degrees were presented to Dr. Glennan and to Minton M. Anderson, Vice President, Aluminum Company of America.

A reception for the Delegates was held in Panel Hall of the Fenn Tower, followed by the inaugural dinner at the University Club. The Very Reverend Frederick E. Welfle, S.J., President, John Carroll University, delivered the invocation, and Minton M. Anderson was the speaker of the evening. His address was on "Doorstep to Life."

The day not only included the inaugural for President Earnest, but also the inauguration of the presentation of the first Distinguished Service Citations in recognition of a quarter-century of partnership in the Fenn Plan of Cooperative Education. Representatives of the following companies which engaged Fenn students on the co-op plan were seated at a second speaker's table at the Inaugural Dinner:

> Aluminum Company of America
> American Steel & Wire Division

Bailey Meter Company
Central Outdoor Advertising, Inc.
The Cleveland Electric Illuminating Co.
The C. O. Bartlett & Snow Company
Fisher Body—Cleveland Division
General Electric Company
The Lincoln Electric Company
The May Company
National Carbon Company, Inc.
National Tube Division of U.S. Steel
The Ohio Bell Telephone Company
The Oliver Corporation
Otis Elevator Company
The Pennsylvania Railroad Company
Perfection Stove Company
Reliance Electric & Engineering Co.
The Sherwin-Williams Company
The Standard Oil Company of Ohio
Swift & Company
White Sewing Machine Corporation

Dean Major B. Jenks was chairman of the Inaugural Committee. Two hundred and eight delegates of colleges and universities and thirty-three representatives of learned societies and professional associations were present in addition to many Cleveland friends of the Board of Trustees and Faculty.

The 1953 commencement convocation was held at Severance Hall on May 29. The Honorable Frances P. Bolton, Representative to Congress, Ohio 22nd District, delivered the address, entitled, "The Responsibility of Opportunity." There were 273 graduates, 33 in Arts and Sciences, 97 in Business Administration, and 143 in Engineering. William A. Quallich of this class was president of the Fenn Alumni Association in 1967 and was elected to a three-year term as a Member of the Fenn Educational Foundation in 1970. Honorary degrees were conferred upon: Claud Foster (L.H.D.), Adrian D. Joyce (D.B.A.), William A. Stinchcomb (D.P.A.), and the speaker, the Honorable Frances A. Bolton (LL.D.).

The Case Institute of Technology conferred an honorary degree, Doctor of Engineering, on President Earnest at its June commencement in 1953. Earlier in the year he had been elected to the office of Vice President-Zone III (nineteen states) of the American Society of Civil Engineers (A.S.C.E.) for a two-year term. As such he was a representative to Engineers Joint Council and Chairman of its Committee on Employment Conditions. At a special meeting sponsored by Case during the summer of 1953, he was a recipient of their Distinguished Service Award.

The Cleveland Commission on Higher Education requested as its first recommendation that Fenn College consider instituting two-year semi-collegiate programs. The following is a copy of its recommendation:

> The Cleveland Commission on Higher Education believes that Cleveland needs a junior college program of studies. This program should offer a two-year collegiate education that will include courses in general subjects such as English and specific training in vocational skills such as Secretarial Science. Both the high school graduates and the businesses of Cleveland will benefit from such education. The Commission is asking Fenn College to experiment with a junior college program.
>
> The Commission believes that a two-year course of studies is what many young people want. They find four years of education beyond high school too long. They are not interested in the traditional college studies leading to a bachelor's degree. They need the skills and knowledge to be gained from some post-high school education. A two-year course should meet their need and their interests.
>
> Cleveland business will use their skills and knowledge. The economic life of Cleveland has become highly technical and complex. Along with many professional men it needs an even larger number of persons educated to work with them. Chemists need laboratory technicians; engineers need tool designers; dentists need skilled assistants; lawyers and business men need capable secretaries. In two years of education beyond high school students can be trained for such work. Cleveland needs good citizens as well as skilled workers. The two-year course of studies should seek to provide both in its combination of general and vocational education.
>
> The Commission is asking Fenn to experiment with a junior college program in addition to its present courses of study. Fenn College meets a basic educational need in Cleveland. This institution of higher education offers a practical curriculum which permits

great flexibility of program. Through its undergraduate cooperative programs during the day, its large part-time enrollment in the evening, its Technical Institute, and its extension work in in-plant training Fenn provided a broad educational service to the community.

Fenn College is therefore the most suitable institution in the city to experiment with a two-year program. It now provides education similar to that of a two-year junior college in the Evening Division certificate programs of its School of Business Administration. It provides sub-professional training in its Technical Institute, also an Evening program. Its educational structure and program is organized to meet Cleveland's vocational demands. The Commission is asking it to determine the nature and extent of the demand for a two-year program and the best means of meeting it. By doing so Fenn College will be continuing its record of service to the community.

This experiment undertaken by Fenn would obviate the danger of an additional four-year college developing in the community. Separate two-year colleges tend to grow into four-year colleges. Cleveland has enough four-year institutions granting bachelor's degrees, and it should not be asked to support another. The Commission believes that a two-year, vocationally oriented education is one for which the student can be asked to pay a normal tuition charge.

For its expanding program in its several fields, Fenn needs and merits the support of the community.

President Earnest appointed a special committee composed of all five Deans, the Registrar, Director of Admissions, and one representative from each of the following: Faculty Development Committee, Women's Advisory Board, Alumni, and three members of the Fenn Corporation to make an extensive study of two-year terminal programs which might prove popular. He warned the members of the new committee that there was a natural anxiety on the campus that a day Technical Institute type of program would reflect negatively on Fenn's academic stature which was growing more favorable year by year. He also recommended that whatever programs are suggested should be entirely at the college level.

The Board of Trustees, on August 10, 1953, approved the experiment in a daytime terminal education program at the college level with the request that it should be inaugurated in September 1954. At this same board meeting Kenneth Jenkins, R. M. Hochner, James H. Bond, and Albert M. Cousins were approved as new appointees to the faculty. These men remained with Fenn and were transferred to The Cleveland State University in September 1965. The following recommendations were also approved on August 10, 1953, by the Trustees:

1. Increase in Evening Division student tuition rates:
   Arts & Sciences and
   Business Administration from $11.00 per credit to $12.00
   Engineering from $13.50 per credit to $14.00
   Technical Institute from $12.00 per hour to $13.00
2. Increase in dormitory rent from $4.50 to $5.00 per week.
3. Increase in parking fee from $5.00 to $7.50 per quarter.
4. A four and one-half percent increase in Faculty salaries amounting to $16,000 for the year.
5. The proposed budget for the ensuing year with an estimated income of $934,042 and estimated expenses of $1,119,513.

The appointment of Dr. V. Richard Gulbenkian as Registrar was approved at the September 28, 1953, board meeting. He later became Director of Admissions and Records and remained on the C.S.U. staff in this same status upon transfer of Fenn to the State of Ohio. Chairman Stilwell announced the appointment of K. F. Akers as Chairman of the Special Campaign Committee. Akers reported that $582,320 had been pledged to the $1,500,000 goal of the new capital development program at Fenn.

The Annual Meeting of the Fenn Corporation was held October 12, 1953. Edward T. Bartlett II, Clarence L. Collens, James H. Coolidge, and Herbert P. Ladds were re-elected for six-year terms. Sydney L. Hall was elected to fulfill the unexpired Trustee term of the late Jacob D. Cox, Jr. William R. Miller, Fenn Alumnus, Class of 1934, was elected to serve as an Alumni Trustee for a three-year term.

Mrs. H. N. White, owner of the White Apartments, located on the southeast corner of Chester Avenue and East 24th Street, informed President Earnest in the fall of 1953 that she was going to put the White Apartments on the market and that the asking price would be about $300,000. It was decided that, the price was too high, it would not be good business acumen to add a second fund raising campaign to the one we were already engaged in to convert the Ohio Motors Building, and that the President should confer with Mrs. White and endeavor to have her postpone placing her apartment building on the market. As it worked out, she agreed to delay selling the apartment for a brief time and to notify President Earnest before placing the property in the hands of a realtor.

The final board meeting for the year 1953 was held on December 15. Akers reported that about $718,000 in cash and positive pledges had been received toward the $1,500,000 goal for rehabilitation of the Ohio Motors Building.

Action was taken by the board for Fenn College to contribute $100 to the Leyton E. Carter Memorial Fund of the Cleveland Foundation. Dr. Carter had passed away November 16, 1953, and his loss was deeply felt by his colleagues on the board because of his generous contribution of his personal time to Trustee activities, especially those relating to academic affairs. In fact, Dr. Carter was a member of the Evening Division Faculty at the College and met his classes until the moment illness overtook him. At this same meeting, the board, by unanimous vote, approved the following resolution to be made a part of the official Minutes and an appropriate presentation of the resolution to Mrs. Carter. President Earnest later presented the bound resolution to Mrs. Carter at her home.

A Tribute to Dr. Leyton E. Carter

Fenn College has suffered a great loss in the passing of Dr. Leyton E. Carter. As a member of the Board of Trustees for twenty years, he gave much of himself to the fulfillment of proper administration of the College. His contagious enthusiasm added materially to forceful leadership, not alone from him, but from the other members of the Board of Trustees. He was deeply interested in the progress of Fenn and our academic standing, and anxious that we should attract men of high quality to our faculty.

As a member of our Evening Divsion staff for 34 years, teaching subjects on economics and government, he attracted many students to our halls of learning because of the richness of his ability to require the student to think for himself. He was always receptive and openminded, both in and out of the classroom, and he was sought as a dinner partner in our cafeteria by both students and staff members.

Dr. Carter was always eager and willing to represent the Board of Trustees at any faculty occasion. His command of the English language, his ready wit and solemn manner of speech beckoned the attention of everyone present.

Fenn College has indeed lost a really great friend, but the imprint present in Dr. Carter's strength of character, his faith in Fenn College, our objectives and brand of education will remain forever as an inspiration to all members of the Fenn Family.

G. Brooks Earnest, President
Fenn College

The Northern Ohio Druggists Association through George Miller, a Member of the Fenn Corporation, requested that the college give consideration to the possibility of establishing a School of Pharmacy. A special task committee was appointed to explore the need and report back to the Development Committee of the Board of Trustees.

Milestones of the year 1953 would have to include the following:

1. Purchase of the Ohio Motors Building, which was temporarily named the West Campus Building (following completion of structural rehabilitation it was dedicated as the Charles J. Stilwell Hall).
2. Option was taken to purchase the lot at the northwest corner of Euclid Avenue and East 24th Street.
3. The first inauguration ceremonies for a Fenn College president were held.
4. A portion of the Fenn Tower parking lot was graded and paved.
5. The Civil Engineering curriculum was accredited by the Engineer's Council for Professional Development.
6. All five Engineering curricula were approved by the University of the State of New York (Regents). As the result of this approval Fenn Engineering Graduates were permitted for the first time to become registered to practice engineering in the state of New York.

1953 was a good year for Fenn, it was a busy year full of accomplishments. The Fenn Family pulled together and was operating as a team.

The Executive Committee of the Board of Trustees met February 9, 1954, principally to hear a report by President Earnest on the proposed affiliation of Huron Road School of Nursing and Fenn College.

A special task committee composed of representatives from the Huron Road Hospital and Fenn College had been working on the details of this new program for several months. The proposed affiliation was unanimously approved and recommended for transmission to the board at its next meeting.

Because of the accelerated, time-consuming, fund-raising activities of the Trustees at the 1953 year's end and during the early months of 1954 the full board did not meet until April 12, 1954. Accordingly, there was a lengthy agenda. Following are some of the actions taken or reported:

1. Approved an increase in tuition for Freshmen Arts and Sciences and Business Administration from $140 per Quarter to $160 to conform to the same rate as Engineering Freshmen had been paying for several years. Approved an increase of $1 per credit hour in all schools, both Day and Evening Divisions, making the Arts and Sciences and Business Administration tuition $13 per credit hour and Engineering $14.

2. Gave tentative approval to the proposed Huron Road Hospital Nursing Program for start-up in the Fall of 1954. The program would (1) provide improved training of nurses in their technical field and in general education, (2) attract more women into nursing and thereby help alleviate the local as well as national shortage, and (3) result in economies of total program through integration of teaching services. The program to be a three year curriculum (co-op) at the end of which the student would receive an associate degree from Fenn and certificate in nursing from Huron Road Hospital. The students resided in a dormitory near the hospital.

3. It was reported that $900,960 in cash and pledges had been received toward the $1,500,000 building campaign known as Phase I to convert the Ohio Motors Building for educational purposes. The architect, Mr. Joseph Ceruti, was preparing working drawings for this first phase.

4. Authorization was granted to start the proposed American Institute of Banking Evening Division program in the Fall of 1954. The courses were taught by Fenn's Faculty supplemented by instructors from the banking profession. It further developed that 500 to 700 students were enrolled in this program each year.

5. Authority was also granted to begin a Graphic Arts Program in the Technical Institute in the Fall of 1954. The Graphic Arts industry

agreed to provide the funds for equipping one room in the quonset huts as a laboratory for this program.

C. De Witt Hardy was the speaker at the May 13, 1954, meeting of the Members of the Fenn Corporation and Faculty. He spoke on the subject "Fenn's Future in the Cleveland Community." The architect's plans for the conversion of the Ohio Motors Building were shown for the first time at this meeting. Representatives from the following Cleveland firms were presented plaques as twenty-five year members of partnership with Fenn College through the engagement of co-op students:

Diamond Alkali Co.	Sears Roebuck & Co.
The Higbee Company	Stouffer Corp.
Hill-Acme Co.	White Motor Co.
The Osborn Manufacturing Co.	Republic Steel Corp.

The 1954 Commencement Convocation was held at Severance Hall on May 28. Dr. John D. Millett, President of Miami University, delivered the address, entitled: "The Obligations of Education." Dr. Millett later became the first Chancellor of the Ohio Board of Regents. There were 219 graduates: 24 in Arts and Sciences; 82 in Business Administration; and 113 in Engineering. Honorary Degrees were conferred upon Clarence L. Collens (D. Eng.), Randolph Eide (D.CS), Miss Belle Greve (L.H.D.), and the speaker, Dr. John D. Millett (LL.D.).

President Earnest was appointed to the Special Committee on Engineers in Industry in 1954 because of his activity as Chairman of the Committee on Employment Conditions of the Engineers Joint Council, headquartered in New York City. He was also elected to a three-year term as a member of the Board of Governors of the Cleveland Engineering Society.

The agenda of the Trustee meeting of August 10, 1954, was largely concerned with faculty personnel affairs. The following persons, all of whom were still with Fenn at the transfer of the College to the State in 1965, were approved for appointment September 1, 1954: Joseph W. Ink, Instructor, Department of History; Leopold W. Haas, Assistant Professor of English; Doretta C. Thielker, Associate Professor of Nursing Science; and Wilfred C. Ahrens, Assistant Professor, Accounting. The 1953–1954 budget was amended to include $11,000 for installation of asphalt driving lanes in a portion of the student parking lot and $2,880 for equipment for the office machines laboratory.

The Executive Committee of the Board met August 23, 1954, to hear reports from President Earnest and Warren L. Morris concerning the status of the White Apartments adjacent to the campus on the southeast corner of Chester Avenue and East 24th Street. A potential buyer had made an offer of $275,000 to Mrs. White for the apartment building. Action was taken directing President Earnest and Warren Morris to contact Mrs. White to determine whether reconsideration might be given to Fenn College as a potential buyer. Discussion hinged around ways and means of financing the purchase inasmuch as the College was already heavily financially obligated with the recent purchase of the Ohio Motors Building. It was felt that it might be possible to establish a syndicate to assume a second mortgage on the apartment property.

Upon meeting with Mrs. White it was determined that she had a bona fide offer of $275,000 for the property, but that she would give the College until Saturday, September 11, 1954, to declare its intention to make an offer. Accordingly, a special meeting of the Board was called for September 8, 1954, at which time President Earnest reported the outcome of his meeting with Mrs. White. He further reported that several profit and non-profit institutions had shown an inclination to take a first mortgage on the White Apartments up to $150,000 at four and one-half per cent interest and that Trustees and other friends of the College had indicated their desire to purchase second mortgage notes up to $135,000 at four and one-half per cent interest. After a brief discussion the following action was taken:

> Mr. Iglauer moved and Mr. Fisher seconded following resolutions be adopted:
>
> RESOLVED: That the officers of this corporation to wit, President and Secretary, be and they hereby are authorized and directed to acquire by purchase for this corporation the Apartment House property located at the corner of East Twenty Fourth Street and Chester Avenue in the city of Cleveland, owned presently by Edna White and Cathryn White Ludwig;
>
> BE IT FURTHER RESOLVED: That the officers be and they hereby are authorized and directed to make such purchase of such property at a price not to exceed Two Hundred Seventy Thousand Dollars ($270,000).
>
> BE IT FURTHER RESOLVED: That the officers be and they hereby are authorized and directed to borrow a sum not to exceed $150,000

at an interest rate not to exceed 4½% per annum to be secured by a first mortgage on the said White Apartment property.

BE IT FURTHER RESOLVED: That in such an event the officers be and they hereby are authorized and directed to borrow an additional sum not to exceed $120,000 at an interest rate of 4½% per annum to be secured by a second mortgage on the said White Apartment property, the notes evidencing such borrowing to mature ten years from a date, provided, however, that in lieu of interest bearing notes in the face amount of $120,000, non-interest bearing notes in the face amount of $174,000, due ten years from date may be issued and sold at a price of $120,000.

BE IT FURTHER RESOLVED: That with respect to such total borrowing of $270,000 the officers be and they hereby are authorized to incorporate in the evidences of indebtedness, and of mortgages securing the same, such other terms and conditions as the officers in their discretion, and with advice of counsel, may deem necessary or appropriate, provided, however, that such second mortgage notes and mortgage shall not obligate the College to appropriate any of its general funds to the amortization of such second mortgage indebtedness, but that such second mortgage notes shall pledge the general credit of the College to the payment thereof and any interest thereon when due.

BE IT FURTHER RESOLVED: That pending the completion of the borrowings herein authorized, funds required for the completion of the purchase of the White apartment property may be advanced from the operating account or any other available funds for interior financing purposes provided that such advance shall be repaid, if other than from the Surplus Fund account, by the proceeds of such borrowing or, if said borrowing is insufficient, from the Surplus Fund Account.

Motion Approved.

Trustee Adrian D. Joyce passed away suddenly on August 25, 1954, and the Board of Trustees, at this special meeting on September 8, passed a resolution in memoriam to Joyce. Through his thoughtfulness and dedication to Fenn College, the College later received a bequest of $10,000 from Joyce's estate.

The 1954 Annual Meeting of the Fenn College Corporation was held on October 11; thirty-eight were present. Charles J. Stilwell, Dr. James C. Hodge, and Sydney L. Hall were re-elected to the Board for six-year terms. Hugh J. Morrison was elected to replace Ralph L. Dickey (class of 1960) who had resigned. H. F. Meyer was elected to fill the unexpired term of Adrian Joyce (class of 1956). Jay W. Collins, Fenn Alumnus (class of 1940) was elected to serve a three-year term as Alumni Trustee. President Earnest presented a brief annual report pointing out the following highlights of the year:

1. The Huron Road Hospital School of Nursing became affiliated with Fenn in the nation's first Co-op nursing program.

2. The White Apartments were purchased.

3. The American Institute of Banking educational program became affiliated with Fenn.

4. The Chemical Engineering Program was accredited by the Engineer's Council for Professional Development.

5. The first summer session in Education established a new curriculum in the School of Arts and Sciences.

6. The Graphic Arts program of Cleveland Lithographic Institute became affiliated with Fenn.

7. Two-year Associate Degree Programs were started in Secretarial Studies and in Accounting.

The board, at its November 17, 1954, meeting, accepted the resignation of recent electee Sydney L. Hall who became Vice President of the Potomac Electric Power Company in Washington, D.C. President Earnest reported that the Ohio Motors Company had presented a complete change in the original agreement for occupancy of the Ohio Motors building by the College and for acquisition of the property at the northwest corner of Euclid and East 24th Street. Under the new agreement the College would occupy the building by November 30, 1956, instead of July 1, 1955; and the College could acquire the corner property at its option at any time between November 30, 1956, and July 1, 1968. The board approved the changes in the original agreement. The board also approved at a fee of $2,500 the retention of the American City Bureau of Chicago to conduct a survey of the fund-raising potential for Phase II of the College's capital development program.

The final meeting of the Board for 1954 was held December 13. Mr. F. E. Killen of the American City Bureau was present to conduct an Attitude Survey of the Trustees present. President Earnest reported that the Winter Quarter enrollment for the Day Division was 894 compared to a budget estimate of 805 and the previous year's Winter Quarter enrollment of 781. Trustee Edward T. Bartlett II presented the following report on the Pharmacy School Study:

REPORT ON PHARMACY

In the fall of 1953, the Northern Ohio Druggists Association through George Miller, a member of the Fenn Corporation, requested that the College give consideration to the possibility of establishing a School of Pharmacy. During the past fifteen months the College administration with the cooperation of the Director of the Cleveland Committee on Higher Education, has studied the Pharmacy education situation as it pertains to the Cleveland area.

The study has included the following:

1. A survey of the membership of the Northern Ohio Druggists Association to determine their educational needs.

2. A meeting with the Director of the American Foundation for Pharmaceutical Education, the organization charged with the responsibility of the education of teachers of pharmacy.

3. A meeting with representatives of the American Council on Pharmaceutical Education, the accrediting agency.

4. Inspection of the Pharmacy schools at Duquesne University in Pittsburgh, and Columbia University in New York City.

The Development Committee of the Trustees met on two occasions, November 11 and December 3, 1954, to review the study and to hear a report on Pharmacy Education in Cleveland prepared by C. DeWitt Hardy, Director of the Cleveland Committee for Higher Education.

At the present time there are four existing Schools of Pharmacy in Ohio (Ohio State, Toledo, Ohio Northern, Cincinnati), one of which (Ohio Northern) is listed as being deficient by the accrediting agency. If this deficiency is not corrected within a reasonable period, understood to terminate in June 1955, the school can be dropped from the accredited list.

The Development Committee is of the opinion that even though the study indicates a need for a local school of Pharmacy, and that Fenn is a possible site for such a school, any action by Fenn should be postponed until a decision is made by the American Council on Pharmaceutical Education regarding Ohio Northern's school of Pharmacy.

As it turned out it was felt that there was insufficient financial support in the Cleveland area to establish a School of Pharmacy at Fenn, so the subject was dropped. W.R.U. had previously closed its School of Pharmacy and transferred its students to Ohio Northern University.

For over a year the Personnel Policies Committee of the faculty had been studying and revising the personnel policies relating to promotion of instructors, terminations of annual appointments, and termination of indefinite tenure, of the Faculty of Instruction and the latter three for Educational Services. Many years had passed since a comprehensive study and revision had been made. The completed recommended changes were approved by the board on March 23, 1955.

Also, for over two years a committee of the Fenn Alumni Association had been working with the College Administration respective to a co-operative program of administration of Alumni affairs and the application of funds contributed by the Alumni. The "agreement" was returned several times for further study and revision by the Finance Committee of the board. Finally, at the March 23, 1955, board meeting the "agreement," with the support of the Finance Committee was unanimously approved by the Board.

The board at its meeting on April 27, 1955, passed a resolution to modify the original lease agreement with the Ohio Motors Company and the Motors Realty Company dated May 12, 1953, by eliminating the right of the Motors Realty Company to compel the exercise of the option to purchase in advance of a final date and to extend the time to July 1, 1968, during which Fenn could exercise the option to purchase the Euclid-24th Street corner property on six months notice. Included also was the extension of rental leases beyond June 30, 1955, on certain portions of the Ohio Motors building (later Stilwell Hall) which were rented to three different companies.

It appeared that there would be a surplus at year end, August 31, 1955, so the board at this same meeting approved the following capital expenditures recommended by President Earnest and approved by the Board Finance Committee:

1. $10,000 toward the removal of the balcony in the gymnasium to make the area practicable for basketball and other intercollegiate and intramural practice.

2. $11,500 to complete paving and drainage of the student parking lot. The previous year $11,000 had been applied to grading and paving the first portion of the lot.

3. $10,000 for additional pointing and caulking of the Fenn Tower. Over the past two years $34,000 had been spent on this project which had an overall estimate for completion of $75,000.

4. $23,847 to fully construct six temporary classrooms in the northeast area of the first floor of the Ohio Motors Building. A large increase in Evening Division registration required additional classroom space, and it was estimated that the income from tuition would cover the cost of this construction in less than two years.

Also at this same board meeting the recommendation by President Earnest that a new administrative office of Dean of Academic Service and Director of the Evening Division be created was approved. C. DeWitt Hardy, Director of the Cleveland Commission for Higher Education, was appointed to this office. This move permitted the president to apportion more of his time to the Capital Development Program. Fenn was experiencing growing pains. The Day Division Fall enrollment for 1954 was twelve per cent over that of 1953, and the Evening Division Spring enrollment for 1955 was six per cent over that for 1954.

Dr. Wilson Compton, President, Council for Financial Aid to Education, Inc., was the guest speaker at the May 9, 1955, meeting of the members of the Fenn Corporation and Faculty. Plaques in recognition of twenty-five years' partnership in Fenn's co-op program were presented to representatives from the following companies:

> The Austin Company
> Cleveland Crane and Engineering Company
> Cleveland Diesel Works of G.M.C.
> Electric Controller & Manufacturing Company
> Hertner Electric Company
> The Ohio Rubber Company
> The Parker Appliance Company
> Rola Company
> Sterling-Lindner-Davis
> Wellman Engineering Company
> The Yoder Company

The 1955 Commencement Convocation was held at Severance Hall. Dr. Carlton S. Proctor of the consulting firm of Moran, Proctor, Mueser and Rutledge, New York City, delivered the commencement address.

His subject was "Delusions of Security." The graduating class numbered 183 distributed as follows: 27 in Arts and Sciences, 74 in Business Administration, and 82 in Engineering. James E. Maisel of this class joined the Faculty of the Department of Electrical Engineering in September 1958 and at the date of this writing was Associate Professor of Electrical Engineering at The Cleveland State University.

The following received Honorary Degrees at the 1955 Commencement:

Howard Edwin Isham, Doctor of Commercial Science (D.CS)
Carl Frederick Wittke, Doctor of Laws (LL.D.)
Elbert H. Baker, Jr. Doctor of Engineering (D.Eng.)
Carlton S. Proctor, Doctor of Engineering (D.Eng.)

The budget for the fiscal year September 1, 1955, to August 31, 1956, was approved at the July 26, 1955, meeting of the board. It showed an estimate of income from all sources other than gifts of $1,566,203 and expenses of $1,686,254. The balancing deficit of $120,071 was to be met by contributions. This compared with deficit budgets of $130,000 in 1954–1955 and $185,000 in 1953–1954, yet Fenn closed each year in the black. The estimated income from tuition and fees was $1,220,257 with 55 per cent derived from the Evening Division and 45 per cent from the Day Division.

Dr. Walter R. Van Voorhis was promoted to Chairman of the Department of Mathematics at this same board meeting and Emil J. Stefancic was promoted to Librarian, both filling vacancies caused by resignations.

Since about 1930 Fenn had been offering a course in Transportation in the School of Business Administration in the Evening Division. The course started with one semester offerings and developed in about fifteen years to a full certificate program in Transportation. In 1954–1955 there were 186 students enrolled in the program. The movement of people, raw materials, and manufactured goods plus the training required by traffic departments of industry, and transportation companies in the economics, procedures and regulations applying to the movement of people and goods created a demand for a full bachelor degree program in Transportation in the Evening Division. One of the highlights of the year 1955 was the approval by the board on July 26 of a seven-year baccalaureate degree program in Transportation.

The 1955 Annual Meeting of the Fenn Corporation was held November 15. The following amendment to the Regulations of Fenn College was approved:

> Section 7.(e)   The members of the Corporation may from time to time elect Honorary Life Trustees who shall continue as such Trustees during their natural life. Such Honorary Life Trustees shall not be considered for quorum purposes and shall have no vote as Trustees.

Another highlight in the year 1955 was the election at this Corporation meeting of Clarence L. Collens and Justice Harold H. Burton as the first Honorary Life Trustees of Fenn College.

Other items of business at the meeting included the re-election of Ellwood H. Fisher, Clayton G. Hale, and Allen T. Perry for six-year terms, Class of 1961. James W. Corey was elected to the same Class. Arthur S. Armstrong was elected to fulfill the unexpired term of Justice Burton, John S. Wilbur to fulfill the unexpired term of Collens, and Norman F. Smith to fulfill the unexpired term of Sydney L. Hall. Martin H. Huge, Fenn 1938, was elected as an Alumni Trustee, Class of 1958. Curtis Lee Smith, President, Cleveland YMCA became an *ex-officio* Trustee. The election of the following as Members of the Fenn Corporation, representing certain business, industrial and professional groups also took place:

> Joseph E. Adams, White Motor Company—Automotive Manufacturing
>
> Harry Allen, Republic Steel Corporation—Steel Manufacturing
>
> Karl F. Bruch, Jr., Hill Acme Company—Machine Tools
>
> Warren H. Chase, Ohio Bell Telephone Company—Communications
>
> George Dively, Harris-Seybold Company—Graphic Arts
>
> Carl W. Evans, Gray Drug Company—Drugs
>
> J. R. Hoover, B.F. Goodrich Chemical Company—Chemical Manufacturing
>
> Lynn F. Jennings, Dairyman's Farmers Milk Company—Dairy Products
>
> Chester H. Kimmel, Ohio Crankshaft Company—Industrial Equipment
>
> William G. Laffer, Clevite Corporation—Non-ferrous Metal
>
> H. J. McGinn, Eaton Manufacturing Company—Automotive Parts Manufacturing

Donald L. Millham, General Electric Company—Electrical Equipment

Robert C. Overstreet, Tinnerman Products, Inc.—Fastenings

C. E. Smith, Towmotor Corporation—Materials Handling

A. W. Steudel, Sherwin-Williams Company—Protective Coatings

Douglas O. Yoder, The Yoder Company—Metal Working Equipment

Following the business session President Earnest prefaced annual reports of staff members with the following statement:

The individual annual reports you are going to hear tonight represent, of necessity, a summary of activities and a resolution of problems for the fiscal year 1954–1955, ending last August 31st. Combined they represent a magnificent story of the response of a group of people to a great challenge. It is a story of coordinated efforts of Trustees, Corporation members, Administrative Staff, Faculty, Students, Alumni and citizens of greater Cleveland. It is a story of the support of the adage that the moral, academic and spiritual tone of college life can be elevated by hard work and loyal whole-hearted cooperation.

Fenn College, like any other institution of higher learning, is composed of three main segments: (1) people, (2) physical plant, and (3) invested funds. The latter two are inanimate and valuable only as they are made useful to people. You will hear much about all segments this evening.

"The People" of Fenn College are divided into five groups— the students, the faculty and staff, the alumni, the Board of Trustees plus its constituency known as the Fenn Corporation. This collection of groups we call the Fenn Family, and it must be my goal, as President of the College, to give full service to each of them.

The students are our "raw material" and constitute a most important element of our family. The faculty and staff are the "core" of the College and their responsibility is to instruct, inspire and manage. The alumni are the "finished product" and down through the years a college reputation has been measured by the composite of achievements of its alumni. Fenn is a relatively young college, and we are growing rapidly in alumni strength, however, 70% of our alumni graduated since 1947. The Board of Trustees of Fenn College is a unique organization in its loyalty to the college and its earnest efforts in fund raising, both capital and operating. The Fenn Corporation also is unique in that it is a complement of leaders in the various walks of life in metropolitan Cleveland interested in higher education in their community. This genuine active interest by the Trustees and Corporation members adds real zest to the operation of the College and inspires the faculty to better performance.

Fenn College cannot escape from the influence of and dependence upon the community and constituency which shelters it. Without the understanding and financial support of such a constituency neither Fenn College nor any other college can long stay in business. The Trustees may be considered on the community side of the ledger also. They serve as guardians of the property and investments and assume the responsibility for determining policies and for engaging administrative personnel to assure that such policies will be carried out—and all this without pay. A "labor of love," so to speak, with about the only reward the satisfaction which comes from assuming the responsibility for a civic essential.

These facts about the Fenn Family are reviewed here lest we become forgetful of the important roles and essential contributions of one another in the life of this great institution which we represent here tonight. It is the joint responsibility of all to see that the heartening progress of the past year is maintained. *Success depends on full harmony of purpose* and, of course, pure, unadulterated hard work.

Details of this past year's activities and progress will be recited by members of our staff in responsible charge. Our keynote is expansion—expansion of our services to our students, to business, to industry, and to the community. You will hear reported the accelerated expansion of our enrollment, expansion of our curriculum, expansion of staff, expansion of our co-op program, expansion of our physical plant, and expansion of our annual budget.

We have experienced growing pains in attempting to resolve the urgent need to expand our manpower, plant and other facilities. We have not been able to increase our faculty and expand our plant at the rate we would like. We have had to compromise with our hopes and dreams. Our decision to build these temporary classrooms in which we are meeting tonight is an example of the manner in which we have tried to meet our problems within the limits of our resources.

I do not want to steal any of the thunder of the members of our staff reporting this evening, but I do wish to compliment each of these key people engaged in the business of administering Fenn College. They have lightened my load and worries by making correct decisions in their own individual areas and assisting me in the decisions I have had to make. The composite of their annual reports is essentially my annual report. The credit is theirs, and my only request is that you listen attentively to each staff member and at the close of the meeting I'm sure that you will be proud, as I am, that you are associated with Fenn College. . . .

In closing our Fall Corporation Meeting on annual reports, I will sum up the emphasis in four facts reflecting a satisfying positive movement forward:

1. Our growing capacity to examine ourselves critically
2. The multiplying and stretching forth of more hands to give the college added support
3. Better teamwork, both on the field and in the stands
4. The frank and earnest acknowledgement and recognition that, good as we may be in manpower, equipment and other resources, we must be better henceforth.

The following staff members presented annual reports:

Dr. V. Richard Gulbenkien, Registrar

M. C. Herrick, Director of Admissions

Dr. Major B. Jenks, Dean, School of Arts and Sciences

Paul R. Anders, Dean, School of Business Administration

Dr. Wm. A. Patterson, Dean, School of Engineering

Max B. Robinson, Dean, Cooperative Education

C. DeWitt Hardy, Dean, Academic Services

Arthur P. Loegler, Director of Finance

Following the staff reports and the adjournment of the meeting the group toured the new classrooms in the Ohio Motors Building and several of the rehabilitated floors in the Fenn Tower. Fifty-five were in attendance at the meeting.

The final board meeting of 1955 was held December 12. The following officers were re-elected for the ensuing year:

Charles J. Stilwell, Chairman

Ellwood H. Fisher, Vice Chairman

James H. Coolidge, Treasurer

Howard R. Taylor, Jr., Secretary

The engagement of Harold R. Glaze as Superintendent of Buildings and Grounds was approved. Glaze later transferred to The Cleveland State University with the same responsibility. His father had been Superintendent of Buildings and Grounds at the YMCA from 1911 to 1927.

Nineteen hundred and fifty-five had turned out to be a very good year. By means of a telegram received December 12, the president was notified that the College would be the recipient of a grant from the Ford Foundation, the income from which for the ensuing ten years was to "be used only to increase faculty salaries."

The board took action December 12 to prepay the principal payments on the Ohio Motors Building for a two-year period ending September 30, 1957. Action was also taken to appropriate $40,000 of the 1954–1955 operating surplus, plus the net earnings of the White Apartments (after the first mortgage principal and interest had been met), to purchase some of the second mortgage notes held by the Trustees.

Yes, 1955 was a good year for Fenn College in many ways; not the least was the first undefeated season in the history of the College in an intercollegiate sport—soccer. But, many additional pleasant and beneficial events took place at Fenn in 1956.

X

---

*Education should be as gradual as the moonrise,
perceptible not in progress but in result.*

George J. Whyte, 1821–1878.

H. R. Taylor, Director of Development, submitted his resignation early
in 1956 to join the public relations department of a local industry.
Taylor's final report on the capital campaign to raise funds to rehabilitate the Ohio Motors Building was, as of February 10, 1956, as follows:

Cash received*	$997,793	
Balance due on pledges	86,233	
		$1,084,026
Expected further payments	$290,880	
Total		$1,374,906

Murray M. Davidson succeeded Taylor as Director of Development
and Public Relations and remained in this office until the date of his
resignation, August 31, 1965, the day before Fenn College was transferred to the State of Ohio.

The first board meeting for 1956 was held March 8 at the University
Club. President Earnest presented the enrollment report for the Spring
Quarter as shown in Table 1.

President Earnest also reported the discontinuance of the long-standing Veterans Administration Testing Program:

Early in January, 1956, the Regional Office of the Veterans Administration requested a re-negotiation of our contract for testing

---

* Includes $41,695 from Trustees.

TABLE 1

ENROLLMENT REPORT

DAY AND EVENING DIVISIONS, SPRING TERM 1956

A. *Day Division Enrollment Spring Quarter*

	Enrolled	Co-op.	Total	Spring 1955
Arts and Sciences	106	29	135	132
Business Administration	206	108	314	278
Engineering	339	174	513	447
Nurses	42	—	42	39
Total	693	311	1,004	896

NEW STUDENTS

	Freshmen	Transfers	Part-time	Total	Spring 1955
Arts and Sciences	9	5	3	17	16
Business Administration	14	7	2	23	36
Engineering	27	10	2	39	44
Total	50	22	7	79	96

B. *Evening Division Enrollment Spring Semester*

	Enrollment Spring 1956	Enrollment Spring 1955
Arts and Sciences	788	694
Business Administration	1,777	1,603
Engineering	795	765
Technical Institute	1,026	1,084
Total	4,386	4,146

Day Technical Institute	
Cleveland Graphite Bronze	4
Fisher Body Co.	51
	55
Off-campus—Euclid	
Foremanship	8
Real Estate II	28
Industrial Psychology	14
	50
American Institute of Banking	466
Lithographic Arts	40
Total Spring Enrollment	4,997

(Evening Division)

of veterans. In the re-negotiating procedures the head of the VA Regional Office in Cleveland arbitrarily decided to modify the interpretation of one of the sections of the VA rules and regulations. This particular section has existed since the beginning of our contractual arrangements with the VA office. The new interpretation prohibited our staff members, who were assigned to veterans' testing, to do other testing or teaching for the College. We explained that it would not be economically sound for us to comply to this interpretation as there were not enough veterans assigned to our office to keep our men busy.

The result of our re-negotiation survey, therefore, called for termination of our contract. The effective termination date of the contract was February 29, 1956. It was unfortunate that the head of the Regional Office suddenly decided to change the interpretation of the ground rules, for we have had splendid relations with this organization for over eleven years. We do feel proud of the fact that we have had a hand in counseling over 24,000 veterans during this period.

Termination of our contract with the VA Regional Office will not result in a surplus of manpower in our Department of Personnel Development because we have had two of this staff leave us for industry within the past six weeks. We will still carry on the personnel testing for industry and business and our own students at Fenn. In addition, the members of the staff assist in the teaching of orientation courses as well as in the Department of Psychology.

Arthur P. Loegler, Finance Director, was elected Secretary of the Board of Trustees and the Corporation, succeeding H. R. Taylor. The Group Insurance Program, established in February 1951, had experienced sizeable dividends, and because of no deaths of employees in the program, it was possible to double the coverage, effective March 1, 1956, at no extra cost to the employees. The board voted this action.

The distribution of the faculty in the various ranks was: seventeen full professors, twenty-one associate professors, nineteen assistant professors, and ten instructors. Most colleges held a preponderance of instructors. Because of Fenn's problem in obtaining faculty at the instructor rank, President Earnest presented the following report and recommendation:

Since we are located in a large metropolitan area, including four other major institutions of higher education, we do compete for services of young men entering the teaching profession. We are handicapped, not only by our modest salary scale and our four-quarter teaching year, but also by the fact that we have no provision in our Personnel Policies for financial assistance to those of our faculty engaged in graduate study.

The colleges and universities with graduate schools are in a favored position to attract young teachers into their employ, for their staff members are permitted to carry on graduate work free of tuition charge in their early years of teaching when their salary scale is lowest. Most able young men going into college teaching are vitally interested in the opportunity for additional academic training because they realize that in order to progress in the professional field of teaching it is essential to acquire advanced degrees.

In order to make our prospects brighter for engaging and retaining able young teachers, it is recommended that our Personnel Policies provide some financial assistance to faculty members doing graduate work. Accordingly, the following recommendation is submitted:

That the College adopt the policy of granting to full-time faculty members (1) one-half the tuition cost for up to 6 hours of graduate credit per term for the purpose of obtaining an advanced degree, and (2) a grant of up to one-half the tuition cost of graduate study while on a quarter's leave of absence with pay, both subject to the approval of the President of the College.

The board approved the recommendation.

The board approved the retirement of Professor Mouck. The Minutes read thus:

HAMLIN MOUCK—Professor, Accounting, School of Business Administration. Part time 1914–35; full time 1935–56. Effective date of retirement June 8, 1956. Professor Mouck is the oldest member of the faculty in term of service. In the book entitled "The Story of Accountancy," copyrighted in 1954 by the Ohio Association of Certified Public Accountants, there appears the following statement: "Undoubtedly more students have been taught accounting by Professor G. Hamlin Mouck of Fenn than by any teacher in Cleveland for he has been teaching continuously since 1914. Many of our early CPA's and private accountants studied under Professor Mouck. He is and always has been held in high respect by his students." Professor Mouck once served as Chairman of the Accounting Department and for several years was a member of the

Board of Managers of the Cleveland Y.M.C.A. Institute of Technology, which Board was a forerunner of the Board of Trustees of Fenn College. In accordance with our retirement practice he would hold the title of Professor Emeritus of Accounting.

Employing the 1954–1955 educational costs as a working basis the costs to teach Fenn's students on a credit-hour basis resulted as follows:

	Cost per Credit Hour	
	Day Div.	Eve. Div.
Overhead costs, including administration and general, library, all student services (coordination, guidance and activities, health and physical education, personnel development), and plant operation	$ 8.12	$ 7.09
Instructional costs for the three schools (Arts and Sciences, Business Administration, Engineering) and the Technical Institute ...	$ 8.79	$ 5.48
Total cost per unit, including instruction and overhead	$16.91	$12.57

The tuition rate for an upperclass student was $13 per credit-hour in both the Day and Evening Division in the Schools of Arts and Sciences and Business Administration, and $14 per credit-hour in the School of Engineering. The Evening Division was self-supporting, inasmuch as the tuition income of $13 or $14 per credit-hour compared favorably with the $12.57 cost per credit-hour; however, the Day Division was obviously not self-supporting. Assuming an average tuition of $13.50 per credit-hour, the upperclass students paid approximately 75% of their total educational costs.

In the freshman year, Fenn was subsidizing the cost of education of the students to a much higher degree. For the year 1954–55 the freshman in Arts and Sciences paid $9.60 per credit-hour; in Business Administration $8.42 per credit-hour; and in Engineering $8.56 per credit-hour. Fenn College for many years had been employing the policy of giving freshmen three quarters of education for the price of two. (President Earnest referred to this policy frequently as Fenn's "cut-rate freshman year.")

The 1955–1956 tuition rate for the freshman year was $480, or $160 per quarter. The unit costs to teach Freshmen were not much less than the unit costs to teach upperclassmen.

Based upon the above study the board voted to increase the freshman year tuition to $600 for students in Arts and Sciences and Business Administration and to $630 for students in Engineering. This action projected a gross increase of $54,000 for 1956–1957 based on the anticipated freshman enrollment of 400 students.

The May 1, 1956, meeting of the Board of Trustees was one of the most significant board meetings in all of Fenn's history, especially in the point of view of the faculty. Just a glance at the brief Minutes of the meeting will indicate the volume and variety of important business transacted:

Present:

Chairman Stilwell; Trustees Akers, Bartlett, Burns, Case, Collens, Collins, Earnest, Hodge, Huge, Lees, Miller, Norman F. Smith, Stecher, Taylor, Woodling, and Messrs. Davidson and Loegler

Chairman Stilwell called the meeting to order at 4:12 p.m.

1. The minutes of the meeting of March 8, 1956, were approved as distributed.
2. Items of General Information

    a. President Earnest announced that Mr. J. Carlton Ward, president of the Vitro Corporation of America, would be the speaker at the annual Faculty-Corporation banquet to be held Tuesday, May 8, 1956, and urged the Trustees to be present.

    b. Distinguished Service Awards, Alumni: President Earnest presented the names of the alumni who are to receive distinguished service awards.

    c. President Earnest expressed the appreciation of the Faculty for the action taken by Trustees at the March 8, 1956 meeting with regard to financial aid granted to those taking graduate work and the increase in Group Insurance coverage.

3. Report of the Personnel Policies Committee

    a. On motion of Mr. Case, duly seconded, it was voted to accept the resignations and approve the new appointments and leaves of absence.

    b. On motion of Mr. Case, duly seconded, it was voted to approve the recommendations of the faculties of the Schools of Arts and Sciences, Business Administration, and Engineering and grant degrees to the candidates.

4. Report of the Development Committee

   a. President Earnest announced the distribution of the brochure "Financing Fenn's Future," an analysis of Fenn College from the standpoint of the future fund raising approach.

   b. Mr. Bartlett then presented the recommendations of the committee.

   c. On motion of Mr. Bartlett, duly seconded, it was voted to authorize the Chairman to appoint a Standing Committee on Public Relations, a special Appraisal Committee, and a special Building Committee.

5. Report of the Finance Committee

   a. On motion of Mr. Case, duly seconded, it was voted to approve the expenditure of $2,400.00 for painting laboratories and classrooms in the Prospect Fenn Building.

   b. On motion of Mr. Bartlett, duly seconded, it was voted to approve the transfer of $2,927.81 expended for architect's services, from the Current Fund to the Development Fund.

   c. Mr. Loegler reported that the bequest [$15,000] received from the estate of Mrs. Stella Antisdale had temporarily been invested by the Finance Committee, in 90 day U.S. Government paper.

6. Recommendations for Honorary Degrees

   On motion of Mr. Collens, duly seconded, it was voted to grant honorary degrees at the 1956 Commencement to Messrs. Alfred A. Benesch, Harry D. Sims, Clayton G. Hale and Mr. Arch T. Colwell, the Commencement Speaker, as recommended by the Faculty.

7. Recommendation for "change in calendar" and "three-quarter teaching year"

   On motion of Mr. Case, duly seconded, it was voted to change the present college calendar, postponing the opening date approximately 3 weeks later than at present; to adopt the three-quarter teaching year, maintaining present individual annual salaries and to pay an additional fee to instructors who teach during the Summer Quarter as recommended by President Earnest.

8. Recommendation for change in "Founding Date" of the College

   Hearing no objections the Chairman authorized the College to adopt the year 1923 as the "Founding Date" of the College.

The meeting was adjourned at 5:47 p.m.

s/*A. Loegler*, Secretary

President Earnest had previously appointed a committee composed of representatives from the administration, faculty, and alumni to study and report on the presentation each year of some form of award to a few distinguished alumni. The committee recommended the presentation of up to three Alumni Distinguished Service Awards each year at an annual Alumni banquet. The first three recipients approved by the Trustees were:

HIRAM BROWN, B.S. in Metallurgy, 1937, President of both his Freshman and Senior classes at Fenn, honored as outstanding man in his graduating class, Chief Metallurgist, Solar Aircraft, Des Moines, Iowa, and author of over forty articles in technical and professional journals.

HELEN LOBDELL, B.A., 1942, in Social Sciences, graduate work at Columbia University, American University, University of Michigan and Western Michigan College, teacher of art and history in Watervliet, Michigan high school and author of a number of historical novels for readers of high school age which have won national recognition for her.

MAURICE J. STRUCHEN, JR., 1943, Bachelor of Business Administration, *cum laude*, 1943, M.A. in Business Administration "with distinction" from Wharton School of Finance, 1947, youngest Vice President, National City Bank of Cleveland. (Later, 1970, President, Society National Bank of Cleveland, Member of Fenn Educational Foundation and Chairman of the Board of Trustees of The Cleveland State University.)

The three new committees appointed by the board were given the following duties:

Appraisal Committee; to estimate potential gifts from prospective donors to enable establishment of a realistic campaign goal.

Building Committee; to assess the feasibility of the total building program.

Standing Committee on Public Relations; to assure the creation of an integrated public relations program designed to strengthen Fenn's position in the community and facilitate fund raising efforts of the College.

Two of the far-reaching actions approved by the board at the May 1, 1956, meeting were the revision of the College Calendar and the adoption of the three-quarter year for the teaching faculty. Many of the faculty expressed their viewpoints on the adoption of the three-quarter teaching year as the most important and far-reaching decision that the board had made thus far in the history of Fenn College.

There were few occasions in the past when the faculty of an institution have expressed appreciation to the Administration for actions contributing to the support, security and well-being of the Faculty. One such instance at Fenn was as follows:

> The following resolution was submitted by the Personnel Committee of the Faculty and adopted at the March 22, 1956, meeting of the General Faculty:
> "That the Faculty compliment the Administration on its generous and forward-looking policy in two recent decisions affecting the welfare of the Faculty: (1) The liberalization of the group insurance protection, and (2) the provisions to assist faculty members with the expense of graduate study; and that the President be instructed to so inform the Board of Trustees."

Shortly after Professor Simon retired as Professor Emeritus of Speech, August 31, 1952, President Earnest appointed a Committee on Historical Records and reappointed Professor Simon as Archivist to carry on the recommendations of the committee relating to gathering and preserving historical records of Fenn. Professor Simon established his office in the Johnson Building and set about gathering memorabilia and drafting a chronological record of facts concerning the College. Upon completion of the Ohio Motors Building in 1959, a special air-conditioned archives room was provided off the library on the third floor.

President Earnest, being relatively new at Fenn, wondered what prompted using 1881 as the founding date. He put the question to the Committee on Historical Records. As noted in the following report the committee was not very helpful, for the result of its efforts ended in a tie vote and the President's Advisory Committee broke the tie in favor of the 1923 date which received unanimous Trustee approval:

Changing the Founding Date of Fenn College

> The 1881 founding date of Fenn College has been in question for several years. Most members of the staff were of the opinion that it was the year in which the YMCA instituted courses of instruction. Several months ago our Archivist, George Simon, re-

ported that he could not find any historical record respective to courses of instruction being started in 1881, nor could he find any historical record concerned with the establishment of that year as the founding date by officials of Fenn College.

I requested the Committee on Historical Records to explore the subject and submit a recommendation for the founding date. The Committee made an exhaustive survey of factual data and found that there are only two possible realistic dates of origin. These are 1870 and 1923, the first being the date of the first classes offered under the YMCA (and these were French and German taught by Professors LeVassner and Esch respectively), the second, 1923, being the date of matriculation of the first class ever to receive bachelor degrees from Fenn.

It is recommended that the Board of Trustees of Fenn College give every consideration to changing the founding date of the College to 1923, reasons being: (1) Realistically, college courses toward a degree program began in 1923, which led to the first graduating class of five students four years later, in 1927; (2) It would be much more appropriate to celebrate our 50th Anniversary in 1973, than our 100th Anniversary (or Centennial) in 1970; and (3) In keeping with founding dates of other institutions of higher education in metropolitan Cleveland, it would be more modest for us to assume the 1923 date than to endeavor to stretch our founding date prior to Case's (1880).

It will undoubtedly be of interest to the Board to learn that the Committee on Historical Records was divided evenly between the two dates, 1870 and 1923, and that the President's Advisory Committee voted unanimously in favor of the 1923 date.

The sixth annual Faculty-Corporation banquet was held May 8, 1956, at the University Club. J. Carlton Ward, Jr., President, Vitro Corporation of America, presented the address, titled, "The Impact of Nuclear Energy on Industry." The following awards were presented: Honorary Life Member to Clarence L. Collens and Justice Harold H. Burton; twenty-five year Trustee Award to Ellwood H. Fisher (He was the first trustee so honored.); the first Alumni Distinguished Service Awards to Helen Lobdell, 1942, J. Maurice Struchen, Jr., 1943, and Hiram Brown, 1937; twenty-five year Co-op awards to Thompson Products, Inc., and Westinghouse Electric Corporation; the first Distinguished Service Awards were presented to those members of the Faculty and

Staff who had been with the College for twenty-five or more years. The following were recipients:

Miss Almeda Rothrock, Payroll Secretary (44 years of service)

Miss Ann E. Sharrow, Assistant Registrar (31 years of service)

Miss Ola I. Twerell, Purchasing Agent (30 years of service)

Dean Paul R. Anders, School of Business Administration

Professor Millard Jordan, Chairman, Department of Sociology

Professor Donald C. Fabel, Chairman, Department of Mechanical and Metallurgical Engineering

Professor William C. Davis, Chairman, Department of Electrical Engineering

Professor Homer Woodling, Chairman, Department of Physical Education

Professor Virgil Hales, Chairman, Department of Engineering Drawing

Professor Randolph Randall, Chairman, Department of English

Professor Donald Tuttle, Department of English

Professor Lad Pasiut, Department of Chemistry

Professor G. H. Mouck, Department of Accounting

Professor George Simon, College Archivist

The above Faculty and Staff members' collective service to the College in 1956 totalled 411 work-years, an amazing record of loyalty for a small college which was never able to compete with salaries of faculties of private colleges in large urban areas.

The thirtieth commencement convocation (the war years having produced more than one convocation per year) of Fenn College was held May 25, 1956, at Severance Hall. Trustee Arch T. Colwell delivered the commencement address on the subject, "Approach to Opportunity." A class of 157 graduates received diplomas: 13 from the School of Arts and Sciences, 66 from the School of Business Administration, and 78 from the School of Engineering. The following received Honorary Degrees: Alfred A. Benesch, Doctor of Laws (LL.D.), Harry D. Sims, Doctor of Humane Letters (L.H.D.), Clayton G. Hale, Doctor of Laws (LL.D.), Arch T. Colwell, Doctor of Engineering (D.Eng.). Carl J. Volk of this class later became Assistant Finance Director of Fenn College and transferred to C.S.U. as such in 1965.

The College received a shock on June 13, 1956, upon the sudden death of Professor William C. Davis, Chairman, Department of Electrical Engineering since 1928. Professor Davis created the department, led in the planning of its curriculum, developed the laboratory, and even built much of the equipment himself. He planned the new electrical engineering laboratories which were later constructed in Stilwell Hall (former Ohio Motors Building). He was never too busy to concern himself with the problems of the students, faculty, and alumni.

Chairman Stilwell announced the following Trustee committee appointments at the July 16, 1956, board meeting:

Development Committee
Sub-Committee on Building: Paul E. Lees, Chairman; Clarence M. Taylor, Clarence J. Beller.
Sub-Committee on Appraisal: George S. Case, Chairman; Harry F. Burmester, L. Carl Weiss.

Standing Committee on Public Relations
Clayton G. Hale, Chairman
H. F. Meyer
Hugh J. Morrison
Vernon B. Stouffer
Jay W. Collins

The Sub-Committee on Building held four meetings during June and July 1956, embracing three major areas of study, namely: (1) Possible alternative usages of the West Campus building,* including the land should the building be razed. (2) Existing plans and specifications for the building. (3) Initiation of the conversion program. The committee asked the administration to study the area needs in the West Campus building with the thought of postponing completion of certain areas until 1960–1961. The committee likewise requested that the architect submit a report on the cost of refurbishing the Tower after all the necessary moves to the West Campus building had been completed. The architect later presented an estimate of $251,000.

Following is a summary of the findings of the Building committee:

The Committee has concluded:

a. The ultimate use of the West Campus building should be for college classrooms, laboratories, student services, and offices.

---

* The West Campus building was a temporary name authorized for use in referring to the Ohio Motors building.

b. The existing specifications are generally sound but some substitutions may be authorized by a building committee to effect economies.

c. Authority should immediately be given architect Joseph Ceruti to start working drawings on the West Campus building.

d. The building or conversion project should be conceived as a single project but with postponement of interior completion and equipping of those areas designated as deferrable.

e. Deferrable areas should be walled and their utilities stubended.

The Committee believes its conclusions produce the following results:

a. Approximately 75% of the Building Program will be initiated without further delay, meeting the anticipated need.

b. The space most urgently needed will be provided first and the expense of the Prospect-Fenn buildings will be eliminated.

c. The penalty which the architect anticipates for doing the job in two "phases" will be partially overcome.

d. Avoiding further delay will forestall further cost increases.

As a final exercise in thoroughness, one more re-study was made of all possible alternatives which included:

a.   Sale of the building.
b.   Demolition of the building.
c.   Use as student-faculty parking garage.
d.   Lease of entire property.
e.   Immediate partial conversion to college use and lease of balance.
f.   Immediate partial conversion to college use without leasing balance.
g.   Convert 100% to college use immediately.

The Committee is unanimously agreed the West Campus building's ultimate use should be for college classrooms, laboratories, student and faculty services, and offices.

It was reported at this same board meeting that the first $225,000 of the Ford Foundation grant to increase faculty salaries had been received. Upon becoming a private college in 1952 Fenn's investments were authorized by the Board Investment Committee. James H. Coolidge, Chairman of this committee in 1956 recommended, and the board approved, that henceforth the Ford grant of $225,000 plus the Stella

Antisdale Scholarship Fund of $15,000, plus an accumulated current fund surplus held in savings accounts in several banks, be pooled into a new portfolio in one bank, creating Fenn's first Endowment Fund. The College budget for the academic year 1956–1957 was approved at this meeting. The estimated income was $1,652,710 and the estimated expenses were $1,837,002 which called for contributory income of $184,322 to balance the budget.

The September 24, 1956, board meeting was held in one of the temporary classrooms in the West Campus building. President Earnest reported that the pointing and caulking of the Fenn Tower was completed during the summer of 1956. This five-year project was completed in four years. Work had started on the painting of all exterior window frames and other metal work. The gymnasium and handball court had been repainted. A resolution was passed accepting an agreement to place the College portfolio in custody of The Cleveland Trust Company, and following committee reports, President Earnest showed slides of the proposed layout of floor plans for the West Campus building. Following adjournment of the meeting President Earnest conducted the Trustees on a tour of the building.

The board met prior to the Corporation meeting, in the former new-car showroom of the West Campus building, on October 29, 1956. The entire meeting was concerned with planning for the fund raising campaign to convert the building for academic purposes. President Earnest requested that, as a first step, the Trustees set for themselves a goal of $125,000, which was 6.7% of the total proposed goal of $1,883,000. Alan R. Blackburn, the new public relations and fund raising consultant, was introduced, and he emphasized the need for conviction on the part of those concerned with fund raising in order to properly interpret Fenn's contribution to industry and business. On motion of Clayton G. Hale, Chairman of the Board Public Relations Committee, the following resolution was unanimously adopted:

> RESOLVED That the Board of Trustees of Fenn College agrees to accept the following course of action for the Fund Raising program of Fenn College:
>
> I. Realizing that the success of the campaign will in large measure depend on the effective manner in which the Fenn story is made known to our prospects, a full scale, intensive public relations effort will be initiated and continued. The administration

will set up tour meetings to which groups of prospects will be invited. Board members will be asked to take responsibility for issuing invitations and hosting these meetings.

II.   The Administration and Board of Trustees will intensify efforts to seek operating monies for the fiscal year 1956–57. A Board Committee will be appointed with a Chairman to make the personal contacts. All companies who regularly give operating money and those who have given irregularly during the past five years will be approached.

III.   A personal approach will be made before the end of 1956 to those companies who are already familiar with the program of Fenn College and are favorably disposed toward it, with the thought in mind that these companies may wish to take advantage of tax benefits at the year's end, making some portion of their contribution to Fenn's capital needs at this time.

A letter will be written to each company by the Chairman of the Board and a personal follow-up of each letter will be made by a Board member assigned to the company. This effort will be complete before November 30, 1956. No company will be sent a letter unless we have assurance there will be a personal follow-up.

IV.   The capital campaign will be held as soon as, but not before, top leadership has been effectively cultivated and enlisted.

A.   The steps to be taken to secure this leadership are: (1) The Public Relations program as prepared by the administration will be put into action to make Fenn better known, especially to the community leaders; (2) A three-year goal of $125,000 will be set for personal contributions from the Board; and (3) Each Board member will agree to accept a responsible position in the campaign organization.

B.   In this capital campaign we shall approach all large corporations who gave in 1953 for leadership giving. In addition, the effort will be a full-scale campaign in which all sources of potential money will be solicited.

C.   Our immediate goal will be $1,883,000. This sum is sufficient to remodel the West Campus building to the extent that a move completely from the Fenn-Prospect Building can be made.

The immediate need for the entire West Campus Building including $251,000 for remodelling Fenn Tower after moving is $2,832,500.

The Development Committee is requested to draw up a plan and estimates for Fenn's long-range needs.

At the annual Corporation meeting, following the board meeting, action was taken to amend the Regulations of Fenn College increasing the number of elected Trustees from twenty-four to thirty; five Trustees being elected, each year for a six-year term. Other actions approved at the meeting included the election of Elbert H. Baker, Jr., as an Honorary Life Trustee. Arthur S. Armstrong, H. F. Meyer, Dr. Robert M. Stecher and Vernon B. Stouffer were re-elected to six-year terms, ending in 1962. Warren L. Morris was elected to fulfill the unexpired term of Elbert H. Baker, Jr. (class of 1958). John R. Hoover (1959), Harry F. Burmester (1960), C. E. Smith (1961) and Donald L. Millham (1962) were elected for terms ending as indicated, and M. J. Wurzbach, '37, was elected to a three-year term as an Alumni Trustee.

Annual reports were presented by President Earnest and his staff members responsible for academic and business affairs. Following the meeting the members of the Corporation were conducted on a tour of the West Campus building.

The following officers were elected at the December 27, 1956, meeting of the board:

Charles J. Stilwell, Chairman
Ellwood H. Fisher, Vice Chairman
James H. Coolidge, Treasurer
Arthur P. Loegler, Secretary

President Earnest reported that the Trustees had subscribed $100,000 of their goal of $125,000 to the Development Fund.

And so, a lot happened at Fenn during 1956. Here are some of the highlights recapitulated:

Faculty teaching year reduced from four quarters to three, and calendar adjusted to coincide with other colleges.

Faculty graduate study subsidized.

First endowment funds received (from the Ford Foundation).

Board of Trustees enlarged; electees from 24 to 30, total Board from 32 to 36.

School of Nursing selected to offer pilot program for veterans with military nursing experience.

Founding date of College changed from 1881 to 1923.

Awarding of first Alumni Distinguished Service Awards.

First awards to Trustees, Faculty and Staff for twenty-five years of service.

First Faculty Handbook published.

The highlights at the end of each year for the five years are undoubtedly an indication that "all charts went up" for all phases of college activity. For instance Day Division enrollment grew from 690 in 1951 to 826 in 1956, not including students on co-op. The total number of day students in 1956 including Co-op was 1,280. Evening Division enrollment grew from 3,660 to 5,274. Total operating income of the College grew in five years from $1,276,000 to $1,738,000 and the College ended each year "in the black."

The accompanying roster includes those individuals of the "Fenn Family" composing the Board and Corporation at the close of 1956.

The Trustees, the President, and the staff of the Department of Development were so arduously involved in the Fenn Capital Development Program that no meeting of the board was held in 1957 until June 10. Board committees did hold meetings, however, and one item of business recommended by the Board Personnel Committee was officially approved by a letter ballot after receiving authorization from the Board Finance Committee and the Executive Committee. The allocation of the anticipated income of $229,700 resulting from increased tuition effective September 1, 1957, was approved as follows:

For salary increases	$104,081
For additional Faculty	59,105
For scholarships	20,000
For other expenses	46,514
Total	$229,700

It was estimated that the amount allocated to salary increases would provide for an average increase of 9.7% for all employees and 11.7% for the full-time faculty.

The Annual Corporation-Faculty meeting was held May 21, 1957. Peter Viereck, eminent educator, historian, and poet, of Mount Holyoke College addressed the assemblage on the subject, "The Unadjusted Man: A New Hero for America." He ended his speech with the following

statement: "Most curricula reflect an atomic age which puts a new premium on the technician and on practical outer applications of inner theory. Yet without the understanding of man's inner nature which impractical art and literature gave us, and without the inner ethical restraint which religion gives us, our outer practical and mechanical progress is paving our road to hell with good inventions." Chairman Stilwell presented Elbert H. Baker, Jr., with an Honorary Life Member Award and a co-op award for twenty-five years of service by Baker's company—The Locke Machine Company—at this Corporation dinner, and Clayton G. Hale presented the College with a set of volumes, "The Opinions of Justice Harold H. Burton" (those opinions of the Court which were written by him; and only three sets were printed— one for his family, one for his own Alma Mater, Bowdoin College, and one for Fenn College). Justice Burton of the United States Supreme Court was an Honorary Life Member of the Fenn Board of Trustees. Librarian Emil J. Stefancic accepted the books for the Fenn Library.

The first order of business at the June 10, 1957, board meeting was the ratification of action taken on March 28 by the Executive Committee (followed by letter ballot) relative to the distribution of additional income of $229,700 resulting from an increase in tuition. Action was also taken at this meeting to add a new curriculum in September 1957 leading to the degree of Bachelor of Science in Chemistry and to replace the ongoing degree program in Metallurgical Engineering with a modified curriculum leading to the degree of Bachelor of Science in Metallurgy.

The commencement convocation for 1957 was held in Severance Hall on June 18. Harold Terry Clark, prominent Cleveland attorney and civic leader, was the speaker of the day. His subject was "The Challenging Future." It was the shortest commencement address on record at Fenn—only ten minutes. One hundred-ninety graduates received diplomas, thirty-eight in Arts and Sciences, seventy-five in Business Administration, and seventy-nine in Engineering. Richard A. Epaves of this class became an Instructor in the School of Business Administration in 1962 and transferred to C.S.U. in 1965 as Assistant Professor in Accounting. James A. Chesebrough, James B. Skellenger, Dolores M. Boduroff, and George F. Quinn, Jr., of this class spent several years in various staff positions at the College, but none was with Fenn at the time of the transfer to the State of Ohio.

The following eminent Clevelanders were recipients of honorary degrees at this 1957 Fenn College commencement:

Harold T. Clark, Doctor of Laws (LL.D.)
Edward D. Lynde, Doctor of Humane Letters (L.H.D.)
James L. Myers, Doctor of Engineering (D. Eng.)
Whiting Williams, Doctor of Laws (LL.D.)

Seldom does a college completely drop a curriculum, but Fenn was forced to do so in the fall of 1957. Lack of interest and enrollment in the subject of Home Economics occasioned the discontinuance of all of those courses. Trustee Vernon Stouffer was particularly interested in this program, but few Day Division students elected to take it. The laboratory equipment was sold, and the vacated space was converted to classrooms and faculty offices.

On June 26, 1957, the College received its second installment from the Ford Foundation. The amount was $228,000 making the total grant $453,000 which was $3,000 more than expected, and this was added to the Endowment Fund. The annual income from this total grant was restricted to increasing faculty salaries for ten years.

Only two meetings of the Board of Trustees were held in 1957. The second meeting was held on October 1. President Earnest reported that the fall Day Division enrollment totaled 1,315 as against 1,280 for the fall of 1956, and that the enrollment for the Evening Division dropped from 5,274 in 1956 to 5,164 in 1957. School distribution of the student body is shown in Table 2.

The operating budget for the fiscal year September 1, 1957, to August 31, 1958, was approved. The proposed budget income was $2,154,847 including prospective contributions totalling $103,272. The proposed budget expenses totaled $2,154,847 with a $50,000 reserve for contingencies. It was noted that 70.8% of the proposed expenses was for salaries and other personal services.

Chairman Stilwell emphasized the rapid growth of the College, the need for a survey of all functions and the creation of new trustee committees to obtain a closer relationship between the trustees and the administration. It was voted to request Chairman Stilwell to appoint a trustee committee to study and determine whether a management survey of the College should be made by an outside agency. It was also voted that the Chairman should appoint a five-man Trustee Committee on Buildings and Grounds.

TABLE 2

SCHOOL DISTRIBUTION OF THE STUDENT BODY

DAY DIVISION

| | Fall 1957 | | | Fall 1956 | | | |
	School	Co-op	Total	School	Co-op	Total	% Change
A. & S.*	130	47	177	130	36	166	+7%
B.A.**	212	97	309	218	121	339	−9%
Engr.	549	220	769	478	217	695	+11%
Nurses	39	21	60	51	29	80	−25%
Totals	930	385	1315	877	403	1280	+2.7%

EVENING DIVISION

Fall 1957		Fall 1956		% Change
A. & S.	893	A. & S.	967	−8%
B.A.	2217	B.A.	2095	+6%
Engr.	873	Engr.	918	−5%
T.I.	1181	T.I.	1294	−9%
Total	5164	Total	5274	−2%

* Arts and Sciences.
** Business Administration.

Trustee Vollmer Fries, Chairman, Operation Fund Committee, reported $123,239 in gifts for the 1956–1957 fiscal year just closed which was an increase of twenty-four percent over the previous year's gifts. Trustee James W. Corey announced that thirty-one solicitors had raised a total of $935,862 in capital gifts. Alumni Trustees Jay W. Collins, 1940, and William R. Miller, 1934, reported that $76,000 had been pledged by 1,100 Alumni and that a total of 3,350 Alumni will be contacted. Chairman Stilwell reported that $110,000 in firm pledges had been received from the trustees toward their goal of $125,000. Verbal assurance was given for the balance.

Chairman Stilwell announced the appointment of a Civic Sponsoring Committee numbering ninety of Cleveland's civic leaders under the chairmanship of Charles M. White, Chairman of the Board, Republic Steel Corporation. Two luncheon meetings were held shortly thereafter in the private dining room of Republic Steel Corporation at which President Earnest described the development program of the College and showed slides of the proposed use of each of the five floors in the West Campus building.

The number of various committees working in behalf of Fenn's fund raising program as of the Fall of 1957 were: Capital Development Committee, Appraisal Committee, Foundation Committee, Special Gift Committee, Business and Industry Committee, Alumni Committee, Civic Sponsoring Committee, Public Relations Committee, Building and Grounds Committee, and Finance Committee.

The 1957 Annual Business Meeting of the Fenn College Corporation was held at the University Club on the evening of November 19. Trustees K. W. Akers, H. F. Burns, G. S. Case, and G. V. Woodling were re-elected to six-year terms. Van H. Leichliter, President, American Steel and Wire Division of U S. Steel Corporation, was elected to fill a vacancy in the class of 1963 and W. J. Hunkin II, Vice President, Hunkin-Conkey Construction Company, was elected to fill a vacancy in the class of 1958. George B. Davis, 1941, was elected an Alumni Trustee to fill the unexpired term of Milton J. Wurzbach, 1937, who was transferred to the Pittsburgh office of the U.S. Steel Corporation. Madison H. Dods, 1934, was elected for a three-year term as an Alumni Trustee.

President Earnest presented a digest of the 1956–1957 Annual Report which was distributed to those present. The speaker of the evening was Ralph M. Besse, who at that time was Executive Vice President, Cleveland Electric Illuminating Company. (He later went through the chairs as President and Chairman of the Board.) His subject was "Methods to Match the Money."

The Cleveland *Plain Dealer* on November 26, 1957, carried the following editorial concerning Fenn College:

FENN'S REPORT

In his extensive annual report on Fenn College's operations, President G. Brooks Earnest detailed many of the downtown school's achievements and listed an illuminating financial statement.

Total income was $1,974,450.30; total expenses were $2,040.04 less than that. This proud accomplishment was brought off, President Earnest explained, through gifts totaling $123,239.35. Without such gifts the college would have been forced to curtail drastically its salaries or its activities. The president commented:

Fenn depends absolutely on grants for current expenses, capital funds and endowment. The sources are Cleveland business corporations, individual donors, alumni and foundations. . . . The college is grateful for this evidence of its worth. The measure of its gratitude shall continue to be the fulfillment of its responsibilities to all constituencies to the fullest extent of its resources.

In another part of the report he refers to the fact that most Fenn graduates go to work in Cleveland—and that students generally earn here while learning, some of them doing so well on the job that they don't finish their full course of study.

The need for continued, and increased, support by business of Fenn and the other privately run colleges here is obvious. In a time when there is a slackening of production in some lines, in what is to be hoped will be a temporary condition, company managements should not withdraw or cut financial backing. If they do they may be injuring the education of young people they will be needing several years from now.

Some of the highlights of the year included the fact that 167 of the 190 June graduates found jobs in Cleveland; that programs in nursing, Business Administration, and the Technical Institute awarded associate degrees or certificates of completion to 128 successful candidates, all employed in Cleveland; and that the Faculty numbered 77 full-time and 186 part-time. The final payment of The Ford Foundation grant ($228,000) was received making the total grant $453,000.00. Total gifts to year's operations amounted to $123,239. Professor Donald R. Tuttle led in the movement to raise state certificate standards for high school teachers of English. Professor Frank De Marinis, Chairman, Department of Biology, was one of a group of scientists selected to study radioactive fallout in populated areas. The tests were conducted in Nevada. A second edition of her book *Bridges and Their Builders* by Dr. Sara R. Watson, Professor of English, was published. A new course in Nursing Science was developed by Doretta C. Thielker, Associate Professor of Nursing. A study, "Impact of the St. Lawrence Seaway on the Port of Cleveland—Estimated General Cargo" was published by the School of Business Administration's Bureau of Business Research. Two new degree programs were instituted in the School of Engineering, namely, B.S. degree in Metallurgy and B.S. degree in Chemistry. A record breaking enrollment of 2,685 was achieved in the Technical Institute. The first students in the Huron Road Hospital School of Nursing at

Fenn College, numbering 28, were graduated. The 1,566 man-quarters of employment was supervised by the Department of Cooperative Education. This is equivalent to 391.5 man-years of work. The total amount earned during the year by co-op students was $1,479,000. The first complete inventory of Library since 1949 showed a total of 37,185 volumes. Important gift library acquisitions for the year were: The United States Supreme Court Opinions (3 volumes) from Justice Harold H. Burton, The International Yearbook and Statesman's Who's Who, from Clayton G. Hale, and Digest of International Law (8 volumes) from Royal M. Hochner, Assistant Professor of Mechanical Engineering. One thousand one hundred ten individuals were tested for Fenn, industry, and high schools by the Personnel Department headed by George A. Leech. The highest spring Evening Division registration in Fenn's history was achieved—4918. One hundred and twenty-two students participated in 87 dual intercollegiate contests, of which Fenn won 27. Bohdan Huryn, a member of Fenn's soccer team, was voted "All-American" in a nation-wide poll of coaches, Fenn's third All-American (Robert F. Busbey was All-American in swimming, and Ben Firth was All-American in fencing). Intramural sports were participated in by 843 men and 233 women. The Fenn Alumni Association with William J. Pugh, 1941, President, and Richard H. Stanse, 1953, Executive Secretary, placed first among Ohio co-educational institutions in percentage of alumni contributors (40% participation) and ninth in the United States according to a survey by the American Alumni Council.

During the year President Earnest was appointed Chairman of the Engineers Council for Professional Development Committee of the Cleveland Section, American Society of Civil Engineers. He served in this capacity through 1960. He was also elected to a three-year term as a Trustee of the Cleveland Council on World Affairs and a three-year term as Chairman of the College Division of the Cleveland Community Fund which later became the United Appeal.

Although the Board of Trustees met only twice during 1957, it was a year of many accomplishments, really the start of a series of busy years each progressively becoming more productive.

The calendar year ended with a "bang." Certain committees had been meeting furiously in 1957 relative to the final design space allocation in the West Campus building. Working drawings were prepared by Architect Joseph Ceruti, employing these space allocations. Building specifications were also prepared by Mr. Ceruti. Upon approval of the working drawings by all committees involved, including the Board of Trustees, the plans were distributed to five general contractors, and to three sub-contractors of each of the mechanical trades, plumbing-heating, ventilating and air-conditioning, and electrical. Receipt of bid date was set as January 10, 1958, so 1958 was to start with the same "bang" with which 1957 had ended.

The Trustee Buildings and Grounds Committee met January 11, 1958, the day following the receipt of qualified bids from five general contractors and three sub-contractors for conversion of the West Campus building. Bids were actually requested for two specific methods of construction: the cost of conversion of entire building and the cost of converting only the basement, first, and fourth floors as a first stage, thus deferring the second and third floors until a later date. The bids disclosed that the prudent decision to make was the conversion of the building in one project, for there was only a difference of $160,000 (by the low bidder) in the cost of converting the entire building in one construction project over the cost of the first stage.

The committee reviewed all the bidding, including the alternatives and unanimously recommended the following:

Contractor	Area of Contract	Bid Price
The A. M. Higley Co.	General	$1,171,550
Feldman Brothers	Plumbing	212,460
Feldman Brothers	Heating, Ventilating and Air-Conditioning	323,721
Martien Electric Co.	Electrical	296,000
	Total	$2,003,731

The board met on January 14, 1958, and unanimously accepted the recommendations of the Building and Grounds Committee. Harry F. Burmester, Chairman of the Board Finance Committee, reported that there was $1,366,000 in capital cash and equivalent on hand and an additional $708,200 in written pledges so it appeared feasible to proceed as far as the cost of construction of the building was concerned. However, about an additional $1,000,000 would be required to furnish and equip the West Campus building and renovate vacated areas in the Tower Building. An estimate of total cost was as follows:

West Campus building	$2,004,000
Balance of architect's fee	35,000
Kitchen and dining room equipment	100,000
Laboratory and classroom equipment	400,000
Alterations to Fenn Tower	251,000
Contingencies	210,000

Total $3,000,000

With the board voting to award the contracts for complete rehabilitation of the West Campus building, Chairman Stilwell emphasized the fund raising task ahead to meet the expenses of all of the above projects.

President Earnest announced at this board meeting that representatives of the School of Engineering met with the Board Development Committee to discuss the advisability of purchasing a computer for more sophisticated engineering instruction analysis and for modernizing several of the College record procedures, but it was decided that a suitable type would be too expensive to warrant consideration at that time.

The following slate of officers was placed in nomination and unanimously elected to serve for 1958:

Charles J. Stilwell, Chairman
C. E. Smith, Vice Chairman
Harry F. Burmester, Treasurer
Arthur P. Loegler, Secretary

The January 16, 1958, *Plain Dealer* carried the following editorial respective to the action taken by the Board of Trustees at its January 14 meeting:

FENN MOVES AHEAD

Over a period of many years the leaders of Fenn College have been on their toes to meet opportunities and responsibilities. Now the trustees have approved an immediate start on a 4-million-dollar reconversion of the former Ohio Motors Building on E. 24th Street. When completed late next year, this will almost double Fenn's present instructional space, from 192,000 square feet to 370,000.

Thus the college is preparing for the two-for-one tidal wave of students expected in the future—for the not-too-distant time when there will be twice as many college applicants as there are now. The trustees show full confidence in their institution and in this community in starting now, rather than waiting to see how things develop later. They are going ahead even though the college needs 1½ millions or so more than it now has to pay for the reconversion job.

There would be no question of adequate funds for Fenn, if it were a state-supported school. Because it has no claim to tax money it deserves all the more tribute—and voluntary financial backing from alumni, friends and businesses. Cleveland, as Ralph M. Besse told a Fenn audience last November, should do as well for Fenn as Fenn has done for Cleveland.

Sorrow struck the Fenn Campus on April 1, 1958, upon the sudden death of Arthur O. Loegler who had served as Director of Finance for twenty-two years. Three successive Fenn presidents trusted his judgment—so did the students. He felt he was obligated to advise the students about their financial affairs, believing that part of education was learning financial responsibility. At times during his regime his duties also included responsibility for dormitory policy, administration of the Student Loan Fund and Secretary to the Board of Trustees. His colleagues remember with respect his prudence, his discretion, his rigorous personal honesty, and his strong loyalty and faithfulness to the College. One aspect of a good administrator was made clear—he sought, engaged, and trained Vernon H. Davis, 1939, as his assistant, and upon his death Mr. Davis was eminently qualified to step in and carry on the full obligations as Finance Director, in which office he remained upon the transfer of Fenn to the State of Ohio.

The annual Fenn Corporation-Faculty meeting was held May 20, 1958, at the University Club. The Trustee 25-year award was presented to Clayton G. Hale by Chairman Stilwell. The Faculty 25-year award was presented to Dean Max B. Robinson and the 25-year awards in partnership with Fenn's cooperative education program were awarded to representatives from the following companies or organizations:

Cleveland Board of Education
National Copper and Smelting Co.
New York Central Railroad
Western Automatic Screw Machine Co.
The Harshaw Chemical Co.

Cleveland Switchboard Co.
Young Men's Christian Association
Fisher Bros. Co.
Jones and Laughlin Steel Corp.
General Motors Corp., Euclid Division
Clevite Corp.
The Halle Bros. Co.
Electric Storage Battery Co.
Ohio Department of Highways

Alumni Distinguished Service Awards were presented by President Earnest to Jay W. Collins, 1940; William R. Miller, 1934; and Clarence O. Poleni, 1929. The speaker on this occasion was Maurice B. Mitchell, President, Encyclopedia Britannica Films, Inc. His subject was "Education—A New Era Begins." He gave an illuminating address concerning the future of education in America and some of the new teaching techniques being perfected for future generations

Construction activity on the West Campus building got under way February 1, 1958, with the completion date set at July 1, 1959, to permit installation of laboratory equipment before the start of the Fall term. However, in early May, the Building Trades Unions called a strike, and James W. Corey, Chairman of the Trustee Buildings and Grounds Committee, reported to the board on June 4 that, due to the strike only ten percent of the contract work was thus far performed.

At the same board meeting the low bid for equipping the kitchen ($93,000) was approved and also $150,000 for immediate purchase of fixed laboratory equipment requiring mechanical connections.

The Ohio Department of Highways was preparing plans to widen Chester Avenue on the south side by 32 feet from just east of East 21st Street to East 40th Street. This construction would encroach on the White apartment building and the vacant land to the north of the West Campus building. It would put the College out of the apartment business. The State offered Fenn $326,147 for the land and damages. Trustee Warren L. Morris had an independent appraisal made which approximated the offer by the State. At the June 4, 1958, board meeting, Morris moved the acceptance of the offer from the State and unanimous positive action was taken on the motion. This income materially increased the funds available for conversion of the West Campus building.

Morris assisted also in obtaining a tax refund for the West Campus building property for the years 1956 and 1957. This amounted to $16,663.22.

Dorothy Binion was officially engaged as Assistant Director of Public Relations at this same board meeting. For years she had been very active in the Cleveland Council on World Affairs. Following the transfer of Fenn College to the State of Ohio, she became Director of the Cleveland Council on World Affairs.

The 1958 commencement was held at Severance Hall the evening of June 4. Dr. Edward R. Sharp, Director, National Advisory Committee for Aeronautics, Lewis Flight Propulsion Laboratory, gave the address. He was a Member of the Fenn College Corporation. The subject of his address was "The New Age of Exploration."

There were 204 graduates in the Class of 1958 distributed as follows: School of Arts and Sciences, 32; School of Business Administration, 74; School of Engineering, 98. The following men were recipients of honorary degrees: Fred W. Ramsey, Doctor of Laws (LL.D.), Clyde T. Foster, Doctor of Laws (LL.D.), William Hunt Eisenman, Doctor of Science (D. Sc.), posthumously, and Edward R. Sharp, Doctor of Engineering (D. Eng.).

The Board of Trustees met August 21, 1958, in Room 213 of the Fenn Tower to review and take action on the proposed budget for fiscal 1958–1959, to hear a report from the Buildings and Grounds Committee and to tour the West Campus building to note the splendid progress on construction, now that the strike was settled.

The proposed operating budget totalling $2,083,866 (slightly exceeding the estimated 1957–1958 budget) included $126,748 for unrestricted gifts on the income side and $20,000 for contingencies on the expense side. The Buildings and Grounds Committee reported that payments on the contract amounted to $524,332.80 to September 1, 1958, and the cost of fixed laboratory equipment on order amounted to $146,061.79 and kitchen equipment on order amounted to $95,923.50. Also that the best bid for disposition of furniture and appliances in the White apartments amounted to $1,950. Occupants were notified to vacate by October 1, 1958.

Stephan Tracey, Civil Engineer with the American Steel and Wire Company, was made available on a full-time basis by Trustee Van Leichliter, President of the Company, to provide a daily check and inspection on the construction of the West Campus building to insure that all specifications were adhered to. Tracey proved to be an invaluable asset to the College because of his lengthy tenure in construction activities and his knowledge of the relationships between the written specifications and actual construction, especially where change orders were involved. Tracey was also most helpful to Architect Joe Ceruti, in checking the monthly billing submitted by the A. M. Higley Co., contractor.

Harry F. Burmester, Chairman of the Trustee Finance Committee, reported at the same meeting that even with all the pressure that is being applied to the capital development fund campaign contributions were not being received in sufficient quantity to accumulate the necessary total at the completion date of the various projects under way. Accordingly, the board moved to grant the Finance and Executive Committees authority to borrow to an upper limit of $1,400,000 at the lowest possible interest rate.

The board met at a special breakfast meeting at the University Club on Friday, September 26, 1958, to take positive action on the following:

    a. Arrange for financing, with the five major Cleveland banks, for a $1,130,000 unsecured loan at 4½% per annum to mature December 31, 1962. (Note this maturity date with later reference as to when the total loan was finally paid off.) This loan was to be taken in amounts of $100,000 or greater prior to July 1, 1959.

    b. Payment in full of the remaining balance of $208,000 on the 1st mortgage on the West Campus building. (It was purchased for $650,000 on May 12, 1953.)

    c. Payment in full of the remaining balance due on the White Apartments from funds obtained from the Ohio Department of Highways for the property purchased by them for the widening of Chester Avenue.

The above action placed all of the College's debt obligations with the five major Cleveland banks.

The board met prior to the annual dinner meeting of the Fenn Corporation at the University Club on November 18, 1958. Chairman Stilwell discussed the proposed amended Code of Regulations of Fenn College. The intent of the changes was to bring more interested people into closer relationship with the College. This was accomplished via providing for increased turnover of Trustees and Corporate Members. The board remained the same size, but instead of classes of five Trustees serving six-year terms, there would be classes of six Trustees serving five-year terms, with a limit of ten years of service. The Corporate Members were elected for three-year terms with a limit of six years of service. The Minutes of the meeting state: "For the first time machinery is provided for graceful retirement from the governing bodies of the College."

At the annual Corporation meeting following the board meeting the resolution amending the Code of Regulations was adopted. In addition the following Trustees were elected to a five-year term: Vollmer W. Fries, William J. Hunkin, II, Paul E. Lees, Warren L. Morris, and Clarence M. Taylor. Mr. Karl F. Bruch was elected to the board to fill a vacancy and Charles R. Day, 1945, was elected to a three-year term as an Alumni Trustee succeeding H. Martin Huge, 1938.

In line with increasing the membership of the Fenn Corporation the following Corporate Members were elected for three-year terms:

> D. C. Adams, Treasurer, Addressograph-Multigraph Corp.
> Bertrand J. Belda, Resident Partner, Ernst & Ernst
> Donald S. Carmichael, Attorney
> A. T. Colwell, Vice President, Thompson Ramo Wooldridge Inc.
> Irving S. Dow, Works Manager, Aluminum Company of America
> Herbert T. Florence, Exec. Vice President-General Manager, The
>   Cleveland Crane & Engineering Co.
> Wade N. Harris, President, Midland-Ross Corp.
> Herbert S. Ide, Jr., Vice President & Treasurer, Eaton Mfg. Co.
> Frank R. Kohnstamm, President, Jack & Heintz, Inc.
> James M. Lister, Director, Urban Renewal & Housing Dept., City
>   of Cleveland
> Sam S. Mullen, President, Cleveland Pneumatic Tool Company
> Thomas F. Peterson, President, Preformed Line Products Co.
> Robert W. Ramsdell, President, The East Ohio Gas Company
> T. Laurence Strimple, President, National Acme Company
> H. E. Widdell, President, Arthur G. McKee & Company
> Lee Wilson, Chairman of the Board, Lee Wilson Engineering Co.,
>   Inc.

Chairman Stilwell introduced the speaker of the evening, Mr. James Lister, Director, Urban Renewal & Housing Department of the City of Cleveland, who presented an illustrated talk on metropolitan planning especially relating to freeways and their effect on traffic patterns. Much of the talk was directed to Fenn's relative position respective to planning in downtown Cleveland and therefore was of especial interest to the group

In President Earnest's annual report for the school year 1957–1958 chief attention was directed to the students. He said as a preface: "I have not touched upon the salient quality of the Fenn student, which is his academic worth." In regretfully referring to Fenn's attrition of carefully admitted students, he quoted a portion of his talk directed to the entering Freshmen at the opening convocation of the College in the Fall of 1957, thus:

> Brains are the ultimate U.S. resource in the space age. You have brains. You were selected from many others to join this Freshman class at Fenn College. If you fail, this is folly, and your own. If you drop college to get married, this is a weakness you and your spouse may both live to regret the rest of your natural lives. If you drop out to accept a job which looks good right now, you may be sure it won't look good five years hence. That's the time when your colleagues will be graduating into jobs with futures open only to the learned, with the highest positions in their fields in the prospect before them. If you drop out because friends of yours who didn't make college are getting good jobs and driving flashy cars, there is a fatal flaw in your character we somehow missed. And your days even for driving flashy cars will be already numbered by your decision. I do not care what reason you have for dropping your academic career at Fenn or any other institution you may attend—this, for you, in this day and age, is sheer folly. Ignorance is not bliss. For people with good minds it is misery— the miseries of a dead-end job, the miseries of a blighted life, the miseries of always thinking what might have been.

Highlights of the year appearing in the annual report included:

1.   Thirty-one percent of the Faculty held Ph. D. degrees and 56% showed evidence of scholarly productivity.

2.   The retirement of Miss Almeda Rothrock, Payroll Secretary, who had been with the institution since 1912 (46 years). She was succeeded by Mrs. Mary B. Jenkins who transferred to C.S.U. in the same capacity.

3.   The graduation of 18 nursing students from The Huron Road School of Nursing at Fenn College.

4.   A total enrollment of 2,288 in the Technical Institute with part-time Faculty of 54.

5. Co-op students employed for 1593 man-quarters at average quarterly rate of $906, therefore earning a total of $1,743,258 for the school year.

6. Library circulated 24,698 items for the year. Catalogued books totaled 39,617 with a net gain of 2,432.

7. Sixty-five Day Division students, including forty-five Freshmen, received $30,000 in scholarship grants.

8. Selma M. Montasana, Dean of Women reported Day Division women enrollment increased from 188 to 197.

9. Ruth L. Pattison, Director of the Audio-Visual Center secured and loaned 783 films for lecture purpose. There were 28 showings of the Fenn College film, "A College Meets A Challenge."

10. One hundred and four students participated in 84 dual inter-collegiate contests. Fenn won thirty-eight and tied one. The Fencing Team was undefeated and the Swimming Team lost only to Carnegie Tech. Seventy varsity letters were awarded. Two hundred and fifty-six men and sixty-four women students participated in intramural sports.

11. The Fenn Alumni's cash contributions of $30,590 exceeded the previous year's total.

12. President Earnest was appointed a member of the national Task Committee on Administrative Procedure, of the American Society of Civil Engineers, and the Committee on Development of the Young Engineer, of the Engineers Council for Professional Development.

XI

Sometimes, I think, the things we see
Are shadows of the things to be;
That what we plan we build.

Phoebe Cary, 1824–1874.

The Board of Trustees did not meet in 1959 until March 30. The incumbent officers were re-elected, namely:

Charles J. Stilwell, Chairman
C. E. Smith, Vice Chairman
Harry F. Burmester, Treasurer
Vernon H. Davis, Secretary

The board took favorable action in giving the United Food Service Management, Inc., exclusive rights to operate all food services on the Fenn Campus. The new large cafeteria, faculty dining rooms, and kitchen in the West Campus building increased and greatly enhanced the College's ability to feed the growing student body and the enlarged Faculty and Staff. The management fee was five percent of gross receipts, and the contract was for one year.

President Earnest reported that the total billing to date on the West Campus building stood at $1,597,509.95 which included about a one percent increase over the original contract price for extras. Also, that the contractor moved his completion date for the building ahead from July 1 to May 1, 1959.

Chairman Stilwell reported that fund raising had been benefited by campus luncheons with small groups and that increased attention should be paid to small companies, some of whom had never contributed to Fenn. He urged the trustees to pledge 50% to 75% of their previous gifts as a further goal by mid–1959.

431

On the recommendation of Trustee Karl Bruch, reporting for the Development Committee, the board authorized the engagement of Charles L. Knight, planning consultant and landscape architect, to collaborate with Architect Ceruti and the Director of Development on the creation of a master plan for the College, illustrated with accurate maps reflecting the campus in 1962, 1965, and 1975, the cost of the study not to exceed $5,000.

The board also approved a renewal contract with Huron Road Hospital. Since certain new laboratory and classroom facilities were being built into the West Campus building, a new organizational pattern was envisaged for the management of the nursing program. More responsibility was being turned over to Fenn College with coordinating committees established at Fenn and at the Hospital, in curriculum, clinical experience, conduct of co-op work quarters, and finance. The Director of the School of Nursing was responsible to the Director of Huron Road Hospital for the administration of the Diploma Program in Nursing and to the President of Fenn College for the administration of the program leading to the Associate Degree in Applied Science.

On recommendation of President Earnest, the trustees took action to increase the tuition effective in the Fall Quarter of 1959 as follows:

DAY DIVISION

Freshman Year

School of Arts and Sciences	from $660 to $720
School of Business Administration	from $660 to $720
School of Engineering	from $780 to $900

Upperclass Years

School of Arts and Sciences	from $15 to $16 per credit hour
School of Business Administration	from $15 to $16 per credit hour
School of Engineering	from $17 to $19 per credit hour

EVENING DIVISION

All classes, including Freshmen, subject to the same increase as the upperclass years above.

TECHNICAL INSTITUTE

Same as upperclass years above for School of Arts and Sciences.

TABLE 1

TOTAL COST OF DEGREE PROGRAM

	Arts & Sciences	Business Admin.	Engineering
Fenn College	$2975	$3247	$4155
John Carroll University	2755	2755	....
Baldwin-Wallace College	3327	3327	....
Western Reserve University	3476	3476	....
Case Institute of Technology	....	....	4830

The total cost for an entire degree-program at Fenn College and the other four major institutions of higher learning in Metropolitan Cleveland is given in Table 1 for the academic year 1959–1960. It must be noted, however, that Fenn's program is for five years and the other four are for the conventional four-year programs:

The Special Survey Committee submitted its first report to the board at this same meeting. The report as follows was received:

A Survey Committee was appointed in October, 1957, to establish whether or not a survey of the organization would make a more effective college operation. The Committee concluded the first step was a statistical study showing quantitatively, the present status of the College.

Professor Russell L. Ackoff, head of the Operations Research Group at Case Institute of Technology, was engaged to prepare an objective statistical basis providing the Administration and the Board of Trustees with the facts necessary for making judgment decisions involving the college operation.

The *Statistical Study Providing an Objective Basis for Planning at Fenn College* was completed, and the Committee met on March 16, 1959, with Dr. Ackoff for a discussion of the *Report*, and felt, upon verification, the *Report* would provide the essential fundamental data.

With statistical data of future enrollment and plant equipment on hand, the Committee recommended that the data be used to project the quantitative objectives for 1965, 1970, and 1975. With the objectives clearly stated, the Committee would then entertain a proposal from a management consulting firm to recommend the most effective organizational structure to fulfill the future objectives.

The Survey Committee plans to meet again as soon as the President is prepared to present

a. the philosophy of the College, and

b. the quantitative objects for 1965, 1970, and 1975.

If the Committee then considers a survey appropriate to the most effective operation of the College, a recommendation will be made to the board for action and subsequent responsibilities transferred to the Development Committee of the board.

The annual Corporation-Faculty meeting was held at the University Club on May 20, 1959. Philip H. Coombs, Secretary, The Fund for the Advancement of Education, was the principal speaker. The title of his address was "The Future of the Liberal Arts College in America."

Chairman Stilwell presented an award to Harold H. Burton, Associate Justice, retired, United States Supreme Court, for twenty-five years of distinguished service as a Trustee of Fenn College. Mrs. Burton accompanied Justice Burton. President Earnest received a letter from Justice Burton shortly after his return to Washington.

President Earnest presented awards to representatives from the following firms or organizations which had completed twenty-five years of partnership with Fenn in providing co-op jobs for students:

Otis Elevator Company (Baker Industrial Trucks Div.)

City of Cleveland (City Hospital)

Glidden Company

Harris-Intertype Corporation

Iron Fireman Mfg. Company

Leisy Brewing Company

St. Luke's Hospital

Warner & Swasey Company

The following were recipients of the Alumni Distinguished Service Award: Edward J. Hrdlicka, 1938, H. Martin Huge, 1937, and Theodore S. O'Konski, 1934. Walter O'Konski of the Class of 1932 was President of the Fenn Alumni Association for the school year 1958–1959.

The board met May 26, 1959, and spent considerable time in discussing Trustee Bartlett's report as Chairman of the Board Development Committee. He reported that Knight had submitted site plans for Phases 1 through 3 for the future physical planning of the College. Some of the areas contemplated in the five-year duration of Phase 1 included:

May 26, 1959

My dear President Earnest:

      This is just a line to record my appreciation
of the cordial reception which you gave me at the meeting of your trustees and corporate members at the University Club in Cleveland on May 20.

      I thank you for the artistic plaque which you
caused to be presented to me in recognition of my 25 years
of service as a member of the Board of Trustees.

      Please accept again my congratulations upon the
constructive policies of Fenn College and its effort to
adapt itself to the particular needs of the City of Cleveland. The College has met with exceptional success and
I am sure that this is in large part due to the thoughtful
and aggressive leadership which you have given to the institution.

                  Cordially yours,

                  Harold H. Burton

President G. Brooks Earnest
Fenn College
Cleveland 15, Ohio

a. Acquisition of the property on the northwest corner of Euclid Avenue and East 24th Street under option with the Motors Realty Company.

b. Acquisition of the Sadd restaurant property.

c. Removal of the two quonset buildings.

d. Construction of a dormitory and a service building.

e. Vacation of East 24th Street between Euclid and Chester Avenues as a public street.

f. Grading and landscaping of the campus.

The board took the following actions respective to future phases submitted by Knight:

a. Trustee Warren Morris investigate price on various parcels of land on the south side and to the south of Euclid in the vicinity of East 24th Street for possible acquisition by the College.

b. President Earnest approach the Administration of the Cleveland Automobile Club concerning its plans for the future and inform them of Fenn's interest in this property between the College's east boundary and the Innerbelt Freeway should the Club ever plan to relocate.

The properties were investigated and appraised by Warren Morris, and it was amazing the interest created in the sale of properties to the south of Euclid to Fenn College. Of course, with the on-going financial obligations held by Fenn at the time, the College was in no position to negotiate immediately to increase its land and building holdings.

Trustee James Corey reported for the Buildings and Grounds Committee that only $251,728.22 remained to be paid on the total contract (plus extras) of $2,030,740.40 and that equipment and furniture could be moved in about July 1. Dining service would start in the West Campus building on June 22, and remodeling plans for the Tower would be ready for bids within two weeks.

A revised budget for the academic year 1958–1959 was approved. The income side totalled $2,083,866 including estimated gift income of $146,748, and the expense side was balanced with an amount of $20,000 reserved for contingency. A tentative 1959–1960 budget carried proposed increases in salary averaging five percent and with the attendant fringe benefits would increase the College's expenses about $70,780.

The commencement convocation for 1959 was held at Severance Hall on June 16. George Gund, President, The Cleveland Trust Company, delivered the address titled "A Banker Looks to College Graduates." Diplomas were distributed to two hundred and forty-five graduates as follows: 32 from the School of Arts and Sciences, 96 from the School of Business Administration, and 117 from the School of Engineering. Honorary Degrees were conferred on the following: Frederic McConnell, Doctor of Humane Letters (L.H.D.); Louis Carl Weiss, Doctor of Laws (LL.D.); Henry E. Widdell, Doctor of Engineering (D. Eng.); George Gund, Doctor of Laws (LL.D.). David C. French and Donald A. Campbell, Jr., of this class, returned to the campus for a few years in staff positions: French in charge of the Audio-Visual Department and Campbell as Director of the Alumni Association.

A special luncheon meeting of the board was held in the West Campus building on June 19, 1959, specifically to hear reports and recommendations of the Board Committees on Buildings and Grounds and on Finance. Action was taken to proceed with remodeling the Tower as proposed by the administration for a cost not to exceed $250,000, also to expend approximately $13,000 additional for stainless steel doors to the 24th Street entrance to the Tower Lobby. The Tower and Foster building conversion and rehabilitation program included the following:

Basement:
  Relocate Print Shop
  Stock rooms for Print Shop and Bookstore
  Buildings and grounds service area
  Hydraulics Lab expansion

First Floor:
  Offices for Finance, Registrar, Admissions, Cooperative Education
  Facilities for Bookstore
  Expanded Mailroom in Lobby
  New Front Entrance with revolving door
  New door on east side of lobby

Second Floor:
  Replace partition doors with permanent wall in Room 205

Third Floor:
  Offices for Dean of Women and Dean of Academic Services
  Student activities including Snack Bar

Fourth Floor:
  Offices for Psychology, Room 412

Eighth Floor:

Offices for Alumni, Room 809

Sixteenth Floor:

Convert all offices to dorm rooms

Eighteenth Floor:

Convert all space to offices

Foster Building:

Offices for math department

It was voted to award the above remodeling of the Tower as a general contract to The Albert M. Higley Company on a cost-plus-fixed-fee basis, not to exceed the $250,000 as previously authorized by the board.

Discussion ensued relative to financing the Tower conversion resulting in an approved resolution authorizing and directing Treasurer Burmester to negotiate an amendment of the existing loan agreement with the five major Cleveland Banks with the object of borrowing an additional sum of $200,000 to be applied specifically to the Tower rehabilitation program.

The Board of Trustees meeting of September 14, 1959, was an historical one in that it was the very first one held in the new Board Room on the first floor of the West Campus building. President Earnest announced the expectation of the largest Arts and Sciences and Engineering entering classes in Fenn's history, also, the largest total fall enrollment. This forecast was based on the experience in applications as of September 1, 1959, versus 1958 on the same date, as shown in Table 2.

TABLE 2
ENROLLMENT FORECAST

	Accepted or eligible applicants		In process		Denied		Cancelled		Total	
	1959	1958	1959	1958	1959	1958	1959	1958	1959	1958
Arts & Sci.	76	47	18	16	72	43	21	18	187	124
Nursing	41	39	9	9	29	40	15	27	94	115
Bus. Admin.	99	82	12	19	102	131	17	22	230	254
Engr.	281	181	24	28	152	178	63	84	520	471
Total	497	349	63	72	355	392	116	151	1031	964

As the result of the Ackoff report touched on earlier, the Survey Committee met with the Board Executive Committee August 17, 1959, and heard a proposal from Ernst & Ernst respective to a Fenn College organization-accomplishment program. Ernst & Ernst agreed to study the following two areas (over a five-month period) for a fee of $15,000:

1. To establish a sound administrative plan of organization including the functional relationships between the Board of Trustees and Fenn executives, to describe the basic functions and activities necessary for accomplishment, and to provide the rationale and techniques through which this integral plan may be attained.

2. To appraise present and additional personnel requirements on an immediate and long-range basis to assure adequacy of the human resources for attainment of the approved program.

A Motion was made and passed to ratify this action at the September 14, 1959, board meeting.

The Department of Public Relations and Development had been studying for some time the application of the Ruml plan of operating a college, to the operation of Fenn. This plan recommended class sizes and student-teacher ratios which with a certain tuition rate would create a balanced budget each year. In other words the student would be paying 100% of the cost of his education through tuition instead of 90% that the Fenn student was paying in 1959–1960. Trustee Bartlett reported on some of the ramifications of such a proposal at the September 14, 1959, board meeting.

Ratification was also obtained at this same meeting on the borrowing of $150,000 instead of the previously approved $200,000 to finance the remodeling of the Tower. This reduction was made possible because of increased capital gifts.

The final budget for 1959–1960 was also approved balancing out at $2,262,162. Included in the income side were anticipated gifts of $149,852 and in the expense side a reserve for contingencies of $20,000.

Chairman Hale of the Trustee Public Relations Committee received the board's endorsement for the dedication of the West Campus building during the last week in January 1960.

A very special meeting of the Board of Trustees was called for 5:00 p.m. November 17, 1959, in the Library of the University Club. This was in advance of the annual business Corporation dinner meeting to be held the same evening. The reason for the special meeting was to hear the important recommendations of the Trustee Development Committee, chaired by Edward T. Bartlett II on the study by the President's Cabinet which had come to be known as "The Integrated Plan of Fenn College." Herewith is the full report as exhibited in the Minutes of the board meeting:

For several months members of the Development Committee individually and as a group have spent much time in studying material prepared by President Earnest and his staff in connection with our planning for the future of Fenn over the next ten to twelve years. We felt that it was vitally important to give careful attention to the proposed size and character of the Fenn of 1970 before tackling plans for the physical development. This we have done.

We have finally approved and recommend to you, the objective of a total day enrollment of 3,600 in 1970. This is considerably less than a figure we seriously considered for a while. It is the President's recommendation. While it is somewhat more than the Faculty Advisory Committee would have recommended, they have indicated their support of it as an objective. It compares with an actual figure of 1,324 for 1958—a planned 171 per cent increase. Be sure you understand that this is an objective, the accomplishment of which will require effort in many directions. It is not an estimate of what will naturally come about if we sit back and let the future unfold on its own.

This enrollment objective is not recommended just in order to create a bigger college, but because we believe that only by attaining a size of this order can we achieve the academic and operating economies that will permit a substantially larger percentage of our income to go to faculty salaries. That will mean substantially higher salary ranges which in turn will enable us to compete in the scarcity market that everyone sees ahead in the teaching field. The hope and aim is to produce a better quality of education at Fenn in 1970—not just more of it.

The economies we refer to will in the academic area be achieved through a major change in class sizes. There will be far fewer of today's conventional classes—with over 16 but less than 100 students. Large lecture, discussion and demonstration courses, some with as many as 500 to 600 students, will be introduced in fields of study where the deans have already indicated they think this type of teaching would be appropriate. Hand in hand with these will come a big increase in the number of smaller seminar and laboratory groups, probably averaging around 12 or 13 students. There will be some reduction in the number of class teaching hours by the faculty and also in the number of hours spent in class by the students. In operations and administration more detailed studies and forecasts are required and are being undertaken, but we are presently proceeding on what seems like a reasonable general assumption, namely, that our overhead need not increase at the same rate as our volume of business. We are assuming for 1970 an average day student tuition charge of $843 compared with $568 in 1958, an increase of 48 per cent in twelve years.

To achieve the 1970 broad objective of a better education, more efficiently produced for more students, we must have more plant. You have in your folders a tentative schedule of plant additions and changes phased through 1970. This, along with projections of our hoped for financial operating results in future years, is due for a lot more study and will undoubtedly change many times through the years. However, we need your blessing for some overall plan such as this so that we can proceed with site planning and the development of specific, firm, short-term plans for our next step into the future.

Recommend approval to going forward with academic, financial and physical planning based on a day enrollment objective of 3,600 in 1970 and Further Recommend approval for present planning purposes of the Schedule of Physical Facilities presented in Table 3.

Comments relative to the 1961–1963–1965–1967–1970 physical objectives appear in Table 5.

An illustrative pamphlet on the various elements of the "Integrated Plan" was prepared. Important segments of this pamphlet included statements on:

1. What Fenn does for the community.
2. How the community and the college work together.
3. What the community does for Fenn.
4. Increasing the Fenn contribution to the community.
5. Aims of the College.
   a. Distinction
   b. Low unit costs

TABLE 3

1958 STATUS AND 1970 OBJECTIVES
PHYSICAL FACILITIES

Item	Year	Objectives
Instructional facilities and equipment	1958	Engineering and Science Hall
		Fenn Tower
		Foster Hall
	1961	Auditorium and lecture hall seating 600
		Instructional equipment
	1963	Instructional equipment
	1965	Lecture hall for 300
		Instructional equipment
	1967	Instructional equipment
	1970	Extension of Library reading room facilities
Administrative facilities and equipment	1958	Tower conversion
	1963	Administration building
	1965	Service building and tunnel
Residential facilities and equipment	1958	Tower for 192 students
	1961	Hall for 350 students
		Tower for 232 students
	1963	Hall ready for 350 students ready by October 1964
		Tower for additional 72 students
		Conversion of floors 2–7 for student union and athletic purposes
	1967	Hall for 350 students
Land aquisition and site improvements	1961	Fringe parking for 485 cars
		Option property
		Sadd property
		Site improvement
	1963	Fringe parking for 485 cars by October 1964
	1965	Site improvement
	1967	Fringe parking for 500 additional cars
		Site improvement
Athletic	1967	Gymnasium land and building
		Alumni project

6. The problem.
   a. Enrollments are rising.
   b. Teachers are in short supply.
7. The 6-point program.
   a. Drastically increased enrollments.
   b. Increase student-faculty ratio.
   c. Reapportion class sizes. (lecture & seminar)
   d. Lower unit cost of instruction.
   e. Increase faculty salaries.
   f. A logical and sound building program.
8. Short and long range land, building, equipment and furniture needs.

Slides were made of the illustrations in the pamphlet, and President Earnest gave many illustrated talks before Boards of Directors, officers, and fund committees of industries, banks, commercial, and philanthropic organizations. "The Integrated Plan of Fenn College" was well received by all who viewed the slide presentation or read the pamphlet. It created a renaissance in capital income to the College. The conception, thought, and man hours of study and discussion in preparation of the plan proved to be of inestimable value—a wise investment which increased Fenn's assets, not only monetarily, but also from the standpoint of enlightening many Clevelanders (who knew little or nothing about Fenn) concerning Fenn's place and prospect for growth in the higher educational sun of Cleveland and its environs.

At the annual Corporation dinner meeting following the board meeting of November 17, 1959, Dr. George H. Baird, Director of the Educational Research Council of Greater Cleveland, spoke on the subject, "The Future High School Graduate: A Problem of Quality."

During the year 1959 President Earnest was elected President of the Cleveland Engineering Society for a one-year term at the 79th Annual Meeting of that organization. He was elected a Trustee of The Cleveland Automobile Club. He was also Chairman of the Reception Committee for the National Convention of the American Society of Civil Engineers held in Cleveland.

Looming as a busy year and one really filled with much progress for Fenn College, 1960 turned out to be a "banner" year in the life of the College.

The first Board of Trustees meeting for 1960 was held January 19 in the Board Room of the West Campus building. In fact, all future board meetings were held in this Board Room.

The first order of business was the re-election of the following officers:

Charles J. Stilwell, Chairman
C. E. Smith, Vice Chairman
Harry F. Burmester, Treasurer
Vernon H. Davis, Secretary

Smith presented the following recommendations of the Executive Committee:

> As Vice Chairman of the Board and a member of the Executive Committee, I wish to state that the Committee has arrived at its recommendation on the naming of the new building on the Fenn campus, formerly known as the Engineering and Science Building and as the West Campus Building.
>
> Our criteria, as to the man to be so honored, were: (1) a distinguished career in a substantial field; (2) distinguished service to Fenn College; (3) a good name; and (4) a respected and admired person among the elders of the community.
>
> Gentlemen, it is our well-considered recommendation that Fenn's new building be named in honor of Charles J. Stilwell whose distinguished career culminated as president and chairman of The Warner & Swasey Company; whose distinguished service to the College has spanned 22 years as a Trustee, 16 of them as Chairman of the Board; and whose good name is widely respected and admired by all in the Cleveland community.
>
> It is our recommendation that the name of said building shall henceforth and perpetually be Charles J. Stilwell Hall and shall be commonly referred to as Stilwell Hall.

The Minutes of the January 19, 1960, meeting read thus:

> Upon motion of Mr. Smith and being duly seconded, the Engineering and Science Building was named "Charles J. Stilwell Hall" with unanimous standing vote and enthusiastic applause. Chairman Stilwell thanked the Board for the honor accorded him and stated his appreciation for the sentiments expressed.

Leichliter reported on the summarization of statistics and costs on the completed remodeling of Stilwell Hall. These were itemized in the following letter from Ceruti:

Dear President Earnest:

While the final payment is being processed for the construction of your West Campus Building, I thought you might like to have a summary of the costs for your Board Meeting.

Total Sq.ft.	Total Cu.ft.	Total Cost	Cost/sq. ft.	Cost/cu. ft.
184,214	2,336,818	$2,032,913.13	$11.05	$0.87

The land value assumed at $5.00 per sq. ft. (142' $\times$ 430' $=$ 61,060 sq. ft.) $\times$ $5.00 $=$ $305,300.00. Cost of property $650,000.00 minus $305,300.00 $=$ cost of building structure or $344,700.00. Transposed into unit costs this would amount to $1.87/sq. ft., or $.15/cu. ft., for a total building cost of $12.92/sq. ft. and $1.02/cu. ft. Considering the complex nature of this structure and the amount of equipment it accommodates this seems like a very reasonable cost and a real value for the college.

We estimate that the cost due to contingencies is estimated at $10,000.00, or approximately ½ of one per cent. This also seems to be a very reasonable sum since the average allotted for contingencies in alteration projects is usually 10 per cent which in this case would be $200,000.00.

All this would not have been possible without a good team of contractors and for this we had The Albert M. Higley Company and the prime sub-contractors Feldman Brothers Co. and Martien Electric Company.

In addition the continuous supervision given by Mr. Tracey was of inestimable value to avoid complications and keep the construction running smoothly.

We trust that you and your Board will be satisfied and that the College will have many fruitful years in the use of the West Campus Building.

Sincerely yours,

s/*Joseph Ceruti*, A.I.A.

The board then took action by the following resolutions expressing its appreciation for the professional services of Ceruti and Tracey in carrying to a most successful completion the conception, design, and construction of the rehabilitation of Stilwell Hall:

WHEREAS, Joseph Ceruti was Architect of Charles J. Stilwell Hall; and

WHEREAS, the conversion of this property posed multiple problems of great difficulty which were solved with economy, ingenuity, and professional acumen; and

WHEREAS this building is proudly accepted into the facilities of the college well within contemplated limits of both time and money; therefore

RESOLVED, That this Board convey to Joseph Ceruti its unanimous appreciation and thanks for distinguished service to the college.

s/*Charles J. Stilwell*, Chairman
s/*G. Brooks Earnest*, President

Signed at Cleveland, Ohio
January 29, 1960
The second resolution:

WHEREAS, Stephen E. Tracey did ably and faithfully represent the interests of Fenn College on site during the construction of Stilwell Hall; and

WHEREAS, He brought to this work qualities of tact, perseverance, professional acumen and humor rare in degree; and

WHEREAS, These qualities in combination with his learning and experience have assisted so markedly in bringing to fruition the combined skills of many; therefore,

RESOLVED, That this Board convey to Stephen E. Tracey its unanimous appreciation and thanks for special service to the college.

s/*Charles J. Stilwell*, Chairman
s/*G. Brooks Earnest*, President

Signed at Cleveland, Ohio
January 29, 1960

Action was also taken to revise Article 16(b) of the Personnel Policies of Fenn College to permit tuition remission of (a) all Faculty and Staff members including their wives (or husbands) in any course offered by the College, (b) Faculty and wives (or husbands) in Evening Division for any Evening Division courses, and (c) full-time YMCA employees in any course offered by the College.

For some time the Administration had been working on a ten-year program, as previously mentioned. The detailed academic and financial aspects of the plan were presented at the January 19, 1960, meeting. As the result thereof a resolution was adopted authorizing the Development Committee to enter into negotiations with neighboring property holders and also with the City of Cleveland concerning their interests respective to parking, traffic, and other urban improvements.

Action was taken directing Trustee Warren Morris to negotiate with Sadd *et al.* to acquire their bar and grill facing on East 24th Street opposite Stilwell Hall and surrounded by the Fenn College Campus, and if negotiations were successful, to empower the Executive Committee to consummate the purchase.

Action was also taken to retain Architect Ceruti to prepare preliminary plans for a 350-student dormitory, and Finance Director Vernon Davis was instructed to keep posted on possible government financing and to prepare an application as the elements of preliminary drawings and other data became available.

One of the outstanding events ever to be held on the Fenn Campus was the dedication of Stilwell Hall on Friday evening, January 29, 1960. Over 400 Faculty members, guests, and spouses attended the dinner and ceremony. Ellwood H. Fisher served as toastmaster. Reverend Dr. Yoder P. Leith, Pastor, Forest Hill Presbyterian Church, delivered the invocation. Mayor Anthony J. Celebrezze responded on the value of Fenn College to the City of Cleveland. President Earnest welcomed those in attendance and described the details leading to the naming of the building. Stilwell, Chairman of the Board of Trustees, responded, expressing his appreciation to his Trustee colleagues for the honor and their trust in him and their counsel throughout the years. The main event of the evening was a slide presentation by President Earnest of the proposed ten-year development program for Fenn College, following which, Phillip Porter, of the Cleveland *Plain Dealer*, presented a large framed painting of The Fenn Tower and surroundings, a copy of which was used in color as the front cover of the *Plain Dealer* rotogravure section. Following the benediction by Rabbi Silver, the guests were invited to tour the building with the faculty serving as guides. All in all, it was a most gala occasion.

However, gala as the occasion was, following the formal ceremony, the board met at 9:30 p.m. in a very special meeting to adopt unanimously a resolution to authorize the officers of Fenn College to execute an agreement between the College and John Sadd and George Sadd as sellers for the purchase of the Sadd Building on the easterly side of East 24th Street for $105,000. This was the only item of business taken up at this meeting—the close of a very important day in Fenn's history.

At the February 26, 1960, meeting of the board, Trustee Warren Morris reported that Sadd's attorney refused to honor the purchase agreement. In as much as the College had fulfilled all of its commitments under the purchase agreement there was no breach or failure on its part, so there was nothing to do on the part of Fenn but to await developments.

President Earnest reported at this meeting that the Spring Evening Division enrollment would be in excess of 4,600 as compared to a budget forecast of 4,425 which would result in an increase of approximately $13,000 more tuition income than the $380,700 budgeted. The President also mentioned receipt of an inquiry from Cleveland-Marshall Law School relative to the possible affiliation with Fenn College. A Board Task Committee was appointed to study and report on this subject.

This February 26, 1960, meeting of the Board of Trustees was really an historical one for Fenn College, for Stilwell announced that after much consideration he had reached a decision to resign as Chairman of the Board but desired to continue in the status of Trustee. The President felt that no formal action was considered necessary.

President Earnest accepted Stilwell's resignation on behalf of the Trustees and expressed the regret thereof. He, likewise, expressed the deep gratitude on the part of the members of the board for the outstanding leadership Stilwell had generously given to the College through his twenty-two years of loyal and faithful service as a Trustee. Special tribute was paid him for his accomplishments as Board Chairman over the past sixteen years and the signal progress made by the College during this era. Trustee Warren Morris responded concerning his personal association with Stilwell back to their college days at Dennison University, and several anecdotes of their long-standing friendships. He read the following resolution of the Council of the City of Cleveland as published in the City Record on the occasion of the naming and dedication of the Charles J. Stilwell Hall:

> WHEREAS, this Council was pleased to learn of the announcement that Fenn College's new Engineering and Science building was named Charles J. Stilwell Hall last week; and
> WHEREAS, the building of this educational edifice was primarily made possible by the dedicated work of Charles J. Stilwell, Fenn's

Board Chairman and a Director of Warner and Swasey Company; and

WHEREAS, under the spirited leadership of Charles J. Stilwell, a staunch advocate of the cooperative program in higher education, the college has made great strides toward academic excellence and completion of its splendid instructional facilities; now therefore,

BE IT RESOLVED, that the Council of the City of Cleveland congratulates Mr. Charles J. Stilwell on the occasion of this great honor and tenders to him the gratitude of the entire community for his years of faithful service in behalf of the advancement of education.

BE IT FURTHER RESOLVED that the Clerk of Council be and he hereby is requested to transmit a copy of this resolution to Mr. Charles J. Stilwell, 20814 Brantley Road, Cleveland, Ohio.

Adopted February 1, 1960.
Effective March 13, 1960.

Trustee Clayton G. Hale read a resolution of the Board of Trustees as follows:

WHEREAS Charles J. Stilwell has served this Board, Corporation, and College for sixteen years as Chairman and for twenty-two years as Trustee; and

WHEREAS Mr. Stilwell has now indicated his desire to retire as Chairman;

NOW THEREFORE BE IT RESOLVED that this Board, by its standing vote, do hereby signify its appreciation and gratitude to Mr. Stilwell for his firm, energetic, and far-sighted leadership as Chairman of this Board, all of which by intention and in result has produced a steady and remarkable advance by the College towards excellence; and

BE IT FURTHER RESOLVED that this Board, continuing to number Mr. Stilwell among its members, shall exert its full powers to continue the advancement of the College towards the distinction and dimension envisioned by the policies adopted during the incumbency of Mr. Stilwell with the same energy and sound judgment he has so long and so fully exemplified.

The above resolution was adopted by a standing vote.

Dr. James C. Hodge, Chairman of the Nominating Committee, placed in nomination Trustee Harry F. Burmester to succeed Stilwell as Chairman and Trustee Vollmer W. Fries to succeed Burmester as Treasurer. They were elected by unanimous vote. Burmester, on assuming the Chair, commented in a highly complimentary fashion on the loyal and unstinting services of Stilwell. This was one of the longest meetings in the history of Fenn's Board, and rightfully so, for a great man was turning over the gavel of considerable responsibility to his elected successor.

The Survey Task Committee reported on the scope and objectives of the recently received Ernst and Ernst suggested plan of organization at the May 18, 1960, board meeting. The board passed the following resolution:

> IT IS HEREBY RESOLVED by this Board in regular meeting and upon the recommendation of its Survey Committee:
> THAT the report of the Plan of Organization for Fenn College formulated upon the order of this Board and presented by the firm of Ernst & Ernst be, and hereby is, adopted:
> THAT the President of the College be, and hereby is directed to make provision in the 1960–61 budget for the establishment, in accordance with said report, of the following offices by or before fall quarter, 1960: (1) Provost, (2) Director for Planning (postponable), (3) Director for Fund-Raising (postponable), (4) Coordinator for Administrative Procedures (postponable);
> THAT the President be, and hereby is advised to pursue the administrative policies and philosophy set forth in said report pertaining to appropriate delegations of authority and responsibilities to the line administrators named above, all to the end of the timely accomplishment of the 1960–61 objectives of the College as heretofore approved by the Board.

Chairman Burmester reorganized the Board of Trustee committees in accordance with the Ernst and Ernst recommendations. The total board personnel and new committee make-up are shown in Table 4.

The Survey Task Committee members were also reappointed to serve under the Board Executive Committee to follow through with the recommendations of the Ernst and Ernst report.

Trustee E. T. Bartlett II continued to represent Fenn College as Chairman of the Euclid Innerbelt Committee. This committee was comprised of representatives from the YMCA, the YWCA, the Cleveland Automobile Club, the Arthur G. McKee & Co., the Cleveland Episcopal

TABLE 4

BOARD OF TRUSTEES
STANDING COMMITTEES

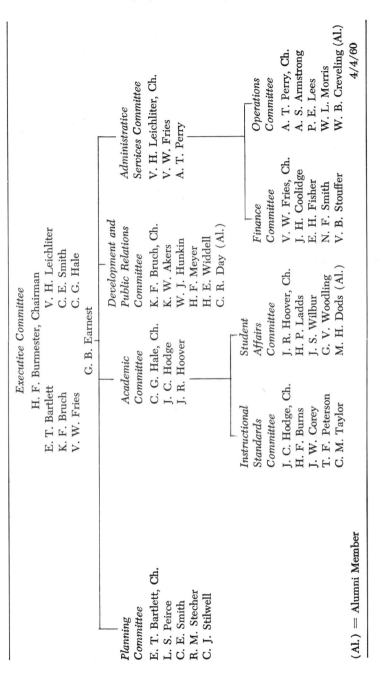

Executive Committee

H. F. Burmester, Chairman

E. T. Bartlett   V. H. Leichliter
K. F. Bruch   C. E. Smith
V. W. Fries   C. G. Hale

G. B. Earnest

*Planning
Committee*

E. T. Bartlett, Ch.
L. S. Peirce
C. E. Smith
R. M. Stecher
C. J. Stilwell

*Academic
Committee*

C. G. Hale, Ch.
J. C. Hodge
J. R. Hoover

*Development and
Public Relations
Committee*

K. F. Bruch, Ch.
K. W. Akers
W. J. Hunkin
H. F. Meyer
H. E. Widdell
C. R. Day (Al.)

*Administrative
Services Committee*

V. H. Leichliter, Ch.
V. W. Fries
A. T. Perry

*Instructional
Standards
Committee*

J. C. Hodge, Ch.
H. F. Burns
J. W. Corey
T. F. Peterson
C. M. Taylor

*Student
Affairs
Committee*

J. R. Hoover, Ch.
H. P. Ladds
J. S. Wilbur
G. V. Woodling
M. H. Dods (Al.)

*Finance
Committee*

V. W. Fries, Ch.
J. H. Coolidge
E. H. Fisher
N. F. Smith
V. B. Stouffer

*Operations
Committee*

A. T. Perry, Ch.
A. S. Armstrong
P. E. Lees
W. L. Morris
W. B. Creveling (Al.)

4/4/60

(Al.) = Alumni Member

Diocese of Ohio, the Trinity Cathedral, and Fenn College. This committee, for many years, concerned itself with the urban development of the area of Cleveland between East 18th and East 30th Streets and between Carnegie and Superior Avenues, but the prime interest was the neighborhood immediately surrounding Fenn College.

The New Integrated Fenn Plan which was presented at the dedication of Stilwell Hall was revised and later adopted at the May 18, 1960, board meeting. The academic objectives and the immediate and long-range capital needs were approved as shown in Table 6.

The Spring Corporation Meeting was held June 1, 1960. Representatives from the following companies received plaques for their twenty-five years of service as employers of Fenn's co-op students:

V. D. Anderson Co.
Cleveland Worm and Gear Division
Eaton Manufacturing Co.
General Industries Co.
Tropical Paint Co.
Bearings, Inc.

There were two particular highlights connected with this particular Corporation meeting. First was the unveiling of an oil portrait of Ellwood H. Fisher for his twenty-nine years of dedicated service as a Fenn Trustee, eleven of which he served as Chairman. The artist was John W. Teyral of the faculty of the Cleveland Institute of Art. Chairman Burmester, in presenting the portrait to the President of the College, asked that it be "given a place of honor and prominence in perpetuity." President Earnest expresseed his personal gratitude to the anonymous grantor of the portrait and to Fisher for his wise counsel as a Trustee, and promised a place of honor and prominence in Panel Hall of Fenn Tower as part of the College's collection of Chairmen of Boards of Trustees and Presidents of the College.

President Earnest then read a statement from Dr. John Dickey, President of Dartmouth College, Fisher's Alma Mater. It read as follows:

ELLWOOD HUFF FISHER

Ellwood Huff Fisher is a rare person. Above and beyond your heavy business responsibilities you find the time and talent to provide needed leadership in many volunteer efforts—and doing all of this exceedingly well.

TABLE 5
1958 STATUS AND 1970 OBJECTIVES
(Revised April, 1960)

Factors	1958	1961	1963	1965	1967	1970
Total Day Division Enrollment	1,324	1,800	2,200	2,600	3,000	3,600
On-Campus Enrollment, Day Division	935	1,260	1,540	1,820	2,100	2,520
(Evening Division)	(187)	(315)	(385)	(455)	(525)	(630)
(Total)	(1,122)	(1,575)	(1,925)	(2,275)	(2,625)	(3,150)
Student Load (clock hours) Day Division	19.4	18	17	17	17	17
Course Registrations, Day Division	14,025	17,010	19,635	23,205	26,775	32,130
Teaching Load, Full-Time Faculty, Per Quarter:						
Day:	12	10	9	9	9	9
Evening:	3	3	3	3	3	3
Total:	15	13	12	12	12	12
Number of Full-Time Faculty	73	79	96	114	131	157
Total Courses Taught, Day Division, 3 Quarters	657	592	648	770	884	1,060
Class Sizes:						
Seminar and Laboratory, 15 or Less	200	550	597	713	834	997
Lecture-Discussion-Demonstration Averaging 125	0	18	21	21	21	21
Lecture-Discussion-Demonstration Averaging 250	0	12	12	18	18	21
Lecture-Demonstration Averaging 500	0	12	15	18	18	21
Conventional Classes in the range 16–99	457	(—	—	—	—	—)*
Evening Division Enrollment	4,814	5,300	5,700	6,100	6,500	7,000

* Represents lecture courses with less than 100 enrolled.

TABLE 6
THE NEW FENN 1960–1970
Physical Facilities, Site Improvements
Including Preliminary Estimates

Completed by Fall, 1961

1.	300-unit residence hall*	$1,200,000
2.	Convert 8–18 floors of Tower—304 students	100,000
3.	Land acquisitions, incl. option & Sadd's	380,000
4.	Site improvements	50,000
5.	Additional instructional equipment & furniture	350,000
	Total	$2,080,000
	*To be financed	1,200,000
	To be raised	$ 880,000

Completed by Fall, 1963

1.	300-unit residence hall*	$1,200,000
2.	Auditorium for 600 and gymnasium	1,300,000
3.	Site improvements	25,000
4.	Additional instructional equipment & furniture	50,000
	Total	$2,575,000
	*To be financed	1,200,000
	To be raised	$1,375,000

Completed by Fall, 1965

1.	Administration Building	$ 800,000
2.	Site improvement & resurfacing for parking	50,000
3.	Additional instructional equipment & furniture	100,000
	Total—To be raised	$ 950,000

Completed by Fall, 1967

1.	Business Administration Building	$ 800,000
2.	Convert 2–7 floors of Tower for student union, athletic facilities, and dispensary	100,000
3.	Site improvement	50,000
4.	Additional instructional equipment & furniture	100,000
	Total—To be raised	$1,050,000

Summary

1961	$ 880,000
1963	1,375,000
1965	950,000
1967	1,050,000
To be raised	$4,305,000
To be financed	2,400,000
Total	$6,705,000

Since your graduation from Dartmouth College in 1921, you have been continuously working and pioneering in the Fisher Brothers Company and in these busy years you have devoted major amounts of time to both educational and civic work in Cleveland, Hanover and elsewhere. Fenn College and Dartmouth are both grateful to you for your outstanding leadership and thoughtful support.

At Dartmouth, you have served as a member of the Alumni Council, the first Dartmouth Development Council, the first Capital Gifts Campaign Committee, and are now Chairman of the important Bequest and Estate Planning Committee of the Alumni Council. Time and again you have come forward to help in major Dartmouth causes. At Fenn, where you served as Trustee and Chairman of the Board, you have been equally helpful.

For your distinguished service, I am delighted on behalf of your Alma Mater to salute you as you receive this additional honor tonight.

s/John Dickey

May 24, 1960

Mr. Fisher, always noted for his humbleness and modesty, responded as follows:

My first words Thank you—for this honor you have bestowed upon me. It makes me humble and proud.

Unlike the old man, who, when asked if he had ever seen Halley's Comet replied, "Yes, but only from a distance," I am one of the few who have seen Fenn from "close-in" for over 30 years. I am grateful for that experience—for the opportunity to associate myself with those who worked at it over the years—saw it grow from a few hundred students encouraged by the YMCA, studying in classrooms located in old Gay Nineties type houses on Prospect Avenue and a 1926 laboratory building, to today's 6,000 students studying in the imposing classrooms on Euclid Avenue—Fenn Tower, Claud Foster Building, and the new Stilwell Hall laboratory building, adjacent on East 24th Street. Meanwhile, the budget has grown from $100,000 a year to this year's figure of over $2,000,000.

Yes, I am grateful, too, since three basic ingredients for success in any enterprise have been, and are, present in Fenn College. They are imagination—belief—leadership—

Imagination to foresee the possibilities for mentally-endowed but financially-handicapped students to earn an education beyond the high school level, through the Co-op Plan of work and study;

Belief that higher education is everybody's business; and to thoughtful people it is the biggest job facing the nation today; and

Leadership of the highest order, supplied by the founder, Dr. C. V. Thomas, and so well carried on these past ten years by the present President, Dr. G. Brooks Earnest, the Board members, faculty, and staff.

With these three basic ingredients encouraged and sharpened, Fenn will fulfill its mission, and I am fortunate to have had a small part in it.

Thank you all!

The second highlight of the evening was the address, "The Confessions of a College Trustee" by Dr. Robert M. Stecher, Fenn Trustee, and like Fisher, an alumnus of Dartmouth College. Dr. Stecher graduated from the Harvard Medical School. He became a clinical professor at the Western Reserve Medical School, a Director of the Cleveland Medical Library, the Arthritis and Rheumatism Foundations, the Kettering Foundation, and the Cleveland Health Museum; he owned one of the finest collections of Darwinian writings and first editions in the United States. Dr. Stecher devoted most of his professional life to searching out the causes of arthritis and the rheumatic diseases which cripple mankind. He died March 14, 1972, while vacationing in Scottsdale, Arizona.

Shortly following the Corporation meeting date, President Earnest received the following letter from Fisher:

Dear Brooks:

With all the genuineness I can muster, I want to use this means to tell you again how proud and happy you made me and my family.

I hear nothing but compliments on the way you handled everything. The commemorative message I shall always keep and cherish.

With it all I am sure Fenn has gained some new stature too. And that, after all, is most important.

With every good wish,

Sincerely,

s/*Ellwood* (Fisher)

The Board of Trustees held a special meeting prior to the Commencement Dinner at the Wade Park Manor on Sunday, June 12, 1960. In Chairman Burmester's absence, President Earnest acted as Chairman. Trustee Howard F. Burns described the negotiations with John and George Sadd for the purchase of the Sadd Bar and Grill, located on the east side of East 24th Street near Chester Avenue. A written offer was extended by the Sadd brothers to sell the property to Fenn College for $110,000 in the form of an option agreement to be consummated over a period of years. A resolution was adopted authorizing President Earnest and Secretary Vernon H. Davis to execute the agreement between Fenn College and the Sadd brothers.

The thirty-seventh commencement convocation was held at Severance Hall following the usual commencement dinner for those who participated on the stage and their wives. Charles J. Stilwell, Director and former President of The Warner & Swasey Company, also Trustee and former Chairman of the Board of Fenn College, delivered the commencement address. He spoke to the graduates on "The Part You Have To Play."

There were 250 graduates in the Class of 1960 distributed as follows: School of Arts and Sciences, 46; School of Business Administration, 84; and School of Engineering, 120. One hundred and eighty members of this class graduated from the Day Division, and seventy members from the Evening Division.

Clayton G. Hale, 1932, T. Gordon McAusland, 1929, and Clifford D. Williams, 1937, were recipients of the Alumni Distinguished Service Awards at the Annual Alumni Association Dinner Meeting held at the

Cleveland Engineering Society. Richard Verba of the Fenn College Class of 1941 was President of the Fenn Alumni Association for the school year 1959–1960.

The following men were recognized for their distinguished professional and public careers by having honorary degrees conferred upon them:

Carl D. Friebolin, Doctor of Laws (LL.D.)
George W. Heise, Doctor of Science (D. Sc.)
Nathaniel R. Howard, Doctor of Humane Letters (L.H.D.)
Charles J. Stilwell, Doctor of Humane Letters (L.H.D.)

On May 9, 1960, representatives of the Cleveland-Marshall Law School submitted a draft of a proposed agreement to affiliate with Fenn College. The new Committee on Instructional Standards under the Chairmanship of Dr. James C. Hodge studied the draft and recommended that the subject be assigned to a Review Committee of the Executive Committee complying with the new Ernst and Ernst plan of organization for such studies. This subject was thoroughly discussed by other interested Board Committees, but it was the consensus that more facts should be obtained prior to bringing it to the board for action.

The Executive Committee of the Board met June 13, 1960 (the day following commencement), to take action on a proposed agreement between Fenn and its adjacent neighbor to the west, Arthur G. McKee & Co., to purchase, and share in the use of, a Burroughs Co. computer system. For some time the administration had been exploring various economical methods for obtaining a computer for use in instruction as well as by the admission and business offices. Rental equipment had been employed for some time for student record and grade posting by the Director of Admissions and the Registrar. The proposed agreement called for Fenn College to be the purchaser of the computer with reimbursement by Arthur G. McKee & Co. In return Fenn was to be assigned certain daily time for use of the computer for whatever usage the College wished. The Executive Committee authorized the execution of the agreement.

The computer was purchased and housed in a specially constructed, temperature and humidity controlled room in the McKee building, adjacent to Stilwell Hall, and a special doorway was cut through McKee's east wall to make access convenient for Fenn faculty and students.

It turned out that the computer was mostly used by Fenn for instruction and the modern solution of engineering problems. It so happened that the time payments on the computer terminated in late 1965 coincident with the transfer of Fenn College to the State. Because of the rapid development in computer hardware, the Burroughs computer became obsolete and inadequate for the services required by Arthur G. McKee & Co. about this same time. The Fenn Educational Foundation, the successor to Fenn College, eventually sold the Burroughs computer (original cost of $450,000) for $250 to a scrap dealer.

The Executive Committee also took action at the June 15, 1960, meeting to engage the services of Alan Blackburn as a consultant to the Department of Development in its fund raising activity. Inasmuch as the board had taken action at the May 18, 1960, meeting to set a two-year fund raising goal of $2,100,000 to initiate the Fenn Integrated Plan, it was felt that professional fund raising counsel was needed.

The last Board of Trustees meeting in 1960 was held on September 22. Secretary Vernon H. Davis informed the board that the necessary papers were in escrow to transfer the Sadd real estate to Fenn College on January 1, 1961.

The resignation of Trustee Paul E. Lees was accepted at this same board meeting. Lees' health required his move to a warmer climate. He was later replaced by C. Bert McDonald, President of McDonald and Company.

Trustee Arthur S. Armstrong in reporting for the special committee on the affiliation of the Cleveland-Marshall Law School with Fenn submitted the following resolution which was adopted: "Whereas Fenn College is launched into an integrated ten-year program of expansion and development which can be expected to absorb all of our thought and energies, it is the considered opinion of the committee that the time is inopportune to develop any new relationships." Copy of this resolution was mailed to Dean Stapleton of the Cleveland-Marshall Law School.

The population explosion of the sixties was already having its effect on the Day Division enrollment which increased 13% in the Fall of 1960 over that for the Fall of 1959. The total Day Division enrollment for the Fall of 1960 was 1,580 and the total Evening Division enrollment was 5,317 (a 5% increase) for a total student body of 6,897.

President Earnest had originally suggested to the Ernst and Ernst consultants engaged in making the study for the reorganization of Board and College administration procedures that an additional administrative officer, i.e., a provost, be considered in light of the anticipated expanding College enrollment. As mentioned previously, this was one of the recommendations in their final report. The President felt that time had arrived to fill this office and recommended that Dr. Wm. A. Patterson, Dean of Engineering, be promoted to this status and carry both the responsibilities of Dean and Provost (in charge of all academic affairs) until a new Dean of Engineering was appointed. The September 22, 1960, board meeting was the first attended by Dr. Patterson as Provost. He attended all board meetings thereafter and assisted President Earnest in presenting the academic affairs of the College.

Alumni Trustee Madison H. Dods informed the board at the September 22, 1960, meeting that the Fenn Alumni Association had raised $20,680 in the year just ended August 31, 1960, with participation of 51.6% of the Alumni. This compared most favorably with the figures for the previous fiscal year of $10,484 from only 27.9% of the Alumni. Dods was later elected a Trustee and Secretary of the Board and Corporation of The Fenn Educational Foundation in December 1970, and a member of the Executive Board of the Fenn Educational Fund of The Cleveland Foundation in 1971.

The work entailed in preparing an annual budget was no sinecure. It required the time and effort of the department chairmen, the deans, the provost, the officials in charge of all administrative and service departments, all numbering approximately 55. In addition there were the various committees of the board which studied the proposed budget and either accepted it or made recommendations for changes before it was brought to the entire board for adoption. The following extract represents the proposed budget material as it was prepared by the Director of Finance, Vernon H. Davis, for the fiscal year September 1, 1960, to August 31, 1961. This budget was approved at the September 22, 1960, board meeting. This was a typical budget. Exhibit C gives a capsule description of the basic elements from which the budget was constructed, i.e., enrollment forecast, projected income and proposed expenses. Table 7 shows the condensed proposed budget for 1960–1961 compared with the estimated for 1959–1960 plus the actual budget for 1959–1960 and the actual year-end statement for 1958–1959. Table 8 shows the anticipated operating income in detail plus the break-down in enrollment for the 1960–1961 and 1959–1960 budgets. Table 9 shows the anticipated operating expenses in detail.

EXHIBIT C

FENN COLLEGE

Proposed Operating Budget for the Fiscal Year 1960–61

A proposed operating budget for the school year 1960–61 is hereby submitted. Total income and expense this year is estimated at $2,501,764., up 11% over 1959–60 actual. For an interesting comparison this is 144% greater than 1951. No provision is made for a contingency reserve.

A. *Enrollment Forecast.* In this budget tuition and fees are 77.1% of total income as against 80.5% in 1959–60. There was no increase in tuition for the coming year; last fall there was a 9.5% rate increase in tuition. "Auxiliary Enterprises" and "Gifts" bulk larger in this budget increasing percentage wise from 13.1% to 15.2% and from 4.6% to 6.2%, respectively over last year's estimated actual.

Day Division. New student estimates for Fall 1960 are 625, and total for Freshmen and Upperclassmen is 1,145 as compared with 1959 figures of 507 and 1,038. This is an increase of 23% and 10% respectively.

Evening Division. Fall semester evening students are estimated at 5,175 this year as against an actual in 1959–60 of 5,068. The Spring semester is estimated at 4,775 as against 4,647 in 1959–60. Total registrations for the year including Summer are 10,225 as against 10,051 in 1959–60—an increase of 1.7%.

B. *Income Budget.* This is the highest to date for the college and as noted above is almost 2½ times greater than it was 10 years ago: $2,501,764.

> *Tuition and Fees.* These are computed to return $112,690 more than the actual this year, which is accounted for by increased enrollments. Tuition and fees provide more than 88% of Educational Expense: $1,928,962.

> *Endowment Fund.* The principal of the Fund remains at $553,000 and is expected to continue to earn about 4%: $22,000.

> *Gifts.* This is the balancing figure in the budget and compares with $149,852 for 1959–60 although that amount was not actually needed and we will probably close the year with a

gift figure of around $112,000 for 1959–60. Gifts for 1960–61 are 6.2% of total income. Ten years ago when the budget was less than half as large as it is now Gifts were $190,023 or 18.5% of total income for that year which indicates a substantial degree of increase in operating efficiency over the period: $154,707.

Departmental Services. Testing service done for outside companies on a fee basis. This is the same as the actual for 1959–60: $17,150.

Auxiliaries. The cafeteria in this, its first year of operation, was unable to carry the charges put against it—principally the charges of $12,684 for rent for the year—and will show a loss of approximately $7,000 for the year. However since the operation steadily gained in efficiency during the year, it is again budgeted to break even after rent charges of $15,000 for the year: $265,125.

The dormitory is expected to bring in $69,600 in room rent and will this year include the 17th and 18th floors as additional residence floors and parts of the 19th and 20th as lounge and study areas. Room rent per quarter is advanced from $75 to $84 for 1960–61. If necessary, additional accommodations can be arranged for at the YMCA to take care of overflow. The bookstore has exceeded expectations this year and is budgeted for a sales increase of $13,508 over the estimated actual for 1959–60 on the basis of more students and additional new lines of merchandise in the coming year.

Other Income (Includes rent charges of $79,200 to auxiliary departments): $113,820.

a. Miscellaneous Sales & Services: $23,700. This is income from parking lot ($16,400), rental of swimming pool, rooms, etc. ($3,600), telephone pay stations ($740) and missellaneous ($2,960). It is budgeted at the actual for 1959–60.

b. *Interest*: $3,720 Bank interest on savings accounts is computed at 3% on approximately $124,000.

c. *Scholarship Income*: $7,200. This is the total of gifts restricted to this purpose and is budgeted at slightly more than actual this year reflecting the increase in numbers of students.

C. *Expense Appropriations* Salary increases for 1960–61 have averaged about 5.8% to the individual. Normal attrition and additions, the increases to the individuals, plus the major addition of the Provost's office account for the $96,310 gross increase over last year's budget for salaries, wages and lectures fees. This amount plus the attendant fringe benefits account for well over half of the $187,000 that Educational Expense increased over last year's budget: $2,501,764.

Personal services continue to be the largest single item of expense and with fringe benefits total $1,770,894 or 73.1% of total expense, excluding inter-department rent charges therefrom. Last year this percentage was 74.47% and in 1958–59 it was 73.68%.

Respectfully submitted,
s/ *G. Brooks Earnest*, President
s/ *V. H. Davis*, Finance Director

September 22, 1960

The 1960 Annual Meeting of the Fenn Corporation was held November 15 at the Union Club. Total attendance was 106. The following were elected as Members of the Corporation:

Guthrie Bicknell	B. W. Maxey
John Burge	Andrew B. Meldrum, Jr.
Fred L. Crossman	Joseph B. Meriam, Jr.
Paul S. Dickey	Frederick T. McGuire, Jr.
Albert E. Dillingham	Karl H. Rudolph
Frank L. Elmendorf	H. E. Russell
Raymond Feldman	Wilbur J. Shenk, Jr.
Max Freedman	John Sherwin
Robert H. Hoge	Glen O. Smith
James A. Hughes	Harry B. Warner
William Irrgang	R. J. Wean, Jr.
Edwin T. Jeffery	A. J. Weatherhead
Elliot J. Jensen	E. Clare Weber
Carter Kissell	H. L. Weiss
The Very Rev. David Loegler	Charles M. White
W. A. Marting	

The following were elected as Emeritus Members of the Corporation:

George C. Brainard	Robert H. Jamison
George A. Bryant	Edward D. Lynde
Thomas F. Dolan	Herman Moss

Dr. James C. Hodge, Norman F. Smith, Karl F. Bruch, Jr., and Harry F. Burmester were re-elected for a five-year term, Class of 1965, and

TABLE 7

SCHEDULE A(1)

Comparative Statements of Operations with Proposed Operating Budget for 1960-61

INCOME	1960–61 Proposed Budget		Act. 1959–60 Est. at 6-30-60		1959–60 Budget		1958–59 Actual	
Tuition & Fees	$1,928,962.	77.1%	$1,816,272.	80.5%	$1,803,637.	79.74%	$1,570,577.	77.3%
Endowment	22,000.	.8	22,726.	1.0	22,000.	.97	21,869.	1.1
Gifts	154,707.	6.2	103,670.	4.6	149,852.	6.62	122,950.	6.1
Departmental Services	17,150.	.7	17,316.	.8	13,822.	.6l	17,201.	.8
Sub-total Educational Income	$2,122,819.	84.8%	$1,959,984.	86.9%	$1,989,311.	87.94%	$1,732,597.	85.3%
Auxiliary Enterprises	265,125.	10.6	228,404.	10.1	203,400.	8.9	244,857.	12.1
Other Income	113,820.	4.6	67,760.	3.0	69,451.	4.16	53,133.	2.6
TOTAL INCOME	$2,501,764.	100%	$2,256,148.	100%	$2,262,162.	100%	$2,030,587.	100%
EXPENSE								
Admin. & General	$ 542,453.	21.6%	$ 502,345.	22.3%	$ 503,196.	22.24%	$ 428,637.	21.1%
Instruction	1,029,045.	41.1	940,274.	41.7	943,352.	41.7	851,830.	42.0
Student Services	167,368.	6.7	152,977.	6.8	154,681.	6.84	151,854.	7.5
Library	51,450.	2.0	45,402.	2.0	45,440.	2.01	43,445.	2.1
Plant Operation	397,361.	16.0	357,154.	15.8	356,877.	15.78	239,028.	11.8
Sub-total Educational Expense	$2,187,677.	87.4%	$1,998,152.	88.6%	$2,003,546.	88.57%	$1,714,794.	84.5%
Auxiliary Enterprises	259,087.	10.4	207,201.	9.2	178,616.	7.90	232,117.	11.4
Other Expense	55,000.	2.2	49,884.	2.2	60,000.	2.65	81,214.	4.0
Res. for Contingencies	–0–		–0–		20,000.	.88	–0–	
TOTAL EXPENSE	$2,501,764.	100%	$2,255,237.	100%	$2,262,162.	100%	$2,028,125.	99.9%
Net Income	–0–		911.		–0–		2,462.	.1
	$2,501,764.	100%	$2,256,148.	100%	$2,262,162.	100%	$2,030,587.	100%

TABLE 8

SCHEDULE A(2)

Detailed Operating Income Budget
Proposed for Fiscal 1960–61

	Budget 1960–61	Budget 1959–60	Numbers of Total Enrollments (Est.) 1960–61	(Actual) 1959–60
Tuition—Day				
Arts & Sciences	$ 168,163.	$ 168,830.	790	771
Bus. Admin.	205,875.	190,400.	840	761
Engineering	640,625.	578,575.	2,115	1,858
Total Day	$1,014,663.	$ 937,805.	3,745	3,390
Tuition—Evening				
Arts & Sciences	169,338.	154,720.	2,300	2,158
Bus. Admin.	351,914.	325,280.	4,200	4,132
Engineering	203,005.	211,090.	1,600	1,637
Tech. Inst.	138,605.	132,800.	2,125	2,124
Total Evening	$ 862,862.	$ 823,890.	10,225	10,051
TOTAL ALL TUITION	$1,877,525.	$1,761,695.		
Misc. Fees	$ 51,437.	$ 41,942.		
Endowment Income	22,000.	22,000.		
Gifts & Grants	154,707.	149,852.		
Departmental Services	17,150.	13,822.		
Sub-total Educ. Inc.	$2,122,819.	$1,989,311.		
Auxiliaries:				
Bookstore	195,525.	153,400.		
Men's Residence	69,600.	50,000.		
Total Auxiliaries	$ 265,125.	$ 203,400.		
Other Income:				
Misc. Sales & Services	23,700.	19,000.		
Interest	3,720.	3,087.		
Rent	79,200.	35,364.		
Scholarships	7,200.	12,000.		
Total Other Income	$ 113,820.	$ 69,451.		
TOTAL ALL INCOME	$2,501,764.	$2,262,162.		

TABLE 9

SCHEDULE A(3)

Detailed Operating Expense Budget

Proposed for Fiscal 1960–61

		1960–61	1959–60
Administration:			
Admissions	10	$ 42,443.	$ 36,305.
Finance	11	59,722.	52,042.
President	12	37,780.	34,150.
Public Relations	13	35,578.	38,675.
Registrar	14	40,969.	38,177.
Graphic Arts	15	64,078.	59,725.
Alumni	17	8,538.	8,790.
Development	18	39,660.	45,735.
Provost	19	19,997.	–0–
TOTAL ADMINISTRATION		$ 348,765.	$ 313,599.
General Expense	16	193,688.	189,597.
TOTAL ADMIN. & GENERAL		$ 542,453.	$ 503,196.
Instruction:			
School of A & S		$ 297,300.	$ 257,995.
School of B. A.		216,518.	210,214.
School of Engrg.		459,403.	420,168.
Technical Institute		55,824.	54,975.
TOTAL INSTRUCTION		$1,029,045.	$ 943,352.
Student Services:			
Coordination	70	$ 50,427.	$ 40,345.
Guidance	71	10,718.	10,157.
Health & Phys Ed	72	50,084.	46,391.
Pers. Develop.	73	23,969.	26,395.
Activities	74	3,728.	3,594.
Dean of Acad Ser	75	12,148.	12,798.
Dean of Women	76	7,138.	6,915.
Audio-Visual	77	9,156.	8,086.
TOTAL STUDENT SERVICES		$ 167,368.	$ 154,681.
Library	78	$ 51,450.	$ 45,440.
Plant Operation:			
Tower	81	200,743.	179,647.
Claud Foster	83	22,647.	19,769.
Stilwell Hall	85	173,971.	157,461.
TOTAL PLANT		$ 397,361.	$ 356,877.
SUB-TOTAL EDUC. EXPENSE		$2,187,677.	$2,003,546.

TABLE 9 (*Continued*)

Auxiliaries:			
Bookstore	92	$ 176,200.	$ 137,671.
Men's Residence	94	82,887.	40,945.
TOTAL AUXILIARIES		$ 259,087.	$ 178,616.
Scholarships	96	55,000.	60,000.
Reserve for Contingencies		–0–	20,000.
TOTAL ALL EXPENSE		$2,501,764.	$2,262,162.

Charles M. White was elected to the same Class succeeding Charles J. Stilwell who was elected as the first Life Trustee. C. B. McDonald was elected to the Class of 1963 to fill the unexpired term of Paul E. Lees who had resigned earlier. Walter B. O'Konski was elected to a three-year term as an Alumni Trustee succeeding Madison Dods.

President Earnest presented a brief review of the past year, including as a most important highlight the occupancy of the new Stilwell Hall. Also mentioned were the new Integrated Plan of Fenn College, a total Day and Evening Division enrollment for the Fall Quarter of 6,897, a total co-op student earnings of $1,529,400 with an average of $1,910 per student for the year, a full-time Faculty of eighty, the purchase of Sadd Restaurant, the establishment of new computer center in collaboration with the Arthur G. McKee & Co. and a balanced budget for the year.

Dr. Patterson (new Provost) spoke on Fenn's thirty-seven years of progress and several of the problems facing the College at that time and steps being taken to resolve them. There was also a premier showing of the new motion picture entitled "Integrated Plan of Fenn College." This film showing activities on the Fenn Campus with actors chosen from all segments of the Fenn Family was shown many times later to key people in most of the corporations in Greater Cleveland in connection with the fund drive.

At a special Case Alumni Banquet during 1960, President Earnest was presented a Certificate of Meritorious Service in the form of a framed illuminated scroll by the Case Institute of Technology Alumni Association.

The first Trustee meeting for 1961 was held on January 4 in the Board room at Stilwell Hall preceded by a tour of the new Computer Center at the Arthur G. McKee & Co. The following Officers were re-elected:

Harry F. Burmester, Chairman
C. E. Smith, Vice Chairman
Vollmer W. Fries, Treasurer
Vernon H. Davis, Secretary

Because of the press of his business, John S. Wilbur resigned from the Board. He was succeeded by William G. Laffer, President of the Clevite Corporation, in March of 1961.

The Sadd property was occupied for the first time on and after January 1, 1961, for educational purposes.

The status of a proposed Ohio community college law was reviewed at this meeting. The State Interim Commission on Education Beyond the High School had just approved the major provisions thereof the last week in 1960. The Provost Cabinet had under way a study of the impact of a community college on Fenn College.

Trustee Karl Bruch announced that $303,181 had been pledged to the Building Fund during 1960 and that $60,121 of the Trustees' goal of $150,000 had been pledged in the same interim.

Architect Joseph Ceruti presented drawings for a proposed dormitory. It was estimated that construction, equipping, and furnishing costs would be $1,976,800 of which there was a federal government loan fund reservation of $1,650,000. It was also estimated that the annual debt service for operating the dormitory would be $43,250. Because of these debt figures the board moved to request a ninety-day extension of time from the Housing and Home Finance Agency (HHFA) for filing a full application. In the meantime Architect Ceruti revised the original design from eleven to nine floors, thereby reducing the total cost, fully equipped and furnished, to $1,640,000. Estimated annual operating deficit was reduced to $30,160 which still did not please the Trustees, so action was taken directing President Earnest and Finance Director Davis to visit the HHFA offices in Chicago and request a second ninety-day extension.

This visit to the HHFA offices was made March 23, 1961, and it was discovered that because the Fenn Bookstore and Dormitory were located in the Tower building, the income from which must be pledged to liquidate the loan, the Tower would have to be mortgaged for the period of the loan. President Earnest, therefore, recommended at the June 7, 1961, board meeting that the College request formal cancellation of its Preliminary Application for a loan of $1,650,000 from the College Housing Program of HHFA. The board accepted.

The board took action at its January 4, 1961, meeting to increase the tuition as follows, effective September 1, 1961:

| | Current | | Proposed | |
	Per Quarter	Per Credit Hr.	Per Quarter	Per Credit Hr.
Arts & Sciences	$240	$16	$280	$18
Business				
Administration	240	16	280	18
Engineering	300	19	330	23
Technical Institute		16		18

Permission was also granted at this same board meeting for a two-year leave of absence to Dr. Frank De Marinis, Professor and Chairman, Department of Biology, to accept an appointment by the U.S. Department of State as Deputy Scientific Attache at the American Embassy in Rome, Italy.

As a Trustee of the Cleveland Automobile Club, President Earnest was able to engender many pleasant cooperative relationships between the two organizations. One of these, approved by a resolution of thanks at the March 20, 1961, meeting of the Fenn Board, included use of the Cleveland Automobile Club's large parking lot by Fenn's Evening Division students. The College's security force policed the lot during the evening. The Club also planted a row of poplar trees on the boundary between it and the College.

The Fenn Alumni Association started a fund raising campaign in March 1961 to furnish the new student union facility on the third floor of the Tower. It was estimated by Harry H. Holzheimer, 1940, of Holzheimer Interiors, Inc., that it would cost about $25,000 to provide the furnishings. Snack bar and mechanical services would require approximately an additional $60,000.00.

Trustee Van H. Leichliter reported at the March 20, 1961, board meeting that all but $351,000 of the original loan of $1,030,000 to construct, equip and furnish Stilwell Hall had been paid back.

The following is a quotation from the Board Minutes of June 7, 1961: "Chairman Burmester directed attention to the honor conferred upon President Earnest by nomination to the presidency of the Ameri-

can Society of Civil Engineers for October, 1961 to October, 1962."
President Earnest, himself a former Professor of Civil Engineering at
Case Institute of Technology, had been nominated by unanimous vote
of the Board of Direction of the Society at the Phoenix meeting held
in April 1961. The American Society of Civil Engineers was the first
non-military professional and technical society in the United States.
It was founded in 1852, was and still is international in scope and
membership, and in 1961, at the time of Dr. Earnest's nomination as
President of the Society, there were 47,571 members. By July 1973
the membership had grown to 67,818, and the annual operating budget
was over $5,000,000.

High-lights of the June 7, 1961, board meeting include an enrollment
forecast for the fall of 1961 showing an eighteen percent increase in
Day Division students and a seventeen percent increase in the Freshman
Class. The projected increase in the Evening Division was less than
one percent. President Earnest appointed a new committee consisting
of Trustee Bruch, Provost Patterson, Davis, and himself to plan for
a ten-year forecast of all of Fenn's needs. It was announced that Fenn
was selected as one of ten colleges to participate in an "operations
analysis," sponsored by the Commission on College Finance of the Association of American Colleges and implemented by the Fund Fulfillment Corporation of Chicago. A grant of $50,000 was contributed by
the U.S. Steel Foundation for this study. The approval of the The
Board of Huron Road Hospital of the transfer of the nursing school
faculty to Fenn was also made known. The Euclid Inner-Belt Association chaired by Trustee Bartlett was newly staffed with F. N. Winkler
as its first Director and Thomas Miller as his assistant. The Cleveland
Foundation gave $10,000 toward expenses to get the Association office
started.

Further highlights of this board meeting included the recommendation of the student officers of the Day and Evening Division Councils
that the Student Activities Fees be increased $5 per academic year
per Day Division student and $.50 per semester for Evening Division
students to assist in financing the rehabilitation of the third floor of
the Tower for Student Union accommodations. This was a generous
action on the part of the Student Council officers. The board moved
to thank the students and granted permission to proceed with the final
decision left in the hands of President Earnest. The president later

decided to accept the recommendation of the Student Council officers effective September 1, 1961. A more detailed and precise estimate of the remodeling and furnishing prepared by Ceruti and Holzheimer turned out to be $89,250. With the Fenn Alumni Association contributing about $25,000, it was determined that it would take about four years to pay for the remainder through the pro-rated income from the Student Activity Fees. Fifty percent of the student fees was distributed toward student activities (weekly newspaper, year-book, and the like), twenty percent was allocated toward athletics, and the remaining thirty percent toward Student Union facilities. It bears reiterating that the students volunteered to resolve a financial need of the College to enhance their campus life, which was contrary to the present attitudes of many radical students on most college campuses.

Each month schedules *A* and *B* were provided the Trustees to keep them in close touch with the financial status of Fenn's Development Program. The schedules in Table 10 for April 30, 1961, exhibit the completeness of this reporting:

William R. Lenga, 1928, Madison H. Dods, 1934, and Richard Zimmerman, 1943, were recipients of the Alumni Distinguished Service Awards at the Annual Alumni Dinner Meeting held at the Cleveland Engineering Society. Donald Goodwill of the Fenn College Class of 1934 was president of the Fenn Alumni Association for the school year 1960–1961.

The 38th Commencement Convocation of Fenn College was held in Severance Hall on June 11, 1961. James F. Lincoln, Chairman of the Board, The Lincoln Electric Company, delivered the commencement address, titled, "The Challenge of the Future." Two hundred and thirty-eight graduates received diplomas, distributed as follows: School of Arts and Sciences, 32; School of Business Administration, 85; and School of Engineering, 121. Honorary degrees were conferred upon the following distinguished civic-minded citizens of Cleveland:

Howard F. Burns, Doctor of Laws (LL.D.)
Frank E. Joseph, Doctor of Humane Letters (L.H.D.)
James F. Lincoln, Doctor of Humane Letters (L.H.D.)
Charles E. Spahr, Doctor of Engineering (D. Eng.)

In May of 1961 the administration of Flint Junior College (Michigan) invited President Earnest to come to Flint and speak to a group of individuals interested in learning about Fenn's Co-op program. The in-

Table 10
SCHEDULE A(4)
Development Program
Budget Control

	Original Estimate	Changes + or −	Current Budget	Expended	Balance
Development Program Phase I (1953–1959):					
Stilwell Hall, Remodeling Tower, Equipment	$3,738,000.	$−38,133.	$3,699,867.	$3,691,551.	$ 8,316.
White Apts.—1st Mtg.	−0−	+112,500.	112,500.	112,500.	−0−
TOTALS PHASE I	3,738,000.	+ 74,367.	3,812,367.	3,804,051.	8,316.
Phase II (1960–1962):					
1881 E. 24th St.	115,000.	−3,000.	112,000.	40,000.	72,000.
North West Corner Euclid-24th St.	300,000.	−0−	300,000.	−0−	300,000.
Instructional Equipment	100,000.	−0−	100,000.	−0−	100,000.
Tower Conversion 3rd Floor	75,000.	−0−	75,000.	−0−	75,000.
Lecture Facility	770,000.	−0−	770,000.	−0−	770,000.
Site Improvement—Dormitory	75,000.	−0−	75,000.	−0−	75,000.
Furnishings—Dormitory	200,000.	−0−	200,000.	−0−	200,000.

TOTALS PHASE II	1,635,000.	−3,000.	1,632,000.	40,000.	1,592,000.
GRAND TOTAL I & II	5,373,000.	+71,367.	5,444,367.	3,844,051.	1,600,316.
Cash on hand					8,316.
Additional loan needed					1,592,000.

Present balance of loans

	4½%	6%	Total
Total Loans	$800,000.	$80,000.	$880,000.
Less Repaid	525,000.	8,000.	533,000.
	$275,000.	$72,000.	347,000.

Maximum anticipated borrowing	1,939,000.
On hand for repayment	6,775.
Balance to be provided for	1,932,225.
Unpaid pledges on hand	286,717.
Additional pledges needed	$1,645,508.

SCHEDULE B
Income & Expenditures—Development Fund
June 1, 1953 thru April 30, 1961

INCOME

Gifts of cash & stock	$3,076,922.78	
Alumni	56,827.23	
		$3,133,750.01
Interest earned on investments	80,414.39	
Net income from commercial operation of buildings & rental State of Ohio	64,682.36	
State of Ohio easement & damages	313,295.00	
		458,391.75
Bank loans		950,000.00
		$4,542,141.76

EXPENDITURES

Phase I (from Schedule A)	$3,804,051.00	
Phase II (from Schedule A)	40,000.00	
		$3,844,051.00
Repaid on bank loans		683,000.00
		$4,527,051.00

UNEXPENDED BALANCE

In Union Commerce commercial account		$ 8,418.69
Due to current fund		(6,672.07)
		$ 15,090.76*

---

* $6,744.62 are pledged to apply on repayment of the bank loan and are included in $23,022.76 of stock which will be converted to cash over a period of time. ($7,932.14) is cash available.

vitation was suggested by Guy J. Bates who had been General Manager of the Fisher Body Plant in Cleveland. Bates had been transferred to Flint and became associated with the members of the C. E. Mott Foundation who were vitally interested in the Flint Junior College and contributed heavily to it. Most of the members of the Mott Foundation attended the dinner meeting at which President Earnest spoke. In addition to the Co-op program, President Earnest detailed the activities of Fenn's Technical Institute. These two programs created so much interest that C. E. Mott and a number of the members of his Foundation Board flew to Cleveland in September 1961 to visit Fenn and attend a luncheon in Stilwell Hall where they heard such dignitaries as Mayor Celebrezze, Charles W. White, and other distinguished citizens extol the virtues of Fenn College and especially the value of the Co-op and Technical Institute programs to Cleveland's commerce and industry.

The following is a quotation from the September 20, 1961, Board Minutes:

> Mr. Colwell stated he was impressed with the number of friends Fenn College has. This comes to his attention in his fund raising activities. He asked Trustees to mention Fenn when talking to their friends. Special mention was made of a luncheon arranged in Pittsburgh by Mr. Leichliter and the contacts Mr. Fisher is making with Foundations.

Following the purchase of the property that became Stilwell Hall, by agreement dated May 12, 1953, supplements were added July 1, 1953, and April 1955 providing for the purchase of the property on the northwest corner of Euclid Avenue and East 24th Street for the sum of $300,000. At the September 20, 1961, board meeting the following resolution was adopted:

> RESOLVED, That G. Brooks Earnest, President, and Vernon H. Davis, Secretary, of Fenn College, a corporation not for profit, be and they hereby are authorized to exercise the option for Fenn College to purchase from Motors Realty Company the property at the northwest corner of Euclid Avenue and East 24th Street in the City of Cleveland as more fully described in the Agreement dated May 12, 1953, and supplemented July 1, 1953, for the sum of Three Hundred Thousand Dollars ($300,000). Also supplemented by Agreement of April 1955.

And said President and Secretary are further authorized to take all steps necessary for the carrying out of said option for the purchase of said property for the purchase price of $300,000 and are further authorized to make the necessary payments under said agreement and to execute a mortgage or make necessary bank loans and to take all further steps which are necessary for completion of said purchase.

Approval was also given for the following at the September 20, 1961, board meeting: The appointment of Burl H. Bush as Dean of Engineering. Dean Bush, former Dean of Engineering at Fenn College, had recently retired as Commander from the U.S. Navy. Emeritus status was granted to Karl D. Kelly, Professor of Mathematics, and Max. B. Robinson, Dean of Cooperative Education, both retirements effective September 1, 1961. An operating budget for fiscal 1961–1962 with a total expense of $3,058,865, requiring $159,145 in gifts to balance, was approved.

Chairman Burmester called for an observance at the same board meeting in memory of the passing of four members of the Fenn Family, James H. Coolidge of the Board of Trustees, Edward R. Sharp, Harold R. Moorhouse, and A. A. Stambaugh of the Corporation. The President was directed to send a resolution to the families on behalf of the Board of Trustees of Fenn College. Coolidge had served as a Trustee since 1941. He died July 14, 1961.

The Annual Corporation meeting for 1961 was held at the Union Club on November 14. It was an historic affair. Seventy Trustees, Members, and guests were present. The first order of business subsequent to the preliminaries was the introduction of Past Board Chairman Ellwood Fisher by Chairman Burmester. Following is a portion of the transcript of the meeting as produced by a stenotypist:

At this point, and not on the agenda, I [Chairman Burmester] have been asked by Trustee Ellwood Fisher for the privilege of the floor. I think you all recall that Ellwood Fisher is Fenn's first Chairman of the Board. And who should I be, as its third, to deny him any privilege of that sort?

Mr. Fisher?

... Applause ...

Mr. Fisher: Mr. Chairman, President Earnest, and Dr. Alter, gentlemen, I have a letter which I should like to read. It is addressed to me, as the Chairman of the Foundations Committee, Fenn College Fund Development Program.

Dear Mr. Fisher:

At a special meeting of the Board of Trustees of the Leonard C. Hanna, Jr. Fund, held on Tuesday, November 7, 1961, a careful review was made of the information which you had kindly furnished relative to the Fenn College Fund Development Program. We are glad to advise you that at the conclusion of this study, the following resolution was unanimously adopted:

RESOLVED, that in order to aid Fenn College in meeting certain needs of special urgency, which are among those included in the Fenn College Fund Development Program, Leonard C. Hanna, Jr. Fund will do the following:

1. Contribute to Fenn College the sum of $300,000, payment to be made at our option in cash or securities, taken at their fair value as of the date of delivery, such date to be on or after January 15, 1962, but prior to September 15, 1962, as we shall hereafter mutually agree with the officers of Fenn College.

2. Provide the Fund, in the sum of $150,000, as a matching fund to be paid to Fenn College at some time after January 15, 1962, in the event that after the date of this letter, but on or before September 15, 1962, Fenn College is successful in raising a like amount from other sources.

You may announce the contents of this letter at such time as you will deem most helpful to the Fenn College Fund Development Program.

We have been deeply impressed by the record of Fenn's outstanding service to the Greater Cleveland Community and by the carefully considered plans which have been made by the officers, trustees, and special committees of Fenn to meet its present and forseeable future needs. We wish for Fenn College Fund Development Program deserved success.

Sincerely, Leonard C. Hanna, Jr. Fund, by Harold T. Clark, Lewis B. Williams and John C. Virden.

. . . Standing applause . . .

Chairman Burmester: Ellwood, would you like the privilege of the floor again?

Mr. Fisher: A little later.

. . . Laughter . . .

Chairman Burmester: Well, I would say that Ellwood has kept this under his belt for 24 hours. This is most gratifying, and it has been pleasing to all of us, as well as being thrilling. And the expression by the Trustees of the Foundation, namely Harold Clark, Lew Williams and John Virden, represents after all exactly how we feel. They expressed to us, as they delivered this check, their belief in Fenn, and it is manifested here tonight by your presence. It will help us further the dreams that we all have for Fenn and its campus.

I should like to add to the comment that was made to us yesterday by the trustees, that they look to this as giving us the opportunity to exercise the option on the property opposite Fenn College on Euclid Avenue. The option price is $300,000, that is the cash that they have given us, and the $150,000 in matching funds, which I honestly believe is no difficulty, means a total of $450,000.

In checking this afternoon, Dr. Earnest tells me that [it] is the largest Foundation gift of this kind that was ever given to Fenn College.

I want to specially thank Ellwood Fisher, who is Chairman of the Foundation Section of the Fenn Development Committee, and assure him of our appreciation of his effort in bringing this wonderful gift to us. He has worked hard on this, and I am sure that it is the forerunner of other generous gifts in the years to come.

At this point, I would also like to make a comment—and this is equally important, because it comes from one of our trustees, who within the last several days—and he wants his name to remain anonymous—[he] has given us an additional gift of $50,000.

. . . Applause . . .

Chairman Burmester: And I also would like to mention to you, in the same spirit—and I know this will please you—that a corporation of this community, which has for years been a modest, but sizable contributor to our welfare, has also given us a gift in kind of $50,000.

. . . Applause . . .

Chairman Burmester: These two that I mention were honestly unexpected. We had hoped that some things like that would happen, and it did happen. But for those of us who are working on the development campaign, I think you can share our glee and our happiness, when we realize that these dollars are coming in. This isn't all that is coming to Fenn since the last time we met. You will be hearing more about that. But I would like to return to the agenda.

The following elections took place at this Annual Corporation meeting: Ellwood H. Fisher as Fenn's second Life Trustee; Arch T. Colwell as a Trustee to fulfill the term of the late James H. Coolidge; the re-election as Trustees, Class of 1966, James W. Corey and C. E. Smith; Wade N. Harris, Edward E. Helm and Paul S. Dickey to the Class of 1966 to replace Ellwood H. Fisher, Clayton G. Hale and Allen T. Perry; Raymond B. Aufmuth as an Alumni Trustee for a three-year term to succeed Charles R. Day; and the re-election to the Corporation for three-year terms, Dr. S. J. Begun, Cornelius E. Eerkes, Dr. Charles S. Higley, John F. Patt, Charles H. Smith, E. Russell Swiler and S. B. Taylor. The election of Elmore L. Andrews, Richard T. Baker, Warner B. Bishop, J. R. Blakeslee, Jr., John R. Dingle, John S. Fangboner, J. G. Fogg, Jr., C. R. Horsburgh, Dr. Abe Silverstein, Sidney H. Smith, Donald R. Spotz, Nelson S. Talbott and Frederick N. Winkler to membership in the Corporation for a three-year term also took place, and Trustees Clayton G. Hale and Allen T. Perry returned to the Corporation in accordance with the Code of Regulations. They were thanked for their long years of service as Trustees. They were eligible for re-election to the board after one year on the Corporation.

Dr. Chester M. Alter, Chancellor, University of Denver, and a distinguished educator, was the speaker of the evening. His subject was, "Call for Forward Planning," a very timely topic with respect to Fenn's then recently inaugurated long range planning program. The following quotation from Dr. Alter's address coincides almost identically with the experience of preparing a ten-year budget at Fenn, but not perhaps in the same sequence:

> We undertook to make annual budgets for each of the next ten years. Let me say this was hard work. It forced us to make many decisions in advance, which otherwise would have been left floating in thin air and unresolved from year to year. This was excruciating, this was painful, it was awful. But psychologically and actually, the process I think, for me and many of my associates, was the most thrilling thing that we have ever experienced.
>
> The first step in this forward budget projection was a review of our own basic and fundamental educational objectives. This was done largely by faculty committees, and by deans and administrative officers. And this was generally subscribed to by the faculty of the university.

And this is important, for let me say it was not subscribed to by all members of the faculty. There are always those who think otherwise, and this we had to live with.

The second step was that the administration had to learn to have respect for these objectives which we set up for ourselves.

The third step that I would mention, a necessity, was that the trustees had to make an honest effort to understand these objectives. And, that may have come hard for some of them.

Fourth, we undertook a constant interpretation of our objectives, our uniqueness as a university, to our various publics.

Our fifth step was that we prepared a list of 52 assumptions, assumptions about the nature of our future as a university. About 15 of these assumptions had to do with the national and regional economy in our society, all of the factors in our national economy and in our national society which affected higher education.

Also, it included many items which had to do with national and regional educational problems themselves. About 37 of these assumptions which we drew up had to do specifically with the University of Denver.

As a result of this comprehensive study and successful campaign to raise $25,000,000, the University of Denver was one of six regionally scattered private institutions in the United States to receive a $5,000,000 unrestricted grant from the Ford Foundation.

The Fenn Executive Committee met December 6, 1961, to hear the agreement submitted by Trustee Burns to exercise Fenn's option to purchase the northwest corner property on Euclid Avenue and East 24th Street.

President Earnest reported at this same meeting that the College had received a gift of an executive DC-3 airplane. Inasmuch as Fenn had no specific use for this plane, it was placed on sale at $60,000. It was finally sold for $50,000. Provost Patterson had reported to the President that the faculty morale and cooperation with the administration was better than at any time in Dr. Patterson's experience at Fenn, and this was mentioned to the Executive Committee. Chairman Burmester spoke to the point that the ground rules had not been established for a community college in Cleveland and without this knowledge Fenn could not defend against specific competition, but could only strive to grow better and stronger. Trustee Fries supported this thesis and added that considerable thought should be given to what character Fenn might assume in order to be of best service to Greater Cleveland. President Earnest further reported that Architect Ceruti had begun the preliminary studies on space needs and other basic data for the new building (administration and auditorium) to be constructed on the option property on the northwest corner of Euclid Avenue and East 24th Street.

A number of honors came to President Earnest during the year 1961, the most important being his election, in October, to the presidency of the American Society of Civil Engineers. Besides representing the society at many Local Sections in the United States, he was the ambassador for the society at engineering meetings in Caracas, Venezuela; London, England; Panama; Puerto Rico; Montreal, Canada; Bogota, Colombia; and Fairbanks, Alaska. At a number of these meetings he was given illuminated scrolls as an honorary member of the foreign engineering societies.

Additional honors are:

A. Guest of the U.S. Air Force on an engineering inspection tour of the Dew Line and Ballistic Missile Early Warning System in the Arctic Circle, visiting Frobisher Bay, Canada; Sondrestrom and Thule Air Bases in Greenland; Elmendorf and Clear Air Bases near Fairbanks, Alaska; and Anchorage, Sparrevohn and King Salmon Dew Line Stations in Alaska.

B. Appointed with two other Cleveland college presidents to the Vernon B. Stouffer Scholarship Committee.

C. Appointed a member of the Advisory Committee to the Cleveland City Planning Commission.

During the year Fenn College finished its first decade as a completely independent private college. A comprehensive ten-year report entitled "A Decade of Achievement of Fenn College, Cleveland" was published. The following chapter will include the highlights of that report.

XII

Let us, then, be up and doing,
With a heart for any fate;
Still achieving, still pursuing,
Learn to labour and to wait.

Henry Wadsworth Longfellow, 1807–1882.
A Psalm of Life, 1839, Stanza 9.

A decade of achievement of Fenn College–Cleveland. This chapter is brief, but it shows, by illustrated graphs and columns of statistics, the records of growth and achievement of Fenn College over its first ten years as a private, independent college. The graphs and statistics are extracted from a 52-page booklet which described the ten year (1951–1960) highlights of the following, in the order shown:

Cooperative Education Program
The Student Body and Academic Services
    Office of Admission and Records
    Office of Dean of Students
    Student Guidance
    Office of Dean of Women
    Department of Personnel Development
    Department of Health and Physical Education
    The Fenn Alumni Association
    The School of Arts and Sciences
    The School of Business Administration
    The School of Engineering
    The Technical Institute
    The College Library
    The Audio Visual Center
Department of Finance

Development
Financial Contributors to Fenn College
Board of Trustees
The Corporation

The following quotation is from the portion of the booklet on the subject of Development: "The development of the Fenn Campus is a tribute to the vision of Fenn's Trustees who, even though funds were short, took advantage of every opportunity to acquire properties crucial to an institution planning to meet its share of the future educational needs in the community."

The opening statement in the booklet titled "A Decade of Achievement, Fenn College—Cleveland" was by President Earnest. It reads as follows:

Ten years ago, in February, 1951, Fenn College achieved independence from its parent organization, the Cleveland Y.M.C.A. During this decade, the College has come to maturity—grown up, so to speak—from a dependent adjunct of the Y to a fully-accredited independent degree granting institution. It is of these last ten maturing years that we wish to tell the story.

The story of Fenn College during the last decade is the story of a small community. It is a history, if you will, of a community of scholars, teachers, and students working together toward common goals.

Historians, I now suspect, must be numbered among the most frustrated of scholars, for men and events will not lend themselves easily to a simple narrative. Much that is vital must by necessity be excluded, even from such a relatively brief history as this. Every person who has been associated with Fenn during the past ten years—faculty, students, administrative staff, trustees, members of the Fenn Corporation—has contributed substantially to Fenn's progress, but space requirements obviously prohibit even the mention of the majority of these names. This being so, how little then can really be said of the hopes, fears, doubts, and dreams that went into the shaping of events we will presently explore. Very little, and this is a great pity.

It is for this reason that we must sometimes read between the lines of what follows. Although in the telling of such a history a sense of inevitability and easy triumph may often appear, we must keep in mind that seldom is progress achieved without a generous expenditure of "blood, sweat, and tears." Hindsight all too frequently tends to ignore or to gloss over the conflicts, the false starts, and the failures—all of which comprise a vital part of the essentially human in any history.

Also—and this is of the utmost importance—we must direct attention to the very great contribution of the City of Cleveland and its environs to the continued healthy development of the College. Without the generous support—both spiritual and financial—of local businesses, industries, civic organizations, and foundations it would be impossible to relate the story of "A Decade of Achievement of Fenn College, Cleveland."

s/*G. Brooks Earnest*, President

The ten-year record of fulfillments is shown by the following tables. Table 1 shows the Fall Quarter Day Division school enrollment for the decade 1951–1960.

Table 1

FALL QUARTER ENROLLMENT FOR DAY DIVISION FOR 1951-1960
(Not including students out on Co-op jobs.)

Total	690	607	620	739	831	877	943	946	1045	1173

Enrollments

	'51	'52	'53	'54	'55	'56	'57	'58	'59	'60
Engineering	394	336	322	405	407	478	553	515	560	579
Business Administration	197	185	186	190	237	218	212	244	231	304
Arts & Sciences	99	86	112	98	130	130	139	128	196	207
Nursing				46	57	51	39	59	58	83

Year '51 '52 '53 '54 '55 '56 '57 '58 '59 '60

☐ Nursing   ■ Arts & Sciences   ▨ Business Administration   ⣿ Engineering

TABLE 2

Year	Arts & Sciences	Business Administration	Engineering	Technical Institute	Total
1951	510	1391	779	980	3660
1952	639	1371	742	958	3710
1953	739	1590	765	1081	4175
1954	777	1681	808	1167	4433
1955	858	1874	867	1105	4704
1956	967	2095	918	1294	5274
1957	893	2217	873	1181	5164
1958	962	2121	753	978	4814
1959	1100	2099	784	1085	5068
1960	1200	2100	800	1075	5175

Table 2 shows the Fall Quarter Evening Division school enrollments for the Fall Quarters from 1951 through 1960.

Table 3 shows the geographical distribution of Day Division Freshmen for the Fall Quarter of 1960.

TABLE 3

State or Country	*Arts	% of Total	B.A.	% of Total	Engr.	% of Total	Total	% by State
Ohio	109	86%	119	93%	205	82%	433	86.2%
Pennsylvania	8	6%	7	5%	17	7%	32	6.3%
New York	6	5%	0	0%	22	9%	28	5.6%
Florida	0	0%	2	2%	0	0%	2	.5%
California	0	0%	0	0%	1	.5%	1	.2%
Illinois	1	1%	0	0%	0	0%	1	.2%
Massachusetts	0	0%	0	0%	1	.5%	1	.2%
Michigan	1	1%	0	0%	0	0%	1	.2%
Virginia	1	1%	0	0%	0	0%	1	.2%
West Virginia	0	0%	0	0%	1	.5%	1	.2%
Foreign Students	0	0%	0	0%	1	.5%	1	.2%
Totals	126		128		248		502	

* Nurses included.

Table 4 shows the average monthly Co-op earnings for the various Schools and Departments for 1960–1961. The total Co-op earnings for all students was $1,726,755 for this same year.

Table 4

AVERAGE MONTHLY CO-OP STUDENT EARNINGS FOR ACADEMIC YEAR 1960-1961

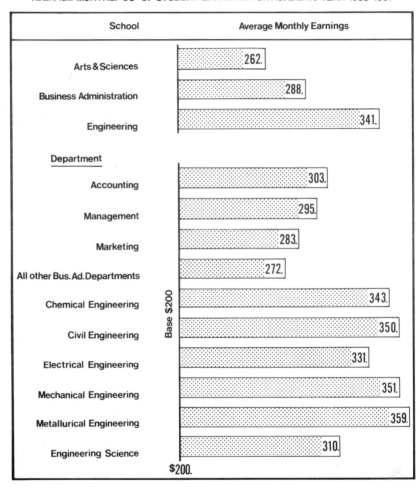

School	Average Monthly Earnings
Arts & Sciences	262.
Business Administration	288.
Engineering	341.
Department	
Accounting	303.
Management	295.
Marketing	283.
All other Bus. Ad. Departments	272.
Chemical Engineering	343.
Civil Engineering	350.
Electrical Engineering	331.
Mechanical Engineering	351.
Metallurical Engineering	359.
Engineering Science	310.

Base $200

$200.

Table 5 shows the number of Fenn College degrees conferred in the three Schools during the decade.

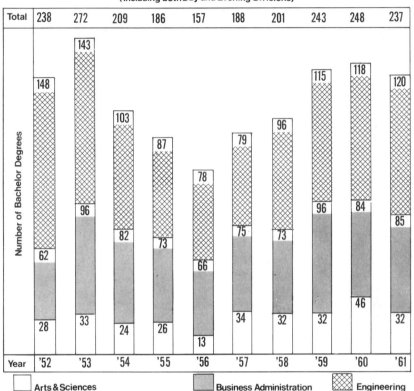

Table 5

NUMBER OF FENN COLLEGE DEGREES CONFERRED FROM 1952 to 1961
(Including both Day and Evening Divisions)

| Total | 238 | 272 | 209 | 186 | 157 | 188 | 201 | 243 | 248 | 237 |

Number of Bachelor Degrees

| Year | '52 | '53 | '54 | '55 | '56 | '57 | '58 | '59 | '60 | '61 |

☐ Arts & Sciences   ▨ Business Administration   ▧ Engineering

Table 6 shows the changes in tuition rates per credit hour during the decade.

TABLE 6

Year of Change	Arts & Sciences	Business Administration	Engineering
1952	$14	$14	$14
1954	13	13	14
1957	15	15	17
1959	16	16	19
1961	18	18	23

Table 7 shows the average faculty salaries for the decade. The year 1956 does not reflect the fact that the teaching year was reduced from eleven months to nine months with little change in previous 1955 annual salaries. Faculty members were paid on a credit-hour basis for teaching the Summer Quarter, whereas in all the previous years of Fenn College's existence the Summer Quarter teaching load was included in the annual salary. This action taken by the board, as mentioned in Chapter X, had the same effect as a significant increase in the annual salary of a faculty member.

Table 7

AVERAGE ANNUAL FACULTY SALARIES FROM 1951-1961

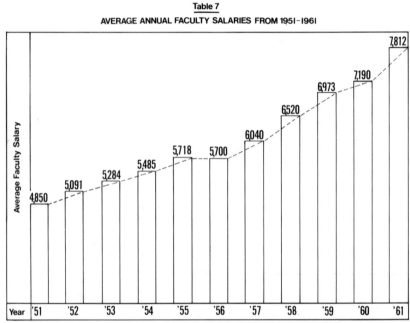

Does not reflect the reduction of base teaching year from 11 months to 9 months in 1956

Table 8 shows the total contributions by the Alumni each year for the decade, and Table 9 shows the percent of participation of Alumni contributors (of total living Alumni) for the decade. In 1960 and 1961 this percentage was amongst the highest in the United States for all alumni-giving to colleges.

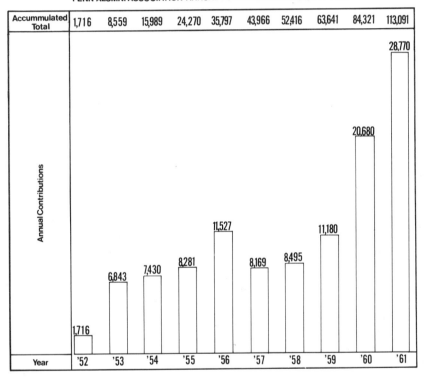

Table 8
FENN ALUMNI ASSOCIATION ANNUAL CONTRIBUTIONS FROM 1951 – 1961

Accummulated Total	1,716	8,559	15,989	24,270	35,797	43,966	52,416	63,641	84,321	113,091
Year	'52	'53	'54	'55	'56	'57	'58	'59	'60	'61

Annual Contributions: 1,716 · 6,843 · 7,430 · 8,281 · 11,527 · 8,169 · 8,495 · 11,180 · 20,680 · 28,770

Table 9

FENN ALUMNI ASSOCIATION PERCENT PARTICIPATION IN ANNUAL CONTRIBUTIONS
FROM 1952 to 1961

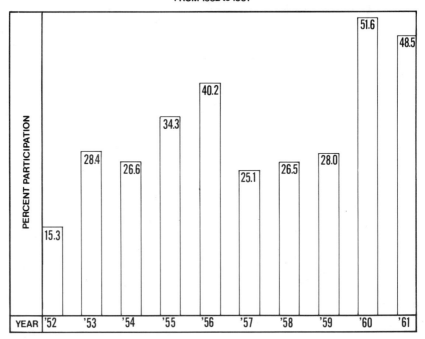

Table 10 shows the comparison of tuition and total operating income for the decade.

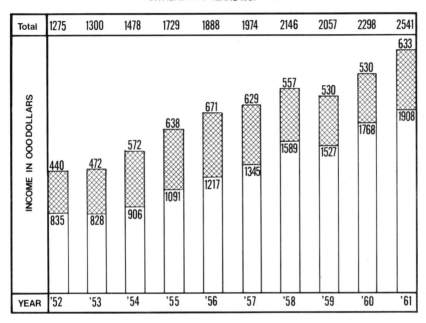

Table 10

COMPARISON OF TUITION AND OTHER OPERATING INCOME
FOR ACADEMIC YEARS 1951-1961

Total	1275	1300	1478	1729	1888	1974	2146	2057	2298	2541

INCOME IN 000 DOLLARS

| | 835 | 828 | 906 | 1091 | 1217 | 1345 | 1589 | 1527 | 1768 | 1908 |
| Other | 440 | 472 | 572 | 638 | 671 | 629 | 557 | 530 | 530 | 633 |

| YEAR | '52 | '53 | '54 | '55 | '56 | '57 | '58 | '59 | '60 | '61 |

☐ TUITION INCOME   ▨ OTHER OPERATING INCOME

Table 11 shows the comparison of operating gift income and capital income for the decade.

Table 12 shows the comparison of plant values for the years 1951–1952 and 1960–1961.

Table II

COMPARISON OF CAPITOL AND OTHER OPERATING CONTRIBUTIONS
FOR ACADEMIC YEARS 1951 to 1961

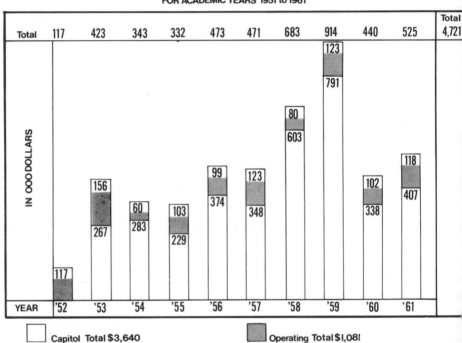

											Total
Total	117	423	343	332	473	471	683	914	440	525	4,721

Capitol Total $3,640   Operating Total $1,081

Table 12

COMPARISON OF FENN COLLEGE PLANT VALUES FOR ACADEMIC YEARS 1951– 1961

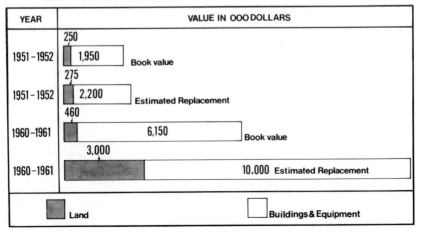

YEAR	VALUE IN OOO DOLLARS
1951–1952	250 / 1,950 Book value
1951–1952	275 / 2,200 Estimated Replacement
1960–1961	460 / 6,150 Book value
1960–1961	3,000 / 10,000 Estimated Replacement

Land   Buildings & Equipment

Table 13 shows the cumulated increases in plant and equipment.

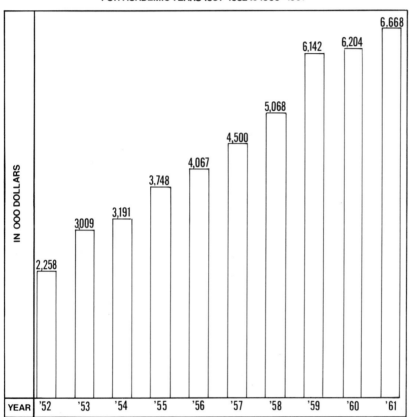

Table 13

CUMULATED INCREASES IN PLANT AND EQUIPMENT FUNDS
FOR ACADEMIC YEARS 1951–1952 to 1960–1961

Table 14 shows the book value of endowment for the decade.

Table 14

BOOK VALUE OF ENDOWMENT FOR ACADEMIC YEARS 1951 to 1961

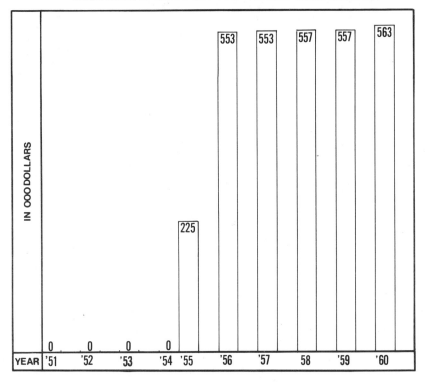

Table 15 shows the income and expense statements for the decade.

Table 15

FENN COLLEGE STATEMENT OF INCOME AND EXPENSES
(Year's end August 31)

Income	1952	1953	1954	1955
Educational and general:				
Tuition:				
Day Division	$ 412,094	$ 394,818	$ 363,353	$ 445,551
Evening Division	422,626	433,418	542,734	645,383
Endowment fund income	—	—	—	—
Miscellaneous fees	5,894	9,133	23,012	30,106
Departmental services	27,562	41,643	59,574	69,622
Gifts	119,123	155,668	113,234	102,913
Total Educational	987,299	1,034,680	1,101,907	1,293,575
Auxiliary enterprises:				
Bookstore	107,186	95,901	97,432	111,258
Restaurant	78,435	83,071	87,302	91,944
Dormitory	30,335	30,066	33,106	34,641
Total Auxiliary	242,263	209,038	217,840	237,843
Other non-educational:				
Rent	12,750	18,907	107,008	150,339
Scholarships	24,000	—	11,644	6,989
Interest	—	2,103	4,888	2,793
Miscellaneous	9,952	11,522	16,908	16,885
TOTAL INCOME	$1,276,264	$1,276,250	$1,460,195	$1,708,424

Expenses	1952	1953	1954	1955
Educational and general	$ 960,907	$ 991,522	$1,118,904	$1,260,395
Auxiliary enterprises	219,461	195,605	200,044	216,259
Other non-educational expenses	25,748	33,912	115,109	138,293
TOTAL EXPENSES	$1,206,116	$1,221,039	$1,434,057	$1,614,947
EXCESS INCOME BEFORE SPECIAL CHARGES	70,148	55,221	26,138	93,477
Transfers to plant funds:				
Current expenditures for plant	29,127	42,458	23,704	66,673
National Defense Student Loan Fund	—	—	—	—
Net income-properties	—	—	—	21,858
Net Income after Special Charges	$ 41,021	$ 12,753	$ 2,434	$ 4,946

TABLE 15 (*Continued*)

1956	1957	1958	1959	1960	1961
$ 509,114	$ 594,479	$ 751,797	$ 761,050.20	$ 919,327.90	$1,031,222.65
707,536	750,283	837,701	766,227.40	848,943.33	877,250.70
–	9,299	21,696	21,868.97	22,529.18	22,763.87
35,862	41,136	39,587	43,299.18	53,392.20	54,446.27
39,824	16,599	16,476	17,201.35	18,841.29	18,365.91
99,283	123,239	85,683	122,950.08	102,154.83	117,584.24
1,391,619	1,535,035	1,752,940	1,732,597.18	1,965,188.73	2,121,633.64
129,284	140,395	148,461	143,938.76	182,686.01	210,816.21
95,717	93,588	78,902	56,871.59	–	–
39,998	39,950	38,698	44,046.50	52,936.50	65,530.65
264,999	273,933	266,061	244,856.85	235,622.51	276,346.86
170,906	90,443	69,411	20,250.00	35,364.00	79,200.00
10,762	15,306	13,743	9,363.17	7,994.18	6,172.48
4,066	3,372	3,859	3,093.09	3,687.82	3,830.56
20,704	30,421	21,900	20,426.37	23,964.20	30,410.66
$1,863,056	$1,948,510	$2,127,914	$2,030,586.66	$2,271,821.44	$2,517,594.20

1956	1957	1958	1959	1960	1961
$1,391,499	$1,548,551	$1,719,849	$1,714,794.87	$2,001,613.53	$2,150,963.35
239,393	255,974	257,794	232,119.74	211,937.32	272,307.85
162,440	98,855	79,254	55,496.91	52,235.80	40,856.20
$1,793,332	$1,903,380	$2,056,897	$2,002,408.93	$2,265,786.65	$2,464,127.40
69,724	45,130	71,017	28,177.73	6,034.79	53,466.80
54,272	28,652	48,789	24,967.45	1,092.56	47,953.25
–	–	–	749.89	3,012.11	3,870.67
13,824	14,438	17,977	–	–	–
$ 1,628	$ 2,040	$ 4,251	$ 2,460.39	$ 1,930.12	$ 1,642.88

Table 16 shows the balance sheets for the decade.

TABLE 16

FENN COLLEGE BALANCE SHEET
(Year's End August 31)

ASSETS

	1952	1953	1954	1955
CURRENT FUNDS				
Cash	$ 243,334	$ 66,976	$ 35,441	$ 272,003
Notes receivable	3,412	2,458	1,426	—
Due from endowment	—	—	—	—
Marketable securities	—	201,848	214,883	9,849
Accounts receivable	38,990	38,055	43,712	35,411
Inventories	54,347	60,952	69,228	83,118
Prepaid expense and deposit	9,800	11,424	10,421	14,240
Total Current Funds	349,883	381,713	375,111	414,621
STUDENT LOAN FUNDS				
Cash	14,547	17,037	17,665	18,746
Marketable securities	—	—	—	—
Notes	8,916	6,654	6,170	5,286
Total Student Loan Funds	23,463	23,691	23,835	24,032
ENDOWMENT FUNDS				
Uninvested cash on deposit with agent	—	—	—	—
Marketable securities	—	—	—	—
PLANT FUNDS				
Cash	49,917	106,742	239,251	457,209
Marketable securities	259	9,498	320	6,031
Fenn Tower	1,200,000	1,200,000	1,200,000	1,200,000
Apartment land and building	—	—	—	272,959
Other land and buildings	631,158	1,284,576	1,297,289	1,338,314
Building improvements	66,765	86,375	111,270	112,653
Furniture and equipment	310,123	321,713	343,017	360,769
Total Plant Funds	2,258,222	3,008,904	3,191,147	3,747,935
AGENCY FUNDS				
Cash	4,773	4,155	10,967	12,031
Marketable securities	7,221	7,278	7,244	7,238
Total Agency Funds	11,994	11,433	18,211	19,269
TOTAL ASSETS	$2,643,562	$3,425,741	$3,608,304	$4,205,857

ASSETS (*continued*)

	1956	1957	1958	1959	1960	1961
	$ 283,738	$ 205,789	$ 175,472	$ 295,535	$ 219,643	$ 268,473
	—	—	—	—	—	—
	—	15,000	15,000	15,000	15,000	15,000
	24,758	9,713	9,656	9,659	9,681	9,681
	13,494	15,507	13,532	14,105	9,848	24,563
	87,077	38,898	42,918	36,439	44,294	45,265
	16,111	17,314	22,160	23,572	30,403	29,495
	425,178	302,221	278,738	394,310	328,869	392,477
	21,463	21,480	19,867	24,509	35,583	49,615
	—	—	—	8,607	8,607	8,607
	2,695	2,754	4,480	7,724	27,361	52,609
	24,158	24,234	24,347	40,840	71,551	110,831
	—	—	—	83	220	98
	225,450	568,024	568,255	571,725	571,752	578,273
	309,686	386,385	553,726	468,121	110,908	29,853
	439,813	759,007	507,286	—	—	22,950
	1,200,000	1,200,000	1,200,000	1,200,000	1,200,000	1,200,000
	272,959	272,959	272,959	—	—	—
	1,338,314	1,351,459	1,980,221	3,532,019	3,571,967	3,684,919
	112,653	112,653	112,653	146,065	342,297	393,806
	394,059	417,053	440,851	796,135	978,397	1,336,863
	4,067,484	4,499,516	5,067,696	6,142,340	6,203,569	6,668,391
	9,136	11,896	13,774	15,731	17,645	18,805
	8,238	10,213	10,173	11,041	11,724	15,573
	17,374	22,109	23,947	26,772	29,369	34,378
	$4,759,644	$5,416,104	$5,962,983	$7,176,070	$7,205,330	$7,784,448

LIABILITIES AND FUNDS

	1952	1953	1954	1955
CURRENT FUNDS				
Accounts payable	$ 31,597	$ 54,958	$ 43,557	$ 72,981
Scholarship funds	24,858	30,784	33,409	32,865
Deferred income	12,500	1,600	1,340	7,025
Undesignated gifts	25,639	26,330	26,330	26,330
Operating capital	100,000	100,000	100,000	100,000
Accumulated income	155,289	168,041	170,475	175,420
Total Current Funds	349,883	381,713	375,111	414,621
STUDENT LOAN FUNDS				
Principal of fund	23,463	23,691	23,835	24,032
ENDOWMENT FUNDS				
Due to current fund	—	—	—	—
Principal of fund	—	—	—	—
Undistributed income from securities transactions	—	—	—	—
Total Endowment Funds	—	—	—	—
PLANT FUNDS				
Mortgages and other notes payable	39,080	586,894	346,642	578,821
Contract retention	—	—	—	—
Gifts	1,527,261	1,730,129	1,989,865	2,280,301
Provided through operations	—	—	162,759	196,932
Excess appraised value of Fenn Tower	691,881	691,881	691,881	691,881
Total Plant Funds	2,258,222	3,008,904	3,191,147	3,747,935
AGENCY FUNDS				
Principal of funds	11,994	11,433	18,211	19,269
TOTAL LIABILITIES AND FUNDS	$2,643,562	$3,425,741	$3,608,304	$4,205,857

LIABILITIES AND FUNDS (*continued*)

1956	1957	1958	1959	1960	1961
$ 72,485	$ 51,739	$ 35,744	$ 124,695	$ 60,347	$ 117,047
41,324	36,144	29,552	52,007	45,330	47,773
7,992	8,922	6,355	8,060	11,714	14,537
26,330	26,330	26,330	26,330	26,330	26,329
100,000	100,000	100,000	—	—	—
177,047	79,086	80,757	183,218	185,148	186,791
425,178	302,221	278,738	394,310	328,869	392,477
24,158	24,234	24,347	40,840	71,551	110,831
—	15,000	15,000	15,000	15,000	15,000
225,450	553,024	553,000	553,000	553,000	553,000
—	—	255	3,808	3,972	10,371
225,450	568,024	568,255	571,808	571,972	578,371
456,931	414,967	345,429	822,314	657,119	643,383
—	—	58,259	103,016	—	—
2,635,467	3,048,339	3,575,501	4,103,535	4,431,882	4,862,487
283,205	344,329	396,626	421,593	422,686	470,639
691,881	691,881	691,881	691,882	691,882	691,882
4,067,484	4,499,516	5,067, 696	6,142,340	6,203,569	6,668,391
17,374	22,109	23,947	26,772	29,369	34,378
$4,759,644	$5,416,104	$5,962,983	$7,176,070	$7,205,330	$7,784,448

The following is the president's closing statement in the ten-year report for the decade 1951–1961—a report which speaks for itself.

This has been a decade of achievement. We have seen in detail the steady growth and development of the various schools and departments of the College. We have witnessed the changes in curricula and the initiation of new academic services to the community. And we have observed the planned improvement and expansion of Fenn's physical facilities.

A college is no better than its Faculty and Student Body. Thus, if achievement there has been, the lion's share of credit must be given to these two vital groups. It is true that Fenn's growth would have been impossible without the generous moral and financial support of the Greater Cleveland community, but it is equally true that this support would not have been forthcoming were it not for the singular efforts of its Faculty and Student Body.

Fenn presently faces a number of severe problems, and the future will no doubt pose many more. We must take steps to retain in upper-division studies more of our intellectually capable underclassmen. We need to become more efficient as an institution, always striving to utilize more thoroughly and wisely our fine talent and our well-equipped educational facilities. We must become ever more competitive financially so that we can attract and hold younger teachers of promise with the doctorate. We must maintain a sufficiently flexible policy so that we can react quickly and effectively to the ever changing educational needs of the community. But above all, we must continue to provide the highest possible quality of education, seeking always to approach more closely that excellence which is the goal of Fenn College.

XIII

Forward, as occasion offers.
Never look around to see whether any shall note it. . . .
Be satisfied with success in even the smallest matter,
and think that even such result is no trifle.

Marcus Aurelius Antoninus, AD 121–180.
Meditations, VIII, 29.

Nineteen hundred and sixty-two was the beginning of a second decade for Fenn College as a private institution of higher learning. But, as the reader will soon discover this status was short-lived. Fenn never reached the end of a second decade as a private college. In fact, extenuating circumstances were already arising that created questions relative to the place of Fenn in the future higher educational activities in Greater Cleveland. The first of these circumstances was the planning for a junior or community college which was underway, led by Ralph M. Besse, Chairman of the Cleveland Commission on Higher Education. President Earnest felt, however, that "Fenn could exist under the conditions calling for a public Community College established in 1965 with good facilities and centrally located." He said so in his report titled "Ten-year Fiscal Projection of Fenn College" which had been mailed to the Trustees early in January.

The first meeting of the board in 1962 was held on January 29. Following is an excerpt from the Minutes of the meeting:

> President Earnest discussed the background of the position he had taken with the Cleveland Commission on Higher Education when the local colleges were asked to go on record concerning a community college. He felt then, and is of the same opinion today, that the only course open to Fenn was to vote for it along

503

with all the other Cleveland colleges. To do otherwise would have resulted in local feelings to Fenn detrimental to its long term interests and could not possibly have affected the results any more favorably to us.

Chairman Burmester also commented in similar vein and added information concerning the position of the Cleveland Commission. He had been advised that some Board members were not sufficiently clear as to Fenn's position relative to the community college— that possibly the College (Fenn) was not sensitive to the threats posed by this. The ground rules have not been established nor the form or locations of such college or colleges. Without this knowledge Fenn cannot defend against specific competition and can only strive to grow better and stronger in general.

Trustee V. W. Fries "suggested that continued thought be given to Fenn's place in the community (because of the community college) and if necessary, what character the College might assume to be of best service to greater Cleveland."

The Motors Realty Company requested that Fenn exercise the option on the purchase of the property on the northwest corner of Euclid Avenue and East 24th Street set at $300,000 at the time of the purchase of the Ohio Motors building, later, Stilwell Hall. This proved to be excellent timing in light of the recent $300,000 grant from the Hanna Fund plus an additional $150,000 matching grant from them (which latter was accomplished by contributions within four months). The board adopted a resolution at this same meeting thanking the trustees of the Hanna Fund.

A one-story used-car sales building occupied a portion of the option property. For some years Lou Cohen had rented the building and the remainder of the lot for his used-car business. The board authorized renewal of a lease agreement with Cohen providing for rental at $14,100 per year with termination upon three-month's notice by either party. There was no outlay of any operating expenses while the College was in the process of acquiring the parcel.

Now that the College owned outright all of the property on both sides of East 24th Street between Euclid and Chester Avenues, consideration was given to vacating this portion of East 24th Street inasmuch as it reached a dead-end at Euclid Avenue anyway. The Euclid

Innerbelt Association (EIBA), under the chairmanship of Fenn Trustee
E. T. Bartlett, requested the Director of Traffic, City of Cleveland,
and the EIBA Planner to study the effect of such closing. In addition
President Earnest requested the Traffic Engineer for the Cleveland
Automobile Club to make traffic studies at the two intersections of
East 24th Street with Euclid and Chester Avenues. As the result of
these three studies, the Director of Traffic, City of Cleveland, considered
it unwise to press for closing the street because East 24th Street was
carrying a large amount of traffic in addition to Fenn-generated traffic.
Furthermore, the Upper Euclid Avenue Association had already taken
steps to oppose the closing of the street. To close it, there would have
to be a suitable alternative such as the opening of East 22nd Street
between Euclid and Chester Avenues.

The following officers were elected at this January 29, 1962, board
meeting:

Harry F. Burmester, Chairman
Dr. James C. Hodge, Vice Chairman
Vollmer W. Fries, Treasurer
Vernon H. Davis, Secretary

Chairman Burmester announced the Board Standing Committee structure for 1962; it is shown in Table 1.

Provost Patterson reported that rapport between students and faculty
and the cooperation with the administration was at an all-time high
since his joining Fenn in 1936. President Earnest presented the final
enrollment statistics for the Day Division of the Winter Quarter of
1962 as shown in Table 2.

The Ten-year Fiscal Projection of Fenn College prepared by the
Provost's Cabinet was submitted to the board at this meeting for later
review and consideration. The College was still awaiting the ten-year
10-college study from the Fund Fulfillment Corporation. However,
there was sufficient information in the Provost's report to request Architect J. Ceruti to proceed with preliminary studies on space needs and
other basic data toward planning for a new building to be constructed
on the newly acquired option property.

TABLE 2

WINTER QUARTER 1962 DAY DIVISION ENROLLMENT
STATISTICS

	ACTUAL			BUDGET			WINTER QUARTER 1961		
	School	*Coop*	*Total*	*School*	*Coop*	*Total*	*School*	*Coop*	*Total*
Arts & Sciences	256	90	346	250	85	335	193	63	256
Business Admin.	285	132	417	285	140	425	266	105	371
Engineering	500	258	758	510	260	770	511	277	788
Nursing	117	11	128	115	10	125	86	17	103
	1158	491	1649	1160	495	1655	1056	462	1518

Following are excerpts from the Provost's ten-year study:

INTEGRATED PLAN

During 1959 the Department of Development of the College was active in planning for the ten-year future physical needs. On the occasion of the dedication of Stilwell Hall in January 1960, the result of this planning, known as the Integrated Plan, was presented to the audience and the mass media.

A new campaign was immediately instituted to raise funds for effecting the Integrated Plan. However, late in 1960 there was increased movement toward legislation for community colleges in Ohio. The Integrated Plan did not include the effect of community colleges in the Greater Cleveland area in its basic assumptions. The Trustees, therefore, asked the Administration to study the effect of one or more community colleges in Cuyahoga County on the future of Fenn College.

Following the announcement of the Integrated Plan a faculty committee was appointed to study ways and means of effecting the plan from an academic standpoint. . . .

COMMUNITY COLLEGE

Late in 1960 legislators were working on a Community College Bill, and the minutes of the Fenn Board of Trustees for their meeting of January 4, 1961 show this comment:

"The status of the proposed Ohio community college law was reviewed and it was reported that the State Interim Commission on Education Beyond the High School had approved the major provisions thereof the last week in 1960. Much discussion ensued. The Provost's Cabinet is studying the impact of a community college on Fenn College and will submit a report about February 15, 1961. . . ."

In summarizing the situation Chairman Burmester again requested those present to refrain from speculating in public that the private status of Fenn College could change lest our position be affected adversely."

THE NEW TEN-YEAR PLAN

Starting back in April 1959, various departments of the College were assigned tasks of gathering basic data to project a new ten-year plan based upon Sidney Tickton's [Ford Foundation] recommendations and containing several assumptions regarding a community college. Certain specifics were requested by the Special Committee on the Ten-Year Plan, and this Committee met at least once per month to hear progress reports and discuss special elements of the Plan.

The 1959–60 academic year was chosen as a base year to explore all basic data because this was the latest year for which we had full and complete records of all kinds—academic and fiscal. The following statistics were gathered and will be obtained for each year hence:

a. Quarterly enrollment for academic work
b. Quarterly enrollment for cooperative work
c. New students to schools of Day Division
d. Number of men and women enrolled in Day Division
e. Number of veterans and non-veterans in Day Division
f. Geographical distribution of Day Division students
g. Distribution of Day Division students in Cuyahoga County high schools
h. Semester enrollments for Evening Division
i. New students in Evening Division
j. Number of veterans and non-veterans in Evening Division
k. Number of degrees and titles conferred by each School in Day and Evening Divisions.

Other base data for the year 1959–60 were obtained to determine certain comparisons where economies may be suggested for future years. These are:

a. Number of teaching faculty by rank (3 qtr. yr. and summer)
b. Average teaching load of full-time faculty members
c. Average number of students per credit-hour taught over a three-quarter year

d. Average student load per quarter in credit hours
e. Student-faculty ratio
f. Teaching cost per student credit-hour
   1. for all courses taught by full-time faculty
   2. for all courses taught by part-time faculty
g. Total cost per student credit-hour
h. Average number of students per credit-hour taught in Day and Evening Divisions throughout year.

Coincidental with the study being made by the Special Committee on the Ten-Year Plan, the Faculty Committee on Curriculum and Instruction is exploring ways and means of reorganizing curriculum and class size to effect better economy of operation while still striving for improvement in quality of instruction.

The Provost's Cabinet prepared "Recommended Assumptions for the Fenn College Ten-Year Financial Plan"—first, for the United States as a whole, secondly, for the Greater Cleveland area and, thirdly, for the College itself. They also prepared Estimates of Future Fenn Enrollment for:

1. Actual for base year 1959–60
2. For 1969–70, assuming no community college in area, but does include Euclid Branch of Kent State University
3. For 1969–70, assuming competition from a community college established in 1965 with good facilities and centrally located
4. For 1969–70, assuming competition from community college plus State University Branches in suburbs
5. Competition from a four-year tax assisted institution which would offer no engineering program (no year given).

Item 3 above appears to be the most probable community college possibility for 1969. The estimated Fenn enrollment, assuming a community college established in 1965 with good facilities and centrally located is as follows:

School	Day Division	Evening Division
Arts & Sciences	450	750
Business Administration	500	1200
Engineering	1300	650
Technical Institute	—	700
Total	2250	3300

ASSUMPTIONS FOR THE UNITED STATES AS A WHOLE

1. Characteristics of the U.S. Economy
    a. High employment will continue.
    b. No war or other national disaster will occur.
    c. Inflationary tendencies in prices will continue—1% a year.
2. Need for College-Trained Manpower
    a. Steady increase in next ten years.
3. Number of Students in All Colleges and Universities
    a. Number will approximately double, 1959–1969.
    b. Urban institutions will grow in greater proportion than non-urban.
    c. The increase will continue after 1970.
    d. A greater portion of the increase will occur in mid-Western colleges because of pressure from the East.
4. Faculty Salaries
    2. Will double on the average, 1959–1969, based upon the conclusion of the President's Commission and most studies.
5. Student Aid
    a. Volume of government funds for scholarships and loans to students will grow.
    b. Nevertheless, colleges will continue to provide a growing amount of student aid.
    c. Growing amount of loan funds available from other agencies.
6. Funds for Construction
    a. Government and private loans will be available for construction of revenue-producing facilities.
    b. Private gifts will finance the major portion of other college facilities.
    c. Federal funds will also become available (grants or loans) for non-revenue-producing facilities.
7. Government Aid
    a. The cost of higher education will increasingly become a public rather than a private responsibility.
8. Private Support
    a. The financial support of corporate industry in higher education will increase.

ASSUMPTIONS FOR THE GREATER CLEVELAND AREA

1. Characteristics of the Greater Cleveland Economy
   a. The economic growth will continue to be above the national averages.
   b. Cleveland will continue to be a high cost of living area compared to other centers.
2. Need for College-Trained Manpower
   a. Steady increase in next ten years will exceed national average.
3. Number of Students in Greater Cleveland Colleges and Universities
   a. Will approximately double, 1959–69.
   b. Public tax-assisted institution will be established at least by 1965.
   c. Major competition will be provided by 1965 to Fenn and other private institutions by a public institution.
4. Faculty Salaries
   a. Increase will need to equal or exceed national average because of the high cost of living in the area.
5. Student Aid
   a. Any state distribution of federal scholarship funds will discriminate against Cleveland and Cuyahoga County students. (This is based on the present practice of reserving at least one scholarship for each county.)
6. Funds for Construction
   a. Government and private loans will be available for construction of revenue-producing facilities.
   b. Private gifts will finance the major portion of other college facilities.
   c. Federal funds will also become available (grants or loans) for non-revenue-producing facilities.
7. Urban Renewal
   a. The general effects of urban renewal will be a general improvement in the area of the College which will increase the value of property.
   b. There will be continued commercial development of the area immediately adjacent to the College.
8. Private Support
   a. The financial support of Cleveland corporate industry in higher education will increase.

    b. This increase might well be greater than the national average.

ASSUMPTIONS FOR THE COLLEGE ITSELF

1. Purposes and Objectives of the College
   a. Academic Objectives
      1) Quality of students will remain approximately the same. Probably cannot and should not raise quality substantially but should seek to admit better motivated and better prepared students.
      2) Continue our efforts to attract an able faculty through improved working conditions and better salaries.
      3) Continue to provide sound undergraduate education in arts and sciences, business administration, and engineering, and to collaborate with the Huron Road Hospital and perhaps other hospitals in nursing education.
      4) Continue to improve techniques for securing adequately prepared students for college-credit evening courses.
      5) Continue to operate an evening technical institute until other adequate provision for such training is available in the community.
   b. Co-operative Education—The College will continue to adhere to the co-operative plan of education with possible changes in the requirement in the School of Arts and Sciences.
2. General Characteristics of the College
   a. Coeducational—day and evening.
   b. No graduate programs.
3. Curriculum—We foresee a trend to a larger body of core courses and as a result a smaller number of programs as a means of achieving greater efficiency and quality in our educational program. Also in the interest of efficiency we foresee the need for improved scheduling of course offerings to provide for more uniform teaching loads throughout the 3-quarter year.
4. Teaching Methods
   a. Adaptation to larger class size.
   b. Greater experimentation with independent study.
   c. Increased use of student assistants in laboratories.
   d. Expansion of the role of audio-visual services.
5. College Calendar—unchanged (Now operating round the clock and year round)

The space-need study being executed by Ceruti and the administration resulted in the identification of a primary need for a large lecture hall and centralized administrative offices. A building on the northwest corner of Euclid Avenue and East 24th Street (option property) combining these two facilities would permit conversion of the 8th, 9th and 10th floors of the Fenn Tower for dormitory space housing ninety students, plus additional faculty offices, and expansion of the bookstore on the first floor. At the April 18, 1962, board meeting the Trustees voted to proceed with the working drawings of a new Administration-Lecture Hall building.

During the discussion on the national trend in decreasing enrollments of engineering students Trustee G. J. Woodling, partner in a firm of patent attorneys, made the following comment: "Fenn graduates are able to begin inventing within one or two years following school, whereas graduates of schools where pure science is emphasized require 6 or 7 years to become inventive. He ascribed this to Fenn students having more exposure to learning involving the use of their hands."

Louis S. Peirce was re-nominated by the Board of Trustees of the YMCA to be its representative on the Fenn Board of Trustees, to which he was duly re-elected.

The nursing program in conjunction with Huron Road Hospital had been under study for several months. The Board of the Huron Road Hospital was desirous that the College assume all responsibility for the academic activities including all teaching personnel. The clinical laboratory work would still be executed at Huron Road Hospital, and the students would still be housed in the dormitory near the hospital. However, the rigid prerequisites for national accreditation and a decrease in applications for the following Fall Quarter induced the Fenn Trustees to drop the program. It reverted to a diploma program under Huron Road Hospital with courses given at Fenn under a contract basis. Those nursing students who had already started the three-year Associate Degree program were permitted to continue to graduation.

The 1962 Annual Spring Meeting of the Corporation was packed with history. It was held on May 22 at the Union Club, and it was designated the "Decennial Corporation Dinner" on the invitations. Chairman H. F. Burmester presided and in introducing the guests at the speakers' table lingered a little longer on the introduction of the newly appointed Dean of the School of Engineering, Burl H. Bush.

The reader may remember that Dean Bush was formerly Dean of Engineering prior to his departing in 1941 at the beginning of World War II to serve his country, being a graduate of the United States Naval Academy at Annapolis. For twenty-one years he had been associated with the Navy in shipbuilding, research activities, engineering, and education. He had just retired as Commander, and President Earnest, although he had never met Dean Bush, was successful in persuading him to leave San Diego and rejoin the Fenn Faculty. It could be said that Dean Bush and his charming wife, Eloise, were officially piped aboard the good ship "Fenn" at this Decennial Corporation Dinner.

Appropriately engraved medallions with the Fenn College seal on one face were awarded to Harry Anderson and Ronald Bender, Fenn Alumni, who tied for the highest grade in Structural Engineering in the Ohio State Registration Board Engineers-in-Training Examinations taken by over 400 applicants, and had the highest score of all applicants in all branches of engineering in the Cleveland area in 1962; George Bergold who made the highest grade in Structural Engineering for full registration certification; Terrence Telzrow, a chemical engineering senior who won first prize for a research paper entered in the American Chemical Society's Mid-Central Regional Student Contest (the second time this trophy was won by a Fenn Student; a third win would bring permanent possession to Fenn). Trustee Allen T. Perry was awarded a plaque faced with a Fenn medallion and an inscribed plate in recognition of his twenty-five years of loyal service as a Fenn Trustee. He had served on a number of Trustee committees and had been the Chairman of the Personnel Committee for a number of years.

President Earnest was then called upon to pay tribute to Stilwell in the unveiling of an oil portrait. Following is his introduction of Stilwell:

> Chairman Burmester, Members of the Fenn Family and honored guests;
>
> I have asked for the privilege tonight of honoring a truly great man and a staunch friend of Fenn College—Charles J. Stilwell. All of you are aware of Mr. Stilwell's long and devoted service to Fenn. He has given of himself in every way to build a permanent place for the future generations of Cleveland's youth.
>
> Charles, while you have a long record of community service, we, at Fenn, feel we have a prior claim upon you. You are as much

a part of Fenn as Fenn is a part of the community and we intend to make doubly sure that this alliance shall continue to exist in a permanent way.

Proud as we were of having a building named in your honor, we felt the College should have something more personal. Last Friday, in the studios of the distinguished artist, Edith Stevenson Wright, I had the privilege of seeing the portrait I am about to unveil, and to this audience, I must admit the thrill of the first view of Mrs. Wright's magnificent portrait of Mr. Stilwell was one I shall never forget.

This is a moment of personal gratification to me because of my personal respect for the man and what he has meant to Fenn College. The College is honored to salute you, Charles, and we shall own and display in perpetuity this portrait of you, a gift of an anonymous donor and friend of long-standing of the College.

At this point President Earnest unveiled the portrait, and Stilwell was given a standing ovation, both before and following his brief response. And, upon introduction, the artist, Edith Stevenson Wright, was greeted with a ringing round of applause. She had earlier won international acclaim through her portraits of Winston S. Churchill, Field Marshall Ferdinand Foch, President Calvin Coolidge, and Ambassador Myron T. Herrick. She had also done a portrait of Sereno Peck Fenn.

Since this was the Decennial Corporation Dinner, the main theme was the presentation of a report on a decade of achievement. Following is Chairman Burmester's introduction thereof:

Now, I want to talk to you about our President, G. Brooks Earnest. As most of you know, Dr. Earnest enjoyed a long teaching career at Case Institute of Technology, achieving the rank of a full professor, before coming to Fenn College.

In 1951, he came to Fenn as Dean of the School of Engineering and a year later—to the day—was appointed the third president of the College. For the past decade, Dr. Earnest has provided the leadership under which Fenn has achieved its present position.

He has brought many honors to Fenn, the most recent of which is his election as President of the country's oldest professional and technical society—the American Society of Civil Engineers. As President of this Society, he has caused attention—both national and international—to be focused on Fenn College.

Dr. Earnest is a man of wide civic, cultural, and educational interests. Since an institution is often the lengthened shadow of a single man, Fenn has indeed been fortunate in having a man of Dr. Earnest's talents.

It is my pleasure to give you Dr. Earnest who will present his report on a decade of achievement of Fenn College under his inspired leadership.

President Earnest's talk was an illustrated record of the first ten years of Fenn's existence as a private and independent institution of higher learning. Year by year highlights were described, and the charts shown in Chapter XII were enlarged on the screen with pertinent comments thereon. A résumé of the reasons for modifying the 1960 Integrated Plan to a cut-down structured ten-year plan was given, the main reasons being the proposed proliferation of branch campuses of the tax-supported state universities and the popular ground swell of the community colleges. Enrollment projections and faculty size were modified, and the nature and sequence of priorities were changed. The newly planned Administration and Lecture Hall structure was described, of course, with the continued need for financial support.

President Earnest praised the support of the Trustees, the Members of the Fenn Corporation, the Women's Advisory Board, the Civic Sponsoring Committee, the Faculty, Staff, Alumni and Students. He closed his remarks with the following statement: "I am confident that we *can* and *will* obtain the necessary financial support. If there is one certain thing that I have learned during my term as President of Fenn College, it is this: If a college tries persistently to serve the most vital needs of both the students and the community, *that* college will attract the support, both spiritual and material, to carry on this most essential endeavor."

The 1962 Decennial Corporation Dinner had many highlights. Chairman Burmester closed the meeting with one of them. He announced that through the efforts of Past Chairman Ellwood H. Fisher the Trustees of the Beaumont Foundation, through its Chairman Edgar Hahn, had pledged a gift of $100,000 to the Fenn new-building fund. He also thanked "Arch Colwell, Karl Bruch, Fred Crawford, Herb Ladds and Charlie White for their magnificent help as members of the Funds Development Committee." He announced that Fenn was in good financial health, new challenges lay ahead and that the College's sole ob-

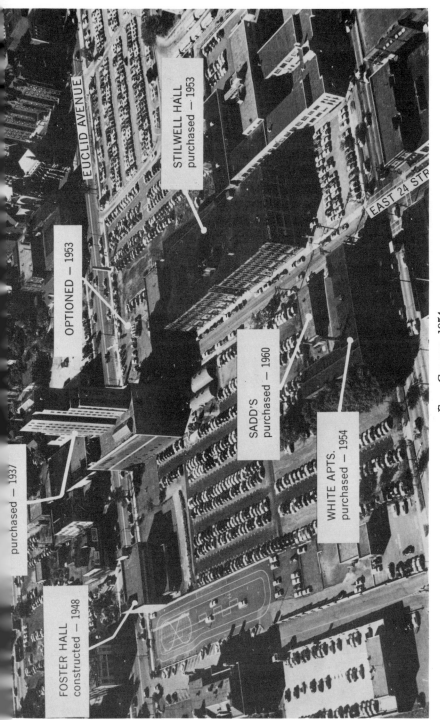

EUCLID AVENUE

EAST 24 STR

STILWELL HALL
purchased — 1953

OPTIONED — 1953

purchased — 1937

SADD'S
purchased — 1960

FOSTER HALL
constructed — 1948

WHITE APTS.
purchased — 1954

Fenn Campus—1954

Ohio Motors Company Building prior to conversion as Stilwell Hall

Stilwell Hall following conversion

Moving books from library in Fenn Tower to third floor in Stilwell Hall in September, 1959

New Stilwell Hall Library

Panel Hall, third floor of Fenn Tower

Annual meeting of Fenn College Corporation, November 20, 1956

Almeda J. Rothrock, Secretary to Dr. C. V. Thomas and
Assistant to Finance Director from January 12, 1912 to September 30, 1958
George B. Simon, Chairman, Department of Speech and Archivist

Air view, Fenn College campus in foreground (1963).
Downtown Cleveland in background.

Volunteer assistance by members of the Fenn College Women's Association

Board Chairman, Charles J. Stilwell and President G. Brooks Earnest study remodeling plans for Ohio Motors Building.

Paul R. Anders, Dean, School of Business Administration
Major B. Jenks, Dean, School of Arts and Sciences
William A. Patterson, Dean, School of Engineering; Provost, 1960–1965

Harold H. Burton, Justice, Supreme Court of the United States
and President G. Brooks Earnest

Graduation ceremony of Huron Road Hospital–Fenn College School of Nursing, September 15, 1960, at Forest Hill Presyterian Church.

The President's Cabinet

William A. Patterson, Provost; Vernon H. Davis, Finance Director; Murray M. Davidson, Director of Development.

President's Cabinet—1959
Standing, left to right: Dean of Engineering, William A. Patterson;
Dean of Business Administration, Paul R. Anders
Seated, left to right: Dean of Women, Selma M. Montasana; President,
G. Brooks Earnest; Dean, School of Arts & Sciences, Major B. Jenks

Twenty-Year Club—November 2, 1964

From top, left to right: A. Fazekas, J. Pease, Provost Patterson, B. Crider, R. Randle, Dean Herrick, H. Woodling, H. Morgan, D. Fabel, T. Dolson, M. Jordan, P. Earl, J. McGrew, C. Topp, Dean Jenks, E. Stefancic, R. Shindler, P. Bloomquist, M. Faust

N. Rimboi, K. Sherman, D. Theodore, M. Glaze, G. Simon, O. Twerell, I. Willoughby, J. McNeill, Dean Bush, W. Dilworth, G. Parmelee, F. Gallo, G. Leech, W. VanVoorhis

Not included in picture: Dean Anders

Professor Millard L. Jordan, former Chairman, Department of Social Studies. Upon retirement, Archivist of Fenn College and Cleveland State University.

jective was the enhancement of Greater Cleveland's intellectual, moral and social resources. A printed ten-year report was distributed at the close of the meeting.

Severance Hall was the setting for the 1962 Commencement Convocation held the evening of June 10. As usual the auditorium was filled to overflowing with graduates, relatives, friends, faculty, trustees, and alumni. The Honorable Anthony J. Celebrezze, Mayor, City of Cleveland, delivered the Commencement Address, entitled "Countdown for Tomorrow." There were 219 graduates distributed as follows: School of Arts and Sciences, 32; School of Business Administration, 76; and School of Engineering, 111.

Honorary Degrees were conferred upon the following:

> Dr. Robert M. Stecher, Doctor of Humane Letters (L.H.D.)
> Hassel Tippit, Doctor of Laws (LL.D.)
> Eugene W. Kettering, Doctor of Science (D. Sc.)
> Anthony J. Celebrezze, Doctor of Laws (LL.D.)

Milton J. Wurzbach, 1937, Charles R. Day, 1945, and Ernest C. Harris, 1939, were recipients of the Alumni Distinguished Service Awards at the Annual Alumni Dinner Meeting held at the Cleveland Engineering Society. Donald Susat of the Fenn College Class of 1937 was President of the Fenn Alumni Association for the school year 1961–1962.

The Minutes of the board meeting of September 19, 1962, opened with a sad note. The board observed the deaths of two members, Elbert H. Baker, Jr., a member since 1932, who had died August 16, 1962, and Thomas F. Peterson, a member since 1959, who had died August 24, 1962. A resolution, proposed by President Earnest, was passed providing for the establishment of a Trustee Memorial Collection in the Fenn Library to perpetuate the names of those Trustees who pass away during their terms of service to the College. On the occasion of the addition of each volume to the collection, notice thereof together with the resolution of the Trustees was tendered the family of the deceased as an expression of sympathy from the Board. The resolution is quoted here:

> A. Proposed resolution for institution of a Trustee memorial collection of books for the Fenn College Library
>> Be It Resolved that a Trustees' Memorial Collection be established in the Fenn College Library to perpetuate

the names of those Trustees who may pass away during their term of service to the institution, and that a suitable bookplate be designed to distinguish the memorial book.

B.   Proposed resolution for action by Board of Trustees for specific individuals

Whereas, the Trustees of Fenn College desire to record their deep sorrow at the death on
of their associate   who since
served as Trustee of this College, be it
Resolved, that the memory of
be perpetuated by a specific volume in the Trustees' Memorial Collection at the Fenn College Library.

Resolved Further, that a notice of such action be tendered to his family as a humble expression of the Board's deep sympathy.

C.   Proposed message for card to be tendered to the family of the deceased Trustee

In warm appreciation of his sincere effort as a Trustee of Fenn College, the Board of Trustees unanimously resolves to honor   by the addition of a new volume to the Trustees' Memorial Collection in the Fenn College Library. This gift is intended to perpetuate his memory by enriching the educational resources of coming generations.

President Earnest visited Eugene Kettering and Mr. Cessna of the Kettering Foundation in Dayton, Ohio, to request financial assistance for the Lecture Hall complex. Aid was refused because the foundation contributed for buildings only when used for science. Kettering suggested, however, that despite heavy financial commitments for the year, the Distribution Committee would entertain a request for laboratory equipment. Itemization of needed equipment in detail including catalog number was promptly submitted, and in a very short period authorization was given by the Kettering Foundation to purchase $50,000 worth of the scientific equipment requested.

President Earnest had also made several trips to Flint, Michigan, to describe the Fenn Co-op program to members of the Mott Foundation, which had been a generous contributor to the Flint Junior College. During these excursions he asked for a grant from the Mott Foundation toward the Lecture Hall complex, but in the end the Foundation decided to hold to its policy to contribute to physical facilities only in the Greater Flint area.

About this time Dr. Charles E. Chapman was appointed President of the newly legislated Cuyahoga Community College. He was introduced to the presidents of the Greater Cleveland colleges at a luncheon hosted by Ralph M. Besse, Chairman of the Cleveland Commission on Higher Education. Dr. Chapman stated that he expected to have day and evening classes in the Fall of 1963 in downtown rented facilities and evening classes only in the suburban areas, possibly east, west, and south. Kent State University still maintained three branches in Cleveland and Euclid, and Ohio State University had a branch in Lakewood High School. The Cleveland Foundation had made a grant to the Cuyahoga Community College toward start-up operating expenses. Money for physical facilities had to come from the voters' approval of a bond issue.

The Fund Fulfillment Report financed by the U.S. Steel Corporation (mentioned earlier) had submitted its ten-year report, and it was full of inaccuracies because of misunderstanding of the Fenn five-year Co-op Program. The other nine colleges being studied were on the usual four-year degree program and largely in liberal arts. Fenn College apparently proved quite complex because its five-year program was not reducible to the formula and computerization being used on the other nine colleges. The report was returned for revision.

Also discussed or approved at the September 19, 1962, board meeting were the operating budget for the fiscal year 1962–1963 with a total expense-income figure of $2,881,445 of which $247,758 were needed in gifts to balance the budget. The enrollment forecast for the Fall Quarter was 1,735 for the Day Division and 5,080 for the Evening Division. There was a slight drop from the Fall of 1961 because of the decrease in 18-year-olds and the increasing activity in the public college branches in the evening. A contract with the Federal Government for use of Fenn buildings for fall-out shelters was approved. The Euclid Innerbelt Association had just completed a report and plat on a portion of the downtown area including Fenn College for the request of urban renewal funds. A certain area of the plat adjacent to Fenn's property was designated as "Educational" assuming that Fenn would expand its campus in the years ahead. Also, the project depended upon educational use of certain of the area to gain matching federal funds.

Preliminary plans for the new Lecture Hall complex had been completed by Architect Ceruti and were ready for submission to the Trustee Planning Committee. Chairman A. T. Colwell of the Funds Development Committee plus seven Trustees called on twenty-two solicitors who in turn visited 150 corporations to raise development capital to build the Administration-Lecture Hall building. The Trustees quota was $250,000. Tentative arrangements were made for a future event to terminate the end of Phase II and kick off Phase III of Fenn's building program.

Professor Chester J. Kishel, Department of Mechanical Engineering was granted a two-year leave of absence to accept an assignment by Michigan State University at the Polytechnic School of the University of Sao Paulo, Brazil, South America, to consult, instruct, and advise concerning the establishment of IBM computer facilities under the sponsorship of the United States International Cooperative Administration.

One of the first orders of business at the November 13, 1962, Trustee meeting was the formal acceptance of and thanks for a gift of real estate, including completely furnished and equipped buildings thereon from Mr. and Mrs. Clayton G. Hale. Following is the resolution adopted by the board:

RESOLUTION

WHEREAS, Clayton G. Hale, a Trustee and long-time friend of Fenn College, has offered to convey to Fenn College as a gift a certain tract of land described as follows:

Situated in the Township of Medina, County of Medina and State of Ohio, and being a part of Lot 57 of said township, and bounded and described as follows: Beginning at a point in the center line of County Road 21 a distance of 1093.3 feet N. 89 deg. 38 min. E. along the center of said road from the west line of said lot; thence S. 0 deg. 10 min E. along the west line of lands formerly owned by J. Failor, and lands formerly owned by Alicia Clark, et al., 1315.4 feet to an iron pin; thence west 165.7 feet to an iron pin; hence N. 0 deg. 10 min. W. 1314.3 feet to the center line of County Road 21 and 30.0 feet north of an iron pin set on the southerly side of said road; thence N. 89 deg. 38 min. E. 165.7 feet to the place beginning, and containing within said boundaries 5.00 acres of land, as surveyed Aug. 12, 1946 by W. W. Anderson and A. W. Nettleton, Registered Surveyors, be the same more or less, but subject to all legal highways, together with all of the improvements on said property and the household and other furnishings, tools, benches, tables and other personal property of said Clayton G. Hale located on said premises which premises consist of approximately 5 acres of land located on County Road 21 in Medina Township, Medina County and State of Ohio.

NOW, THEREFORE, be it resolved by the Board of Trustees of Fenn College that said gift be accepted and that the President and Secretary of the Corporation be requested to express to Mr. and Mrs. Clayton G. Hale the very great appreciation of Fenn College for this generous gift.

This property, known as Hale's Hollow, adjoined a lake on a neighbor's property and cordial arrangements were made between Mr. Hale and the neighbor to pump water from the lake for shower and toilet purposes. The property, its physical facilities and the attractive view proved to be a wonderful retreat for the Fenn faculty and staff and their families. Many restful hours were spent there by the president's cabinet during planning sessions.

The Director of the Fund Fulfillment Association's ten-college 10-year financial study committed suicide, so the final report for Fenn College was never completed to the satisfaction of the Board Planning Committee. Louis Peirce, Chairman of this committee, announced at the November 13, 1962, board meeting that the report was "valuable for forward planning." President Earnest and his cabinet members had made preparations for a ten-year plan for Fenn, but had postponed their study awaiting the Fund Fulfillment report. There was no purpose in further delay, so President Earnest announced that his aim was to have a plan extending through 1973 completed by March 1963. Some of the material from the Fund Fulfillment report was revised for use in Fenn's ten-year report.

The preliminary plans for the new lecture hall complex were displayed and described. Action was taken to further explore the layout and acoustics to establish feasibility prior to starting the detailed working drawings. Of significance was the fact that the 600-seat auditorium was planned to be divided into two 300-seat lecture halls by a newly designed, acoustical, movable partition.

Trustee Edward Bartlett informed the board that the Euclid Innerbelt plan for development of the area had been presented to the city officials

and civic leaders and that the project depended on the educational
use of a portion of the area to make the plan eligible for matching
federal funds. Albert Levin, who owned the land occupied by Perry
Parking Company (between East 21st Street and Arthur G. McKee
property from Euclid Avenue to Chester Avenue), was originally opposed to the Innerbelt Plan, but he decided to support it since it allocated all of his property to educational usage, not withstanding he
had a client for early disposal of the property. There was even a thought
by the Euclid Innerbelt Association of projecting the new community
college campus on the Levin property, but the Fenn Trustees felt it
would not be good policy to have the two educational institutions in
close proximity.

Other items of information from the Minutes of the November 13,
1962, board meeting are as follows:

1. The receipt of the Wynonah E. Thompson bequest on October
    1 amounting to $6,384.63 toward scholarships and $27,979.25
    unrestricted for a total of $34,363.88. The board designated
    the unrestricted amount as "Acting Endowment Fund."
2. Through payment of $2,000 in October, the College completed
    the last installment on the Sadd property. The only remaining
    mortgage balances were $145,000 on the northwest corner of
    Euclid-East 24th Street (option property) and $13,983.23 on
    the Warters parcel (a long term mortgage). These, plus $74,000
    on a bank note, comprised the entire indebtedness of the Col-
    lege as of that date.
3. Chairman Burmester proposed the following "resolution of com-
    mendation of President Earnest for his work in carrying the
    name of Fenn College to the membership of the American
    Society of Civil Engineers while President of the Society." It
    was unanimously adopted:

Gentlemen, I propose a resolution of commendation of Brooks
Earnest for his fine accomplishment as President of the American
Society of Civil Engineers. In that position he headed a board
comprised of the nation's distinguished civil engineers, governing
the affairs of the oldest professional and technical society in the
Western Hemisphere. He traveled tirelessly more than 45,000 air
miles. He made appearances throughout the United States and also
in Canada, Europe, Central and South America, representing the So-

ciety and Fenn College. From the speaker's rostrum and the printed page he reached the Society's 50,000 members, as their presiding officer and—in his person or his words—as President of Fenn College. He should be commended not only for the fine job he did for the American Society of Civil Engineers, but for his splendid achievement in the role of ambassador extraordinary for Fenn College. Brooks, we thank you.

The last Fenn Family meeting of 1962 was the Annual Corporation meeting held at the Union Club on December 4. Trustee William J. Hunkin, II, Chairman of the Nominating Committee moved the nomination of the following who were officially elected: Arthur S. Armstrong, Trustee, Class of 1967; Clayton G. Hale and Allen T. Perry, Trustees, Class of 1967, to succeed Dr. Robert M. Stecher and Vernon B. Stouffer, who returned to the Corporation; Richard T. Baker, Class of 1967, to succeed H. F. (Fritz) Meyer, who retired at the completion of his term; Frank L. Elmendorf, Class of 1967, to fill the term of Thomas F. Peterson who died August 24, 1962; Alfred G. Hose, Alumni Trustee, to succeed Wilson B. Creveling (3-year term); Donald C. Adams, Bertrand J. Belda, Donald S. Carmichael, Irving S. Dow, Herbert T. Florence, Herbert S. Ide, Jr., Sam S. Mullen, Robert W. Ramsdell, T. L. Strimple for reelection to the Corporation after having been retired for one year; and George P. Bickford, Merrill Cox, Francis A. Coy, Charles L. Goldsword, Robert D. Hickok, Jack W. Lampl, Jr., David C. Lincoln, Raymond S. Livingstone, Galen Miller, John R. Ruhlman, Ellery Sedgwick, Jr., Curtis L. Smith, Chester A. Thompson for election to the Corporation for three-year terms expiring in 1965.

President Earnest reported at this Corporation meeting that the figure at the bottom of the Fenn balance sheet of $8,683,000 had increased by $898,500 over the past year, of which $826,000 was in plant funds. Total operating income for 1962 was $2,949,000 and just ten years ago it was under $1,000,000. Day school enrollment was reported as 1,681 against 1,663 the previous year and for evening school 5,384 against 5,111.

Trustee Arch T. Colwell informed the group that one-third of the $1,800,000 goal was in sight for Phase III of the Development Program.

The address of the evening was given by Ralph M. Besse, Chairman of the Cleveland Commission on Higher Education and President of the Cleveland Electric Illuminating Company. It was entitled "The

Status of Education in Cleveland" and proved to be exceptionally timely and suitable to the occasion.

Additional highlights for the year included the opening of a new Management Laboratory in the School of Business Administration under the leadership of Professor Harry M. London and through the cooperation of the Fenn Chapter of the Society for the Advancement of Management and the generous business and industrial friends of the College. Drs. Walter Van Voorhis, Frank Bockhoff and Paul Olynyk received special grants for research projects during the year. The Department of Cooperative Education provided jobs for 2,125 students, who earned a total $2,033,000 during the year. The average monthly wage for all students was $331. Fifty-five different companies were represented by 79 officers at luncheons on the campus to hear Fenn's story on Co-op education. The Technical Institute under the able direction of Nicholas Rimboi had a total enrollment of 1,130 students. It sponsored two seminars during the year, one on Top Management and one on Fluid Power. Fenn had its first wrestling team since 1935 and its best basketball season for many years with 9 wins and 9 losses. Professor Robert F. Busbey was chosen to coach the United States Olympic Women's Swimming Team which participated in the 1964 Olympic Games in Japan.

An important area of development in the School of Arts and Sciences, under the direction of Dean Jenks, during 1962 was in the fine arts. The growth of the fine arts program of the College through the scheduling of assembly programs, musical events, art exhibits, fine films, plays, and poetry activities showed a growing concern with the total education of the student with special emphasis on his extracurricular influences. Increasingly, the College sought to create a community in which faculty and students joined in developing an atmosphere of learning and culture.

The School of Business Administration, under the able direction of Dean Anders, extended on an experimental basis the use of large lecture and smaller quiz sections in its classes in Economic History and Principles of Economics. This method was designed to increase the effectiveness of teaching, which Fenn would be able to use more extensively upon completion of the new lecture hall-administration building. A workshop in Economic Education was conducted on sixteen Saturday mornings with twenty teachers of social studies from Cleveland high schools.

The annual report of the Fenn Bureau of Business Research received statewide recognition. It was prepared at the request of the Cleveland Chapter of Independent Garage Owners of Ohio to provide a cost study of garage services. The report proved to be so useful that the State Association requested copies for state and national distribution.

The School of Engineering, under the able direction of Dean Bush, revised and up-dated its curricula of Chemistry and Chemical Engineering. The development of the Unit Operations Laboratory was practically completed. The Meriam Hydraulics Laboratory was completely remodeled. The $50,000 grant from the Kettering Foundation aided materially in the expansion of the advanced laboratory program in physics.

President Earnest was appointed to the John Fritz Medal Board of Award and the A.S.C.E. Task Committee on Appointments. An unusual number of honors were bestowed on the President during the year 1962 largely because of his being President of A.S.C.E. Some of these included:

1. Highest citation of the Ohio Society of Professional Engineers.
2. Honorary Membership, Cleveland Engineering Society.
3. Honorary Member, La Sociedad Panamena de Ingenieros y Architectos. (Panama)
4. Honorary Member, Colombia, South America, Professional Engineering Society. (Bogota)
5. Honorary Member, Student Chapter, A.S.C.E., University of Puerto Rico. (Maraquez)
6. Honorary Commendation, first Water Resource Engineering Conference, Omaha, Nebraska.
7. Presidents' Plaque, A.S.C.E.
8. The Ritual of the Calling of an Engineer, Iron Ring of Canada.
9. Huesped de Honor, Universidad Central de Venezuela, Caracas, Venezuela.

The encumbent officers were re-elected at the first Board meeting in 1963, held on January 30, namely:

Harry F. Burmester, Chairman
Dr. James C. Hodge, Vice Chairman
Vollmer W. Fries, Treasurer
Vernon H. Davis, Secretary

As of the date of this board meeting, the only indebtedness of the College was a $70,000 mortgage to the Motors Realty Company and a $13,000 mortgage on the Warters property.

The greater part of this meeting concerned the Euclid Innerbelt Association plan for the neighborhood based upon Urban Renewal legislation. Trustee Bartlett, Chairman of the Association, explained that about thirty parcels of land were involved, and that it was essential that either a hospital or another college become a party to the plan in order for it to qualify for the type of federal financial assistance required.

Chairman Burmester indicated the Executive Committee, which had met on January 21, 1961, was not opposed to a community college or to the Euclid Innerbelt Plan. The community college organization had already been formed, and, whereas the locations of the college were first thought of as being in Euclid and Parma, a downtown branch thereof had already been started in the former Brownell School building at East 14th Street near Bolivar Road. The community college was also negotiating for the Crile Hospital property in Parma Heights.

Most members of the board felt that the community college should not be located near Fenn College, and that it would be preferable to have it located in the St. Vincent area if there was to be a downtown unit, but, under no circumstances should the board oppose a community college. As the result of the board's action the Euclid Innerbelt Plan was doomed, for no hospital or other college was considered for the site.

Chairman Burmester announced that a bill was then pending to create a Board of Regents which would be in responsible charge of all administrative, academic, and financial affairs of all public higher education in Ohio. The bill was enacted into law, and Dr. John D. Millett, President of Miami University, Oxford, Ohio, was appointed Chancellor of the Board of Regents. Richard T. Baker, Trustee of Fenn was appointed to the board by Governor Rhodes.

The Trustee Planning Committee and Executive Committee had met with Architect Ceruti and were assured through his contact with a firm of Boston consultants that the proposed auditorium with movable partition dividers was feasible from architectural, acoustical and esthetic viewpoints. As a result, the board authorized Ceruti to proceed with the working drawings for the projected Lecture Hall-Administration building.

XIV

It is the beginning of the end.

Charles Maurice de Talleyrand-Périgord, 1754–1838.

You will soon understand the reason for the quotation at the beginning of this chapter, i.e., "It is the beginning of the end."

President Earnest was in attendance at an A.S.C.E. Board of Direction meeting in Milwaukee, Wisconsin, May 13, 1963, when he was called out of the meeting about 11:00 a.m. (Cleveland time) for an emergency phone call from Warren H. Chase, Director of Commerce, State of Ohio. Chase had previously retired as the Vice-President for Engineering, of the Ohio Bell Telephone Company and was a friend of long standing of President Earnest. The following was the information reported by Mr. Chase:

1. Governor Rhodes wants to do as much as he can for private colleges.
2. The Governor is not sold on community colleges.
3. The Governor feels there is a need to bolster higher education in *practical* areas, especially engineering.
4. The Governor inquired whether Fenn would like to be a state university. There is a need for one in this area. The same management would continue, there would be an expansion in physical facilities, the school would fall under the jurisdiction of the Board of Regents like other state universities.
5. Only three people know about this discussion; Governor Rhodes, Warren Chase, and President Earnest.

What President Earnest did not know was that about an hour before the call from Mr. Chase, Provost Patterson had received a call from Richard L. Maher, Politics Editor, *The Cleveland Press*, who stated that key men in the Rhodes administration had recommended that Fenn

GIVE LIGHT AND THE PEOPLE WILL FIND THEIR OWN WAY

The Cleveland Press

A Scripps-Howard Newspaper

LOUIS B. SELTZER, Editor   GEORGE E. CARTER, Business Manager

Net Paid Circulation for the year ending Sept. 30, 1963

351,065

OHIO'S LARGEST DAILY NEWSPAPER

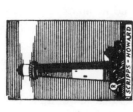

KEY RHODES AIDES URGE STATE TO TAKE OVER FENN COLLEGE

By RICHARD MAHER
Politics Editor

Key men in the Rhodes administration at Columbus have recommended that the state take over Fenn College and develop it into a major state university concentrating on engineering and scientific research, it was learned today.

CP, May 14, 1963

The recommendation follows a survey of educational institutions made at the direction of Governor Rhodes.

Rhodes asked for the survey in January with a view toward determining where the state could step up its efforts in the field of nuclear sciences and new technological methods to meet space age competition.

Top men in his administration, it is understood, are almost unanimous in recommending that a new state university be set up in Cleveland.

Most in Taxes

They point out that Cleveland, the largest city in the state, contributes most in taxes to state-supported universities, that it has the largest single student group at Ohio State and that it is the ideal place for a space age engineering school because of such facilities as the NASA laboratory here.

Fenn was pegged by those who have made the recommendation because of these conditions:

AN EXCELLENT engineering school, and a policy of educating without frills.

ITS CLOSENESS to downtown and its availability to public transportation.

THE POSSIBILITY that it could be expanded through urban renewal or eminent domain as a state university.

As yet no approach has been made to Fenn by the state, it was learned.

However, it is known that Rhodes long has believed that the Cleveland area is entitled to more state education money and that it should have a state institution of its own.

Funds for the takeover of Fenn — if it can be arranged with the trustees — would come from a proposed $200,000,000 bond issue for education purposes which it is expected the Legislature will place on the fall ballot.

Reports are that upwards of $15,000,000 would be needed to acquire the property. Fenn is owned by the Fenn College Corp., which is composed of a group of businessmen of the community.

The survey sent on to the governor recommends that no immediate change be made in the school's setup if the state should be successful in making it a state university.

It is planned that the present board of trustees, composed of prominent business leaders of the community, remain.

Harry F. Burmester, chairman of the Fenn trustees, said he had not heard of the proposal.

★

★

★

★

★

★

CP, May 14, 1963

State Hasn't Talked To Fenn's President

By BUD WEIDENTHAL

Fenn College president G. Brooks Earnest said today he was "amazed and surprised" to learn that the Rhodes administration is considering converting Fenn to a state institution.

"We're a private institution and making extensive plans to stay that way," said Earnest in a telephone interview. He is in Milwaukee attending a meeting of the American Society of Civil Engineers.

The educator was commenting on a story in yesterday's Press revealing that leaders in the state administration had recommended that Fenn become a state university concentrating on engineering and scientific research.

News to Him

Earnest said he had never been approached by members of the administration, and so far as he knew a state takeover had not been discussed with the Fenn board.

But sources here reveal that board members have been approached informally and that some of them expressed interest in the proposal.

It is said negotiations in such a deal would be long and detailed, possibly taking two years or more. The deal, it was suggested, might be similar to the transfer of the University of Buffalo from a private to a state-operated institution.

Also Surprised

Ralph Besse, chairman of the Cleveland Commission on Higher Education, said he had not heard of the Fenn proposal. He said that such a move should be given careful study in relation to the total needs in Greater Cleveland.

He stressed that it was important that studies already made be consulted and that the development of the new Cuyahoga Community College not be overlooked.

The commission had backed the new community college in the hope that it would be able to serve the higher education needs of the county.

If the Buffalo pattern is followed in a transfer of Fenn to the state, the college trustees would give the buildings and equipment to the state in return for a promise of a major increase in operating funds and a state-sponsored building program.

The Fenn plant is valued at $14,000,000 and its annual operating budget about $3,000,000. An endowment of slightly more than $500,000 would be turned over to the state.

Tuition would be reduced to compare with other state universities — a decrease of about $600 per year. And faculty salaries would have to rise sharply.

★

★

★

★

★

★

City Doesn't Need a State College, Commission Here Tells Rhodes

By BUD WEIDENTHAL

Cleveland does not need a new state university now, the Cleveland Commission on Higher Education said today in a statement directed at the Rhodes Administration.

The commission urged the governor and his advisors instead to move ahead rapidly in developing a strong county-wide community college "which, if properly supported, would be able to accept twice as many students as a new state university at a fraction of the cost . . ."

The commission issued the statement after reports that the Administration was considering converting Fenn College into a state university. Fenn is a member of the commission.

The commission, composed of six civic leaders and presidents of the five major colleges and universities in Cleveland, commended Rhodes for his concern for higher education.

But it urged him to refer to the four major surveys of higher education needs in the state made during the past decade.

"Each of these surveys was made by competent people," said the statement. "Each contains a good deal of data, much of which is specific to Cuyahoga County. Each has recommendations which should be carefully analyzed in the light of the Cleveland community's long-term higher educational planning.

"None of the existing reports advise or advocate a new state university for Ohio or for Cleveland at the present time."

"Cleveland's problem," the commission said, "is to develop a diversified program of higher education in private and public colleges."

It urged that colleges be available for all income groups.

CP, May 16, 1963

Commission president is Ralph Besse, Illuminating Co. president. Other members are Mrs. Robert Jamison, vice president; Harry Burmester, Union Commerce Bank president, treasurer; attorney Frank Joseph, secretary; Nat Howard, former editor of the Cleveland News, and Edward Sloane, president of Ogelbay Norton Co.

Burmester is also president of Fenn trustees.

CP, November 12, 1963

The County and the State

Details of Governor Rhodes' proposal for making Fenn College part of the state system disclose two things:

TWENTY-FIVE MILLION DOLLARS, which the governor says he can spend here, is a lot of money. No community would wish to turn down an educational grant of that size.

A TECHNICAL INSTITUTE, which is what Rhodes is proposing for Cleveland under the wing of Fenn College, would probably force Cuyahoga Community College and Fenn to exchange roles.

The Community College was set up to provide two-year higher education for Greater Clevelanders, with its curriculum to include

Fenn Hesitates on Rhodes Offer

By BUD WEIDENTHAL

A proposal by Governor Rhodes to build a $25,000,000 institution for Fenn College in the St. Vincent Urban Renewal area and turn over the present Fenn building to the Cuyahoga Community College met with hesitant response today from Fenn trustees.

Said trustees President Harry Burmester: "So far as we are concerned Fenn College will continue to be a private institution." He said the board is considering the Rhodes offer but has reached no conclusion.

"We must base our decision on what is best for all the people of Cleveland," said Burmester. He added that he would have no further comment.

Other board members said they were surprised and confused at the Rhodes offer but indicated their readiness to study the plan.

★

Rhodes made his offer at a meeting last night at the Union Club attended by the governor, three members of the Board of Regents and the Fenn executive committee.

THE GOVERNOR said the state was interested in contracting with Fenn to operate a major technical institute for the training of technicians for industry. This kind of technician is badly needed in the Cleveland both liberal arts and technical courses. A state technical institute would duplicate much of CCC's function.

Governor Rhodes' motives are commendable and understandable. He wants to provide educational facilities for training people to get jobs, the kind of jobs Cleveland industry needs now and will need more in the future.

However, the governor is the greatest proponent of eliminating duplication in services paid for by tax money. And Cuyahoga County has already voted to tax itself to support something closely akin to what the governor proposes.

The new state Board of Regents should have the ultimate say on establishment of a new school. The Regents were set up by the Rhodes administration to direct Ohio's educational development and to minimize overlapping and excess facilities.

Let's hear what the Regents think of the new Fenn proposal. Civic, educational and industrial leaders of Greater Cleveland also should be heard on a matter of such importance.

★

CP, 11-12-63

land area, the governor said.

The present Fenn program of business, liberal arts and engineering would remain the same under the Rhodes proposal. But they would be housed in the state financed campus.

The offer to pour state funds into a Fenn technical institute brought bitter criticism from Robert Lewis, president of the Cuyahoga Community College trustees.

"I am angry, frustrated and surprised," said Lewis. "We have labored mightily for two years to bring a new public college to Cleveland which would serve the needs of the community.

"One of our major objectives has been to provide the kind of technical program that the business leaders of the city told us they wanted. We have hired a director of technical education who is among the most experienced and best in the nation. We have been building a competent staff.

"WE ARE A STATE institution and we have kept the state officials fully informed of our progress. We are ready with the backing of the people of Cuyahoga County to move ahead.

"And now without ever discussing it with us, the governor is saying that we must cancel one of our major objectives. I call this poor planning. I think this is bad for the future of education in Ohio."

Bartunek Charges Betrayal by Rhodes

Democratic State Sen. Joseph A. Bartunek charged today that "the people of Cleveland have been betrayed by Governor Rhodes."

"Many of us have supported the Community College on the understanding it was designed to meet the special needs of Cleveland. We are going to fight for this all the way down to the wire.

"There is no logical reason," said the senator, "why the governor should now propose to set up a separate state-financed technical institute to be run by Fenn."

Bartunek said he would seek support of the six-member Cleveland delegation in fighting the Rhodes proposal when it comes to the Senate during a special session next month.

Bartunek pointed out that he broke from his party and supported the 250-million-dollar state bond issue on the understanding that $12,000,000 would go to the Community College.

Press, 11-13-63

Fenn Teachers Split on Ohio's Tech Offer

The Fenn College faculty was reported divided today on the offer by Governor Rhodes to have Fenn operate a $25,000,000 technical institute here.

The professors discussed the state proposal at yesterday's regular faculty meeting, presided over by President G. Brooks Earnest.

While guarded in their comments faculty members interviewed by The Press expressed considerable concern about the plan.

There was, however, much interest in the possibility of Fenn becoming a full state university.

The governor had proposed that Fenn operate a technical institute for the state on a 40- to 50-acre campus to be financed by the state in the St. Vincent urban renewal area. The present Fenn buildings would then be turned over to the Cuyahoga Community College.

GOV. RHODES had told Fenn officials of the great need for trained technicians in the state. Industry is seeking employees who have been trained as engineering assistants, draftsmen, electronics aides and the like, said Rhodes.

Rhodes told of plans to build at least seven such institutes in Ohio. He said he believed Fenn was the most likely college in Greater Cleveland to operate an institute.

He said it could be closely tied to Fenn's engineering school. Rhodes insisted Fenn would not lose its identity but would operate the technical institute as an adjunct to its present curriculum.

THE NEED for technicians to work with professional engineers has been mentioned often by business leaders in the Cleveland area. At a meeting earlier this year, executives said that three to five technicians were needed in certain areas for every trained engineer or scientist.

A survey by the Cuyahoga Community College last year found there was demand for thousands of persons with such training.

Harry Burmester, president of Fenn trustees, said that Fenn's executive committee will meet to consider the governor's proposal.

Not a Rush Decision

Fenn College officials are following proper procedure in placing the school's future before the state Board of Regents.

The question arises because of Governor Rhodes' interest in founding a technical institute here, under the direction of Fenn. Eventual state investment of $25,000,000 for a new campus is promised by the governor.

Rhodes' proposal—attractive in itself—dims the future of the sprightly new Cuyahoga Community College for which 215,029 county residents voted tax support last week. Another new publicly-supported, two-year school offering technical courses would be a strong competitor for the community college, particularly with the state treasury behind it.

"We want to determine what is best for Fenn and what is best for Cuyahoga County," said Harry Burmester, president of Fenn's trustees. That goes for everybody, particularly when $25,000,000 for education is involved.

The Little Hoover Commission's analysis of state universities said this week: "The limited funds available for education must be wisely directed toward the most productive educational use." The commission notes that the Board of Regents has this responsibility.

Surely the decision on how best to spend the $25,000,000 here—if that sum is available—does not have to be made overnight. Nor even before the brief Legislature session in December.

Cuyahoga County wants and deserves its fair share of Issue #1 proceeds, but the money should be invested in education on a sound, long-range basis.

THE PLAIN DEALER

Ohio's Largest Morning and Sunday Newspaper

HERMAN L. VAIL,
President

F. WILLIAM DUGAN,
Vice President and General Manager

THOMAS VAIL,
Publisher and Editor

PHILIP W. PORTER,
Executive Editor

Daily 328,314   Net Paid Circulation for 6 months ending Sept. 30, 1963   **Sunday 485,237**
as filed with the Audit Bureau of Circulations, subject to audit.

CPD, May 14, 1963

TAKEOVER BY OHIO AT FENN 'PREMATURE'

Gov. James A. Rhodes and his cabinet have been discussing means of helping Fenn College turn out more graduates in the physical sciences, but talk about Ohio taking over the school is "premature."

This information came yesterday from Warren H. Chase, Ohio director of commerce, who has been assigned by the governor to survey the state's technical education facilities. Object of the survey, he said, was "to see what we can do to improve the engineering and science image of Ohio."

Commenting on published speculation of Fenn becoming a state college, Chase said he was "disgusted" by the report, "because Fenn has not been talked to." He added:

"I am all in favor, if it can be worked out.

"But as to whether it ever comes to fruition, your guess is as good as mine."

CHASE, a Clevelander and a retired vice president of the Ohio Bell Telephone Co., said "Gov. Rhodes' idea is to have a state college in this area."

How to lose a delicious fish dinner.

One possibility, he said, was for a training school for technicians, or "engineers aides," in various fields. This plan, however, would not necessarily be feasible for Fenn. Chase said the college "has great possibilities in the next 20 years or so."

"Whether it (Fenn) goes this way or whether it goes its own way, it should some day get university status," Chase, a member of the Fenn College Corp., said.

"Because Fenn is a good school, we have been trying to help it out. But when the state starts helping one private school, it's like opening Pandora's box," he added.

"There are other difficulties. I would like to see Fenn's co-operative plan keep on going, but this would make it different from any other state college in Ohio."

While a state college appears in the offing for the Cleveland area, and while Gov. Rhodes intends "to establish several technical institutions throughout the state," the notion of Fenn becoming a state college "is just a glint in somebody's eye," Chase said.

PD, November 12, 1963

State Offers Fenn New $12-Million Institute

Technical Course Granted and Shift in Site Proposed

By ALBERT C. ANDREWS

An offer of state affiliation with Fenn College that might involve moving the school's downtown campus was proposed last night to Fenn trustees.

An initial state grant of $12 million was offered, it was learned by The Plain Dealer. This aid might rise later to $25 million.

Goal would be to create what one high state official called "the finest technical institute in the country."

Among those taking part in a meeting at the Union Club were Gov. James A. Rhodes; Roger Cloud, speaker of the Ohio House of Representatives, and Richard L. Krabach, state finance director. Also president were Harold W. Oyster, chairman of the new State Board of Regents, Warren H. Chase, board secretary, and James O. Ford, board member.

They conferred with Harry F. Burmester, Fenn board chairman; other trustees, and President G. Brooks Earnest.

HIGH POINTS of the state's proposal:

• Fenn might become a full four-year state university.

• A state program, on the other hand, might be operated under contract. Fenn would thus retain its own name, trustees and administration.

STATE GRANT OF $ MILLIONS TO ENLARGE LEARNING FACILITIES

TOP NOTCH TECHNICAL CONTRIBUTION TO THE COMMUNITY

AMMUNITION $1- GRAND

FENN COLLEGE

Interested in big game?

The main part of the Fenn College campus, looking west on Euclid Avenue. The Foster Engineering Building is in the foreground and Fenn Tower, at E. 24th Street, in the background.

State and Fenn College officials as they met here last night. From left: James O. Ford, State Board of Regents member; Harold W. Oyster, regents chairman; Harry F. Burmester, Fenn board chairman; Roger Cloud, house speaker; Gov. James A. Rhodes; G. Brooks Earnest, Fenn president, Richard L. Krabach, state finance director.
Plain Dealer Photo (Norbert J. Yassanye)

● The initial state program probably would cover a two-year sequence for engineering technicians. Other Fenn departments would not be affected.

● Space requirements probably would make it necessary to move the campus from its present location at Euclid Avenue and E. 24th Street. The campus was said to be so located that further expansion there would be impossible.

AFTER THE MEETING, neither state nor Fenn officials wanted to be quoted on details.

Gov. Rhodes termed the session "a very interesting exploratory discussion."

Burmester said most of the conference had concerned the proposed technical institute.

He added that a decision would have to await discussion by his board of trustees. The trustees plan to confer further with the State Board of Regents, he said.

A STATE OFFICIAL suggested that a new Fenn campus location be found in a downtown urban renewal area and that the present campus be made available to Cuyahoga Community College.

The community college, now in temporary quarters, has an option on a permanent site at E. 30th Street and Scovill Avenue S.E. in the St. Vincent Urban Renewal Area.

State officials said they would make available to Fenn $12 million from the $250-million bond issue approved by voters last week. An appropriation covering this and other educational needs would first have to be made by the General Assembly, which is to meet in an adjourned session on Dec. 2.

ADDITIONAL FUNDS, it was hoped, would come from other sources.

A state spokesman said the plan could be put into full effect in two years if

Fenn trustees approved.

The initial level of training to be offered, that of engineering technician, would be comparable to that of medical technician. The two-year graduate receives a diploma as an associate rather than a bachelor's degree. He is sometimes termed "semi-professional."

A state official called the lack of such technicians one of the most pressing problems in Ohio. He said industrial firms are threatening to move to other states because of inability to obtain such employees.

THIS OFFICIAL called Erie County Technical Institute, two-year college near Buffalo, N. Y., the finest such school in the country now.

"We can do better than that," he said.

Erie County offers programs in such varied fields as construction and industrial technology, dental hygiene and food service.

TUITION FOR THREE quarters at Erie County is $270. Fenn tuition is about $1,000, depending upon the student's program.

Operation by contract would be somewhat similar to a plan used by some branches of the State University of New York, SUNY, for example, has several contract branches at Cornell University.

PD, 11-14-63

KEEP PRESENT FENN SETUP, STUDENTS SAY

By ALBERT C. ANDREWS

Fenn College students, debating possible state aid to their college, want no change in their present program.

The cooperative plan, in particular, was endorsed strongly by students polled yesterday by The Plain Dealer.

"This school survives on its co-op plan," one student said of the program which schedules alternate three-month periods of work and study.

Quizzed on state aid in general, some students favored and others opposed it.

THE STUDENT newspaper, the Cauldron, said yesterday in an editorial:

"It is quite obvious to everyone that we have ever talked to at Fenn that the school can use more money . . . "We all prefer private schools; but better a good state college than a struggling private institution on its way down."

The editorial was written by Cauldron Editor Richard A. Ellis, a senior from Dayton.

"There is a great deal of feeling here that if there is going to be a state university in Cleveland it had better be Fenn," Ellis told The Plain Dealer. "If the state opens a separate university, Fenn won't be here."

GOV. JAMES A. Rhodes and other state officials, in a meeting Monday with Fenn trustees suggested that the state finance a two-year technical institute to be operated by Fenn. The college would retain all of its present programs and its name, trustees and administration.

It was suggested that Fenn move from its present campus to a larger site in an urban renewal area.

However, Dale Baldwin, senior accounting major of 1628 Pleasantdale Avenue S.W., felt the present site offered ample room for expansion.

Other student comments included:

SHARON HOBART, senior nursing student, 6947 Hilton Road, Brecksville: "I think state assistance would be all right as long as the college is allowed to retain its present program and even though our program is actually better. But I am afraid that with state aid we will have the state telling us what to do."

TOM ROYER, freshman mathematics major, 3113 W. 100th Street: "If Fenn became a state university it probably would help prestige. It's easier now for an Ohio State graduate to get a job than a Fenn graduate, even though our program is actually better. But I'm afraid state aid affiliation would lower our standards."

AMY KOSSUTH, evening English major, 4430 Barrett Road, Olmsted Township: "As long as they don't try to confine Fenn to a technical institute, it would be all right. We should retain our liberal arts and cooperative programs."

STATE SEN. Anthony O. Calabrese, D-Cleveland, backed the state proposal. He warned that an argument might jeopardize Greater Cleveland's chances of getting any educational aid.

Earlier, State Sen. Joseph W. Bartunek, D-Cleveland, opposed the governor's suggestion. Bartunek said he favored creation of a four-year state university here. He believed a technical institute should be operated by Cuyahoga Community College rather than separately.

PD, 11-20-63

★ ★ ★ ★ ★ ★ ★ ★

READERS SAY
Fenn College Board Wise

You censure, and properly, workmen in New York who, without conscience, became part of a large jewel robbery.

In a preceding editorial you castigate "some quarters" in our community for not grabbing at the money Gov. Rhodes has offered the community for education . . . an offer not without strings.

The same conscience that should keep us in moral bounds also requires that any responsible organization carefully count the cost of accepting such an offer. The trustees of Fenn College are behaving as responsible stewards when they consider carefully every implication of Gov. Rhodes' offer before accepting. We must believe that these trustees will consider not only their own interests and purposes but also those of the entire community.

In this editorial you have prejudged the decision of this group of men. This is not worthy of your responsibility to the community.

R. J. BERRY

1831 Richmond Road,
Cleveland 24

P.D., 11-12-63

Rhodes on the Move

In his offer to Fenn College, Gov. James A. Rhodes demonstrates his sincere interest in advancing the allied causes of higher education, industry and the Cleveland area.

The state-assisted technical training school which the governor wants added to Fenn would provide the technicians so urgently needed in modern industry.

If Ohio, the Cleveland area in particular, is to keep the industry it now has and attract new industry, it must supply these technicians in quantity in the years to come.

Wisely, the governor has not laid down an inflexible set of conditions that Fenn would have to meet in order to qualify for the proffered millions of dollars in state assistance.

He would have the college's present board of trustees continue in full control.

He would have the college continue all the courses and degrees it presently provides. As a supplementary and new impor-

tant function, however, he would have Fenn become one of the nation's centers for technical training.

Some of the Fenn trustees may be fearful of any kind of a tie-up with the state. Some may be hesitant about any change affecting the basic purposes of the college.

Against this they must weigh the rare opportunity that is presented, the demonstrated need of industry for trained technicians and the future of metropolitan Cleveland.

Some friends of Cuyahoga Community College fear that the offer to Fenn, if accepted, means that the community college will get nothing. We think their fears are exaggerated. Present Fenn quarters might be turned over to the community college if the state builds new and bigger quarters for Fenn.

In total concept this could be something big for Cleveland.

It deserves utmost consideration.

LET'S NOT MUFF THIS CHANCE

It would be unthinkable for Greater Cleveland to lose the opportunity it now has to receive up to $25-million in new state funds for higher education facilities.

But it could happen.

In view of the pettiness and bickering that have been the reaction in some quarters to Gov. James A. Rhodes' offer, the Cleveland area could end up with nothing.

The negative thinkers and those with axes to grind are dissatisfied with the way the money would like to see the money allocated. They want to see it go to their own pet projects. They are creating confusion, muddying up the waters.

Out of this needless confusion, one fact stands eminently clear. Neither the private college status of Fenn nor of any other college would be disturbed by acceptance of the governor's generous offer.

The situation calls for straight thinking, clear thinking and quick action.

On Dec. 2 the Ohio Legislature will meet and will enact legislation to provide for the distribution of at least a substantial part of the $175 million that the voters have approved for higher education facilities.

There are demands from all over the state for a share of the bond issue money. And those demands have been growing every day since the issue was approved.

It would be helpful if Fenn College could reach a speedy decision as to whether it wishes to take advantage of the governor's offer.

We are hopeful that the decision will be to seize this opportunity to widen Fenn's already substantial area of service to the community.

Work for Agreement

Now that Gov. James A. Rhodes has come up with a refinement of his original plan for giving a financial shot in the arm to higher education in Greater Cleveland, let us hope that action by all concerned is not too long delayed.

With large sums of money involved and with many important things at stake, it is understandable that a natural tendency exists among those involved to take plenty of time for study and appraisal.

But the danger of lengthy delay is obvious. Demands upon the recently approved bond issue funds for higher education are coming from all over the state. They will easily exceed the amount of money available.

Gov. Rhodes wants to make Cuyahoga County a major center of state supported or assisted higher education. He has correctly sized up the need and opportunity here.

But he has to deal with a rurally dominated legislature in at least one house of which Cuyahoga County's population is vastly under-represented.

Leaders in the field of higher education in this community knew that money would be available if the November bond issue passed. They must have formed some ideas as to how it should be used. The offer of funds certainly did not suddenly burst upon them like a bombshell, even though the details of the governor's original proposal, and now his altered plan, may have been somewhat of a surprise.

The Plain Dealer urges that the educators involved, working with the governor and the state board of regents, strive mightily to reach agreement as quickly as possible. It will be most regrettable if Cuyahoga County goes to the bond issue money barrel too late and finds it empty.

★   ★   ★

Takes Effect Sept. 1
FENN BECOMES CSU AS BOARDS APPROVE

By HARRY LENHART JR.

The vows tying Fenn College to Cleveland State University were pronounced yesterday with a flurry of laudatory speeches and handshakes.

Present for the historic State Board of Regents swap were Gov. James A. Rhodes, State Finance Director Richard L. Krabach, Mayor Ralph S. Locher and Dr. John D. Millett, chancellor and director of the

The vows, however, will not take effect until Sept. 1. That is when Fenn, the 83-year-old privately supported institution, situated on a 7.7-acre campus at Euclid

Avenue and E. 24th Street, will officially become the nucleus of CSU.

UNTIL THEN, the school will be jointly administered by Fenn and CSU officials.

The agreement between CSU and Fenn culminated negotiations that began 71 days ago.

A number of steps remain to be taken. Among them are approval by the 80-member Fenn Corporation, which holds title to the college facilities; completion of a legal document embodying the agreement, and approval of the contract by Common Pleas Court. But the biggest hurdle has been cleared.

THE TERMS of the transaction were approved first by the Fenn board of trustees yesterday and then by the CSU board, in separate meetings.

Yesterday's agreement modified a contract proposal worked out by negotiating committees for both boards and approved by the Fenn trustees three weeks ago.

As in the first proposal, the $15-million Fenn campus will be turned over to CSU as a gift and a $260,000 payment will be made for furniture and equipment at Fenn.

But, in the earlier proposal, CSU would have taken over Fenn on July 1 rather than Sept. 1.

THIS LED to a Fenn request that it be permitted to keep some $240,000 in tuition and other fees collected from students attending the summer school. The summer term would have begun under Fenn administration but would have been carried on by CSU.

Lawyers in the Ohio attorney general's office pointed out the problems this might create. Would credits earned during the summer term be Fenn or CSU credits? Could a student sue for the difference between the tuition he paid Fenn when he started the summer term and the much lower tuition that would go into effect when CSU took control?

TO SATISFY Fenn's insistence for some payment beyond the $260,000, which in reality represents Fenn's current operating deficit, yesterday's agreement also provided for an additional $114,000 payment labeled as the amount needed to pay certain administrative expenses at Fenn between now and the date of the transfer.

There was no change in the plan to reorganize the Fenn Corporation as a nonprofit foundation, using whatever assets remain after the transfer. Assets are expected to amount about $1.5 million.

HARRY F. BURMESTER, chairman of the Fenn trustees, said yesterday the foundation, to be known as the Fenn Education Foundation, would help CSU do things a state university cannot do with state money. This could include scholarship assistance, fellowships, and the endowment of professorships. But this aid will not be limited, he said, to CSU.

At a luncheon following the two board meetings yesterday, Dr. Millett emphasized that although Fenn was becoming a state school, that does not mean that henceforth all support will come from the state. He urged community support as well.

GOV. Rhodes predicted CSU would become an architectural showcase of the Midwest and with proper management one of the finest schools academically in the country.

The CSU board also announced yesterday the selection of Outcalt, Guenther, Rode & Bonebrake as architects and planning consultants for the new institution. This firm also is drafting a master plan for Cuyahoga Community College's new campus.

CPD, Mar. 11, 1965

CSU, FUTURE 'SHOWCASE,' IS BORN

The doors of Cleveland State University have been opened figuratively, even though the institution's classes will not assemble until autumn under the new banner.

Ratification of transfer agreements between the boards of Fenn College and CSU marked the end of a long period of formal deliberation and the beginning of a bright new era in state-sponsored higher education in Cleveland.

Gov. James A. Rhodes pointed toward a star-spangled future of CSU when he stated here yesterday that it "could be the showcase of America." Certainly few institutions start with the outlook of CSU, the fine base of Fenn College plus $7 million in previously approved bond issue money and an additional $37 million for expansion if the $290 million bond issue, Issue #2 on the May ballot, passes.

Rhodes described CSU as "bringing a university to the people," citing the great advantage of a central, downtown location. Mayor Ralph S. Locher correctly maintained the importance of CSU in the city's future cannot be overemphasized.

Beginning with the fall term, CSU will consist of Fenn College of Engineering and the colleges of business administration, arts and sciences and education. From this the proposed growth is such as to make Cleveland the site of one of the nation's most complete universities.

The final changeover was not without humor. Harry Burmester, Fenn board chief, said the trustees felt they were "not giving away a daughter but were gaining a son" through the amalgamation. James Nance, head of the CSU board, replied that CSU would "try to be a good son."

But behind the gay repartee were months of serious study and hard work by members of both boards and by the State Board of Regents, all for the ultimate benefit of the state, the city and the taxpayers.

The "marriage" starts out with confidence and a great sense of satisfaction. CSU represents action, not idle words.

become a state university. Therefore, the long distance phones were busy all that day between President Earnest in Milwaukee, Chairman Burmester, Provost Patterson, and Davidson, Director of Public Relations at Fenn, in Cleveland and Chase in Columbus. Nevertheless the home edition of *The Cleveland Press* carried a story by Richard L. Maher on the front page.

Chase was flabbergasted to learn from President Earnest about the *Press* story. At 3:15 p.m. of the same day, Chase told Provost Patterson that just ten minutes previously he had told the Governor that only three people had any inkling of this idea, i.e., the Governor, President Earnest, and Chase. Upon renewing contact with the Governor, Chase called Provost Patterson and informed him that the Governor had admitted that two legislators from the Cleveland area had made the suggestion to the Governor. So, the story was released. Action had to be taken immediately because of the *Press* story. As the result of more long distance phoning with President Earnest, the following two memoranda were mailed to the respective important constituents of the Fenn Family.

MEMORANDUM

May 13, 1963

TO: All Members of the Fenn College Board
FROM: Chairman H. F. Burmester
SUBJECT: CLEVELAND PRESS Article, dated May 13, 1963.
    Copy attached.

This memorandum is to apprise you that the article appearing in today's PRESS suggesting Fenn become a State University, raises an issue that has not been discussed either officially or unofficially by any Fenn Trustee or administrative official.

If and when the Government of the State of Ohio submits a proposal to the Fenn Board, through proper channels, we shall be prepared to give the consideration to which it is entitled.

Be assured you will be fully informed if there is any such proposal.

s/Harry F. Burmester, Chairman

MEMORANDUM

May 13, 1963

TO: The Fenn College Faculty and Staff

FROM: W. A. Patterson

In the Home Edition of today's *Cleveland Press* there is a front page story with the headline "Key Rhodes Aides Urge State To Take Over Fenn College."

Fenn College has not been approached by the Rhodes administration concerning this matter. No members of the Administrative Staff or the Board of Trustees have participated in discussions with state governmental officials concerning the possibility of Fenn College becoming a state university.

Of course the subject was of a nature which generated much newsprint with articles in *The Cleveland Press* and The Cleveland *Plain Dealer*.

The Cleveland Commission on Higher Education comprised of the presidents of the five major colleges in Greater Cleveland and six lay people, chaired by Ralph Besse, President of the Cleveland Electric Illuminating Company, was greatly concerned about this turn of events because it had strongly recommended and nurtured the recent establishment of the Cuyahoga Community College and had also been instrumental in the preparation of a survey titled "The Future of Higher Education in Cleveland." The Commission prepared the following statement, dated May 16, 1953, for publication:

May 16, 1963

A STATEMENT BY THE CLEVELAND COMMISSION

ON HIGHER EDUCATION

This week's news items indicate that Governor Rhodes is studying Cleveland's need for higher educational facilities. The concern of the administration in Columbus for higher education is to be commended. It is to be hoped, however, that no recommendations affecting Cuyahoga County will be made by the administration without taking full advantage of the data developed in prior studies and the know-how of existing organizations.

Four major surveys of higher education by four separate organizations have been made—Governor O'Neill's Ohio Commission on Education Beyond the High School, Governor DiSalle's Interim Commission on Education Beyond the High School, The Ohio College Association's Report by Dr. John Dale Russell, and the Cleveland Commission on Higher Education's "The Future of Higher Education in Cleveland."

Each of these surveys was made by competent people. Each contains a good deal of data, much of which is specific to Cuyahoga County. Each has recommendations which should be carefully analyzed in the light of the Cleveland community's long-term higher educational planning.

None of the existing reports advise or advocate a new state university for Ohio or for Cleveland at the present time. Cleveland's problem is currently to develop as fast as it can a diversified higher educational program of both public and private colleges so that any ambitious young student can find a higher educational program appropriate to his abilities and objectives.

All of these reports strongly support a vigorous development of a two-year community college program for technical institute training, sub-professional engineering courses, and the arts and sciences. This program is now in the course of development. As a matter of orderly planning it ought to be given priority by all forces until it is well established.

The community college program, if properly supported, would be able to accept fully twice as many students as a new state university and at fraction of the cost of constructing facilities for an equal number in a university setting.

The Cleveland Commission approves and applauds the state administration's concern for education. It suggests, however, that in processing its investigation of this vital subject it seek the advice and counsel of the local people and organizations who have given years of study and spent many thousands of dollars to obtain a proper perspective and an orderly development of plans for our higher educational expansion and development. The Commission believes that higher education in Ohio needs the administration's leadership in developing a long-range program for the state so that decisions affecting the education of our youth will not be made in isolation but with full understanding of the total problem.

The Commission is confident that there would be an instantaneous response if the state administration were to seek the expert advice and counsel of our distinguished Ohio educators and their various organizations.

The first meeting of the Board of Trustees following the amazing announcement by Governor Rhodes of May 13, was held on Tuesday,

June 4, 1963. Extracts of several of the important items appearing in the minutes follow:

1. A resolution was passed tendering the humble expression of sympathy of the board to the family of Herbert P. Ladds who had died on April 6, 1963. Ladds had served as a Trustee since February 7, 1945 (over eighteen years).

2. Fifty-five companies had participated during the academic year in luncheons at Stilwell Hall in groups of five or six at which a co-op student reported on his work experience with one of the companies. The company representatives were very impressed with these meetings so it was decided to continue them in the next academic year.

3. President Earnest announced that the ten-year fiscal study in process of revision to reflect the effects of both a community college and a State University on Fenn would be completed near the year end, and that the end of the ten-year plan, 1973 would be the fiftieth anniversary of the founding of Fenn College.

4. Trustee Louis Peirce, Chairman of the Trustee Planning Committee, explained that no part of the news story concerning the State's intention to buy Fenn was the responsibility of anyone connected with the College—no member of the Fenn Family had been officially approached. The only direct (but unofficial) contact was in the idea expressed by Warren H. Chase to President Earnest by phone on May 13, 1963.

5. On May 1, 1963, a Trust Deed of Gift and Agreement between Fenn College and Whiting and Dorothy Rogers Williams was established through a gift of 300 shares of Cooper Industries, Inc. common stock valued at $9,450. The College was to pay the donors, during their lifetime, the earnings of the fund after which the fund would be available for the general purposes of the College.

6. The New Building Committee of the Board consisting of Chairman James C. Hodge, Ray B. Aufmuth, Edward E. Helm and Allen T. Perry was reported. President Earnest announced that the construction drawings for the new Administration and Lecture Hall would be completed about December 1,

1963, and that bids would be taken early in 1964 with the view that actual construction would begin about March 1.

7. The Kulas Foundation presented a gift of $17,460 to Fenn for the construction and equipping of three music listening rooms in the library in Stilwell Hall. The Albert M. Higley Company was the low bidder and was awarded the contract.

8. Action was taken on recommendation of the Engineering Cabinet and the Engineering Faculty to change the names of two degrees, Bachelor of Science in Chemistry and Bachelor of Science in Metallurgy, to Bachelor of Engineering Science with the appropriate word Chemistry or Metallurgy appearing on the diploma in smaller print beneath the degree. This was in line with the national trend in engineering schools and in addition dispels the concern of prospective employers and the state boards of registration for engineers about the lack of the word "engineering" on an engineering graduate's diploma.

9. Trustee Louis S. Pierce submitted a résumé of the Euclid Innerbelt proposal and how Urban Renewal worked. President Earnest displayed the plan for Phase I of the Euclid Innerbelt proposal. No action was necessary.

10. Through a visit to Detroit by Trustee Arch T. Colwell and President Earnest, the Kresge Foundation made a grant of $25,000 toward the $1,800,000 projected Administration and Lecture Hall provided that a total of $1,775,000 was raised by 1966.

The fortieth commencement of Fenn College was held at Severance Hall on June 16, 1963. Dr. Algo D. Henderson delivered the commencement address titled, "Talent for Tomorrow." He was Director of the Center for The Study of Higher Education of The University of Michigan. There were 266 degree recipients, distributed as follows: 51 in Arts and Sciences, 74 in Business Administration, and 141 in Engineering. The following were recipients of Honorary Degrees:

Algo D. Henderson, Doctor of Laws (LL.D.)
Warren L. Morris, Doctor of Laws (LL.D.)
Curtis Lee Smith, Doctor of Laws (LL.D.)
Malcolm B. Vilas, Doctor of Laws (LL.D.)

John G. Janssen of this class received his Ph.D. at the University of Michigan and was engaged as a professor in the Department of Civil Engineering in the Fenn College of Engineering at C.S.U. in September 1968.

Clifford Graves, 1941, William J. Pugh, 1941, and Eleanore J. Bouguard, 1940, were recipients of the Alumni Distinguished Service Awards at the Annual Alumni Dinner Meeting held at the Wade Park Manor. Nicholas DiCello of the Fenn College Class of 1949 was the President of the Fenn Alumni Association for the school year 1962–1963.

The first order of business at the September 11, 1963, meeting of the board constituted announcements of Ray Aufmuth's resignation as a Trustee because of his transfer to San Francisco and Richard Baker's appointment to the Ohio Board of Regents. Because of this appointment Baker resigned from the Fenn Board.

The proposed operating budget for the fiscal year 1963–1964 was approved at this meeting. The budget called for contributions amounting to $244,049 to close the estimated total expense for the year of $2,971,-674. Trustee Colwell reported that over one-third of the total $1,800,000 for construction of the Lecture Hall complex had been contributed. Trustee Hodge, Chairman of the Task Committee on Building, moved and the board approved proceeding with the architectural drawings and to give Lou Cohen the required ninety-day notice to vacate the option property at the northwest corner of Euclid Avenue and East 24th Street.

The President reported that the three music listening rooms made possible through a gift of $17,460 from the Kulas Foundation would be completed in the south end of the library about September 16, 1963.

Chairman Burmester stated that Governor Rhodes had suggested an exploratory talk with himself and President Earnest, but later, because of the appointment of the Board of Regents and the $250,000,000 proposed bond issue, the Governor chose to postpone the discussion. It was decided that until the Governor states his plans, Fenn should continue to grow stronger, although with all the newspaper statements it may be difficult to raise operating funds through contributions. Trustee Hale stated the Lecture Hall should be completed to serve Cleveland.

Provost Patterson reported that the 1972–1973 annual operating need of $1,103,000, as determined by his Cabinet, did not take into account competition from a new local tax-supported state university. President Earnest proposed to have such information for the November meeting of the board, but he felt "it would result in a picture for the future that would take some doing."

A special meeting of the Executive, Planning, Development, Public Relations, and Finance Committees was scheduled for 4:00 p.m. November 11, 1963, to hear the administration's report on the projected ten-year program. A meeting of the board was to follow immediately. However, on Saturday, November 9, Warren Chase called Chairman Burmester about 10:00 p.m. and informed him that the Governor and several Regents wanted to meet with representatives of Fenn College at 6:00 p.m. on the same evening, November 11. This situation limited the time in which the Fenn Board Committees and Board were able to meet.

Chairman Burmester opened the Special Meeting by indicating that Governor Rhodes was under pressure concerning the distribution of the proposed $250,000,000 provided by the outstanding voter approval of the state bond issue. Newspaper publicity indicated $175,000,000 would go for capital support of public higher education. Intimation was that $25,000,000 would be allocated to a new tax-supported university in the Cleveland area and that $10,000,000 would be allocated for a technical institute.

Dr. Patterson then described the ten-year projected program (see Table 1) and there followed much discussion especially concerning line A on the Table, "Gift Income Required to Balance Operating Budget," for the ten-year period through 1972–1973.

Most of the Trustees expressed the viewpoint that they would like to see Fenn remain private and small, but with a state university in the Cleveland area it would be more difficult to obtain operating funds because corporations would consider their tax dollars were helping to support the state university and therefore they would be doing their part for higher education in Greater Cleveland.

The November 26, 1963, board meeting proved to be a very important one. President Earnest first presented "The Fenn College Ten-Year Financial Plan as a Private College." The remainder of the meeting was held to a general discussion of Fenn's plight. Following are abstracts from the Minutes of the meeting:

TABLE 1

PROJECTED GIFT INCOME REQUIRED EACH YEAR, 1962–1963
THROUGH 1972–1973, TO MEET ESTIMATED ANNUAL
OPERATING COSTS AND CAPITAL NEEDS*

Operating Budget	1962–1963	1963–1964	1964–1965	1965–1966
Income				
Tuition	$2,171,000	$2,259,933	$2,210,061	$2,483,720
Other Net-Income	196,701	205,500	202,000	198,500
Total	$2,367,701	$2,465,433	$2,412,061	$2,682,220
Expenses				
Academic & Student Services	$1,562,901	$1,643,134	$1,714,770	$1,891,400
President, Finance & Devel.	267,970	287,885	330,326	367,783
General Expense	196,440	210,210	248,643	271,085
Building & Grounds	384,015	395,722	386,307	455,999
Alumni	12,875	14,100	15,228	16,500
Scholarship	55,000	60,000	65,000	80,000
Total	$2,479,201	$2,611,051	$2,760,274	$3,082,767
A. Gift Income Required To Balance Operating Budget	$ 111,500	$ 145,618	$ 348,213	$ 400,547
Capital Gifts Required:				
For Physical Facilities	$ 407,000	$ 500,000	$ 500,000	$1,000,000
For Endowment	—	—	—	500,000
B. Gift Income Required To Meet Capital Needs	$ 407,000	$ 500,000	$ 500,000	$1,500,000
Total Gift Income Required To Meet Operating Costs and Capital Needs, A. + B.	$ 518,500	$ 645,618	$ 848,213	$1,900,547

* Based upon the following assumptions.

1. Enrollment estimates are based upon current college age population figures, the predicted continued increase in the percentage of college students enrolled in tax-assisted institutions, and increased competition from other colleges, public and private. However, the likelihood of a new state university in our immediate area has *not* been taken into account.

2. Increases in tuition fees, salaries, fringe benefits, non-salary costs, etc., are consistent with forecasts of economists in the field, the plans of other institutions, our past experience, and the increases in the cost of living for the past five years.

3. Capital needs are to provide for the following:

1963–1965	Completion of Lecture Hall		$ 1,000,000
1965–1968	Gymnasium	$1,000,000	
	AAA Property	1,700,000	
	Instruct. Equipment	200,000	
	Endowment	1,500,000	
			$ 4,400,000

Table 1 (*Continued*)

1966–1967	1967–1968	1968–1969	1969–1970	1970–1971	1971–1972	1972–1973
$2,541,073	$2,801,850	$2,847,625	$3,148,944	$3,233,568	$3,569,593	$3,676,270
215,000	231,500	248,000	260,500	273,000	285,500	298,000
$2,756,073	$3,033,350	$3,095,625	$3,409,444	$3,506,568	$3,855,093	$3,974,270
$2,026,990	$2,202,770	$2,348,720	$2,562,400	$2,737,490	$2,914,050	$3,108,200
386,183	409,904	429,381	455,743	480,751	503,411	533,500
291,476	313,460	337,162	362,719	390,278	419,998	435,415
601,178	728,107	800,074	830,943	864,884	899,995	1,086,825
17,800	19,000	20,600	22,000	22,500	23,000	24,845
95,000	110,000	120,000	130,000	135,000	140,000	145,000
$3,418,627	$3,783,241	$4,055,937	$4,363,805	$4,630,903	$4,900,454	$5,333,785
$ 662,554	$ 749,891	$ 960,312	$ 954,361	$1,124,335	$1,045,361	$1,359,515
$1,000,000	$ 900,000	$1,000,000	$1,000,000	$1,000,000	$1,000,000	$1,000,000
500,000	500,000	400,000	400,000	400,000	400,000	300,000
$1,500,000	$1,400,000	$1,400,000	$1,400,000	$1,400,000	$1,400,000	$1,300,000
$2,162,554	$2,149,891	$2,360,312	$2,354,361	$2,524,335	$2,445,361	$2,659,515

1968–1973	Levin Property	3,200,000
	Dormitory Furnishings	200,000
	Instruct. Equipment	300,000
	Parking Deck and Site Improvement	1,300,000
	Endowment	1,900,000
		$ 6,900,000
1963–1973	Total	$12,300,000

4. No provision is made for graduate programs which are likely to eventuate.

5. No provision is made for:
   a) Interest expense on property acquisition or construction.
   b) Contingencies.
   c) Repairs, maintenance, and replacements of a major nature.

a. Events have been happening so fast that memos on the subject are out of date before distributing.

b. A point in question was the propriety of the Governor in giving so much attention to a technical institute.

c. Recommendation was made that the Administration visit the University of Buffalo which had recently changed from private to public status. (This visit was later made by the President and Patterson, Davis, and Davidson).

d. Question was broached by a member of the Ohio Board of Regents whether the State could take over the Engineering School only.

e. President Earnest was called from the meeting to receive telephone information from Warren Chase, Secretary of the Board of Regents, that the Regents were recommending $1,000,000 to the County Community College, $750,000 to begin a Technical Institute and $3,000,000 for Engineering Education.

f. One Trustee made the following comments: "It is shocking the way the situation changes. All the publicity has been damaging, and it has not originated with us. It appears we have no choice in the matter. We prepared for a rush of students in 1965 which will now not materialize."

Several Trustees felt there would be much competition between Fenn and a new state university because each would attract the same type of local students, but, in order to make ends meet, Fenn's tuition would have to be two or more times the tuition of a state university. It was generally agreed by a number of the Trustees—not all—that because Fenn had little endowment to supplement annual requests for operating grants and furthermore because the Fenn Alumni had not yet developed a comprehensive program of giving, exploratory steps should be taken leading to state affiliation to obtain the best arrangement possible. Trustee Howard Burns pointed out that it was legally possible, but not probable, that if Fenn's property was wanted badly enough it could be obtained by eminent domain. He also suggested that, should Fenn eventually become affiliated with the State, many things could be written into the first contract document that may be impossible to add later. It was decided not to adopt any resolutions at this meeting, but to wait and see what the Governor had in mind later in the evening.

It so happened that the Governor completely surprised the members of Fenn's Executive Committee at the evening meeting by offering a grant of $12,000,000, which might be extended later to $25,000,000, to create a two-year technical institute either as a full four-year state university or under contract with the State, Fenn remaining private. Suggestion was also made at the meeting that Fenn move and expand its campus elsewhere and the existing Fenn campus be turned over to the new Cuyahoga Community College.

The Fenn Trustees and especially the administration took lightly to Governor Rhodes' proffer, the reason being that Fenn's faculty and staff had worked many years to raise Fenn's quality of education to a level whereby the curricula were accredited in a number of important areas. A day-division technical institute would undo these years of genuine effort because the academic standards of such curricula were far below the requirements for accreditation in baccalaureate degree curricula. Much newsprint developed immediately as the result of the Governor's offer. See pages following 545.

A Trustee commented that "politics will force a state institution to this area. Only the financially strong have a chance of surviving. Co-op should continue. We should sell the College and establish a foundation." Others commented, "We should not become a technical institute. We should remain private. The State does not seem to know what it wants. Fenn would undoubtedly be affected more than any other Cleveland university or college should a state university be located in Cleveland."

The following resolution was adopted unanimously:

> BE IT RESOLVED that the Board of Trustees of Fenn College be requested to extend the authority of the Executive Committee so that it may continue to study the possible relationship of Fenn College to the State of Ohio, and, further, that the Board authorize the Executive Committee to negotiate with the Board of Regents concerning the status of the College.

It was felt that affiliation with the State was now inevitable although many of the Trustees were reluctant to support this move. The meeting ended with a statement from Trustee Dickey that, "Higher education should be our first consideration and bricks and mortar second. If we do become state-supported, we should endow a foundation with the proceeds of our holdings." A number of the Trustees heartily agreed with Dickey.

The Annual Corporation meeting of Fenn College was held at the Union Club December 9, 1963. The following ninety-four members and guests were present.

Adams, J. E.*	Harris, W. N.*	Miller, M. D.*
Anders, P. R.†	Helm, E. E.*	Morris, W. L.*
Armstrong, A. S.*	Henninger, J. G.*	Norton, J. A.
Auld, R. B.†	Herrick, M. C.†	Nuss, G. G.*
Baird, G. A.	Herzog, G. R.	O'Konski, W. B.*
Belda, B. J.*	Hickman, W. B.*	Patterson, W. A.†
Bicknell, Guthrie*	Hickok, R. D.*	Peirce, L. S.*
Bishop, W. B.*	Hoffman, E. K.	Perry, A. T.*
Bruch, K. F.*	Hoge, R. H.*	Perry, P. B.
Burmester, H. F.*	Hoover, P. J.	Ramsdell, R. W.*
Burns, H. F.*	Horsburgh, C. R.*	Rosenberg, Sam
Calkins, Hugh*	Hose, A. G.*	Ruhlman, J. R.*
Carmichael, D. S.*	Irrgang, William*	Silverstein, Abe*
Channock, R. E.	Jamison, R. H.*	Smith, C. E.*
Chase, Warren*	Jenks, M. B.†	Smith, Kent
Collens, C. L.*	Joseph, F. E.*	Smith, S. H.*
Collens, J. L.	Kilroy, E. A.*	Sparling, W. S.
Cox, Merrill*	Leichliter, V. H.*	Stecher, R. M.*
Coy, F. A.*	Laffer, W. G.*	Steinebach, F. G.*
Davidson, M. M.†	Lincoln, D. C.*	Strnad, J. J.*
Davis, V. H.†	Littman, A. L.*	Swiler, Russell*
Dingle, J. R.*	Livingstone, R. S.*	Taylor, C. M.*
DuBois, P. G.	Lloyd, E. B.	Taylor, S. B.*
Elmendorf, F. L.*	McDonald, C. B.*	Thompson, C. A.*
Feldman, R. V.*	McGuire, F. T.*	Turben, C. F.
Foster, C. T.	Maxey, B. W.*	Ware, K. E.
Gibson, Hugh*	Meldrum, A. B.*	Watkins, H. T.*
Goldsword, C. L.*	Meriam, J. B., Jr.*	Weber, E. C.*
Greene, J. A.	Miller, Galen*	Widdell, H. E.*
Hale, C. G.*	Miller, W. C.	Williams, Whiting*

Winkler, F. N.*   Woodling, G. V.*

---

* Indicates members of Board of Trustees or Corporation.
† Indicates members of The College Administration.

Chairman Burmester reported that in the past year the Board of Trustees had met three times, the Executive Committee nine times, and that he had met with President Earnest an additional nineteen times in conducting the affairs of the College.

Trustee Allen Perry, Chairman of the Nominating Committee, presented the following nominations.

A. Re-election of Trustees and Emeritus Member, Corporation Final Class of 6-year terms, elected 11/57, eligible for election 12/63 as Class of '68. (Figures preceding names represent initial year elected.)

'38 George Woodling	(1 additional year)
'51 Ken Akers	(4 additional years)
'52 Howard Burns	(5 additional years)
'57 Van Leichliter	(5 additional years)
'59 Henry Widdell	(5 additional years)

Original Class of 5-year terms, elected 11/58, eligible for election 12/63 as Class of '68

'40 Clarence Taylor	(2 additional years)
'45 Volmer Fries	(3 additional years)
'56 Warren Morris	(5 additional years)
'57 William Hunkin	(5 additional years)
'61 Bert McDonald	(5 additional years)

B. Election of new Trustees
   a. Dr. Abe Silverstein to serve the unexpired term of Ken Akers (4 years).
   b. Dr. Robert M. Stecher to serve the unexpired term of H. P. Ladds (Class of 1964).
   c. B. W. Maxey to serve the unexpired term of R. T. Baker (Class of 1967).
   d. C. E. Smith for election to Honorary Life Trustee.
   e. Galen Miller to serve the unexpired term of C. E. Smith (Class of 1966).
   f. John H. Henninger, Alumni Trustee, for a three-year term replacing Walter B. O'Konski.
   g. Walter B O'Konski to serve the unexpired term of Ray B. Aufmuth (Class of 1964).

C. Election of Corporation Members
    V. K. Smith re-election after one year retirement;
    H. A. Anderson, G. P. Bakken, Hugh Calkins, Earle A. Chan-
    ner, William H. Eells, George E. Enos, Mervin B. France,
    Hugh R. Gibson, W. Braddock Hickman, Frank E. Joseph,
    Joseph F. Keithley, E. A. Kilroy, Jr., David F. Leahy, Alan L.
    Littman, William A. Lloyd, Harry T. Marks, M. D. Miller,
    James J. Nance, Wallace M. Pattison, D. D. Scarff, James J.
    Strnad, Richard B. Tullis, Thomas V. H. Vail, Hays T. Watkins,
    Jr., Lewis B. Williams.

Chairman Burmester stated that the ten-year outlook, and the interest
of the State in acquiring Fenn College were two important factors
affecting the future of the College as a private institution. He then
called upon President Earnest as the speaker of the evening to present
Fenn's Plan for Unified Public Higher Education in Cleveland-Northeastern Ohio, as follows:

> Metropolitan Cleveland is by far the most productive region
> of the State in goods, services, and income. Its people pay for,
> but do not have, the advantages of a local state university to
> which they can send their children at low tuition rates and have
> them live at home. This is unquestionably the outstanding need
> in public higher education in the State, and its fulfillment carries
> the greater promise of returns in educated people, new knowledge,
> and useful applications in all areas of human productivity. Now,
> in the light of modern technological developments, Cleveland citi-
> zens realize the area needs well-coordinated public higher educa-
> tion on all levels. Cleveland now has public higher education on
> a random basis—i.e., six branches of two state universities, a com-
> munity college, which will incorporate a technical institute pro-
> gram, and a technician's program under the Cleveland Board of
> Education, plus a law which provides for autonomous Technical
> Institute Districts. These all operate under different unrelated gov-
> erning and administrative authorities, and with different sources
> of revenue.
>
> Fenn proposes a plan to the Board of Regents for a coordinated
> system of the elements of public higher education, which will pro-
> vide greatly needed education at lower cost for the youth of our
> community. The plan includes the development of a state univer-
> sity from Fenn's present assets, together with a coordinated system

of community colleges which may or may not include technical programs. Each element operates under its respective Board of Trustees—all coordinated by the Ohio Board of Regents.

A PLAN FOR UNIFIED PUBLIC
HIGHER EDUCATION IN
CLEVELAND-NORTHEASTERN OHIO

The objective of this document is to present a plan for the orderly development and coordination of public higher education in the Cleveland-Northeastern Ohio region, and to delineate Fenn's role as a State University cooperating in the plan.

The problem is this: There is a miscellany of public institutions for higher education in the County, each of them with promise, but each operating independently. This potential duplication or triplication of facilities, faculties, and curricula, results in inadequate support from the public for any one or all of the institutions.

1.   At this time Kent State University operates five branches in the Cleveland Metropolitan area and is considering a future graduate program in Parma.

2.   The Ohio State University has a branch in Lakewood, now in its second year of operation.

3.   The Cuyahoga Community College began classes in September, 1963, with a day enrollment of 1,000 and an evening enrollment of 2,000.

4.   The Max S. Hayes Industrial School, under the administration of the Cleveland Board of Education, offers two-year post high school Technician Training Programs.

5.   The Ohio Code has been revised, authorizing community colleges to offer technical institute programs.

6.   The Ohio Code also permits creation of Technical Institute Districts in the State.

Each of the institutions of higher education thus far established is under separate authority and separate administration. Each pursues its own plans and none has a stated policy about its relationship with the others. All of this suggests there is need for better coordination of public higher education in Northeastern Ohio, and well organized effort toward this end is now highly essential because of the charge given the new Board of Regents.

There is an immediate opportunity for getting agreement on these relationships, which may be crucial to all. The community is now awakened to the relationship of public higher educational opportunities and the area's intellectual, economic, industrial, financial, and social resources. It has indicated its willingness to pay for public higher education. The General Assembly has passed permissive legislation covering the full range of education beyond the high school.

In line with the foregoing, Fenn College herewith proposes the following plan of action to aid in resolving the effective and efficient coordination of public higher education in Northeastern Ohio so that educational opportunities will be available to all.

The plan calls for two basic elements:

(1) A comprehensive state university to be developed on the present site of Fenn College, utilizing its facilities and personnel as a nucleus.

(2) An autonomous system of community colleges and technical institutes, operated by the appropriate governing boards.

The basic idea of the plan calls for a comprehensive state university which would be part of this system.

The community college system in Cuyahoga County is an essential part of this idea to unify public higher education, for it is through the community college and its branches, spread throughout the County, that at least 75 per cent of public education in the freshman and sophomore years will be accomplished. Students satisfactorily completing this pre-university program could transfer with full credit to accredited colleges or universities.

The branches of the state university and of community colleges, with their technical programs, should be spread throughout the entire Northeastern Ohio region. In them initial instruction would be conducted in the humanities, social sciences, natural sciences, and applied sciences. These branches, of course, would not impinge upon the areas served more logically by other state universities or community colleges. Students successfully completing pre-university programs would complete their baccalaureate degrees at the central campus of the university. Admission policies for the freshman classes at the state university, university branches, and community colleges would be coordinated.

The Curriculum

Based on the successful California Plan, joint faculty committees on curriculum can coordinate state university and community college courses. Such close cooperation in matters of curriculum will result in easier transfer of two-year college students to other colleges and universities.

Although coordinated planning in curriculum is essential, there are distinct curricular advantages to maintaining separate governing boards for the state university and the community colleges. Each element in the system must serve different curricular needs, and separate administrations are essential where different educational objectives are to be achieved. The community colleges will be concentrating on education of freshmen and sophomores for transfer to the state university, on semi-professional training, on technical training, and on adult education, and the state university will be concentrating on the undergraduate, graduate, and professional levels.

The Faculties

The assembly of a community college faculty that meets the standards established by the North Central Association is greatly enhanced if there is an affiliated university to which they may look for graduate work.

The opportunity to keep up with one's professional field, to do research, and to have college or university status is expected by all able faculty members. Salary is only one of the factors affecting a faculty member's choice of institution. Equipment, facilities, freedom for research, and academic status are other important determinants. The years to 1970 and beyond, according to the United States Office of Education, offer no foreseeable prospect of change in the mounting demand for faculty people in any field, including the social studies and the humanities; therefore, qualified faculty will be scarce. The community college-state university affiliation, provided by this plan, would be a real asset to this region.

In support of this idea, Ralph R. Fields, Professor of Higher Education, Teachers College, Columbia University, in his book, *The Community College Movement*, says:

"Provisions for encouraging scholarship among the community college instructors seem meager. Teaching loads are heavy. With no regular secretarial service and no teaching assistants, the average instructor finds himself with precious little time during the academic year to keep up in his field of scholarship. . . . Relatively little stress is placed upon research, either in the academic fields or on teaching problems. . . ." (McGraw Hill, 1962, p. 253.)

Dr. Fields is speaking of the plight of presently organized two-year colleges without a university atmosphere, and whose courses may or may not qualify for accreditation at other institutions. This situation notably does not pertain at the Community College located near the University of Bridgeport, an example of a two-year college operating successfully in cooperation with a university.

If faculty membership on the Community College staff meant a college-university environment, where younger faculty members could, without fee, complete work for their advanced degrees, the recruitment prospects would be far less difficult. The public institutions in Northeastern Ohio could offer the same advantages to faculty as public universities do everywhere.

Fenn as the State University—Its Assets and Advantages

If the Board of Regents sees in this unified plan the possibility for accomplishing its educational goals in Northeastern Ohio, it will face the task of establishing a state university in Cleveland at an early date. The fact that Fenn College in many ways lends itself to filling this essential role may greatly reduce the magnitude of the task.

The excellent relationship with the Cleveland business and industrial community that Fenn College has developed over the last 40 years through its Cooperative Plan acts as a stabilizing influence in keeping Cleveland-trained alumni in the Cleveland area. Fenn would hope to continue to employ the best aspects of the Cooperative Plan should it become a state university

Fenn's location, adjacent to downtown Cleveland, is within one hour's commuting distance for one-fourth of Ohio's population. Thus, its readily accessible location is ideal for becoming the nucleus of a state university. Among its other assets are accreditation in important areas, a well-qualified faculty (full and part-time) plus administrative and maintenance-operating staffs. It has a university-type organization with Schools of Arts and Sciences, Business Administration, and Engineering, offering 30 baccalaureate degree programs in Day and Evening Divisions. The campus consists of 371,000 square feet in three buildings on a 7.7-acre campus, with ample room for expansion.

Fenn is fortunate in that an approved preliminary survey is already completed for an urban renewal program linking the St. Vincent and Erieview projects. This plan contains more than 200 acres and would, therefore, provide the land necessary for all needs of a major public university.

Section 112 of the Federal Housing Act permits a city to receive matching funds from the Federal Government for related urban renewal projects for qualified university expenditures. Therefore, Fenn, the only institution in this particular area that can generate these funds, could provide the City with a multi-million-dollar area development program.

This type of program for higher education is precisely what Metropolitan Cleveland needs. For this Cuyahoga County-Northeastern Ohio area, which is the major tax-producing and population center of the State, and which now has no coordinated program for higher education, this plan provides not only what the people need, but what they deserve—the finest and most comprehensive system of public higher education in the country.

This was the final Board and Corporation meeting for the year 1963, a frustrating and exasperating year for the Trustees and administration of Fenn. Chairman Burmester adjourned the meeting by calling for continued financial support to keep the College going through this most difficult time.

The Executive Committee met December 23, 1963, and Chairman Burmester reported on his deliberations with Dr. Harold Oyster, Chairman of the Ohio Board of Regents. Dr. Oyster had requested projected enrollment and budget figures for Fenn as a State University. Richard Baker, who had resigned as a Fenn Trustee, was being most helpful as a member of the Ohio Board of Regents. It appeared that some clarification was finally being made and that the Fenn Family might enjoy a cheerful Christmas, just two days hence.

XV

If life had a second edition,
how would I correct the proofs.

John Clare, 1793–1864.

The first Fenn College fraternities were founded in 1926, Iota Eta in the Day Division and Lambda Tau Sigma in the Evening Division. Iota Eta became national Sigma Tau Gamma in 1961. Beta Beta Alpha, a Day Division fraternity, was founded in 1932 and chartered as Fenn's first national fraternity, Tau Kappa Epsilon, in 1953.

Three Day Division fraternities, i.e., Kappa Delta Phi, Lambda Tau Delta and Pi Sigma Tau were founded in 1929. Pi Sigma Tau became national Delta Sigma Phi in 1963, and Lambda Tau Delta became national Sigma Tau Epsilon in 1964. Lambda Iota Delta was founded as an Evening Division fraternity in 1933.

Gamma Nu Sigma, Fenn's first Day Division sorority, was founded in 1937, and Kappa Sigma Upsilon, Fenn's first Evening Division sorority was founded the same year. A year later, in 1938, the Iota Tau Lambda Evening Division sorority was founded and a Day Division chapter of the same sorority was founded in 1954, but it was changed to Chi Delta Theta in 1964. The Beta Sigma Omicron sorority, also founded in 1954, was Fenn's first National Panhellenic Sorority.

The fraternities and sororities participated in many campus activities including various traditional balls, playnites, intramural sports, aid of needy families, picnics for orphans, homecoming dances, smokers, floats for parades, mixers, ski parties, proms and many others. Usually such activities were co-sponsored by specific fraternity-sorority combinations. There was a lot of healthy competition amongst the Greek letter societies in intramurals, scholarship and other activities. The fraternities and sororities added much to the enjoyment of obtaining a college education and to the all-around college life of the student body.

The Trustee Building Committee met January 7, 1964, and expressed its satisfaction with the plans of the proposed Lecture Hall-Administration Building. Although in a state of quandary, it seemed logical to proceed with internal planning in order to be prepared to act when a decision was made concerning the private versus public status of Fenn College. Accordingly, the committee voted to recommend to the Executive Committee, or the board, that it be authorized to proceed with obtaining bids.

President Earnest and Provost Patterson met with Ohio Regent Ford in Sandusky on January 8, 1964, and with Dr. Oyster (Chairman, Board of Regents) in Columbus on January 10 to submit and discuss the report on operating, planning and financial projections which had been requested by Dr. Oyster.

The Board Finance Committee met January 31, 1964, and it was reported that excellent fall and winter quarter day registrations exceeded the original estimate and that the resulting income exceeded the budget by $34,000. Evening registrations, however, were below the estimate and resulted in an underrun of the budget by $55,000. The prospects for the year had been assessed, and it appeared that the reserve of $115,000 would be sufficient to meet the deficit, assuming no State interference prior to August 31, 1964, the end of the fiscal year. The dollar contribution picture for the year looked very gloomy. As of January 31, 1964 (the date of the Finance Committee meeting), the complete contributions for the first five months of the fiscal year as compared with the first five months of the previous fiscal year were as follows:

	Sept.–Jan. *1963–1964*	*Sept.–Jan.* *1962–1963*
Capital Gifts	$133,185	$246,993
Eliminate special restricted foundations	60,024	
Direct comparison	$ 73,161	$246,993
Add operating gifts	91,943	67,260
	$165,104	$314,253

This sharp decline of 47½% in contributions in one year's time bespeaks the effect of the publicity concerning the possibility of Fenn becoming a public university. Many corporations did not contribute to state universities because they felt they were providing their share of state educational funding through taxation. The Fenn administration and the trustees were working with a serious handicap.

On February 21, 1964, the Cleveland Commission on Higher Education sent the following letter to Dr. Harold W. Oyster, Chairman of the Ohio Board of Regents:

CLEVELAND COMMISSION

ON HIGHER EDUCATION

325 Superior Avenue, N.E.   *Cleveland, Ohio 44114*   *Telephone: 241-7583*

February 21, 1964

Dr. Harold W. Oyster
The Ohio Board of Regents
State House
Columbus, Ohio

Dear Dr. Oyster:

For reasons set forth in a proposal to the Board of Regents, the Trustees of Fenn College are in the process of exploring the feasibility of qualifying for state support - in effect, becoming a publicly controlled and financed higher educational institution. The Fenn Trustees have asked the Cleveland Commission to review their proposals and to express an opinion thereon. The expansion of publicly supported higher education in this area and the effect of such a change on the educational pattern of metropolitan Cleveland and Northeast Ohio has been a continuing concern of the Commission.

The Commission believes that the independently supported colleges and the universities and the publicly supported institutions, should together, constitute a broad and comprehensive higher educational program for Cleveland and Northeast Ohio. Consistent with this belief, the Commission took the first step in sponsoring and helping to develop the Cuyahoga Community College, which today is a vital reality. As you know, it provides instruction to over 3,000 individuals in its first semester of operation - individuals, many of whom could not afford to attend any other kind of college, many who want instruction of a non-credit variety for specific vocations, and those who wish, and are qualified, to continue their academic careers through the junior and senior years. The Commission expects that the College will enroll as many as 10,000 students by 1970.

The proposal of Fenn College to become a state-supported institution has the support of the Commission. While supporting Fenn's proposal for conversion to a state-controlled and tax-supported institution, the Commission believes that the role of Fenn as an integral part of this educational complex should continue as a four-year institution offering undergraduate curricula in the various arts and sciences, engineering and business.

The Commission therefore urges:

1. That the state's responsibility for higher education in the Cleveland area be concentrated in the Cuyahoga County Community College and Fenn College.

2. That the program of Fenn College be maintained at a level of quality adequate to permit the acceptance of transfer students from the Community College and other institutions, and entering students on a selective admissions basis.

3. That immediate steps be taken with Governor Rhodes to place the matter on the agenda for a Special Session of the General Assembly to be scheduled for May, 1964.

4. That Fenn College continue as a four-year institution; that programs beyond the baccalaureate level be established only in conformity with a state-wide plan for the development of graduate facilities.

The Commission makes these four points, knowing of the forthcoming study of higher education in Ohio, for these reasons:

1. The establishment of Fenn College as a state institution and the further development of the Community College would permit the simplificiation of the state higher educational system in Cuyahoga County by the closing of the so-called "state university branches" in local high schools.

   The branches, three in number and under the supervision of Kent State and Ohio State are inadequate to accommodate the large numbers of students who will be applying for college admission in the coming years, while the Community College, as an autonomous county-wide, tax-based institution under single administrative super-vision, can expand its program and facilities as the need develops. The "branches" are not equipped or prepared to give technical institute or other than traditional courses while the Community College will provide comprehensive educational opportunity in response to community needs.

2. The Commission believes that Fenn College should
    be maintained as a quality institution. The
    compulsory "open" admissions policy of the state
    universities has resulted in the admissions of students,
    patently unprepared and unqualified for college
    level work, who should never have been admitted. This
    policy of providing post-high school opportunity for
    all who qualify can be broadened in the combined
    programs of Fenn and the Cuyahoga Community College.

    In Cuyahoga County there is full opportunity for
    any high school graduate to try his hand at higher
    education in a comprehensive community college,
    offering not only college level academic work as do
    the state universities, but in addition, a wide variety
    of technical courses, training programs and part-time
    instruction.

    Under these conditions, there is the opportunity
    for Fenn College to continue its selective admission
    of qualified students as a state institution
    without, in any way, depriving a high school
    graduate of his opportunity to attend college.

3. There is urgent need for immediate consideration of
    Fenn's proposal. Its current financial integrity
    has been drastically diminished by untimely publicity.
    Normal income from gifts, grants and contributions has
    been severely curtailed. Furthermore, its plans for
    expansion have to be rescheduled to await a decision
    by the legislature and the Board of Regents. The
    Commission urges the Board of Regents to expedite the
    proposal with all possible speed and urge the
    Governor to include the proposition in his call for
    a Special Session in May, 1964.

4. The Commission believes that the development of Fenn
    College should be centered on a solid four-year
    baccalaureate program. The Commission strongly be-
    lieves that the unplanned dispersion of graduate
    programs in every state institution in Ohio has re-
    sulted in a heterogeneous collection of graduate
    departments and schools and has prevented the
    development of top grade graduate programs in Ohio's
    state universities.

    The Commission urges a thorough examination, state-wide,
    of the graduate programs in state supported institutions

]

and that any decision regarding Fenn's development
as a state university be made in the light of such
findings.

It may well be that the Regents will conclude that the
proposal contained in numbered paragraph three on page two of
this letter will seriously limit the freedom of The Tickton Group
in their efforts to develop a sound, comprehensive plan for higher
education under public auspices in the State of Ohio. In that event,
we would strongly urge, as an alternative, that ways and means be
found to provide state funds to Fenn College in sufficient amounts
to permit Fenn College to continue its present operations unimpaired
during the course of the study and until definitive actions can be
taken as a result of the study. This alternative proposal should
be viewed as a stop-gap only, since the Commission continues to
believe that Fenn's proposals should form the base on which to
build a tax-supported institution of higher education in Cleveland.

The Commission is the coordinating body for higher education
in Cuyahoga County representing the general public (6 members) and
the five largest local colleges and universities (5 members). It
offers its help in every possible way to bring to this area and Ohio
the best system of higher education we can devise.

Sincerely,

Evan B. Lloyd
Executive Director

This letter has been approved by each member of the
Commission.

EBL:jm

Much work was carried on by board committees early in 1964 so the
first meeting of the board was not held until March 2. The encumbent
officers were re-elected, namely:

Harry F. Burmester, Chairman of the Board

Dr. James C. Hodge, Vice Chairman

Vollmer W. Fries, Treasurer

Vernon H. Davis, Secretary

The Standing Committees of the Board as appointed by Chairman
Burmester are given in Table 1.

The Federal Government, immediately prior to this time, had taken
action to make grants to States to aid in financing capital improvement
needs to meet the space requirements on college campuses for the expanding enrollment of students. Ohio's share was reported as $11,000,000
of which it appeared the new lecture hall complex at Fenn would be
eligible for a "loan" of three or four hundred thousand dollars. Accordingly, the board took action at its March 2, 1964, meeting to establish

TABLE 1

BOARD OF TRUSTEES
STANDING COMMITTEES

Executive Committee

H. F. Burmester, Chairman

J. C. Hodge, V. Ch.	C. G. Hale
K. F. Bruch	E. E. Helm
V. W. Fries	L. S. Peirce

G. B. Earnest

Planning Committee

L. S. Peirce, Ch.
C. G. Hale, V. Ch.
E. T. Bartlett
C. J. Stilwell
E. H. Fisher
H. E. Widdell
V. H. Leichliter

Academic Committee

C. G. Hale, Ch.
P. S. Dickey
J. R. Hoover

Instructional Standards Committee

P. S. Dickey, Ch.
F. L. Elmendorf
A. G. Hose (Al.)
R. M. Stecher
A. Silverstein

Student Affairs Committee

J. R. Hoover, Ch.
G. V. Woodling
C. M. Taylor
W. B. O'Konski (Al.)
W. J. Hunkin

Development and Public Relations Committee

K. F. Bruch, Ch.
A. T. Colwell
A. T. Perry
C. M. White
W. G. Laffer
J. G. Henninger (Al.)

Finance Committee

E. E. Helm, Ch.
C. B. McDonald
W. L. Morris
B. W. Maxey
W. N. Harris

Administrative Services Committee

V. W. Fries, Ch.
A. S. Armstrong
E. E. Helm

Operations Committee

A. S. Armstrong, Ch.
J. W. Corey
H. F. Burns
G. Miller
N. F. Smith

2/25/64

(Al.) = Alumni Member

a list of prospective bidders for construction of the new Administration-Lecture Hall building, to proceed with obtaining bids, and be ready to start construction as soon as assurance was obtained from the Ohio Board of Regents that financing for same would be forthcoming from the State.

Chairman Burmester appointed Trustees Peirce (Chairman), Bruch, Hale, and Fries as Fenn's Trustee Committee to represent the College in deliberations with the State. Chairman Burmester and President Earnest were to be *ex-officio* members. After the first meeting of the Committee, Peirce resigned and Fries was appointed Chairman. Dr. Hodge replaced Peirce on the Committee. Chairman Burmester had been keeping Dr. Oyster informed of Fenn's interim problems by phone and personal contact.

The Ohio Board of Regents had contracted for a proposed Master Plan for Higher Education with outside consultants. The first step by the consultants was to request a host of information in a complex multi-page questionnaire to be submitted to the Board of Regents in successive intervals within ninety days. President Earnest presented the status of the Master Plan at the March 2, 1964, board meeting and also indicated that Fenn's legal counsel was working on material for deliberations with the Regent negotiators.

The Executive Committee of the Board met March 23, 1964, and adopted the president's recommendation for increases in faculty and staff salaries effective September 1, 1964. Also at this meeting Chairman Fries presented a résumé of the status of the situation to date in Negotiating Committee activities. He suggested that the staff move ahead with its plans on the assumption the Ohio General Assembly would meet in special session in May 1964. He estimated that we should proceed on the premise the transaction will be a sale of the College and that payment in some amount will be received for the assets. It was felt for several years that there would be a *quid pro quo* exercised by the State for at least the physical facilities of Fenn which approximated $15,000,000 in value, which would be the basis for a supporting foundation—a concept about which more follows.

The Executive Committee met again April 27, 1964, at which time Chairman Burmester reported on his recent chat with Governor Rhodes. The Governor told Burmester that there would be 20,000 students in a short time on the Fenn Campus. Also that he would not make a firm decision on a special session of the Legislature until after the election scheduled for May 5, 1964. Governor Rhodes informed Burmester, "You need 25 million dollars fast and I will get it for you." In his address at a Chamber of Commerce luncheon the Governor remarked that Fenn was presently negotiating with the Regents to become a state university.

President Earnest informed the board that he had attended a meeting of the Ohio Board of Regents held at Kent State University where Chairman Oyster informed the Regents that he had had a satisfactory meeting at Fenn. Dr. Millett, Chancellor of the Board of Regents, informed President Earnest at the same meeting that Fenn had made a good presentation, and that the cash consideration for the purchase of Fenn College was the only problem.

Chairman Burmester called the board's attention to the fact that Albert Levin had approached him concerning Fenn's interest in a property extending from Euclid Avenue to Chester Avenue between East 21st Street and The Arthur G. McKee & Co. property. If Fenn was uninterested Levin was either going to build a high-rise apartment on it or sell it. The property was a real asset to the College's expansion plans either as Fenn College or as a state university. Chairman Burmester felt that Levin was really not going to build on the property and might desire to sell an option to Fenn as "a public spirited gesture." Deliberations concerning this property had been proceeding for some time between the Administration, Chairman Burmester, Trustee Fries' Negotiating Committee and Rorick of the firm of Baker, Hostetler, and Patterson. Levin had set a price of $3,700,000 on the property.

Chairman Burmester read excerpts from the option prepared by Rorick to the Executive Committee at the April 27, 1964, meeting. It was indicated that an option undoubtedly could be procured covering the period until the Ohio General Assembly met in May, and probably a system of renewals for extension could be obtained should the General Assembly not meet as planned. It was thought that an option with extensions would strengthen our hand in Columbus for more expeditious action. Accordingly, Trustee Fries was given the authority to negotiate an Option Agreement with The 2100 Euclid Company (Levin and syndicate) for the purchase of the aforesaid property for $3,700,000 with the sum of $10,000 to be paid for said option, and that President Earnest and Secretary Vernon H. Davis be authorized to execute such option on behalf of Fenn College. The option was executed with Levin's company under the above terms for a period of 120 days after a law was passed making Fenn a state university, or for 30 days following a session of the Legislature in which a Fenn bill was defeated or one was not even introduced.

The Board of Trustees met June 9, 1964, at which time the actions of the previous interim Executive Committee meetings were approved. In addition to the usual board agenda items, Trustee Fries reported that the Fenn Negotiating Committee had met with the Negotiating Committee of the Ohio Board of Regents on April 9, 1964, and discussed the "Proposed Plan for Establishment of Fenn College as a State University" and that the Regents seemed to accept the major premises with no great area of disagreement. At that moment, the thinking in Columbus was that Fenn would be the nucleus for a state university. The Regents thought an interim policy on selective admissions could be arranged and problems of fringe benefits worked out for faculty and other employees. Trustee Fries told the Fenn Board that if certain Fenn employees lost something in the process, the Fenn Trustees might make it up through the proposed "foundation" which was under consideration.

The report of the "Master Plan for Higher Education" by the consultants headed by Sidney Tickton, formerly with the Ford Foundation, would not be submitted in time for the June 12, 1964, meeting of the Regents at Central State College so it was not expected that a recommendation would be forthcoming from the Regents at this time to Governor Rhodes on the Fenn situation.

One of the most important actions taken by the board at its June 9, 1964, meeting was the acceptance of the retirement of Dean Paul R. Anders of the School of Business Administration effective August 31, 1964. He was awarded the title "Dean Emeritus of Business Administration." Dean Anders had served the College professionally and faithfully since his initial appointment on August 1, 1930. Later, upon the loan of Dr. Patterson to the new administration for the planning of The Cleveland State University, Dean Anders returned for a period of about nine months to aid President Earnest with the administrative affairs of terminating Fenn College. He served without compensation. He passed away Sunday, December 11, 1966, at age 72, while watching a football game on television in his home.

The forty-first commencement convocation of Fenn College was held Sunday, June 14, 1964, at Severance Hall. Frederick C. Crawford, Chairman of the Executive Committee of Thompson, Ramo, Wooldridge, Inc. delivered the address, entitled, "America's Two Secrets of Success." There were 288 graduates, distributed as follows: 65 from the School of Arts and Sciences, 85 from the School of Business Administration, and 138 from the School of Engineering.

Honorary Degrees were conferred on the following:

Perry Brooks Jackson, Doctor of Laws (LL. D.)

John C. Virden, Doctor of Laws (LL. D.)

Abe Silverstein, Doctor of Science in Administration (D. Sc. A.)

Frederick C. Crawford, Doctor of Science in Administration

(D. Sc. A.)

The Trustees' next meeting was held September 28, 1964. It was not known at this date that Fenn College had less than a year to live. The following excerpts from the Minutes of this meeting will prove this point:

1. Chairman Burmester mentioned the letter previously mailed to Trustees entitled "Review of Fenn's status since last Board meeting of June 9, 1964," and said there wasn't much to add or much that currently appeared to be done between now and November 9 when the special session of the Ohio General Assembly was to meet.

2. President Earnest presented the Day Division enrollment report for the Fall Quarter; this information is given in Table 2.

TABLE 2

DAY DIVISION

ENROLLMENT REPORT—FALL QUARTER, 1964

	FALL QUARTER, 1964			BUDGET FALL, 1964			FALL QUARTER, 1963		
	School	*Coop*	*Total*	*School*	*Coop*	*Total*	*School*	*Coop*	*Total*
Arts and Sciences	331	116	447	310	125	435	291	149	440
Bus. Administration	367	167	534	350	160	510	331	171	502
Engineering	545	213	758	515	185	700	486	246	732
Total	1,243*	496	1,739	1,175	470	1,645	1,108	566	1,674

* Approximately 530 new students are included in this Total.

3. On Mr. Bartlett's motion it was voted to pay off the remaining balance on the Warters mortgage (at present $8,000)) at the convenience of the Administration.

4. Chairman Burmester announced appointments of Hale, Dickey, and Peirce to the Fenn College Foundation Committee with Hale, Chairman, and President Earnest, *ex-officio*, and that the first meeting was scheduled for September 30, 1964.

5. In a status report on the proposed Cleveland State University, Burmester said our relationship with the Regents was prime. The Chamber of Commerce, Cleveland Growth Board, and Cleveland Development Foundation Board were currently engaged in planning to insure that the proposed new university be located in downtown Cleveland. Some reports indicated influence from down-state legislators not to establish the major campus on our present location but rather in the suburbs.

He also reported negotiations for taking over Fenn had to cease because of lack of legal authority of the Board of Regents. Negotiations cannot be resumed until the board for the new university is appointed. We are thus, under present interpretations, in the position of being asked by the State to give away Fenn's physical assets without any of Fenn's present board being appointed to the new board for reasons of conflict of interest. This matter is being further studied.

The Regents are awaiting the Tickton Report due at uncertain date, probably November or December 1964. The question at the moment is how much the State will pay for Fenn College. Burmester thought the present Fenn location would always be an important one for a university but not necessarily the only one in the future.

President Earnest reported that Dr. Millett, Chancellor of the Board of Regents, had the legislative bill drafted by his office. Essentially the form of the Bill is to add "Cleveland State University," as applicable, to Ohio code dealing with the existing universities. Dr. Millett was optimistic about capital funds to C.S.U. in the next five years.

Chairman Burmester also stated the administration had been talking to people knowledgeable in the legislative process to gain information and it would be appreciated if the Trustees would convey any thoughts they had to us respecting lobbying or our positioning.

6. The operating budget for the fiscal year, September 1, 1964, to August 31, 1965, was approved. The total budgeted income was $2,870,450 including $176,000 as gift income. The total budgeted expense was $3,165,198 thereby establishing a budgeted deficit of $294,748 which was to be paid out of the accumulated surplus of the College unless there was a definite agreement with the State or the gift income was more optimistic than expected.

The 1964 Annual Meeting of the Fenn College Corporation was held at The Union Club on Thursday, December 10. Seventy-two members and guests were present. Following the introduction of those at the speakers' table and the approval of the Minutes of the previous year's meeting, the Chairman called for those present to rise in memory of The Honorable Harold H. Burton, Honorary Life Trustee, who had passed away October 28, 1964.

Because of the turmoil the College was experiencing due to the uncertainty over a State University in Greater Cleveland, the board decided to amend the Code of Regulations of the College to extend the term of office one year for each Trustee and Member of the Corporation, rather than to change personnel on these two policy-making bodies during this period of stress.

Trustee George V. Woodling was presented a plaque in recognition of twenty-five years of service on the Fenn Board of Trustees.

For the first time in the history of Fenn College the net operations for the previous fiscal year terminating August 31, 1964, resulted in a deficit amounting to $10,213.48. The College, however, had a balance of accumulated income retained for future use amounting to $305,160.52 against which this deficit was charged. Again, the deficit resulted from lack of contributions brought about because of the vague and equivocal situation in which the College found itself regarding State status.

Chairman Burmester then presented the following remarks to those present:

> Members of the Fenn Corporation and guests, I extend my personal welcome to you as we gather tonight for this meeting which has historic significance for the institution we serve.

The steady guidance of many hands, the inspiration of many minds and hearts have moved Fenn College to perform a vital function in its community. Each of you has had a part in the College's achievements, a voice in establishing its direction. Your active interest and dedicated effort have helped carry Fenn to the threshold of a new role in higher education.

How Fenn can seize the challenges of this new role, expand its dimensions, and preserve the College's hard-won heritage are things we should be thinking about tonight. Now, at the outset, I am going to advance the proposition that we cannot deny this new role, any more than we can deny our exploding population, the changing patterns of higher education, and a society that hungers increasingly for knowledge.

Forces outside our sphere of influence have thrust this new role on Fenn. There may be a temptation to let these forces make our decisions for us, but that is a course we cannot risk. Our responsibility compels us to use these forces to shape the ends we have already espoused. I submit to you that this is precisely what we have done. I am certain that there are learned professors at the College who could trace the origin of these forces to the great depression or World War II, or perhaps even to Ancient Rome.

For my purposes, however, I need go back only as far as May, 1963, when Governor James Rhodes suggested that Fenn College operate as a technical college under the aegis of the State. At that moment the College had to face these emerging forces. I think we faced them squarely. Through the summer and autumn of 1963, we took a hard look at the College, its present position and its aims for the future. There was need also for a broader appraisal. What did our community need? What did business, industry and government require? The young people themselves—how was this burgeoning new generation to have the opportunity to maximize its potential? And what about our urban problems—blighted neighborhoods, water and air pollution, swelling welfare rolls and tangled mass transportation?

Through those months we witnessed the shaping of these forces when in June, 1963, the Ohio Legislature passed a law creating the Ohio Board of Regents, and later when the Regents were appointed in September.

When the time for decision came, Fenn said no to State-financed technical school status. Instead, it said on December 9, just one year ago last night in this very room, that what Cleveland and

Northeast Ohio need is a comprehensive state university, and the College submitted a plan for unified public higher education in our region. The plan pointed out that Ohio's most productive region in goods, services, and income did not have the advantages of a local state university to which its citizens could send their children at low tuition rates and circumvent the high cost of living away from home. It outlined the miscellany of public institutions in Cuyahoga County, emphasizing the need for better coordination of public higher education in our region and the relevance of that need to the charge given the new Board of Regents.

Fenn's Unified Plan called for the development of a comprehensive state university to be developed on the College's present site, utilizing its facilities and personnel as a nucleus. The Fenn Plan, though it was created by a private institution for a public institution, was consequently limited by its sphere of influence, but drew much attention from the press and the public. The lasting importance of the plan is not that it provided solutions for every problem Cleveland faces in higher education, but that it raised a community's sights. Everyone from professional educators to day laborers with a family to raise had a stake in this question, and the simple logic was there for all to grasp.

The proposition is simple enough. Cleveland is an urban center with an exploding population of college-age citizens. These young people require education beyond the high school in order to equip themselves for a productive place in our increasingly complex society. Conversely, the community's business, industrial, governmental and professional activities need the boundless resources of their imagination and creativity. In the parlance of political circles, we need them and they need us. And because private colleges do not possess the plant or the financial base to cope with this breaking wave of young people, the burden must be shouldered by public higher education. Conservative estimates indicate that a scant 15 years from now, public higher education will have increased its share of the enrollment pie from its present one-half to 80 per cent. Now if 8 out of 10 students enrolled in college will be attending a publicly supported institution in 1980, I think it is clear enough to everyone in this room that public higher education faces the challenge to achieve new levels of excellence.

All of this, of course, reinforces Fenn's basic position that Cleveland needs a comprehensive state university, rising from the quality and academic integrity Fenn has already created. Now I won't pretend that any of us two or three years ago foresaw what our position would be in December, 1964, but I do believe that by holding firmly to the things we believed in, we performed a great service to our community, our College, to higher education and to ourselves.

Our position was materially reinforced by the action of the Academy for Educational Development. If you will recall, when the Board of Regents engaged the Academy in February of this year to undertake preparation of a Master plan for higher education in Ohio, John R. Everett arrived in Cleveland the next month to begin to document immediately this area's needs, and ours became a top-priority study. By the time the snow had disappeared this City was solidly behind the creation of a Cleveland State University.

On May 19, twenty leading organizations pledged their support of the Fenn plan in a meeting sponsored by the Cleveland Commission on Higher Education. Several weeks later a public hearing of the Legislation Committee of Cleveland City Council elicited overwhelming support for the plan, and in that same month, the Regents directed a letter to Governor Rhodes calling for the creation of Cleveland State University, legislative action and appointment of a Board of Trustees.

This last autumn emergency legislation was drafted and presented to the Ohio Legislature, which convened in special session on November 9. This bill was passed by the House on November 12, 109 votes to 2. That same week the Board of Regents recommended that $37.5 million of a proposed Bond Issue be reserved for public higher education in Cuyahoga County.

On the 17th of November, the Senate Educational Committee unanimously approved the bill for Cleveland State University. Final Senate action is still pending, but once the bill clears the Senate, Governor Rhodes can sign the bill into law within a week. The Governor will appoint a board of nine trustees who can then begin negotiations with Fenn College for the acquisition of its land and facilities to serve as an operating nucleus of Cleveland State University.

Throughout the last 500 days, the word nucleus has appeared hundreds of times, signaling the growth and changing patterns that are to come.

Ohio college enrollment last year totaled 213,889 students, 42 per cent in private institutions, 58 per cent in public. A thoughtful projection of the conservative Thompson Study indicates that by 1975, some 435,000 students will be enrolled in higher education. Private enrollment will increase by 51 per cent, but public enrollment will grow *139 per cent*.

Based on the number of children alive today and a sound review of the increasing number who will look to higher education to prepare for productive livelihoods, another conservative projection predicts an enrollment of 20,000 students at Cleveland State University by 1974, and nearly 50,000 ten years later.

Last Friday evening on a television panel discussion, Dr. John Millett, Chancellor of the Board of Regents, projected a total of 70,000 Greater Clevelanders seeking enrollment in some form of higher education.

If Fenn College is to shape the forces of our time, this institution faces a dual responsibility. It must make decisions that will preserve its heritage and traditions, laying foundations for increased academic achievement, and at the same time, provide educational opportunities for the growing number of young people it must serve. Fenn has already carved out important traditions in providing quality education for young men and women possessed of more brains than hard cash. The only major change in the College's new role is that it must enlarge one factor in its formula. It must serve an increasing number of students.

Now, changing the value of any factor can wreak havoc in a given formula. It is obvious that the remaining factors must be readjusted. That adjustment will come in the years ahead. Our charge now, as we near negotiations, is to make decisions that will preserve an important heritage on the one hand, and create the kind of viable climate that will enable Fenn College to flower into a full-scale university with a boundless future. We owe a debt to the past and obligation to the future.

In two-score years the seed of a one-room school house has blossomed into the institution we cherish today. Now, as we enter 1965, this College prepares to do some impressive growing; we near the bearing of its fruit. Our harvest will come when Cleveland has a state university that nourishes the integrity of knowledge, imparts that knowledge to those who seek and need it, and employs that knowledge to power our progress and provide solutions for the complex problems of the 20th century.

Many of us will live to see that harvest, and each of us should take a special pride in its coming. It took many hearts and hands to come this far; it will take many more to achieve this fruition. The time has come for Fenn to tap the potential that confronts it. This is an age when small plans fall by the wayside, when only those who strive for greatness will prevail.

But this is the way life should be—a series of new horizons, wider than we know, somehow designed to demand the energy and the wisdom of man that drive him to new dimensions of greatness.

Those horizons are here, and Fenn College has the spirit and the character to conquer them. Fenn College is now endowed with the brightest of futures.

The other principal speaker on this occasion was President Earnest. Following is his address on the subject "The Position of Fenn College with Respect to State University Status":

On December 9, 1963, at the annual meeting of the Corporation, Fenn College announced 'A Plan for Unified Public Higher Education for Cleveland-Northeastern Ohio.' The plan proposed that the staff, the organization and the physical assets of Fenn College become the nucleus of a new state university in this area.

The College never intended that its proposal be thought of in terms of its location and physical assets alone; by far the most important part of the proposal was the utilization of the academic resources of the institution which have been developed over the past 41 years.

In a remarkably short time, through the efforts of an able and conscientious faculty and administration and a devoted Board of Trustees, Fenn College has grown from a most humble background into a fine institution with a well-established reputation for sound curricula and high academic standards. For many years Fenn has proudly held full accreditation by the North Central Association and approval of its engineering curricula by the Engineers' Council for Professional Development.

This rapid progress has been possible because of the recognition by the trustees and the administration of the need for faculty self-government and faculty prerogative in academic affairs; because of a concern by faculty, administration, and trustees for effective teaching and earnest scholarship; because of the concern by the whole institution for the welfare of the student; because of the total and continuous commitment of the College to the cooperative program of higher education; because of a selective admissions policy which seeks to relate the capacities of students to the requirements of the curriculum; because of a constant striving toward excellence on the part of the institution; and because of the contributions of the Board of Trustees, members of the Corporation, the alumni, and the community to the financial support of the College.

It was precisely because Fenn has achieved this distinction in higher education that the College felt it could offer the State the opportunity, at the very inception of a Cleveland State University, to operate an accredited institution with a promise of ultimate greatness. In the proposal to make Fenn the nucleus of a state university, it is important to emphasize these invaluable assets which Fenn has accumulated over the years. Thousands of Clevelanders have contributed to the building of this institution. The well-being of Fenn and of the community requires that these assets be protected and enhanced.

The young men and women of Cleveland are not less deserving than those of other Ohio communities, and Clevelanders are not less proud than residents of other regions of Ohio. The city merits a university which catches the imagination of its citizens and enlists their pride and their energy.

It would be illogical to replace one of Cleveland's fine private institutions with a mediocre public university or with one founded on principles which would become heavy obstacles to its development into an excellent institution.

Therefore, in weighing state university status the College shall hold fast to the principles which distinguish Fenn. In particular, this includes carrying out our commitments to our present students, maintaining the essential rights and privileges of the faculty and staff, retaining the cooperative program wherever feasible, making provision that in the beginning and thereafter the admission requirements will be consistent with those of the existing state universities, and keeping the enrollment growth of the institution consistent with the recruitment of an able faculty and the expansion of physical facilities. These principles shall form the basic guidelines in any consideration of Fenn's becoming a state university.

The President informed the members that at a meeting held that noon the faculty had endorsed unanimously his "Position Statement." Then member Frank E. Joseph moved that the Fenn Corporate Trustees and Members endorse the "Position Statement" as presented by President Earnest. The motion was passed unanimously.

Reflecting upon the foregoing, it can readily be discerned that the rugged path the Fenn Trustees walked down for 500 days provided the basis for their endorsement of the President's Position Statement. Without question, the eventual transfer of the physical assets plus faculty and administrative staff to The Cleveland State University was imposed upon the Fenn Board of Trustees and Members of the Corporation.

Just a brief recapitulation: The State (through Governor Rhodes) initiated the concept of a state university in the Metropolitan Cleveland area. It was a most appropriate concept because Cleveland was the largest city in Ohio without a tax-supported state university. From the very date of the announcement of the concept (May 13, 1963) Fenn College was considered as the nucleus for the proposed state university. Fenn was a going concern and rapidly growing in stature. Governor Rhodes had even complimented the College on its efficient management.

It was certainly proper (and in line with Ohio's very poor comparison with other states in relation to the percentage of funds allocated annually to higher education) for Ohio to increase its support of higher education. The obvious way to increase Ohio's status was to provide such funds for benefit of students who reside close to private colleges in densely populated areas. The actions finally taken, however, side-stepped the larger question. The Fenn trustees readily granted that the families of the Cleveland area were entitled to greater return from their taxes toward their higher education needs. It was also obvious that a small (though vigorous and financially sound) college could provide much greater services, in numbers and in program, if given some annual State financial assistance. This would not have gotten into the parochial question at all. The financial aid could have been related to student enrollment, or student financial aid requirements. The management of the college would have remained in the capable local civic hands which had brought it to the status of attracting the Governor's favorable attention and complimentary comments.

It was an opportunity to set an advanced pattern. The Fenn Board of Trustees repeatedly urged its exploration, but were met with an almost stereotyped response that it probably would be unconstitutional.

That seemed to be a handy phrase from some (but not all) of the Attorney-General's staff, for saying the State administration did not want to be bothered.

A trend of eliminating any significant number of the nation's successfully operated private colleges gives rise to thoughts of those countries where the colleges become the pawns of politics, and are opened and closed with the tides of governmental factions. This is the larger question. The Fenn trustees were on solid ground in preferring to explore the broader solution because it had long been done that way in neighboring Pennsylvania, New York and, indeed, even at Oxford and Cambridge in England.

Statements were being offered to the effect that State support to the Cleveland region could turn Fenn into one of the finest technical institutes in the country. Proposed amounts of financial assistance to Fenn as a state university were being publicized in the news media. The Trustees of Fenn College responded to these importunings and for many months they cooperated to the fullest extent with the Ohio Board of Regents respective to the consideration of Fenn College becoming a state university. Much information regarding Fenn's proposed plans to become State-supported was requested by the Regents and presented to them. A meeting of the Regents and Fenn's Trustees and Corporate Members was held in Stilwell Hall on Fenn's Campus. But, in due course, all this cooperation led to a point of no return.

Fenn was steadfastly losing control over the affairs of the original concept as deliberated with the Regents that the newly proposed state university would retain Fenn's Board of Trustees as a policy governing body. And, with the passing of time, there was an increasing variance in agreement from other sources in Columbus.

It finally reached a status where great damage was being inflicted upon the affairs of Fenn as a private college. Fenn had no previous financial difficulties. The College never experienced a deficit budget. However, suddenly with all the publicity of the possibility of Fenn becoming a tax-supported institution, many former faithful business and industrial organizations and generous individuals either dropped or greatly curtailed their operating and capital gift support which had been increasing over the past twelve years. These contributions were very important to Fenn's subsistence as a private college, but it now appeared that Fenn would soon become a tax-supported institution.

In addition to financial woes, there was mounting on the campus an unrest amongst the faculty and student body, kindled by the many uncertainties.

The author wishes to stress the fact that the State initially approached Fenn's trustees, not the antithesis. The college administration had already prepared its own ten-year operating and capital improvement plan as a private college and had completed two years of the program. It is also important to point out to the reader that the State finally received a $15,000,000 debt-free campus (including buildings, furnishings and equipment), a talented faculty of inestimable value, a "ready made" Day Division student body from freshmen through seniors numbering about 1,800, a large Evening Division student body numbering approximately 4,000, plus 6,000 alumni, and all this as an outright gift made possible through Fenn's Board of Trustees.

Within a week after the 1964 annual Fenn College Corporation meeting Governor Rhodes signed the bill creating The Cleveland State University and on December 18, 1964, he appointed the following as Trustees of the new university:

James J. Nance, Acting Chairman (Chief Executive, Central National Bank)

Curtis Lee Smith (President, Cleveland Chamber of Commerce)

Warren H. Chase (Retired Vice President, Ohio Bell Telephone Co.)

Dr. Abe Silverstein (Director, Lewis Research Laboratory NASA)

Joseph Bartunek (Member, Ohio State Senate)

Ernest R. Johnson (1st Vice President, Republic Steel Corp.)

Dr. Middleton H. Lambright (Surgeon and President of the Cleveland Academy of Medicine)

Edward W. Sloan, Jr. (President, Oglebay Norton Co.)

Wm. W. Taft (Member, Ohio House of Representatives)

The board held its first meeting Tuesday, December 22, at which time the following officers were elected:

Chairman, James J. Nance

Vice Chairman, Curtis Lee Smith

Secretary, Warren H. Chase

During the year 1964 President Earnest served on the Inter-Society Relations Committee of The National Society of Professional Engineers and was presented the Distinguished Service Award at the Annual Banquet of the Cleveland Technical Societies Council. He also served as President of the Presidents and Deans Section of the Ohio College Association.

The meetings between the Fenn College and C.S.U. Negotiating Committees reached a stalemate and finally in acquiescence the Fenn College Negotiating Committee submitted the following proposal dated February 8, 1965, to the C.S.U. Negotiating Committee:

> The Fenn College Negotiating Committee has been most reluctant to accept the frequently repeated contention of the CSU Negotiating Committee that CSU can negotiate for Fenn only on the basis of CSU receiving Fenn's fixed assets as an outright gift. These fixed assets are on Fenn's books for $7,500,000, and conservatively have a replacement value to CSU of at least $14,000,000. CSU's Negotiating Committee continued to reject Fenn's proposals, that even some nominal sum be paid Fenn for these assets, which Fenn would then put into a foundation that would devote itself to educational activities at CSU that cannot, by law, be supported with public funds. The Fenn Committee continues to be convinced that its proposals in this regard have been sound and wholly in the interests of the growth and success of CSU.
>
> The Fenn College Negotiating Committee is unanimous in its convictions that the young people of the Cleveland area sorely need the low-cost downtown university educational facilities that CSU can provide; and further, that Fenn's facilities, faculty and staff, all becoming the immediate nucleus of CSU, is the only practical way to fulfill promptly this long over-due need. The need is patent and the need is now, and it is in the full recognition of the seriousness of this situation that the Fenn College Negotiating Committee feels compelled to recommend to Fenn's Board of Trustees and Corporation Members that each in turn act favorably and promptly on the following proposal:
>
> 1. That Fenn make a gift to CSU of the land and buildings at the site of its present campus, and that the terms of the gift provide for a reversion clause should CSU cease to use the facilities as an active part of the educational activities of the University.
> 2. That Fenn sell to CSU all furnishings and equipment used in Fenn's operations on the campus for the sum of $260,000,

which represents the estimate of Fenn's current operating deficit, and which overlooks entirely the very sizeable shrink in gifts of at least $1,000,000. to Fenn since the CSU-Fenn story broke in the press nearly two years ago.

3. That CSU shall accept the transfer of the faculty and staff of Fenn, and that CSU is to make provisions which will hold Fenn Trustees and Corporation Members harmless from liabilities that might arise out of termination of employment by Fenn College, resulting from the fact that Fenn ceased to be a functioning academic institution.

4. That CSU is to provide personnel so transferred from Fenn with the same or improved salary arrangements, at least the equivalent in the area of so-called fringe benefits when they cannot be duplicated in kind, and in general, CSU is to alleviate any personal hardship that arises solely out of the transfer from Fenn to CSU.

5. In view of the immediate need for administrative planning and the immediate need for administrative commitments involving the completion of this school year and the up-coming new school year, it is proposed that the CSU Trustees join with the Fenn Trustees in joint administration of the operations of Fenn College immediately so that CSU can assume its rightful responsibilities in commitments and decisions that must be made in the immediate future. Surely the CSU Trustees as well as Fenn's faculty and staff can each derive great benefit thereby, recognizing of course that all legal phases of the transaction would follow to completion in due course.

6. At the time when all formal actions have been taken and transfer of properties is made, Fenn College will reorganize and become The Fenn Educational Foundation . . . a charitable foundation . . . to administer whatever liquid assets remain with Fenn. It will be the duty of Fenn's Trustees to program the future of the Fenn Educational Foundation when the Trustees determine what if any significant assets remain for them to administer after all responsibilities have been discharged.

7. That CSU is to agree that the Fenn name will be carried on by designating the activities in engineering education as *Fenn College of Engineering*, as one of the colleges of the University. It is to be further agreed that CSU will continue the Fenn Plan for Cooperative Education as a program offered by the University.

If the CSU Negotiating Committee finds the features outlined in this proposal acceptable, and if it is willing to recommend it to its Board of Trustees for approval, the Fenn College Committee will thereafter promptly recommend it to its Board of Trustees and Corporation Members at a special meeting to be called by the Chairman. If the Fenn Board and Corporation Members act favorably upon the recommendation, it will then be necessary for Fenn to instigate appropriate legal proceedings to obtain approval of the Court to the action of its Members in giving its fixed assets to CSU, and approval to its action to terminate Fenn College, neither action having been contemplated by the founders of the College, nor by the donors of the funds which made the College possible.

The proposal outlined above for the sake of brevity has been restricted to a listing and a noting of bare essentials. The Fenn College Committee suggests that if agreement of principles has been reached each side bring together its legal people with instructions to cooperate in the drafting of a formal Contract or Agreement.

> Submitted by
> The Negotiating Committee
> FENN BOARD OF TRUSTEES

February 8, 1965
GBE:jlm

Although this is jumping ahead a month in the Fenn deliberations, the above proposal was accepted by the Trustees of C.S.U. through the following letter of March 8, 1964, to Chairman Burmester, signed by James J. Nance (Chairman, C.S.U. Board) and Ernest R. Johnson (Chairman C.S.U. Negotiating Committee).

In wrapping up the work of the Fenn College Negotiating Committee and exhibiting the mark of an excellent chairman, Trustee Fries submitted the following condensed report to Chairman Burmester on the over-all deliberations between the two Trustee Negotiating Committees of Fenn College and C.S.U.

As you know, our physical assets stand on our books at approximately $7,500,000. The replacement value exceeds $14,000,000. We also have approximately $1,500,000 of potential liquid assets on our books. One of our notable assets, not measurable in dollars, is a fine faculty and staff which as a "going concern" is daily impregnating a fine student body with a quality of college training that is highly accredited. Still another is a fine ever-growing alumni

THE CLEVELAND STATE UNIVERSITY
P. O. BOX 5578
CLEVELAND, OHIO 44101

March 8, 1965

Mr. Harry F. Burmester, Chairman
Board of Trustees
Fenn College of Cleveland
Cleveland, Ohio

Dear Harry:

The Trustees of The Cleveland State University hereby express their acceptance of the proposal of the Trustees of Fenn College dated February 8, 1965, and their willingness to consummate that proposal provided:

1. The effective date of the agreement and the date of take-over of The Cleveland State University is to be on September 1, 1965, or as near thereafter as the completion of the Fenn College summer quarter. If you have not received appropriate court approvals at that time, we shall proceed with a mutually acceptable interim agreement, and,

2. That any subsequent contractual document between the parties to this agreement shall be limited to the seven points of your February 8 proposal unless there is mutual consent to the contrary.

The total direct cash cost of this transaction to the State of Ohio shall be $260,000 as per your proposal.

However, I am happy to advise you that the Trustees of The Cleveland State University are able and willing to employ the administrative and clerical staff, including the heads of academic departments of Fenn College for the months of July and August and meet the expenses of this group if you so desire, providing that the total expense shall not exceed $114,000 for this period. This offer is made in order to accomplish two ends:

1. Assist the Trustees of the Fenn College to restrict their total operating deficit as they conclude their operations, and

2. Assist the Trustees of The Cleveland State University in having adequate staff for planning the 1965 academic year.

The details of the transfer which have been unofficially presented
in draft form dated February 22, 1965, and modified February 25,
1965, by the legal counsel of Fenn College are neither affirmed
nor denied by this letter. The legal form and detailed actions
involved in consummating this agreement shall be made, as usual, with
the counsel and agents of all interested parties being adequately and
fairly represented. Legal counsel in the case of The Cleveland State
University is by law the Attorney General of the State of Ohio.

In the interest of the students who will be affected by the transfer
of Fenn College from private to public status this offer is extended
until 10:30 A.M., Wednesday, March 10, 1965. At that time at the
regular meeting, which is by law a public meeting, of the Trustees
of The Cleveland State University, it is considered necessary in the
public interest that we should agree on implementing your February 8,
1965, proposal as modified with this letter so that a public announcement can be made as to whether CSU shall start the 1965-66 academic
year with or without the Fenn College as the core. At that time,
as you and I have discussed, a public announcement must be made which
will hopefully be a joint announcement that your proposal is to be
implemented.

                                        Cordially,

                                        James J. Vance
                                        Chairman
                                        Board of Trustees

                                        E. R. Johnson
                                        Chairman
                                        Negotiating Committee

group that is working for Fenn's interests. Without Fenn as a nucleus, which can give Cleveland State University a running start, I am sure that starting a new university from scratch would be a very time-consuming and costly project.

When the subject was first discussed with the Board of Regents about a year ago, we felt we would be giving the State of Ohio a bargain in fixed assets if we sold them for their book value, particularly so because we proposed that the purchase amount would go into a Fenn Foundation which in turn would sponsor necessary educational projects at CSU that normally cannot be done with public funds. Even then we were warned from many quarters to the effect that "Columbus" expected the fixed assets as a gift, and that money could not be appropriated to buy our fixed assets.

The new CSU Trustees were appointed in December, and a negotiating committee was established, with which our committee first met on January 13th. We were informed at that meeting that it would be impossible to appropriate any money for our fixed assets. This position was maintained by the CSU Committee in all subsequent meetings. Willingness was expressed, however, to take our fixed assets as a gift and to take over faculty and staff, and insofar as possible hold them free of personal hardship arising out of the transfer.

Our committee made a series of proposals, all of which were rejected. Throughout our so-called negotiations, our team maintained that CSU, just as other state supported schools, needed a foundation of adequate size to devote the income therefrom toward projects which the University cannot do for itself with publicly appropriated funds. The more Fenn could get for its fixed assets, to add to its liquid assets, the greater the benefits to be bestowed upon CSU at its very beginning. It was also pointed out that such a foundation of reasonable magnitude administered primarily by Fenn Trustees would probably cause many of the Fenn group to transfer their civic efforts undiminished to CSU, which personal efforts otherwise would possibly be transferred to other community activities.

The proposals with respect to our fixed assets made by our team in the order listed were as follows:

1. Sell to the State for book value of $7,500,000 and add this to our potential liquid assets of $1,000,000 to $1,500,000 making a healthy foundation of $8,500,000 to $9,000,000 that could do much for CSU.

2. Sell to the State for a smaller amount—just enough so that when added to our potential liquid assets of $1,000,000 to $1,500,000 there would be the minimum amount to make a foundation worthwhile—which we arbitrarily set at $3,500,000.

3. Make a ten-year lease to CSU, with an option for purchase, on a net net basis at a nominal rental per square foot for buildings and equipment—such rentals less any costs to administer the lease to go into the foundation, which presumably would not limit itself to activities at CSU. The rate we proposed was $2.00 per square foot per year, which is surely nominal even though the maintenance was theirs.

4. Make a net net lease of the property and equipment to CSU for $1.00 a year for three years or four years so they could get CSU going promptly, and during the lease build the kind of buildings and facilities they want adjacent to the present Fenn property, or elsewhere. When their new facilities come into use and they have vacated Fenn property, then Fenn Trustees would dispose of the property on the open market and add the funds to the foundation fund, which presumably would not limit itself to activities at CSU.

All of these proposals by our team, having to do with the fixed assets phase of the negotiations, were rejected by the CSU Negotiating Committee. Our team then asked that the CSU team prepare a proposal, which it was hoped would reflect understanding of the points our team felt to be so important. On Monday, February 1st, we met and received their proposal. In essence it was as follows:

1. Accept our physical assets as a gift.
2. Take over our faculty and staff.
3. Use the name of Fenn as the Fenn College of Engineering— continue co-op training for the time being.
4. Take over all of our liquid assets with the exception of our securities and give us a check for $1,250,000, which when added to the market value of our securities of $793,000 makes a total of $2,043,000; which amount was to constitute a Fenn Foundation which was to be controlled at the time of origin

by seven trustees—four from CSU and three from Fenn. Future trustees of the foundation were to be elected by the Trustees of CSU.

What this really means is they proposed to add to our potential liquid assets of $1,500,000 about $500,000 as mainly operating deficits, from which we would start a foundation, and then turn the control of the foundation over to the CSU Trustees. This we have flatly rejected, even though we were informed that the control of the foundation was open to some discussion.

We then prepared an entirely new proposal dated February 8, 1965. This proposal was submitted to the members of the CSU Negotiating Committee on Monday, February 8, and after much discussion the CSU Negotiating Committee members agreed to give the proposal further consideration, which they did the same evening. Furthermore, this same proposal was discussed by the CSU Board of Trustees at a special session on Tuesday, February 9.

Following further deliberation between the Chairmen of the two negotiating committees concerning clarification of a fiscal detail, the Chairman of the CSU Negotiating Committee expressed agreement of his committee and other parties representing CSU with the Fenn proposal of February 8, 1965.

It is agreed by the Negotiating Committees from both Fenn and CSU that July 1, 1965 would be the date of transfer of Fenn College operations to CSU.

The first Board of Trustees' meeting in 1965 was held on Tuesday, February 16. The board noted with regret the resignations of Trustee Dr. Abe Silverstein and Corporate Members James J. Nance and Curtis L. Smith, who had been appointed on the previous December 18 to the Board of Trustees of C.S.U. Trustee Fries officially submitted the February 8, 1965, proposal of the Fenn College Negotiating Committee and reported that it had been approved by both the C.S.U. Board and proper authorities in Columbus.

Alan G. Rorick, Counsel with Baker, Hostetler, and Patterson, explained that Fenn could bring action for a declaratory judgment to terminate the Fenn Corporation. Fenn would be the plaintiff and the Attorney General of Ohio and the C.S.U. Trustees would constitute the defense. All transfer agreements would be presented to Common Pleas Court as a test of their legality.

The C.S.U. Trustees had engaged Dr. Harry Newburn, of the University of Arizona, as a consultant to handle administrative affairs of the proposed new university while they sought a president. There was an urgency about all kinds of C.S.U. operating problems such as admission standards, tuition, faculty, fall enrollment, and budget. Dr. Newburn requested the services of Dr. Patterson, Provost, on a half-time basis to help resolve these operating problems, C.S.U. to pay half of Dr. Patterson's salary. It turned out that all of Dr. Patterson's time was demanded for this planning task.

Many questions were raised at this February 16, 1965, board meeting, such as:

> What about the tax considerations of our donors who provided our endowment and building funds?
>
> When would C.S.U. actually take over?
>
> What about assurances that the faculty and administrative staff members would be protected through engagement by C.S.U.?
>
> What about President Earnest's security?
>
> What about provision for an indemnity clause holding the Fenn Trustees harmless?
>
> Should there be a reversion clause in the agreement?
>
> What if the State Legislature refused to pay Fenn College the stipulated amount?

There was much discussion concerned with making an outright gift of Fenn's physical facilities, but it appeared that to do otherwise at that late date would harm Fenn's future as a college. As one Trustee put it at the meeting, "We had the option of being shot or hung."

At the close of the meeting the following Resolution was adopted:

> RESOLVED: That all actions of the Executive Committee and the Negotiating Committee of the Executive Committee with respect to the negotiations with the Board of Trustees of The Cleveland State University, and in particular the Proposal from the Negotiating Committee, Board of Trustees, Fenn College to the Negotiating

Committee, Board of Trustees of The Cleveland State University dated February 8, 1965, are hereby ratified, adopted, and approved.

The Executive Committee, with the assistance of counsel for the Corporation, is directed to cause to be prepared in cooperation with representatives of the Board of Trustees of The Cleveland State University and such other representatives of the State of Ohio as may be required, an Agreement between Fenn College and the Board of Trustees of The Cleveland State University and/ or the State of Ohio, as may be appropriate, incorporating the features contained in the said Proposal. Such Agreement shall be contingent upon appropriate approval of the court as to the transfer of assets and the termination of the College. Contingent upon such court approval the consummation of this transaction shall be July 1, 1965.

Such Agreement shall be presented as soon as possible to this Board of Trustees and the members of Fenn College for formal approval.

Pending formal approval of such an Agreement the members of the staff of Fenn College are authorized to consult with such representatives of the Board of Trustees of The Cleveland State University as may be appropriate, to the end that joint administrative planning contemplated in the Proposal may be commenced.

The above motion was voted unanimously but, as was said by most Trustees, "reluctantly."

Dr. Hodge then stated that it was his view as a Trustee to preserve Fenn and to this end he had spoken to the President of Case Institute of Technology regarding a possible merger of the two institutions but found that this would not be possible at this time. Trustee Fries reported that the newspaper stories seemed to indicate a leak in information possibly from Columbus because he and Trustee Johnson of C.S.U. had agreed to give joint releases. It was decided that henceforth, the Fenn people should present a cheerful front and voice no misgivings.

There was, nevertheless, still a question in everyone's mind on the final outcome of all negotiations. Chairman Burmester discovered through conversation with Chairman Nance of C.S.U. that, because of the urgent desire to begin classes in the fall of 1965, Nance had considered and assessed possibilities of the Kent State and Ohio State branches doing the job for C.S.U., if a final agreement for Fenn's physical facilities could not be consummated in time.

A special meeting of the Executive Committee was held March 4, 1965, to receive a specific document from Nance and further discuss Fenn's plight. Prior to reading his and E. R. Johnson's letter of March 4, 1965, to the Executive Committee members, Nance pointed out that he had tried to stay on the sidelines and lend Johnson support during the negotiations. He said there were acute money problems because the law creating C.S.U. provided only for operating funds and proceeds from the first bond issue provided only for capital funds, but all funds were subject to approval by other state agencies, making negotiating difficult for the C.S.U. committee. However, he had never heard in Columbus anything but that Fenn should be the nucleus for C.S.U.

Following is Chairman Nance's and Johnson's letter to Chairman Burmester.

As a result of the general agreement of the items in the above letter, the Fenn Board of Trustees held an 8:30 a.m. breakfast meeting at the College on Wednesday, March 10, 1965, at which Chairman Burmester opened the meeting with the statement, "It appears we have now evolved the best solution to the transfer of Fenn College to C.S.U. status." Trustee Frank L. Elmendorf's resignation because of recent conflict of interest was accepted with regret.

Trustee Fries reported in detail the resolution of certain problems leading up to Chairman Nance's letter of March 8, 1965, and referred to a new resolution which Rorick then read to those present. The resolution, as follows, was voted unanimously:

> RESOLVED: WHEREAS, at a meeting of these Trustees on February 16, 1965, the actions of the Executive Committee and the Negotiating Committee of the Executive Committee with respect to the negotiations with the Board of Trustees of The Cleveland State University were adopted and approved and the Executive Committee, with the assistance of counsel, was directed to cause to be prepared a draft of a proposed Agreement with the Board of Trustees of The Cleveland State University with respect to transfer of certain assets and personnel to The Cleveland State University, and
>
> WHEREAS, since the meeting of February 16, 1965, continuing negotiations between the Executive Committee and the Board of Trustees of The Cleveland State University have taken place, culminating in a letter of March 8, 1965, from the Chairman of the Board of Trustees of The Cleveland State University and the Chair-

THE CLEVELAND STATE UNIVERSITY
P.O. BOX 5578
CLEVELAND, OHIO 44101

March 4, 1965

Mr. Harry F. Burmester, Chairman
Board of Trustees
Fenn College of Cleveland
Cleveland, Ohio

Dear Harry:

You have asked that I reduce to writing the tentative agreements that you and I have reached concerning the transfer of the Fenn College operation to the State of Ohio as the core of The Cleveland State University. As you requested, this letter is addressed to you but has been reviewed and is co-signed by Mr. Johnson of our Negotiations Committee who is familiar with all of the discussions which have been held. This writing represents the long and effective work of the Negotiations Committees of both sides as well as the several recent discussions between you and me.

The official proposal of the Fenn Negotiating Committee, dated February 8, 1965, and transmitted to us by the Fenn Trustees' Resolution of Ratification, dated February 16, 1965, is an effective outline for this writing, and permits me to record the tentative agreements item by item. We both recognize, of course, that this series of proposals shall serve as the principal outline of the necessary formal, legally phrased and detailed agreement which must be prepared following mutual acceptance of these basic points.

My understanding is that you and I have agreed that upon advice from you that the Fenn Trustees have approved in principal the agreements listed below, then they shall be presented for immediate similar approval by the Trustees of The Cleveland State University.

As we have discussed, it is quite probable that any public monies which are transferred to Fenn Trustees will come from the operating appropriation to CSU because there are no specific funds provided for the purpose. This decision, and others during the course of our negotiations, has been necessary because of the various and stringent rules and precedents existent on the use of state funds. Because of these conditions, as well as the specific characteristics of the law which created CSU, it has been and is necessary for various agencies of state government, other than the CSU Trustees, to approve our negotiations. This has made the task doubly difficult and tedious, and I wish to express for the CSU Trustees our appreciation of the understanding which you and all others from Fenn have extended to us during the past sixty days.

Now, as to our item by item tentative agreements, in terms of the items of the previously mentioned proposal.

ITEM 1
The CSU Trustees will, of course, be delighted to accept, on behalf of the State of Ohio, your offer of lands and buildings of the present Fenn College Corporation without compensation. This, we believe, is a major community contribution to The Cleveland State University. This Board is mindful of the value of these properties and that such a gift will help greatly in encouraging the rapid development of the new state university.

ITEM 2
The CSU Trustees agree to pay to the Trustees of the Fenn College Corporation the sum of $260,000 which represents the estimate of Fenn's current operating deficit. This sum shall be paid for furnishings and equipment or to extinguish all external property

claims owed by Fenn, whichever phrasing suits the technicalities
of the formal document of agreement.

ITEM 3
The CSU Trustees shall agree to accept the transfer of faculty
and staff of the Fenn College Corporation for initial appointment
to the faculty and staff of The Cleveland State University, and
to hold the Fenn College Corporation harmless from liability that
might arise from termination of their employment.

ITEM 4
The CSU Trustees shall agree to provide transferred personnel the
same or improved salary arrangements upon initial appointment and
to continue such fringe benefits as are permitted by state law,
and this be met from available income.

ITEM 5
The Board of Trustees of The Cleveland State University appreciates
the proposal for joint administration, but believes that this
arrangement is potentially unfair to the students of the summer term
in that it may create difficulties in the assignment and transfer
of credits and other academic matters. Therefore, this Board
proposes that the Fenn College Corporation shall operate the
institution through the summer term and that the actual transfer
of all properties shall take place after the completion of that
term but as near to September 1, 1965 as possible. The Board of
Trustees of The Cleveland State University proposes that it have
access to the Fenn College Corporation property and staff between
July 1, 1965 and September 1, 1965 for the planning purposes as may
be necessary in order to arrange the start of The Cleveland State
University operations in September, 1965. We understand that the
monthly payroll of this administrative and clerical staff, including
the heads of the academic departments, is $57,000 per month. There-
fore, we propose to pay the Fenn College Corporation the sum of
$114,000 for the use of this staff during July and August, 1965.
This Board expresses it hope that the Fenn College Corporation
will provide appropriate office space for the Board of Trustees
of The Cleveland State University from the date of acceptance
of this proposal.

ITEM 6
I express the hope of our entire Board when I say we are very
conscious of the many benefits which such a Foundation can
bring to an academic institution and we hope the activities of
the Fenn Educational Foundation will be devoted to the progress
and growth of The Cleveland State University.

ITEM 7
The CSU Trustees agree to designate the activities of the
university in engineering as the Fenn College of Engineering,
The Cleveland State University, and to continue the cooperative plan of engineering education until such time as further
evaluation of it, including faculty recommendations, can be
considered by those agencies involved.

The financial proposals above represent the maximum possible agreement. The
effect of the potential removal of the $364,000 from the operating funds
of CSU, on such things as the number of students enrolled and the tuition
is not yet known by us. However, we have, as you know, elected to so
encumber our operating funds to this extent in an effort to resolve our
negotiations immediately so that we can move into the essential planning
for the 1965 academic year. The operating funds for CSU are presently a
part of the appropriations bill before the Ohio General Assembly. This bill
will be enacted prior to the July 1, 1965 beginning of the next fiscal year.

The above proposals are all phrased as they have been cleared with the appropriate public officials and agencies involved, and we have every reason to believe that they will be approved.

As you and I have discussed, we are all in agreement that the time for action must be now. We hope, therefore, that your Executive Committee will take affirmative action today. Assuming that such is the case, and that your Board of Trustees accept the recommendation of you and your Committee, we will, upon hearing from you, go ahead with the schedule as discussed. The Cleveland State University Board Meeting will be scheduled for 11 AM, Wednesday, March 10th, following your meeting of the Fenn Trustees earlier the same day. We hope you, and as many other Fenn Trustees as possible will join us in our public meeting to be held in the Sheraton-Cleveland Hotel, so that a joint press conference can be held immediately following our CSU action. We hope to have Governor Rhodes and Dr. John Millett present at this meeting. We have agreed that it is in the best interest of all of us, and certainly the best public image for the community, to present the most united, cooperative and optimistic front possible to all news media on the occasion of this significant agreement.

Following the session, the writer will host a reception and luncheon for as many as choose to stay. This will include the state officials as well as others who have an interest, particularly the press. Will you extend an invitation for me to your Trustees to be my guest at this luncheon affair?

Cordially,

James J. Nance
Chairman
Board of Trustees

E. R. Johnson
Chairman
Negotiating Committee

man of the Negotiating Committee of that University addressed to Harry F. Burmester, Chairman, Board of Trustees of Fenn College, and

WHEREAS, said letter of March 8, 1965, expresses acceptance of the proposal of the Trustees of Fenn College dated February 8, 1965, as modified by the provisions of the March 8, 1965 letter, and

WHEREAS, it is now desired to indicate the approval of these Trustees to the February 8, 1965 proposal, as modified by the understanding set forth in the March 8, 1965 letter,

Now, THEREFORE, the proposal from the Negotiating Committee Board of Trustees of Fenn College Corporation to the Negotiating Committee of the Board of Trustees of The Cleveland State University, dated February 8, 1965, together with the understanding set forth in the aforesaid letter of March 8, 1965, is hereby approved upon the basis that such proposal and modification shall be reduced to contractual form mutually acceptable to both parties and their counsel. The aforesaid approval is expressly conditioned upon the approval of the members of Fenn College Corporation of the transaction contemplated by such proposal as modified by the understanding set forth in said March 8, 1965 letter. The Executive Committee, with the assistance of counsel, is directed to work with the Board of Trustees of The Cleveland State University and its legal counsel to arrive at an acceptable form of legal agreement to be submitted to this Board of Trustees and the members of Fenn College Corporation for their respective approvals.

Trustee Fries also mentioned that Columbus requested the actual turn-over date of the College to the State to be moved from July 1 to September 1, 1965, and that $114,000 would be paid to Fenn representing July and August payrolls for administration and clerical staff to aid in planning for the fall term. The legal "Agreement" between Fenn and the State had reached the third-draft stage. It had verbal approval by the Ohio Board of Regents, Finance Director Krabach, and Governor Rhodes. The biggest hurdle had now been cleared.

The final paragraph of the Minutes of the March 10, 1965, Board meeting is as follows: "Trustee Fisher projected the appreciation of the members of the Board to Messrs. Burmester and Fries and the members of Fenn's Negotiating Committee for their time, effort and energies spent in bringing to fruition the agreement between the Fenn and C.S.U. Boards on the use of the present Fenn College Campus as a core [nucleus] for the new C.S.U."

The public approval of both boards was announced at a luncheon at the Sheraton Cleveland Hotel at noon followed the morning meetings of both boards. Fourteen trustees of Fenn College attended the luncheon.

The following is the statement prepared by President Earnest on the agreement:

The agreement reached this morning between the Fenn Trustees and the Trustees of The Cleveland State University gives Cleveland a good start toward the creation of a comprehensive state university.

By using Fenn College as a nucleus, The Cleveland State University can open next fall with three buildings, a 7½-acre downtown campus, and a faculty of 280 full- and part-time teachers. Fenn's role in providing quality higher education without frills and its location make the College especially well suited for the work that lies ahead.

As President of Fenn, I can tell you that the faculty and administrative staff are very excited about the prospects of becoming a full-scale state university. We have been devoting our energies and time to study and planning for the future of this new institution.

Many Clevelanders may not yet realize the impact this University can have on our community. Our young people need higher education these days to find a productive place in our society. This region needs the skills, brainpower and creativity of its citizens. This exchange can revitalize our area, stimulating employment and economic expansion.

This modern age is powered by knowledge. The great challenge of our time is to put that knowledge in the hands of people who can put it to work. That is what we will be doing at The Cleveland State University in the years ahead.

The urban university today is not a cloistered institution playing a passive role in its environment, but a viable organism in its community. It is our hope that C.S.U. will continue in Fenn's tradition and enhance its position as a knowledge-nerve center of Cuyahoga County.

Its major goal will be to educate citizens who have a knowledge of their spiritual and cultural heritage, and a sense of responsibility for worthwhile application of their learning.

It will continue, as Fenn has in the past, to attract students of broad intellectual and cultural backgrounds, and to reach a goal of greatness toward which Fenn has always striven.

The Ohio Board of Regents met March 19, 1965, and approved the transfer of Fenn College to the State. For the next two months much time was spent in discourse and debate concerning the wording of the agreement and plan of transition between Fenn College and C.S.U. Important areas of resolution were:

Acceptance of all Fenn College employees by C.S.U. for a minimum period of one year and a signed mutual release agreement from each employee waiving any claims, duties, debts, responsibilities, liabilities in law or in equity against Fenn College resulting from the transfer of the College to the State.

Status of President Earnest through to at least his sixty-fifth birthday.

The problem of fringe benefits for the employees of Fenn College for July and August 1965. At the time of transfer they were automatically to go on the public employees retirement system.

Reimbursement to Fenn for operating deficit resulting from reduction of operating grants because of "transfer to State" publicity.

A hold-harmless clause in behalf of Fenn's trustees.

The disposition of specific restricted funds held by Fenn College.

The disposition of monies received by Fenn as gifts for capital expenditure.

A reverter clause in the event C.S.U. does not remain in the Fenn College area.

The method of conveying Fenn's real estate to C.S.U.

The method of conveying Fenn's furniture, fixtures and equipment to C.S.U.

C.S.U.'s purchase of bookstore inventory from Fenn.

The effective date of transfer.

All the above items were discussed many times (Fenn's Executive Committee met May 14, 27, and June 9 on the subject) and eventually resolved by the attorneys and trustees of Fenn and C.S.U. and the Attorney General of Ohio, who at that time was William B. Saxbe. The final Agreement and Plan of Transition was dated July 9, 1965.

While all of the concerns and deliberations were under way leading to the decision literally to give Fenn College's physical assets (including land, buildings, furnishings, and equipment) plus its faculty and staff to the State of Ohio, the Fenn Trustees were reflecting on what to do about the College's liquid assets which as final figures became available, including outstanding student loan values and other special accounts, approximated $2,000,000.

At the board meeting of September 28, 1964, Chairman Burmester had reported that he had appointed a Fenn Educational Foundation Committee composed of Trustees Hale, Dickey, and Peirce with Hale, Chairman, and President Earnest, *ex-officio*. This committee had held its first meeting September 30, 1964. Chairman Hale, in his opening statement, commented that he presumed a likelihood that the proposed foundation would be entirely separate from the new university and that it would have its own Board of Trustees and perhaps other official personnel. He intimated purposes of such a foundation should further the effectiveness of C.S.U. and perhaps other area colleges.

Trustee Dickey described the Purdue Foundation on which he had served as a director. It was started about 1924 with a grant of $250,000 and had grown to $25,000,000 in about forty years. Its operating income in 1963 was approximately $1,500,000. President Hovde of Purdue had stated it was the most important instrument for growth that Purdue had. It provided funds for projects for which State funds were not forthcoming.

Preliminary purposes of the proposed foundation included the following:

1. To strengthen academic programs.
2. Assist faculty and students to further their educational growth.
3. Provide scholarships, fellowships, professorships, and other financial aid to students and faculty.

Inasmuch as the University of Buffalo had had a similar transfer of status, i.e., from private to public, and a foundation resulted from the transfer, it was decided to invite Dr. William J. O'Connor, Director of The University of Buffalo Foundation, Inc. to the next meeting of the Fenn Foundation Committee. This meeting was held November 23, 1964, at which Dr. O'Connor stated that from a $28,000,000 endowment held by The University of Buffalo with private status, the surviving foundation was able to keep only $2,000,000 which was augmented by a loan of an additional $1,500,000 by the State without interest. The balance of the endowment remained with the University to serve to reduce State appropriations where necessary.

Dr. O'Connor disclosed that there was a considerable alienation of the alumni of the University of Buffalo because of the manner of the negotiations and that in an endeavor to heal some of the wounds the offices of the foundation were housed in University buildings, rent free, and the accounting work was done by the university. There was no doubt that problems existed in the transfer to State status.

The Foundation Committee met December 21, 1964, and summarized its findings to date. The committee felt the Foundation should be independent of C.S.U., having its own trustees and administration, and the offices should not be on the C.S.U. Campus. It was probable that the Foundation would not need as large a board as the then existent Fenn College Board, but there appeared no necessity for immediate reduction because there was value in wide representation during the transition period. The Committee urged harmonious relations with the Fenn Alumni. It was recognized that the Alumni were maturing, and that there would be no more Fenn Alumni after the transfer of the College to the State. Increased assets of the Foundation prior to transfer would serve as a substantial force to attract gifts on a broad basis long before C.S.U. could do the equivalent. This would be the best possible seed money for the benefit of C.S.U. in the future.

Because of the pressure of board and board committee meetings the Foundation Committee did not meet again until June 24, 1965. It was decided that the new organization would be known as the Fenn Educational Foundation inasmuch as the C.S.U. Board was agreeable to naming the School of Engineering of Fenn the "Fenn College of Engineering at C.S.U." Discussion ensued concerning the wording of proposed letters to all donors to Fenn College, first with respect to a gift of the physical assets of the College to the State and secondly, with respect to allocating all endowment and other liquid assets to the new Foundation with a minimum of restrictions. Although this letter might not be legally necessary, it was decided that as a matter of courtesy, good faith, and astute public relations, as well as an assistance to the court in judging all aspects of the matter, all donors should be asked to express their official approval of Fenn's plan to retain all such gifts in the Fenn Educational Foundation. Individual letters were prepared, approved and mailed to all donors, numbering approximately one hundred. All donors, but one, complied with the request to transfer their gifts to the newly proposed Foundation.

One of the largest of the gifts ever made to Fenn College was in June 1957 by The Ford Foundation in the amount of $453,000. The income was restricted toward increases in faculty salaries until July 1, 1966, at which time the principal and/or income from the grant could be used for any educational purposes of the institution. Inasmuch as the grant had approximately one year left before expiration of the terms of the restrictive clause, a Resolution of Intention was prepared by Fenn's legal counsel which was approved by The Ford Foundation permitting the principal to be transferred to the Fenn Educational Foundation as noted in the following copy of the Resolution:

WHEREAS, Fenn College Corporation was the Grantee of a grant of $453,000 made by The Ford Foundation on June 24, 1957, the income from which was to be used by the Grantee until July 1, 1966 for the purpose of increasing faculty salaries; and

WHEREAS, it is now anticipated that as soon as Court approval therefor has been obtained, now contemplated to be on or about October 15, 1965 Fenn College Corporation will transfer to or for the use of The Cleveland State University all of the real and tangible personal property presently used by it in the conduct of its educational activities and thereafter will terminate its operations as a college; and

WHEREAS, Fenn College Corporation intends, as soon as reasonably practicable following termination of its operations as a college, to file Amended Articles of Incorporation with the Secretary of State of Ohio and thereafter, in accordance with and pursuant to the terms of said Amended Articles, to continue its existence and operations under the name Fenn Educational Foundation solely for the purposes set forth in said Amended Articles, including, within the scope of said purposes, the assistance of said The Cleveland State University; and

WHEREAS, Fenn College, and upon and after the filing of the aforesaid Amended Articles of Incorporation, Fenn Educational Foundation, desires that the fundamental intent of the June 24, 1957 Ford Foundation grant to Fenn College be fulfilled by it;

NOW, THEREFORE, BE IT RESOLVED:

1. That so long as Fenn College Corporation continues to operate an educational institution, as it did at the time of the June 24, 1957 grant to Fenn College by The Ford Foundation of $453,000, it will continue to follow the original Terms of Grant specified in writing by said The Ford Foundation under date of June 24, 1957.

2. That upon the transfer by Fenn College Corporation to or for the use of The Cleveland State University of all real and tangible personal property presently used by it in the conduct of its educational activities, said Fenn College Corporation, and upon and after the filing of Amended Articles of Incorporation, Fenn Educational Foundation, agrees to hold as Principal the aforesaid Ford Foundation grant of $453,000, either in cash or other property having an equivalent value at such time, in accordance with and subject to the following terms, limitations, uses and conditions:

(a) Until July 1, 1966 all income realized on said Principal shall be used to supplement or increase salaries of the faculty of The Cleveland State University in accordance with the intention expressed in the June 24, 1957 Terms of Grant from The Ford Foundation to Fenn College.

(b) On and after July 1, 1966 said Principal and all income realized thereon shall be paid only to or for the use or benefit of The Cleveland State University in such manner, for such purpose or purposes, and at such time or times as the Board of Trustees of Fenn College Corporation, and upon and after the filing of Amended Articles of Incorporation, Fenn Educational Foundation, shall, from time to time, determine.

(c) Fenn College Corporation, and upon and after filing of Amended Articles of Incorporation, Fenn Educational Foundation, shall report to The Ford Foundation from time to time on its use of the aforesaid Principal and income realized thereon, when and if reasonably requested by The Ford Foundation, and in such reasonable detail as The Ford Foundation shall request.

3. If Fenn College Corporation, and upon and after the filing of Amended Articles of Incorporation, Fenn Educational Foundation, loses or is denied exemption from Federal income tax under the provisions of Section 501(c) (3) of the Internal Revenue Code of 1954, as amended, or terminates operations, or fails to comply with the commitments and intentions set forth in this Resolution, then the unexpended balance of said Principal and income realized thereon shall be returned on demand to The Ford Foundation or its successors or assigns.

Trustee Hale informed the Fenn Board at its June 11, 1965, meeting that the Fenn Educational Foundation (F.E.F.) charter had been approved by the Internal Revenue Service as a charitable foundation and by the Ford Foundation for the retention of its 1957 grant money. The charter was broadly drawn for the operation of F.E.F. in the educational field in Greater Cleveland. It was contemplated that the Trustees and Corporate Members remain in a similar capacity with the new F.E.F.

Trustee Fries also announced at this board meeting that the reverter clause for the transfer agreement assumed lesser importance because C.S.U. was committed to develop in the Fenn College site. Also, the hold-harmless clause had less importance because the proposed approval of the transfer of Fenn's physical assets and staff to the State by the court included such protection. Chairman Burmester brought the board up-to-date on three recent meetings of the Executive Committee and indicated that if legal closing arrangements proved impracticable by August 31, 1965, an interim arrangement would have to be established until the court had acted and a firm closing date was set. The Fenn Board and Corporation would have to vote their approval to the final Agreement prior to the case going to court.

Likewise, the Board was informed that the Internal Revenue Service reported that upon formal and legal establishment of the foundation, it would be exempt from Federal income tax under the provisions of section 501(c)(3) of the Code.

The Fenn College Faculty, at its May 13, 1965 meeting ,passed unanimously the following resolution:

> Be it hereby resolved that, whereas Fenn College shall become Cleveland State University on September 1, 1965, the members of the Faculty of Fenn College do hereupon express their appreciation for the dedicated service of the Fenn Corporation and its Board of Trustees.
>
> Throughout its two score and two years, Fenn College has been honored by the spirited leadership of this city's leading citizens who have served as corporation members and trustees. Their inspiration and thoughtful guidance spearheaded the creation of an urban college which contributed importantly to its community.
>
> Be it further resolved, that this document stand as testimony of the gratitude and high esteem the faculty of Fenn College holds for the members of the Fenn Corporation who have so diligently served the cause of an institution we have cherished.

The forty-second and final Commencement Convocation of Fenn College was held Sunday, June 13, 1965, at 8:00 p.m. in Severance Hall. In accordance with custom for a number of years, Professor George W. Srail was Director of Convocation, Dean Meriam (Bud) C. Herrick was Marshall, Vernon H. Davis, Lee A. Marshall, George B. Simon, and Chester W. Topp were Assistants in the Academic Procession and Student Assistants were provided by Alphi Phi Omega and the Co-ed Association of Women Students.

This final commencement address was given by Trustee Clayton G. Hale, A.V., B.B.A., LL.D., President, The Hale and Hale Company. His subject was, "He Who Cuts His Own Wood Warms Himself Twice," the very wording of which constitutes something of a summary of the cooperative or work-study program of education. Hale's trusteeship of Fenn College dated back to 1933. There were 311 graduates in the final graduating class of Fenn College, distributed as follows: 85 in The School of Arts and Sciences, 109 in The School of Business Administration, and 117 in The School of Engineering.

Inasmuch as this was Fenn's final commencement, a greater number of Honorary Degrees were conferred, largely to trustees and administrative members. The following were recipients:

Harry F. Burmester, Doctor of Commercial Science (D.CS)
Dr. James C. Hodge, Doctor of Engineering (D.Eng.)
Edward T. Bartlett, Doctor of Commercial Science (D.CS)
Karl F. Bruch, Jr., Doctor of Laws (LL.D.)
Vollmer W. Fries, Doctor of Engineering (D.Eng.)
Paul R. Anders, Doctor of Laws (LL.D.)
William A. Patterson, Doctor of Laws (LL.D.)
Dr. G. Brooks Earnest, Doctor of Laws (LL.D.)

The program for the final (1965) commencement convocation is reproduced here:

Throughout its 42-year life span Fenn graduated a total of 5,951 students (just 49 shy of 6,000). Of this total 3,258 received diplomas from President Earnest at fourteen commencements. In other words, 55% of the diplomas granted by Fenn were signed by President Earnest during one-third of the life span of the College.

Philip Perry, 1948, was President of the Fenn Alumni Association in 1965. He was an Alumni Trustee of Fenn College. He became Vice-President of Operations for the Cleveland Electric Illuminating Com-

COMMENCEMENT CONVOCATION

G. BROOKS EARNEST, D. Eng., *Presiding*
President

PRELUDE: "Les Cloches" (The Bells) . . . . *Le Begue*
"Andante Cantabile" (Fifth Symphony). . . . . *Widor*
"Meditation—Priere" . . . . *Jongen*
"Bell Benedictus" . . . . *Weaver*

PROCESSIONAL: "Psalm XIX" . . . . *Marcello*
*(The audience will please remain seated while the academic
procession enters the auditorium)*

NATIONAL ANTHEM: "Star Spangled Banner" . . . . *Key*

INVOCATION: Professor W. FRANKLIN MOORE, PH.D.
Director, Religious Education

FENN COLLEGE CHOIR: "The Builder" . . . . *Cadman*

COMMENCEMENT ADDRESS:
"He Who Cuts His Own Wood Warms Himself Twice"
CLAYTON G. HALE
A.B., B.B.A., LL.D.
President
The Hale and Hale Company

FENN COLLEGE CHOIR: "The 100th Psalm" . . . . *Murray*

CONFERRING OF DEGREES IN COURSE

FAREWELL TO GRADUATES:
PRESIDENT EARNEST

CONFERRING OF HONORARY DEGREES

ANNOUNCEMENT OF HONORS AND AWARDS

FENN ALMA MATER: "When First We Greet the Dawn of Day" . . *Novak*

BENEDICTION: PROFESSOR MOORE

RECESSIONAL: "Postlude in G Major" . . . . *Handel*
*(The audience will please be seated while the academic
procession leaves the auditorium)*

MRS. THELMA MERNER GOLDSWORD, *Organist*

DR. JULIUS DROSSIN, *Director of Music*

THE CLASS OF 1965

THE SCHOOL OF ARTS AND SCIENCES

Candidates presented by Dean MAJOR B. JENKS, PH.D.

The Degree of Bachelor of Arts

CAROL ANNE BLAHA

MARIAN ALBERT BOCZEK

DARLA ANN BRINSKY

DANIEL PATRICK CAFAZZO

KEITH MALCOLM DAVIE

GEORGE W. DEMAREST, JR.

RICHARD ALAN ELLIS
cum laude

RITA JANE ERNE
cum laude

CHARLES FLYNN

LILA GANDOLF
cum laude

MARILYN ANNE GRANDE

KENNETH HANSJORG GREINER

JAMES BLANCHARD HELD

JOHN ALVIN HOWARD

RONALD JOSEPH HUDAK

JAMES JEROME JANDIK

CHARLES BRUCE KALAN

JOHN EDWARD KOHLER

EUGENE JAMES KOZAK

ILGA KRUMINS

JOAN ELEANOR LASKY

BURTON W. LEE III

CAROL BARBARA LOUDON

PRANAS S. MASIOTAS

THEODORE CLYDE MILLER

LOIS FENTON MISKOE
cum laude

RONALD JOHN MOHNICKEY

BARBARA J. MOYSEY
summa cum laude

COLLINS ROOSEVELT MUNNS

LINDA LOUISE PAGON

JAMES W. RICE

KENNETH PAUL ROTHGERY

RUSSELL Y. SALAMON

ORIJANN SLIWINSKI

JOSEPH MICHAEL STERN

ANTHONY J. TORTORICI

MICHAEL A. TRYBY

JOHN JOSEPH UHRIN

GALE K. WARD

DANIEL A. WEITZEL

KATHRYN GASIOR WILMER

THOMAS F. WILMER

DONALD G. WINTON

DONALD R. WRENTMORE

THE SCHOOL OF ARTS AND SCIENCES

The Degree of Bachelor of Science

Anne Marie Bourcier

Steven Anthony Buckner

Joseph E. Colizoli

David Delano Cope
summa cum laude

James Frederick Egan

Donald Lynn Fairhead

Denis Peter Hogya

William Gerald Loucka

Donald L. Mokren, *in absentia*

Joseph James Ochaba

James Frank Opalek

Joan Lee Remle

Harvey D. Schneider

Roger Lee Stone

Bruce C. Strnad

John A. Svigelj

Donald L. Thompson

Dennis Turkall

Nelson H. Wittstock

The Degree of Bachelor of Science in Education

Madeline Ruth Barnett

Glen Joseph Blabolil

Hollie M. Bush

Ann T. Chulak

Judith Melanie Cogen

Catherine Ruth Ellis
cum laude

Judith Margaret Esterhay

Marcy E. Evans

Sharon Bernice Ghelman

Barbara Ann Hoch

Rosalyn N. Kalinoski

Lucille Anne Kamps

Toivo Thomas Karjus

Gayle Marie Maracz

Jean Ann Merritt

Marjorie Ellen Pearce

Sybil Judy Reinthaler

Caroline Ann Salamon

Patricia A. Schweitzer

Judith Ellen Stevenson

Donald Stanley Stralka

Dianne C. Williams

THE SCHOOL OF BUSINESS ADMINISTRATION

Candidates presented by Dean Emeritus PAUL R. ANDERS, A.B.

The Degree of Bachelor of Business Administration

GERALD STEPHEN BAKSI

DOUGLAS W. BALL
  summa cum laude

ANDREW M. BALUNEK

NORMAN T. BAXTER
  cum laude

PAUL M. BEHAL

ATIS A. BILMANIS
  cum laude

PETER STEVEN BODONYI, JR.

ROBERT FRANK BRADACH

DONALD ROBERT BRUSK

MARVIN DALE BUBAN

ROBERT T. CIESICKI

RICHARD A. CONKLIN

KENNETH J. DEMKO

JAMES DIORIO

JAMES DOSS DONOGHUE

RALPH L. DUNN

EDWARD ROBERT DYE

GLENN R. EBEL

CONRAD JAMES FALKENBERG, JR.

MICHAEL ROBERT FINLEY

ANDREW ANGELO FINOTTI

DAVID J. FORSYTHE

ALBERT JOHN FOWLER

VERNON R. FRANKS

PATRICIA L. FRANZ
  cum laude

JEROME PAUL FREEMAL

JACK E. FRIEDMAN

JOSEPH H. FUCHS, JR.

THOMAS RICHARD FUSSNER

JOHN GEORGE GALLOVIC

JAMES NELSON GEDDES

RICHARD GOODWIN GIBSON, JR.

FRANK EDWARD GILMORE

JAMES WALTER GREENE

ELLEN RUTH GUTERMUTH

NICHOLAS HALUTICK

THOMAS M. HANSON

ALBERT ROY HART

RONALD A. HEMBERGER
  cum laude

RALPH A. HEPBURN

RICHARD WAYNE HINKLE

GUENTHER HOEGLER

JOSEPH T. HOLBROOK

BETTY JANE HORNAK
  cum laude

EDWARD F. HUDAK, JR.

DENNIS MICHAEL HYER

GERALD CLARENCE JACOBSON

ROY RAYMOND JONES

JOHN WEST KEMPER

THOMAS A. KERN
  cum laude

THOMAS ALAN KISSACK

WILLIAM PAUL KOBALLA

THE SCHOOL OF BUSINESS ADMINISTRATION

The Degree of Bachelor of Business Administration (continued)

WILLIAM JOSEPH KONYVKA

JOHN P. KOVACH

JOSEPH H. KOVACH

DAVID E. KRESS

RICHARD G. KREUZER

RAYMOND ALLAN KUDLAK

ROBERT CRISPINO LaFRANCE

HUBERT JAMES LaMOREAUX

JAMES JOHN LARVA

PRESTON D. LATTIMER

TIMOTHY A. LEU

RONALD F. LINDEN

CHARLES W. LUCAS

MICHAEL J. MARTIN

ROBERT LAWRENCE MATEJKA

RICHARD F. McCLEMENT, JR.

DONALD ALLEN McWILLIAM

ROBERT EDWARD MERRICK, JR.
  magna cum laude

KEITH EDWARD MILES

THEODORE CHARLES MISKOE

ANDREW S. MOHNICKEY

RONALD M. MOZZETTI

THEODORE L. NARAZINSKI

HOBBY EARL NELS

JAMES R. NEMETH

MARTIN W. O'MALLEY

ROBERT L. ORLANDI
  cum laude

JOSEPH RAYMOND OZIMEK

WILLIAM J. PALEK, JR.

JAMES V. PATTON

JOHN EDWARD PELKO

THEODORE RUDOLPH PESTEL

GARY PLOSKER

JOHN FRANCIS ANTHONY PODRACKY

MICHAEL STEPHEN POTOSKY, JR.

WILLIAM JAMES RAMSEY

LARRY MARSHALL RIGAL

ROGER LEONARD ROALOFS

THEODORE RUSNAK, JR.

JUDITH ANN SAMARIN

JOHN H. SCHULLER

ADAM SCHUMACHER

MARCIA JOAN SEGAL

HELMUT EUGENE SEMS

RICHARD ALLAN SIDAWAY

RONALD ANTHONY SONEGO

JAMES R. STAUFFER

THOMAS GEORGE STEINKE

JOHN EMIL TALAN

TED N. TANNEHILL

CARL TENK, JR.

WILLIAM MICHAEL JOHN USKO

JAMES R. VOLLAN

GARY DANIEL WEIRICH

DON A. WEISHEIT

JAMES WILLIAM ZEITZ

THE SCHOOL OF ENGINEERING

Candidates presented by Dean BURL H. BUSH, M. S.

The Degree of Bachelor of Chemical Engineering

JACK S. ATEN
LESTER EDWARD BROWN
WILLIAM D. CAVE
ROBERT P. DOLESH
  B.M.E., University of Detroit
DONALD CARL FERCH
JEROME J. GERDA

RONALD C. KAMINSKI
JOHN ADAM KREMER
WILLIAM ROBERT LULL
CHRISTIAN JOHN ORSBORN, JR.
EDWARD J. PETERS
RICHARD ALLEN RAYMOND
HENRY GEORGE ROGERS

The Degree of Bachelor of Civil Engineering

ALAIN Y. BAYOUD
LEO CEKADA
GARY SCOTT CREAGER
GEORGE EDWARD HLAVACS
THOMAS W. KLINGENBERG

CHARLES J. MEYER
MICHAEL PAUL NEYLON
ARTHUR O. PAETH
SEPPO J. RANTALA
ROBERT NORMAN TORNOW

The Degree of Bachelor of Electrical Engineering

NORMAN ADAM ADAMS
VICTOR BABENKO
LAWRENCE B. BALACH
JAMES EDWARD BONNER
FRANK ALLAN BURGETT
GARY LAWRENCE COUSIN
RAYMOND C. DUNHAM
JOHN JOSEPH FERCHILL
REGIS B. FISHER
ROBERT PAUL GEDEON
ALAN ARTHUR GRAMBO
RONALD JAMES HALSEY
RUDOLF HERMES
MAC ARTHUR HOWARD
DENNIS RAYMOND HUDECEK
MAX FARRELL HUYCK
ALAN JON KIRSCHNER
NORMAN JOHN KRIEGER

ALEXANDER KRINICKAS, JR.
ALAN R. KRONENWETTER
DAVID V. KUNKA
PAUL MICHAEL MAISTROS
GARY MICHAEL MARRACCINI
WILLIAM HENRY McKENNA
  B.C.E., Polytechnic Institute of Brooklyn
CHAD Z. MOORE
DENNIS JAMES OBLAK
GERALD JOSEPH OSWALD
RICHARD JAY PARKER
JOHN C. PAULOSKI
  summa cum laude
RAJARAM G. PAWAR
RICHARD L. PLAS
ELMER E. RABEK
DALE G. SAUERS
WILHELM SCHMIDT DE FOELDVAR
WILLIAM R. SELF

THE SCHOOL OF ENGINEERING

The Degree of Bachelor of Electrical Engineering (continued)

THOMAS E. STEIGERWALD
MARK FREDERICK TILLMAN
DOROTHY VALENCICH
GARY WAYNE VEST

RICHARD C. WAGAR
WILLIAM P. WAIWOOD
ANDREW WEBER
DAVID CHARLES WIDRIG

The Degree of Bachelor of Mechanical Engineering

JOHN CHARLES BARRETT
  cum laude
GEORGE HARRISON BLAKE
DWIGHT DAVID BROWN
WAYNE SCOTT BUSDIECKER
MICHAEL D. CASELLA
FRANK ALBERT CINADR
  magna cum laude
DENNIS WAYNE CLEM
DONN RICHARD COLBRUNN
NEAL JOHN FEDAK
JOHN L. FRATER
CHARLES A. GALLETTI
ALFRED JOHN HESS
DON J. HEUER
GERALD RAYMOND KOLAR

DIETER HERBERT KULICKE
JOSEPH LIKOZAR
WILLIAM NORMAN LITTELL
ELMER ANDREW MARTIN
DAVID STANLEY NEIGE
ELMER ALBERT NICKELS
MELVIN J. NICOULIN, JR.
WILLIAM CLAIR ROWLES
EDWARD SZEWCZYK
HENRY JAMES VOLDRICH
RAYMOND D. WALDORF
  magna cum laude
DONALD RICHARD WELLS
ROBERT AUGUST WENZLER
DONALD L. WISCHMEIER
DAVID ANTHONY WOOD

CARL H. ZEHNDER

The Degree of Bachelor of Engineering Science

CHARLES FREDRIK BARTH
JAMES CHARLES COLARIC
HENRY EDWARD BUTLER FAIRMAN
THOMAS JAMES FINN
LAWRENCE F. FUNDZAK
THOMAS JOHN HOUSEHOLDER
JOSEPH ALAN JERDONEK
ERNEST JOSEPH KERZICNIK
JOSEPH JOHN KRUPAR, JR.
RALPH J. LENNERTH

JEROME LUCAS
THOMAS EDWARD NASMAN
TERRY PERKO
THOMAS WILLIAM PIETROCINI
JEAN EMILY SETELE
JOHN THOMAS SIMONE, JR.
PETER DEAN SMITH
ANTHONY JOHN SUMODI
FRANK J. URBANCIC, JR.
KURT ALLAN WILL

HERVEY ALLEN WILLIAMS

COMMENCEMENT HONORS

SCHOLARSHIP

summa cum laude

DOUGLAS W. BALL

DAVID DELANO COPE

BARBARA J. MOYSEY

JOHN C. PAULOSKI

magna cum laude

FRANK ALBERT CINADR

ROBERT EDWARD MERRICK, JR.

RAYMOND D. WALDORF

cum laude

JOHN CHARLES BARRETT

NORMAN T. BAXTER

ATIS A. BILMANIS

CATHERINE RUTH ELLIS

RICHARD ALAN ELLIS

RITA JANE ERNE

PATRICIA L. FRANZ

LILA GANDOLF

RONALD A. HEMBERGER

BETTY JANE HORNAK

THOMAS A. KERN

LOIS FENTON MISKOE

ROBERT L. ORLANDI

PRESIDENT'S AWARDS

outstanding achievement and scholarship

DAVID DELANO COPE

JOHN ADAM KREMER

THEODORE CHARLES MISKOE

RICHARD JAY PARKER

COOPERATIVE WORK

GLEN JOSEPH BLABOLIL

LESTER EDWARD BROWN

JUDITH ANN SAMARIN

ATHLETICS

DENNIS TURKALL

ALFRED A. BENESCH ENGLISH AWARD — $100

BARBARA J. MOYSEY

pany in 1971. He was later elected a member of the Fenn Executive Board and in 1973, a Vice Chairman of the Fenn Advisory Committee of the Fenn Educational Fund. Dr. Stanley J. Czyzak, 1937, William J. Franz, 1927, and John G. Henniger, 1939, were recipients of the Fenn Alumni Distinguished Service Awards in 1965.

The July 27, 1965, meeting of the Fenn Board was one of the most important in the history of the College, for it was at this meeting and the meeting of the Fenn Corporation which immediately followed where practically all of the resolutions were approved relative to the legalities of transferring the College to the State of Ohio. These resolutions were earlier mailed to all Board and Corporation Members to provide them the opportunity to digest appropriately all of the salient matters in advance of the board meeting, and be sufficiently knowledgeable of the importance of the meeting.

The first order of business at the meeting was to accept formally, with regret, the immediate resignation of Trustee Louis S. Peirce and also that of Trustee James W. Corey effective on the date of transfer of the College to the State.

The minutes of this board meeting recite best the consequential and memorable highlights and are therefore excerpted as follows:

> The Agreement and Plan of Transition, with Exhibits A, B, C and D attached thereto, which was mailed to each Trustee and each Member of the Corporation in the notice of the meetings dated July 19, 1965, was presented for consideration. The correspondence between Mr. Burmester and Mr. Nance, including Mr. Nance's letter of July 13, 1965, was read to the Board and Mr. Fries reported on negotiations with Mr. Nance and Mr. Burmester reported that Mr. Nance had assured him that C.S.U. would meet the cost of the insurance policy to protect the Trustees, Officers, and Members of Fenn College. Thereupon, on motion duly made and seconded, the following Resolution was unanimously adopted by the votes of all fourteen Trustees present:
>
> RESOLVED:
> WHEREAS, there has been prepared, after extended negotiations and study, and duly presented to this Board of Trustees, a proposed "Agreement and Plan of Transition" (referred to hereinafter as the "Agreement") whereby the Fenn College faculty, staff and certain of its real and personal properties would be transferred to the Board of Trustees of The Cleveland State University (said

University being referred to hereinafter as "CSU") and the State of Ohio; and

WHEREAS, it is believed to be in the best interests of Fenn College as well as in the public interest for such Agreement to be executed and consummated; and

WHEREAS, such Agreement has been approved, in the manner indicated in the Agreement, by the Ohio Board of Regents, the Attorney General of Ohio and the Board of Trustees of The Cleveland State University; and

WHEREAS, the Trustees have considered and do rely upon the representations set forth in a certain letter dated July 13, 1965 from James J. Nance, Chairman of the Board of Trustees of CSU, addressed to Harry F. Burmester, Chairman of the Board of Trustees of Fenn College.

Now, THEREFORE, BE IT FURTHER RESOLVED:

1. That the "Agreement and Plan of Transition" in the form enclosed with the Notice of this meeting is hereby approved, and is recommended to the Corporate Members of Fenn College for their approval. Upon approval of such Agreement by the Corporate Members the Chairman of the Board of Trustees is authorized to execute such Agreement on behalf of Fenn College and to date the Agreement as of the date of approval by the Members of the Corporation.

2. That the officers and counsel for Fenn College are authorized to file forthwith on behalf of Fenn College, its Trustees and Members, the legal proceeding referred to in Paragraph 6 of the Agreement, and to maintain such proceeding until a final judgment has been obtained.

3. That as soon as a final judgment of the Court finding the Agreement valid and legal has been obtained a meeting of this Board of Trustees shall be called for the purpose of determining whether there will be adequate provision in the remaining assets of Fenn College after conveyance of the Assets to be Transferred (Agreement, Paragraph 10(e)), and to authorize the officers to complete and consummate the Agreement.

4. That, it appearing that the final judgment of the Court in such legal proceeding will not be obtained prior to August 31, 1965 and thus it becomes necessary and desirable to authorize the Interim Arrangement referred to in Paragraph 6(c)(iv) of the Agreement, now, therefore, the Interim Arrangement in the form substantially as presented to this Meeting (and referred to

hereinafter as the "Interim Arrangement") is approved, and the Chairman of the Board of Trustees, is authorized to execute such document in substantially such form. It is understood that the Interim Arrangement has not been formally approved by the Board of Trustees of CSU, and if that Board requests changes of a substantial nature, or if after such Interim Arrangement is executed, it becomes desirable in light of experience or unforeseen contingencies to modify the Interim Arrangement, the Executive Committee of the Fenn College Board of Trustees is authorized to approve such changes or modifications.

5. All actions of the Executive Committee and the Officers to date in negotiating the Agreement and the Interim Arrangement and the preparation for carrying out the Agreement and the Interim Arrangement, including the arranging for certain of the personnel of Fenn College to become employed by the Board of Trustees of CSU effective September 1, 1965, the execution of releases on behalf of Fenn College and its Board of Trustees with such personnel, and the making available of certain of Fenn College personnel and office space to assist the Trustees of CSU to plan for the start of CSU's operations September 1, 1965, are hereby ratified and approved. The Officers are authorized to take all action necessary or desirable, consistent with the Agreement and the Interim Arrangement, to prepare for and carry out such agreements, including without limitation thereon, the notification of such Fenn College personnel as have not been notified that pursuant to the Interim Arrangement their employment by Fenn College will terminate August 31, 1965.

6. The Officers are authorized to terminate the operations of Fenn College as a functioning academic institution effective August 31, 1965, and to make necessary arrangements for office space and personnel for carrying on the reduced operations of Fenn College Corporation commencing September 1, 1965.

In connection with the discussion of the foregoing Resolution Mr. Rorick explained that owing to various delays which have occurred in securing the approval of the Attorney General and counsel for CSU, it will not be possible to complete the Agreement and Plan of Transition prior to August 31, 1965; and that it will, therefore, be necessary to enter into an Interim Arrangement between Fenn College and the Trustees of CSU for the use of the Fenn College property during the period from September 1 until the consummation of said transfer and transition, and accordingly the Interim Arrangement referred to in paragraphs 4 and 5 of the foregoing Resolution is necessary to enable CSU to commence operations promptly on September 1, 1965 and the Resolution to be adopted would authorize that Interim Arrangement.

Following a discussion and report by Mr. Hale as to amending the Articles of Incorporation of Fenn College to provide for a change of name to Fenn Educational Foundation and an enlarged scope of activities for such Foundation, Mr. Hale moved and Mr. Galen Miller seconded a motion to adopt the following Resolution; said Resolution was unanimously adopted by the votes of all fourteen Trustees present.

RESOLVED: That the proposed Amended Articles of Incorporation in the form enclosed with the notice of this meeting are recommended to the Members of Fenn College Corporation for their adoption; providing, however, that formal approval of such Articles by this Board of Trustees is reserved for consideration at the meeting called for September 14, 1965.

Following the adoption of said Resolution, it was explained that a further action by the Trustees will be necessary in view of the provisions of Section 1713.25 of the Revised Code of Ohio providing that a change in name and purpose of a college corporation can be authorized only after thirty days' notice to every Trustee and an affirmative vote after such thirty days' notice.

Upon motion by Mr. Fries, seconded by Mr. Bartlett, the following Resolution was unanimously adopted by the votes of all fourteen Trustees present, providing for an amendment of the Code of Regulations to provide for indemnification of Trustees and Officers in accordance with paragraph (E) of Section 1702.12 of the Ohio Non-Profit Corporation Law. The said Resolution provides as follows:

RESOLVED: That the proposed amendment to the Code of Regulations of Fenn College in the form submitted with the notice of this meeting is hereby recommended to the Members of the Corporation for their adoption, said amendment and addition to said Code of Regulations reading as follows:

Indemnification of Trustees and Officers

16. The Corporation shall indemnify each trustee and officer of the Corporation and each former trustee and former officer of the Corporation against expenses actually and necessarily incurred by him in connection with the defense of any action,

suit, or proceeding to which he is made a party by reason of being or having been such trustee or officer, except in relation to matters as to which he shall be adjudged in such action, suit, or proceeding to be liable for negligence or misconduct in the performance of duty. Such indemnification shall not be deemed exclusive of any other rights to which he may be entitled under the articles, the regulations, any agreement, vote of members, or otherwise.

Dr. Hodge raised the question as to the arrangements to be made concerning restricted funds which have been given to the College by various donors; and on motion made by Dr. Hodge and seconded by Mr. Helm, the following Resolution was unanimously adopted by the votes of all fourteen Trustees present:

RESOLVED: That with reference to those restricted funds held by Fenn College which counsel recommends be discussed with the donors, the Officers are authorized to work out mutually satisfactory arrangements with such donors for the purpose of providing suitable provisions for the future retention of such funds or the termination of holding of such funds, as a result of the Interim Arrangement and the Agreement. Such proposed new arrangements shall be approved by either the Executive Committee or the Board of Trustees.

The question was raised as to the employment of Mr. Vernon Davis by The Cleveland State University and the necessity of replacing him as Secretary of the Board of Trustees of Fenn College. On motion duly made by Mr. Hoover and seconded by Mr. Burns, the following Resolution was adopted by the unanimous votes of all fourteen Trustees present:

RESOLVED: That, Whereas, Vernon Davis, Secretary of the Board of Trustees of Fenn College and of the Corporation, will become an employee of the Board of Trustees of CSU effective September 1, 1965, it is necessary that a new Secretary be elected; and

WHEREAS, Vernon Davis has submitted his resignation as Secretary of the Board of Trustees and of the Corporation effective this date;

Now, THEREFORE, BE IT FURTHER RESOLVED:

1. That the resignation of Vernon Davis as Secretary of the Board of Trustees and of the Corporation is accepted with great regret; and

2.   That Karl F. Bruch, Jr. is hereby elected as Secretary of the Board of Trustees and of Fenn College Corporation to serve until his successor has been elected.

3.   That Vernon Davis is commended for his faithful and excellent discharge of his duties as Secretary for a period of many years.

Chairman Burmester reminded the Board of Trustees of the meeting to be held on September 14, 1965, as required by law, in order to authorize the change of the name and purposes of the Corporation; and requested all Trustees to be present at said meeting.

All fourteen of the Trustees present remained throughout the meeting and voted affirmatively on all Resolutions submitted to and hence adopted by the board. There were no dissenting votes on any Resolution. The trustee meeting adjourned at 3:55 p.m. which was just in time for the Corporation meeting which had been called for 4:00 p.m.

Trustees Howard F. Burns and Vollmer W. Fries were appointed as tellers to count the proxies to report the number of Trustees and Members present in person or by proxy at the Corporation meeting. They reported that there were twenty-six Corporate members present in person (fifteen Trustees and eleven Members) and that forty-two Corporate members had given Burmester and Earnest voting power to act for them at the meeting of Members (fourteen Trustees and twenty-eight Members). Chairman Vollmer W. Fries of the Negotiating Committee presented a résumé of deliberations with key representatives of C.S.U. since February 1965. Alan Rorick (Baker, Hostetler, and Patterson) announced that two copies of the proposed Agreement with C.S.U. had been signed by Nance, Saxbe (Attorney General of the State of Ohio), and by Dr. Millett (Chancellor of the Board of Regents of the State of Ohio).

The following Resolutions were unanimously adopted by the vote of all those present with Chairman Burmester and President Earnest voting the forty-two proxies in favor of each Resolution. There was no dissenting vote from any one as to any Resolution presented at said meeting:

RESOLVED:
WHEREAS, there has been prepared, after extended negotiations and study, and duly presented to this meeting of Corporation Members, a proposed "Agreement and Plan of Transition" (referred

to hereinafter as the "Agreement"), a copy of which Agreement was enclosed with the Notice of this meeting, whereby the Fenn College faculty, staff and certain of its real and personal properties would be transferred to the Board of Trustees of The Cleveland State University (said University being referred to hereinafter as "CSU") and the State of Ohio; and

WHEREAS, it is believed to be in the best interests of Fenn College as well as in the public interest for such Agreement to be executed and consummated; and

WHEREAS, such Agreement has been approved, in the manner indicated in the Agreement, by the Ohio Board of Regents, the Attorney General of Ohio and the Board of Trustees of The Cleveland State University; and has been authorized by the Board of Trustees of Fenn College and recommended to the Corporation Members for their approval; and

WHEREAS, The Corporation Members have considered and do rely upon the representations set forth in a certain letter dated July 13, 1965 from James J. Nance, Chairman of the Board of Trustees of CSU addressed to Harry F. Burmester, Chairman of the Board of Trustees of Fenn College.

Now, THEREFORE, BE IT FURTHER RESOLVED:

1. That the "Agreement and Plan of Transition" in the form enclosed with the Notice of this meeting is hereby approved. The Chairman of the Board of Trustees is authorized to execute such Agreement on behalf of Fenn College and to date the Agreement as of the date of this approval.

2. That the officers and counsel for Fenn College are authorized to file forthwith on behalf of Fenn College, its Trustees and Members, the legal proceeding referred to in Paragraph 6 of the Agreement, and to maintain such proceeding until a final judgment has been obtained.

3. That the officers and the Board of Trustees are authorized to take all action necessary or desirable to effectuate the Agreement, including without limitation thereon, the termination of the operations of Fenn College as a functioning academic institution effective August 31, 1965 and the adoption of an Interim Arrangement as referred to in Paragraph 6(c)(iv) of the Agreement.

There was a discussion and explanation of the proposed Amended Articles of Fenn College to be adopted after the consummation of the transfer of the property to The Cleveland State University, and on motion made by Mr. Bruch and seconded by Mr. Hoover, the following Resolution was unanimously adopted by the vote of all Members present:

RESOLVED: That the Articles of Incorporation of Fenn College upon the consummation of the transfer of the property to The Cleveland State University shall be amended by the adoption of Amended Articles of Incorporation.

There was a general discussion as to the distribution of funds, the transfer of personnel, and the reaction of students to the present project, and President Earnest replied to questions from the floor.

There was further general discussion as to the work done by the officers, trustees and the various committee members of the Board of Trustees to effect the Agreement and Plan of Transition, and on motion made by Mr. Whiting Williams and duly seconded, the following Resolution was adopted by the vote of all Members present:

RESOLVED: That it is the sense of this meeting that the officers, trustees and the various committee members of the Board of Trustees have performed a significant service in working out the Agreement and Plan of Transition and all related matters, and the membership commends them for their fine work in bringing this complicated transaction to a virtual conclusion.

Under the provisions of the Agreement it was expressly agreed to transfer the following to the State of Ohio:

Premises and property by quit-claim deed

Furniture, fixtures, and equipment by bill of sale

Official school and departmental records and files including financial

Fenn's option agreement to purchase the Levin property at Euclid Avenue and East 21st Street

All personnel employed at that time by Fenn, if they so desired, at the same or improved compensation and fringe benefits

Not included in the above were three items expressly mentioned in the Agreement, namely:

A 5-acre tract of land with buildings in Medina County, Ohio, a gift of Trustee Clayton G. Hale and known as Hale's Hollow.

A Burroughs 205 Computer owned by Fenn but located in the Arthur G. McKee & Company premises.

Personal files and records of the faculty and administrators.

As soon as possible after the execution of the Agreement the Trustees of Fenn were charged to consummate the appropriate legal proceeding to be filed in the Court of Common Pleas of Cuyahoga County and to obtain approval of the Court to effect a final judgment as to the validity and legality of the agreement. Following the judgment of the Court, a fixed time (thirty days) was granted for appeal on behalf of all parties thereto.

Fenn's legal counsel prepared a "Memorandum of Law in Support of Petition for Declaration Judgment and Equitable Relief" completely describing full details of the Agreement plus the fact that Fenn would then file amended Articles of Incorporation to become the "Fenn Educational Foundation" and that all of the assets remaining after the transfer of said assets to the State were to be devoted by Fenn in furtherance of its purposes as the Fenn Educational Foundation.

A comprehensive study was made concerning the extent donors restricted Fenn in its use of their gifts. It was found that a considerable number of gifts were restricted. In every instance the donors in question either (a) waived any interest in, or restrictions upon said donations, or (b) agreed to a specific future use of the donations by the Fenn Educational Foundation.

The final paragraph in the "Memorandum of Law . . . " indicated that "none of Fenn's property is subject to any legal restrictions which preclude the Court from granting the relief prayed for in the petition." The Attorney General of Ohio in endorsing the Agreement signed a statement that he found "nothing in the statutes or the Constitution of the State of Ohio to restrict the Board of Trustees of C.S.U. from entering into the Agreement."

The case (No. 816,473) was tried in the Court of Common Pleas, Cuyahoga County, on September 27, 1965. Donald F. Lybarger was the presiding judge. Fenn College, *et al.*, were the plaintiffs and Nance, *et al.*, were the defendants.

Judge Lybarger in his comprehensive "Memorandum of Opinion" stated, "At the outset, the Court has not the least difficulty in deciding the question of jurisdiction. The Court finds that the facts are as alleged in detail in plaintiffs' petition."

The Memorandum of Opinion further stated:

> With the aid of many employers in Greater Cleveland Fenn has maintained a Cooperative Education Program that has enabled

students to earn their way while getting a college education. It has, throughout the passing years, served many young men and women and also folks beyond the usual college age who but for its ministrations might have lacked the boon of higher education. Fenn, therefore, has had a deep impact upon the life of Greater Cleveland that can never be erased. Appropriately the Court may paraphrase the language of the Latin poet Horace and say that Fenn has "builded a monument more lasting than bronze."

With the proposal to create C.S.U., and now with its establishment as a university supported by the State of Ohio, it has become obvious that Fenn's financial contributions have been curtailed. It is a logical conclusion of fact from the evidence that, with Fenn lacking an adequate endowment, depending largely on student fees and facing rising costs of operation, the change of functions by Fenn and the adoption of active educational functions by C.S.U. is highly desirable not only from the standpoint of both but also because it is in the public interest in promoting the cause of education in northeastern Ohio. It will make possible a strong university built upon the foundation laid by Fenn and having a much higher potential in the field of public education in the future.

The Court has studied the Agreement and Plan of Transition and finds that it is carefully drawn fully to protect the interests of Fenn and C.S.U. and to accomplish the transition between the two institutions in an efficient manner.

Granted that present conditions suggest the desirability of the Agreement, and that its terms are fair in every respect, a pertinent legal question is whether Fenn has authority to make a contract transferring most of its physical assets and merging its faculty, staff and facilities with those of another institution?

As a non-profit corporation Fenn has the wide general authority granted it in R. C. Chapter 1702. The Court need not belabor the fact that Fenn, under R. C. 1702.12 may make donations for "charitable, scientific, literary, or educational purposes." It may "sell, exchange, transfer, and dispose of property of any description." It may make contracts and do all lawful things incidental to its general purposes. Fenn's Articles of Incorporation give it broad purposes and plenary power to accomplish them. R. C. 1702.39 specifically gives a corporate body such as Fenn power to transfer any assets "without the necessity of procuring authorization from the court." Since the transfer here involves by far the larger part of Fenn's assets and the change of Fenn's name and functions, Fenn has complied with the requirements of R. C. 1702.39 as a corporation not for profit and has also complied with the express requirements of R. C. 1713.25 in giving more than thirty days actual notice to each Trustee of a special meeting of the Board, at which meeting more than a majority of said Board of 34 members attended and voted for such changes without a single dissenting vote. Finally, the 105th General Assembly gave statutory authority to the Trustees of C.S.U. specifically to make a contract with Fenn such as is now embodied in the Agreement.

The evidence establishes that the Ohio Board of Regents, in the exercise of the authority granted in R. C. Chapter 3333, has approved the Agreement and found it to be in accord with its regulations, as contemplated by Sec. 2 of H 2 (130 v Pt. 2).

It is abundantly clear that Fenn has full and complete legal authority and its Trustees and Members ample discretion to enter into the Agreement and thereby transfer most of its assets to C.S.U. It need not even have resorted to the Court to have such action sanctioned.

May Fenn legally carry on by changing its name to "Fenn Educational Foundation" and by modifying its purposes and powers as proposed in amended articles of incorporation. The answer is an unequivocal "yes." R. C. 1702.38 gives such authority to Fenn, as a corporation not for profit and R. C. 1713.25 dealing with changes of name and functions of a college was fully complied with in the meeting of September 14, 1965 as pointed out above, and as noted hereafter equity sanctions it. The evidence establishes that under its new name Fenn will carry on as a non-profit corporation supporting worthy educational, literary, charitable and scientific endeavors.

But what of Fenn's donors of past years? Do they have any present interest in Fenn's assets? May any givers be heard to complain that the carrying out of the Agreement and subsequent change of name and program of Fenn violate either the spirit or the terms of their donations? In spite of the fact that the representative general donors in their answers have disclaimed any interest in Fenn's property, and that those who have made gifts for specific purposes have almost unanimously waived the observance by Fenn of their former conditions, the litigants deserve an answer to the questions just raised.

There is nothing more certain in life than change. As a wise man has said: "New occasions teach new duties; time makes ancient good uncouth." What is reasonable and helpful today may not remain so with the passing of the years. No man can accurately anticipate the needs of the next generation. Equity has long recognized this, and in dealing with trusts, both private and charitable, has not hesitated to exercise its inherent power over the administration of trusts in order to perpetuate the purposes of settlors in the face of changed conditions. This has been especially true as to charitable trusts.

The Court concludes that Fenn is fully justified not only by statute but also under the equitable doctrine of deviation (1) in amending its charter to change its name, modify its purposes and alter its program of operation as proposed; (2) in transferring its property to or for the use of C.S.U. as called for in the Agreement, and (3) in taking all steps necessary and incidental to effectuating the Agreement. Finally it is clear that those who have been so generous to Fenn in the past have the assurance that their charitable intents will be perpetuated, and, although they have no legal title or interest in any of Fenn's assets, that their donations will continue to advance the cause of education.

For the above reasons the Court grants the prayer of the plaintiffs' petition and has this day rendered a declaratory judgment accordingly. [Dated September 27, 1965]

The Effective Date for the Agreement to be consummated was established in the Agreement and Plan of Transition "to be not later than 30 days after the final judgment." On this date, Fenn was to deliver to C.S.U. and C.S.U. to deliver to Fenn all items and evidence in the Agreement and Plan of Transition assuring each party that all terms of the Agreement have been successfully and faithfully consummated.

Accordingly, the final, and therefore historic, meeting of the Fenn College Board was held in the Board Room at Stillwell Hall at 4:00 p.m. on Wednesday, October 27, 1965. The following information was presented and business transacted:

Alan G. Rorick explained in detail the decrees included in Judge Lybarger's final judgment.

Vernon H. Davis presented the report of audit by Ernst & Ernst as of August 31, 1965, and an interim financial report from September 1, 1965, to date of meeting. Approximately $2,000,000 would be available as the assets of the new foundation.

The transaction contemplated by the Agreement was authorized to be consummated on behalf of Fenn College, and the officers were authorized and directed to take all action necessary or desirable to consummate such transaction. The effective date of closing was set as November 1, 1965.

Resolutions were authorized concerning the disposition of certain funds held by Fenn.

Authorization of a resolution to retain all Fenn Trustees as Fenn Educational Foundation Trustees.

Authorization of a resolution to terminate all former Fenn Trustee Committees except the Executive Committee.

Authorization of a resolution to establish a new Planning Committee and a new Investment Committee for the Fenn Educational Foundation (F.E.F.), including the duties of each committee.

Action was taken to remove the records, property and office of F.E.F. from C.S.U.

Action was taken to employ bookkeeping and accounting personnel.

Trustee Paul S. Dickey was appointed to the Executive Committee to fill the vacancy created by the resignation of Louis S. Peirce.

Ernst & Ernst were designated as auditors of F.E.F.

Dr. G. Brooks Earnest was elected as a Trustee of F.E.F. to fill out the unexpired term of F. L. Elmendorf and the office of President of Fenn College was terminated upon filing with the Secretary of State of Ohio the Amended Articles of Incorporation changing the purposes of the (College) Corporation and its name to Fenn Educational Foundation.

Election of Clayton G. Hale and Dr. G. Brooks Earnest as Vice Chairmen of the Board of Trustees of the new (F.E.F.) Corporation.

Establishment of new banking arrangements for F.E.F.

The following committee appointments were made by Chairman Burmester:

Because of the historic significance of the above meeting a photograph was taken of those in attendance and is shown with proper identification in Figure 1.

The meeting adjourned at 5:40 p.m., thereby closing for all time the deliberations of the Trustees of Fenn College following a very fruitful forty-two years of business in the higher educational world. Fenn provided an educational haven both during the day and evening for literally thousands of students, nearly 6,000 graduates, and thousands of non-graduates. Thus Fenn astonishingly created an effective imprint on the life of Cleveland, of Ohio, and other states as well, through its educational programs and especially its day cooperative education program which gave the graduates a "cutting-edge" of applied know-how which provided a spring-board for them into the business and professional world. An era of YMCA and privately supported higher education had come to a close, but there was really no wake for Fenn's buildings and all other physical assets together with its highly qualified faculty and staff which were already supporting C.S.U. as the nucleus for the new state university. How fortunate the Trustees of C.S.U. were that they did not have to seek temporary quarters (as Cuyahoga Community College did), seek its own starting faculty, wait at least four years for its first graduating class in order to become accredited by important academic accrediting bodies, and the start of its alumni association, and find

Standing: P. S. Dickey, B. W. Maxey, A. G. Hose, W. J. Hunken, n, Galen Miller, E. T. Bartlett, E. E. Helm.
Seated: A. T. Colwell, E. H. Fisher, H. F. Burns, A. G. Rorick, C. G. Hale, G. B. Earnest, H. F. Burmester, K. F. Bruch, Jr., G. V. Woodling, V. H. Davis, V. W. Fries, W. B. O'Konski.
The following Trustees were absent: Arthur S. Armstrong, Norman F. Smith, Wade N. Harris, John R. Hoover, William G. Laffer, C. Bert McDonald, Warren L. Morris, Dr. Robert M. Stecher, Charles J.Stilwell, Clarence M. Taylor, Van H. Leichliter, Charles M. White, John G. Henninger, H. E. Widdell.

a permanent campus on which to construct its future buildings and establish all the administrative personnel required to manage a large university. Through the gift by the Trustees of Fenn College, of a ready-made and operating campus with the essential personnel for teaching, management and operation, C.S.U. gained at least a six-year head-start as a public institution in Greater Cleveland. In addition, by accepting Fenn's Alumni, nearly 6,000 strong, C.S.U. acquired an earnest, loyal group ready and willing to assist the university in its educational, business, and fund-raising activities. For these reasons, and many more, the Trustees of C.S.U. should forever be grateful.

Herewith ends Fenn College's history—to become the nucleus of a much larger university (State tax supported) which will shape the destiny of many youths residing within and outside of Greater Cleveland. The former Trustees and Corporate Members of Fenn College, and especially this author, extend every best wish to the Trustees of C.S.U. in their endeavors to further illumine the educational torch at the university with learning of highest order.

Now the effect of the foregoing is being felt in Metropolitan Cleveland and other areas of the United States by the successes of Fenn alumni. Here are just a few who have had a hand in guiding the business, spiritual and industrial complex of Cleveland and other cities;

> J. Maurice Struchen, 1943, President, Society National Bank of Cleveland, Chairman, Board of Trustees, The Cleveland State University
>
> John G. Henninger, 1939, President, Euclid National Bank
>
> Jay W. Collins, 1940, Executive Director, Euclid General Hospital
>
> Wilson B. Creveling, 1937, President, Midwest Screw Products, Inc.
>
> Edward J. Hrdlicka, 1938, Consultant, Hydraulic Equipment
>
> H. Martin Huge, Vice President, Lorain Products Corporation
>
> Roy L. Jensen, 1937, President, The Hale & Hale Company
>
> John T. Patton, 1955, Judge, Court of Common Pleas, Cuyahoga County
>
> Philip B. Perry, 1948, Vice President of Operations, The Cleveland Electric Illuminating Company
>
> Charles R. Day, 1945, former dean of Cleveland newscasters, Regional Public Relations Director, Ohio Bell Company
>
> Kenneth D. Hughes, 1948, Treasurer, Scott & Fetzer Company

T. Gordon McCausland, 1929, Vice President and Treasurer, Reliance Electric Company (retired)

Donald Wise, 1943, Senior Vice President, Cuyahoga Savings Association

William J. Franz, 1927, President, The William J. Franz Co.

Madison H. Dods, 1934, President, Allied Power Transmission Co.

Raymond B. Aufmuth, 1939, Vice President, Arthur G. McKee & Co., San Francisco, California

Dr. Robert E. Chable, 1944, Pastor, United Church of Christ, Venice, Florida

Dr. Leonard R. Stone, 1947, Head-Nucleonics, Republic Steel Corp.

Reverend Paul R. Balliett, 1939, Pastor, Maple Heights United Methodist Church

Mary Ann Dorsch, (1950) Buyer for Halles

Richard J. Verba (1941) Owner, R. J. Verba Equipment

George V. Parmelee, (1933) Chairman, Department of Mechanical Engineering, Fenn College and The Cleveland State University

Vernon H. Davis, Director of Finance, Fenn College

Clayton G. Hale (1932) President (Retired), Hale & Hale Co.

Ernest C. Harris (1939) Chairman, Department of Civil Engineering, Fenn College; Senior Staff Engineer, Ken R. White and Co., Denver, Colorado

Clifford D. Williams (1937) President and owner, C. D. Williams and Associates, Augusta, Georgia

William A. Quallich (1953) Comptroller, Gould, Inc.

XVI

There is nothing permanent except change.

Heraclitus (*floruit* 513 B.C.)

As indicated in Chapter XV, the Board of Trustees of Fenn College at a Special Meeting held September 14, 1965, amended the Articles of Incorporation of the College to serve as the Amended Articles of Incorporation of the Fenn Educational Foundation. The Foundation, not C.S.U., was really the successor to Fenn College inasmuch as the Articles of Incorporation of the College were amended to serve a different purpose than theretofore and the same Trustees and Officers were continued at least for an additional year. The same Members of the Corporation were elected for another year also.

Not certain of how the thirty-nine special funds of all descriptions held by the College were to be administrated, these funds were transferred by a court order to the Fenn Educational Foundation (F.E.F.) September 27, 1965. However, over the course of the first year of operation approximately half of these funds were turned over to C.S.U. because they were either too small or required too much attention and paper work for the part-time staff of F.E.F. Eventually, most of the funds remaining with F.E.F. were lumped into one corpus with the sole restriction remaining for the Ford Foundation Grant fund that the income from this specific grant be paid to C.S.U. for purposes recommended by F.E.F.

Because of the difference in the operation of a relatively large college versus that of a small foundation, it was foreseen that the Fenn Executive Committee could administer most of the operational and policy affairs with the need for an entire Board of Trustees meeting perhaps only once or twice per year.

The first meeting of the Executive Committee of the Fenn Educational Foundation was held Wednesday, December 8, 1965, in the Board Room of the Union Commerce Bank with Chairman Burmester presiding.

Trustee Hale reported that through the courtesy of Dr. James A. (Dolph) Norton, President of the Greater Cleveland Associated Foundation (G.C.A.F.), F.E.F. could share office space with the Associated Foundation in the National City Bank Building at Euclid Avenue and East Sixth Street, available December 15, 1965, with secretarial and phone service, all on a pro-rata-of-expense basis. Unanimous action was taken "that Mr. Hale proceed firming up the office space and furnishings to put F.E.F. in business in cooperation with G.C.A.F."

Trustee Hale had also assumed the responsibility of obtaining a part-time experienced individual to keep books for F.E.F. He subsequently obtained Henry J. Kubach, retired Assistant Treasurer of the Cleveland Hardware Company (later by acquisition, Controller of H. K. Porter Company, Cleveland Forging Division).

It was agreed that all checking accounts excepting that of the the Union Commerce Bank be closed out and henceforth such activity be concentrated at the Union Commerce Bank.

Ernst & Ernst had agreed to update gratis the audit from September 1, 1965, to current date for final determination by the Internal Revenue Service for 501(c)(3) status and to set up books to provide proper financial records for F.E.F. Chairman Burmester offered free rental of a safe deposit box at the Union Commerce Bank for the first year of F.E.F.'s operation.

Action was taken on the first scholarship aid offered by F.E.F. at this first meeting of the Executive Committee. Rolf E. Lehming, a C.S.U. student from Germany was awarded $500 in the form of a tuition grant. He was not only the "first Co-op" student (not to be confused with the later category of "Fenn Co-op Scholars"), but also, the first foreign student to receive support from the Foundation. F.E.F. was now an actively functioning foundation.

The name of the Planning Committee was changed to the Long Range Planning Committee with the idea in mind that the Fenn Executive Committee would handle short range details to provide a base for F.E.F. Hale, Chairman of this newly named committee suggested that public relations counsel be sought on a month-to-month basis to aid in establishing the image to which F.E.F. should aspire in most effectively fitting into its community role.

At the January 7, 1966, meeting of the Fenn Executive Committee, Hale reported that furniture had been purchased and all other preliminaries, including fidelity bonding, were accomplished to establish an office headquarters with G.C.A.F. Also, action was taken to grant a requested $25,470 to C.S.U. for scholarship support for the academic year 1966–1967. The terms of the grant, however, were to be negotiated by Chairman Burmester and Dr. Earnest with the appropriate officials at C.S.U. that this fund be used mostly for students of the Greater Cleveland area who were participating in the cooperative program.

The Long Range Planning Committee met for the first time January 13, 1966, and inasmuch as there was present a non-member of the Fenn Executive Committee plus a guest as a public relations counsel, Chairman Hale reviewed the activities of the Fenn College Board of Trustees including the actions necessary to establish F.E.F. and the deliberations of the Executive Committee at the two meetings held thus far. He further reported on the establishment of an F.E.F. headquarters in the offices of G.C.A.F. and that the Executive Committee had decided to limit the geographical area of grantees to that of Metropolitan Cleveland.

The following decisions resulted from this lengthy meeting:

1. It was too early to pursue long range planning.
2. F.E.F. should distribute income only, not principal.
3. F.E.F. should be an innovative foundation, not merely a custodial one.
4. As F.E.F.'s objectives became crystallized, contributions could be sought from persons and corporations interested in those objectives.
5. F.E.F. should not limit its interest to C.S.U.
6. The public relations counsel suggested that if F.E.F. was to mature, it must support private needs not met by others, and have, preferably, an exclusive purpose.
7. The Trustees and Corporate Members should be up-dated on the activities of the Fenn Executive and Long Range Planning Committees as soon as possible.

Accordingly, under date of March 7, 1966, Chairman Burmester mailed to all Trustees and Members of the Fenn Educational Foundation a progress report, expressing, in detail and with dates, the activities of the Fenn Executive Committee from September 1, 1965, through March 7, 1966. He indicated that the assets of F.E.F. as of December 31, 1965, totalled $2,109,748.52.

Executive Committee meetings were held on June 7, July 26, and August 2, 1966, largely concerning investment of the assets of F.E.F., change in banking operations and procedures, requests for grants, receipt of IRS approval of F.E.F.'s tax exempt status plus considerable discussion on both short and long range plans. It was finally decided to invite certain college presidents and other educationally active lay people (individually) of Cleveland to a series of meetings to explore and discuss possible alternative purposes for F.E.F. and resolve the wisest course and methods for charting its future.

Through a series of eight Executive Committee meetings between August 9 and November 9, 1966, the following were invited to present their viewpoints relative to Cleveland's need for financial support of various aspects of higher education:

Ralph M. Besse, President, Cleveland Commission on Higher Education, and Chairman of the Board, Cleveland Electric Illuminating Company

Dr. Charles E. Chapman, President, Cuyahoga Community College

Father Hugh E. Dunn, President, John Carroll University

Dr. Harold L. Enarson, President, The Cleveland State University

Dr. John S. Millis, President, Western Reserve University

Frank E. Joseph, Partner, Jones, Day, Cockley and Reavis

Dr. A. B. Bonds, Jr., President, Baldwin-Wallace College

Dr. Robert Morse, President, Case Institute of Technology

Ellwood H. Fisher, Trustee, Fenn Educational Foundation (Past Board Chairman, Fenn College)

If there was one element of agreement which resulted from these sessions with leaders of higher education in Cleveland, it was that F.E.F.'s purpose would fill a need unsupported by other foundations in Metropolitan Cleveland. Father Dunn felt that F.E.F. should continue to fulfill its educational mission in the community and that since cooperative education was Fenn College's mission, the Trustees of the Foundation should strongly consider perpetuating the image of Fenn by financially supporting cooperative education at both the undergraduate and graduate levels. Others on the above list of invitees expressed similar uses for F.E.F.'s income. Most felt that state universities were not generally enthusiastic about the cooperative plan of higher education because it required an additional administrative expense which many trustees of state universities thought did not relate to the usual budget items for direct teaching. Therefore, F.E.F. could at least help lift this onus from the C.S.U. budget by lending financial support to continue Fenn College's Co-op program in partnership with Greater Cleveland's business and industry.

At the November 9, 1966, meeting, Hale and Dickey submitted the report of the Long Range Planning Committee, and following suggestions for final editing, action was taken to submit the revised final edition to the Trustees and Members by mail with an enclosed ballot requesting them to reply likewise as to whether they were favorable or unfavorable to the Proposed Program for the Fenn Educational Foundation. The crux of one of the items of the long range plan was the inducement of other colleges and universities in the Cleveland area to incorporate some measure of Co-op education into their on-going programs. Dr. Earnest visited with presidents or deans at each institution, but the only one who, at that time, felt co-op programs could be started was Dr. Chapman of Cuyahoga Community College.

The voting on Hale and Dickey's proposed program by mail ballot was so preponderantly favorable that the charge to the Long Range Planning Committee to proceed with a formal presentation to the F.E.F. Board of Trustees seemed very clear. Accordingly, a special meeting of the board was called for Wednesday, February 1, 1967, in the Board Room of the Union Commerce Bank. Inasmuch as this was the first Board meeting since October 27, 1965, Chairman Burmester reviewed the activities of the Fenn Executive Committee resulting from fourteen meetings of the committee in the interim. A resolution ratifying all actions of the Executive Committee during the interim was unanimously passed.

Trustee Dickey highlighted the new Fenn Co-op Scholar Program and stressed that to make it effective the following five-point program would be necessary:

1. Develop a prime interest in our program in the commerce, industry, and professional people in the Greater Cleveland community. Retain broad corporate membership but organize Board of Trustees around especially interested individuals. The

Executive Committee should be an active working committee of 6 to 8 persons who have time to devote to the program.

2. Engage a full-time Director for the Foundation to develop interest throughout commerce and industry, counsel with high schools and colleges to select suitable co-op candidates, and work with the colleges and universities in the community to develop suitable programs of study.

3. Plan our first few years on an exploratory basis and with a limited number of participants. Keep our administration expenses plus grants for tuition-aid, etc. within the annual income of the Foundation fund.

4. Avoid fund raising campaigns until the value of the program warrants such. Check no ambitious impulses, however, to receive voluntary contributions.

5. Assign specific duties and responsibilities to the Executive Committee. Areas of service should be explored, selection of candidates need be approved and awards granted to them, the investment portfolio needs constant attention, and Trustees and Corporate Members need frequent reports.

The board then unanimously voted in favor of the following resolution concerning the Proposed Program for the Fenn Educational Foundation. It was prepared by the Long Range Planning Committee under the guidance of Trustees Hale and Dickey.

RESOLVED: WHEREAS, the Executive Committee has conducted a thorough study for approximately one year of the possible areas of activity in which the Fenn Educational Foundation (hereinafter the "Foundation") could make a significant contribution to the needs of higher education in the Greater Cleveland area; and

WHEREAS, the Executive Committee has made a written recommendation as to a particular future program, such recommendation having been sent to all Trustees and Members of the Foundation under a covering letter of December 12, 1966 by Harry F. Burmester, Chairman, Board of Trustees (said recommendation being referred to hereinafter as "Proposed Program for Fenn Education Foundation"); and

WHEREAS, it is desired to authorize hereby an implementation of such recommended program as well as to authorize the Executive Committee to take certain other action;

NOW, THEREFORE, BE IT FURTHER RESOLVED: That the Proposed Program for Fenn Educational Foundation is hereby approved as the primary educational program of the Foundation, and that the Executive Committee is given hereby broad powers to implement such program through such specific operations, procedures and employment of personnel as it deems necessary. The Executive Committee shall report to the Trustees from time to time on the progress of implementation of such program.

The first Annual Meeting of Members of F.E.F. was held May 9, 1967. In addition to the items which were approved at the Trustee meeting on February 1, 1967, the Members approved (1) the new Code of Regulations for F.E.F., (2) the action taken by the Executive Committee since the October 27, 1965, meeting, and (3) the current financial reports on the affairs of F.E.F. The fiscal year was changed to terminate June 30.

The Code of Regulations called for a report of the Nominating Committee on officers at the first meeting of the board following the Annual Meeting of Members. This meeting took place on June 6, 1967, and the following officers were elected:

Clayton G. Hale, Chairman
Paul S. Dickey, 1st Vice Chairman
Dr. James C. Hodge, Vice Chairman
Dr. G. Brooks Earnest, Vice Chairman
B. W. Maxey, Treasurer
Karl F. Bruch, Jr., Secretary

A By-Law provision concerning the Investment Committee was adopted at this meeting outlining the size, term of office, and duties of the members. Alan G. Rorick, legal counsel, warned the board that F.E.F. might face a problem with the Internal Revenue Service regarding accumulated income. He proposed a motion to distribute to one or more of six specified Cleveland colleges all accumulated income as of June 30, 1967, within the period expiring June 30, 1972. The motion was passed. The said accumulated income was actually distributed a year ahead of this deadline.

The Cleveland State University held a very special convocation at Severance Hall on June 10, 1967, at which time all Fenn Alumni (degree holders) were issued C.S.U. diplomas by President Enarson thus making them alumni of C.S.U. This was in compliance with the contract between Fenn College and C.S.U. relative to Fenn College graduates.

On June 22, 1967, the Executive Committee of the Fenn Educational Foundation unanimously adopted the following resolution regarding the immediate Past Chairman of the Board of Trustees:

> WHEREAS, WE, the members of the Board of Trustees of the Fenn Educational Foundation have a profound respect for Harry F. Burmester; and
>
> WHEREAS, as Chairman of the Board of Trustees of Fenn College from 1960 to 1965, and the Board of Trustees of the Fenn Educational Foundation from November 1st, 1965 to June 6th, 1967 he has given freely of his time, interest and energies in the advancement of affairs of the College and the Foundation; and
>
> WHEREAS, special cognizance is taken of the leadership and direction given by him in the difficult two years of deliberations concerning the possible use of Fenn College as a new State institution of higher learning in Greater Cleveland through to the actual transfer of the College to the State of Ohio;
>
> NOW, THEREFORE, BE IT RESOLVED: That we, the members of the Board of Trustees of the Fenn Educational Foundation record our high esteem for Harry F. Burmester, and our lasting appreciation and gratitude for his sincerity of purpose, his clear judgment, his accomplishments, and his many major contributions to Fenn College, the Fenn Educational Foundation and the community.

It was further resolved that this Resolution be prepared in the form of an illuminated scroll, to be signed by the officers and to be presented to Mr. Burmester at a luncheon with the Executive Committee. Also, the following resolution was unanimously approved:

> RESOLVED: That the Executive Committee recommends to the Board of Trustees for action by the Corporate Members at their next meeting that the Code of Regulations be amended to provide for a third Life Trustee; and further recommends that Mr. Harry F. Burmester be elected as the third Life Trustee of the Foundation.

Action was also taken at this meeting to extend an offer to Dr. G. Brooks Earnest as the full-time Director of the Fenn Educational Foundation. Dr. Earnest had been giving a third of his time to the Foundation activities in the capacity as Consultant to the Cleveland State University and was planning to terminate this association at C.S.U. as of October 31, 1967.

As the result of the June 22 meeting of the Fenn Executive Committee the Cleveland *Plain Dealer* carried the following article on June 25, 1967.

> New plans for promoting the "cooperative plan" of education in Cleveland have been announced by the executive committee of the Fenn Educational Foundation.
>
> "During the summer the foundation will consult with each of the six local institutions of higher learning regarding the September term, with continued emphasis on the cooperative plan," said Clayton G. Hale, newly elected chairman of the foundation.
>
> The six institutions are Case Institute of Technology, Western Reserve University, Baldwin-Wallace College, John Carroll and Cleveland State Universities and Cuyahoga Community College.
>
> Continuous consultations will be going on with Cleveland industrial and commercial firms which have historically constituted the backbone of support of the cooperative concept, Hale added.
>
> The foundation's funds now amount to $2,125,000. They represent the assets of Fenn College remaining after the transfer of the campus property to CSU in November, 1965.
>
> The former Fenn College was a pioneer in cooperative education—simultaneous employment and education. Through the foundation the trustees of old Fenn are continuing to develop this concept.
>
> Foundation officers who will serve with Hale for the coming year are Paul S. Dickey, first vice chairman; Dr. G. Brooks Earnest, Dr. James C. Hodge and B. W. Maxey, vice chairmen, and Karl F. Bruch, Jr., secretary.
>
> C. B. McDonald is chairman of the foundation's investment committee.

Upon recommendation of Chairman Hale, action was taken at the October 23, 1967, meeting of the Fenn Executive Committee to engage the firm of Winter and Winter as public relations and publicity counsel. The Committee also approved the printer's proof of a proposed brochure which was prepared under the direction of Trustee Dickey. The brochure is shown here.

The November 7, 1967, meeting of the Fenn Executive Committee was a very special one as noted by the Minutes published as follows in total.

FENN
EDUCATIONAL
FOUNDATION

Projects a NEW DIMENSION
in higher Education
Combining . . . .

WORK

STUDY

**FINANCIAL
GRANTS**

● Having an employee who is interested not only in his job and his pay envelope but in his employment as a possible future career.

● Having a worker whose employment is more meaningful because of the academic work periods alternating with full-time employment.

● Having Fenn Co-Op Scholars on a "matching plan" so that during periods when one is enrolled full-time in college, another is employed full-time without any job interruption as far as the employer is concerned.

● An opportunity to participate in the total educational process of Fenn Co-Op Scholars.

● Grants for all or part of the cost of academic study.

● Employment on a full-time basis, alternating with periods of full-time study in a field closely related to his field of study.

● Concentrated attention, while enrolled as a student, upon the curriculum of the educational institution.

● Full attention upon, and interest in the work done and all of its components while employed.

● Opportunity to make a wise choice of a career by becoming familiar with the vocational possibilities of the chosen field of study.

● An opportunity to offer a co-op, work-study program for carefully selected students, a program now offered by more than 60 colleges or universities in the United States.

● A method of assisting students to benefit by the alternating of academic study and employment, without disruption of present schedules and curricula, but merely by prolonging the student's degree-seeking program.

● Co-operation with highly motivated students to enable them to participate in the Fenn Co-Op Scholar Program and to benefit by the grants awarded to students, and the important influences of the Program in career selection.

FOR THE EMPLOYER
PROVIDES VALUABLE
EMPLOYEES . . . .

BENEFITS OF
THE FENN CO-OP
SCHOLAR
PROGRAM. . . . .

FOR THE STUDENT
PROVIDES FINANCIAL
GRANTS . . . .

FOR THE COLLEGE
OR UNIVERSITY
PROVIDES HIGHLY
MOTIVATED STUDENTS . . . .

HOW THE
PLAN
DEVELOPED . . . .

THE FENN EDUCATIONAL FOUNDATION

The Fenn Educational Foundation provides a plan of support and assistance to a limited number of highly-motivated young people to undertake programs of co-op education at undergraduate or graduate levels.

The Foundation is a non-profit corporation, established for the purpose of administering funds remaining from Fenn College after the transfer of the major assets of the College to The Cleveland State University, in 1965. The foundation has adopted a plan for the use of the income from the funds in its trust for the benefit of higher education in this area. While the income from the trust is not large, the Trustees of the Foundation have adopted a plan to fill a need not now being met in this area.

FENN COLLEGE PIONEERED THE CO-OP PLAN IN CLEVELAND

To make clear the functioning of the plan which, for ease of recognition, is called the Fenn Co-Op Scholar Program, it is necessary to review briefly part of the history of Fenn College, up to the date of its absorption into The Cleveland State University in 1965. In 1923, when Fenn College was founded, it initiated in Cleveland the cooperative program of higher education. Throughout greater Cleveland, and in many other important centers of the U.S.A., are Fenn graduates who can and do attest to the effectiveness of higher education acquired under the co-op program.

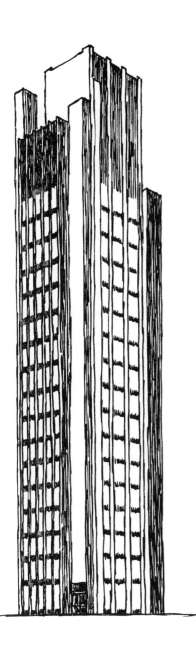

C.S.U. CONTINUES
THE CO-OP PLAN

Effective in September, 1967, The Cleveland State University has not only continued but has given new stature and recognition to the co-op, work-study plan. The C.S.U. proposed to appoint a businessman's advisory committee to the Co-operative Education Program. The Cleveland State University also plans to promote the co-op program within and without the University. The Fenn Educational Foundation has made a grant, renewable for two more years, to assist the co-op program to grow and flourish at The Cleveland State University.

THE FENN EDUCATIONAL
FOUNDATION ENLARGES
THE CO-OP PLAN

The Trustees of the Foundation are confident that colleges and universities of the area, in addition to The Cleveland State University, will be willing to co-operate by permitting full-time students to enroll for a program in which full-time employment for a designated period will alternate with full-time enrollment in a designated semester, quarter, two semesters or two quarters, as may be best for the student, his college or school and his employer.

During the student's employment period, he is considered to be a student of his educational institution and his work should be co-ordinated with his studies. Students in such a plan are awarded financial grants by the Fenn Educational Foundation during the periods of study based upon demonstrated need. Other conditions that must be met are:

Possibilities

of Education for Undergraduate and Advanced Degrees through the Fenn Co-Op Scholar Program

In Business Administration

In Education

In Engineering

In the Humanities

In Languages

Charles F. Kettering said

"What gives co-operative education its strength is that it lap-welds theory from the classroom with practice on-the-job. It creates a weld that is much stronger than the butt-welding of a college degree followed by employment, the two touching at only one line of contact."

In Law

In Natural Sciences and Mathematics

In Social Studies

In Social Work

High motivation of scholar
Better than average academic records
Serious interest in attaining a degree from an
accredited college.

Candidates for selection as Fenn Co-Op Scholars are chosen without regard to race, creed or color, solely upon the criteria quoted above.

Candidates for the Fenn Co-Op Scholar Program may be recommended by the educational institution in which they are currently enrolled; by high school guidance counselors for recent or current secondary school graduates; and by employers who have in their employ men or women with secondary school diplomas or with some college background who could benefit by a college education, particularly on the co-op plan, or men or women with bachelor's degree who could be benefited by working for an advanced degree.

Supporting colleges or universities are asked only to be willing to permit Fenn Co-Op Scholars to work and study on a staggered plan, alternating regular enrollment periods with periods of full-time employment, thus, prolonging the customary time to complete graduation requirements.

In order to implement the employment phase of the student's co-op program, the Trustees of the Fenn Educational Foundation recommend the enlistment of a group of companies, as supporting commerce, industry and professional members of the Fenn Co-Op Scholar Program. Executives of these companies would be encouraged to select one or more present employees for the Fenn Co-Op Scholar program, or to offer employment to co-op students currently enrolled at a local college or university.

An important feature of this plan of working closely with the supporting commerce, industry and professional members could be called the "matching plan." For each student employed on a periodic basis, the office of the Fenn Educational Foundation will try to find another student in an appropriate field of study so that two students might alternate as full-time employees and full-time students, thus equalling, for the employer, one full-time, year-'round employee. The Trustees of the Fenn Educational Foundation are sure that this "matching plan" of Fenn Co-Op Scholars can succeed with the co-operation of employers, scholars and the educational institutions.

In summary, the Fenn Educational Foundation, with the financial resources at its command, is launching a Fenn Co-Op Scholar Program to make possible all of the advantages of combining academic study with education through work related to the field of study chosen by the Co-Op Scholar, and to make such a program possible in any college or university in this area.

• WORK
• STUDY
• GRANTS

Minutes of Meeting of Executive Committee
Fenn Educational Foundation
Union Club, Parlor 14—12:00 Noon—November 7, 1967

Present: All members of the Executive Committee: Clayton G. Hale, Chairman; Paul S. Dickey, First Vice-Chairman; Dr. James C. Hodge, Vice-Chairman; Dr. G. Brooks Earnest, Vice-Chairman and Director; B. W. Maxey, Treasurer; Karl F. Bruch, Jr., Secretary; and C. Bert McDonald, Chairman of Investment Committee; Harry F. Burmester as honored guest of this occasion; and, by special invitation, Vollmer W. Fries as former Chairman of the Negotiating Committee.

Absent: None.

Chairman Hale suggested that this meeting of the Executive Committee, set on a day when every man could be present, be devoted exclusively to the purpose for which it was called: a recognition and appreciation of Harry F. Burmester and his seven years as Chairman of The Fenn College and The Fenn Educational Foundation Boards, with special reference to his leadership in the relations with the State of Ohio incident to the creation of Cleveland State University; that all other business be dispensed with.

This ceremonial occasion was decreed by the full Board of Trustees, which authorized the Executive Committee to prepare a suitable resolution (heretofore reported to all Trustees in the Committee's Minutes of June 22, 1967); have it lettered upon a scroll; and make presentation of it in a small meeting specifically devoted to this purpose.

Accordingly, this meeting consisted of informal conversation and reminiscences over the luncheon; the presentation of the framed scroll; and the taking of a photograph. There then appeared a reader, with a wreath of ivy 'round his head, who rendered from the Greek historian Thucydides those passages known as the Melian Dialogue. This was followed by a brief noting of certain similarities between Harry Burmester's term of service as leader of the Fenn Men, and the problem of the Men of Melos 2,383 years ago.

Luncheon adjourned (with no expense to the Foundation) at 1:45 P.M.

s/*Karl F. Bruch, Jr.*, Secretary

Resolution

WHEREAS, WE, the members of the Board of Trustees of the Fenn Educational Foundation have a profound respect for Harry F. Burmester; and

WHEREAS, as Chairman of the Board of Trustees of Fenn College from 1960 to 1965, and the Board of Trustees of the Fenn Educational Foundation from November 1st, 1965 to June 6th, 1967 he has given freely of his time, interest and energies in the advancement of affairs of the College and the Foundation; and

WHEREAS, special cognizance is taken of the leadership and direction given by him in the difficult two years of deliberations concerning the possible use of Fenn College as a new State institution of higher learning in Greater Cleveland through to the actual transfer of the College to the State of Ohio;

NOW, THEREFORE, BE IT RESOLVED: That we, the members of the Board of Trustees of the Fenn Educational Foundation record our high esteem for Harry F. Burmester, and our lasting appreciation and gratitude for his sincerity of purpose, his clear judgment, his accomplishments, and his many major contributions to Fenn College, the Fenn Educational Foundation and the community.

(It was further resolved that this Resolution be prepared in the form of an illuminated scroll, to be signed by the officers and to be presented to Mr. Burmester at a luncheon with the Executive Committee.)

The following extracts from an article in the *Cleveland Press* of December 13, 1967, by Business Editor Ray De Crane, were mailed to all Trustees and Members of the Fenn Educational Foundation:

A new concept in cooperative work and study education, embracing college study at both the undergraduate and graduate level, was unveiled here today by the Fenn Educational Foundation.

FEF is the successor to the Fenn College Trustees. Their resources—totaling $2,274,000—represent assets remaining after Fenn College was converted into Cleveland State University in 1965.

Under the program, . . . students now in college under a financial strain, and employees with a bachelor's degree who recognize the need of higher education will be given financial help.

FEF trustees—industry, commerce and banking executives—have, for the first time, obtained the cooperation of all major colleges in Greater Cleveland.

. . . .

Paul S. Dickey, president of Bailey Meter Co. and first vice chairman of the FEF trustees, said it took more than a year to put the program together. "For the employer, it provides valuable employees, for the student, financial grants; for the college or university it provides highly motivated students," Dickey said.

Earnings from their fund, about $100,000 a year, will finance the FEF program. Details of the program have been mailed to area high schools and colleges and to major employers.

"We hope to start with a small group of about 20 students next fall," Dickey said.

The foundation will give full or partial tuition aid, depending on need, and will provide employment in the field of study for the student. Students and employers will be paired so that while one student is completing a quarter or semester of study his alternate will be on the job.

An innovation is the aid which will be offered to the full-time employee who wants to do graduate work.

Going to night school after working all day dilutes the effectiveness of both the education and the job, the FEF believes. Its program allows employees to go to college for one semester, while working the following semester.

"Too often these deserving people have family responsibilities which make it impossible for them to return to school at their own expense," Dickey explained.

"Under our program it is hoped a way may be worked out between the employer and the foundation to supply that man his regular earnings during the time he is in class," Dickey explained.

Tuition grants and job opportunities will be offered to men and women. No arrangement has been made with women's colleges. But the program may include Ursuline, Notre Dame and Lake Erie colleges, Dickey said.

The January 4, 1968, Minutes of the Fenn Executive Committee indicated that Director Earnest was consolidating all former Fenn presidents' office file records, discarding unimportant papers, and marking all the remainder for historical reference.

On March 14, 1968, a delightful dinner event hosted by C.S.U. was held at the Mid-Day Club on which occasion twenty-five of the forty-seven living recipients of honorary degrees from Fenn College were present to receive honorary degrees from C.S.U., thus fulfilling the contract agreement between Fenn College and C.S.U. relative to all degree holders, both undergraduate and honorary, from Fenn being accepted as C.S.U. degree holders.

The first Fenn Co-op Scholars (A) were selected at C.S.U. They were Hushang Aldad and Manouchehr Movahedi, both Iranians whose personal funds were exhausted at the beginning of their senior year, and who had completed the required number of quarters on Co-op jobs.

Chairman Clayton G. Hale's memo which accompanied the June 17, 1968, Minutes of the Executive Committee carried the following two paragraphs:

> In carrying out the objectives laid down by the Trustees I offer this analysis of our present position: (1) the Fenn Scholar program is developing slowly; (2) the aid to co-operative students in Greater Cleveland is moving briskly; (3) and the support of the co-operative education concept in this area, notably at C.S.U., has been nothing short of vital if it were not to expire with Fenn College.

> Thus, for the first time, I am reporting to you that we do have this Foundation "turned around"; and that we are, under our modification of the old Fenn College charter, usefully functioning along the lines envisioned from the series of inquiring meetings held two years ago.

It was decided at the October 11, 1968, meeting of the Executive Committee that henceforth F.E.F. would publish its annual balance sheet and grant information, together with a list of Trustees and Corporate Members, in both the *Plain Dealer* and the *Cleveland Press*. It was also announced at this meeting that Lakeland Community College planned to establish a cooperative education program.

The first Annual Meeting of the Fenn Educational Foundation Corporation in nineteen months was held at the Union Club on December 10, 1969. Dr. James McConnell, Professor of Psychology, attached to the Medical School, The College of Literature, Science and The Arts, and the Mental Health Research Institute of the University of Michigan was the speaker of the evening. His subject was: "Cannibals, Chemicals and Memory." It was really an interesting illustrated talk on his research activity over a period of fourteen years with so-called "flat worms." The business portion of the meeting consisted of approving three amendments to the Code of Regulations, the report of the Nominating Committee, the reports of the Chairman, Director and Treasurer. It was also reported that Trustees Galen Miller and Wade N. Harris had passed away since the last annual meeting.

The following résumé of grants made or approved by F.E.F. from September 1, 1965, to October 31, 1968, was presented by Director Earnest:

		No. of Grants
To Cleveland State University		
Development of Co-op Program	$ 88,400.00 –	3
Financial aid to students enrolled originally in Fenn College	59,510.30 –	15
Supplemental aid to faculty salaries (Administration of Ford Foundation Grant)	17,538.92 –	1
Cost of new C.S.U. diplomas for all living Fenn alumni and Fenn Honorary Degree recipients	6,525.00 –	2
Study of special Co-op Doctor of Engineering Program	6,000.00 –	1
Fenn Co-op Scholars	3,200.00 –	8
Dean Anders Memorial Scholarship Fund	3,000.00 –	2
Total	$184,174.22	32

To Fenn Co-op Scholar Program

Cleveland Metropolitan college area—Accumulated income as of June 30, 1967 irrevocably committed to the Fenn Co-op Scholar Program at six Greater Cleveland colleges to June 30, 1972 $ 20,673.54

To Baldwin-Wallace College

Tuition aid for Upward Bound Program	$ 11,500.00 –	2

To Cuyahoga Community College

Study and implementation of Co-op Program	$ 10,000.00 –	2

To Cleveland Scholarship Program

Tuition for six needy inner-city high school graduates	$ 4,800.00 –	2

*To the Educational Association of
Metropolitan Cleveland*

Educational TV Program $ 2,500.00   –   1

*To the Cleveland Commission on Higher
Education*

Teacher education improvement project $ 2,000.00   –   1
                                          ───────────   ──
                                                              8

                Grand Total $235,647.76
                                          ───────────

                                          Total Grants   40

Dr. Stecher, Chairman of the Nominating Committee, presented the following slate of officers for the ensuing year. All nominees were unanimously elected:

Chairman, Paul S. Dickey
Vice Chairman, Director, Dr. G. Brooks Earnest
Vice Chairman, Clayton G. Hale
Vice Chairman, Dr. James C. Hodge
Treasurer, Wm. J. Hunkin, II
Secretary, Alfred G. Hose

Former Chairman, Harry F. Burmester, was elected a Life Trustee.

The Fenn Educational Foundation suffered a great loss December 19, 1968, in the death of Howard F. Burns. As a member of the Board of Trustees of Fenn College for thirteen years and its successor the Fenn Educational Foundation for three years, he gave much of himself to the fulfillment of prudent administration of the College and the Foundation. He was deeply interested in the progress of Fenn College, its academic standing, and the execution of appropriate legal actions. Burns gave yeoman's service to the College in the vast amount of legal preparation in the court action to transfer the College to the State of Ohio as the nucleus for The Cleveland State University. He also saw to it that we adhered to the "Code of Regulations" in all matters pertaining to the administration of the College and the Foundation. The "Fenn Men" are grateful for his years of active service, which were of vital significance and most inspiring. His allegiance to Fenn College and the Fenn Educational Foundation will always be remembered. Among Burns' many extra-curricular activities were his service as a Council Member and Member of the Executive Committee of the American Law Institute, and Trustee of Mt. Holyoke College from 1950 to 1960, President of the Board 1958–1960.

Burns was a partner in the law firm of Baker, Hostetler, and Patterson. At a joint meeting of the Executive and Investment Committees on May 7, 1969, Alan G. Rorick, also of the same law firm, and who had assisted him in much of the Fenn legal preparation, was elected a Trustee to fill that vacancy. Following the business meeting a special presentation meeting was held in honor of Director G. Brooks Earnest.

Presentation by Clayton G. Hale

to

G. Brooks Earnest

at

A Joint Meeting of The Executive and Investment Committees
Union Club, Parlor 12 — 12:00 noon — May 7, 1969 — Present:

Executive Committee	Investment Committee
Paul S. Dickey, Chairman	C. Bert McDonald, Chairman
Clayton G. Hale, Vice Chairman	Vollmer W. Fries
James C. Hodge, Vice Chairman	Clayton G. Hale
G. Brooks Earnest, Vice Chairman, Director	E. E. Helm
W. J. Hunkin II, Treasurer	W. J. Hunkin II
Alfred G. Hose, Secretary	J. Maurice Struchen
C. Bert McDonald	

Present by Invitation

Ellwood H. Fisher, Life Trustee, former Board Chairman
Harry F. Burmester, Life Trustee, former Board Chairman
James W. Corey, former Trustee
Alan G. Rorick, Baker, Hostetler & Patterson
Henry J. Kubach, Consulting Controller

At a special pre-luncheon meeting of all members of the Executive and Investment Committees together with several guests noted on the cover page, Mr. Clayton G. Hale, former chairman, Board of Trustees, Fenn Educational Foundation, read the following citation in behalf of Dr. G. Brooks Earnest:

Our Chairman, Paul Dickey, has asked me to say a few words at this time about the last President of old Fenn College. His choice of speaker, from among the present officers of the Foundation, derives simply from length of service to that College—but I am none the less pleased to attempt to carry out his assignment.

An examination of the Minutes of the College serves to remind us of a number of things. Dr. C. V. Thomas, the first outstanding President of Fenn College, fell across his desk at noon on Friday, Nov. 28, 1947. I was one of the pall-bearers.

Dr. J. C. Nichols, Dean, was named by the Trustees as Acting President. A Selection Committee of Trustees, aided by a Faculty Advisory Committee, screened over 100 persons and, on July 2, 1948, agreed upon Dr. Edward Hodnett as the next President. He attended his first Board Meeting on Oct. 29, 1948.

Moving forward, now, through some stormy years, the Board, on Sept. 7, 1950, appointed G. Brooks Earnest as Dean of Engineering —even though we still had a Dean of Engineering who resisted all Board efforts to persuade him to resign. Another Dean's duties and authority had been changed three times and his resignation requested. A Board member had admonished the President about his responsibilities. A nominating committee of the Board itself had reported "no nomination" for Board Chairman, "no nomination" for second vice-chairman, one nomination for first vice-chairman and that nominee thereupon withdrew his name, and soon afterward resigned from the Board. Simultaneously, the College was separating from the Y.M.C.A. at the latter's request. The newspapers were in full cry. Employment termination dates were set, and then reset for later dates to allow individuals more time to seek other employment. Letters were written, ordered written, entered in the records, modified by later letters. There existed great patience and humane consideration—and near chaos. In one meeting (April 25, 1951) the Board accepted the resignations of nine faculty members. The Board became dejected over the endless hours it was devoting to listening to all sides, yet seeming to make little progress toward settling the College down to its real work. On

July 12, 1951, the resignation of President Edward Hodnett was accepted "with extreme regret."

Six months later, on Jan. 28, 1952, a new Selection Committee made an interim report recommending, and the Board appointed, G. Brooks Earnest, Dean of Engineering, as Acting President of the College; and nine months after that, on Sept. 22, 1952, this acting appointment was made a full appointment with the support of the Selection Committee, the Faculty Advisory Committee, the Alumni Advisory Committee, and the Board of Trustees.

It was under these terrible circumstances which had prevailed just 67 days short of 5 years, that Brooks Earnest accepted the charge to become the President of Fenn College. He almost dropped out of sight and turned inwardly to quietly, patiently, courteously and honorably, one by one, mend the lacerations of the remaining loyal faculty and staff. This was the first necessity; and the very calmness and competence with which he slowly brought it about led some to undervalue what he was doing. We were out of our trouble. Ten years later we could look back upon a mighty internal growth and spirit, a doubled budget and tripled assets; and while Brooks Earnest would be the first to give all due credit to the Deans, the Department Chairmen, the Business Officers, the Trustees, Board Chairman Charles Stilwell, and all the other men of goodwill with whom we have been blessed, the fact remains that we found a President who was equal to the time and the place to which he was called.

And now, Brooks Earnest, as evidence of the truly deep respect and affection which are felt for you by your fellow workers in that good cause, we want to present to you the engraved signatures of the 31 Trustees who comprised your Board at the end of your College Presidency, together with several others selected from your colleagues within the College itself; and it is my honor, acting on behalf of all these others, to hand this to you with our blessings.

Dr. Earnest expressed his genuine appreciation for Mr. Hale's wonderful tribute and the handsome tray, indicating that he and Mrs. Earnest would be forever grateful for this fine gift.

The following signatures were engraved on the tray:

Trustees

Arthur S. Armstrong	W. J. Hunkin, II
Edward T. Bartlett, II	William G. Laffer
Karl F. Bruch, Jr.	Van H. Leichliter
Harry F. Burmester	B. W. Maxey
Clarence L. Collens	C. Bert McDonald
A. T. Colwell	Warren L. Morris
James W. Corey	Walter B. O'Konski
Paul S. Dickey	Allen T. Perry
Ellwood H. Fisher	Norman F. Smith
Vollmer W. Fries	Dr. Robert M. Stecher
Clayton G. Hale	Chas. J. Stilwell
E. E. Helm	Clarence M. Taylor
John G. Henninger	Charles M. White
Dr. James C. Hodge	H. E. Widdell
John R. Hoover	George V. Woodling
Alfred G. Hose	

Fenn College Staff

Burl H. Bush, Dean of Engineering

Wm. A. Patterson, Provost

Vernon H. Davis, Director, Finance

Major B. Jenks, Dean of Arts & Sciences

Ernest C. Harris, Chairman, Department of Civil Engineering

Presentation of sterling silver tray to Dr. G. Brooks Earnest by Ellwood H. Fisher, Paul S. Dickey, Clayton G. Hale, and Harry F. Burmester.

It was announced at the June 23, 1969, Executive Committee meeting that the Hunkin-Conkey Construction Company had contributed $2,000 to the Fenn Educational Foundation. This was the first direct gift to the Foundation by a Cleveland business firm.

Dr. Harold L. Enarson, President of C.S.U., was a guest at the September 16, 1969, meeting of the Executive Committee. He reported on the progress the university was making as the result of the three-year $88,400 grant F.E.F. had awarded C.S.U. to further develop its Co-op Program of higher education. He reported there were 847 students in the program distributed as follows: Engineering, 402; Business Administration, 223; Arts and Sciences, 157; and Education, 65.

A grant of $1,800 was approved to Mrs. Mary M. Patterson for graduate nursing study at Case Western Reserve University. This was the first scholarship grant made by the Foundation to a graduate student.

It was reported at the same meeting that the Foundation had received a bequest of $18,096.19 from the estate of Bertha C. Fisher, the mother of Ellwood H. Fisher. This was the first bequest received by the Foundation.

The 1969 Annual Meeting of the Foundation was held at the Union Club on December 11. Dr. James A. (Dolph) Norton, Director of The Cleveland Foundation and President of the Greater Cleveland Associated Foundation, was the speaker of the evening. He reviewed the history and significance of the tax reform bill which was being considered by the U.S. Congress. He also suggested rules which he recommended for adoption by foundations in the conduct of their affairs. The Act when passed, as will be seen later, did have a decided effect on the future administration of the Fenn Educational Foundation.

A resolution was adopted at this meeting in appreciation of a gift of $100,000 from The Louis D. Beaumont Foundation in satisfaction of a pledge to the building fund of the former Fenn College. This gift was "allocated to scholarships and other academic needs for students, and to increase the quality of education at Metropolitan Cleveland's colleges and universities."

Director Earnest reported that steps had been taken for the sale of Hale's Hollow, a five-acre property near Medina, Ohio, including a three-room cottage and large two-car garage. This property had been donated to Fenn College by Trustee Clayton G. Hale and Mrs. Hale in November 1962 for use as a retreat for the administrative staff and faculty of the College. It was subsequently sold and the proceeds added to the invested funds of the Foundation.

Many new grants were approved at the June 10, 1970, meeting of the Executive Committee. These grants together with previously and later approved grants are summarized at the end of this chapter.

At this same meeting, Alan G. Rorick, legal counsel, advised the members of the Executive Committee concerning the pros and cons of being a "private" versus a "public" foundation. It was decided that a study should be made relative to whether F.E.F. should apply for "public" foundation status.

The greater part of the September 10, 1970, meeting of the Executive Committee was spent on discussion of prospective limitations affecting F.E.F. as a private foundation and what problems would arise and what would be the involvements should F.E.F. decide to convert to a public foundation or public charity. Clarification of all questions was impossible at that date because the Internal Revenue Service had not issued its final regulations relating to the Act.

At the Annual Meeting held December 8, 1971, the Board and Corporate Members of F.E.F. were brought up-to-date on the deliberations of the Executive Committee throughout the year 1971, especially relating to the study being made concerning "private versus public" status. As per custom, copies of Minutes of all Executive Committee meetings had been mailed to all Trustees and Members so that they had the opportunity to keep abreast of all Executive Committee activities.

Dr. Wayne Rodehorst, President of Lakeland Community College, was the speaker on this occasion. He gave a very informative and interesting talk on the academic and physical progress being made on their new campus and stressed the programs of cooperative education which they had already instituted and planned to institute as soon as funds were available.

It was reported at this meeting that Trustees James W. Corey and Henry E. Widdell and Member W. Braddock Hickman had passed away during the year.

Inasmuch as 1971 was the last full calendar year for operation of the Fenn Educational Foundation the roster of officers, trustees, standing committees and members for that particular year was as follows:

FENN EDUCATIONAL FOUNDATION
700 NATIONAL CITY BANK BUILDING
CLEVELAND, OHIO 44114

Memo to: Trustees and Members, Fenn Educational Foundation (F.E.F.)

From: Clayton G. Hale, Chairman

Re: Progress report on the Fenn Co-op Scholar Program

        You have received copies of the brochure describing the new Fenn
Co-op Scholar Program. We thought you may wish to be informed concerning
the distribution of the brochure to date. Besides the 29 Foundation Trustees,
copies were also sent to:

                    51 F.E.F. Foundation members
                    16 Cleveland high school principals
                    32 Suburban high school principals
                    29 Additional corporations with
                       extensive co-op experience at
                       Fenn College and C.S.U.
                     5 Greater Cleveland College Presidents
                    16 Copies to Cleveland Board of
                       Education Counselors
                    20 Copies to C.E.S. Counselors
                       and students

In addition a number of interested individuals have been sent copies. In
all 536 copies have been mailed to 169 different individuals, corporations
and educational institutions.

        The enclosed copy of an article in the November 13 issue of the
Cleveland Press augers well with our purpose to unostentatiously tell our
story to as many as possible. We are looking for highly motivated, above-
average students to spring-board our Program at two or three of Cleveland's
institutions of higher education. We are hopeful that a source of several
of the initial recipients of the scholarship will be the corporate structures
managed by our Trustees and Foundation members. There must be some alert,
bright young men in your organizations whom your supervisory personnel feel
a college education would make much more valuable to you.

        Dr. G. Brooks Earnest, now full time Director of the Foundation,
with office at 700 National City Bank Building (phone 579-0030), is
particularly qualified to be of assistance and will welcome inquiries from
you.

January 2, 1968

During the latter part of 1970 and early in 1971 the major subject
at Executive Committee meetings hinged around the disadvantages
which were eventually going to be imposed upon private foundations
by the Tax Reform Act of 1969. Early in 1971, Director Earnest presented F.E.F.'s problem to Dr. James A. (Dolph) Norton, Director

of The Cleveland Foundation, and was informed of a method or plan whereby F.E.F. could establish its assets with The Cleveland Foundation (a public foundation) as a Special Fund and still maintain the essentials of its existing structure and policies for recommending grants to higher educational institutions in the Greater Cleveland area, toward studies or programs in cooperative education or scholarships in behalf of designated co-op students.

This plan would call for the F.E.F. funds to be transferred to the responsible control of The Cleveland Foundation. The existing Trustees and Members of F.E.F. would be organized into a single unit known as the Fenn Advisory Committee and a smaller Executive Board similar to the existing Executive Committee would be impowered to carry on the affairs of the Advisory Committee between annual meetings of the full Committee. The Executive Board would make recommendations for grants to the Distribution Committee of The Cleveland Foundation. All Minutes of meetings of the Executive Board would promptly be mailed to every Member of the Advisory Committee and, of course, furnished to The Cleveland Foundation.

This plan would have all the advantages of public foundation status and, as a practical matter, still permit F.E.F. to function almost as theretofore, but without the disadvantages imposed upon a private foundation by the Tax Reform Act of 1969.

Dr. Earnest informed the Executive Committee of his consultation with Dr. Norton at a meeting held February 8, 1971. Following considerable discussion the following resolutions were unanimously passed:

RESOLVED: That the Executive Committee approves, in principle, the proposal presented in general terms to this meeting that Fenn Educational Foundation ("FEF") terminate its present private foundation status under the Tax Reform Act of 1969, pursuant to the special termination rule of section 507(b)(1)(A), by dissolution and distribution of assets to The Cleveland Foundation ("CF"), such assets to be held and designated as the Fenn Educational Fund of the CF with such special Fund to be administered by CF, on the advice and recommendations of a Fund Committee composed of persons who are now Trustees or Members of FEF, in substantially the same manner and for substantially the same purpose as FEF now operates, subject, however, to whatever overriding conditions, limitations and restrictions on the Fund and its operation may be imposed or required by the Resolution and Declaration of Trust creating the CF;

FURTHER RESOLVED: That the firm of Baker, Hostetler & Patterson is employed and authorized to study this proposal, determine what actions, court orders, rulings, agreements and procedures are necessary or desirable in order best to protect the interests of FEF, its Trustees and Members, and effectuate said proposal, and to prepare all pleadings, briefs, ruling requests, trust agreements, resolutions and other documents which said firm deems appropriate for submission to the Board of Trustees and Members for their approval and final authorization;

FURTHER RESOLVED: That the officers are authorized, with the counsel of Baker, Hostetler & Patterson, to negotiate with CF a draft of such agreements and other documents as are appropriate to carry out the above proposal and for submission to the Board of Trustees and Members for their approval and final authorization.

The above resolution simply granted the approval for F.E.F. legal counsel to proceed with a comprehensive study including all ramifications of the plan. Then if the plan proved to be feasible and desirable, the F.E.F. officers (with assistance of counsel) would negotiate with The Cleveland Foundation a draft of all essential documents for presentation to a full meeting of F.E.F. Trustees and Members.

Chairman Dickey indicated at the May 14, 1971, meeting of the Executive Committee that all reactions to the proposal for dissolution of F.E.F. and the distribution of assets to The Cleveland Foundation had been most favorable under the new circumstances.

Counsel Rorick reported that a form of trust agreement had been prepared and had received the approval of the members of the Distribution Committee of The Cleveland Foundation, and that The Cleveland Foundation had agreed to retain Dr. Earnest as a consultant to its Distribution Committee.

It was also decided at this meeting that upon consummation of the plan of dissolution of F.E.F. its net assets would be divided into five substantially equal parts, and that each of the five banks participating in The Cleveland Foundation's Multiple Trustee Plan would be designated as a Trustee under a separate trust agreement. The five banks were: The Cleveland Trust Company, The National City Bank of Cleveland, Central National Bank of Cleveland, Society National Bank of Cleveland, and Union Commerce Bank.

After considerable discussion of all of the ramifications involved with the preparation of all the essential documents for dissolution of F.E.F. the following resolutions were adopted:

> RESOLVED: WHEREAS, by action taken at the Executive Committee meeting of February 8, 1971, the officers and counsel were authorized to negotiate with The Cleveland Foundation ("CF") a draft of such agreements and other documents as are appropriate to carry out the proposal presented in general terms at the meeting referred to, relating to the assets of the Fenn Educational Foundation being held as the Fenn Educational Fund of CF; and
>
> WHEREAS, the officers and counsel have carried on such negotiations and have presented to this meeting a form of Trust Agreement which has been approved by representatives of the Distribution Committee of CF; and
>
> WHEREAS, counsel has advised the Executive Committee that a ruling request from the Internal Revenue Service should be filed at the earliest possible time and has prepared and presented such a request and related documents at this meeting; and
>
> WHEREAS, the Executive Committee wishes to authorize the filing of such a ruling request and to approve the form of Trust Agreement referred to above.
>
> NOW, THEREFORE, BE IT RESOLVED: That the Trust Agreement between the Fenn Educational Foundation and a bank or banks, as Trustee or Trustees, establishing a trust under The Cleveland Foundation Resolutions and request for ruling of the Internal Revenue Service relating to same are hereby approved in substantially the form and content presented at this meeting;
>
> That Mr. Paul Dickey, Chairman, is hereby authorized to execute on behalf of this Foundation a Power of Attorney in favor of counsel (Norman A. Sugarman, Alan G. Rorick, David R. Fullmer and Richard H. Leukart, II), to represent the Foundation in matters involving the Foundation relating to such ruling request; and
>
> That subject to the receipt of a favorable ruling on the above-mentioned ruling request and confirmation by the Board of Trustees and Members of the Foundation of all actions and documents necessary to carry out a Plan of Voluntary Dissolution and Distribution of Assets to effectuate the proposal approved at the Executive Committee meeting of February 8, 1971, and further contingent

upon approval by the Court of Common Pleas of Cuyahoga County, Ohio, the Chairman and Secretary are authorized to execute the Trust Agreement and take all other action necessary or desirable to effectuate such Plan.

That the Chairman or any Vice-Chairman is authorized to call a meeting of the Board of Trustees and Members to consider and act upon the proposed Plan of Voluntary Dissolution and Distribution of Assets as approved at the meeting of the Executive Committee, February 8, 1971 and in these resolutions.

FURTHER RESOLVED: That counsel is authorized to prepare and file a complaint with the Common Pleas Court, Cuyahoga County, Ohio seeking the direction and approval of the Court to consummate the Plan.

A special joint luncheon meeting of Trustees and Corporation Members was held at the Union Club on June 28, 1971, to discuss the proposed Plan of Voluntary Dissolution and Distribution of Assets of the Fenn Educational Foundation, copies of which had been enclosed with the "call of the meeting." David R. Fullmer, of the firm of Baker, Hostetler, and Patterson, answered questions on possible alternatives and outlined restrictions and possible penalties if the Foundation continued as a private foundation.

Unanimous action was then taken to adopt the following Plan of Voluntary Dissolution and Distribution of Assets and to instruct counsel to complete the necessary legal steps precedent to the consummation of the Plan by the Executive Committee of the Board of Trustees:

Plan of Voluntary Dissolution and Distribution of
Assets (hereinafter referred to as the "Plan")

WHEREAS, contingent upon obtaining the approvals referred to hereinafter, Fenn Educational Foundation desires to terminate its present private foundation status under the Tax Reform Act of 1969, pursuant to the special termination rule of Section 507(b)(1)(A) of the Internal Revenue Code, by a voluntary dissolution under Chapter 1702 of the Ohio Revised Code and distribution of its assets in trusts to be administered by the several trustee institutions who have adopted the Resolution creating The Cleveland Foundation under the Multiple Trusteeship Plan, said Resolution having been supplemented by a Resolution adopted by the Distribution Committee of The Cleveland Foundation and approved by the Trustees Committee of The Cleveland Foundation on April 14, 1967 (said Resolutions creating The Cleveland Foundation and as supplemented being referred to hereinafter as "The Cleveland Foundation Resolutions").

NOW, THEREFORE, IT IS RESOLVED: 1. Subject to satisfaction of the conditions set forth in Paragraph 2 below, Fenn Educational Foundation and the Members of Fenn Educational Foundation elect to be dissolved and wind up its affairs.

2. The election to dissolve and wind up referred to in Paragraph 1 above is contingent upon:

a. The obtaining of a ruling satisfactory to counsel for Fenn Educational Foundation, upon a request to the Commissioner of Internal Revenue that upon consummation of the Plan, Fenn Educational Foundation will meet the requirements of Section 507(b)(1)(A) by the end of the 12-month period (as extended by Amended Temporary Regulation Section 13.12(a)(4)(i), T.D. 7085, 36 *Fed. Reg.* 150 [1-6-71]) beginning with its first taxable year which begins after December 31, 1969, and thereby terminate its private foundation status pursuant to the special rule of Section 507(b)(1)(A), effective as of July 1, 1970;

b. The obtaining of an appropriate final order from the Court of Common Pleas, Cuyahoga County, Ohio approving the Plan;

c. The obtaining of appropriate consents of donors, settlors or other parties, with respect to disposition of restricted or trust funds of Fenn Educational Foundation, as approved by the Executive Committee of the Board of Trustees and as required or authorized by the Court of Common Pleas, Cuyahoga County, Ohio in the proceeding referred to in Paragraph 2(b) above; and

d. Completion of arrangements with the Distribution Committee of The Cleveland Foundation satisfactory to the Executive Committee of the Board of Trustees with respect to (i) contract of employment between the Distribution Committee and Dr. G. Brooks Earnest upon consummation of the Plan, and (ii) assumption by the Distribution Committee effective upon consummation of the Plan of the liability of Fenn Educational Foundation for deferred compensation due to Henry J. Kubach under his employment contract with Fenn Educational Foundation.

3. Upon dissolution of Fenn Educational Foundation, its net assets after the payment of or the adequate provision for the payment of all known obligations, shall be distributed as follows:

a. All unrestricted assets in trust to be held under a Trust Agreement (hereinafter "the Trust Agreement") by the several trustee institutions co-operating in the said Multiple Trusteeship Plan of The Cleveland Foundation, such assets together with the restricted assets referred to in Paragraph 3(b) below which are to become part of such trusts, to be divided among such trustee institutions in a manner to be approved by the Executive Committee of the Board of Trustees, with the objective of having five substantially equal trust estates, each trust estate being administered by a separate trustee institution, it not being intended, however, to divide a single restricted fund or trust of Fenn Educational Foundation into more than one trust estate.

b. All restricted or trusts assets of Fenn Educational Foundation upon consummation of the Plan to be distributed as approved or ordered by the Court of Common Pleas, Cuyahoga County, in the proceeding referred to in Paragraph 2(b) above, it being the desire of the Members and Trustees of Fenn Educational Foundation that such restricted or trust assets form a part of the trust estates of such trusts under the provisions of Article II, subparagraph(a) of the Trust Agreement relating to assets subject to currently effective restrictions.

4.   The Executive Committee of the Board of Trustees shall determine in their discretion when the conditions in Paragraph 2 above have been satisfied, and upon such determination:

a. the Chairman, any Vice Chairman and the Secretary of the Board of Trustees and of the Corporation be, and they hereby are, authorized and directed to execute and file in the office of the Secretary of State of the State of Ohio a Certificate of Dissolution verified by their oath as required by law, and to do, or cause to be done, all such other acts and things as may be necessary or proper in order that the dissolution of this Corporation may be forthwith accomplished;

b. the Chairman, any Vice Chairman and the Secretary of the Board of Trustees and of the Corporation be, and they hereby are, authorized and directed to take any and all actions as may be necessary or desirable to effectuate the distribution of assets contemplated by the Plan and the winding up of the affairs of Fenn Educational Foundation, including but not limited to (i) the execution of Trust Agreements, in substantially the form and content of the Trust Agreement, with the several trustee institutions cooperating in the said Multiple Trusteeship Plan of The Cleveland Foundation, (ii) the transfer to such trustee institutions of the assets of the Corporation as approved by the Executive Committee of the Board of Trustees, and in connection with such transfers to execute all necessary stock powers and/or assignments, and (iii) the execution and filing of any returns or reports required by the United States Internal Revenue Laws;

c. until further action by the Board of Trustees, the Executive Committee of the Board of Trustees is authorized and directed to take such other and further actions as may be necessary or desirable to completely wind up the affairs of this Corporation.

The following memorandum accompanied the Minutes of this meeting:

Memo to: Trustees & Members, Fenn Educational Foundation (F.E.F.)
From: G. Brooks Earnest, Director
Re: Joint Meeting, Trustees & Corporate Members, and the following Executive Committee meeting, June 28, 1971.

The Joint Meeting of the Trustees and Corporate Members was historical in the sense that it well might be the last meeting of this group under the aegis and name of the Fenn Educational Foundation.

You received the "Plan of Voluntary Dissolution and Distribution of Assets" of F.E.F. with the Call of the Meeting dated June 15, 1971, and because this "Plan" was officially approved at the June 28, 1971, meeting, we are enclosing another copy because it should be a part of the official minutes of the meeting.

The term "Dissolution" does not imply that we are going out of the foundation business. We are merely establishing a new type of operation with the Cleveland Foundation (a public foundation) in order to continue doing the same things we have been doing all along and not be susceptible to the penalties imposed upon a private foundation through the Tax Reform Act of 1969.

The present Trustees and Members will be known as the Fenn Advisory Committee, and the present Executive Committee of the Board will be known as the Executive Board. We will continue to hold meetings and select grantees as we have in the past. The primary change will be that our present corpus will be distributed between five Cleveland Banks in trusts and our recommendations for grants must be submitted to the Distribution Committee of the Cleveland Foundation for approval and payment.

August 5, 1971

The final meeting of the Executive Committee of the Fenn Educational Foundation was held October 6, 1971. The very last grant approved by the Executive Committee was for a scholarship fund honoring the late Dr. C. V. Thomas, the first President of Fenn College. Following is the article from the Minutes of the meeting concerning this grant:

> Mr. Hale reported on a Memorial Scholarship Fund proposed by Baldwin-Wallace College (as a part of their 125th Anniversary Program) to honor Dr. C. V. Thomas, the first President of Fenn College. He stated that it seemed to be the last opportunity to do this, that Cleveland State University showed little indication to do so and that Baldwin-Wallace College was an appropriate institution to receive the Fund since it had awarded an honorary degree to Dr. C. V. Thomas. The amount suggested for the memorial Scholarship Fund is $25,000. Mr. Hale stated that if the Foundation would be willing to provide one-half of the amount, he and other friends of Dr. Thomas would make up the difference. After some discussion, Mr. Hunkin moved that the Foundation make a grant of $12,500 to establish the proposed Memorial Scholarship Fund memorializing Dr. C. V. Thomas, on the basis of an additional sum of $12,500 to be provided from private sources, it being understood that the scholarships from the income of this fund would be for students in co-operative or work-study programs at Baldwin-Wallace College. Dr. Hodge seconded the motion and it was unanimously passed.

At this same meeting Rorick advised the committee that various steps had been completed as contemplated by the plan, including the receipt of the requisite ruling of the Commissioner of Internal Revenue, the obtaining of an appropriate final order from the Court of Common Pleas, Cuyahoga County, Ohio, on September 22, 1971, approving the plan and other necessary actions to consummate the plan, the obtaining of appropriate consents of donors, settlors and other parties with respect to the disposition of certain assets of the Foundation. Rorick also indicated that it is proposed to transfer, on a temporary status, the assets comprising the Whiting and Dorothy Rogers Williams Fund to Dyke College.

Action was then taken by the Fenn Executive Committee to liquidate and distribute all of the assets of the Fenn Educational Foundation at or prior to the close of business on the same day, October 6, 1971. Accordingly, following the Executive Committee meeting representatives of the Foundation met at stated times with representatives from each of the five banks acting as trustee institutions under the Multiple Trusteeship Plan of The Cleveland Foundation and delivered certain afore-determined securities to the respective bank representatives. The Fenn Educational Foundation thus expired at the close of business on October 6, 1971, to become The Fenn Educational Fund of The Cleveland Foundation on the following day.

Under the date of October 12, 1973, Chairman Paul S. Dickey informed the Trustees and Members of the former Fenn Educational Foundation of the many facets involved in the transfer of assets and in arriving at the Foundation's new status, by means of the following well phrased memorandum:

To: The Members and Trustees of Fenn Educational Foundation

This letter will report that on October 6, 1971 all of the assets of Fenn Educational Foundation were distributed in accordance with the Plan approved by the Members and Trustees at their meeting on June 28, 1971. The net assets were divided among each of the five Cleveland Banks participating in the Multiple Trusteeship Plan of The Cleveland Foundation, namely Central National Bank of Cleveland, The Cleveland Trust Company, The National City Bank of Cleveland, Society National Bank of Cleveland and Union Commerce Bank, under a form of Trust Agreement which had been approved by the Members and Trustees at their meeting on June 28, 1971. These Trust Agreements established what will be known as "The Fenn Educational Fund." All of the assets distributed to The Cleveland Trust Company relate to a grant originally made to Fenn College by The Ford Foundation and are subject to the restriction worked out with The Ford Foundation and approved by the Court of Common Pleas that the trust estate shall be paid only to or for the use or benefit of The Cleveland State University or its successors. Of course, all assets comprising The Fenn Educational Fund are subject to the overriding conditions of the Resolutions providing for The Cleveland Foundation.

In addition to the distribution of net assets to create The Fenn Educational Fund, the value of the Wunsch Foundation Fund in the amount of $27,655.96 was transferred to The Cleveland State University under an agreement wherein CSU will continue to hold the Wunsch Foundation Fund and use the income for awards to members of the student body in the Fenn College of Engineering for the best papers on the subject of Materials Handling and design projects reasonably related to the subject of Materials Handling. The Wunsch Foundation Fund was transferred to CSU with the approval of the Wunsch Foundation and the Court of Common Pleas.

An agreement was entered into with Dyke College under which Dyke College will hold the Whiting and Dorothy Rogers Williams Fund, pay the income therefrom to Whiting and Dorothy Rogers Williams during their lifetimes, and upon the death of the survivor of Whiting Williams and Dorothy Rogers Williams the balance of the Fund will become a part of The Fenn Educational Fund. This arrangement was made necessary by reason of the terms of the original instrument under which the gift was made and the requirements of the Internal Revenue Service.

The distribution of assets was carried out with the approval of the Court of Common Pleas, Cuyahoga County, Ohio, Case No. 896335 in a Final Judgment of Judge John V. Corrigan entered October 6, 1971. An appropriate ruling from the Internal Revenue Service had also been obtained providing for the desired approval of the transfer of net assets under the Plan.

Appropriate arrangements were effected with the Distribution Committee of The Cleveland Foundation for the retention of Dr. G. Brooks Earnest as a consultant to the Distribution Committee with respect to matters involving The Fenn Educational Fund of The Cleveland Foundation. Also appropriate arrangements were effected with the Distribution Committee of The Cleveland Foundation for the payment to Henry J. Kubach of deferred compensation which is owed to him by Fenn Educational Foundation.

Having completed the above transfer of assets, our Fenn Educational Foundation Corporation will be legally dissolved and future grants of income will be effected exclusively through The Fenn Educational Fund. As you all have been previously advised, an Advisory Committee known as the Fenn Advisory Committee, comprised initially of all of the present Members of the Fenn Educational Foundation, will make recommendations from time to time to the Distribution Committee of The Cleveland Foundation with respect to disposition of net income of The Fenn Educational Fund. In addition to the Fenn Advisory Committee, there is established an Executive Board under The Fenn Educational Fund agreements, which is intended to operate in much the same way as our Executive Committee of the Board of Trustees has operated. Until the first organizational meeting of the Fenn Advisory Committee the Executive Board will consist of those persons who are presently members of the Executive Committee of the Board of Trustees.

The unique roles of Fenn College and Fenn Educational Foundation in promoting and assisting co-operative and work-study programs in institutions of higher education in the Greater Cleveland area has evolved now into a new chapter under the renowned The Cleveland Foundation.

I am happy to report the successful conclusion of the above transaction which has entailed a great deal of work by the Executive Committee, Dr. G. Brooks Earnest, Henry J. Kubach and our attorneys.

Sincerely yours,
s/*Paul S. Dickey*, Chairman

October 12, 1971

The purpose of the original Fenn Educational Foundation as determined by the Board of Trustees and Corporate Members was to provide support and assistance to a significant number of highly motivated young people to gain higher education (undergraduate or graduate) through a combined schedule of study on Greater Cleveland campuses and practical experience through off-campus jobs; in other words, to perpetuate the influence of Fenn College whose stock-in-trade was the mandatory cooperative program of higher education.

When on October 6, 1971, the Fenn Educational Foundation became the Fenn Educational Fund of The Cleveland Foundation, the former Trustees and Corporate Members became the Fenn Advisory Board, and the former Executive Committee, comprised of seven members, became the Fenn Executive Board. Dr. G. Brooks Earnest, formerly Director of the Foundation, became Consulting Director of the Fund. The original purpose noted above was continued.

Over the six-year period of operation of the Fenn Educational Foundation, most of the grants were directed toward the development of co-op programs in several of the Greater Cleveland colleges and universities and toward scholarships for students enrolled in co-op programs. The latter were known as Fenn Co-op Scholars. Following is a résumé of all the grants approved by the Trustees and Members of the Fenn Educational Foundation and awarded from September 1, 1965, to June 30, 1972.

1. $64,570 to 523 students at C.S.U. for scholarships prior to the institution of the Fenn Co-op Scholar Program.

2. $30,615 to 64 Fenn Co-op Scholars (A) at C.S.U. This program was adopted in 1966 and most of the recipients were seniors.

3. $32,686 to 173 Fenn Co-op Scholars (B) of which 92 were enrolled at C.S.U., 78 at C.C.C., and 3 at C.W.R.U. This program was started in 1969 with a group of businessmen at Calvary Presbyterian Church.

4. $19,000 to 32 Fenn Co-op Scholars (C) at Notre Dame College. This program was adopted in 1969 and the recipients were engaged in a work-study program at the College.

5. $12,730 to 24 Fenn Co-op Scholars (D) at C.S.U. This program was adopted in 1970 and is restricted to students enrolled in the Bachelor of Engineering Program in the Fenn College of Engineering.

6. $10,600 to 6 Fenn Co-op Scholars (E) taking graduate work at C.W.R.U. in the Departments of History and American Studies. The students carry on archival work for The Western Reserve Historical Society for which they also receive academic credit. This program started in 1970.

7. $5,000 to 9 Fenn Co-op Scholars (F) of which 5 were enrolled at C.W.R.U., 3 at C.C.C. and 1 at Lakeland Community College. This program, in conjunction with the Cleveland Area League for Nursing, started in 1971.

8. $88,400 to C.S.U. toward development of its Co-op program.

9. $17,539 to C.S.U. for faculty salaries in accordance with the Ford Foundation Grant.

10. $3,000 to C.S.U. for the Dean Paul R. Anders Memorial Scholarship Fund.

11. $24,600 to C.S.U. toward a study for a special Doctor of Engineering degree program. (Intern)
12. $32,340 to C.S.U. to institute a Bachelor of Engineering Technology program. (Co-op)
13. $15,000 to C.S.U. toward planning for a doctoral program in Chemistry. (Intern)
14. $12,205 to C.S.U. to institute a new course in Engineering Concepts for Freshmen.
15. $1,000 to C.S.U. for Senior awards for material handling papers.
16. $4,800 to C.S.U. in conjunction with the Cleveland Scholarship Program, Inc. for 6 inner-city high school graduates.
17. $6,525 to C.S.U. toward C.S.U. diplomas for former Fenn College graduates.
18. $3,800 to C.W.R.U. for graduate tuition of Mary M. Patterson.
19. $55,000 to L.C.C. for development of Co-op programs.
20. $10,000 to C.C.C. to implement its Co-op programs.
21. $11,500 to Baldwin-Wallace College toward Upward Bound program.
22. $12,500 to Baldwin-Wallace College toward Dr. C. V. Thomas Memorial Scholarship Award for work-study students.
23. $8,000 to the Cleveland Commission on Higher Education toward Teacher Improvement Education Projects.
24. $10,000 to The Educational Association of Metropolitan Cleveland (WVIZ) toward its higher educational T.V. activities.

A summary of the total funds granted during the six years of existence of the Fenn Educational Foundation is as follows:

To C.S.U.	$329,916.00
To C.C.C.	18,874.00
To C.W.R.U.	16,820.00
To Baldwin-Wallace College	24,000.00
To Lakeland Community College	55,000.00
To Notre Dame College	19,000.00
To Cleveland Area League for Nursing	5,000.00
To Cleveland Scholarship Program, Inc.	4,800.00

    To Cleveland Commission on Higher Education   8,000.00
    To Educational Television (WVIZ)   10,000.00
                                                  _____

                                    TOTAL $491,410.00

One amazing statistic of tremendous importance is that at least 839
carefully screened students, enrolled in Greater Cleveland colleges and
universities, had benefited from outright scholarship grants totaling
$227,654.22 during the six years of existence of the Fenn Educational
Foundation. Therefore, the Fenn Educational Foundation provided a
genuine and greatly needed operations service to the colleges and universities located in Metropolitan Cleveland and especially to the students enrolled in co-op or work-study programs. In perpetuating the
image of Fenn College most of the grant funds each year were directed
to unusual areas of need not customarily supported by other local foundations.

There appears to be a ground swell of colleges and universities adopt-
ing co-op or work-study programs in the United States. Until 1953
the concept of Cooperative Education was applied basically in the
pre-professional programs of Engineering and Business Administration
with a few notable exceptions, Antioch, for one instance, in the Liberal
Arts disciplines. As of 1953 there were thirty-five institutions of higher
education in the United States offering cooperative programs.

In 1953 the only national voice of cooperative education was the
Cooperative Education Division of the American Society for Engineering Education (A.S.E.E.) which came into being in 1929. By 1962 it
was felt that a national organization should be formed because the
co-op concept had spread to all professional disciplines in the colleges
and universities, to the junior and/or community colleges, to the technical institutes, to graduate programs, and into secondary school programs.

Accordingly, by means of a grant from the Kettering Foundation
and with administrative support from the Thomas Alva Edison Foundation, the National Commission for Cooperative Education (N.C.C.E.)
was formed in 1962. Dr. Charles F. (Boss) Kettering was a staunch
supporter of cooperative education, both at the University of Cincinnati
and as a trustee of Antioch College. Since 1962, largely through the
efforts of N.C.C.E. and A.S.E.E., there have been outstanding develop-

ments in cooperative education. Today, in 1973, over three hundred institutions of higher education employ some form of co-op work-study program, a phenominal 760% increase in the number of institutions over a period of nineteen years.

At one time Fenn College was the only institution in the Greater Cleveland area engaged in the Cooperative Program of higher education. As of 1972 the following institutions had developed or had plans for developing some form of co-op or work-study programs:

1. The Cleveland State University—both undergraduate and graduate
2. Lakeland Community College
3. Cuyahoga Community College
4. Notre Dame College
5. Dyke College
6. Baldwin-Wallace College
7. Case Western Reserve University—graduate
8. John Carroll University

It is obvious that as the popularity and demand for co-op or work-study programs grows in Metropolitan Cleveland, there is a greater need for increasing the corpus of the Fenn Educational Fund of The Cleveland Foundation to satisfy the scholarship needs of the students and the co-op curriculum developmental needs of Cleveland's institutions of higher education.

In the years ahead it will be interesting to follow the trend in higher education to see whether the co-op principle of immediate marriage of practical application with theory will expand as rapidly as it has over the past two decades. Those who have been associated closely with Fenn College, commonly known as the "Fenn Family," may well be proud of the fact that Fenn was one of the country's early pioneers in cooperative education at the college level.

FINIS

Portrait of Dr. G. Brooks Earnest

EPILOGUE

Members of the Association of Cleveland State University Women (formerly, Association of Fenn College Women, A.F.C.W.) and guests, I must publicly express my gratitude to Dorothy Srail, Barbara Small and other members of your Association for your courtesy. Mary joins me in this expression. I should also express my appreciation to certain former Trustees of Fenn College for their support of your project, and especially to Nancy Bunch Sheridan, the artist.

I am sure that those present this evening who have never seen me or who have seen me only since about 1961 will say that the portrait does not resemble me. But those who have known me for many years will admit there is a striking resemblance as I appeared during most of my years at Fenn. Anyway, I am pleased that your portrait committee preferred to have me portrayed with hair.

At the time of the transfer of the College to the State, Fenn had four oil portraits: Dr. C. V. Thomas, Fenn's first President; Ellwood H. Fisher, Fenn's first Chairman of the Board of Trustees; Harold H. Burton, Justice of the Supreme Court of the United States and a member of Fenn's Board of Trustees for forty years; and Charles J. Stilwell, Fenn's second Chairman of the Board of Trustees. I had the distinct pleasure of unveiling the portraits of Messrs. Fisher, Burton and Stilwell. I humbly join this select group.

I have been writing the history of Fenn College in my spare time. At this point in time (a common expression) I have proof-read galleys for eight of the sixteen chapters. It now appears that the book will be published in April or May of 1974. I have spent hours on end reading the Fenn Board Minutes, and other Fenn publications (Millard Jordan and his Secretary, Ethel Hamilton will vouch for my explorations in your Archives Office).

701

I find the writings of Dr. Thomas (Tommy) mark him as a learned man. I have quoted much of his philosophy on education in my book. Here are just two of his quotations: "The purpose of Fenn College is to equip young men and women to live useful and more abundant lives," and the second; "It is the obligation of the College to teach the student the knowledge, skill and attitude required for living." (Co-op)

The Fenn Educational Fund of The Cleveland Foundation, with which I have been associated since the transfer of Fenn College to the State, has made grants totaling $346,000 to C.S.U. between September 1, 1965 and June 30, 1973. These grants were for the development of co-op programs and for scholarships for Fenn Co-op Scholars. During the same interim nine other institutions in Greater Cleveland shared in grants totaling $199,000. So C.S.U. has received 63.5 percent of total grant funds ($545,000).

Our purpose is to endeavor to perpetuate the image of Fenn College through supporting cooperative programs of higher education in Metropolitan Cleveland.

Again, many thanks to the members of your Association. I am most grateful, proud and humble for your kindness.

INDEX

Ackoff, Russell L., 433
Adams, Charles E., 15, 16, 21, 25, 37, 38, 88
Adams, Donald C., 428, 541
Adams, Joseph E., 392, 576
Addams, Judge George S., 38
Ahrens, Wilfred C., 384
Aiken, Dr. Samuel C., 2
Akers, Kenneth A., 347, 366, 372, 380, 402, 419, 577
Albert M. Higley Company, 314–15, 422, 438, 569
Aldad, Hushang, 674
Allen, A. F., 38
Allen, Harry, 392
Alter, Dr. Chester M., 479–80
Aluminum Company of America, 218, 376
Alumni Bulletin, 231
American Multigraph, 14
American Steel and Wire Company, 46, 218, 225, 376
Amme, Professor, 5
Anders, Paul R.: Fenn faculty member and dean, 85, 111, 156, 196, 212, 236, 237, 259, 260, 262, 270, 301, 347, 367, 376, 395, 407, 542, 576; career summarized, 120; retired, 593; honorary degree conferred on, 628; Memorial Scholarship Fund, 696
Anderson, H. A., 578
Anderson, Harry, 514
Anderson, Minton M., 369, 376
Anderson, Newton M., 6
Andre, C. P., 44
Andrews, Albert C., 556–59
Andrews, Elmore L., 479
Antisdale, Stella, 403; Scholarship Fund, 409–10
Armstrong, Arthur S., 392, 412, 459, 541, 576, 680
Armstrong, John W., 71

Arthur G. McKee and Company, 458–59, 467, 468, 644
Association of American Colleges, 227
Aufmuth, Raymond B., 205–6, 479, 568, 570, 577, 653
Auld, Robert B., 270, 576
Austin Company, 390
Ayres, Col. Leonard P., 52

Babcock, E. S., 8
Bailey Meter Company, 377
Baird, G. A., 576
Baird, Dr. George H., 443
Baker, Elbert H., 18, 38
Baker, Elbert H., Jr.: Fenn College Trustee, 18, 110, 149, 174, 175, 199, 207, 216, 235, 252, 257, 259, 265, 267, 280, 287, 292–96 *passim*, 344, 366, 374, 375; honorary degree conferred on, 391; Honorary Life Trustee, 412, 416; death of, 535
Baker, Newton D., 38, 41
Baker, Richard T., 479, 541, 544, 570, 577, 583
Baker Motor, 13
Bakken, G. P., 578
Baldwin, Fred C.: Fenn College Trustee, 203, 216, 231, 235, 256, 280, 298, 338, 343, 344, 347; death of, 353, 366
Baldwin-Wallace College, 675, 697
Balliett, the Rev. Paul R., 206, 653
Bartlett, Edward T.: Fenn College Trustee, 216, 231, 235, 256, 280, 286, 292–96 *passim*, 338, 343, 366, 374, 375, 380, 388, 402, 403, 434, 439, 440, 450, 470, 505, 539–40, 544, 595, 640; honorary degree conferred on, 628; Fenn Educational Foundation Trustee, 650, 680
Bartunek, Joseph, 605
Bates, Guy J., 475
Battey, M. M., 2

703

Waltemade, Robert C., 254
Walter, John W., 273
Ward, J. Carlton, 402, 406
Ward, Samuel, 25, 72, 74, 87, 111, 123–24, 273
Ware, K. E., 576
Warner, Harry B., 463
Warner & Swasey Company, 46, 63, 208, 215, 216, 218, 434
Watkins, Hays T., Jr., 576, 578
Watson, Dr. Goodwin B., 60, 63, 71, 82, 84, 119
Watson, Dr. Sara Ruth, 232–33, 273, 420
Wean, R. J., Jr., 463
Weatherhead, A. J., 463
Weatherhead Company, 218
Weber, E. Clare, 463, 576
Weidenthal, Bud, 548–49, 550–51
Weiss, H. L., 463
Weiss, Louis Carl, 408, 437
Welfle, the Very Rev. Frederick E., 376
Wellman, Gerald S., 55, 71, 111, 119, 124, 132, 166, 195; tribute to C. V. Thomas, 301–2
Wellman Engineering Company, 390
West Campus Building. See Stilwell Hall
Western Automatic Screw Machine Company, 424
Western Reserve University, 33, 41, 348; Cleveland College of, 48. See also Case Western Reserve University
Westinghouse Electric Corporation, 406
Weygandt, Judge Carl V., 19, 56, 62, 72
Whalon, George, 326
Whitcomb, Cecil B., 63
White, Bertram W., 273
White, Charles M., 418, 463, 467, 475, 516, 680
White, Harry, 126
Whitehair, J. C., 217, 231, 236, 256
White Motor Company, 384
White Sewing Machine Corporation, 377
Wickenden, Dr. William E., 74, 80
Widdell, H. E., 428, 437, 576, 577, 650, 680, 683
Wilbur, John S., 392, 468
Williams, A. B., 9
Williams, Clifford D., 187, 188, 195, 199, 205, 206, 212, 325, 457
Williams, Dorothy Rogers, 568, 692, 694
Williams, E. M., 41
Williams, George, 1

Williams, Lewis B., 41, 477, 478, 578
Williams, Paul E., 58, 71, 113, 118–19
Williams, Whiting, 417, 568, 576, 644, 692, 694
Williams (Whiting and Dorothy Rogers) Fund, 568, 692, 694
Willingham, Miss (librarian), 62, 74, 187
Willis, the Hon. Frank B., 43
Wills, D. C., 25, 26, 39
Wilner, Theodore J., 206
Wilson, Lee, 428
Wilson, S. M., 44
Winkler, Frederick N., 470, 479, 576
Wise, Donald E., 234, 653
Wittke, Dr. Carl F., 198, 391
Woodling, George V.: Fenn College Trustee, 217, 235, 256, 259, 280, 292, 330, 332, 347, 402, 419, 513, 576, 577, 680; plaque awarded to, 596
Woodling, Homer E., 64, 72, 111, 124, 217, 262, 273, 407
Wright, Edith Stevenson, 515
Wright, John David, 217, 235, 257, 258, 267, 280, 324, 331
Wunsch, J. W., 347
Wunsch Foundation Fund, 694
Wurzbach, Milton J., 188, 412, 419, 535
WVIZ (Educational Television), 697, 698

Yeager, Robert F., 204
Yoder, Douglas O., 393
Yoder Company, 390
Young, E. F., 2
Young Men's Christian Association of Buffalo, 68–69
Young Men's Christian Association of Cleveland: founded, 2; "Old Association," 2; "Modern Association," 2; Constitution, 3–4; Board of Managers created, 5; Centerville Mills Camp purchased, 14; Board of Trustees (1925), 38–39; Diamond Jubilee Anniversary, 61; 25-year award presented to, 425
—Educational Committee: created, 3; in 1882, 5
—Schools (Educational Branch): incorporated, 26; first Board of Governors of, 27; name changed, 27
—Cleveland YMCA School of Technology (Y-Tech): named, 27; Board of